The Lone Star

The Lone Star

★ THE LIFE OF ★

John Connally

James Reston, Jr.

1817

An Edward Burlingame Book

HARPER & ROW, PUBLISHERS, New York
Grand Rapids, Philadelphia, St. Louis, San Francisco
London, Singapore, Sydney, Tokyo, Toronto

FIRST EDITION

Designed by Karen Savary
Picture insert researched, edited, and designed by Vincent Virga

---

Library of Congress Cataloging-in-Publication Data

Reston, James, 1941–
    The lone star: the life of John Connally/James Reston.—1st ed.
        p.   cm.
    "An Edward Burlingame book."
    Bibliography: p.
    Includes index.
    ISBN 0-06-016196-5
    1. Connally, John Bowden, 1917–   . 2. Presidential candidates—United States—Biography. 3. Cabinet officers—United States—Biography. 4. Texas—Governors—Biography. I. Title.
E840.8.C66R47   1989
973.926′092—dc20
[B]   89-45060

---

89 90 91 92 93 AT/RRD 10 9 8 7 6 5 4 3 2 1

For
J. B. R. and S. F. R.

★ CONTENTS ★

Illustrations follow p. 404.

★ ACKNOWLEDGMENTS ★

OVER THE TWO AND A HALF YEARS in which this book was written, I have benefited from the generously given time, advice, and wisdom of countless people. The written record of the life and the work of John Connally is vast and illuminating, but it is spread through three presidential libraries, a number of libraries within Texas, and the National Archives. I am deeply grateful to these individuals who helped me find the often-elusive materials through which I could fashion this narrative.

The most helpful was the staff of the LBJ Library in Austin. Its director, Harry Middleton, was unfailingly cordial and receptive to my requests—and solicitous of my occasional complaints. Harry was instrumental in releasing certain materials that had hitherto been closed to research. His archivists, Claudia Anderson, Bob Tissing, Nancy Smith, Linda Hanson, and Michael Gillette, were always responsive and professional and often made suggestions about certain areas for research that had not occurred to me. For materials on Connally's early life, particularly his days at the University of Texas, the Barker Texas History Center was essential, and its director, Don Carleton, was a real friend to the book.

On matters relating to Watergate, which I couch in its broad definition, I could not have been better served than by Steve Tilley at the National Archives. Besides guiding me through the voluminous trial transcript of *U.S. v. Connally* and the files of the Watergate Special Prosecution Force, he too helped to secure the release of previously closed materials. His colleague at the National Archives, Marion Johnson, shared with me his encyclopedic knowledge of the Warren Commission files and pointed me toward fruitful avenues of investigation. Equally, at the JFK Library in Boston, Henry Gwiazda was always supportive. I will treasure the memory of him tossing boxes around late one afternoon until, at last, we came upon the Jerry Bruno diary of the preparations for Kennedy's fateful Texas trip.

The experience at the Nixon Project in Alexandria, Virginia, was rewarding in a different way. Because of the adversarial relationship between Nixon and the Nixon archivists, in which the former president fights disclosure as the archivists press for it, research at the Nixon Project can be emotional and frustrating for everyone. For all the pink sheets that indicate a Nixon decision to withhold documents, the boxes of open materials inevitably contained the few documents that illuminate the fascinating alliance between Connally and Nixon—a relationship that was so different from the one between Connally and Lyndon Johnson. Within the constraints imposed upon her, Joan Howard was nearly saintly in her desire to help. No less revealing were certain documents I received from the Gerald Ford Library, and I am particularly grateful to former president Ford himself for helping me to understand them.

I cannot forget those who, like Ross Milloy, Lowell Leberman, Creekmore Fath, Liz Carpenter, Lawrence Wright, John Henry Faulk, and Philip and Linda Hardberger, gave me sustenance and shelter and much good conversation on my research trips to Texas. Fath, in particular, was essential to conveying a rich picture of the University of Texas in the 1930s and the raucous ambience of Texas politics in the 1940s and 1950s. I spent many enlightening and often boisterous hours with him. Largely because of controversial work that has been done previously on Lyndon Johnson, I understood the ambivalence of the close Connally associates toward working with me and appreciated that a spirited debate over whether or not to cooperate was under way within the circle of Connally friends. Therefore, I'm particularly grateful to Golfrey and Merrill Connally, Bill Stinson, George Christian, Julian Read, Robert Strauss, Mickey Gardner, and Lady Bird Johnson for their willingness to share their time and their memories.

Finally, my dear friend and colleague of twenty years, Alfreda Kaplan, labored valiantly as always in the preparation of the manuscript. The book is much improved by her incisive recommendations.

The Lone Star

Youth

Toward the end of the nineteenth century, Wilson County, on the upper coastal plain of South Texas, was still wild and untamed. In the wake of Reconstruction, the town of Floresville had been established upon two hundred acres belonging to Josefa Flores de Barker, a native of the Canary Islands, near the center of the county and not far from the San Antonio River. It was incorporated in 1874, and its courthouse was a three-room frame house located on the public square; near it, the jail, a blockhouse of red stone, was added in 1875, just in time for the troubles that civilization would bring in the 1880s.

At first, the commissioners of the new county put their minds to rudiments of transportation. The county roads needed to be surveyed, and in 1886 the San Antonio and Aransas Pass Railroad came to Floresville. Wildcats were an issue. When one Francisco Charles was paid fifty cents for a wildcat scalp, a lengthy debate over the rightness of bounty hunting ensued, and it was decided that the government would cease to pay for scalps. Antagonisms between men were more emotional. Wilson County lay upon the southern fringe of the open cattle range, once the hunting grounds of the Comanche, the Tonkawa, and the Lipano-Apache. For years its free grassland had been grazed by herds belonging to landless cattlemen. But the barbed wire fence had been invented in 1873, and that revolutionized the West, for "bob wire" was to the cattle industry what the cotton gin became to the raising of cotton. The new invention found its way to Wilson County by the early 1880s, and its arrival caused considerable excitement, as the free-grass forces watched the clodhoppers gobble up their range.

The drought of 1883 brought the conflict between the free-grass men and the fence men to a head. As small landholders erected fences, they were dubbed "outside sharks." At dusk bands of nightriders who called themselves "javelins," "owls," and "blue devils" began to roam the range, cutting the fences. The forces armed themselves on both sides. It was a problem that extended throughout the central portion of Texas, and it forced the governor of Texas, John Ireland, to convene a special session of the legislature in 1884. The legislature proceeded to approve a law which made it a felony to destroy a fence, but it also required that a gate be provided every three miles, a quaint concession to the open-range men. The fabled Texas Rangers enforced the law.

As Wilson County moved into the twentieth century, it boasted that more Texas Rangers came from the rolling countryside around Fairview, not far from the fields where young John B. Connally, Jr., worked his father's spread, than from any other area of Texas. In due course, the strife over fences receded, and the open range gave way to small farms. "The genius of the unfenced world," as J. Frank Dobie called it, withered away.

The soil of Wilson County was rich, more an extension of the loamy Louisiana lowlands than of the dusty Texas brushland to the west. Its reddish-brown, sandy loam, streaked with waxy black contrails, lent itself splendidly to the cultivation of cotton. Despite bumper crops, the price of cotton was low—four cents a pound in the 1880s—and this led the farmers to organize a Farmers' Alliance. A new method of pulling cotton relieved the worry over low prices for a short time, when the Winslett family arrived from Alabama and began to pick cotton by dragging heavy sacks between the rows rather than by the old method of filling an apron and emptying it frequently into a central basket. With the new method, pulling seventy-five pounds of cotton was considered a good day's work. One bale per acre was the average yield.

The cotton prosperity of Wilson County seemed assured when the San Antonio and Gulf Railroad brought the second spur into Stockdale, east of Floresville, as the end of its New Orleans line. But in 1903 insects destroyed the cotton crop and came again the following year, and the farmers gradually diversified their operations into corn and sorghum, flax and melons. By the time the towering figure of John Bowden Connally, Sr., settled on his tenant farm east of Floresville, it was toward the end of King Cotton's reign and before the more predictable rule of the plebeian peanut took over.

The elder Mr. Connally was six-foot-five, with a well-chiseled, angular, leathery face that narrowed into a strong chin, and a strong, forceful personality. When he grew older, it was often remarked that old man Connally looked like Old Man Texas himself. He had grown up in Union Valley, in the northeast corner of Wilson County. During World War I, drawn by the lure of the Chisholm Trail, he had left home at the age of fourteen, striking out for New Mexico to do some real cowpunching. When he returned to Union Valley, the new schoolteacher was Lela Wright from Fairview, who had landed the job by virtue of having completed high school. She was a woman of average height, with a shy, retiring nature, and when she married Connally she was quite content to become a farmer's wife and defer to her powerful husband. Health, above all, was a strong inducement to this marriage on the receding Texas frontier. For there was heart trouble on Connally's side of the family, whereas his wife, Lela, came from a family of eight, with a reputation for hardiness and longevity. In fact, after bearing eight children her mother would live to the age of 102. Mrs. Connally herself, with eight children to her credit, made it to only 93.

Life on a South Texas farm before the Depression was stark and unforgiving. Cooking was done on an iron woodstove, fueled by footlong splits of wood, or in a baking oven built into the fireplace. The diet was simple: chicken and dumplings was a summer standard, with the wife usually the one who chased down the chicken, delivered the *coup de grâce*, and plucked the bird for the pot. Winter meals were less appetizing: bacon and beans generally, complemented by whatever had been canned from the summer garden. In the yard there was the wash kettle, a huge iron pot whose water was brought to a boil by a fire underneath and whose load would be agitated by a long pole. Soap was homemade, a greasy combination of lye and cracklings. Heat came from the fireplace and light from lamps fueled either by kerosene or by carbide, a chemical that sat under the house produced acetylene gas, which was then piped to standards on the walls and gave off a soft, pleasant white light.

John and Lela Connally began their family quickly, as was the custom in rural America, and they had every intention of making the numbers large. Their start was not auspicious. The first child, a son named Wyatt, was born in their first year of marriage. Months later, as his mother tended to her many chores, the child fell in the hearth fire and was burned to death. Thereafter Wyatt was scarcely ever mentioned. A son and a daughter followed in quick succession before, in 1917, the third son, the namesake, was born. Three more sons and a daughter followed him.

The tragedy of the farm did not end with the death of Wyatt. Once, when her boys were still toddlers, Lela Connally went out to bring in the milch cow, and an angry Jersey bull attacked her. She was badly roughed up and saved only by the intervention of their English bulldog, Major.

In the Wilson County of Johnnie Connally's upbringing, work on the farm began early in life. By the time they were five years old, the Connally boys were dispatched into the cotton rows, not perhaps with the massive cotton sacks that the Winsletts had introduced, but with more appropriately sized flour sacks. Teams of horses and mules worked the soil, and the brothers and cousins labored together in the fields. When there was socializing, it was usually at the house of Connally's grandmother in Fairview, for Grandpa Wright had died early, and the family gathered there in raucous, generous feasts to please the grand old lady. During those times there was generally competition among the barefoot boys as to who could eat the most roasting ears. The Connallys were not an especially pious lot. Methodist by tradition rather than practice, the Connally boys were active in the Epworth League, the church's Sunday night gathering for young people, largely as an antidote to the dreary routine of farm life and, later, as a place to meet the local girls.

In the 1920s, old man Connally took what work he could on the side to supplement his meager income. He worked as a barber and a grocer and a freelance butcher. When ranchers wanted their steers slaughtered, Connally would throw his knives, cleavers, and butcher's saws into his battered Model T, pile his namesake in with him along with his Mexican helper, Carlos Estrada, and off they would go to the unpleasantness. Young John's job at this impressionable age was to carry water to the men as they hacked and carved, but also to coddle the steers' blue brains, which in those days were a farmer's treat. The shuddering memory of this childhood practice contributed to John Connally's abstemiousness later.

In 1926 the elder Connally gave up farming and moved his family to San Antonio. Plagued with debts, which for a tenant farmer could only mount, he acquired an old stretch Buick and inaugurated the Red and White Ball Bus Line. The old Buick became a familiar sight upon old Highway 16 between San Antonio and Corpus Christi, its cheerful pennants streaming from its back fins as it picked up its passengers in Calaveras, Elmendorf, and Poth. At first, Mr. Connally himself drove, unfolding his lanky body in the back seat of his bus at night to save the cost of a hotel. When the eldest son, Stanford, became of age, he took over the driving.

The family settled in Harlandale, the southern suburb of San Antonio and now a Mexican neighborhood. For the first time, the Connallys enjoyed the luxury of electric light and an indoor bathroom. They were not likely to go soft with these creature comforts, however. Young Johnnie arose at 2:00 A.M. to deliver milk by truck to have a little pocket change. At the Harlandale public schools he was drawn naturally to debating and to dramatics, as was, half a continent away, his future boss and promoter, Richard Nixon. All five years that the Connally family remained in San Antonio, John represented Harlandale in declamations at the County Meet. His talent for "exclaiming" was evident to his family, and at the family table, dominated by his politically astute father, the opinions of young John were accorded early respect. At his public performances he delivered his florid orations without a note. The words poured out of him. "The Siege of the Alamo" was his standard topic at declamations. In a big, round voice, hand clutched to his breast, he boomed out profoundly, "Santa Anna came storming in, as a storm might come. . . ." and the audience bristled with excitement.

As he made his way through Harlandale High School, he soon became identified as a boy with promise. He knew he was handsome, and it led to a fastidiousness about his appearance which was unusual among his peers. It was not a trait he learned from his father, who was casual, if proper, in his dress, or from his barefoot brothers and cousins. His narcissism came together with his energy and his ambition and formed a combination that was altogether his own. It became important to him to impress.

In the theater, young John Connally found the place to exhibit his talents, and he was cast early as a leading man. The school plays cultivated his voice and his sense for the dramatic gesture, but they also brought out a talent for comedy.

In his senior class play, Connally took the part of Jarvis, the enterprising butler who rents the mansion of his aristocratic master to a few Hollywood types upon the family's apparent departure for Europe, only to have the owners return home unexpectedly. In this Katherine Kavanaugh three-act farce, "Johnnie" Connally, as his local stage billing called him, was supposed to be a character of sober countenance and totally lacking in a sense of humor, whose big moment in the play comes with a spectacular pratfall amid luggage and hatboxes on the stairs when his mistress surprisingly reappears. As much of a challenge surely was the need for Jarvis to drop all his *h*'s. What a sixteen-year-old Floresville youth with a Cockney accent sounded like—" 'Eaven 'elp us, if yer mother ever 'ears of this!" Jarvis exclaims at one point—one can only imagine.

In 1932 the Connally family had returned to Wilson County. For young John Connally—by now, an imposing six-footer himself and a future Peanut King in the local parade—it was not a welcome move. To return to the open countryside, to cattle and hayseed, to kerosene and carbide lamps, was a comedown from the wonders of San Antonio. But for his father, the return was a triumph. The bus company had put him on his feet financially. He had sold the old Buick to the Greyhound Company and he had returned to Floresville to realize a Texas dream. West of town, the 1,200-acre Coughran ranch—infested with mesquite but dotted with stately live oaks— was for sale, and Connally bought it for $30 an acre, a low price even in Depression times. He was now a rancher rather than a sodbuster or a clodhopper. He was aristocracy. His stature soared, especially as he paid off his longstanding debts in the community. He decided upon Herefords as his breed and began to build a herd. If he was about to lose John to college, he still had three sons, Golfrey, Wayne, and Merrill, to help out. In due course he was advertising his breeding bulls on the local market, nothing of champion stock, but sound and hardy.

In Wilson County in the 1930s there were two dominant figures, A. B. Carnes and Sam Fore, Jr. The most prominent was Carnes, the easygoing sheriff of the county for seventeen years. The problems of law enforcement in those days were of the garden variety for a small Texas farming community. Occasionally there was a rowdy bunch at the Floresville saloon, or the regular dog- and cockfights out in the county, or the odd horse thief and cattle rustler or bootlegger during Prohibition, who slipped north from the Mexican border and loaded his cargo into high-speed cars bound for San Antonio.

During World War I, when John Connally's father was a vaquero in New Mexico, Sheriff Carnes had kept an eye on the German community in Poth, for there were reports of German spies making their way north from Mexico. Later, in the early 1930s, the worry was the terror that such bloodthirsty characters as Bonnie and Clyde instilled in rural Texas communities, as the Model T replaced the horse and the Browning automatic rifle replaced the six-shooter. So bad had the epidemic of rural bank robberies become that the Texas Bankers Association was offering $5,000 for the dead body of a bank robber and not a dime for the culprit alive, and this brought into being an almost worse scourge—that of the bounty hunter.

To assist Sheriff Carnes, if he needed help, were the Texas Rangers, who claimed Wilson County as their special breeding ground. As a force they had deteriorated from the noble days of Captain L. H. McNelly, whose Rangers caught a group of Mexican cattle bandidos red-handed near the border and "naturalized" thirteen of them. If there was still a hero among the Rangers during the 1920s and a model for growing boys to emulate, it might have been Captain Will L. Wright, who was a distant relative of Lela Wright Connally. Captain Wright had made a name for himself at the end of World War I, when he tracked down Mexican horse thieves and draft evaders around Laredo, stalking them through the chaparral of the border country for days. When he slept, he draped a horsehair rope around his torso so rattlesnakes would not be tempted to climb into bed with him and warm themselves against his back. But his chief fame came from wild shootouts he had had with bands of Mexican bootleggers in 1921 and 1922 around Las Animas. In the first, on November 22, 1921, he had captured 37 horses laden with 3,000 quarts of tequila, but on December 22, 1922, he had "naturalized" a Mexican "general" as he captured 800 bottles of tequila, sotol, and imported Scotch and rye, bound for the Christmas trade.

In his routine duties, Sheriff Carnes had to be concerned with the security of the Saspamco plant, the only industry in the county, which had been shaping clay sewer pipe since the Civil War and whose whistle at the end of the workday was a welcome sound as it wafted over the fields where the Connally boys worked. In the southern part of the county there were a few modest oil operations to watch over. They had been made possible after 1854, when slaves, digging for water, had discovered a black, unpleasant-smelling substance seeping from the ground and had quickly covered the hole.

In 1936 Sheriff Carnes ran into trouble himself, as he became embroiled in a dispute which in those days passed for a major scandal. The Commissioners Court had paid the sheriff $7,000 in fees, an enormous sum then, payments which the county now declared to have been illegal. A lawsuit resulted, and it was an outrage to see the sheriff himself in the dock as the accused. Not long before he ran for reelection in the Democratic primary in 1936, the sheriff went to trial. Though he was found innocent, the court required him to pay $28. Simply to be charged, even if one were declared not guilty at trial, was politically catastrophic—a lesson Johnnie Connally would learn bitterly himself thirty-nine years later.

A side effect of the scandal was to lure John Bowden Connally, Sr., into politics. For the county clerk, one J. T. Houston, was implicated with Sheriff Carnes, and it was whispered that some $4,000 of county funds were missing. The clerk's job was one of the most secure and steady-paying jobs in those bleak Depression days, and Connally matched up with a Stockdale man as the candidate for sheriff, to run against the courthouse "ring." There were two voting boxes in Wilson County in that period, and one of them was heavily Mexican-American. This box generally ran as high as five to one for the ruling clique in the courthouse because the sheriff, together with the commissioners, controlled the county jobs on the roads. To win, Connally had to draw heavily in the Anglo box. To call it *Anglo* was a misnomer, for the white population was composed largely of Eastern Europeans—the Germans down in Poth, the Poles in the eastern part of the county, the Czech Bohemians not far from the Connally ranch around Fairview. Often taking his sons along, Connally stumped the beer halls and the dance halls of these groups, finding himself, a man who never danced, out of place in the raucous setting of beer and polka, bratwurst and guttural languages. Among the Polish Catholics he expected to do well, because a Catholic priest had endorsed him as the candidate of honesty. Connally promoted this quality. His advertisement in the *Floresville Chronicle-Journal* read, "He is a man thorough in action, honest in character, and one who is insistent upon equal rights for all. Vote for him. Justice for all . . . partiality to none."

In the statement that the *Chronicle-Journal* requested from all local candidates, John Connally, Sr., with humble modesty, wrote, "I offer for this important office on my own merits and ask the support of the voters on that basis. If elected, I feel I possess the necessary qualifications to give people the service they expect from the official holding this position. I shall appreciate the votes of all who see fit to support me, but I shall bear no ill will against anyone desiring to vote for another." Connally swept into office with a plurality of 430 votes, and his running mate beat old Sheriff Carnes by 400.

The other prominent figure in Wilson County, Sam Fore, Jr.,

was the publisher of the local weekly newspaper. An immensely fat man, well over 300 pounds, who had the added problem of persistent hernias, Fore managed somehow to carry his weight with dignity, and he was an intellectual force far beyond his own community. In local political matters, such as the sheriff and county clerk races, he maintained a strict neutrality. But he was an engaged Democrat, even a "brass collar Democrat," and he was not given to journalistic pretension about objectivity. He had actively supported Democratic candidates throughout his life, not simply with passionate editorials but in political contacts as well. He had attended his first Democratic Convention in 1928, when Franklin Roosevelt had struggled to the podium with leg braces, supporting himself on two canes, to nominate Al Smith; and again in 1936 Fore had acquiesced when John Nance Garner (old "Cactus Jack") had nominated his daughter to be queen of the convention.

In 1931, the Fourteenth District had elected to Congress a wealthy socialite named Richard Kleberg. Corpus Christi, in the southern part of the district, was his stronghold, for his family owned twenty percent of the fabled King Ranch, centered in Kleberg County south of Corpus. Adept at polo and golf, but awkward in politics, Kleberg was strong in "Kleberg country," where, as the scion of the King Ranch aristocracy, he had been dealing with vaqueros all his life. He spoke Spanish fluently, and he knew how to run an effective campaign in the southern part of his district. But he was weak with the small farmers of the Hill Country and with the ethnic minorities of Wilson County. From the venerable state senator, later undersecretary of the interior, Alvin Wirtz, Kleberg had heard about a "live wire" from Johnson City, a gangly, twenty-three-year-old schoolteacher named Lyndon Johnson. Kleberg hired Johnson as his congressional secretary and dispatched him to the northern towns to do political spadework. Soon after the special election of 1931, Johnson visited Sam Fore in Floresville.

It was an evening that Fore would always remember vividly and about which, later, he loved to reminisce when he visited the White House of Lyndon Johnson. After dinner, young Johnson had kicked off his shoes and stretched out on the Fores' living-room floor in stocking feet. Propped up by a pillow and sustained for hours by a jar of Mrs. Fore's cookies, Johnson talked on and on into the night, for more than four hours, as he consumed the cookies one by one. The intensity and determination and apparent brilliance of the young congressional aide impressed Fore considerably, and they began a lifelong friendship. As they came to know one another better, it was particularly Johnson's determination never to take no for an answer that impressed Fore. It was an instinct that Fore liked to think he shared with Johnson. From that first day when Lyndon Johnson lay on his living-room floor next to the oil stove that had a "giant burner," Fore felt Johnson had a similar mechanism within his makeup. For years to come, Fore's standard line in getting Johnson focused on a political problem was, "Now, Lyndon, turn on that giant burner!"

In the coming few years, Johnson returned to Floresville regularly for other "sock-foot reunions." He quickly got to know all the important personages in the town, such as the county clerk, and he would enfold them in his long arms on the street, in loud, unmistakable greeting. To Fore, it became quickly clear who, at least for the northern part of the district, was the real congressman. When Congressman Kleberg himself came to town, Lyndon Johnson led him around by the nose, whispering into the congressman's ear the names of those they encountered and occasioning Kleberg's duckfooted salutations. As Fore remembered it, Johnson would say with a hint of patronizing contempt, "Now, Mr. Dick, don't make any mistakes. On your left is Miss Patty Jo Craighead. Over there is Reverend Heacock. . . ."

In 1936, on the day John Connally, Sr., was elected to be the clerk of Wilson County, Johnson returned to Floresville once again. But he was now in Austin as the Texas director of Roosevelt's youth employment agency, the National Youth Administration. Young John Connally was away at the University of Texas, and he had gone to college, in part, because a stipend from Johnson's NYA had made it possible. Like over 900 UT students who had NYA grants, he earned seventeen cents an hour, but his job was better than most: he shelved books and typed at the library of the Texas Supreme Court. He knew well where his sustenance was coming from and who provided it. It was natural that the beneficiaries of the NYA stipends would view Lyndon Johnson as their hero, and John Connally was no exception. But there was a nine-year difference in their ages. Between the ages of seventeen and twenty-six, that was a huge gulf.

As he entered the University of Texas, Connally was just another tall, straight seventeen-year-old, with a fine face, a deep voice, and a shock of black hair. If his upbringing had been stark and full of hard work, it had been robust and healthy, and it imparted to young John Connally his expansiveness and his sense of fun. His awareness of poverty, to the extent that he had it at all, was subliminal, for there had been little in Wilson County to envy, little that was better than what the next family had. Still, he had developed a powerful drive to rise above the station of his tenant father, to amass land and wealth and power to protect himself from a return to the hard-scrabble existence of his youth. For now, that lay dormant in his subconscious.

Humble virtues had marked his early life: hard work, honesty, patriotism, the sort of values which later, when he presented them in a booming voice from the stump, were regarded by sophisticated listeners as the empty platitudes of a politician who had no real convictions. His upbringing also nurtured the view that the world was a dour, treacherous place, where adversity was the rule and where one rose above his given station only through merit and excellence and strength. That was the way it was supposed to be. The best would rise to the top. In the drive to be "number one," that tiresome and oft-repeated exhortation of politicians and football coaches, the greatness of America lay. If you became "number one" against the stiff and unforgiving competition, you were entitled, unabashedly, to the fruits. You were justified in protecting hard-won rewards against the host of less talented, less honest, less hard-working who were ready to snatch them from you.

★ 2 ★

University of Texas

IN THE 1930s, the University of Texas was a vibrant, rambunctious, sometimes outrageous place to be. It was The University, a grand mix of social classes, political ideologies, and religious beliefs that served as a powerful unifying force for the vast state of Texas. It was caught up in the frenzy of the New Deal. The social revolution that gripped America galvanized the students as well, and when Franklin Roosevelt spoke to the nation in a Fireside Chat, all the radios in Austin, including the students', were tuned in and the dulcet tones of the president's voice wafted through the trees.

The student body had topped 8,000 in 1933, when a well-groomed, excited, distinctly rustic John Connally arrived. The school seemed huge and daunting to him, as he stood in line next to an equally countrified boy from Rockwall, Texas, named Henry Wade. He laid down his thirty-dollar matriculation fee and an additional five dollars for the "blanket tax" which entitled him to a host of delights, including tickets to the football games and the productions of the main theatrical group, the Curtain Club, as well as subscriptions to the daily campus newspaper, the *Daily Texan*; the humor magazine, the *Ranger*; and the campus yearbook, the *Cactus*. The *Daily Texan* was already an unusually distinguished campus newspaper. Its quality came from the passion and the talent and the rowdiness of its student writers, rather than from any assiduous faculty guidance. The paper was totally independent, the more so for the good fortune that the journalism department on campus was

12

weak and incapable of helping or meddling. The *Ranger* attracted a handful of writers who later rose to national prominence. Robert Eckhardt was its editor in 1936–37 and later became the stalwart liberal congressman from Houston, and Charles Black wrote wicked, satirical poetry for the magazine before he got serious about constitutional law and became one of the nation's leading legal scholars. And John Henry Faulk, Johnnie Faulk then, wrote light pieces as the *Ranger*'s far-flung correspondent in such exotic places as Canebanks, Texas, before he went on to become well known as a humorist and folklorist.

Campus politics was, as at other state universities, a training ground for future politicians. Traditionally, the high posts in student government, such as the presidency of the Student Association and even the editorship of the *Daily Texan*, the *Cactus*, and the *Ranger*, were traded back and forth among members of the two most fashionable, and socially prominent, men's fraternities, Phi Delta Theta and Kappa Sigma. Votes were cast on personality and demeanor and style rather than on burning issues, although a pocketbook issue such as whether the blanket tax should be raised from $5 to $5.50 could exercise the campus. The exuberance and the humor and the excesses of youth were manifold.

As a response to the triviality of campus issues, a rowdy physics major named Jimmy Dibble, who was considered one of the two or three certifiable geniuses on campus, organized the Taciturnians. He ran for student office on the platform that, if elected, he would abolish student government forthwith and forever. To be elected as editor of the *Cactus* entitled the victor to the serious joy and prestige of choosing the Bluebonnet Belles, for the sizable beauty section of the yearbook, and the Good Fellows, one of the highest student honors.

John Connally threw himself into this lively swirl enthusiastically. He had a farm boy's pleasure and profound gratitude at being presented with such a grand array of delights. He gravitated immediately to the dramatic clubs: the Curtain Club and the Wesley Players, a national Methodist dramatic organization. For his oratorical interests, he joined the Atheneum Literary Society, and became its president in his second year of college. He proceeded to win the campus oratorical contest that year in competition against all the other literary societies on campus.

When Connally joined the Atheneum Literary Society he took part in a rich tradition. Forensic societies had been vital at the University of Texas since its inception. Indeed, the story was oft repeated that the Atheneum Society had held its first meeting the day before the first classes at the university convened in the wing of the Old State Capitol in 1883. In its earlier days, the members wore tuxedos for their sessions, which made all the more ridiculous the fare that was devoured so eagerly. It was a society whose earnest claim to existence might be to nurture poise under pressure, fast thinking, and clever disquisition, but it made no pretense to seriousness. The society convened once a week in the basement of the Law Building, and always began with one member stepping into the hall and proclaiming in his best and most important voice, "Oyez, oyez, oyez, the honorable Atheneum Literary Society is now in session." It was a signal honor to be chosen as the herald in the hallway, and an even greater honor to reenter the room and not be vilified for a weak and unworthy performance. John Connally was remembered as one of the best and least vilified of these heralds.

Connally's election as president of the society might have been a dubious distinction. The president was, by longstanding tradition, the target of impeachment proceedings at least twice a year. Generally, the offense was for the flagrant or inadvertent violation of Article 10, Section 2, of the Constitution. Since no one had ever read such an article in the Constitution or, for that matter, even knew what constitution was being referred to, Article 10, Section 2, became anything the hounds of impeachment divined it to be. Connally made a particularly good target as an official in the dock, for he was already cultivating his jutting jaw, his scowling expression, and his icy stare. He listened impassively, aloofly, coldly, as he was vilified as John "Bow-Down" Connally. In the face of charges, he adopted the thoroughly self-righteous pose of a man who would never lower himself to answer such scurrilous and unfair claptrap. He was equally dignified and humble when his defenders rose to eulogize his integrity and his sacred honor in flowery, stirring phrases. Then, in the moment everybody waited for breathlessly, the president would rise, but once and briefly, to defend himself.

Only occasionally was there ever a formal topic, such as the respective virtues of the English parliamentary system versus the American system of separation of powers. Instead, the society was more keen on such burning subjects as the best cure for cockroaches or, better, whether there was such a thing as a virtuous woman— and, if so, what could be done to cure that. When they could think of nothing to dispute, which was often, members were given to reciting heroic passages of their favorite poems. The themes of these perorations generally had to do with drunkenness and other youthful excesses (Hugh D'Arcy's poem "The Face on the Barroom Floor" was one favorite) when they were not exhortations to noble sacrifice or lofty principle. One member at this time, Jesse Villar-real, who later went on to become a distinguished professor of speech at UT, had adopted Longfellow's "Excelsior" as his standard, and he often set the tone for the meeting with grand flourishes and a rising voice that came to a crescendo with the sad and noble verse:

> "Oh stay," the maiden said
> "And rest
> "Thy weary head upon this breast!"
> A tear stood in his bright blue eye
> But still he answered, with a sigh,
> > "Excelsior!"

Connally's favorite was no less rousing nor melodramatic, for he combined a ditty called "The Hermit of Shark Tooth Shoal" with Robert Service's "The Shooting of Dan McGrew," and he could put the room into boisterous excitement.

In his third year Connally decided upon law as his formal course of study and began law school, for this melding of undergraduate with professional education was still possible in those days. At last, he joined a fraternity, a legal one. As a rube from Floresville he had scarcely been an exciting prospective pledge to the fraternities of "the better sort." Class sensibility was an aspect of university life that rankled not only Connally but other bright stars from the Texas hinterland. Jake Pickle from Big Spring in West Texas—later a congressman from Lyndon Johnson's original district—had organized a place on campus called Independence, and from that redoubt the bucolic upstarts staged a coup against the fraternity clique. Members of this rebellion included Bobbie Strauss from Lockhart (better known as Robert Strauss when he became the treasurer of the national Democratic party). He belonged to a poor boys' fraternity called Tejas, the first Spanish name of Texas. There was Joe Kilgore, from Brown County, then considered an ultra-liberal, before he went off to the war, but who turned sharply to the right and eventually gained the reputation of being one of the more conservative members of the U.S. Congress.

And there were two brilliant economics graduate students, C. Wright Mills and Creekmore Fath. Fath was a member of the Associated Independents, a group that enjoyed its working-class label as the "barbs"—short for "barbarians," a name given to them by the sophisticates of the fraternity clique. Fath would go on to be a youthful Roosevelt adviser during World War II and to hold other high posts in Washington, as his competitor, C. Wright Mills, went on to a literary calling. Pitted against these assorted barbarians, hicks, rubes, and upstarts were a smooth Phi Delt named Joe Greenhill, who edited the *Cactus* in 1937 and later became the chief justice of the Texas Supreme Court, and John V. Singleton, Jr., a frat man who was "pinned" to a lovely Tri Delt and Austin belle named Idanell Brill. Idanell Brill later threw him over to marry John Connally, and Singleton went on to become a Houston federal judge.

In sum, it was a talented crowd.

The intellectual life of the campus was dynamic. In the rare circumstance of Austin, shared only with Madison, Wisconsin, where the dominant, well-regarded state university is situated in a small state capital, academics and politics mixed in a heady brew. Jimmy Allred, the last and perhaps the only truly liberal Texas governor of this century, was in office. He was a passionate New Dealer and personally close to a number of university professors. Regularly, the governor entertained students from the university for dinner at the governor's mansion. Usually, their escort was Dr. Robert H. Montgomery, a highly popular, outgoing economics professor whose cult following included Creekmore Fath and C. Wright Mills. A black Scotsman who often talked of brandishing his old shillelagh whenever there was a world war or a Republican administration, Montgomery had an enormous, prominent nose and a magnificent orator's voice. He was known to the students as "the Doctor," and his course in corporate finance was one of the seminal experiences that all bright students of the day like John Connally considered a must. Montgomery's economic philosophy was distinctly New Deal, liberal but pragmatic, and he presented Roosevelt's social engineering to his classes favorably but without ideological dogmatism. He was a popular speaker at local organizations, and if he railed against monopoly in America, he invoked Lincoln and Jefferson rather than Marx or Norman Thomas on how the era of corruption would ensue when the wealth of the nation was concentrated in a few hands. "There is a lot of talk about the absurdity of plowing up cotton and killing pigs," he told the Austin Lions Club in 1936. "I agree with most folks that the idea is silly, but we must remember that before we had killed one pig, the US Steel Company had killed eighty-seven percent of its pig iron. Before we plowed under two rows of cotton, International Harvester had plowed under eighty-three percent of the cotton planters."

Montgomery's style, rather than his economic philosophy, fascinated students. His lectures were held in the largest auditorium of the university, and they were often attended by spectators who were there only for the show. He had long sideburns and a great shock of red hair; he wore concho belts and bolo ties, and his fingers were weighted with enormous bishop's rings, silver studded with turquoise, that had been given him by a Russian sword dancer who performed at the Troika night club in Washington, which Montgomery had frequented during his two-year stint at the beginning of the New Deal in Henry Wallace's Agriculture Department.

As he lectured, Montgomery would stride back and forth across the stage, and his lectures, laced with allusions to the Greeks and the Elizabethans, were often prompted simply by a student's question on some economic point at the beginning of the hour. By the mid-1930s, he fretted to friends that he was losing his grip on the students' affections, because the current crop no longer understood, much less appreciated, his allusions to Milton, or Greek mythology, or even the King James version of the Bible. At his home on Dillman Street, Montgomery and his wife, Gladys, often held soirees with his coterie of student disciples. He referred to his small cult as his "golden lads," a phrase he borrowed from Shakespeare's *Cymbeline*, but he never quoted the whole, sad line: "Golden lads and girls all must, / as chimney-sweepers, come to dust." Connally was not one of these golden lads, not one of Montgomery's anyway, for no one mistook him for an intellectual. But he did attend Montgomery's class, as did his future wife, Idanell Brill, as a necessary rite of passage.

There were more radical members of the faculty than Montgomery, even of the economics faculty. Among them was Clarence Ayres, an institutional economist who put the expansion of technology at the center of his economic analysis. He wrote a minor classic called *The Theory of Economic Progress*, whose theory of economic value was more influenced by Thorstein Veblen than by Karl Marx, as well as a shocking, libertine tract advocating free love. Ayres was in constant, if civil, conflict with the one avowed Marxist on the economics faculty, Edward Everett Hale (no kin to the nineteenth-century preacher and author of the Civil War classic *Man Without a Country*). But Hale was dry as dust, and he was careful to ground his course in comparative economic systems in solid scholarship, out of an abundance of caution. Texas was infamous for its political interference in academic affairs, and Hale knew it. He had no desire himself to become a man without a country. (Indeed, three economists would be fired from the UT faculty before World War II for the sin of attending an AFL-CIO convention.)

In October 1936, when John Connally presented himself as a candidate for the student assembly for the first time, two issues of academic freedom came to a climax in Austin. They riveted the campus, and both provided memorable lessons in democracy. The *Daily Texan* plugged away in its fine tradition of insolent and impertinent editorializing, evincing a healthy contempt for the shenanigans of Texas legislators. The term "leeches" was in political vogue on campus, and students freely applied the label to politicians and lobbyists who were seen as sucking dry the blood of Texas. When the *Daily Texan* ran an editorial savaging Congressman "Buck" Buchanan, Lyndon Johnson's predecessor in the Fourteenth District, under the headline LEECHES DON'T LIKE LIGHT, certain legislators had had enough. Under pressure from the capitol, the Board of Regents declared it would install a faculty supervisor to control excessive student opinion. On October 14, the faculty voted unanimously for the censorship, professing with grand sanctimony, "The Regents would much prefer a fine sense of editorial propriety to the restrictions that had to be imposed." The issue of a free press in a democracy was to be played out in the pure laboratory of the university.

About the harness of censorship, one would expect the students to be earnest and lacking in humor. In the Law School, where Connally labored as a second-year student to master First Amendment cases and participated in the moot court proceedings of the Hildebrand Law Society, the action by the regents became an object lesson. In moot court, the *Daily Texan* was sued for libel. The case arose when the *Texan* announced, incorrectly, the secret marriage of one Eva Belle Zale to J. A. Strut in Round Rock, Texas. When the paper discovered it was in error, it printed a retraction the next day. But the damage had been done. It was submitted that the fictitious Miss Zale was really engaged to a Mr. Alan Jones, and Jones, hearing the Strut rumor, turned a cold shoulder to the distraught Miss Zale. Engaging the firm of Nesbit, Connally, and Butler, Zale sued for libel. The characters and the plot were all made up, but the issue was real.

Nothing was too serious for the humor magazine, the *Ranger*, however. It reported that at great expense and labor it had solicited comments on the censorship of the *Daily Texan* from famous people. King Edward VIII was then breathless in his relationship with Mrs. Wallis Simpson, but Mrs. Simpson took time to comment, "I think it's disgraceful. If I ever did anything so low, I should expect to be crowned." And though Alf Landon had managed to carry only two states in the election of 1936, he rested up from his defeat and was quoted as saying of the *Daily Texan* censorship, "They couldn't get away with that in Maine—or in Vermont—the people are too intelligent!" The comments of Ernest Hemingway, Mae West, Shirley Temple, and Donald Duck, said the *Ranger*, had been censored.

Emerging in tandem with the censorship issue was another one, which brought out the uproarious, high-spirited bent of the student body. The purveyor of the good cheer was one Roy Miller, the notorious mayor of Corpus Christi, who was also unabashedly the chief lobbyist for the Texas Gulf Sulphur Company. If sulfur was the brimstone of biblical ill repute, it had also brought heavenly profit to a small cult of Texas prospectors. Shortly after the turn of the century, oil prospectors had discovered the Big Hill Sulphur Dome in Matagorda County, south of Houston, one of the richest and most chemically pure deposits ever found. As the uses of sulfuric acid multiplied, especially in the manufacture of weaponry in World War I, Texas Gulf Sulphur Company came to have a virtual monopoly on sulfur extraction, and it had an interlocking directorate between the house of J. P. Morgan and the house of Andrew Mellon. When the Texas legislature met, Roy Miller was the industry's wirepuller. Before the convening of each legislative session, Miller's practice was to engage a bank of forty rooms in the old Victorian Driskill and Austin hotels, and offer them free of charge to the convening legislators. In the days when legislators made five dollars a day for a 120-day legislative session, this briny generosity was much appreciated. Through little more than an outright payoff in kind, Miller and Texas Gulf Sulphur felt secure that its tax-free status would be protected.

Dr. R. H. Montgomery, who came from the county next door to Matagorda, Wharton County, where the huge Boling Dome and Long Point sulfur plants were situated, proposed a sulfur tax, for he found the Gulf Western Sulphur Company to be a paradigm of the monopoly system that was bad for America. (He developed this argument in a book entitled *The Brimstone Game*.) Roy Miller was mortified, and declared this suggestion to be nothing short of dangerous socialism. He persuaded his pocketed friends in the legislature that Reds were running wild on the UT campus. Not merely Montgomery, but the whole of the University of Texas should be investigated. If the students were not Communists—who would deny that some rapscallion had run across the football field that year flourishing a red flag?—well, then, by God, they were certainly atheists.

The *Ranger*, of course, was overjoyed with this sudden windfall of rich material. Under the naughty editorship of future U.S. Congressman Bob Eckhardt, the magazine saw a good chance to fulfill its charter: to "tweak our noses at the statues in our local park, to throw an occasional grenade, and to print our little propaganda sheet." In October it published its Communist number. Its cover was a scandalous taunt: a huge hammer and sickle against a red background; inside, it contained such useful features as a Communist alphabet: ("D is for dictator, a man of affairs / who'd kick his own grandmother down the stairs. . . . H is for hammer, which swung by the fist / deeply impresses the Capitalist. . . .") and a piece called "What Is Communism?" by Billyski Boonski, who had purportedly just returned from two days in Russia, where at the border "twelve long-bearded guards confiscated my grandmother (thinking this was a camera), tattooed a red flag on my forehead, sang the Internationale, and shot the conductor through the stomach."

On October 13 the committee to investigate un-Americanism on the UT campus convened. It was chaired by Joe Caldwell, a humorless, hatchet-faced attorney from Dimmitt County, whose mouth seemed to be forever frozen into a mean snarl. To students, he was the Torquemada of the piece. Caldwell professed to find it acceptable if professors merely taught the comparative principles of Communism and Fascism. (The lines between the two forms of government were blurred in the inquisition.) But he believed some professors were actually pointing out advantages of these foreign scourges, and at this practice he frowned. "If a complete vindication is returned," he exclaimed to the press, "parents will feel better about sending their children to the university." Upon this point there was to be considerable disagreement.

Students and townspeople thronged to the galleries, as the investigation was proclaimed to be, if not the greatest show on earth, certainly the greatest show in Texas. Even the governor, Jimmy Allred, did not want to miss it and took his place in the gallery at the opening session. Before the gavel came down, the students in the gallery broke into a boisterous chorus of "The Eyes of Texas," the university fight song. When Caldwell tried to stop this outrageous challenge to the dignity of the proceeding by calling in the sergeant at arms to quell the disturbance, a near-riot broke out.

Catcalls and boos poured over the proceeding, as a semblance of order was restored.

Among the first witnesses were students from a group called Progressive Democrats. They were questioned closely about their views on private property, a subject that made the Progressive Democrats especially touchy, since certain letters, later used as evidence in the hearing, had been stolen from their campus office, in a kind of harbinger of FBI activity in the 1960s. The first student on the stand freely admitted that he had once expressed the opinion that if oil was discovered on his farm he would give it all to a central store. In the Texas where huge oil reserves had just been discovered by enterprising wildcatters, this was a shockingly radical opinion. Had not the student once written a letter to a Dallas man who was "recognized as one of the leading radicals in Texas?" Caldwell asked.

"Well, that depends on who recognizes him," the student replied acerbically to thunderous cheers.

"When Norman Thomas spoke last year in Austin, did you hear him advocate racial equality for Negroes?"

"No, I didn't hear him say that," the student responded. "I do recall that he protested against the unfair treatment of the Negro race."

"Do you believe that there is a drift of the present form of government toward Communism or Fascism?"

"Well, I believe that when a legislature is directed by lobbyists, it's not my idea of an ideal democracy."

"What is your program for ending these things you say you don't like?"

The student pulled from his pocket his membership card in the Progressive Democrats and received permission to read its statement of purpose. It was language influenced by Dr. Montgomery, who was an adviser to the group and whose pamphlet entitled "Salvaging Democracy" was its inspiration.

"The function of our industrial order is to produce the most generous quantities of goods and services and to distribute them to the largest possible number of people. The individual's share in these goods and services should be determined by his efforts in producing them."

"Then you would have the actions of the individual dictated by government?" Caldwell prodded.

"The greatest political good is liberty," was the reply.

"Then instead of controlling the individual, you would have government control business?"

"Yes, to the extent that private monopoly is against public interest. The Supreme Court has been promoting this principle, but I would like to see it done by the Texas legislature."

"Then you believe in the abolition of the system of checks and balances?"

"No, sir. I believe that the people should have the final say."

"What he means," said another of the five-man panel, "is that there should be more balances and less checks."

The student was uncowed. "What I mean is that equality of opportunity in securing the essentials of life, health, education, and economic advancement must be provided for all."

It was no contest from the beginning. Several calmer, brighter heads in the legislature tried to stop the burlesque, for they were concerned that the legislature had opened itself to ridicule. "This investigation has done more to bring the Legislature to ridicule— and righteously—than any other ten acts in this session," exclaimed Roy Hofheinz (later a Houston judge and the builder of the Astrodome). "Last night I heard that young student give the platform of his organization. If that is Communism, then ninety-five percent of the members of this House are Communists!" But Hofheinz was roundly voted down, and the inquisition proceeded for two weeks.

Its high point was the calling of "the Doctor," Dr. Montgomery. He had received his summons to the hearing when he was in the midst of a lecture. A Texas Ranger had entered from the rear of the auditorium and marched to the lectern. Now, Montgomery was ushered into the capitol as a conquering hero by a phalanx of admirers, and when he entered the legislative chamber he received a standing ovation. From the opening shot, it was clear that Dr. Montgomery would not be an easy target.

"Dr. Montgomery, do you belong to any subversive organizations?"

"Just four."

"What are they?"

"The Methodist Church, the Masonic Lodge, the Rotary Club, and the American Legion."

"Now, Dr. Montgomery, is it true that your field of expertise is public utilities?"

"Yes."

"Have you ever worked for a utility?"

"No. And I have never laid an egg either, but I can make a hell of an omelet!"

The gallery burst into cheers. This was not going as Caldwell had hoped, so he attempted other avenues of inquiry. Montgomery stoutly defended his belief in democracy, denied that he ever espoused any of the "isms" under review, and asserted that he feared Fascism more than Communism in America.

"Dr. Montgomery, do you believe in private property?"

The question was a mistake. "I most certainly do," Montgomery replied. "There is no greater advocate of it in the country. I would like to see it extended to one hundred million people." The house broke into thunderous applause and cheers.

The proceeding droned on for days without drawing blood, and it was criticized as a canard in the press. Finding no evidence of Communism on campus, the inquisitors shifted to atheism and decided to call Dr. Clarence Ayres. Ayres's economic views were liberal, but his views on morals were positively radical. Besides his dry book on economic programs, there was his unrepentant book on sex, defending his dumping his first wife to run away with his secretary.

"Dr. Ayres, do you believe in God?" Caldwell began.

"Mr. Caldwell, do you mean a pantheistic or an anthropomorphic God?"

In late October, the house adopted a report clearing the university of all charges and denying Caldwell the right to extend the charade, or even to write a report. But the vote did not come until Dr. Montgomery was recalled as a witness, where he surprised the committee by presenting affidavits both charging the committee with receiving stolen property and exposing the whole proceeding as the brainstorm of sulfur lobbyist Roy Miller to get "his scalp" for his advocacy of a tax on sulfur.

This circus amused the students and compelled their attention, but it also conveyed a false impression. The student body as a whole was neither as liberal as the Progressive Democrats nor as sardonic as Dr. Montgomery. In fact, the majority tended to the conservative side, and that included the independents like John Connally, who gained their reputation for liberalism only by challenging the fraternity establishment, not for promoting any vision of a more egalitarian society in the wider world. Even Lyndon Johnson, who came to Austin in 1935 to become the Texas director of Roosevelt's youth employment agency, the National Youth Administration, and to nourish contacts for a congressional race in two years, was far from a pure liberal, although he cast himself as a Roosevelt man.

John Connally fell easily in with the majority consensus of the student body. He was no crusader for a conservative society, nor was he particularly displeased with the world as he found it. He wanted to rise out of the stratum of society where he began, not to be consumed with the problems that plagued that stratum. He had the good looks and the charisma to do it. To him, politics was a game. Personality and technique, style and political alliances were the main factors in winning, and winning was everything. By 1937 Connally had become a glamorous figure on campus, for he was beautiful to look at. He spoke well, in a deep, confident voice. He dressed well, often in tailored three-piece suits. Altogether, he projected a commanding, if occasionally arrogant, presence. A future political foe, Maury Maverick, Jr., would never forget the first time he saw John Connally. Maverick was not easily impressed. He was the son of the curmudgeon congressman from San Antonio, and he was himself a youthful curmudgeon. Maverick remembered a sweltering September day in 1938 when he attended an opening convocation of students, and Connally appeared, cool and unruffled, before the freshmen in one of his three-piece wool suits: "He was a striking man, vastly more impressive than anyone else, extraordinarily impressive." Maverick liked him immediately, and this feeling would stay with him grudgingly for the rest of his life. "I've fought every crazy conservative in this state," Maverick would say, "but John Connally never had the self-righteousness of the normal reactionary. He'd kick the shit out of you and later he would laugh about it. He would never invoke Jesus. To him, politics was a game, and he meant to win." It was an attitude cemented in college.

Besides declamation, Connally's other love in college was the theater. In 1936 he was elected president of the Curtain Club—the group that also featured Zachary Scott and Eli Wallach—and he was reelected to two successive terms. Quickly, he became a glamorous leading man, generally in plays that displayed a comic sensibility. He cut figure eights as Curly in Lynn Riggs's boisterous folk play *Green Grow the Lilacs* (the precursor of the classic *Oklahoma!*) and in an S. N. Behrman play, *Biography*, which two years earlier had featured Ina Claire on Broadway. In *Biography* he took the role of Kurt, a debonair but vindictive editor who was supposed to rant and rave in the best manner of comfortable radicals. In defining the spine of his character, Behrman imparted traits to which Connally could relate: an essential audacity which comes from having seen the worst happen, the hardiness of one who can be devastated by pity, the bitterness of seeing justice thwarted and tears unavailing in a youth, the intensity of a fanatic, and the carelessness of a vagabond. At everything else, instructed Behrman, Kurt was supposed to laugh.

Opposite Connally in *Biography* in the role of Slade Kinnicott, the role Una Merkel had in the film version of the play, was a lively campus beauty named Idanell Brill. In 1936 she had been voted a Bluebonnet Belle, and in 1937 the Texas Relay Queen as well as the representative of the University of Texas to the Sugar Bowl. Brill came from a large Austin family. Her father was a mild-mannered man who owned a saddle shop and was as often fishing on Lake Austin as selling leather in his shop. Her mother was a large, expansive woman who filled their rambling Austin home with games and fun and old costumes. Nellie Brill had lived the charmed life of a popular beauty with brains and spunk. She pledged the fashionable Tri Delt sorority when she arrived at the university, and soon after became "pinned" to the charmer from Delta Tau Delta and Waxahachie, Texas, John Singleton. ("Pinning" was that arcane preliminary to engagement, where the frat man bestows his bejeweled fraternity pin upon his beloved in a solemn ceremony of devotion.) In the theater, Nellie Brill took roles in *Post Road* and *Biography*. In a play called *College Widow* she played a wicked seductress who vamps the football hero on the way to a football game, and then she was a star socialite in *First Lady*, which spoofed Washington social life and which she may have remembered some years later when she became the brightest star in the otherwise bland cast of wives in Richard Nixon's cabinet.

Biography was a predictable success. The review in the *Daily Texan* took off with an unfair comparison to the Hollywood movie version. "The cinema schooled us to think that Robert Montgomery was Richard Kurt. John Connally is not Robert Montgomery, but why bring that up? Connally is as effective a Richard Kurt as we could ask from the Curtain Club, for Kurt has a mind poisoned with cynicism and only Marion Fronde could get beneath the surface of it. . . . Idanell Brill takes Una Merkel's role of Slade Kinnicott. She does just what you would expect: she gives the role the vigor and American feminine insouciance that is required." It did not take many Curtain Club productions before Nellie Brill had given back the pin to her frat man and was on the arm of the new Curtain Club president. This heightened Connally's stature further on campus.

In 1936 Jake Pickle had been elected president of the student body as the first independent to overcome the power of the frat clique. The independents were reelected in 1937, and when John Connally became the independent candidate in 1938 it appeared that a political dynasty was in the making. His announcement for the election was a mirror of the simple, direct statement his father had made in offering himself as the clerk of Wilson County. Young Connally thought he was qualified for the post he sought and, if elected, promised an honest, independent administration. Bobbie Strauss became his campaign manager. If Connally was opposed by Robert Eckhardt and Creekmore Fath, he was supported by Joe Kilgore and Jake Pickle and a host of other political activists. Though they could not know it, the real significance of the process lay in the forging of enduring political friendships, as later these men fell into the service of Lyndon Johnson.

On April 6, from a seven-man field, Connally lost the election by 18 votes to the candidate of the frat clique, but two days later, in the runoff, he swamped his opposition by 1,100 votes.

On the day the Connally victory was announced, another election was to be held on campus, and in many ways, it interested the student body more. There were five candidates for Sweetheart of Texas. For this distinction, no electioneering or campaigning was allowed, and the polls on campus were open for only five hours on the morning of the annual Roundup Ball. That morning the *Daily Texan* profiled the contenders. Each was allowed a two-adjective description of her qualifications under her picture. There were "sweet and delightful!," "poised and charming," "merry and scintillating," and "gracious and intriguing." The fifth was "gay and vivacious": Idanell Brill, five-foot-three, with blond hair and sparkling blue eyes.

The Roundup Ball featured one of the best Hollywood bands, George Hamilton and his "Music Box Music," and the theme was a musical retrospective. It began with the tango of 1913, moved to the Charleston of 1923 and the Black Bottom of 1928, and climaxed in the current rage, the "Big Apple," before the lights went down and George Hamilton swung into "You Are My Sweetheart" and then "The Eyes of Texas." Nellie Brill emerged to greet her court and her subjects. In the years to come there would be many other star-studded evenings when she and her future husband, John Connally, would enter the spotlight at Gregory Gym.

When in September 1938 the commanding figure of John Connally assumed the presidency of the student body, world events, hardly visible in Texas, were clouding the future. Connally appeared majestically before Maury Maverick and the other freshmen to wax poetic about Texas, and to dedicate his administration to instilling a new school spirit at the university and to avenging the loss in football to Texas A&M the year before. As he did so, half a world away, Adolf Hitler appeared in the Nuremberg night amid Albert Speer's cathedral of light to exhort thousands of well-disciplined Nazi soldiers to restore the Sudetenland to the Third Reich. As Hitler marched, Connally succeeded at long last in getting the city of Austin to put additional traffic lights on the "drag" of Guadalupe Street alongside the campus, in the interest of student safety, and in getting coeds as cheerleaders.

Hitler's rumblings impinged little upon the real concerns of the campus. The United States remained a neutral nation. Roosevelt himself had signed the Neutrality Act of 1935, which legitimized America's isolation and left the president constrained in his ability to support the Allies in the face of the Nazi menace. Of course, there was no draft. Nevertheless, the debate over American isolation was intensifying, and on the UT campus there were students who sensed what was coming. One of them was Charles Black, the future scholar of constitutional law. Black published a poem in the *Ranger* which trembled with youthful passion:

> Oh sirs! Oppress us till we squeal and howl
> With loathsome fees and levies monstrous foul!
>
> . . . .
>
> But do not, sirs, we humbly pray
> Force us to look upon the cursed day
> When strutting braggarts on our college hill
> Perform that silly mummery called drill!
>
> . . . .
>
> Plant not here to stink upon our breath
> The Tree of War, whose blood-red fruit is Death!

Most students could not imagine a military emergency affecting them. To them, Hitler was a ridiculous figure, and John Connally was among those who saw how funny Hitler was.

In early October, after the Munich Agreement had been signed, and Hitler had taken charge triumphantly of the Sudetenland, a student named Jimmy Dibrell lost the chairmanship of the student Judiciary Council, and as a result he announced that he was "seceding" from the Student Association to form the "Studaten Party." He promptly declared himself to be "Der Furor" and dispatched a telegram to Hitler in Berlin which read, "Aid badly needed for Studatenland! [Signed] Der Furor."

John Connally, as president, was not about to ignore this fun and rushed to the aid of Der Furor. He issued a statement which began, "In order that my stand shall be questioned no longer, and that my name shall never again be linked with the majority seeking to oppress the plebiscite, I humbly beseech His Excellency, Der Furor, Minister Plenipotentiary of Herr Hitler, to Stewed-Aten-land to accord me the pleasure and privilege of being numbered among the Stewed-Atens. . . . —JOHN CONNALLY, Candidate for Der Furor of Studatenland."

By early 1939 Connally had been at the University of Texas for nearly six years. His pursuit of the student body presidency had required a lighter academic load, and the consequence was that he had to stay at the university an extra year. Still, if he felt he was slipping behind his contemporaries, it did not show. He worked at a breakneck pace, scurrying about from one activity to the next. When the secretary of an Austin law office tried to contact him on the university campus, it took her three days. Message after message was left at a host of campus offices. Connally had been seen recently at them all, but no one knew for sure when he would turn up again. In a comment that was meant to conjure up a bawdy image, Jake Pickle once remarked at a black-tie roast of Connally that John Connally always came to class from a different direction.

Meanwhile, in January 1939, the outrageous Pappy O'Daniel was inaugurated as the governor of Texas in the UT football stadium. A crowd of 65,000 turned out for the lurid display of cornpone virtues. O'Daniel was a wildly successful flour salesman who went on the radio singing the praises of his product, called Hill Billy Flour. The broadcasts became a Texas staple, and their opening line, "The Light Crust Dough Boys Are on the Air!," became a standard greeting. Over time, the broadcasts expanded into sentimental commentaries on various homespun subjects, generally with a simple religious exhortation, and Pappy accompanied his message with sad hillbilly songs. Now an energetic forty years old, Ole Pappy was said to have the knack for making people laugh or cry at will. It is small wonder that Connally saw all politicians, including Hitler, as slightly ridiculous.

O'Daniel's political career had begun when he read a letter on the air from a blind man who urged him to run for governor, and Pappy asked his audience whether he should. Fifty-five thousand letters poured in that week to beseech him to make the race. So he hitched up the sound truck he had used in advertising his flour and made a thirty-six-day campaign swing. Superb businessman that he was, O'Daniel knew that whatever happened to his dalliance in politics, it would be great for business, and it was. Preaching the

Ten Commandments and the Golden Rule, he attracted enormous crowds, outdrawing his "experienced" competition forty to one. He financed the campaign by sending his children, Micky-Wicky and Molly, into the crowd with small flour barrels marked FLOUR NOT PORK to take up a collection, and the coins poured in.

As an impressionable political neophyte who supported O'Daniel's opponent, young John Connally had attended an O'Daniel rally in Waco, and he was impressed. "When I saw twenty-five thousand people assembled, and I saw those little flour barrels passed around, and I saw the money come out of those pockets of people who didn't have much to begin with, I knew everyone else was in trouble."

At one speech, O'Daniel spied a twenty-dollar bill in the bucket, held the bill up, and wanted to know who gave it so he could return it. "Nickels, dimes, and quarters only, please," he demanded. (Of course, *he* had put the twenty-dollar bill in the barrel himself.) When the swing was over, he was $800 in the black, a sum which he ostentatiously donated to a flood relief program. The papers excoriated him. The professional politicians spurned him. It was hard to find any decent, intelligent person who would admit that he was for Pappy. When criticized, he fell into the hillbilly song "Please Pass the Biscuits, Pappy," and this led to much grinding of teeth among his opponents. After his election, which he won with an outright majority against eleven opponents, thereby claiming the governorship without a runoff, O'Daniel asked the people of Texas to try him for two years. "I'm not saying all Mr. Roosevelt's plans are sound and right," he said, "but as long as he has the national grab bag open, I'm gonna grab all I can for Texas."

At the conclusion of the inauguration ceremony at the university, O'Daniel's Hillbilly Boys, with his son Patty-Boy on the fiddle and Micky-Wicky on the banjo, gave a rousing rendition of "The Old Rugged Cross" and then of the song composed by the new governor, called "Beautiful Texas." If one had been fortunate enough to witness this remarkable spectacle, he had the honor to invoke a much-used line in Texas: "I've been to everything now—the World Series, Barnum & Bailey's Circus, the inauguration of W. Lee O'Daniel to be Texas governor, and to Molly's wedding, too."

For John Connally, life on campus had become frantic and glamorous and distracting. How driven and overextended he was showed when the first semester grades came out. Even in his university days, Connally was a polarizing figure. He had intense rivals, and they included Creekmore Fath, the future Roosevelt adviser, and Robert Eckhardt, the future congressman. When Eckhardt and Fath noticed that Connally had not passed the requisite ten hours needed to participate in campus activities, they went immediately to Joe Greenhill, the future chief justice of the Texas Supreme Court, who was then getting his groundings on the student judicial council. Fath and Eckhardt demanded a meeting of the council to consider this violation of Article 10, Section 2, of the Constitution.

Before the hearing could take place, Connally resigned his presidency. His resignation statement was both sad and pompous. He hoped only that he had not offended anyone and that he had treated everyone fairly, but circumstances beyond his control (studying?) had conspired against him. In handing in his resignation, he said, "I do so with a feeling of bravery I do not possess. I do so with a reluctance that only I can feel. Perhaps I can best explain by quoting Petain at Verdun: 'Here I stand. I can do no other.' " For someone who was being forced to quit because he had flunked a few courses, it was indeed a grand construction of the events.

His departure from student politics might have been ignominious, but there were grander opportunities brewing in the real world. Lyndon Johnson was in his second term in Congress, and he was fretting about his Washington staff. A demanding, overbearing boss, Johnson was not satisfied with the team he had first gathered in his Capitol Hill office—he was rarely satisfied—and he badly needed an energetic "secretary" (as legislative assistants were still called) who could stand up to the pace. In the spring of 1939, President Roosevelt had called a special session of Congress to consider the Neutrality Act, and Johnson felt that his staff problem was more acute than ever. He went to Austin to do some scouting.

At the Stephen F. Austin Hotel that spring, Lyndon Johnson had lunch with J. R. Parten, an oilman and a member of the university's Board of Regents, and complained about his problem. "Major" Parten was a fascinating contradiction of a man, who combined his multimillion-dollar oil, ranching, and sulfur businesses with ardent New Deal politics. In two years Parten had gotten over the poor first impression that Johnson had made on him. Parten had been introduced to Johnson in then-Governor Jimmy Allred's office, and asked the new congressman what his platform was. "Oh, I'm going to Washington to help Roosevelt pack the Supreme Court," LBJ replied, and Parten, a Jeffersonian in all matters except oil and gas, was horrified.

In 1939 Parten, as the chairman of the Board of Regents for the university, had some acquaintance with the outstanding students on campus. He had met young John Connally at a number of university functions and had been impressed with him. In the summer of 1938 Parten had observed Connally when the youth did volunteer work in the runoff campaign of Gerald Mann to be the Texas attorney general. (Mann, too, was a fascinating figure. Known in Texas as the star of the SMU football team, where he was the "Little Red Arrow," he had worked his way through Harvard Law School before he returned home to become one of Governor Allred's assistant attorneys general.) Thus, when Johnson complained to J. R. Parten and asked for a recommendation, Connally came to Parten's mind. As it happened, the congressman had had another recommendation, this time from the dean of the university, for another UT student, named Walter Jenkins. When Jenkins was approached on campus, he had to ask who Lyndon Johnson was.

Connally, at least, was better informed. He had his preliminary interview with the old Austin fixer, Alvin Wirtz, and then, at Wirtz's suggestion, he wrote to Congressman Johnson directly. He stressed his many scholastic achievements, including the fact that he was one of only seven UT students in the *Who's Who of American Colleges and Universities* and that he had been inducted into the honorary campus organization known as the Friars, a "signal honor," as Connally put it, which anyone from the University of Texas would appreciate. He stressed his typing and his stenographic skills as well, and wrote:

"Mr. Johnson, I feel that it would be a distinct privilege to work for you and with you, and though at the present time I am unacquainted with all of your duties and responsibilities, I assure you that it would be a pleasure as well as a duty of mine to become conversant with them and aid you in their fulfillment to the best of my ability."

Stiff and formal though the letter may have been, it was effective. Johnson called Sam Fore, Jr., in Floresville.

"Sam, I've got a boy from your town who has applied to me for a job. His name is John Connally. What do you know about him?"

"He's a mighty fine boy, and he's got lots on the ball," Fore replied. "You'd better take him quick."

Lyndon and John

MANY YEARS LATER, when John Connally presented himself to Congress for his confirmation to be secretary of the navy and, later, to be secretary of the treasury, he noted in passing that as a young man he had worked in the "Neutrality Congress." Mentioning this only in passing minimized the significance of the item in his vita. To be in Washington from 1939 to 1941, to be young, politically active, and bright, was an extraordinary and deeply formative experience. When Connally came to Washington to join the adult world, an epoch of American history was drawing to a close.

For a century and a half the United States had enjoyed its remoteness from the rest of the world, luxuriating in the safety of the oceans, flattering itself that in its youth and vibrancy it represented a model of peace and justice, consoling itself that its mere geographical size deterred foreign aggression. America was, in fact and in spirit, a neutral nation. Its historic shunning of foreign entanglements was central to the national sensibility. Once in American history—in the passage of the Embargo and Non-Intercourse acts in the early 1800s—the zeal to avoid foreign entanglement had produced the opposite effect. In those acts, the use of economic embargo against the belligerents in the Napoleonic Wars had actually brought war upon the United States, the War of 1812. More recently, the involvement in World War I had come only after German U-boats had deliberately sunk three American ships in March 1917, apparently leaving the American president no choice after such a brazen act of belligerence. Between the years 1939 and 1941 that was all to change.

Another event in August 1939 signaled a change in the course of human events. On August 2, Albert Einstein wrote a letter to President Roosevelt raising the possibility of an atomic bomb. Citing the work of Enrico Fermi and Leo Szilard, he wrote, "This new phenomenon could also lead to the construction of bombs, and it is conceivable—though much less certain—that extremely powerful bombs of a new type may thus be constructed. A single bomb of this type, carried by boat or exploded in a port, might very well destroy the whole port together with some of the surrounding territory." But the opportunity to construct a doomsday weapon was not the compelling aspect of the Einstein letter. Rather, it was the worry that Germany had the technical skill, the scientists, the laboratories, and the uranium to go forward with the weapon, and, Einstein suggested, she was going forward. Years later Einstein deeply regretted this letter, calling it the "one great mistake of my life." As his biographer, Ronald Clark, points out, Einstein's was a double mistake, for the German competition never materialized, while the American efforts, in part prompted by this letter, led directly to the nuclear world as we now know it.

Still, in 1939, neutrality was the central issue of the time for Americans, and it would be vigorously debated in the United States Congress. In signing the Neutrality Act four years before, Roosevelt had worried about the law's "inflexible" arms embargo section, which made it illegal for the United States to ship any arms or munitions to belligerent nations in a state of war, for he recalled the boomerang effect of the Embargo and Non-Intercourse acts of the early nineteenth century: "It is conceivable that the wholly inflexible provisions of this act might have exactly the opposite effect from that which was intended. In other words, the inflexible provisions might drag us into war instead of keeping us out." These were the words of his 1935 statement, which he would accent in the summer of 1939, but he had signed the Neutrality Act and pronounced its overall purpose as "wholly excellent." Indeed, in the year of its passage, when Mussolini invaded Abyssinia, FDR invoked it immediately.

The following year, in 1936, when the civil war in Spain broke out, Roosevelt invoked the act again, even though a domestic civil war in Spain was technically outside the strict purview of the act. And in May 1937, in a joint resolution, Congress not only overwhelmingly reaffirmed the Neutrality Act, but specifically extended it to cover the Spanish conflict.

In Congress, there were two ringing voices of isolationism: in the Senate, William Borah of Idaho, and in the House, the elegant Mr. Hamilton Fish of Westchester County, New York. During the debate over the widening of the Neutrality Act in 1937, Fish had given a radio address in which he drew the comparison between an energetic, peace-loving, noble America and the "old nations" of Europe, intent upon blood feuds. The savagery of the Spanish Civil War was akin to the Duke of Alva's purge of the Dutch in the 1500s, Fish suggested, adding, "You can almost hear the beating of the wings of death this evening as she hovers over Europe." War had returned to barbarism, and the tragedy, to Fish, was that instead of promoting peace, nations were building up their supplies of weapons, presaging a war of even greater savagery. "If the old nations of the world insist on arming to the teeth and going to war, it is their war and not ours," he said. "We are prepared to spend millions for defense but not one dollar to send American soldiers to foreign lands to fight other peoples' battles. We are opposed to all entangling alliances, entrance into the League of Nations, war sanctions and commitments. We propose to avoid taking part in all ancient blood feuds and boundary disputes or picking the chestnuts out of the fire for foreign nations. Our policy is and must be to mind our own business, stay at home, and try to solve our own problems for the best interest of all the American people."

After Congress passed the extension of the Neutrality Act in 1937, Senator Borah rose to point out that the congressional sentiment was nearly unanimous, that it had the approval of the executive branch, that it represented the will of the great majority of the American people. The United States stood as a symbol for peace in the world, said Borah, "a power standing not for force, not for cruelty and injustice, but for fair dealing among nations, for reason and justice. We will not only have added honor to our own national happiness, to our own people, but we will have rendered to all nations and to all peoples a service far greater than it will ever be possible for us to render by joining any nation or nations in carrying on war."

Senator Borah overstated the case. The neutrality bill of 1937 was an intensely controversial matter, and it occasioned impassioned debate and dissension within a significant segment of the press and the public. The *Washington Post*, for example, asserted that the bill was rigid and restrictive, unfair in its application, and immoral in not drawing a distinction between the aggressor and the victim in a foreign conflict. The so-called neutrality bill was a "compound of ignorance, timidity, and ineffective isolation," wrote the *Post*. Sharp-tongued Dorothy Thompson railed even more acidly against the proposed legislation. It would, she said, "tie our hands, limit our influence, and restrict our power which now in the time of peace may be used to help prevent such a war from occurring." Time and again the opponents invoked the Kellogg Briand Pact of 1928, which condemned aggression. Wrote Dorothy Thompson, "We, the greatest, strongest single nation on earth announce, by inference, that there is no such thing as 'right' or 'wrong' and no such thing as morality. In advance of all possible hostility we perform the greatest Pontius Pilate act in history."

In attempting to undercut the critics who were claiming that American inaction in the face of foreign war was to favor the land-based power of Germany, the proponents of the measure put in a cash-and-carry provision, providing that a belligerent power could buy American goods only on a cash basis, carrying away its American purchases in its own ships. This was meant to tilt the balance back in favor of Britain, for she had the cash, the ships to transport the American goods she bought, and the strong navy to protect those ships on the high seas. But if this provision favored Britain over Germany, it equally favored Japan, which itself as an island nation had an impressive and fast-expanding navy. Japan had invaded China and in 1937 was slaughtering millions of Chinese in Nanjing.

Thus, for the most powerful nation in the world to remain strictly neutral in any meaningful sense was a very complicated matter indeed. Neutrality was scarcely a simple scale which might remain in equilibrium by adding no weight to either side. It was a woefully complicated gadget, made up of many parts that did not necessarily mesh, where dense bulk on one side was meant to equilibrate with slippery fluid on the other. It might exist only in the mind of the imaginative but naive policymaker, and, more broadly, in the collective romanticism of America.

"Suppose there is a war involving Japan and England, and Japan manages to blockade British and Dutch possessions in the Far East, which is the chief source of our rubber supply," Dorothy Thompson hypothesized. "Without rubber our automobile industry collapses. Will we stand by in such a case?"

As events in Europe moved quickly in the summer of 1939, FDR began a campaign to repeal the Neutrality Act, particularly its arms embargo section. In June the House turned this campaign aside, voting to retain the embargo. FDR went to the Senate. On July 18 he invited Senate leaders to the White House. "I made a terrible blunder signing the Neutrality Act in 1935," he confessed. "We base our need for changing the present law on the ground that it works in Hitler's favor. War may come at any time." By a narrow vote of twelve to eleven, the Senate Foreign Relations Committee tabled the measure, putting it over to the next session, which was not to start until January 1940. In early August, Neville Chamberlain personally requested that Britain be able to purchase the secret American bombsight called the Norden, and FDR was forced to reply, "Britain's request can not be granted unless the sight desired by the British Government is made available to all other governments at the same time."

On the day after Hitler invaded Poland, Roosevelt spoke of the historic precedent of American neutrality that went back to the days of George Washington. In a Fireside Chat he warned against anyone who would talk "thoughtlessly or falsely" about American armies going to Europe. He promised an official reaffirming proclamation on neutrality. But he meant the opposite, for the worm was turning, and it turned within one phrase in the speech—a phrase against which his own secretary of state, Cordell Hull, had vehemently argued: "This nation will remain a neutral nation, but I cannot ask that every American remain neutral in thought as well. Even a neutral has the right to take account of facts. Even a neutral cannot be asked to close his mind or conscience."

In the words of the FDR biographer Ted Morgan, FDR was "a navigator attempting to turn a large ship around in a narrow channel against a stiff current." The president could not wait until January for Congress to take up the Neutrality Act again, because the arms embargo provisions were now "vitally dangerous." Britain needed arms and ships and bullets fast. The best way to keep America out of war might be to ensure that the defense of Britain was successful. On September 21 the president called for an extraordinary session of Congress. It was to convene solely for a great debate on the arms embargo, for that provision was not consistent with traditional American neutrality but an aberration from it, akin to the Embargo and Non-Intercourse laws that had sucked America into the War of 1812.

"Let no group assume the exclusive label of the peace bloc," Roosevelt told a joint session. "We all belong to it."

The days ahead were perilous, and there was now the probability, rather than the mere possibility, of wide-scale global warfare. To repeal the arms embargo would return America to a real and traditional neutrality. A repeal offered a greater chance for the country to remain at peace.

The stage was set for a grand, noble, and ennobling debate.

★

But John Connally was not to be ennobled by it. There was no great awareness on his part that he was blessed, at this critical, formative moment in his life, to be present at a turning point in American history. He was coming to work for Lyndon Johnson, a junior congressman only nine years older than Connally, whose understanding of foreign policy was rudimentary at best and whose interest in it was almost nonexistent. Lyndon Johnson in 1939 was a kid on the make. He was brash and loud and overbearing, a braggart who wore his ambition for higher office a bit too openly, and he was not infrequently a liar. In his first two years he had managed to alienate many in the Texas delegation, as he talked much in the hallways and the cloakrooms, but did virtually nothing of note on the floor of the House. As a youthful freshman with no power or influence, he had attempted to ingratiate himself with Roosevelt, writing sweet notes to the president and requesting meetings which somehow were never held. On the Naval Affairs Committee, he had a bit more success with its chairman, Carl Vinson, who seemed more susceptible to Southern syrup, as a fellow freshman legislator put it, but Johnson remained an "ensign" on the committee, allowed to ask only the occasional brief question of committee witnesses.

It was not until July 1939, just as Connally was getting settled in the Johnson office, that Johnson succeeded in seeing Roosevelt in the White House. Even then he was a last-minute add-on to a meeting scheduled for the wealthy Texas newspaper publisher Charles Marsh.

In his constituency as well, Johnson was isolated, for he represented the only district of Texas which could loosely be described as liberal. At this stage of Johnson's career, he possessed no passion toward the poor, the weak, or the colored. To be sure, he made the occasional statement that later was widely invoked by biographers in attempts to show an early genesis for his presidential accomplishments in the field of civil rights. In a radio address on January 23, 1938, for example, he was high on slum clearance. "Last Christmas, when all over the world people were celebrating . . . I took a walk here in Austin, and there I found people living in such squalor that Christmas Day was to them just one more day of filth." The photograph of Johnson strolling around the Santa Rita public housing project in Austin, whose construction he had supported, was given wide circulation. And it is true that Johnson was mildly upset when Mary Bethune came to Austin in the mid-1930s and could find a place neither to eat nor to sleep. To a colleague, Johnson quipped, "Oh, hell, what can you do about it? Just try to do the best you can."

To Luther Jones, who worked for Johnson in his first term but who was anxious to escape to the Justice Department as soon as possible, Johnson's posture toward minorities was "pure expediency." Jones admired Johnson's drive and executive genius but he remained clear-eyed amidst the posthumous perfuming of Johnson's historical reputation. He felt that Johnson became "enamored" of civil rights only when he became a national figure, and then did "wonderful things for the country." But not early on. Creekmore Fath, the scholarly Austin attorney who was deeply involved in Democratic party politics in Texas all through the Johnson era, was more blunt: "If you look at Lyndon Johnson's voting record from 1937 to 1957, it was racist. He was horrified that his maid, Ophelia, had to pee on the side of the road in John Stennis's Mississippi, and that's what got him into [civil rights]."

In those days Texas remained distinctly Southern. In Congress, the Texas delegation was dominated by titans—Sam Rayburn and Roosevelt's vice president, John Nance Garner. Rayburn was the son of a Confederate cavalryman, and he took this heritage seriously. A picture of Robert E. Lee always had an honored place on his office wall, and to him, the Republican Party remained the party of Generals Sherman and Grant. "As long as I honor the memory of the Confederate dead and revere the gallant devotion of my Confederate father to the Southland, I will never vote for electors of the Republican Party, which sent the carpetbagger and the scalawag to prostrate the South with saber and sword," he once said. It would become a widely accepted commonplace in Texas that Sam Rayburn set his sights only on the speakership as his ultimate goal because he was convinced that the presidency was foreclosed to him and any other Southerner.

Garner, in turn, manifested his racial attitudes in his treatment of the Mexican-Americans who worked on his vast pecan ranch in

Uvalde, Texas. Hispanics made up more than half of Uvalde's population, and the rubicund Garner, with big hat and lash, was the classic overseer. "They are not troublesome people," he once observed of his laborers, "unless they become Americanized." But that was not likely to happen, not in Uvalde, anyway. "The sheriff can make them do anything." In Garner's pecan operation the sweatshop paid a penny a pound for shelled nuts, enabling a good man to make a dollar a day at knuckle-busting work.

In 1939, however, Garner seemed to be the likely successor to Roosevelt, if Roosevelt decided not to challenge the American tradition of a two-term presidency. In the early polls to determine preferences without Roosevelt in the race, Garner had forty-five percent. Had his candidacy ever become really serious—it was truncated by Roosevelt's decision to run again—his methods on his Uvalde ranch would surely have undercut him, showing him as the tyrannical Texas foreman who cared nothing for the common man.

The rest of the Texas delegation provided no other elevating model for young John Connally. Richard Kleberg, of the King Ranch, was still in Congress and as concerned as ever about his handicap on the golf course at the Burning Tree Country Club. Maury Maverick, the only genuine liberal voice of the Texas delegation, was gone, having been defeated for reelection in 1938. Martin Dies, Jr., represented an East Texas district and was becoming a Texas harbinger of Senator Joseph McCarthy. In 1939 he became the first chairman of the House Un-American Activities Committee, whose proceedings Roosevelt called un-American and sordid, as Dies charged first that 500 government employees were Communists and then upped the figure to 1,800. Harold Ickes would observe that the names were always the same and redoubled themselves, and that Dies was like the man who stuck his chewing gum under the desk and periodically brought the same piece out to chew again.

In Lyndon Johnson, Connally found himself in the presence of the quintessential political animal. Johnson was totally absorbed in political technique rather than substance. Nothing that did not have some political objective seemed to interest him. He could not sit still at the movies and generally left early. He did not go to plays. He did not read books about religion or philosophy, not, as Luther Jones pointed out, because these subjects did not interest him but rather because they did not apply to anything he needed to do. Johnson was the doer, not the dreamer. He was concerned with the present, not the future. "He was keeping his eye open for the main chance always," Luther Jones observed, and he was happiest when he was dead on in the middle of the political spectrum, for he had embraced the political maxim that you should never get "too far out in front of the people." Parochial matters dominated. A dam on the Lower Colorado River of Texas was far more central in his constituents' consciousness than Nazi troops in the upper steppes of Russia. Since a Texas dam was the most important thing to Johnson, so it must be to those around him. If he did not dream, they were not to do so either. If he did not worry about the future, why should they? If political technique was all-important, so be it.

When Johnson lived at the Dodge Hotel and was a congressional secretary for Congressman Kleberg, he was an inveterate talker. The most memorable discussions were not about the New Deal program that was changing America so profoundly but about the political figures who knew how to sway the masses. Huey Long was his special fascination. When Long's book *Every Man a King* came out, it was the only book that his friends ever remembered Johnson discussing chapter and verse, for, as Luther Jones remarked, there was much in Long that attracted Johnson. Only Long's penchant for overspending distressed Johnson, not his demagoguery. Besides Long, Johnson's heroes were scarcely men of substance and vision. Nor did his heroes have common qualities, apart from their ability to sway men toward any end, regardless of its merit. If Johnson admired Long, who built his career on challenging Standard Oil, he equally admired Senator Joe Bailey, the Texas senator at the turn of the century who had allowed himself to be bought by Standard Oil. Another scandal-ridden Texan interested him, "Farmer Jim" Ferguson, the governor of Texas in 1917 who had faced impeachment when Johnson's father was in the state legislature. What Johnson seemed to draw out of these three cases was that here were men who knew how to overcome scandal through the force of their personalities, the power of their oratory, the solidity of their political friendships.

Within the Texas political culture surrounding John Connally at this time of his life, the values of bald political ambition, of political technique over substance, of obsessive anticommunism, of simplistic xenophobia, of Southernness, of patrician and even racist attitudes, and of bare-knuckled political power plays were transcendent.

The preeminent value, however, was loyalty. To Johnson, loyalty was a living, breathing, pulsating verity. It was the foundation of political life, its chief tenet, the very glue of the process. He talked about it. He insisted upon it. He never forgave its transgression. "Everything was subordinate to loyalty," said Luther Jones. "You must be loyal. That dominated Johnson's thinking. He could forgive you if you were stupid, but he'd never forgive you if you displayed disloyalty. That was a cardinal, a mortal sin. This was reiterated many, many times in different ways." Johnson had never forgotten a moment in the spring of 1935, when he was still secretary to Richard Kleberg, and he had contracted a virulent pneumonia that might have killed him. As he awoke in his hospital bed, dizzy from a drug haze, he perceived first the glow of a cigarette end, and then a bald pate, and finally the harried, distraught visage of Sam Rayburn. Rayburn had been there all night, so distracted that he had smoked one cigarette after another through his vigil, and his front was littered with ash.

"Now, why would this man, Sam Rayburn, one of the most powerful men in Congress, come to the bedside of this young man, this lowly secretary?" Johnson had asked himself, and then answered. "Loyalty. Loyalty is what counts in politics."

There was to be one other lesson Connally would learn in the drama that was played out before his impressionable eyes in 1939 and 1940. Sam Rayburn had sought to maintain a collegiality among the Texans in Congress, and the vehicle for this home-state solidarity was his well-known Wednesday luncheon in the Speaker's Dining Room for the Texans, known wryly as the "Board of Education." Besides the two senators and twenty-one representatives from the state, Vice President Garner was always welcome as the Texan of highest distinction in government and now, in 1939, a very real possibility to become the first Texan and the first Southern president. But if Garner was high in the national polls, he was very low in the esteem of Franklin Roosevelt. In fact, the two had fallen out so completely that they were no longer on speaking terms. Garner spent a considerable portion of his year planning his takeover from his living room in Uvalde. (Each corner of that living room was piled to the ceiling with cases of Jack Daniel's whiskey, gifts of lobbyists who knew his taste. He drank a quart every day, starting around seven in the morning.) When Garner was in Washington, he worked to undercut the president's policies in Congress, with the exception of his help in the attempt to repeal the Neutrality Act. Late in 1939, the ruddy-faced Garner announced formally for the presidency. Roosevelt's comment to his cabinet on the announcement was: "I see that the Vice President has thrown his bottle—I mean his hat—into the ring."

The real public attack on Garner came not from Roosevelt but from the bushy-browed labor leader John L. Lewis, however. Just as Connally was becoming Johnson's first assistant in the congressional office, Lewis created a sensation in Congress with an appearance before the House Labor Committee. The committee was considering bills that would weaken labor support on wages and hours, and Lewis knew where the impetus for such antilabor moves originated. "The genesis of this campaign against labor is not hard to find. It emanates from a labor-baiting, poker-playing, whiskey-drinking evil old man whose name is Garner," Lewis bellowed. "Some gentleman may rise in horror and say, 'Why, Mr. Lewis has made a personal attack on Mr. Garner.' Yes, I make a personal attack on Mr. Garner because Garner's knife is searching for the quivering, pulsating heart of labor!" The Texas delegation did rise in horror and hastened to the defense of its most distinguished citizen. Meeting in Rayburn's office, they drafted a resolution which denied that the vice president was either a heavy drinker or an enemy of labor.

For Lyndon Johnson, a man who forever declared loyalty as the glue of politics, here was an awkward case of divided loyalty, and he pondered which way to go. On the one hand, he desperately wanted to be Roosevelt's main man in Texas. If Johnson went with the president against the Speaker, his standing with the White House could take a quantum leap, even if he found himself isolated still farther from the Texas delegation and from his mentor. On the other hand, he was a Texan and a protégé of Sam Rayburn, and Rayburn was counting on a solid show of Lone Star chauvinism. Johnson refused to sign the statement. He told the delegation he could not subscribe to the language of the statement because everyone knew Garner was a heavy drinker and was bitterly opposed to labor. To deny this would make the delegation look foolish. The dramatic moment of the confrontation came when Rayburn took the young congressman aside and tried to force him to sign. Rayburn lost his temper and fell into one of his terrifying white rages.

"Lyndon, I am looking you right in the eye," Rayburn seethed.

"And I am looking you right back in the eye," Johnson replied.

Later, Johnson would cast this episode as an elaborate tale of political courage.

The lesson, of course, was that in a conflict between state loyalty and presidential demands, the state comes second—if you want to get ahead. And Johnson was to get way ahead by this one stand. Access to the president and to the White House suddenly opened up. Though Johnson had been unable to get into the Oval Office for two years, now, suddenly, he was there frequently and almost at will. Indeed, he was beyond the Oval Office and into the presidential bedroom.

Dorothy Jackson (soon to be Dorothy Nicols) has described how Johnson treated his White House visits. "He went in the back door, which was his favorite way of going, and he would go before the president was up, seeing him in his bedroom. The Boss always typed a little thing for [the President] for whatever project he was up there on. It was always one page and just as short as it could be, because Mr. Johnson said that if you can't say it on one page, you're just no good."

One of the little things that Johnson wanted from the president in this period was support for a naval air station at Corpus Christi, and for his friends George and Herman Brown, of the Brown and Root construction company, to build it. This Johnson got in the winter of 1939. Brown and Root got the contract without the hassle of competitive bids. From that point forward, Lyndon Johnson never had to worry about funds for his political campaigns. Brown and Root was always there. This nexus between access, power, and money was a lesson John Connally also took to heart.

★

Connally came to Washington with another University of Texas recruit, the studious, intense, buttoned-down Walter Jenkins from Wichita Falls, who had worked in John Connally's presidential campaign at the university, but whose knowledge of the wider political world was limited. The graduates took up residence in the Dodge Hotel, a musty old Washington institution which catered to aging widows and young congressional assistants and which was located kitty-cornered from Union Station. The basement of the Dodge was reserved for the congressional types. Lyndon Johnson himself had lived there six years before. The place represented a certain initiation to Washington life. Popular with congressional aides for its rate of twenty-five dollars a month and its convenience to the Capitol, it had a basement segregated by sex, with the bachelors rooming on one hallway and the single women on another unconnected hallway. It was notorious for its clanking steampipes, which kept up a steady drumbeat through the winter, and the noise was matched only by heated, excited political talk that filled the ducts late into the night.

Even the occasional congressman lived there, like the colorful Maury Maverick from San Antonio, who loved to take a gaggle of congressional secretaries around the corner to dinner at Child's Restaurant and shock them with his radical views. But Maverick had been defrocked in 1938, and was about to stand trial in San Antonio for fraud.

Connally took up residence at the Dodge with an exalted status. He had a car, which made him something of a man about town, especially once a month, when the Texas Society held its formal dances at the Mayflower Hotel. Dorothy Jackson (whose brother had been Connally's roommate in college) arrived in September 1939, and Connally felt that she, too, deserved a special initiation to Washington life. On her first night in town, he and Jenkins insisted upon taking her to the Gayety, a scandalous burlesque house owned by the scurrilous impresario of the tease, Colonel Jimmy Lake, otherwise known as the Mayor of Ninth Street. It was said that no other burlesque house in America played to such a distinguished audience of diplomats and legislators (Oliver Wendell Holmes had been a regular in the 1920s), but not everyone in Congress was amused. Senator Theodore Bilbo, of Mississippi, did his bit for public morals by trying to shut the place down. "It is driving our boys to evil," Senator Bilbo told a public hearing on child welfare. "Even Senate pages are frequenting the place. I cannot speak too much of its elaborate evil. I wish you women would do something about it."

"Senator, we women are trying to do something about it," replied the proper witness at the hearing, the president of a women's organization, "but you will find when you go into the matter further that our city fathers give us little encouragement."

In times past, the titles of the shows had tended to the camp—*Anatomy and Cleopatra, Follies Brassiere,* and *Panties Inferno*—but the Gayety had been a start for some greats like Bert Lahr, Gypsy Rose Lee, Al Jolson, Joe E. Brown, and Will Rogers. The centerpiece of the Gayety in those days was a platinum blonde named Hinda Wassau, whose real name was Wausauskas, and the Mayor of Ninth Street would profess that Hinda had actually originated striptease. Hinda had been acclaimed as "Washington's Adopted Daughter," and she had, according to the management, "that strange something" which brought her out of the back line. Nor was she above wrapping herself in the flag, as was, and is, the fashion in Washington. A few years later she would join the WAACs. The report in the *Washington Post* read:

> That homey little lady of the Gayety, Hinda Wassau, one of the few people in overcrowded Washington who is really

taking up space by public demand, was touched by the naked white flame of patriotism yesterday.

The thought has been shimmying through her mind for a long time and yesterday, while dressing after an act at the Gayety, where she periodically builds public morale by removing the world's cares, she announced her decision to join the WAACs. It isn't boredom in her success that is making La Wassau restless. "I don't want to hold any office," she announced. "I just want to start fresh from scratch and go as far as I can."

"I don't know whether we ought to do this or not, Dorothy," Connally said with mock modesty. "It's rough. I warn you. It's *rough!*" Rough by 1939 standards. The Gayety closed in 1950, the victim, so the commentators said, of television and the plunging neckline.

But Dorothy Jackson, prim and correct with her hair pulled back in a librarian's bun, was a good sport. She survived her initiation, going on to live at the Dodge for the year and a half before her marriage, along with Jenkins, Connally, and two other Johnson staffers before them, Luther Jones and Gene Latimer.

Around the Dodge, Connally became somewhat notorious for his narcissism. He was particularly fascinated by his own hair, and he would, by Luther Jones's account, stand for hours before a mirror brushing it. "He'd look at his hair, and he'd brush it, and he'd brush it, and he'd brush it. Oh boy, he'd lovingly caress it. If we'd kid him about it, he'd say, 'Well, this will guarantee that it will never come out. It will never be thin. I'm going to keep it like this all my life.' " When Luther Jones made this observation years later, it was after Connally was a well-known figure, and he added, "That is his hair today, I think. It's not a wig, is it?"

Connally, Jenkins, and Jackson were to learn early that Lyndon Johnson was using up his staff like paper clips and then discarding them. For a time before these three arrived, Sherman Birdwell had been Johnson's first secretary, and the Boss had hounded him unmercifully about the slowness of his typing, working him so hard that his weight dropped from 165 to 130 pounds. When it was clear that Birdwell was about to crack up, he was dispatched back to Texas and put out to the pasture of the Texas civil service. The bard of the Johnson office was a former Oklahoma newspaperman and Maury Maverick speechwriter named Herbert Henderson. Considered brilliant and indispensable, he wrote the sensitive letters like condolences to the wealthy and the powerful as well as Johnson's speeches. The latter was something of a thankless task, since Johnson seemed to freeze up with a printed text no matter how poetic the words, and he lost all his personal warmth. Henderson was an alcoholic, whose drinking grew worse in the Johnson operation, and not infrequently he would drop from sight for weeks. Once when that happened, Johnson asked the FBI to find him. Latimer, in turn, had been a debating student of Johnson's when LBJ was a teacher in Cotulla, Texas, and he was Johnson's secretary when Connally and the others joined the staff in the summer of 1939. But in August 1939 Latimer had a bona fide nervous breakdown and had to be relieved. In a tearful, childlike departure, he said to Johnson, "You never said I did anything wrong, but you never said I did anything right. It seems as if in a year you might have said . . .," and his voice trailed off.

Latimer's breakdown was the event that propelled Connally into the position of first secretary to Johnson earlier than might have been expected. There were those who saw Connally, even at the age of twenty-two, as a younger Lyndon Johnson. Physically, they had similarities, at least in height and elephantine ears, although Connally was considerably more beautiful to look at. They had the same confident, brassy air, and it would not be long before the younger, malleable Connally would adopt the physical mannerisms and gestures of Lyndon Johnson. They came from similar roots, although Connally's were more humble. In entering this dizzying maelstrom, Connally's strength was that he knew who he was. He had none of Johnson's raging insecurities. In his presidential years, Johnson was given to prefacing some complaint to the Ivy League products from the State Department with the line: "I'm just a poor country boy who went to a small state teacher's college, but . . ." John Connally would never utter such a thing, for he wished to forget, rather than remember, his roots. He had risen to the very top of the prestigious state university, not some parochial teacher's college, and at *his* university, he had exchanged his provincial rawness for a studied elegance. He was highly sought after for employment when he graduated—by top Austin law firms and by the state attorney general. If Johnson did not treat him properly, he had other immediate prospects. Hard work was one thing; lack of respect was another. It was Johnson's intuition that in Connally he had a special find whom he could not exploit contemptuously, if he wished to keep him, and it was Connally's unspoken understanding that he could quickly move laterally if he had to. This understanding between them started the relationship off on the right foot, and made it last a lifetime. It was a relationship of equals. Indeed, John Connally is the only individual in the Johnson circle whom Johnson ever treated as an equal, and he did so from the beginning.

Still, in that very commanding presence that Connally projected early lay the basic problem of his career. People looked at him, and they saw Lyndon Johnson nine years younger. This helped Connally in his early career, but plagued him fatally later on.

It began in 1939. After Johnson made Connally his secretary, the congressman received a congratulatory note from Judge S. S. Slatton, a Civil Appeals judge in San Antonio. Judge Slatton praised LBJ on his wise selection and added, "John reminds me of Lyndon at Cotulla"—a reference to Johnson's teacher days—"and I know you two will render a great service." It was as if they were the Tenth District's political twin towers.

"John is with me now in Washington and is doing a fine job," Johnson replied to the judge. "I feel I have someone with me who will grow and progress and increase his usefulness as he grasps the opportunity which lies before him to serve our Texas folks."

What Lyndon Johnson lacked in vision, he more than made up for in sheer physical energy. Long hours, from early in the morning to past midnight, were the norm, as well as time on the weekends. Letters were his obsession. From his days as Kleberg's secretary, Johnson had enshrined an inflexible rule: letters were to be answered on the day they were received. "It was worse than adultery to leave a letter unanswered," Gene Latimer said. In marked contrast to the stiff, patrician Kleberg, Johnson had a talent for the informal letter. His missives had an almost oral tone, as if the congressman were there grabbing your lapels, and he wished to impart the style to his staff. They were expected to learn his pet phrases and, once they were learned, the congressman did not have to dictate his letters at all. "Ultimately no dictations were required," Luther Jones observed. "He'd just sit there and make a few comments. 'Say yes.' 'Say no.' 'Put him off.' 'Butter him up.' In due time, we developed a set of systems, so that I knew what he wanted. But at first I wrote literally hundreds of letters over. And he had no compunction at all about making you write them over, even if you had to stay until midnight. You handed him fifty, sixty letters at five o'clock, and he might mark out every one of them."

Johnson's technique was to make his staff members compete, pointing out to one staffer that another was working faster. Pitting one underling against another was an aspect of what later, within the Johnson cult, became known as the Johnson "treatment," but pitting a young man against himself was also part of the treatment. The Boss might wander by a young assistant's desk and say, "I hope your *mind* is not as cluttered as that." When, in terror, the assistant had swept the desk clean, Johnson might return later and say, "I hope your mind is not as *empty* as that."

When the regular correspondence was finished, Johnson initiated a separate mountain of it altogether: congratulatory cards and letters to new mothers and newlyweds, to award recipients at Rotary and Kiwanis clubs, and even to the graduates of the high schools in the district, meaning that each letter had to be unique, lest the kids compare them.

Connally fell right in with the system, and soon oversaw it. It was just the way the Boss wanted it. When the congressman was out of town Connally generally led his communications to the Boss with the all-important "letter count." March 8, 1940: "Dear Boss: We have put out 56 letters today. We answered every letter we have received. . . ." March 9, 1940: "Dear Boss: Today was a rather uneventful day here in the office. We put out 54 letters. We haven't left the office all day—despite the fact that we haven't turned out the biggest day's work by any means. . . ."

So comprehensive was the Johnson letter mill that it even included a weekly letter from Johnson to his mother, Rebekah. These letters have become of particular interest to Johnson biographers, especially those with a psychological bent. But the documents expose the perils of biography. "There have been a lot of ridiculous ideas about Lyndon Johnson's mother . . . about her influence, about his need to please her," Gene Latimer has said. "Doris Kearns, for example, she must be absolutely out of her mind! Kearns talks a lot [in *Lyndon Johnson and the American Dream*] about that relationship and his letters to her. Well, what Kearns didn't know was that he never had time to write his mother from Washington. That was my job. I was assigned every week to write a two-page letter to his mama . . . you know, a family letter like I'd write to my own mother. It was typewritten. He'd sign it and away it would go."

With so much paperwork to churn out, a regular congressional staff did not suffice. So Johnson began to muster a cadre of bright UT graduates and put them in patronage jobs around Capitol Hill to supplement his regulars. It was a group that would support Johnson for many years to come; naturally its members became associated with him. But it was as much a Connally crowd as a

Johnson crowd, if not more. Connally was the recruiter, the catalyst, and the sergeant major. Connally friends were hired as elevator operators, Capitol policemen, and gallery doorkeepers. When they had finished their hours at the gallery door or the button panel, they went to their real jobs in Johnson's office. Jake Pickle and John V. Singleton, Jr., the latter being Connally's old rival at the university for the attentions of Nellie Brill, came into the fraternity this way.

If Johnson's superhuman office demands drove some to drink and others to the sanitarium, they scarred still others in milder ways. During this time John Singleton, for example, would have an experience that would permanently affect his personal habits and permanently tarnish the image of Lyndon Johnson in his mind, even though Johnson eventually became his benefactor. Brought to Washington as a jackleg Capitol policeman, Singleton lived in the Dodge Hotel with Pickle, who was also a cop. Given his bent for organization, Singleton proposed to reorganize the chaotic office files and was given the go-ahead. It was, of course, a tedious, time-consuming job, and after midnight he got tired and retreated to the Dodge for a few hours' sleep, stacking the remaining files on the floor between two chairs. He expected to be back before 6:00, since Johnson generally called in at 7:30, when Singleton was expected to have read the morning mail and be ready to report on it. Predictably, the young man overslept and, so the legend goes, woke up in a cold sweat. When he raced to the office he found the office floor bare.

"Where are all the papers?" Singleton cried in stark terror.

"We don't know. Where are our files?" Pickle shot back.

Soon enough, it was clear that the maid had come in at six and swept up the files, throwing them in the trash. Lyndon Johnson stormed in and came "absolutely unglued," to use Singleton's phrase, and his rage at Singleton's negligence was shared by the normally gracious Lady Bird. The upshot was that the young lawyer rushed frantically to the huge trash bin in the basement of the Cannon Building, and for the next three days stood waist deep in trash, searching for the precious Johnson letters, finding one here and there, and failing to recover most. Lyndon Johnson never forgot, much less forgave, the transgression (although he did appoint Singleton to the federal bench). Into his retirement, Judge Singleton has a visceral abhorrence of leaving anything important on the floor.

This story notwithstanding, it is the testimony of those who survived his rages that Lyndon Johnson could be fun to be around. The testing often had a jocular, kidding edge. For those who objected that some Johnson wish could not be fulfilled, he established the "I Can't Do It Club," or ICDIC, which had a membership card and even an elaborate citation. This served to prod the honoree (or to shame him) to greater heights of effort, and it often worked wonders.

To all who are present shall come greetings:

Recognizing his recent achievements and reposing confidence and trust in the abilities and qualifications of Charles Marsh consistently to discover the fire escape down which he can run, the forty reasons why it can't be done, thereby demonstrating that nothing can be done:

Now, therefore, I hereby anoint and welcome him to the venerable and mystic order of the I.C.D.I.C. by and in virtue of Section 17 of the ancient fraternity of I Can't Do It Club.

By which appointment, he is now entitled to all the disabilities, immunities, and impotencies appertaining to the brotherhood.

In testimony hereof I have hereunto signed my name and caused the great seal of the Order to be affixed, this third day of April in the year of laissez faire 1940.

_____

Grand Exalted Pish Posh

Attest_____
Administrative Assistant to the Grand Exalted Pish Posh

The Pish Posh was a consummate mimic who could adopt the mannerisms and basso profundo voices of all the dominant figures on the Hill. He was a skilled storyteller whose standard tales grew more elaborate in their repetition. In their embellishment the stories were transformed to make an apt point, until they became three times as long over the years. To the sophisticated Northeasterners, Johnson sought to make the Texas Hill Country into a mythical Oz-like place, and at Washington parties he dominated with his romanticization of his homeplace, giving quarter to no one else in the room. Johnson dominated in the way that, years later, Connally could electrify a room with his sheer masculine, sculptured presence.

Johnson was also a good dancer who always made sure to dance with and charm the wives of those he wished to impress. His enthusiasm was boundless and contagious, and it instilled in his office a sense of challenge and mission, as well as the profound feeling that here was a young politician going places, if in the end those were places where no one wanted to be.

To Luther Jones, who worked for Johnson in his freshman term, Johnson had "an extra something" that made him appear a "man of destiny." It was chemical, Jones thought, probably due to an "overactive thyroid" . . . or mechanical, for to the staff Johnson was a "jet engine in pants." And Johnson had another quality that made the survivors in his entourage adore him. In those who were loyal to him, Johnson overlooked weakness, and he stuck with many of them through incompetence and stupidity.

Even those who had been done in by Johnson could love him later. Gene Latimer, for example, who had been driven to the psychiatrist's couch, would later accentuate Johnson's sensitivity and sympathy during Latimer's emotional distress. "Biographers and news media alike have libelously stated that Lyndon Johnson treated his staff with demands amounting to inhumanity and brutality," Latimer said later in an impassioned apologia. "If this below-the-belt charge had any foundation, I wonder why we have not heard more about it from those who worked for him. Lyndon Johnson was hard and tough, extremely so, but no one under him worked harder than he did himself. Far from being ruthless to his employees, their welfare was very important to him. He was extremely sentimental about people who were close to him. I wish those carpers could have seen him as I did, driving himself late at night, his right hand wrapped in a hand towel to keep blood from dripping from a gash, signing a mountain of letters, when each signature made him suffer."

There is, of course, another way to look at this. By alternately driving and soothing, berating and entertaining, browbeating and charming and overwhelming his staff, Johnson instilled in them a crippling dependency. It is a method of control, salting love and commitment with fear, that in modern times we have understood best in the methods and the madness of religious cult leaders. To work for Lyndon Johnson was to join a cult. It was to become Lyndon's boy, and to stay Lyndon's boy into your dotage. The obverse was Lyndon, the father. Just as Johnson himself sought in powerful, older men like Sam Rayburn a son-to-father relationship, so to his younger staff did he advance his own position as the collective father. That could be shattering, and it could be debilitating. It made one feel part of something special, just as it robbed one of the ability to think for himself.

After World War II, Connally was to receive a letter from

Norman Heine, who had worked peripherally in the Johnson congressional office during the Neutrality Congress, but who had decided he could not return after the war.

"Really, John, as much as I admire and respect LBJ, I [can not] go back to work for him," Heine wrote in 1946.

> I felt before I left that I was treated not as an adult and an intelligent person, but as a child and an inferior. I've found that you either love LBJ and take him or you love LBJ and you don't take him. To me, there are many in his entourage who are weaklings and too content to depend on him and his ability to supply their means of living. Too many of them, I've felt, care honestly nothing about the man, but they're too damned scared to show their feelings because they might have to shift for themselves. While I was in the Navy, I often wondered whether I could get along on my own or not. It became something of an obsession with me that I must. The only way I'd ever work for Lyndon again is to feel, beyond a shadow of a doubt, that I was actually needed by him, and be sure in my own mind that it was not I who needed him.

Heine was not the only person who understood the perils of dependency. Most of the Johnson staff understood it. The question was how to deal with it. Sherman Birdwell, Connally's predecessor as Johnson's secretary, was to compare Johnson's role with his staff to the Texas system of the *patrón*, where the owner of a vast ranch had his peons over whose welfare he exercised total control, tyrannically or benignly. " 'You stay with me and instead of social security, you can depend on me for medication and care, food and shelter the rest of your life,' " Birdwell said of Johnson's management style. "He meant it. I'm sure as long as he had anything, I would share in it. But you don't want to have this feeling of dependency, and that's the reason I wanted to get into something that I owned a part of, and as it grew, I could grow with it."

How Connally could grow as long as he remained the overseer of Johnson's congressional ranch was now his problem. In two years on Capitol Hill, he had learned the rules of politics according to Lyndon Johnson. He accepted them simply as the way things were. It was a narrow education, which overlooked larger lessons to be drawn from the sweeping events of the time, events which were being influenced by bigger Texans than Lyndon Johnson.

★ 4 ★

"If Jack Were Only Here"

DURING THE GREAT NEUTRALITY DEBATE, Texas was represented from an unlikely quarter by the formidable Sam Rayburn. After his early years in Congress, Rayburn rarely took the floor to address the House, and almost never to speak at length, much less with churning passion. Rather, he was rightly known for his parliamentary maneuvers, his backstage horse-trading, his ceremonial raps of the gavel, and his grim, balding presence as part of the backdrop for a presidential speech to Congress. But when he was some months away from realizing the dream of his life—to become Speaker of the House—he entered the neutrality debate with a force and an eloquence that were extraordinary. His speech was a bona fide event. In arguing that the president be liberated from the binding strictures of the Neutrality Act, he brought the House membership to its feet.

In the summer of 1939 the House had first considered a repeal of the arms embargo section of the Neutrality Act, as President Roosevelt requested, and Rayburn and Hamilton Fish were to engage in a clash of giants over it. The exchange took place a month before Fish was to make an utter fool of himself by trundling off to Germany, meeting with Nazi leaders, and vacationing in Ribbentrop's castle. Over there, he was to proclaim Germany's claims to be just, and, once back, he was to promote an organization called National Committee to Keep America Out of Foreign Wars. At a convention of the group in October 1939, Fish would ask rhetorically, "Who made our foreign policy? Where did it originate?" But the response was not rhetorical. The audience roared back, "The Jews! The Yiddies! The Kikes!"

In the debate in the summer of 1939, however, Fish's voice of isolation had to be reckoned with, and Rayburn meant to do it. For the rapt House, Rayburn recalled that he had been a member on April 6, 1917, when war was declared at three o'clock in the morning. That night and that vote remained the most anguishing of his career. Now, they approached a vote no less anguishing. Moments later, Fish would bring the other side of the House to its feet when he agreed with the gentleman from Texas on only one thing—that the world was on the verge of war. Again, Fish conjured up his avian image of the angel of death flapping its wings loudly over Europe. Rayburn took up the issue of national morality: "Is it immoral to ship a gun to China so that a Chinaman may protect his sacred fireside from invasion and from the murder or ravage that may be committed upon his wife and upon his children?" If the applause was thunderous for that, it was no less so when Fish put forward the counterargument: "If we must go to war, it must be in defense of the United States of America and not in the defense of the munition makers and war profiteers."

That had been in July. Now it was late October, and the mood of the country was changing. Hitler was firmly entrenched in Poland, and though the American people still wanted to stay out of the European war, the question was whether the arms embargo provision of the Neutrality Act helped or hurt that goal. On October 27, the Senate voted sixty-three to thirty to repeal the embargo. Bowing to the concerns over the parallel to the American entry into World War I, the Senate bill specifically barred American ships, as well as American citizens, from the war zone. It was now up to the House of Representatives to transform the Senate proposals into law.

Again Sam Rayburn took the rostrum, and he admonished the members not to interrupt him, for he did not intend to yield. He was a magnificent, intimidating figure. He began with a change of argument from the August colloquy with Hamilton Fish; this time he asserted boldly that he did not believe America to be on the verge of war or "anywhere near it." Upon the parallel to the American entry into World War I, Rayburn was especially eloquent, for he spoke as one who had been in the chamber during the debate twenty-two years before: "When [in 1917] there occurred a loss of life and the violation of rights we then claimed, I saw this country converted from a peace to a war mind in sixty days. Five million men were called to arms, and two million of them went across the sea. We stand today in the backwash of that great conflict. Hopes were blasted and the faiths of lifetimes were blotted out, and they never returned. I pray God that as a member of this body I may never be called on again to move an army under this flag."

The repeal of the arms embargo in November 1939 marked the first major turn by the United States toward becoming an active player in the effort to stop Hitler. The next—a mandatory peacetime draft—would be taken a year later in the summer and fall of 1940. The selective service was naturally of particular interest to a towering twenty-two-year-old man in his prime. Congress was debating his future. Legislation for the draft was introduced in Congress in June 1940. Given the still-strong isolationist sentiment, Roosevelt wanted to tread lightly. A military buildup had been under way since May. It amounted to over a billion dollars in the form of tanks and guns—tanks and guns with no men to man them.

For Connally, the president's statements were clear enough. The politicians were shifting the country onto a war footing. Furthermore, Roosevelt's language was an elegant appeal to a young man's patriotism. American men were soft and needed to be physically hardened. In Europe there were armies seven times as large as America's, and their troops could march thirty miles in a day. The president doubted that the jackleg American forces of 500,000 could march fifteen miles in a day. This was, said the president, the cause of youth. It was a bold challenge to American manhood.

On September 16 Congress finally passed the Selective Service Law. In signing the law, the president sought to tie it to basic traditions of American history and of common law, conjuring up the image of the tough American youth in Revolutionary times, rallying to the defense of his fireside. "In colonial times, the average American had his flintlock and knew how to use it," Roosevelt said. Modern life did not emphasize the skills and the toughness demanded of soldiers. The draft also broadened and enriched the American concept of citizenship, the president asserted, as it became a fundamental obligation in a democracy. To John Connally and his generation, this appeal had an irresistible ring.

During the bitter debates over selective service, Connally had begun a campaign of his own. He sought a commission in the Naval Reserve. His boss, Lyndon Johnson, was already a lieutenant commander in the Naval Reserve and a member of the Naval Affairs Committee of the House. There was a Texas tradition of serving in the navy, and with Johnson behind him, a commission seemed assured. A portfolio of favorable letters from distinguished Texans was gathered to recommend him, and they were sent directly to the secretary of the navy, Frank Knox. Among his recommenders were the ex-governor of Texas, Jimmy Allred; Congressman Carl Vinson; the senator from Texas, Morris Sheppard; Ernest O. Thompson, the commissioner of the Texas Railroad Commission; J. R. Parten, the oilman; and, of course, Lyndon Johnson himself, who wrote of Connally's "executive potentialities" and of the "unusual amount of responsibility and authority" that Connally had borne in the Johnson office: "In my experience as a Member of Congress, I have naturally come into contact with hundreds of outstanding young men from all over our country, and of all of them, I consider John Connally the most promising. John has worked closely with me in my duties as a member of the Naval Affairs Committee and has received valuable insight into the problems and objectives of the United States Navy. He has shown himself to be brilliantly capable of meeting any situation."

In the summer of 1940, when it might have seemed to John Connally that the entire American government—perhaps the entire world—was pondering his fate, other things were on his mind. He had become engaged to Nellie Brill, and she was coming to Washington! Lady Bird Johnson was going to drive back to the capital from Texas in the Johnson jalopy toward the end of the summer along with Sugar Critz Pickle, the talkative wife of another Johnson aide, Jake Pickle, and it was suggested that Nellie travel with them. It was a merry, zany trip. Sugar Pickle never stopped talking; Lady Bird was transported by the beauty of the Ozarks and the Great Smokies; and Nellie Brill, this prom queen by whom the other two were fascinated, seemed quiet and shy and a bit guarded, as she wondered what kind of crowd this was which she had agreed to join.

In Washington, Nellie found her fiancé deeply engaged in the process of raising money for Democratic candidates who were up for election in the fall, and she joined him in an empty office with scarcely more than a typewriter, and began her political education. Lyndon Johnson had been assigned this important fund-raising job by Sam Rayburn, and he saw its potential to advance his stature among his Democratic colleagues. To the extent that he could muster large political contributions, Johnson appreciated the debt and gratitude in which he would be held by successful Democratic candidates. John and Nellie became the central figures in the effort. It was here that Connally first proved himself effective in persuading businessmen to open their pocketbooks, the talent that was to serve him well throughout his political career. And it was also here that he learned to drop zeroes when he spoke of political contributions, for that was the way the real professionals, like Lyndon Johnson, talked about them. "Paul has sent five," Johnson wrote Rayburn in October about an anonymous contributor. "I had hoped he would send five times as much." To the outsider, this could become confusing, and once in a future campaign, that confusion redounded very handsomely to Connally's benefit. For he would go to see one Harris Melasky, an attorney from Taylor, Texas, who represented a number of East Texas wildcatters.

"How much do you need, John?" Melasky asked.

"Ten," Connally replied with uncustomary modesty, for the campaign was so strapped that it needed a thousand dollars immediately.

"Well, my partner is out hunting in the West, and I can't get in touch with him by phone," Melasky said, apparently taken aback. "I feel I have to talk to him first."

"But Harris," Connally protested, "we can't even pay the rent!"

"Well, okay. If that's all you need." And he wrote out a check—for $10,000! "There's more when that's gone," the donor added.

As John and Nellie did the spadework, Johnson gained the recognition as a master of the political process. The Johnson "treatment" was becoming better known, in which its practitioner would stand up in your face and simply wear you down with the sheer dogged relentlessness of his argument. Bruce Catton, the columnist and Civil War chronicler, wrote after the election in which the Democrats unexpectedly gained rather than lost seats, "The Democrats gained in strength in the House instead of taking the heavy loss they were doped to take. The chief reason was that the party found a new miracle worker—the youthful and energetic Congressman Lyndon Johnson."

In the Johnson office on Capitol Hill, high spirits reigned after the election of 1940, and the addition of Nellie Connally to the circle had much to do with it. She was funny and independent and a bit zany, a "frustrated actress" as she would sometimes confess, and she would work her frustrations out by involving herself with a community theater and even shaming the various players in the office into office skits. Taking her material from a book of melodramas and dragooning even the normally shy Lady Bird into her productions, Nellie became the exacting director of such office classics as "My Mother Was a Lady, or . . . If Jack Were Only Here," which were immortalized on film, set to the ragtime piano of silent movies, and later narrated by Lady Bird. Lady Bird starred in a skit called "Heaven Will Protect the Working Girl," the story of a farm girl who goes to seek her fortune in the big, wicked city, where she has her first date with a hefty, mustached dandy (played drolly by a colleague with the fine stage name of J. B. Brumbelow). Dressed in a tight-fitting, floor-length lace gown and a huge Edith Wharton hat tilted at an alluring angle—a costume for which Nellie had scoured the attics of Washington—Lady Bird was directed sternly and hilariously by Nellie through the climactic scene where the villain, Brumbelow, with a decidedly wicked gleam in his eye, first reaches over and pats Lady Bird's hand and then suggests the unthinkable! In shock, Lady Bird stands up, eyes skyward and jaw turned away, at the effrontery. "He had asked me if I would like a *demitasse*," the narrator says. "I didn't know what it was, but I assumed it was something dreadful." The director orders a cut to a Victorian snapshot. Brumbelow must have assuaged her. "Believe it or not, heaven did protect the working girl, and so they were married."

And so, in December of 1940, John Connally and Nellie Brill were married as well. The ceremony was in Austin's First Methodist Church, and the society column in the Austin paper reported importantly that Congressman Lyndon Johnson was the best man. In fact, Johnson had encountered a last-minute hitch and wired his apologies profusely, adding, "There is no one who has greater affection for you both than I or who wishes you both greater success. Have a grand honeymoon and a Merry Christmas." If the Austin paper was wrong about the best man in the Connally wedding, it was at least right about the bride's dress. She wore ivory Duchess satin, drawn along medieval lines and appointed with a sweetheart neck of corded puffing and leg-of-mutton sleeves.

Actually, the Boss was not sentimental about such ceremonies if they conflicted with work. After all, Johnson himself had had no formal society wedding but had forced his marriage to Lady Bird on an impulse, using a dime-store ring. Connally at least escaped the lot of Walter Jenkins. When Jenkins got married a few years later, Johnson abruptly ordered him back from his honeymoon to attend to more pressing matters. Johnson would not have dared to try such a thing with Connally.

When the newlyweds returned to Washington and set up in a small apartment, there was no escape from global problems. All the major congressional business seemed to deal with the mobilization of youth. The bald political compromise that Roosevelt had accepted with the Selective Service Law of 1940—providing for only twelve months of training and allowing for an extension only by congressional action—was now nearly half up, and a bruising battle about that lay ahead.

Connally's authority in the Johnson office was now established and unchallenged. He had also become a well-known figure among the congressional aides across Capitol Hill, having been elected the speaker of the Little Congress, a mock congress of congressional staffers, a post that Lyndon Johnson had also held when he was an assistant to Congressman Kleberg. Connally's intimacy with Johnson had deepened. There was something almost chemical about their friendship. The fact that Connally had taken on the mannerisms of Johnson imparted an eerie physical aspect to his surrogacy. Johnson began to entrust Connally with the tough-guy jobs (or hatchet-man jobs, as the opponents preferred to call them), and even though Connally was only twenty-three, he handled them, including dealing with money and dispensing it where it might be needed, without qualms. When a record existed of such transactions, which was rarely, it was cryptic. "LBJ: delivered $300.00 in cash to Maury on the floor today. jbc."

But Connally was getting itchy. A part of him seemed to know that in a year and a half he had learned the main lessons of the job. He bridled in the subordinate's role, and he began to explore other options in Texas.

In March 1941 Congress took the first major step to aid Great Britain directly. The Lend-Lease Act appropriated the enormous sum of $7 billion for war matériel to "any country whose defense the President deems vital to the defense of the United States." Isolationists charged that the bill would mean "ploughing under every fourth American boy."

Once again Sam Rayburn, now the Speaker of the House of Representatives, was a powerful Texas voice for the legislation. Yet even Rayburn continued to argue that the Lend-Lease law was a measure to avoid war. After Lend-Lease passed the House, Rayburn delivered an eloquent radio address: "The lease-lend bill is not, as some people are trying to make us believe, a bill to put America into war; it is a bill to keep war from America. It is based on the common sense proposition that it is better to give those nations which are fighting to stop Hitler in Europe the sinews of war with which to fight, rather than to let them go unaided down to defeat, leaving ourselves isolated and alone in an unfriendly world . . . to fight Hitler on the Rio Grande." Nevertheless, Rayburn had not forgotten the branch of the government of which he was a leader. The law granted to the president extraordinary powers. While Rayburn conceded such power in a world crisis, he strutted his jealousies over the prerogatives of Congress. It must set the policy, and the president must carry that policy out.

In these debates Lyndon Johnson had remained idle, his concerns domestic and parochial, but the threat of Hitler could no longer be ignored and finally, on San Jacinto Day, April 21, he made a major speech to a joint session of the Texas Legislature. To Johnson, the situation was a schoolyard fight, with big guys and little guys; wily tricksters, bullies, and weak sisters; loud mothers and slick talkers; namby-pambies and cowards. The United States was in this fix, he asserted, because its friends—the European democracies—had fallen down on the job. As military commemoratives go, it was not a bad speech. It combined ardent praise for Roosevelt, a round warning of the danger, and some worthwhile statistics, such as the fact that by 1941 Germany had spent $230 billion on weapons, while America had spent $30 billion, part of which was still on paper. But it was when Lyndon Johnson personalized the situation that he revealed his basic instincts.

"Certainly, I am not defeatist," he told his fellow Texans. "I just like to know the size of the fellow I have to whip, where he came from, what he thinks about, and how he slugs."

The speech, however, was little noticed. San Jacinto Day in 1941 was to be Governor Pappy O'Daniel's day, not Lyndon Johnson's— it was the governor who made headlines statewide. Eschewing the statehouse for the shrine itself, the San Jacinto battlefield, there, with his flair for the startling, dramatic gesture, he appointed the octogenarian son of Sam Houston to fill the vacant seat of U.S. Senator Morris Sheppard. Houston was to serve until a new senator could be elected in a special election (but he promptly died after he arrived in Washington).

Lyndon Johnson, however, would not be outdone. Two days later he announced his candidacy for the senate seat and he made John Connally his campaign manager. The staging of his announcement was vintage Lyndon Johnson. As a congressman little known outside his district, he had one claim to national office. That was his relationship with the president, and what better place was there to accentuate that tie than the White House itself? In fact, Roosevelt had called him to the White House to encourage him to make the race. At this point it looked to the White House as if Martin Dies would be the next senator from Texas, and Dies, whom the president disliked personally, had been a profound embarrassment to the administration with his House Un-American Activities Committee and his charges of Reds in the executive branch. By Johnson's own account, the president had said to him, "Martin Dies is going to be the next United States senator, and he will be a disgrace to the United States and to Texas."

After his conference with the president, Johnson strode out onto the White House lawn and told reporters that he was running. He trumpeted yet again his ardent support of Roosevelt and cast that support in the tradition of the dead Senator Sheppard, whom he wanted to succeed. A few minutes later, FDR held a regularly scheduled press conference, and of course he was asked whether he was endorsing Johnson. Feigning surprise, the president professed to have heard the news only a few minutes before the press heard it. While Texas Democrats must choose their own candidate, all he could say was that "Lyndon Johnson is a very old, old friend of mine." About a year and a half old, to be exact. The *Dallas Morning News* got the message: FDR PICKS JOHNSON TO DEFEAT DIES.

For Connally, the Senate race of 1941 was the political equivalent of an Arctic growing season. At twenty-four years old, he found himself at the head of a statewide campaign with national significance. There were many other, more experienced political operatives available for the job. Senator Alvin Wirth, for example, resigned as undersecretary of the interior to join the campaign, and the newspaper publisher Charles Marsh stood ready to assume control. Furthermore, this was not going to be the relatively easy proposition of Johnson the Roosevelt man against Dies the apostate. A far more formidable adversary soon entered the race: the governor himself. O'Daniel was considered nearly unbeatable. He carried a magical aura, which confounded the political experts, for his constituency was invisible and impossible to identify. Texans simply loved him, no matter how outrageous his actions or statements. Few would confess openly to being for him. They just voted for him in the privacy of the booth.

Yet O'Daniel's aura seemed to be tarnishing ever so slightly. (Even his Hollywood-bound daughter, Molly, was said to be losing her looks.) This was the feeling of the Johnson camp, but it was only a feeling, and it was not backed by hard evidence. Johnson entered the race with only nine points in the polls. A few weeks after the White House staging, this showing doubled, but LBJ remained the underdog.

Given this situation, Johnson's reasons for appointing Connally to the top campaign post were shrewd. The campaign was to become a youth movement, even a crusade of sorts. The candidate himself was thirty-three years old, and the goal was to portray him as the coming Texas legislator, O'Daniel as fading and silly, and Dies, a one-issue man. Let O'Daniel and Dies split the anti-Roosevelt vote. Texas knew whom President Roosevelt wanted. But the task was not so simple. O'Daniel was magic, and Dies was one of the greatest stump speakers in Texas political history. Johnson, by contrast, was a bellower. If Johnson was to win, he had to win on organization. With Connally at the helm, his troops would be recruited from youth, their platoon leaders, statewide, coming from the ranks of Johnson's old NYA beneficiaries. They would be young men just out of college, who had gotten an education only because Johnson's NYA had provided the pennies from the make-work jobs that had made higher education possible. For those who had benefited from the NYA while at the university that Connally had dominated, the campaign had a double claim on their loyalties and their energies.

John Connally was the natural leader for this group. He had an addictive quality that made the young gravitate to him. Robert Strauss, one of his followers in the 1941 campaign, was to say, "We were all Connally contemporaries, but he was always chairman of the board. He had the unique quality of having leadership without being resented for it. Everyone just assumed he was in charge." Connally's eminence had been fairly achieved at the University of Texas, not some provincial state teachers' college, and, therefore, he dignified Johnson.

Nellie's presence enlivened and brightened the campaign. At one point with Johnson out of town and the campaign rhetoric heating up, she passed along a little poem to cheer Johnson up:

Now Pappy would really love this; and Molly would like it too,
If one by one we'd fall aside and lose a vote or two.
The man would say we're quitting: we cannot win this race
The Trojan Horse that Dies brought in might quicken up his pace,
But we won't let you do it. We're pulling for you too strong
We miss you lots and need your smile to pull this thing along.

Johnson chose his alma mater, Southwest Texas State Teachers College at San Marcos as the site for his formal declaration in Texas. Connally dispatched Strauss, Pickle, Singleton, and others throughout Hays County to drum up a big crowd. The gymnasium was draped with bunting, and the campaign staff was deployed throughout the audience to generate a wave of cheering at the applause lines. They knew what was coming. It was to be a statement that touched the universal resentment of youth: that old men always think up the justifications for war and send young men off to do the fighting and dying. "If the day ever comes when I cast my vote to send your boys to war," Johnson told the crowd, "that day will I resign my seat in the United States Congress and join your sons." There was no doubt in the minds of his youthful followers that Johnson's promise was sincere. The nobility of it made them swell with devotion and commitment. He was one of them. It personalized the world situation and broke down the barrier between the generations. It was a statement that neither the cigar-chomping Dies nor the flour-dusted, portly O'Daniel could make, and it produced big headlines in the state the next day.

It also signified a historical seed. Here was a crucial moment of patriotic commitment that the generation of Johnson and Connally could remember for a lifetime. The country was in crisis, and they, the young men of the nation, stood ready to answer their country's call. The threat to their country was so clear, so palpably evil. Their readiness to sacrifice came willingly, unquestioningly. It was broadened and fixed into a grand principle. This was what American youth was supposed to do whenever and for whatever reason their country got into trouble. They were responding.

★

A month into Johnson's senatorial campaign, Roosevelt declared an unlimited national emergency.

Once again, as Connally watched, Johnson responded immediately to the alarm. He wired Roosevelt that he was ready to return to Washington right then. Perhaps this was grandstanding, for it was scarcely likely that the president would pluck a good Democrat away in the heat of his campaign. In any event, Roosevelt declined the offer. Johnson was performing a higher service by his campaign, but the president added, "Please return immediately after the election."

Connally ran the Johnson campaign from the sixteenth floor of the Stephen F. Austin Hotel in Austin. He had plenty of money to work with, since the Brown and Root firm had benefited handsomely from the construction of the Pedernales electrical cooperative and from the Corpus Christi Naval Air Station, and was ready to return the favor. A substantial contribution also came from Sid Richardson, one of the five wealthiest independent oilmen in Texas.

In long and excited conferences, the young staff settled upon several themes for the campaign. "Peace, Progress and Preparedness" captured the high ground. "Roosevelt and Unity" and "Franklin D and Lyndon B" accentuated the White House tie. "He gets the job done" stressed the candidate as a doer.

Connally helped write Johnson's speeches. The speeches outdid each other, one to the next, in their alarming tone about impending war, the threat to democracy, the urgency of mobilization. Overblown rhetoric predominated, and phrases rolled around like loose cannonballs, clanging against one another: "We sent a dove of peace across the Pacific, with a roll of poetical gush in his beak, when we should have dispatched a dozen frowning warships to carry the message. Japan laughed and moved south."

The isolationists in the Senate became the regular targets in these diatribes. Johnson flailed away at Charles Lindbergh in particular, the darling of the America First movement. Lindbergh was "a once daring sea adventurer turned lay-down artist," and Texas preferred "a brave Roosevelt any day to the Lindberghs, . . . under the bed to escape the lightning."

As the ultraconservative business town in the state, Dallas was hopeless for the Johnson campaign. So they concentrated on liberal Houston and on the small towns where Johnson was at his best. There, the crowds were filled with men in sweaty overalls with huge mustaches, who could bend the candidate's ear on how it ought to be done in Washington, and the audiences usually contained at least one old Confederate veteran and one old trail driver from the Chisholm Trail. "Glad to see ya, partner," was his standard greeting, as he would sweat down three or four suits in a day of twenty speeches. The campaign courted the publishers of the rural newspaper chains. Besides Charles Marsh and his eight papers, Houston Harte and his eight papers that included San Antonio, Corpus Christi, and San Angelo came aboard, as did Charles Woodson from Brownwood and his small chain. The small papers furnished the quotations that Connally ballooned in the campaign literature. "It is time for Roosevelt and Unity," wrote the *Waco News-Tribune.* "With our commander-in-chief desiring Lyndon Johnson to be one of his generals in the United States Senate, these newspapers stand ready to obey his desire." To the *San Marcos Record,* Johnson was "the administration leader in the House." "Other good men are in the race," wrote the *Abilene Reporter-News.*

"None of them, however, has the experience, coupled with the entree to the New Deal councils that Lyndon Johnson has."

In the meantime, the opposition was making mistakes, and Connally was learning how to capitalize on them. Dies had localized his crusade against Reds, shifting his aim from the national government to John Connally's alma mater. Johnson nailed him. To the cheers of his UT cadre, the candidate said that far from being "a factory grinding out communist comrades," the university instead was producing "red-blooded Texas boys to command navy ships." Meanwhile, O'Daniel was touting his proposal for an independent Texas armed force. At Johnson campaign headquarters, a wire from FDR to Johnson was invited, which read, "My reply to the Governor [about his proposal to create a Texas army and navy] was intended to be courteous, thus avoiding calling the scheme preposterous, which it undoubtedly is." O'Daniel proclaimed Roosevelt nothing more than a backslapper who could scarcely run a peanut wagon, not a particularly deft move when the commander-in-chief had just declared an unlimited national emergency. "It must have comforted Hitler to hear the governor talk like that," Johnson retorted.

Although the Johnson campaign staged a strong finish, on election night Connally knew the election would be close. But how close? Dies had faded and would come in a poor fourth, behind the little red arrow, the football star–cum–attorney general, Gerald Mann. The race was between Johnson and O'Daniel, with the congressman seemingly comfortably ahead by 15,000 votes (with only 40,000 votes yet to be counted). The Texas Election Bureau declared that, short of a miracle, Johnson was the winner, and the Austin headquarters fell into raucous jubilation, with the victorious candidate being hoisted into the air by several leathery supporters with a fistful of victory telegrams held high to the ceiling.

But Connally and his buddy, Jake Pickle, were to learn a bitter lesson. "You don't celebrate until it's finally finished," Pickle was to say later. "We went to bed after a gay party with our man, the new senator from Texas. By the time we got down the next day at noon to try to get to work and pick up the pieces, the reports were coming back in that we hadn't won. There had been some change."

Political races down to the wire are like close games in professional basketball: the coaches, rather than the players, determine the outcome. That's when the professional managers earn their pay. In Texas, on the days when votes were stuffed into cylinders locked with padlocks, the process was dishonest. To John Connally's credit, he did not come to the practice of vote stealing and election fraud comfortably, but perhaps this was what it meant to grow up. This was a winner-take-all election where the margin of victory was likely to be counted in the hundreds, by a handful here and there. When Connally got back to work, Johnson's lead had dwindled first to 5,000 on Sunday and then to 77 votes on Monday. The election had become a grab bag, a power play, with friendships, especially those with dishonest bosses, to mean the difference.

The voting pattern was changing mysteriously. Whereas on Sunday O'Daniel was getting four out of ten votes from East Texas, on Monday he was getting seven out of ten. In Dies's own district, Johnson's percentage of the vote was strangely shrinking, as O'Daniel's soared. On Sunday, Connally took a call from one of Johnson's political heroes, the former governor, "Farmer Jim" Ferguson.

"It'll take money to stop stealing in Dies's district," Ferguson said. Connally was offended, and hung up. Perhaps he knew that a bribe to Ferguson wouldn't work; Ferguson was a pawn of the beer interests, and the beer interests wanted O'Daniel, a teetotaler, out of the state house and into the U.S. Senate, where he would be rendered harmless. Connally knew that the beer boys could top any bribe that he might offer.

But then Connally made a real mistake. The East Texas counties were in the pocket of his opponents, but the Johnson campaign had the border blocs of South Texas, especially Duval County and its notorious "Duke," George Parr. Johnson wanted to create the appearance of victory early in the tabulation, for that in itself could create a wave, and since Parr could deliver vote margins of 100 to 1, the tide of victory might originate there, with Duval County.

"Should we report our votes?" the South Texas bosses asked Connally.

"Yeah, bring 'em in," he ordered.

They were caught, for the fix was in. "As soon as all [our South Texas blocs] reported, the opposition knew our total," Jake Pickle was to say. "The thing began to erode. It was a question of the opposition knowing."

"What can we do?" a desperate Johnson asked his lieutenants. "Can we do anything in South Texas?"

"No. Duval's in, all the others are in," came the answer. "We'll have to wait to see what comes in from East Texas."

As victory slipped away, the Johnson forces came together at the candidate's home on Happy Hollow Lane. Connally and Pickle were scandalized and demanded a challenge. To use Pickle's term, they were "electrified" by the prospect that fraud could overturn the result. Johnson listened quietly to the arguments back and forth.

"Well, boys, I've listened to all the arguments and I've heard all these figures," he said finally. "It looks to me like we've been beat. You just don't turn one of these elections over. I don't see how we can do it. We'd better just admit that we're defeated and be a good loser. There might be another time."

It was not quite as noble nor philosophical a posture as it sounded. Johnson was looking to the future, and he knew that if he challenged the result and lost, he was finished. This election was cost-free in political terms. He not only remained a congressman, but with his impressive showing against the all-time vote-getting champion, he became, even in defeat, Texas's premier congressman. This had been a race for one year in the Senate; the regular election was coming up in 1942. (Only Pearl Harbor was to undercut his plan.) In defeat, the candidate took the high road. In a reference to O'Daniel's prior calling, Johnson commented engagingly, "I got flour in my eyes."

Connally and the young Turks had learned a few lessons. The first was that in the final tabulation of a razor-close election, you needed to be slightly ahead, no matter how you got there, for, as Jake Pickle put it, when vote fraud occurs in Texas and the final count is in, "You'd better put salt and pepper on it, and go your way." O'Daniel had won by 1,311 votes.

Exhausted and deeply disappointed, Connally retreated to Floresville. Outdated congratulatory messages continued to pour in, prolonging his despondency, but the telephone, the one-wire party line with its wind-up handle, was silent. He vowed one thing. His friend, Lyndon Johnson, was owed one. He had a term in the Senate coming.

★

As Sam Rayburn labored masterfully in Congress for the Roosevelt policy, he also prodded his protégé, Lyndon Johnson, to make, at long last, a real speech on the House floor. Early on, Rayburn, remembering his own loquacious indiscretions as a young House member, had counseled caution and silence, obedience and deference, almost as an archbishop would counsel a novitiate. In his first four years, Johnson had learned so well that he had nothing to show for his presence, but he could no longer submit the excuse that he was still learning the rules.

Finally, on August 8, 1941, as the bitter debate over the extension of the draft began, he bestirred himself. The vote over the draft was certain to be close. The whole of Roosevelt's preparedness policy turned on a strong military posture. The entire weight of America was being thrown behind Britain, but if the extension bill failed, that weight, at least as measured by its standing army, would be reduced by two-thirds. The stakes were enormous: a token force of 400,000 or a well-trained force three times as large.

As the debate began, Roosevelt was steaming to Placentia Bay in Newfoundland to have his first face-to-face meeting with Churchill. Lyndon Johnson took the floor early. As there was little poetry in him, he underlined the familiar Roosevelt position: the national interest was in peril; enlistments should remain in force until the "emergency" was over; it was absurd in the present situation to send two-thirds of the army home just as it was getting on its feet. If there was anything original about what Johnson had to say, it was his evocation of Texas tradition, and as he spoke of that tradition, he might have been looking directly at John Connally.

"I know how Texas boys feel. I am one of them. Texas boys come from a race of men who fought for their freedom at the Alamo and Goliad and San Jacinto. They fought those battles to establish the Republic of Texas with their strength and their blood. They had little equipment, and what they had was poor. Every time they fought they were greatly outnumbered. But they fought anyway, because they were battling for their homes, for their religion, their liberty of conscience and action."

It was not the last time he would presume to speak for youth, but at least now, at the age of thirty-three, he still qualified more or less as a Texas boy. He had promised in the spring that if ever he had to vote to send American men abroad into a foreign war, that day he would resign from Congress and join them. It was a promise he was to keep, although it was a half-promise. He did not vow to stay the course in uniform if the emergency lasted years. For now, Texas boys from "such stock" were not the slackers; they were not going to require discharge simply because an "arbitrary date" was on their military papers. "Texas boys," he said, "prefer extended service now to slavery hereafter."

With the galleries full of flag-waving mothers and young servicemen, the House passed the extension on August 12 by one vote—203 to 202. A catastrophe for the administration was barely averted. It had been a huge political gamble. The Democrats had bet the store on the outcome. Johnson wanted a scapegoat for the closeness of the vote, and found it in pacifist college editors like

Kingman Brewster, Jr., the editor of the *Yale Daily News*, and in Charles Lindbergh and the other nervous Nellies of the America First movement. (After Lindbergh, the "Lone Eagle," had argued in Des Moines that, because of American air power, Germany could never conquer the United States, that Lend-Lease would only prolong the war and increase the bloodshed, and that the United States had no stake in the defense of Britain, the Texas legislature passed a resolution that Lindbergh was not welcome to speak in the Lone Star State.) Later, Lyndon Johnson would boast that *he* had drummed up the one vote that had won the day, but this, of course, was absurd. The man to credit was another Texan, Sam Rayburn, who had labored hard and long in the cloakrooms and the hallways, calling in favors that had been piled up over the years. When the vote came, the Republicans held back a few votes to see what was needed to defeat the measure. They were outmaneuvered by the Speaker. When the one-vote result was tallied, Rayburn immediately slammed down his gavel and made it final, giving the Republicans no chance to bring in their holdouts. They howled their points of order, but there was nothing to be done, even though Rayburn had stretched the House rules to the limit. The next day, August 13, an irate Hamilton Fish did not mention Lyndon Johnson when he delivered his funeral lesson, according to isolationism:

"The administration won a Pyrrhic victory by one vote through the use of power, patronage, and political bosses. The vote definitely means that no selectee will be sent outside the Western Hemisphere, that there can be no unity and no appropriation to carry out such a personal Roosevelt war. The American people are weary of broken promises, hypocrisy, deceit, and inspired war propaganda. They are overwhelmingly against sending our youth into foreign wars or helping bloody-handed Joe Stalin make the world safe for Communism. Congress can be expected to vote three to one against involvement in wars in Europe, Africa, and Asia . . . unless attacked."

Unless attacked. . . .

A few weeks later, after a German submarine fired two torpedoes at an American ship and missed, Roosevelt told the nation, "If you see a rattlesnake poised to strike, you do not wait until he has struck before you crush him."

Meanwhile, as the clouds of war grew darker by the week, Connally was in Austin, a naval officer in reserve. Technically, he had resigned from Lyndon Johnson's staff in March of 1941, but then the Senate campaign had come along, and after that he remained Johnson's man back home, shoring up the Johnson political machine in the wake of his narrow defeat by Governor Pappy O'Daniel, and preparing for the Senate race of 1942. On November 13, days after Roosevelt swamped Willkie in the general election, LBJ wrote to "his boy," John, in Austin, ordering Connally to travel to each of the nine counties outside Travis to make sure the machine had "representation" even in the smallest places. They would always have people in the larger county seats, Johnson wrote, so Connally was to pay particular attention to such crossroads in the eastern part of the district as Somerville, Lexington, and Dime Box. "Be sure to get the lay of the land in each box before you make a contact," wrote the Boss. "Find out who the most influential men and women in the box are and then contact each of them personally, and get their assurance that they will work for us through the term. This is very, very important, and I am afraid we have neglected it too much in the past. Spare no expense and no time in whipping this thing into shape." The air of urgency about political matters bespoke Johnson's priorities. No such thing as the imminence of global warfare was to distract Connally, for it was not distracting his Boss. "We are burning some midnight oil here these days, but I am becoming increasingly conscious of our failure to have the aggressive, seasoned, local contacts we need. *This is the main justification for your being down there.*"

They communicated almost daily. Often the letters from Washington had the tone of orders from a hard-pressed field marshal, one very uncertain in battle:

"We're going to try to handle our publicity better. If you have not already done so, I want to urge you again that you *personally* know (*rather intimately*) the boys in the Capitol press room. . . . Talk to these fellows every chance you get. Go see them now and show them these stories and ask them if they won't use some stuff on us, and then watch the papers closely. If they do, drop me a note, and I'll write them and tell them. . . . Please, please, please concentrate on making friends of the Capitol press. Go to lunch, talk and visit with the Capitol Corps. Most of them write columns and see if you can't get us mixed up in them pretty regularly."

As the United States inched toward war, Connally, as Johnson's legman, kept to his routine political chores. They toured the Port Arthur military shipyards together, with Johnson loading every statement with the assumption of imminent war. "If that fellow over there doesn't do his job right, you and I and a lot of others will go fight Hitler and die," the congressman proclaimed. "We will take Hitler in 1943." When the report of this came out in the *Brenham*

Banner Press, Johnson liked the write-up so much—especially the portrait of him as a big, energetic country boy who turned up at military shipyards one day and then the next day, in the Capitol, got his shoes shined before he voted for a revision of the Neutrality Act—that he had Connally reproduce and distribute the clipping widely. But there were other, less complimentary brush fires for Connally to contain: the allegation that Johnson had made big stock deals while in office and that he had received campaign contributions from John L. Lewis and his big-labor pals. Connally was to squelch both rumors. In his political travels around Johnson's district, Connally apparently had done his work all too well, and had started a rumor which was fueled by a gossip column in the *Austin American-Statesman*. John Connally, to all appearances ever the faithful Johnson lieutenant, was secretly plotting to run for his boss's congressional seat when the Boss was enticed into challenging Pappy O'Daniel again for the Senate in 1941. The rumor was of the very kind, Connally knew, that might throw Johnson into a rage. On December 3, four days before Pearl Harbor, Connally wrote to Johnson in an effort to squelch the rumor:

> Needless to say, I have absolutely denied and scoffed at the very idea and have consistently replied that I thought we had the best congressman in the United States. I think it is terrible for such a situation to exist, and of course, I am doing everything I can to counteract my part of it. Don't let me overexaggerate the talk. There is no ground swell at all. I, of course, will continue to stop the remarks whenever I possibly can.

Three days later, as the Japanese carrier pilots were getting their final briefings in the Central Pacific, Connally was engaged in getting together Lyndon Johnson's customary gifts of huge turkeys to his friends in high places and ensuring that Speaker Rayburn got a case of his favorite Scotch.

First Lieutenant

On DECEMBER 6, 1941, the University of Texas football team played the University of Oregon in the kind of gloriously bitter grudge match that Texas alums could savor. Coached by D. X. Bible and inspired by the leaping grabs of Noble Doss and the scatback running of Speck Sanders, Texas had a powerhouse team that year. Some were saying it was the greatest team in Texas history. Coming into the final game, UT was ranked fourth in the nation, after drubbing the Aggies of A&M, 23–0. To the outrage of the faithful, however, Texas was passed over for the Rose Bowl, when Oregon State invited the patricians of Duke to Pasadena instead. Early in the week of the Oregon game, Coach Bible, he of the long face, announced that after a difficult conference with his disheartened and angry squad, the University of Texas would accept no bid to a lesser bowl. Thus, it was for the Longhorns to show on December 6—a day which broke clear and fifty degrees, perfect football weather—not only that there had been a gross miscarriage of justice at Pasadena but that the Longhorns were the true national champions.

John and Nellie Connally wanted to make an occasion of it and went to the game with their old UT crowd (which had now become the nucleus of the LBJ crowd): Jake Pickle and his wife, Sugar; John Singleton; and the future governor and senator, Price Daniel. It was a satisfying afternoon in Memorial Stadium as the Longhorns trampled the Ducks of Oregon, 71–7. Jubilantly, the Connally party repaired to the guesthouse out on Lake Buchanan, where they spent a happy night playing dominoes and the word game Ghost.

December 7, 1941, is a day on which every American of that generation seems to remember, minute by minute, with startling vividness, where he was and what he was doing. At the stone guesthouse on Lake Buchanan, the activity was football, the men tossing the ball around on the lawn at lakeside, when Nellie Connally raced out, screaming the news from Pearl Harbor. They all scurried back indoors and huddled around the radio. They knew what it meant for them.

They were a Navy crowd. Connally, of course, was already commissioned in the naval reserve, while Pickle and Singleton were soon to become naval officers in the V-7 or "ninety-day wonder" program. In Washington, meanwhile, Lyndon Johnson rose, on one of the rare occasions as a member of Congress when he asked for the recognition of the chair.

"Mr. Speaker, I ask unanimous consent for an indefinite leave of absence."

Speaker Rayburn savored the moment reverentially, but his parliamentarian's words did not depart from custom. "Is there objection to the request of the gentleman from Texas?" he asked matter-of-factly. There was none. "So be it," he said solemnly, and tapped his gavel. Johnson then rushed off to the White House with his request to the commander of the fleet to assign him immediately to active duty. Their conversation was brief. The president said he understood and wished the congressman good fortune.

For John Connally there was no such grand ceremony about his induction. He stepped forward like millions of other American men without congressional or presidential awareness, and he knew he was in for the duration. Johnson had made a political promise to *leave* with the boys if they were called to a foreign war. *Staying* was a different matter. Connally's promise had no such complexity. It was genuine, unqualified, and sincere, a purely patriotic and unremarkable act with no hidden agenda. Johnson was to stay eight months. Connally would stay more than four years.

There is nothing quite like the moment when a whole nation goes to war. It is full of fear and foreboding, marked with uncertainty, and yet with the nobility and the poignancy brought by the sight of young men donning their starched uniforms for the first time, packing their canvas bags, and boarding their trains or their planes or their ships. It is a time to weep, but it is also a brief moment to feel proud and strong, before reality sets in. So it was for these two Texans, and for those who loved them. Charles Marsh, for example, the Texas publisher who had become so involved with Johnson and Connally in their political battles, was given to sleeplessness in his house in Washington, where he lived with his secretary, the sister of Alice Glass, his future wife. When in his fitfulness a thought seized him, he would knock on his secretary's door and summon her to work in the "cooler," so named in those days of nascent air conditioning because his basement office was the only room of the house blessed with the new contraption. There he would dictate. In the week after Pearl Harbor, around 2:30 A.M., Marsh summoned Mary Glass once again, and in the cooler he dictated a letter to Johnson, but it might have been meant for Connally as well.

> It is all so clear as the flash of truth about you and life ahead woke me a moment ago. Your eye sparkles with a light just a little more mature. Your great emotion is more pure. The clear wisdom is soon to join your great energy. You are not to die young as do so many of great embryo genius: by the heat of its own flame. It seemed sad to see you all buttoned in uniform, that outward thing, but now, I see enough to know even the uniform shall not destroy. You are to learn discipline. You are to take orders. You are to fight with skill and frankness amid the dull, the frightened, the lazy, the vengeful, the jealous, and the sly. . . . As you slash at evil with your very good sword, see a better way through before you cut, so that the marchers behind be not lost in the swamp of doubt and despair. There shall be many around you to applaud mere courage. They are the idle ones. The wise are silent, because they are at work. You shall be welcome home when your face shows that you have not used your sword for self, but when your face shows the sword was used to clear a way with the least cruelty to erring men, as men's needs were met. Even in armor, the truly great are gentle. The gentle man in peace or in war does not walk with cruelty.

Johnson received his orders on December 9. He was to report to the Office of Naval Operations for instructions and to proceed to San Francisco to the commandant of the Twelfth Naval District. From the start, the congressman operated at the top, under the watchful gaze of then–Undersecretary of the Navy James Forrestal, who had personally recruited him into the service. Forrestal issued a terse order that the fresh lieutenant commander, junior in rank though he may have been, was to be given priority transportation.

Johnson left abruptly and without fanfare on December 23 for the West Coast with a mission to observe the training progress of civilians engaged in navy contract work at commercial plants. If there was not much heroic about that, not much political collateral back in Texas, not much that could justify Charles Marsh's nocturnal thoughts, it was emblematic of the nation's industry bending itself toward the colossal exercise of world war.

For Connally, the days of December and early January were spent getting his own life in order and reorganizing Johnson's congressional office for the absence of them both. He went about his chores cheerfully, without fretting about his fate or the world's. To his old theatrical coach in college, Professor James Burton, he wrote on December 18 about the endless motion of his and Nellie's life, back and forth to Texas so often that they could find their way blindfolded: "Perhaps one of these days when I have a long white beard and Nellie has a wooden leg, we can settle down in one spot and enjoy life. For the present moment, however, I have no complaints to speak of."

Before he left for the West Coast, Johnson had seen to it that Connally would be kept close to him as an aide. The Navy Department realized that they would have to take Johnson and Connally as a package. During the Christmas recess, the offices in Congress were closed, with the members all away, but Connally labored on as a one-man transition team. In a letter to LBJ in California, he proposed that Lady Bird become Johnson's stand-in in Congress, and it was done. Already, holed up in a San Francisco hotel, Johnson was feeling anxious and isolated from the Washington scene he desperately, viscerally needed. To Connally he wrote in early January, "Your note was the kind that I want to get every day. If you will just make it part of your daily routine and write every afternoon before you leave for the navy, I think we can keep tuned in pretty well."

Within Forrestal's office in 1942, Johnson and Connally had caught the eye of J. W. Barker, a Columbia professor who was now an assistant to the undersecretary and who was watching over industrial mobilization. Barker was anxious for Johnson to work with him on labor problems in navy shipyards and on civilian training, and he wrote a memo for Forrestal requesting that Johnson and his sidekick be detailed to him after Johnson's return to Washington: "Thank God for our wisdom in grabbing Lyndon Johnson to work in the navy. He's going to be a grand goad stuck in everyone's side including me. . . . He's a live wire of the first water."

But Johnson was not at all sure that touring naval shipyards and analyzing labor problems were quite the stuff of legend. Immediately on his return from the West Coast he began to look around for a change, and made an appointment with Jonathan Daniels, the wily North Carolinian who was then on Roosevelt's staff. Daniels's assessment of Johnson was more canny than Barker's, and he noted in his calendar, "Appt with Lyndon Johnson, energetic and intelligent Texas Congressman who wants for the sake of his political future to get into a danger zone, though he realizes his talents are best suited for handling speakers and public relations." They met for a drink in the Carrolton Hotel, Johnson looking distinctly impressive and chivalrous in his blue uniform and gold stripes. "There is no rest in his dark, bright eyes," Daniels wrote in his diary. "His mood altered easily. Slim and curly haired, smoking and laughing, he looked less like the sea portrait of a congressman than the equally conventional picture of the movie actor in sea-going costume." Months later, Daniels would view Lady Bird similarly, without the sweetness and nobility that most saw: "She is the sharp-eyed type who looks at every piece of furniture in the house, knowing its period and design—though sometimes she is wrong. She is confident that her husband is going places, and in her head, she is furnishing the mansions of their future." Wry as Daniels may have been toward the Johnsons, the congressman would eventually get from Daniels what he wanted.

Johnson's first trip to the West Coast had been so hastily laid on that there had been no time for a ritualized farewell, in which the beloved could properly send their noble men off to war. But in February, Johnson left Washington again, reportedly for the South Pacific. This time Ensign Connally left with him.

At Union Station in Washington in 1942, the heartrending prologue to war was played out. Under the vaulting roof, against the backdrop of classic marble and warm brass, the tread of armies passed across its concrete floor. Young men of every size and description, many who had never left home before, were caught up in the ceaseless march. Duffel bags lay in clusters everywhere, as recruits sat and waited, smoking and laughing, expectantly. Always, the bittersweet farewells, with that gesture almost carved in stone as an emblem of the 1940s: the girl pulled against the soldier in uniform, one of his arms tightly around her, the other hand on the string of the duffel bag, his cap slightly askew, and one of her legs kicked up at right angles for balance as they kissed. So it was for the Johnsons and the Connallys, except that the group included the Speaker of the House. At the statidn, Sam Rayburn was a discreet chaperone, standing like a granite statue off to the side. When the train pulled away, the Speaker stepped forward and took each woman by the arm:

"Now, girls, we're going to get the best dinner in Washington."

If that dinner was on the Speaker, Lady Bird would repay him many times over in the coming months. Lady Bird, that high-toned girl from Karnack who had been pampered by nannies and maids all her life, was finally learning to cook, for she had been taking lessons from Congressman Maury Maverick's wife, starting with how to boil water. Now she had Nellie Connally by her side. When their men went off together to the wars of San Francisco, the wives moved into the same apartment, for suddenly Lyndon was making only $275 a month as a lieutenant commander and John something less as an ensign. The meals Nellie and Lady Bird cooked were simple—they called them meal #1 and meal #2: #1 consisted of a ham casserole, spinach, and black-eyed peas. For they were busy. Lady Bird was also having to learn how to be a member of Congress, and Nellie how to be her first lieutenant.

In effect, their relationship mirrored exactly that of their husbands, with Nellie becoming Lady Bird's "little sidekick." If Lady Bird was sweet and shy and ladylike, Nellie buoyed the office with her congenital cheeriness and sense of fun and pluck. When spring came, she returned to Austin and from there wrote Lady Bird a note about a social occasion that was pure Nellie: "I liked the Judge fine and the madam is a honey, but personally I think the old duck should have stayed in his own backyard. Jimmie A. [ex-governor Allred] said many nice things about my pretty little boss—which is you—as any fool can plainly see." Lady Bird, in turn, was concerned about her little sidekick. "You poor little dear, I certainly have been worried about your health: I do hope you will go at once to a very reputable doctor and get examined from head to toe." For Nellie was pregnant. If Lady Bird was concerned, she might have been a tad envious as well, for she was having miscarriage after miscarriage, four in all, before her first daughter, Lynda Bird, was born in 1944.

When they reached San Francisco, Johnson and Connally took up residence in the Empire Hotel, and from there, they began their observation of manpower and training problems. Johnson quickly tired of it. There was not enough in the assignment to engage his attention, and he could not swallow his demotion in status. He did not quite appreciate yet that he was now in the real military and that the country was really at war. More than once, he had to be instructed sharply on the necessity to salute higher authority. By nature, both Johnson and Connally were men who had to be in charge, but Connally at least did not fight his junior status now. Within days of his arrival in San Francisco, Johnson was complaining to the Navy Department about the lack of direction and the absence of leadership, as if he should be running the show. "There is much that I should be doing that I am not," he wrote his immediate superior in Forrestal's office, Admiral John Gingrich. "One does not function well without authority and responsibility. When and if you or the Boss runs into a problem that requires energy, determination, and a modicum of experience, give me the word. *I need* more work." On the side, Johnson was exploring other avenues for higher rank and more visibility. He had inveigled his Texas adviser, Alvin Wirtz, into approaching President Roosevelt with the proposition that Johnson be detailed to the White House with the rank of admiral.

"I can appreciate how you feel and how much you would like to have more power to get things done," Wirtz wrote him discouragingly in late February, "but I am doubtful whether it would be altogether advisable for you to be called into the White House before summer and before you have some more active service. All of us have to do the things we can do, and we can't all be Roosevelts and MacArthurs."

That he could not be a Roosevelt or a MacArthur was scarcely the kind of thing Lyndon Johnson liked to be told, but Wirtz sweetened his caution with a bit of intelligence. He had spoken to Rayburn, who was then pondering whether to recommend to Roosevelt that all members of Congress on active military status be discharged and called back to political duties in Washington. Rayburn was fretting about the politics of the proposal, and Wirtz had counseled that such a discharge, if it were to be done, not take place until after the summer primaries or even perhaps until after the general election in the fall.

The letters from Wirtz were a "spring tonic" to Johnson amid his frustrations. The discussions with Connally at the Empire Hotel ignored the Russian winter counteroffensive against the Nazis and the Japanese advances in the Pacific at Guam and the Philippines, and centered on whether Johnson should run for the Senate again against Pappy O'Daniel. Should he defer to the former governor, Jimmy Allred, who wanted to run, but would do so only with

Johnson's acquiescence? Johnson's political talk became tedious, and he compelled Connally to listen late into the night. While Connally, of course, was not uninterested, Texas politics for him were not quite so all-consuming, not under the present circumstances, and he tired of Johnson's singlemindedness. California was a new world for him. He wanted to see San Francisco and Los Angeles, to shop among the Oriental stores and go to Hollywood. So he dragged the reluctant congressman along to Japanese shops in North Beach, where they bought pearls for Nellie and Lady Bird. They came to favor a shop whose merchant was himself awaiting reassignment to one of the shameful detention camps for Nisei Americans. More than twenty years later, before Christmas in 1964, when he was governor of Texas and Johnson was president, Connally returned to the same store and was delighted to find the same merchant still behind the counter. Polite as ever, the shopkeeper remembered those days early in the war when two handsome young naval officers had frequented his shop. He was proud to know that Connally's companion had become the president of the United States.

"And tell me, Mr. Connally, what are you doing now?" the man asked.

It is a story Connally enjoyed telling often in the Johnsons' company, especially when foreign state leaders were present, and President Johnson would inevitably reply, "I'm going out there one day soon and say to that man, 'Isn't it wonderful what happened to John Connally?' And then I'll wait and see if he asks, 'Mr. Johnson, what are you doing now?' "

If Connally could get Johnson to shop nearby with him in San Francisco, it was harder to get the congressman to Hollywood. The movies remained a mystery to Johnson, an area of little interest, just as they were to Connally utterly fascinating. At the heart of Connally's fascination for Hollywood may have been the fact that in 1939 he had turned down an invitation to go there for a screen test. (Nellie, too, had been offered and refused the same invitation.) Since Connally had gone on to a higher calling as Johnson's assistant, perhaps he never resolved in his own mind whether he had done the right thing. In any event, he was keen to see Lana Turner, who then reigned as Hollywood's sex symbol. It would forever after become a story told on Johnson that he asked, apparently sincerely, "Who is Lana Turner?"

In mid-March, Rayburn finally put his proposal to President Roosevelt, and the subject of bringing all members of Congress home began filtering to the press. In Texas, a local politician, O. P. Lockhart, had suggested publicly that Lyndon Johnson could render greater service in Congress than in the military. Wirtz dutifully sent along the clipping, believing Johnson would be flattered, but Johnson reacted testily, for he knew he had hoisted himself upon his own petard. "Since I asked the Commander in Chief for active duty, since the Secretary of the Navy ordered me to duty, since the House and the Speaker gave me an indefinite leave by unanimous consent, it must be presumed that when I am needed in the House, the Commander in Chief, the Secretary of the Navy, or the Speaker will direct such action," he wrote. "In wartime, people take orders from the Commander in Chief, not Lockhart."

In May 1942, through the offices of Jonathan Daniels, Johnson finally got his chance for his politically essential plunge into the Pacific. This mission is something of a seedy footnote, a classic example of the political interference in military affairs for which military men have such intense contempt. When he was president, Johnson would try to make his mission heroic, holding it up as a noble example of combat courage which might be a model to American soldiers in Vietnam, showing them that the commander in chief had been there himself. He longed for it to be seen as the equivalent of John F. Kennedy's heroics aboard PT-109.

The Roosevelt White House collapsed to Johnson's insistence that he needed a combat experience to enlarge his stature as a potential rival for the embarrassing Pappy O'Daniel, who was no help at all to Roosevelt and did nothing to dignify the Democratic side of the senatorial aisle. Johnson was ordered to Australia, ostensibly to give the president a firsthand account of MacArthur's state of mind as the general salved his wounds after the surrender of Bataan and Corregidor Island in the Philippines. From his headquarters in southern Australia, MacArthur now planned his counteroffensive for New Guinea and was shoring up the Allied defense of Australia itself. But the army and the navy were feuding openly about the course of the counteroffensive, as the next grand strategic moves became subject to the jealousies between the services. It was not a situation into which the supreme commander of the Southwest Pacific enjoyed entertaining a grandstanding congressman, with ties to Forrestal, who was promoting the naval argument for a thrust west in the Central Pacific, and who had the ear of the president.

Before Johnson left for Australia, even the political justifications for the mission were eliminated. In May, the *Dallas News* printed an item suggesting that the administration was so intent on having Johnson replace O'Daniel in the Senate that a petition to put his name on the ballot was being prepared by a "spontaneous movement" in Texas. Johnson might resign his naval commission to make the race if the president wanted it. But as he prepared to go to Australia, he left the matter, as usual, to John Connally. For Connally had returned to Washington to take up again his triple role as officer in Forrestal's office, as Johnson's unofficial secretary in Congress, and as Johnson's political manager. On April 27, Alvin Wirtz had prepared two documents for Johnson's signature, a filing for reelection to the House and a filing for the Senate race. Connally was to do what he thought best. He huddled with Lady Bird upon his arrival in Washington for extended discussions. Former Governor Jimmy Allred wanted to run against O'Daniel, and there was that friendship to consider. Some felt that Johnson could beat O'Daniel handily this time around. Ever the Johnson cheerleader, Charles Marsh felt that Johnson as the military hero could beat O'Daniel "from Dutch Harbor to Australia." But Connally was not so sure. Reelection to the House was Johnson's for the asking, Connally felt, but running a race from the Pacific was something else.

"I felt at that time that the war had just started," Connally would say later. "Mr. Johnson had just gone overseas. We did not know how long he would be overseas, how long the war would last. I felt he had a right to be reelected to his congressional seat without question. But our ability to run an effective campaign for the U.S. Senate against an incumbent, while Lyndon was overseas . . . well, I thought it was the better part of wisdom just to file for reelection, for which I knew he'd have no opposition."

There was now nothing politically essential about the Pacific plunge, although Johnson would later claim that his real mission for FDR was to determine if MacArthur had political ambitions. When Johnson arrived at MacArthur's Melbourne headquarters in late May, the general was grandly contemptuous. He well understood why the two colonels who accompanied Johnson were there, but, turning to Johnson, he sniped, "But God only knows what you're doing here."

"I have a message from the president," Johnson replied lamely, but the message could not have been much more than a "howdy."

Nevertheless, the commander surrendered to political reality and gave an impressive briefing on the strategic situation before he dispatched Johnson to inspect military installations, with a brigadier general as an escort. Part of MacArthur's mission at this moment was to bolster the defenses of Australia, for the Japanese were moving to make the Coral Sea theirs and to establish a foothold in the northeast part of the Australian continent. A few days after Johnson arrived, Japanese submarines entered Sydney harbor. So Johnson's firsthand observation of the Australian defenses might be useful to President Roosevelt after all, although these developments were somewhat less important than Rommel's dashing campaigns in North Africa, the siege of Stalingrad, or the battle for Midway Island—three critical turning points in the global conflict that then dominated the president's thoughts.

Johnson traveled to Port Moresby in New Guinea in early June, three weeks after a Japanese invasion force, with the port as its objective, had been turned back. The congressman's adventures from this point forward have been recounted in a book called *The Mission,* by Martin Caidin and Edward Humoff. Briefly, this is what happened. Even though MacArthur specifically ordered that Roosevelt's congressman be kept out of harm's way, Johnson insisted once he got to New Guinea that he be permitted to fly on a bombing mission from Port Moresby over Lae, the Japanese base on the north central coast of the island. He needed to go, he professed to his disapproving escorts, so that he could tell the president of the combat conditions from firsthand observation. The mission involved twenty-seven planes. Johnson was to ride in a B-26 bomber, one of twelve, which were to be preceded by several waves of B-25s and B-17s as decoys. At the appointed hour, the planes were ready, but the VIP was late, and the annoyance of the pilots and bombardiers at this political Pish Posh in their midst was intense before Johnson ever arrived. He first boarded a plane called the *Wabash Cannonball,* but as the planes began to rev up, Johnson needed to relieve himself, so the mission needed to wait for that, too. When he returned, his seat on the *Wabash Cannonball* had been taken by one of his colonel escorts, and in this case rank mattered, so Johnson had to scurry about for a seat on another plane. It was, one might say, the luckiest pee Johnson ever took. Johnson ended up in a plane called the *Heckling Hare,* where he blithely accepted the parachute of the tailgunner, and did not notice that the corporal had no other. The conversation between the corporal and the congressman deteriorated from there, as Johnson was told bluntly that he was stupid, and indeed insane, for going on such a hairy mission where he was neither wanted nor needed. Johnson swallowed this insubordination without a retort.

The plan unraveled quickly in the air. Unfooled by the decoys, the Japanese Zeroes quickly dove in to break up the formation and descend upon the bombers behind. The *Wabash Cannonball* went down quickly, exploding when it hit the ocean as Johnson watched, with all hands lost, including one of the colonels escorting Johnson. A dozen enemy planes scattered the B-26s. Worse, the *Heckling Hare* developed engine trouble and began to lag behind. The Japanese fighter pilots, who had an ace in their midst, noticed immediately. Seven Zeroes fell upon the stray, riddling it with bullets. The American pilot jettisoned his bombs and executed a number of skillful maneuvers, as the parachuteless tailgunner blasted away. For fifteen awful minutes the firefight went on, until the Japanese broke it off voluntarily, realizing that in their preoccupation with the wounded *Hare* the other healthy bombers were getting through to Lae. Its wings and fuselage peppered with bullet holes, the *Hare* miraculously survived. It limped back to Port Moresby. On the ground, Johnson attempted to ingratiate himself with the hardened veterans. "It's been very interesting," he said breezily. "You people really need some stuff to fight with."

Back at MacArthur's headquarters a few days later, the general was caustic. Johnson had kept a diary of his Pacific adventures and in it he quoted MacArthur's greeting to him upon his return to headquarters: "Glad to see you two fellows here where three were last." MacArthur bluntly upbraided the congressman for risking his life needlessly. Johnson protested. He had Texas constituents among the New Guinea contingent, soldiers imbued with the spirit of Bowie, Crockett, and Houston. He told the general of the Austin lad he had encountered at Port Moresby, a pursuit pilot. Johnson had just received word that President Roosevelt had ordered all members of Congress on active duty to return to Washington, and he asked the Texas pilot what he could tell the folks when he got home. "Tell them to get us better fighter planes as quickly as you can and get me word whether my baby is a boy or girl," the pilot replied. This story assuaged MacArthur, and he indulged Johnson for over an hour, listening to his observations. No fool about politics himself, the general abruptly announced that he was presenting the congressman with a silver star for bravery. The citation had not yet been composed, said the general, but Johnson could pick his medal up on his way out. Eventually, some flowery prose was generated, praising Johnson for his "coolness" as a passenger in the face of danger, and his gallant action in returning with "valuable information." Within a week of his return to Washington, Johnson wrote grandly to his constituents, "I lived with the men on the fighting fronts. I flew with them in missions over enemy territory. I ate and slept with them; and was hospitalized with them in the Fiji Islands." (Johnson had contracted pneumonia on his return from Australia.) When, two years later, John Connally faced a year of incessant kamikaze attacks aboard a U.S. aircraft carrier and comported himself brilliantly as a fighter direction officer at the hot spots of Iwo Jima and Okinawa, he would receive a medal one notch lower in the index of gallantry.

If most authors in later years received the story of Johnson's Pacific mission uncritically, so too did John Connally. His boss was now a decorated combat veteran—he had a medal from the great MacArthur to prove it—and the details of the mission raised the Boss in Connally's estimation rather than lowered him. Johnson had dallied with the war, and Connally saw nothing wrong with that. There was fun in it, in fact. A year later, Connally was in Algiers, and there, the Germans launched a few light bombing raids as a soft reminder. In writing to Johnson about it, Connally invoked the fun of Johnson's mission in the Pacific:

"The boys have tried to do to us what you did over New Guinea, but just a few times. I am having more fun than a kid at a circus. I am absolutely fascinated at the show." When the show became real for Connally it would fascinate and entertain him somewhat less.

★

Through the latter part of 1942 in wartime Washington, Connally settled into a routine at the Navy Department and at home. Lyndon Johnson had officially returned to the House of Representatives on July 17, happy for Roosevelt's directive to members of Congress to return. Seven members of Congress were affected by the presidential order, but four of the seven decided to resign from Congress and remain on active duty. As it was initially worded, the directive probably would have backfired: it deactivated the members "except those who wish to remain on active duty for the duration of the war." Had the secretaries of the army and navy not objected to the phrase and insisted that it be deleted, it might have been politically impossible for Lyndon Johnson to take advantage of the invitation. In any event, the Boss was back in their midst, his demands as great as ever, and Connally once again had two full-time jobs.

With Nellie's pregnancy progressing, the Connallys took an apartment in the Wardman Towers, on Mount St. Alban, where the Johnsons also lived. Even in wartime and with a baby on the way, Texas hospitality remained in force. When Jake Pickle passed through Washington as a fresh naval officer waiting for assignment, he moved in with the Connallys.

Lady Bird Johnson, meanwhile, was growing tired of the constant motion of her life. She had lived from one campaign to the next, out of suitcases, in temporary quarters here and there. She longed for a permanent nest, for a family. One miscarriage had followed another, and Nellie Connally's enlarged condition was an ever-present reminder, even rebuke. She was growing quietly desperate. She wanted a house, and she had found one, a white brick Colonial in Cleveland Park, with eight rooms. Johnson acquiesced, but even though his wife was putting up the down payment from her inheritance, Johnson continued to haggle over the price with the seller until the purchase fell into jeopardy. Lady Bird seethed and, finally, with John Connally present one day, she exploded.

"I want that house," she exclaimed. "Every woman wants a home of her own. I've lived out of a suitcase ever since we've been married. I have no home to look forward to. I have no children to look forward to. I have nothing to look forward to but another election!" As she stormed out of the room, the men fell into a stunned silence.

"What should I do?" Johnson finally mumbled.

"I'd buy the house," Connally replied tartly. The two men had old-fashioned marriages in which they were usually unchallenged, but Connally, at least, knew when it was time to placate.

As the year progressed, Connally became increasingly consumed with his military work, and he gradually disengaged himself from Johnson's incessant demands. He was growing into a seasoned naval officer, with nearly a year's service, in the great war of his generation. His compatriots from college and even from the Johnson office were drifting away into the real action. Pickle had gone off to a ship in the Pacific. Singleton had left to be a gunnery officer on a destroyer escort. Even the studious Walter Jenkins had spurned a naval commission and had enlisted as a private in the army. Connally was drawn to the Lend-Lease program, which now was the lifeline to Russia and was extending its mandate to the embattled northern coast of Africa. Within the program, a crackerjack team of young men about Connally's age was getting considerable responsibility: Philip Graham, later the publisher of the *Washington Post;* Harding Bancroft, later a top executive of the *New York Times;* Eugene Rostow, later undersecretary of state; Ben Heineman, later a railroad magnate; Lloyd Cutler, later a pillar of the Washington legal establishment and Jimmy Carter's legal counsel; and George

Ball, who acted as general counsel for Lend-Lease under its head, Edward Stettinius (and who later was undersecretary of state under Presidents Kennedy and Johnson).

Acceding to Connally's interest in Lend-Lease, Johnson called Ball. "George, I've got an able young fellow over here. He could go far. He's gone into the navy, and he'd like to get some experience on the executive side."

"Fine, send him over," Ball replied. "We'll give him some work." When Connally arrived, Ball gave him an office and a telephone. "The telephone was a mistake," Ball would say later with a twinkle. "We never got any work out of him after that." Connally was constantly on the phone to the Texas underground.

In December, Lloyd Cutler was dispatched to Algiers to set up the Lend-Lease office there and, at age twenty-four, to work with the brilliant American diplomat Robert Murphy. Murphy, in turn, was working with young French civil servants who also had futures: Jean Monnet, Maurice Couve de Murville, and René Mayer, as well as with the solid Harold Macmillan of Great Britain. The North African situation had developed into a fascinating mix of the military and the diplomatic, and Algiers seemed to be the place to which bright young men with political connections gravitated.

In November, with Operation Torch, General Eisenhower had launched his invasion of North Africa, landing at various points along the coast, with the objective of challenging Rommel and his Afrika Korps in Tunisia. But Morocco and Algeria were in the hands of the Vichy Government, and the initial opposition to the Allied landings was Vichy French rather than Nazi. In short order, however, the Vichy French surrendered, upon the order of Admiral Darlan, the designated successor to Marshal Petain, who had arrived unexpectedly in Algeria. Eisenhower had to deal with Darlan and there ensued a delicate period when the Vichy French and the Free French were on equal footing, a situation that infuriated General de Gaulle and raised something of a stink back in the United States.

Young Lloyd Cutler arrived in Algiers in mid-December, and no sooner had he unpacked his bags than Admiral Darlan was, shockingly, assassinated. Several days later Cutler received a curt summons from the G-2 intelligence officer to come to headquarters at once. He drove up the slope of the scarped hill to the grand Hotel St. Georges and was ushered into the G-2's office, where the stern officer presented him with a telegram that had just arrived.

CONGRATULATIONS! WE DIDN'T THINK YOU COULD PULL IT OFF SO
QUICKLY!   THE HOME OFFICE

Cutler bumbled and stumbled, trying to explain that this was merely the wicked humor of Phil Graham, but the G-2 was not amused.

Cutler took up residence in a villa halfway up the steep slope of the Sahel hills, which overlooked the lovely, crescent-shaped Bay of Algiers. Along with Livingstone Short (who later became a General Motors executive), Cutler's mission was to strengthen the economy of North Africa, since it was the next strategic step in the war as a staging area for the forthcoming invasion of Italy. Under Cutler the Lend-Lease office was to expand rapidly from 2 to over 150 men.

John Connally was soon thrown into this sparkling and brassy crowd of comers. Early in 1943 he got his orders to Algiers and to Cutler's operation there. The night before he left Washington, the great friend of young Texas warriors, Sam Rayburn, turned up at the Connallys' apartment to bid the young officer good-bye. If Connally's connection was to Rayburn and Johnson, he was soon joined by another Texan, the tall, dried-up figure of Bill Kitrell, who had received his appointment to Algiers directly from Edward Stettinius, who was soon to become secretary of state. At the Hotel St. Georges there was another quasi-Texan with real political connections. That person was Elliott Roosevelt, who had become known in Texas beyond his lineage as the manager of radio stations in the Texas State Network. Connally and Roosevelt got along from the beginning. In Algiers in 1943, the old boy network was working very nicely among the young boys as well. It would not be long before Roosevelt, who could arrange anything, was making plans for Connally to take a trip to the Tunisian front, on to the Middle East, and then far south into Africa. But duty and the forthcoming invasion of Italy interceded, and a disappointed Connally had to demur. He would, however, make another trip, a drive of over 350 miles across tortuous mountain and desert roads to search out another Texan, only to find his friend gone when he arrived.

In February the military situation in North Africa was distinctly unsettled. Recently promoted to head the Afrika Korps, Rommel broke through the Allied lines at the Kasserine Pass in mid-February and left the American forces in Tunisia in considerable disorder. Three weeks and a shake-up of Eisenhower's staff were required to rectify the situation. But Rommel's skillful probes and maneuvers continued through March. As Connally arrived, so too did the nucleus of a planning staff for Operation Husky, the code name for the invasion of Sicily. This planning staff took up headquarters in a cluster of three schools, known as École Normale, two miles from the Hotel St. Georges. As that staff grew, Lend-Lease officers, including Cutler and Connally, were occasionally detailed there, making projections about what the Sicilian economy would need in the way of supplies once the Allied force swept across the island.

Life for a young naval officer in Algiers was scarcely all hardtack and combat boots. The villa where Cutler and Short lived and where Eugene Rostow would soon join them became a social center for the Lend-Lease crowd. Among the benefits that Cutler derived from working with René Mayer and Maurice Couve de Murville on economic and financial matters were the cases of fine French cognac with which the French kept the Americans well stocked. Quantities of Hennessy Three-Star were consumed at regular events. The Americans responded by being suitably deferential to their French counterparts. Eugene Rostow, for example, had been advised to speak only French to Couve de Murville, even though Couve's English was far better than Rostow's schoolboy patois. The tactic worked well, and the men established a firm relationship, one which survived into the late 1960s, when Rostow, as undersecretary of state for political affairs, and Couve de Murville, as minister of foreign affairs, went into tough negotiations on foreign trade matters.

The Lend-Lease office consisted mainly of civilians, and John Connally stood out, for he insisted on wearing his starched navy uniform. Again on display was that instinct, bred of an intense appreciation of his own good looks, to stand apart and to adopt almost an air of royalty.

Certain problems were specifically suited to navy expertise, such as the unscrambling of the gridlock in the Port of Algiers, as Admiral Henry Kent Hewitt, the commander of Operation Husky, began to amass the greatest naval armada ever assembled in preparation for the Italian invasion. Lend-Lease supplies began to arrive as well. Not always were they effective or suited to the exigencies of the moment. Someone in "intelligence," for example, had divined that Arabs drank green tea, and bales of the stuff arrived and rotted on a dock. More nourishing to Connally's sense of humor was a large shipment of women's sanitary napkins, which exceeded the level of advancement both of Arab and even French women. (They were still accustomed to old-fashioned linen.) This material ended up being used to scrub down railroad locomotives, although occasionally a whimsical Arab trader in the sixteenth-century Kasbah stitched the napkins together to make an exotic headdress. Such glitches deepened Connally's conservative instincts, and he worried about the losses to the American taxpayer. A Lone Star axiom occurred to him:

"You never achieve your own ends, nor make a friend by letting some guy trade you a blind, sway-backed horse with heaves for a good thoroughbred and hope to get away with it." He longed for someone in his operation like Johnson, with drive and initiative. But he knew he should not protest unduly, for, despite his lonesomeness, he felt lucky. He had been talking occasionally to the "poor devils" back from the Tunisian front, men who had not been home for years. In general he was satisfied with his situation and confident that he could change it if he got bored or too disgusted. He spoke like a young man with political options, one who was not yet quite committed to patriotic duty. "If the time comes when [my situation doesn't suit me], you can expect to see me home," he wrote Johnson. "There's no doubt I can get there by myself. If you hear a whistle, don't turn a deaf ear."

The grand strategy for both the Atlantic and the Pacific in 1943 had been settled at the Casablanca Conference between Churchill and Roosevelt in January 1943, and those decisions would have a bearing on Connally's future military career. In the Pacific, a plan for a naval campaign west through the islands of the Central Pacific won out over MacArthur's preferred course up the New Guinea coast. In the Mediterranean, Sicily, rather than points far north on the ankle or calf of Italy, was chosen for the landing, even though the island was a well-fortified bastion with poor beaches for amphibious assault and a costly and protracted campaign up the Italian peninsula might be the consequence.

In any event, on July 10, Operation Husky was launched. Connally was left behind in Algiers. Without its armada, the city suddenly seemed like a forlorn and empty way station. It was not long before Connally, Cutler, and the other bright young men of Lend-Lease longed to join the real battle. They began to contemplate new assignments and a greater degree of engagement.

One last event, however, would make a lasting impression on Connally and his cohorts. Four days after Operation Husky got under way, Charles de Gaulle rode triumphantly into Algiers. It was Bastille Day. He came as the tall, imperious, courageous, and abrasive hero of the Free French, a symbol of the regeneration of the French nation, the incarnation of "*la Gloire.*" To this magnificent figure, Connally could relate in a profound way. Here was a grand representation of his attitude toward leadership. De Gaulle was the proverbial knight in shining armor, come to rescue a nation and revive a flagging national spirit; he was just the kind of knight which after the war and after Roosevelt Connally would feel America needed. Before the Monument of the Dead, de Gaulle watched his troops march past and saw in his soldiers, "rising like a wall of flame," the burning desire to take part in coming battles. When de Gaulle spoke, he evoked images that electrified young Americans like Connally and Eugene Rostow: France as a tortured captive, the French as a brave people with new destinies, the griefs and the glories of France's 1,500-year history.

But if such a grandiose presentation stirred in the young a pride and a purpose, it did not export well across the Atlantic. John Connally would eventually find that out.

★ 6 ★

Combat

FOR THE FIRST SIX MONTHS of 1944, Lieutenant John Connally prepared to go to war in earnest. On Saint Simons Island in Georgia, he threw himself into his training as a fighter direction officer. This anticipated eventual duty aboard an aircraft carrier, a weapon which had become central to the Pacific strategy. The navy kept him "busy as the devil," studying how to direct fighters in intercepting enemy aircraft that were coming in from 30 to 100 miles away. His job was to put the American interceptor within three miles of the intruder for a daytime "tallyho" and within three-quarters of a mile at nighttime. "It's a ticklish business but darn interesting," he wrote to Lyndon Johnson, and he fretted when he "butchered" one exam on navigation, for it threatened his standing as one of the top men in his class. He knew he was headed for some hot action regardless. "It just gripes me to make a few foolish mistakes and ruin what would otherwise have been a fair grade," he wrote. "It doesn't make much difference, however, so there's not much point in getting upset over it." In fact, his class standing did make some difference, for it would have a bearing on future assignments.

Johnson was forever the home-base cheerleader. He sought to buoy the spirits of his friend with gossip of Lady Bird's pregnancy or Nellie's work at the Johnson radio station in Austin, as well as with news of other Texas soldiers and of his own political doings. The news from abroad was frequently upsetting, such as the report of the fifty-one boys from Caldwell, Texas, in the eastern part of

Johnson's congressional district, who were killed, wounded, or missing when the Texas Thirty-sixth Division was cut up at Salerno. In their frequent and chatty correspondence, Connally and Johnson celebrated together the heroics of Connally's younger brother, Merrill, whose marine outfit had been in the first wave to establish a beachhead at the Pacific island of Bougainville, where Merrill had flown repeated missions as an artillery air observer over enemy lines and had been promoted from buck sergeant to master gunnery sergeant. In March 1944 Merrill was promoted again, receiving a battlefield commission on Guam. "It's a shame it doesn't run in the family," Connally wrote LBJ in mock self-pity, but LBJ would have none of that. "If you follow in Merrill's footsteps, you'll be Admiral of the Fleet when we sail to Tokyo," Johnson responded. It would not be long before the two brothers would come much closer together, in the death struggles of Iwo Jima and Okinawa.

For Connally, political news from Texas became the spring tonic it had once been for Lyndon Johnson, as he went into advanced night fighter training at Quonset, Rhode Island, laboring over his radar, communications, and navigation books, and he badgered Johnson to write more gossip, resorting to the colloquial: "Please rite an tell me if I shude bee fore buck Taylor sens my congresmen will not rite me!"

The Buck Taylor of the piece was Johnson's opponent in the 1944 Democratic primary, and the challenger was to stage a bitter alley fight against the incumbent. Taylor focused upon Johnson's hollow promise to join the boys in the trenches when war came, and his retreat back into the safe corridors of Congress eight months later. Johnson had failed "to keep his promise to serve his country in the trenches beside good soldiers he helped to send to those trenches," Taylor boomed from the stump.

The charge stung the thin-skinned Johnson, more personally than politically, for it touched his sense of guilt. His guilt was implicit in his warm letters to Connally, who now had come to embody the commitment to stay the course. The guilt was never overtly stated, but the awareness that Connally was headed for the real war very soon brought the men even closer, and put some perspective on Johnson's political battles. Connally signed his letters generally, "My love always," and Johnson, in turn, professed his love to "Johnnie."

In May of 1944, the political struggle in Texas was once again between the loyalists and the renegades of the Democratic party. Sentiment ran high against a fourth term for Roosevelt, and one casualty was Sam Rayburn, who was forced to withdraw his name as a possible vice presidential candidate because of the local Texas wars. Johnson found himself in the uncomfortable situation of being heckled and shouted down at the state convention when an anti-Roosevelt chairman was narrowly elected and a near riot ensued. Shouts of "Get that yes-man off the platform" and "Throw Roosevelt's pinup boy out of here!" filled the Texas senate chamber, where the convention was being held. Now near the end of his training in Rhode Island, Connally, despite his focus on the larger matter of the war, wished he could be there for a good, old political fight, Texas-style. He devoured Johnson's news. "It was terrible, but I feared as much," he wrote Johnson about the state convention. "I only wish I could be with you in Chicago [the site of the national convention where Roosevelt was easily renominated]—maybe we could get in a real fight this time."

In early June, Connally finished his training and received his orders. He was assigned to the "mighty *Essex*," the aircraft carrier which would soon enough earn the accolade "the fightingest ship in the Navy." The *Essex* was the flagship of a new fleet of fast carriers that had now become the linchpin of the Pacific war. The Pacific, MacArthur notwithstanding, was the navy's war, while Europe belonged to the army. Congress had authorized the construction of the *Essex* in 1938, and during the summer of 1940, when John Connally walked the halls of Congress, it had commissioned eleven of the *Essex*-class carriers. Now they were coming on line, as Connally made his way to the Pacific. Of the eleven, ten, freshly in the fleet, were assigned to Admiral Halsey. Only with their arrival would the island campaign in the Central Pacific begin in earnest. To be ordered to the *Essex* as its flight direction officer at this critical stage of the war was a plum assignment.

The farther Connally traveled west, the more his letters to Johnson carried a heightened sense of loyalty. It was as if his own impending danger made his defense of his friend more overwrought. Connally found Johnson's opponent in 1944 a "nobody, a ne'er-do-well and political hanger-on," and he felt that Taylor was in the race only to "cut Johnson up." Charges which normally would be dismissed as commonplace by one experienced in politics now became personalized for the soldier, and Connally reacted passionately when Johnson wrote him of the bitter race. "The first round is over," Johnson wrote. "They used everything in the books, Johnnie, and much that never appeared in any books. It was sponsored by money from without." This made Connally livid. As yet, he did not know that Johnson had won the primary election handily when he wrote, "I still have indigestion, and [I have] my mental gyrations (including a nice, clean murder of a low-down, two-bit, chiseling, unscrupulous stooge)."

That Connally was far away and incommunicado increased his anxiety about the outcome of Johnson's race, and he would not get the results of the race for three weeks. He knew only of the lowbrow nature of the campaign, particularly the charge of hypocrisy against Johnson in contrast to the boys like Connally who were staying the full course of the war. The farther he was removed from the scene of the political fray and the closer he came to the war, the more emotional he became. He wrote to Johnson from the *Essex* with a passion and a vitriol that he would rarely ever again exhibit, calling Johnson's opponent "common" and "an illegitimate offspring nurtured by animal excretion. We can't all be common . . . so I better knock off discussing that 'grate' man. . . . God, what a travesty is our democratic process!"

In the summer of 1944, the thrust westward from Pearl Harbor was well under way. With ten new *Essex*-class carriers as its centerpiece, the American armada had taken Midway, Wake, Truk in the Marshall Islands, and Tarawa in the Gilberts. The *Essex* lay off Eniwetok Atoll in the Marshalls when John Connally joined her in mid-July. Preparations for the assault on Guam, Tinian, and Saipan were well advanced. But going for the "bottleneck" of the Philippines, much less an assault on the Japanese islands themselves, still seemed far away. If Connally was in for the duration, the duration appeared to be another two years at least. The Japanese navy had sustained terrible losses, but it remained a formidable force in its Philippine lair and to the north of New Guinea. Similarly, the Japanese air force, with its superb Zero fighter, was still awesome, although American skill and sheer numbers were gradually giving the Allies the command of the skies, especially as the new Hellcats came on line. They were thirty miles an hour faster than the Zeroes and had heavier guns, thicker armor, and self-sealing gas tanks. Increasingly, American naval pilots sensed that the Japanese were throwing green pilots into the air against them, and the kill ratio was shifting substantially in favor of the Americans.

Connally's old boss, James Forrestal, had taken over as secretary of the navy in April upon the death of Frank Knox, and this gave an additional boost to the navy's air force, for Forrestal had himself been a naval aviator in World War I and was more open than Knox to suggestions from aviators. Naval theory was in the process of embracing air power as its chief weapon, further bolstering the importance of the carrier fleet.

Two weeks before Connally joined his ship, and no doubt to his great disappointment, the *Essex* engaged in a spectacular battle that dramatically boosted the growing emphasis on air power. On June 19, a force of fifty Zeroes came south and were intercepted over the Marianas by a squadron of Hellcats from the *Essex*, led by the navy's chief air ace, David McCampbell. The American fighters dove into the Japanese formation and scattered it, and then began to pick off enemy planes. The sky quickly became a jumble of aircraft as both sides threw scores of planes into the fray. The inexperience of the Japanese pilots put them at a terrible disadvantage. Zeroes suddenly became easy pickings. From the moment one jubilant American pilot crackled over air radio, "Hell, this is like an old-time turkey shoot," the battle became known as the Marianas Turkey Shoot. It was the worst single-day slaughter of Japanese aircraft in the war. Of 373 carrier-based planes and another 50 land-based, the Japanese lost about 300, while the Americans lost 30. The blow was nearly fatal for the Japanese air force, virtually obliterating its carrier air strength. From this point, the imperial strategists began to think about new and desperate methods.

Thus, it was a cocky bunch that Connally was joining in July. But the pleasure of it! He would be directing McCampbell and the aces of Air Group 15 from the chaotic communications room below the flight deck known as the Combat Information Center. From that nerve center of the fleet, security for the entire task force was controlled, air strikes were dispatched, and information from the pilots was gathered and disseminated to the fleet.

Before joining his ship Connally was to have one unexpected joy. At Kwajalein in the Marshalls, he had an idle moment, and wandered into a tent where a marine was sorting mail to inquire of the whereabouts of his brother Merrill. Merrill Connally had already seen more dangerous action than any foolhardy leatherneck might ever hope to see. On Guadalcanal he had been a sniper. At Bougainville, he had carried bow and arrow and spear as he tracked the Japanese in the jungle with native scouts. At Guam, he became a forward spotter, flying in light fabric planes that were catapulted off the decks of the battleships, the *Sangamon* and the *Swannee*, and were retrieved upon their return, if they did return, with a boom and cable. But at Kwajalein, as the marine mail sorter reported, Merrill was resting not a mile away, and John Connally soon burst in on him and woke him from a nap.

Once he was on the *Essex,* Connally would have no time for a leisurely apprenticeship. Within days of his arrival, the *Essex* was launching strikes on the jewels of the Marianas—Guam, Tinian, and Saipan—while Merrill was part of the marines' landing force. In September the fleet edged closer to the Philippines with an assault on the Palau Islands. Bombers from the *Essex* struck Mindanao itself. By early October the *Essex* was north of the Philippines, its planes streaking to Formosa and to the Pescadores in the Formosa Strait and even as far north as Okinawa.

By Christmas of 1944, Connally had become seasoned and had been promoted to chief flight direction officer of the *Essex.* His letters home were terse, for he had no time to write. The war was moving into its desperate end game in the Pacific, and Connally was hard pressed. In early December he wrote Lyndon Johnson a tender Christmas letter, which accented the uncertainties of his life . . . where he would be someplace upon the vast Pacific Ocean on Christmas Day itself, and he hoped that, when the next Christmas rolled around in a year's time, he could be with his best friend again. "My faculties for expressing the hope that you have the happiest Christmas ever are necessarily limited by words alone. Where we will be this Christmas, heaven only knows, but I have high hopes that before another Christmas season rolls around, I will be close enough to enjoy at least a part of it with you. . . . if you need one, this is just a reminder that I will be thinking of you as always." Johnson returned the affection prodigiously. He conveyed his terrible worry for his friend in his response and plied Connally with thoughts of a future together. "I need not remind you of how very, very fond I am of you, but in case you have been concerned about what is going to be done when you return, I would like to ease your mind. It may be that the proposition will not appeal to you, but I am certain you will have a lovely modern home with a salary of at least two or three times what you have made before and the kind of job where we can click along together. If you want to practice law, you can do that in your spare time because I am sure of the success of the plan I have in mind."

What Johnson really had in mind was for his friend to be out of there. The shape of what Connally was experiencing on the *Essex* was gradually becoming clear at home. Connally himself was scrupulous to a fault in avoiding a description of the actual combat operations, for security regulations applied. He would only say it was a "great experience." But his generalizations were frightening enough. To Johnson the day after Christmas, he made time to write again, even though the job of a flight control officer had become a twenty-four-hour job. "We have the axe right on our necks continually, and we do our best to keep it from falling. Since last August we have had a tough siege of it. There isn't much we haven't seen or many dangers we haven't been through. Subs, aerial torpedoes, dive bombers, etc. We feel sometimes that we have an overdrawn account with Lady Luck. I can't go into graphic detail here, but I'm sure several instances are sufficiently etched in my memory to allow me to repeat them second by second."

"Subs, aerial torpedoes, dive bombers, etc." It was the *et cetera* that counted. Early in December the *New York Times* had given the home crowd some sense of how the ax lay continually on the neck of the *Essex*. With the chant of wartime propaganda, the *Times* reported that the *Essex* was winning glory as the "fightingest ship in the Navy," with records in every category: leading air group, leading individual ace in David McCampbell, the greatest number of planes shot down in one day, and the greatest overall destruction of enemy planes and shipping. The glory was fully described, but not the horror; the good fortune, but not the sheer luck. On October 24, the *Essex* had had another glorious day equivalent to the Marianas Turkey Shoot in July, and this time Connally was in the thick of it. On October 20, MacArthur had waded ashore in Leyte Bay. Four days later, on October 24, the Japanese launched a ferocious counterattack. In three separate waves of 60 planes each, they came from Luzon airfields. The air plot of the *Essex* was the first to detect them, and with Connally in the midst of it, McCampbell and seven Hellcats scrambled and were first to intercept. With Connally as the control officer on the *Essex*, McCampbell and only his wingman came in above the 60 fighters, bombers, and torpedo bombers and broke up the formation. The Japanese bombers dove into the safety of the clouds, and the fighters began orbiting in a tight circle. Commanding the high altitudes, McCampbell and his squadron waited for the circle to break up and for other American planes from other carriers to arrive. Then it became a field day. Directed from the *Essex*, the air battle lasted for 90 minutes. "During the next hour or so, we followed the formation of weaving fighters, taking advantage of every opportunity to knock down those who attempted to climb to our altitude, scissored outside, struggled or became too eager, and came at us singly," McCampbell wrote in his report later. "In all we made 18 to 20 passes, being very careful not to expose ourselves and to conserve ammunition by withholding our fire within very close range." Only 18 out of 60 Japanese planes remained in the formation when the action broke off. McCampbell had accounted for nine kills himself, a navy record. Elsewhere American planes had dispatched three Japanese heavy cruisers when the main Japanese striking force under Admiral Kurita was discovered.

That is half of the story. Both at sea and in the air, desperation had begun to mark Japanese actions. McCampbell and his aces had proven indisputably that the Japanese were no match for the Americans in the air. Indeed, the Japanese pilots would probably not have qualified for flight by American standards. The Japanese had to come up with some different tactic with a greater chance to wound the American armada. The new and the ugly appeared on October 24, as the *Essex*'s Air Group 15 took potshots above. Near the *Essex*, the carrier *Princeton* had also thrown its air group into the fray, when a lone Judy glide bomber pierced through the overcast and dove into the *Princeton* flight deck. The Judy smashed through three decks, setting off bombs and torpedoes one by one, before its 550-pound bomb exploded in the ship's bake shop. The *Princeton* was a total loss. Hours later, American torpedoes scuttled it. It went down 2,000 yards off the *Essex*'s starboard bow.

In the days ahead, the suicide mission emerged as a deliberate tactic in a new Japanese air strategy. American carriers were its prime targets. Before his mission, kamikaze pilot Yoshi Miyagi wrote his epitaph in haiku: "I am nothing but a particle of iron, attached to a magnet: the American aircraft carrier." The suicide missions were the brainstorm of Admiral Takijiro Onishi, who had toured Japanese air bases in the Philippines and had been appalled by the woeful inexperience of his fliers. As Onishi's Special Attack Corps came into being, the suicide raids grew in November and December. On November 5, in stormy weather preceding a typhoon, several hundred miles northeast of the Philippines, the *Essex*'s radar picked up a kamikaze coming in at wave-top level, and the carrier's guns shot the Judy down well short of the ship.

By late November the Americans had taken out the major Japanese battlefields in the Philippines, but the enemy skillfully scattered and camouflaged its planes in small airstrips throughout the islands. On November 25 the *Essex* was east of Luzon, launching strikes to ferret out the remnants of the enemy air force. Connally sat in the situation room with his executive officer, then-Commander David L. MacDonald (later the commander of the Sixth Fleet and chief of naval operations), when a radial-engine Judy appeared on the scope from the starboard side. Connally and MacDonald watched in horror as the plane got past first the 50-millimeter cannons and then the 20-millimeter guns, bearing down on the ship like a slow, fat bluebottle fly, shot nearly to pieces and yet still coming. This time they knew they were going to be hit. Their luck had run out. The Judy skimmed along the flight deck, crammed with planes fully fueled and ready to take off, but for some reason it did not dive in time. At last it careened into the port-side deck, touching off a gasoline explosion which killed 15 and wounded 44.

Calmly, MacDonald rose from his chair as dust from the rafters settled over them. "Well," he said to Connally, "they finally got our cherry."

The *Essex*'s virginity was technically gone, but its dignity remained intact. The Judy's bomb had not exploded; it probably had not been armed. This suggested pilot error, for the suicide bombers dared not arm their bombs until shortly before impact, lest they explode in the air prematurely. In this case the pilot's error seemed to be that he allowed himself to be killed at the controls, which would account for the fact that the plane had not plowed into the crowded flight line. A dead pilot at the controls of a suicide plane that still managed to hit its mark seemed to increase the horror. The flight deck of the lucky *Essex* was back in operation in thirty minutes.

This was the *et cetera* about which Connally had written Johnson. This was the ax continuously on their neck. The reports of successful suicide attacks were filtering back home both to Japan and to America. The Japanese high command looked at the situation and concluded that their success ratio was far higher with suicide raids than from massive squadron attacks with inferior pilots. Admiral Halsey and the American high command repaired to rear bases over the holiday season to ponder an effective counterstrategy. If only the technology of the guided missile were closer to perfection—but the recent tests had all failed. In January 1945, when MacArthur invaded Luzon, forty American warships were hit by kamikazes.

Lyndon Johnson had had enough of these terrifying reports from the Pacific. He wanted his friend off that fighting magnet, and home. He approached Forrestal directly on the point in a naked effort at favoritism, demanding that Connally be ordered to Washington for a desk job. On January 25, 1945, he got his reply. In a memorandum from the secretary's aide, Connally's return to Washington was stated to be the secretary's eventual desire, but only after Connally had been out there a logical time. Fighter direction is a specialty which requires special talent as well as extended training. A fighter direction officer must not only be good, but must have the confidence of the fighter pilots as well as the ship's personnel. It takes months to gain this. I would say that Connally is just now arriving at a position of maximum value in his special assignment in the Essex. In view of the relative shortage of fighter directors, I do not believe Connally's detachment any time in the near future is justified. He is under 30, and has already had a considerable period of duty in Washington. His return now would lay the Navy Department and you open to criticism on that basis too, I fear. I wish you would agree to let Connally remain in the Essex until he has been in her a year. What do you say?

To this Johnson scribbled a disappointed "O.K.," but only after he had tried, and failed, to persuade Forrestal face to face. To this failure of the Johnson treatment the congressman made only an oblique and teasing reference in a letter to Connally on February 17, 1945, when, as Johnson knew, Forrestal was on his way to the Pacific and to the *Essex:*

"For some reason or another, Forrestal told me that 'John Connally, in my judgment, is one of the top five young men I have seen in the Navy.' I don't know when you will be ordered back here, but I assume they will want to keep you on the *Essex* for a year. That's just six months too long for me, but that seems to be in the cards."

It is doubtful that Lieutenant Connally would have wanted to be yanked home to safety at this point in the war, especially as a reward of political influence, for he was now operating in the nerve center of his ship and of his fleet, at peak efficiency, with eleven officers and eighty men under his command, and his carrier at the center of an epic death struggle. His abilities were starting to get recognition throughout the fleet. Another bright young man with ties to Lyndon Johnson and to Roosevelt was serving on a ship within rifle range of Connally. That was James Rowe, Jr., the former aide to Roosevelt and later an adviser to President Johnson. In the spring of 1945, Rowe would write to Johnson about a conversation he had overheard among radar watch officers, who were debating whether or not John Connally was the best flight director in the fleet. "The large majority were in favor of John, with one or two dissenters, arguing in a jargon I for one could not make head or tail of," Rowe wrote. "But the important point was that he is good enough to make the question an arguable one."

Johnson persisted in his letters, filling them with the kind of home gossip that sailors long for. Nellie was working at the Johnson radio station in Austin now, as was Connally's younger brother, Golfrey. Johnson reckoned that he could run the station "on loyalty plus two Connallys, and I wouldn't be much afraid to do it considering that Kathleen [Connally's year-and-a-half-old daughter] would be willing to take her place at the post just any day she gets big enough to understand that we want her." Nellie, in turn, was trying to keep her spirits up any way she could. In mid-January, as the *Essex* was refurbishing for the assault on Iwo Jima and Okinawa, she wrote Johnson,

"I really threw one last PM. I had six girlies out for a good drink, dinner, and a wild poker game. After drinks, I quit worrying about how my dinner would taste, because I could have fed them steamed grass and mud pies for all they cared. . . . I've still not heard from Big John but I look into the mail box each day hoping." When the letters did come, Nellie described them as "lonesome-sounding," with no mention of the war.

In February, the *Essex* was in Ulithi making ready for the last phase of the war. But even that rear island, 1,200 miles from the nearest Japanese base, was not safe. On March 11, a kamikaze flew the distance and crashed into the carrier *Randolph*, as she was lit at night and taking on ammunition. The *Randolph* was out of action for a month. John Connally was becoming morose, suddenly beginning to worry that the odds were finally catching up with him. He had written to Nellie about an insurance policy that would provide a college education for his daughter, Kathleen, in the event he was not around. (As it turned out, tragically, it was Kathleen, not her father, who was dead when she would have been of college age.)

"I want to put a stop order now on that kind of nonsense," Johnson wrote Connally when he heard this lugubrious talk. "I know you are going to have a million by the time [Kathleen] is ready to enter college and who knows, I might have that much myself," a prediction that would come true on both counts. "But just in case we wanted to invest it all the night before matriculation day, we wouldn't want to be hamstrung with a couple of girls asking where and how they were going to college. So we have worked it out that Kathleen and Lynda Bird can be reasonably independent so far as education is concerned when they are 18, as neither you nor I were.

If it pans out wrong, I'll chalk up one for you, as I have many, many times. So come along, be a good boy and play with me on this one."

If Connally resented this paternalism, he did not show it in his letters. At his distance and in his danger, he was seized with gratitude and love. The Johnson and Connally families were becoming even more closely intertwined than they had been before, the children now as well as the husbands and wives.

★

At Ulithi, in early February, the briefings on the *Essex* took on a different cast. The target now was Iwo Jima, that hunk of rock and volcanic ash which was deemed strategically important as a base from which to launch an invasion of the Japanese home islands, if it should come to that. From the fighter direction officer's viewpoint the problem now was close air support, but as yet there was no real appreciation of how close that support would have to be. Just as the naval commanders longed for the military scientists to perfect missiles to defeat kamikazes, so the marines might have dreamed of napalm as they contemplated the siege of Iwo Jima. But tests of napalm, too, had failed. Honeycombed with pillboxes and underground tunnels and festooned with the awful symbol of Mount Suribachi, Iwo Jima would have to be taken with bullets, grenades, and flamethrowers.

Before the invasion of Iwo Jima, Connally had another warm visit with his brother Merrill, who was now aboard the battleship *Idaho*. He was still one of only four aerial spotters in the entire Pacific, still ready to board his flimsy cloth plane and be flung off like a clay pigeon to fly over enemy territory, inevitably to return full of holes. This time they were joined by Jim Rowe, and the talk drifted naturally into politics and Texas, to Lyndon Johnson and government after the war. They had no notion of what lay ahead in the coming days, of what the next military objective would be, or what role they might play in it. It was a moment in isolation, to be enjoyed for all it was worth, not a moment to dwell on the uncertainties and the dangers. Those were apparent enough. "Out there, you never knew if your brother was dead or alive," Merrill would say later, but it was he who was flagrantly courting death. By any oddsmaker's calculations, it was a miracle that Merrill had made it this far. Within days of this visit, John Connally wrote to Johnson that his brother was in good spirits and healthy, although he was very worried about Merrill's mortal peril. "The boys are having tough sledding," Connally wrote Johnson, "and one of his buddies has cashed in his chips." That had been a kid named Friday, whose wife had had a baby, but who never found out if it was a boy or girl. He was shot down and lost.

On February 19, as the centerpiece of Task Force 58, the *Essex* held a rehearsal with the marines on Tinian, and the marine planes roared over the beaches in low-level strafing exercises, a tactic that in the real battle would have almost no effect. At Iwo Jima, the Japanese waited. They would eschew the fruitless "banzai charges." In their fortified entrenchments, they would let the marines come to them, contesting every inch of the wasted soil. For the *Essex*, there was no break: ten days before the invasion of Iwo Jima the carrier steamed north to within sixty miles of the Honshu coast to launch the first strikes on Tokyo in three years. As an idea, letting Tokyo have it again was sheer pleasure for the American commanders, but as a reality it was a nightmare. The Americans, almost too cocky now with their unbroken string of successes, lost sixty planes. It was a high loss for those used to turkey shoots and field days, and even though the Japanese lost five times as many planes, it was a harbinger of what the invasion of Japanese soil might be. A strategy to defeat the kamikazes still hadn't been developed. The best the American high command could devise was to place picket ships far forward of the carriers to act as lookouts— and as bait—for the human bombs. It was a countersuicide measure that was itself suicide.

After that sour experience, it was back to the waters around Iwo Jima for the *Essex*, where Connally watched the planes take off from his ship, thinking that they might be flying over Merrill's head. In fact, though Connally would not know it for weeks, Merrill lay near death. Two days before the marines hit the beach at Iwo Jima, his plane was making slow passes over the island, searching for artillery targets, when a shell slammed into the plane's undercarriage beneath the spot where Merrill sat, unprotected by any steel plating, and tore into his thighs. The plane went down six miles from any American ship. When Merrill woke up three days later, he was scarcely accorded a hero's reception. He was asked what he would like to drink, and he ordered hot chocolate. He was asked what his religious denomination was, and he angrily objected that he did not want any chaplain—he was not ready to die. The skipper of the *Idaho* heard about this. He stopped by and complained, half-seriously, that the *Idaho* had never had a casualty until they sent a damn marine aboard.

For the *Essex*, there was no time to tarry, no time to absorb.

No sooner had the American flag been raised on Mount Suribachi than the *Essex*, more a strategic than a tactical weapon, was steaming back north to the Japanese coast to try again. On February 25, a raid on the industrial city of Nagoya was planned. But bad weather closed in, and good luck or bad, the raid was called off.

Back at Ulithi, Connally finally had time to write. Discreet as always, he apologized for not relating his adventures in detail. "Many interesting things happen to us each day which would make exciting reading if we were permitted to pass them on," he wrote Johnson, but the congressman could assume that his ship was always "where the fireworks are." For the first time he made an oblique reference to the kamikazes. "We have had to defend ourselves against tactics even more daring than our own. . . . The work is extremely demanding, requiring all your mental faculties and split-second decisions as well as all your physical stamina and endurance. By now, we are all tired. I tire easily, which worries me a little, because I no longer feel like I'm doing what I should do."

He was not given to self-pity, however. He looked around him and saw others, particularly his brother Merrill, who were giving more. Merrill had been home only once in forty months. Three weeks after Iwo Jima, Connally still did not know that Merrill had been severely wounded. As always, political shoptalk was the best distraction he had. "Nellie writes vague hints that you have your fingers in many pies, all of which I knew—knowing you. She, of course, failed to say what pies you have your fingers in and whether you pulled out a plum."

It would not be until sometime after the war when Connally learned that his mentor and friend had made a romantic pass at Nellie. Then he would only grunt at the mention of it, as if to suggest that he expected as much from Lyndon Johnson. "Lyndon was not a daring philanderer like John Kennedy," said George Christian, a close associate of both Johnson and Connally. "He liked to know the person he was flattering with his attentions." (LBJ was not always tender towards Nellie in the office, however. Once when she did not put a telephone call through to him fast enough, he threw a pitcher of water at her.) As for Connally's own amorous adventures, the ones he related, at least for the record, might have been cadged from the benign comedy of *Mister Roberts* or *South Pacific*. After the war he loved to tell the story of a hospital ship that came alongside when the *Essex* sailed into Ulithi in the Pacific. On the deck of the hospital ship, nurses in starched uniforms stood in formation to salute the brave men of the *Essex*, whereupon the tub's skipper appeared in sandals, shorts, a greasy hat, and full beard, and from his bridge he bellowed through a bullhorn: "Things are sure tough, boys. They can say 'No!' in every language—including braille." That applied to Nellie Connally as well.

At Ulithi, Connally finally learned of Merrill's wounds and was able to search him out in a naval hospital. By this time Merrill could hobble about on crutches, and so the brothers stopped by the colossal, makeshift outdoor bar, nearly a mile long, which had been built to serve the men of the huge armada lying offshore. The boys drew their allotment of two bottles of beer each and repaired to the beach to talk endlessly about their family ranch and their futures after the war, before (teetotalers both) they poured the beer into the sand in a giddy ritual.

★

From March 15 to June 1, 1945, the *Essex* stayed constantly at sea, eighty days of relentless, nerve-jangling, exhausting combat, when the desperate, suicidal instincts of the Japanese rose to their most terrifying pitch, not only in the air, but on the ground and at sea as well. The invasion of Okinawa, the bloodiest single battle of World War II, in which 12,000 Americans would die, lay ahead. Prior to the April landing, the *Essex* pounded away at the island. But now, the Japanese had seen from the Iwo Jima experience that they could cut the Americans to shreds if they would only wait patiently in their concrete redoubts and let the enemy come to them. The mentality of the defenders has been enshrined at the monument to the dead in Tokyo, the Yasukuni Shrine, whose entrance is appointed with the graceful calligraphy of a fifteen-year-old Okinawa boy. "I wear the uniform of the Iron Blood Imperial Corps to demolish the United States and Great Britain. There will come a time when Okinawa sees victory."

No day of the entire war was more taxing for Connally than April 6, 1945. In the defense of Okinawa, the use of kamikazes was no longer only one aspect of overall strategy: it was now the central aspect. Suicide planes from Kyushu swarmed over the fleet, varying their tactics of approach, hitting other carriers: the *Hancock*, the *Intrepid*, the *Enterprise*, and 21 other American ships. The *Essex* was anchored between Okinawa and Kyushu, listening for the rustle of the Divine Wind and waiting to take its blow. For 52 straight hours, the *Essex* fended off attacks in a sky filled with random, fanatic, hornetlike attacks, as the enemy staged 389 separate raids. Eight decks below the flight deck, Connally peered through his scopes and directed the defense indefatigably. He worked without respite and, because of it, acquired the label "The Mole."

The sky was not the only danger on that day. Near dusk American submarines spotted the colossal superbattleship, the *Yamato*, steaming out of port near Hiroshima and heading south through the Bungo Straits between Kyushu and Shikoku, accompanied by six destroyers and two cruisers. She was the largest warship ever built; she displaced nearly three times the tonnage of the *Essex*. This was the ultimate suicide mission, for the *Yamato* carried only enough fuel to reach Okinawa. Her goal was to disrupt the American beachhead, unload her eighteen-inch guns on the American fleet, particularly the carriers, and then swoon like some mythic monster. Through the night, the American carriers maneuvered to intercept the suicide flagship at first light. At 8:22 A.M., through rain and heavy cloud cover, a plane from the *Essex* sighted the *Yamato* churning south at twenty-two knots. After noon, the raids from American carriers began, and within two hours the colossus was a wreck and began to list. Her captain ordered his men to abandon ship and then proceeded to lash himself to a beam. As lore has it, a seaman pulled a biscuit from his pocket, broke it, and placed it on his captain's tongue as a last act of reverence and patriotic fervor.

It was for his "heroic achievement during a concentrated attack on the *Essex* on April 6 and 7" that Lieutenant John Connally was awarded his first bronze star, one rank lower than the silver star awarded to Lyndon Johnson for his New Guinea misadventure. (Unlike Johnson, who throughout his presidency generally wore the ribbon of valor in the buttonhole of his suits, Connally made no such vainglorious display.)

This did not end it. Through April, the Japanese suicide attacks on the fleet continued unabated; they lost over a thousand planes. More than a hundred American ships were damaged or sunk, but not the *Essex*, for it was charmed. The job of subduing Okinawa was now left to the ground forces; and over the southern half of the island, where the enemy took its stand, it was a protracted struggle over every square inch. The Okinawa campaign did not officially end until July 2.

In the meantime, in late April, Connally's relief aboard the *Essex* had been ordered, after a harrowing eleven months at sea that he described merely as "damn tough ones." He alerted Johnson to keep a "weather eye peeled." Weeks went by with no relief and no orders. Connally grew despondent as the fleet under Admiral Halsey, now the greatest assembly of naval power in history, moved northward off the Japanese coast, to destroy the remnants of the enemy fleet and to launch strikes in advance of Operation Olympic—the invasion of the home islands themselves. As usual, Connally tried to keep his mind off the war with thoughts of Texas politics. In April, Drew Pearson had predicted in a radio broadcast that Lyndon Johnson would run for governor in 1946. The news excited Connally immensely, for he saw the governorship as a perfect stepping stone for taking on Senator Pappy O'Daniel in 1948. "Two years a governor and Pappy would be a cinch in 1948," he wrote Johnson.

With the unrelieved tension of the war, ennui was beginning to settle in. Letters were becoming harder and harder for Connally to write, "my own personal form of harikari! except it's a milder form of torture," he wrote Johnson. "And V-Day in Europe? Wonderful! Yet *we* see no change and won't for many months to come." He thought in May 1945 that the war would take another year at least, as Operation Olympic was to involve only the invasion of Kyushu. It was to be followed by Operation Coronet, which would invade the plain of Tokyo. He had no orders and saw no relief, and waiting had become excruciating. "After the longest, toughest year of my life, I suppose I can stand a few more weeks."

But relief would be a few more months rather than weeks, and it would hang on the conclusion of the entire Pacific war, not on any defined tour of duty. When Connally's relief finally landed on the *Essex*, Connally was merely shifted to the carrier *Bennington* in charge of the Combat Information Center for the entire task force.

"Word from John does not encourage me," Johnson wrote to James Rowe, Jr., in July. "I think he must have had some rather exacting assignments, and I wish I could see him. We expected him this way in April, but now he will probably stay there until August."

The fleet campaigned up and down the coast of Honshu through July. Waves of American planes flew over Tokyo and ranged as far north as Hokkaido, delivering a Sunday punch every day of the week. The naval base at Yokosuka south of Tokyo was reduced to rubble. The threat to the carriers had abated, as the once frenzied activity around the fleet air plot relaxed. Still, for his conduct from July 1 to August 15, for his "consistently sound analysis of air combat problems," his "superlative skill" in controlling the fighters, and his "brilliant administrative skill," Connally received his second bronze star.

On August 6, the *Bennington* was sailing in waters east of Tokyo when Hiroshima was leveled, and on August 9 had moved several hundred miles north off the Japanese coast when the bomb dropped on Nagasaki. (As this put his ship in the path of the prevailing winds, John Connally became the only presidential candidate of the twentieth century who caught a whiff of nuclear fallout.)

With the news of the bombs and the word that they had compelled the Japanese to surrender, Lyndon Johnson leaped upon the Navy Department to get John Connally home from the Pacific. He wired Connally to get home to Austin as fast as he could. A jubilant Connally wired back curtly the day after the signing of the peace on the *Missouri,* "Dear Congressman: I'm more than ready when you are. Love, John." His orders were cut the next day, and the Navy Department informed Johnson that his friend would be back in a week. But three days later the congressman had heard nothing. He had been pressing the department for two months about Connally, and now he could not contain himself. His excitement mixed with fury. He wired the Navy Department on August 17, "This is extremely urgent, and I am disappointed that the department has not carried out its commitments to me." And on August 20: "Do not want to be insistent or ugly but after you have received verification, will appreciate your personally contacting Air Transport in order no additional time will be lost." Johnson could not appreciate that the entire United States force in the Pacific was trying to get home. More than a week later, he still had no word. Distraught, he began to bandy about the name of the president of the United States on August 28: "Can not understand why, when after more than two months of promises, still have no word about Connally. Is it beyond reason to ask you to see that his orders are delivered and that he is provided priority by air? I have assurances from everyone from the Big Boss down, but they are never carried out. This is a must!"

At last, Connally's voice crackled over the phone from San Francisco. Johnson prepared the welcome. To the Adolphus Hotel in Dallas he telegraphed: MY BOY, LIEUTENANT COMMANDER JOHN CONNALLY, ARRIVES TOMORROW AND WILL LAY OVER IN DALLAS. PLEASE ARRANGE ROOM, ETC.—LBJ

Forty-Cent Cotton & Ten-Cent Beer

JOHN CONNALLY WAS TO BECOME an elegant, dynamic, captivating star of the stump and the screen and the boardroom, but his political groundings were in the old-time Texas politics. Wedded as he was to his friend and master, Lyndon Johnson, the negative aspects of the Johnson stamp were imprinted indelibly on Connally, while Johnson's admirable qualities, especially his concern for the less fortunate, failed to show up in his ward. Connally would never shake that negative association in the national sensibility, and he would himself say, later, that his central problem was that he reminded everyone of Lyndon.

There is, of course, a lot more to it than that. How the country viewed Johnson and Connally had something to do with how it views Texas. That state maintains an identity as distinct and separate as any in the Union. The legends and jokes about bigness and braggadocio, fantastic wealth and vulgarity, are familiar. The big man in big boots, who wheels and deals with wads of cash, whose currency is oil or hotels and whose pleasure is big-game hunting, who owns a spread as vast as most counties and trades Arabian stallions and prize Santa Gertrudis bulls for office buildings, who puts a nearly life-size photograph of himself and his horse over his limestone fireplace or, alternately, a gigantic oil painting by a French artist of his sagging wife when she was a Bluebonnet Belle at the University of Texas, dressed décolleté in a long gown for the Roundup Ball. . . . These are the lurid images that titillate and amuse the rest of the nation. To the wider public there is something vaguely unseemly about Texas style. The rules there are slightly different. It is the American dream carried to excess.

Texas politics reflects the excess and Texas politics is not about ideas or programs but about personalities. When personality matters most, blood feuds develop. The players are thin-skinned, for the obverse of braggadocio is insecurity, and the two poles are usually present in the same supercharged mentality. In a circumstance where gushing praise and withering humiliation are meted out in equal measure, opponents become "personally obnoxious" to one another. Grudges become eternal.

Also, labels stick. In 1946, the label of wheeler-dealer stuck to Lyndon Johnson. Inevitably, it would splatter to the man behind the congressman, that big-time operator who would more and more come to be regarded as Johnson's henchman.

In February 1946, already in Austin, Connally was officially discharged from the navy. He came home as a bona fide war hero and received his proper accolades in the local press. Much was made, of course, of the occasion for which he was awarded his first bronze star—April 6, 1945, when the *Essex* fought off waves of Japanese suicide raids. In the Austin paper he was given credit for being the only flight direction officer in World War II who ever dared to invoke the call "Hey, Rube!" That was the bloodcurdling alarm given to carrier fighters in the air to repair to the close defense of the fleet— lest the fliers have no fleet when they returned—but no one thoroughly researched the point. The notice quickly faded, and Connally did not dwell upon his laurels. He was twenty-nine years old. Nellie was pregnant again. He was looking ahead. As a mature veteran he was not enthusiastic about Johnson's overture to return to his congressional office, though Johnson suggested that he could practice law on the side if he wished, and would be certain of a salary double or triple his old one. He wanted to strike out on his own, and he wanted to make some money, not simply as a salaried man. Johnson kept after him. Knowing the Connallys' love for University of Texas football, the congressman always got them good seats to the games and then during the game itself, about which Johnson cared nothing, he would bend Connally's ear about politics. It drove Connally crazy. After a time, he got lost on the mornings of football games, so Johnson could not locate him. He would find, however, that Johnson was not so easily denied.

Offers came to join local law firms, to manage an oil and gas distributing company, to run a private utility in South Texas at a salary of $12,000. Having been a mediocre student in law school, he was not interested in the straight practice of law. Rather, he gravitated to the business world, where he could apply his law training to his entrepreneurial bent and where he could ply his charm. Some of his old UT classmates got back together, and with nine other veterans, his brother Merrill and Jake Pickle among them, Connally decided to found a radio station in Austin. They called it KVET, and they planned to make a million bucks. It was the course of least resistance. The Johnson station, KTBC, had been acquired three years before, and it was already returning a handsome profit. KTBC had become a way station for the returning veterans of the Johnson circle, and they were impressed with the promise of broadcasting. Austin was a growing market. The Johnsons were not averse to the founding of another station whose competition would be benign. They knew that some other station would enter the market soon enough, and it might as well be a friendly one.

Connally was the moving force behind the new business. Borrowing $25,000 from a local bank, he became the majority stockholder, and as a result became the station's president, lawyer, and general manager. When he told his father that he had borrowed $25,000, the old man leaned back in his chair. "Well, John," he said, "you've finally gone beyond the point where I can bail you out."

"I don't think you'll have to," Connally replied warmly.

Lyndon Johnson helped with the FCC application, which the partners presented to the commission in a classy, leather-bound folder. "John was more interested in providing leadership than going out on the street selling two-dollar-and-forty-cent radio spots," Jake Pickle would observe once the station went on the air. "He used to be up half the night jawing over a pot of coffee and then couldn't get to sleep, so sometimes we didn't have much leadership first thing in the morning." Around Austin, Connally blended into the business world gracefully. He dressed normally in a business suit and had a penchant for colorful ties and silk shirts, although sometimes he was turned out tastefully Western and casual.

By early May 1946 he was "busy as the proverbial cat," splitting his time between KVET and, inevitably, Johnson politics. He seemed well satisfied with the state of things. He regretted that Johnson had drawn his first real opponent in the forthcoming congressional election, but the candidate did not then seem too formidable. He was Hardy Hollers, a longtime Austin resident and lawyer, who had run for elective office only once before, for county attorney, and had been soundly trounced. Hollers was an older man who had served in World War I as a private and then as a judge advocate through World War II in London and Paris. His chief distinction was that he had served with Associate Justice Robert Jackson in preparing the first cases against Nazi war criminals at Nuremberg.

Three days before Hollers opened his campaign, Connally was in high spirits. To his friend Henry Wade in Dallas, whose path he had crossed in the Pacific and who was now running for Dallas district attorney against an opponent with purported ties to Dallas gangsters, he conveyed regret that he had no money to contribute to Wade's campaign. "After sending the Navy $678 this morning which was overpaid me, I couldn't get you more than one vote at a dollar a vote." Since he had no money to send for the purchase of votes, he had an alternate suggestion for his friend: "I would suggest that you bring that hula hula dancer from Honolulu up there and put her to work. I am sure she can get more votes accidentally than you can by yourself on purpose." That was an inside joke between a couple of old salts.

On May 13, Hollers opened his campaign with a savage speech. He picked up where the lesser opponent, Buck Taylor, had left off in 1944 in challenging Johnson's short and showy military service. But Hollers delivered his sally deftly and with greater force. Johnson, charged Hollers, had used his political influence to wangle a commission as lieutenant commander, whereas most people entered as apprentice seamen or were commissioned (like John Connally) as ensigns. "He [Johnson] went on a few months' sight-seeing tour of the Pacific with a camera in one hand and leading his publicity agent by the other. For his distinguished service, Johnson was decorated," Hollers mocked, basso profundo. "I do not believe that you, the people, approve of the barter of your public offices as you would a dozen eggs."

Minding the store in Texas, Connally was mortified. In his view, the Hollers speech was vicious, and if he had taken the opponent lightly before, he no longer did so. A veteran politician now, Connally adopted an almost academic tone as he analyzed both the substance and the style of the speech. He found the quality of Hollers's voice good on the radio, "although he fails to pronounce the end of his words and stumbles on others to the extent of leaving out conjunctions." In view of his own candidate's problem with conjunctions, Hollers's grammatical shortcomings were not likely to be fatal.

"He hit the war record, yours and his, pretty hard," Connally wrote two days later to Johnson in Washington. "He will make some headway with that for a short period of time, but in the final analysis, with two and a half months to go, not only in this race but in all campaigns this year, people are going to be awfully sick of a man publicly and blatantly patting himself on the back about what a great hero he is."

The irony of that comment seemed to escape Connally, for it was Johnson rather than Hollers who had consistently congratulated himself about his battlefield exploits. If, for brazen political reasons, MacArthur had conferred the silver star on Johnson, General Eisenhower had decorated Hollers for more valid reasons, his work at Nuremberg. Moreover, Connally was more a war hero than either of them; yet he demeaned himself now by becoming Johnson's fawning apologist on the stump. To audiences around the district, Connally professed that, as he was a veteran of the Pacific War, his blood boiled at hearing Colonel Hollers's allegations, and that he and others who had fought on the battlefield would turn the "revealing searchlight of truth on Hollers and his purveyors of half-truths." (At least he conceded half the truth.) Unabashedly, Connally quoted the language of Johnson's silver star citation about gallantry and bravery and asked his audiences if that sounded like a sight-seeing tour to them. "Colonel Hollers during his service as an assistant judge advocate reviewing courts martial at European Theatre Headquarters in London and Paris may have been around with a camera. He may even have carried with him a publicity agent. But I assure you, ladies and gentlemen, that no man who served in the Pacific from the time hostilities commenced until the time of the Jap surrender was around with a camera in one hand and led a publicity agent by the other." It would not wash. But Connally was right in his first reaction: there was not much political mileage in a headquarters judge advocate mocking the grandstanding of a politician masquerading as a military officer, and the public quickly tired of it.

There were other charges which Connally could take personally. Hollers hammered away at Johnson's "well-greased propaganda bureau" in Washington, which was constantly giving Johnson credit for the legislative work of others, and at his Austin "click" (*sic*) which he described as a handful of greedy lawyers who found the pickings good during the war and were now profiteering in the economic reconversion after the war. While veterans were jobless and homeless, "the favored few" were getting priorities on building materials like steel, which otherwise might be used to build veterans' homes. These transactions were being conducted on the black market with Johnson's acquiescence, Hollers charged. The ordinary veteran's discharge paper was like a "hunting license in a closed season."

On June 16 Hollers became more specific, alleging that Johnson was a silent partner in KVET. How had the steel for the new KVET tower been acquired when steel was so badly needed for veterans' homes? he asked. The answer was that Lyndon Johnson had a sympathetic interest in the station, so he could monopolize broadcasting in Austin.

To this charge Johnson himself replied, for such a personal attack on his boys hurt. He named the veterans of KVET: Connally, his brother Merrill Connally, Pickle, Robert Phinney, and Homer Thornberry (who would win Johnson's congressional seat after Johnson moved to the U.S. Senate), all honest, upright, idealistic young men, and some of the finest ever to attend the University of Texas. "Every man jack of them went to war," Johnson exclaimed, shaking with emotion. "Did you ever see fifty-four service decorations in a row? Well, I did. On the chests of these men when they came back . . . an average of five apiece: four bronze stars, two silver stars, two air medals, two distinguished flying crosses, one oak leaf cluster, and one purple heart." Of Johnson's offer to help with KVET, he said that "at first, the boys protested. They said, Congressman, your enemies will say you're trying to monopolize the radio business in Austin . . . that you have a hidden interest in the station. It may hurt you politically. My reply is this: I don't believe that my affection and the gratitude which I feel towards you boys will ever hurt any man politically."

Once again, Johnson was using bright and now war-scarred young men around him to distinguish himself, as if their medals would confer validity on his own. But as their support distinguished him, his support, perhaps unwittingly, demeaned them. His constant reference to his "boys" rooted that servile reputation ever deeper, making it harder for them later to grow up in their own right. They were men now, all turning thirty, and yet they were Lyndon's "boys," with Connally as the head boy. If you didn't believe it, you had only to look at how Lyndon himself referred to them. But the boys did not seem to notice. They had a campaign to run.

Of the charges that Hollers semaphored, one concerned the Johnson campaign deeply—the allegation that Johnson was enriching himself personally in his public life. From the beginning of his congressional career, Johnson had been preoccupied, indeed obsessed, with the never-ending demand for money. His hope that no one would oppose him was, in part, motivated by the axiom that with no opposition, one needed no campaign money. For all his campaigns, he had essentially solved his problem through the beneficence of the Brown and Root construction company, his contacts with wealthy supporters like Charles Marsh, and his and Connally's skill at fund-raising. Once again, in the Texas tradition, donations were generally not dispersed along ideological lines. Very often, they were given because the candidate simply was liked. Lyndon Johnson was liked by many, liked for his sheer energy and doggedness, for his reputation as one who got things done, for his forceful personality.

In this era of Texas politics, the money was almost always in cash. With cash, there was no accountability, for the last thing big contributors wanted was public knowledge of their contribution to a particular candidate. With the universal use of cash, it was common for some of it to be siphoned off for personal use.

Siphoning off money from campaign funds for a new suit was one thing. Taking kickbacks from major government contracts for yourself and for members of your family or feathering the nests of your political cronies—that was something else, a something else that could make you a millionaire, not simply a petty thief. It was the mode of the wheeler-dealer. Lyndon Johnson wanted a business besides his congressional salary. Early in his political life he had turned aside the opportunity to invest in oil, for he felt that oil investments would later be fatal politically. The radio station was the Johnsons' oil well.

Now, Colonel Hollers took the radio station and made it the centerpiece of a general charge of personal enrichment from public life. "A public office is bestowed not for the benefit of the individual but for the good of the people," he said in his opening address. "If your servant in public office uses his prestige to obtain special favors, for himself, his family and his inner political click [sic], you are entitled to know why. If this inner political click has feasted off the spoils of war and thereby amassed great wealth, while you are sacrificing for victory, you are entitled to know why. If you are spending your full-time in a foxhole on the beaches of Normandy or at Guadalcanal or as a prisoner in the hands of the enemy or winging your way over the target behind enemy lines, and your servant is spending his time getting quick profits of war from his own business enterprise, then you are entitled to know why." This was an attack that Connally felt had to be answered immediately. The rumors were widespread, and they were believed. But, once Hollers raised them, his political problem was to prove them.

Nevertheless, the Johnson campaign suddenly felt itself in real jeopardy. Negative ions filled the air, and the question was how to deal with such dangerous electricity. A tense meeting of the staff took place, with Connally, Pickle, and Alvin Wirtz among the dozen or so present. The level of outrage among the loyalists was high, for the Johnson radio station had been acquired fairly three years before, they felt, when no one else was interested. It was no crime that the station had made a good profit; in fact it had done so to the surprise of many. A consensus developed early in the meeting that perhaps Lady Bird should answer the charges, for she could state the specifics of the KTBC acquisition, and Hollers would have a hard time answering a woman. And then Wirtz spoke up:

"I'll tell you, boys. I don't believe that the public is going to like you hiding behind a woman's skirts. I think, Lyndon, that you'd better just challenge him yourself. You haven't got anything to hide. Let's just take him on."

This wiser counsel prevailed. But how to take him on? And with what tone? Connally argued for traveling the high road, delivering a rebuttal couched in lofty invocations of the honor, integrity, morality, and responsibility that public life requires. On May 25, Connally drafted some possible language, which exhibited a bit more Connally pomposity than Johnson earthiness. Its only reference to the Hollers enrichment charge was this: "I have never cast a vote to enrich one man or deprive another, and I will never do so. If you wish me as your representative in Congress to vote class legislation, to work for bills which will take care of special groups, associations, and interests, then you do not want Lyndon Johnson as your Congressman, because whether or not I am your Congressman, it is too important to whoever represents you to be fully conscious of the responsibility placed upon him and the power which he exercises." That was a mouthful that Edwin Booth himself could not have rolled off his tongue. Johnson adopted the tone, but not the words.

Hollers could not deliver the specifics. He held folders high, McCarthyesque, alleging "documented charges too hot to go on the air." He called Johnson "an errand boy for war-rich contractors and big-time lobbyists." But the documentation, whatever it was, was never taken from its folders, and as Connally and Pickle fanned out over the district they made headway casting the allegations as lies. After Hollers went into Johnson's boyhood home of Johnson City, Connally got a report and conveyed it to the Boss in Washington. Hollers, wrote Connally, was spreading the same old stuff, but in Johnson City he ran into a buzz saw. "A. W. [Alvin Wirtz] said he sawed him off a little bit and told him the least he could do was not repeat a bunch of damn lies that somebody had told him." Actually, the Johnson camp was spreading more scurrilous lies of its own. It was whispering that Hollers was a homosexual.

While the Johnson whispers worked, the Hollers public posturing was backfiring. As a candidate, Hollers was proving himself clubfooted. In Johnson City, the colonel had approached a marine combat veteran and asked him cheerfully if he had served in Europe during the war.

In the meantime, Connally was finding that some people cared very little whether Lyndon Johnson was crooked or not. Of an Austin contact, he wrote Johnson, "Tom told him he didn't give a damn if you made a million dollars and if you stole every dime of it. That you had been very friendly and very helpful to him and that he didn't know of a single man that had ever gone to you for assistance that hadn't gotten it."

But the money charge was gnawing at Connally. He was convinced Hollers was himself being enriched by his challenge to Johnson, that he was the "12th political whore to be propositioned by Houston oil men" and that he had been promised that he could write his own financial ticket if he challenged Johnson. That did not concern Connally. More, it had the ambience of greed:

"Congressman, I have just become convinced in my own mind that more than ever before, everyone is money-mad. The whole approach to everything is extremely selfish and greedy. I believe that to be true. Assuming it to be true, that fact alone is your greatest weakness. It is not only your greatest weakness, but the greatest weakness of our government."

What was he saying? It was a turning point for John Connally. He seemed to be struggling within himself about the relation of money to politics: how much was needed, how it should be acquired, what favors were expected from it, what in the real world was okay to appropriate for personal use, and perhaps most important of all, what he could personally overlook and accept about the behavior of Lyndon Johnson. His loyalty to Johnson remained blind. If he wondered about Johnson enriching himself on the side or disapproved, he did not say so outright. His job in 1946 was strictly political: to diffuse the charge. "In the final analysis, it is important that you be elected to Congress because of what you can contribute to the welfare of the country." With reelection as the overarching, all-consuming consideration, one could overlook a lot.

It was a measure of his confidence that Lyndon Johnson did not return to Texas until July. He left himself only seventeen days to campaign. It was to prove more than enough. Borrowing a leaf from Pappy O'Daniel's book, the campaign signed up "Johnson's Hill Billy Boys" to begin playing down-home numbers like "Home on the Range" two hours before the candidate arrived to speak. Johnson had learned about the usefulness of Hollywood since the days in the war when he asked Connally to identify Lana Turner. The campaign enlisted Gene Autry for a number of political appearances, and he proved to be a big draw. Then in his heydey as a movie star, Autry would croon his theme song, "Back in the Saddle Again," and submit to the voters that "that's where you're going to put my friend, Lyndon Johnson, because that's where he belongs." Another bright idea of the 1946 campaign was too bright by half. One of Johnson's campaign workers was Willard Deason, who came from Stockdale, in the eastern section of Connally's home county of Wilson, where watermelons were grown commercially. (Deason later became a commissioner on the Interstate Commerce Commission during the LBJ presidency.) It was decided that Johnson would throw a number of watermelon feasts, for iced watermelon in mid-July in Texas was a certain way to draw a crowd, if not a mob. "Come to the political rally. Gene Autry and Lyndon Johnson. Ice-cold watermelons": it was irresistible. The Johnson campaign anticipated some possible problems in good humor. Umpires were appointed to excavate seeds from small ears. Bring a chair if you fear chiggers, they warned. Any small boy caught throwing a rind forfeits his right to seconds. (No appeals.) No squirting seeds at the musicians. If you like salt, put a shaker in your pocket, along with your favorite weapon. Most important of all, no leaving before the speaking.

In Jake Pickle's words, the campaign had outsmarted itself. "When we got ready for the speaking, which, of course, was the purpose of the thing, the boys were already throwing rinds, and they liked to throw them right down in front where they could be seen. Just when Mr. Johnson would get ready to make a special point, some young boy would raise up and *whop!* he would send one flying across the platform, or at some other boy in the front row, and then a little fight would ensue. Several times during these rallies, when Mr. Johnson (Gene Autry beside him) would forget to cover his microphone, he could be heard shouting to me or Connally, 'John! . . . Jake! . . . get those blankety-blank kids out from in front of here. They're driving me crazy. Look out, Gene! Here comes one at you!' "

The Hollers campaign, meanwhile, kept up its offensive with a series of newspaper ads entitled "Should Lyndon B clean up his own Dog House?" One such ad quoted Johnson as saying, "There's no oil on my fingers," and below it appeared a page from an oil and gas lease record from San Patricio County, north of Corpus Christi, showing royalty control by one Lyndon Johnson. This had little effect. The Johnson ads parried with an almost devotional tone, invoking the lofty sentiments of Homer: "He serves me most who serves his country best." The theme for the campaign was adopted from a tune then high on the charts: "Did you ever see a dream walking?" If that made Lyndon Johnson out to be somewhat more romantic than he actually was, Johnson was able to turn it into a romantic vision of America; the dream was for a country where everyone would work and have an education and where there would be no poverty.

While Connally stayed on the phone, schmoozing with the leaders around the district, Johnson made three speeches a day. He was at his best on the street corners of small towns. There, he would simply arrive with his sound truck and begin speaking. A small crowd inevitably gathered, as the shoppers and the shopkeepers poured from their stores to see what the racket was. At other times, he would start at one end of town at the opening of the business day and challenge himself to see how many shops he could visit in an hour or two. (Connally viewed this technique with awe. With his own pride and aloofness, regarded by many since his college days as arrogance, he knew he could never endure such close interaction. But by the time he became a major candidate himself, it was the age of television, and then his good looks and smoothness carried him.) Johnson surrogates went elsewhere with the sound truck. One, Everett Looney, a liberal Austin lawyer, got caught in a drenching rainstorm with the truck, but managed to get himself photographed, looking a bit bedraggled and forlorn. Nevertheless, the picture in the local newspaper carried the caption "Lyndon Johnson, Rain or Shine." This amounted to a coup in itself, and the campaign reproduced the picture by the hundreds and distributed it widely.

Hollers, meanwhile, was showing that he was not totally humorless. In an idle moment Johnson had proposed that the Colorado River in Texas be made navigable all the way upstream to Austin, and the Hollers campaign seized upon a fine way to answer that. "Can't you just hear that steamboat come 'round the bend into Austin?" Hollers would exclaim, and from the back of the crowd one of his men would blast an old steamboat whistle. The audience roared, and Hollers continued jovially, "Commander Johnson is there at the helm, using more steam to blow the whistle than to pull the wheels." The Johnson boys had to acknowledge grudgingly that this was a nice political gimmick, but they had a few gimmicks of their own.

In the Texas summer, where the heat seared and the glare of the caliche was so bright that it blinded the eyes, beer was a close second to watermelons, especially in the Czech and German sections of the Tenth District. Those sections were extensive, and they had never been partial to Johnson, identified as he was with Franklin Roosevelt, no favorite of Germans. At Connally's direction, Jake Pickle set up shop in Brenham, a well-kept town east of Austin in Washington County, full of mid-Victorian houses which had been built by industrious German immigrants who came after the Civil War. Brenham was a cotton and oil center, situated within the extensive Brenham oil field, and the Germans liked to hold their boisterous weekend shindigs in a tabernacle outside Brenham, at a crossroads called La Bahia. These dances suffered from a critical deficiency in 1946: beer was expensive and hard to come by. A year after the close of the war, it still could not be purchased without a coupon. So the Johnson forces threw a party, and Pickle put out the word that there would be free beer. Unlike watermelons, beer, precious as it was, was not likely to be thrown at the candidate. *Free* beer ensured a big crowd. When the time for the speaking arrived, what was said to Johnson is more memorable than what was said by him. A prominent local lumberman and cotton dealer rose to make the introductions.

"We are a lot of simple people here in Washington County," he began. "We don't ask much from our government. We really want to be let alone if we can be. We need a little money . . . not as much as some people, but we don't like a lot of giveaway programs. Now we've got a guest here tonight who's been very active. He's come here tonight to speak and entertain us." He held up a bottle of beer, and the audience applauded appreciatively. "Now this is what we want to tell Mr. Johnson. We don't want much from our government. *All we ask is forty-cent cotton and ten-cent beer.*" The place burst into cheers and dancing. In due course the crowd became receptive even to what this reputed Rooseveltian had to say. Days later, when the voters went to the polls, the returns from Washington County were evenly split—until one precinct out by La Bahia reported a tally of 550 to 25 for Johnson, which gave him the county.

On the last night of the campaign, Johnson finally took on directly the charge of profiteering. The occasion was a rally at Woolridge Park in downtown Austin, and seven thousand people (by the count of the Johnson campaign) stood before him. On the platform was family: Lady Bird; his mother, Rebekah; and his two sisters. The former governor, Jimmy Allred, introduced him, and he set the mood. " 'Did you hear that Brown dealt in the wheat market and made forty thousand dollars?' " he said, invoking an old saw. " 'Why no,' says the other fellow, 'I didn't hear the story that way. I heard it was Smith, and he was dealing in corn, not wheat, and he lost fifty thousand rather than made it.' " The crowd howled.

"Now that's what they've been saying about your congressman, that he was involved in all of these things. But it wasn't Johnson. It was the Magnolia Oil Company. It wasn't a commodity. It was oil. And he hasn't been making it himself. He's been making it for you." The crowd picked up the chant.

When the candidate took the microphone, his text was "I remember and I know you have not forgotten." Images of the Depression rolled out of him: the banks broke, nothing to eat, no jobs, and images of the war: the assault on democracy, hobnail boots, and the like. "I remember and I know you have not forgotten, because we have gone through this together." He spoke of the "hounds of hate," baying at his doorstep, and answered these apparitions with maternal and biblical invocations. "My mother taught me about this with the words, Can a man take fire into his bosom and his clothes not be burned? Keep thy tongue from evil and thy lips from speaking guile. I can not too greatly blame those who have raised their voices against me. The ox knoweth his owner and the ass his master's voice. I know and you know that while the voice was the voice of Jacob, the hands are the hands of Esau. Their words are as water spilled upon the ground, which can not be gathered up again."

In the end, it was no contest. Johnson swamped Hollers by more than two to one. But Hollers had put an indelible curse on Johnson. In the closing days of the campaign, the colonel had even invoked the most powerful and the most dangerous of all political symbols. Upon his return from Nuremberg after pondering Nazi war crimes, "I found my own people with fear in their eyes and fear in their hearts," he said. "They were afraid of the Johnson political machine. We were only one step ahead of the Gestapo system they had in

Germany." Like everything else in his campaign, Hollers was too late and off-center, but this was one area where he had true standing. As he was putting a lasting mark on Johnson, so he was setting a mark on everyone in the Johnson political machine.

★ 8 ★

The Burglary of 1948

IN 1948, JOHNSON AND CONNALLY went into battle once more. They would win again, this time a United States Senate seat, and Lyndon Johnson's course toward the presidency was set. But the victory added to his reputation as an election thief. It has often been remarked that, had Lyndon Johnson not stolen the election in 1948, he would never have become president. His record in Congress, dismal as it was, did not suggest that he would become a perennial contender for higher office. The year 1948 was a crucial turning point. Equally, had Connally not been there every step of the way in 1948, there to share in the spoils, he too would probably have receded into obscurity. At this stage of his career, but for his relationship to Lyndon Johnson, Connally was just another young, politically active Austin businessman.

In the years after the war, Connally had treated politics as a sideline. He stood ready to throw himself into a political campaign every few years, taking off several months from real, gainful employment, and he enjoyed being Johnson's visible surrogate in Austin. But his heart was in his business career. The pattern he established would last throughout his life: brief political forays, cut short when his longing for the comforts of private life became strong. In contrast to Johnson, Connally never gloried in the label "politician."

Furthermore, the calendar was changing the Johnson-Connally relationship. The congressman's campaigns were no longer young men's crusades. In 1948 Johnson was turning forty. He was going nowhere fast in the House of Representatives. His closest younger aides, Connally and Pickle, had abandoned him, and Johnson was giving serious thought to retirement. The age of television was dawning and his wife's radio station had added a comfortable underpinning to his family's business interests. He was even struck with the romantic notion of returning as a teacher to a high school classroom. Abruptly, in late 1947, he had announced to his inner circle that he planned to retire at the first of the year.

But Lyndon Johnson did not announce his retirement on January 1, 1948. Instead, on that day Coke Stevenson announced for the U.S. Senate. Stevenson had been a broadly popular governor during the war, presiding calmly over the great infusion of capital into Texas that the wartime economy brought and leaving the state with a healthy surplus when he departed office in 1946. Built broad and sturdy, he was the paragon of the West Texas rancher, a bit of a plodder perhaps, whose nickname, "Calculatin' Coke," came from his slow, deliberate manner and his habit of constantly puffing upon his pipe. His formal education had ended with the third grade, but he had educated himself doggedly and was reasonably well read. A bank president in his early career, he grew to be known as a skillful infighter and rose rapidly to become Speaker of the Texas house before being elected lieutenant governor in 1938.

Despite his popular standing, Stevenson's decision to run for the Senate came as a surprise, for previously he had declared, rightly enough, that he was ill suited to the Washington scene. Nevertheless, he was a formidable candidate. Under Stevenson, "Texas had developed a big cash surplus," Jake Pickle has said. "He hadn't spent money, didn't have to. The taxes were coming in. He didn't have to try a lot of new changes or meet new challenges. He could be the taciturn, wise, careful, prudent, successful public servant. That was his approach and his philosophy, too. Coke was a hard campaigner to beat because he'd been in the governor's office just riding the waves."

It remained unclear whether Pappy O'Daniel would run again. A fading star, he was ridiculed in private, occasionally in public; he was even bespattered with eggs and rotten tomatoes. Nevertheless, he was hard to miss on the political scene, and his appeal to the poor, the ignorant, and the devout—still a sizable constituency in postwar Texas—was as strong as ever. O'Daniel was keeping his options open. If he decided to pass up a bruising primary in the Democratic party, he might well accept the nomination later from the Dixiecrat party then being formed, or even from the Republican party. What was there in a party label to a flour salesman such as he?

Stevenson's announcement scuttled Johnson's retirement plans, for if both Coke and Pappy (or one or the other) ran and Johnson chose to challenge, Johnson could once again portray himself as the vibrant candidate of youth and energy. That started Johnson's juices flowing again. In March a Belden poll provided further encouragement and Connally analyzed its results point by point. The poll showed that forty-five percent of the qualified voters preferred congressional experience over gubernatorial experience as background for the U.S. Senate. That favored O'Daniel and Johnson over Stevenson. Connally felt that in a three-way race Lyndon would go into a runoff with Coke, but if, by some chance, Coke and Pappy were in the runoff, Pappy would win. Against Coke alone, Connally felt Lyndon had the edge.

More important, the poll suggested that eighty-five percent of Texas voters preferred their U.S. senator to be under fifty years of age. "The revelations clearly demonstrate that the people want a younger man with the aggressiveness, alertness, and the energy that go with comparative youth," Connally wrote on March 12. But if Johnson was encouraged by the voters' views on age, he might be disheartened by their attitude toward Roosevelt's New Deal, with which he was still closely associated. Two years after Roosevelt's death, Texas newspapers still portrayed Johnson as a Roosevelt "favorite" in their headlines.

As Connally wrote Johnson, that was merely a question of voter perception, for Johnson was neither as liberal nor as Rooseveltian as he once had been. He had voted for the antilabor Taft-Hartley Act, for instance. Nor were Coke and Pappy as manifestly anti-Roosevelt as they had been, for with Roosevelt dead, fifteen percent more people were now claiming that they had voted for the former president than actually had. So the poll attempted to separate the personal popularity of Roosevelt from his program. Connally worried about an attempt to pin the New Deal label on Johnson. "If the election turned on the record alone, you should have no difficulty on that score," Connally wrote on March 12. "Of course, it won't."

The purpose of Connally's March 12 letter to Johnson was to help the congressman decide whether to enter a campaign which this time, unlike in 1941, was an all-or-nothing proposition. But the letter said much about the basic political instincts of John Connally himself, instincts that would later be clear in his own political career. In 1948, a time when Joseph McCarthy and Richard Nixon were blazing into the national consciousness, Connally saw the electorate as uninformed and afraid, for the voters, in their hearts, knew they could not control their own personal destiny, much less the destiny of their nation. "We are all afraid of things we can not see or do anything about." Moreover, he applied his beliefs to the presidential race, where Harry Truman epitomized the common man. Fear in the populace was "the greatest reason for resentment against President Truman," Connally wrote. "There is a lack of faith in his *bigness* or his ability to do the job and a lack of faith in the people around him. Conversely, that is Eisenhower's strength. No one even knows which party Eisenhower belongs to, if any. None of us know his political beliefs on any issue. None of us know his basic political and social beliefs, and yet I think he could carry Texas over President Truman, even if he were to run on the Republican ticket. Why? Not because he is a military man, but because they have faith in his courage; they have faith in his forthrightness. They are drawn to him because they feel he is not schooled in the adroit ways of power politics." Eisenhower's glamour was the best attribute a public man could have. With the people of Texas uncertain about their future, "they are extremely ripe for plucking by a knight in shining armor on a big white horse. . . . I think I am a little more intelligent than the average," Connally wrote on March 12, "and I too am looking for a knight in shining armor. I don't mean to say that I think it is Eisenhower, but it is someone who can capture my imagination, [one who] in the final analysis, has captured my faith and my trust. I want someone who has the courage to do what he believes is right for the good of all the people. In other words, a leader."

On May 11, the inner circle gathered under the big oak trees in Johnson's backyard on Dillman Street in Austin. Connally, Pickle, Horace Busby, and Joe Kilgore were among them. Johnson was torn. He knew he had come to a critical juncture in his career and perhaps so, too, had John Connally. The session under the trees was long and animated. Johnson returned over and over to the negatives, for he evidently wanted to be persuaded, even browbeaten into running. Even his most uncritical devotees agreed that the odds were about four to one against winning. If he lost, it was very likely the end. To the nucleus of his University of Texas counselors, Johnson began to protest too much. When for the last time, he said he would not run, someone piped up, "Congressman, that's really the right decision. We really think you ought to step aside and let us put forward a younger man who can carry on this great tradition."

"Yes," said someone else, taken with the new idea. "We'll run John Connally. If you'll just step aside, we'll start running John."

That was a change-up Johnson was not expecting. "Well, just a minute. Let me think about this a little bit," he said.

The following day Johnson announced his candidacy.

The campaign was scheduled to open May 22 with a speech from the band shell in Austin's Woolridge Park. Horace Busby, who was then about to graduate from UT and was the editor of the *Daily Texan,* had worked on the speech with Paul Bolton, who was the news director at the Johnson television station, KTBC. Around 5:30 P.M. that evening, Bolton took the speech out to Dillman Street. As he arrived, a doctor emerged from the house. The candidate was sick, very sick. It was doubtful that he could attend his own kickoff. Bolton handed the speech to the candidate, who had repaired to bed, and left, much distraught, to return to Woolridge Park. At the appointed time, Johnson's car pulled up at the rally, and to his inner circle Johnson looked positively beautiful as he unfolded from the car in a white suit. He bounded up to the band shell, appearing the picture of health and energy.

If from his sickbed he rose the picture of health, so from his purported liberalism he now became the champion of states' rights and the nemesis of big labor. He announced that he was against the repeal of the poll tax, against the antilynching law, and for, with "utmost enthusiasm," the Taft-Hartley Act.

To the inner crowd, his transformation into a neoconservative was unremarkable, for he was, after all, a politician. Generally, his people felt the occasion had gone well, as the speech was warmly received by the crowd, which seemed unaware that an ideological shift had taken place. The following day the press paid little attention to the speech.

Connally, meanwhile, had brought yet another recent UT graduate into the Johnson camp. He was Warren Woodward, an aviator in World War II, who had returned to the university to complete his degree. On the day of the Woolridge Park event, Connally pulled Woodward aside and told him that he was to travel west with the candidate, to Amarillo and Abilene and Wichita Falls. Moreover, the candidate was sick, tormented with a gallstone lodged in his bile tract, and he was having high fevers. Connally pressed some pills into Woodward's palm and gave some vague instructions as to what Woodward was to do if Johnson's condition worsened.

In Amarillo, it did worsen. Thirty-six hours later, Johnson took to his bed and instructed Woodward to keep all visitors away during the evening before they were to board an overnight Pullman coach for Dallas. The candidate knew that he was approaching an important political moment, one which could demonstrate his claim as an effective operator in Washington. In Dallas, he was to meet with Secretary of the Air Force Stuart Symington, an old friend, and then in Wichita Falls that night he was to announce that after tireless lobbying in Washington, he had succeeded in keeping Sheppard Air Force Base, north of the city, from being closed. Through his efforts, it was to be designated a permanent base.

He was determined not to miss this moment. He had had gallstones before, passed them, and rapidly regained his strength. He wolfed the painkillers that Woodward had gotten from Connally and tried to hold on through sheer force of will.

Aboard the Pullman, his condition grew desperate. In waves, freezing chills and a searing fever alternated as he tossed about in the lower berth. "He'd holler for me to come," Woodward remembered. "When he was hot, he'd say, 'Get this window open!' Well, Pullman windows weren't the easiest things to open. I remember leaning over him and yanking, and then getting the porter. The porter and I would take hold at opposite ends of the thing, and finally we'd get it. But then the noise and the outside soot and the clickety-clack of the train didn't help. After a while the fever would pass, and he'd doze off a little bit. Then the chill would come, and we'd go back and repeat the process of getting the window down. Then he'd call for extra blankets. So I'd go get the porter to fetch all the extra blankets. . . ."

Suddenly, seized with a particularly bad chill, Johnson ordered his aide to get into the bed with him. Young and very nervous, Woodward had known Johnson only a few months. He was terrified over what was happening and what might happen to him if he did not do the right thing. Twice in the course of the night Woodward crawled into bed with the Boss, held Johnson close, and tried to impart his body warmth to the freezing man. In the morning Johnson was a wreck, and so was Woodward. Somehow they dragged themselves to the Baker Hotel in Dallas.

Woodward wanted to call Connally immediately to report the situation, but Johnson would not have it. The poison from the gallstone was spreading through his body, and yet he remained convinced that the stone would pass any moment. He refused to let Woodward call a doctor. The situation remained static through the afternoon, as Woodward grew insane with worry. Finally, the time for the meeting with Symington arrived. In Johnson's anteroom Woodward poured out his burden.

"He is a very sick man, and he'll probably fire me for telling you this," he said to the air force secretary, "but I'm here by myself, and I've got to turn to someone. He's determined to go to Wichita Falls. He's determined to have this conference with you. I don't know what to do."

"Are they out there?" Johnson asked groggily when Woodward returned to his bedside.

"Yes, sir."

"Okay, let's go." He struggled to his feet, showered, and dressed. When he opened the door to greet the secretary, he bounded out with a grin and a hearty handshake, and for a time they conducted their conference as if nothing were amiss. But Johnson flagged and could not carry on his pretense any longer. Symington cajoled him back to bed and got him to agree to see a doctor, who wanted him rushed to the hospital. Johnson agreed, but only if he were to enter the hospital under the conditions of absolute secrecy. Woodward knew he was dealing with an irrational man, but what could he do? At the hospital a low comedy developed with Woodward in the middle, as Johnson stressed secrecy at the same time that he was being rolled down the corridors and receiving warm salutations and good wishes for a successful race from the nurses and doctors who recognized him. At one point a nurse pulled Woodward aside to have him fill out the customary forms and, again, the aide found himself on the spot. He tarried for some minutes, unsure whether to enter the congressman's name.

Johnson was furious. "Don't ever leave me again," he raged. Woodward attempted to explain about the nurse and the forms. "I don't care," Johnson interrupted. "You don't work for her. You work for me. So stay here." Later Woodward learned that in his absence, surrounded by unknowns, Johnson had pulled himself out of bed and stumbled down the hall, looking for his aide, whereupon he had vomited. In the years of their association that followed, Woodward came to know that in times of personal travail Lyndon Johnson always insisted that his own people be at his elbow.

As Johnson calmed down, Woodward again raised the subject of calling Connally. "Yes, do that," Johnson said this time. "Call John and tell him what happened, but tell him not to release it to the press. Have him say I'm just going to be here overnight, and they just want to run some tests. Tell him not to say anything to the press about it." Woodward hurried across the street to a pay phone. After explaining the situation, Woodward said boldly, "Don't tell the press. He'll be out tomorrow."

"That's ridiculous," Connally snapped. "You can't have a candidate for the United States Senate, a member of Congress, enter the hospital and interrupt his schedule and not tell the press." Then there was the question of the Wichita Falls speech. "What are we going to say to several thousand people who are gathered in Wichita Falls to hear him?" Connally asked rhetorically. Johnson had settled on the inclement weather as an excuse.

"That's absurd!" Connally said, growing increasingly annoyed. "You go back and tell him that we've got to release this."

Woodward traipsed back across the street.

"Did you talk to John?" Johnson asked.

"Yes, I did, and he said to tell you that in his opinion he thinks . . . we'd be better off if . . . we tell the press you're in the hospital. We can play it down if you like, but he thinks you can't just disappear into a hospital without the press knowing it." Johnson's scorn gathered on his shattered face. "That is his recommendation," Woodward stammered, adopting a hangdog manner.

"No, I don't want that," Johnson said sharply. In his delirium, Johnson was thinking that perhaps he could just drop from sight for three or four days and then be back on the campaign trail, without anybody knowing he was gone. "You go back and tell John to do it the way I said."

So Woodward scurried back across the street, reached Connally, and conveyed the message. Connally's retort was curt: "Tell him we can't do that."

Back in the hospital, he did, and Johnson said, "You just tell him that I *order* him not to tell the press."

"John, he *orders* you not to tell the press," Woodward said minutes later on the phone.

"Well, it's too late," Connally replied. "I've already done it. Since we last talked, a reporter called and said he understood the congressman wasn't going to Wichita Falls, and I told him what the situation was. Go back and tell him that it's already done."

Woodward was mortified.

"What did he say?" Johnson demanded.

Woodward drew his breath in, braced himself, and blurted it out. "Congressman, he said he'd already released it. He said somebody from the press had called inquiring about the cancellation of your appearance in Wichita Falls, and he told them you were in the hospital here."

An eerie silence, even calm, came over Johnson, terrifying and different, more frightening to Woodward than the hurricane he expected.

"Get your book and pencil," Johnson said at last. "If I can't run my own campaign, I might as well get out." Woodward uttered a sound, as if he'd been stung. "No, now is the time to get out," Johnson continued. "I'm going to withdraw right now."

Stupefied, Woodward fumbled for his notebook and scribbled as Johnson dictated.

When he finished, Johnson turned feverishly to his aide. "Call the press and tell them that either I run my own campaign or I'm not going to run at all," he said, and turned away. Woodward hesitated. For an embarrassingly long moment he lingered in the room. He knew that calling the press was not the right thing to do, but he had his orders. Then, with what later he ascribed to divine intervention, he remembered that Lady Bird was coming.

"Okay, congressman, I will certainly do this, but John told me after the first call that he is sending Mrs. Johnson up. She's in the air right now. I know she's always been with you for these decisions. Let's make the announcement, of course, but let's do it after she gets here."

"Fine," Johnson replied. "You go out and pick her up. Then we'll call the press in, and we'll announce this thing together."

Woodward rushed off to the airport, feeling like a genius. Then with a start, another fear flashed through his mind, and he pulled off to find a telephone. Under no circumstances, none, were calls to be put through to the congressman, nor visitors admitted to his room, until he and Mrs. Johnson returned, he told the hospital supervisor. Puzzled, the supervisor began to object, but finally agreed. In the coming hour, she would have to tell several members of the press who called that Mr. Johnson was indisposed.

When Lady Bird Johnson finally arrived at the hospital she took over. She soothed him and calmed him, and his health became the central concern. The subject of a withdrawal from the race began to fade—they would deal with that tomorrow—as the doctors worried about how to dislodge the stone, which had now been determined to be sky high in the bile duct. For a gallstone lodged so high, the usual remedy was surgery, with a six-week recovery period. But the primary itself was six weeks away, and this strengthened

Johnson's determination to find some way other than surgery to cure the situation.

As the doctors conferred, Johnson and Connally continued to smolder. Communication broke down completely as the morning papers carried the news of Johnson's hospitalization. Johnson seethed, and Connally continued to insist that his action had been right. Messages passed through an assortment of intermediaries. Woodward kept Connally informed secretly. Walter Jenkins, in Washington, became a translator. A day later, setting aside his political concern that the people of Texas would say he did not think Texas doctors were good enough for him, Johnson allowed himself to be flown to the Mayo Clinic in Minnesota. He went in style, in the Lockheed Electra of the famous aviatrix, Jacqueline Cochran, who had popped into Dallas to hear the speech of her friend Stuart Symington.

At Mayo, the medical specialists bowed to the political requirements. At first they tried old-fashioned methods, driving their patient along the rough country roads, and then running him up and down stairs in hopes of dislodging the stubborn stone. At length they settled on an experimental procedure of crushing the stone in place. It was a process that had had only limited success in the past. This time it worked. In the hours that followed the procedure, Johnson began to recover rapidly.

It had been over a week since Connally and Johnson had exchanged a word. But the day after the medical procedure had worked, Connally called Woodward and reached him in Johnson's room. Woodward recalled, "As simple as not, I just handed the phone over and said, 'Congressman, John wants to talk to you.' They talked, picking up just as if nothing had happened. There was no reference to the misunderstanding, if that's what you call it. They went right on. It became the free and easy conversation between two devoted friends."

★

In February 1948 the polls had Stevenson ahead of Johnson four to one. In March the margin narrowed to three to one, and after Johnson's much-publicized hospitalization in Minnesota, the Stevenson lead narrowed further. O'Daniel had been persuaded by the brickbats not to seek the nomination of the Democratic party, and so Johnson's attributes of youth and congressional experience drew the contest with Stevenson in sharp contrast. In the first primary there was a third candidate, the Houston oilman George

Petty; "Texas is Ready for George Petty" was his slogan. But when July 24 rolled around, only twenty percent of Texas was really ready for Petty and his dreary radicalism.

Johnson had thought he would win the first primary outright, by more than 100,000 votes, but his prediction was way off. His total was 70,000 less than Stevenson's, and he just barely qualified for the runoff. For several days afterwards the issue was whether or not it was worth the expense, not to mention the humiliation. The realists in the campaign knew that runoffs usually favored the candidate with the lead. That was Stevenson, not Johnson. They thought, at the very least, that Johnson should be within 30,000 votes of Stevenson's plurality as they entered the runoff, and they knew as well that public interest generally lessened the second time around. Still, the young Turks, led by Connally, wanted to go ahead, and they prevailed.

As the campaign contemplated the next round, the high command determined that Johnson would somehow have to get seventy to eighty percent of the Petty vote. That was a tall order, since Petty had centered his message on "Russia's bloody hounds" and had cast Johnson as an appeaser who would share the atomic bomb with the Communists if given half a chance. Also the Johnson campaign would have to perform considerably better in areas of its natural strength, among the Mexican-Americans in South Texas. Embarrassingly, he had been badly trounced in San Antonio, with a deficit of nearly 10,000 votes, and his showing was surprisingly poor in the Hispanic precincts in the western section of the city. That did not make sense, for Johnson was considered a champion of the Latin cause.

This was still the age of rank segregation, when housing projects, bathrooms, and schools were designated by ethnic group, but the depth of segregation went far beyond public accommodations. As late as 1960, it was illegal in Texas for a black to get into the boxing ring with a white man. In that year, a black fighter named Sporti Harvey went to court to challenge the law. Harvey had been fighting south of the border with great success, and he wanted to enter the American ring. Hadn't he fought white men in Mexico? Harvey was asked at his San Antonio hearing. He paused. "I didn't fight no white man," he replied brazenly. "I fought a Spaniard!" Sporti Harvey won his case, with his able defense lawyer, the irrepressible Maury Maverick, Jr. But when he came north to fight, he was summarily knocked out on successive occasions and then scorned for having set his people back another hundred years.

There were, of course, more sinister aspects to South Texas apartheid. The liberal renegade Maury Maverick, Sr., used to treat the situation sardonically. About the sign over the King Ranch which announced that all were welcome, Maverick told his political audiences that the Mexican laborer was welcomed at planting time, and issued a green card that said "plenty of work." At harvest time the words on the back of the card said, "When the crops are harvested, shoot him!"

Johnson was supposed to be different. He had taught Mexican students in Cotulla, Texas, while Stevenson displayed the distant paternalism typical of a West Texas rancher. More importantly, Johnson had interceded in the case of a Latin soldier from Three Rivers, south of Floresville, who, as a victim of stark racism, had been denied burial in the local cemetery. Johnson had arranged for the veteran to be buried with full honors in the Arlington National Cemetery. This act endeared him to the Mexican community throughout the state.

As the master strategist of the campaign, Connally felt that Johnson's showing would be the reverse of what it had been in the 1941 campaign against O'Daniel. Then, Johnson had carried the cities as O'Daniel swept the rural areas. But in 1948, Connally thought Johnson would take the countryside and lose the cities, largely because he had espoused the Taft-Hartley Act so ardently and had thereby alienated labor. But there were the exceptions: Corpus Christi and San Antonio.

In Corpus Christi, Connally's chief contact was yet another standout from the University of Texas, an attorney named Cecil Burney, Jr. It was in the 1948 election that Burney became a consummate Johnson man, unfailingly loyal, amused and awed by Johnson's powerful and extravagant personality. This shrewd point man had never failed to appreciate the transcendent importance of the Latin vote in his region. He lived in the silk-stocking southern section of Corpus, but when elections rolled around Burney spent very little time there. In the Johnson races, many of which he was to be involved in, he knew that if he worked hard on the Anglo vote, the best he might do was to break even, but if he concentrated on the Latin vote he might garner nearly one hundred percent of it.

In San Antonio, the dirty work was left to one Jimmy Knight, the county clerk. In his effort to turn around the 10,000-vote short-fall, Knight's first task was to unite the feuding clans of the city, the Mavericks and the Kildays. His next was to consolidate the Mexican vote into a bloc on the west side. The latter effort began almost immediately after the Johnson defeat in the first primary, and the money began to flow. Not a great deal of money was needed. A few dollars went a long way in those days. But with ten thousand votes to make up, the figure could mount.

In Austin, Connally presided over campaign strategy from the old Hancock Mansion, a two-story colonial house at Eighth and Lavaca Streets. In his personal habits, Connally remained a night person. He preferred to sidle into the office around eleven in the morning, and not to leave until midnight. To him, the evening hours were the productive ones. That was when the real horse-trading went on. Not everyone in the campaign wanted to be harnessed to Connally's routine, however. (No problem with Johnson, of course. He was willing to politic twenty-four hours a day.) Claude Wild, for example, was the administrator of the campaign, and technically Connally's coequal. He was a stubborn man from the old school and preferred to work a normal business day. The contrast in styles caused considerable internal friction, but Johnson was the candidate of youth, and so the power tilted to Connally.

It is Connally who is often, though erroneously, credited for inventing the idea of campaigning by helicopter. Actually, it was Warren Woodward, the junior campaign aide, who first proposed it. He had been a flier in the Eighth Air Force, and in the budding stage of his relationship with Lyndon Johnson, during the spring of 1948, they spent many hours discussing the advances in aviation, including the advent of the helicopter. In the course of those discussions, Woodward had suggested that the newfangled machine might be useful in political campaigns.

In 1948 the chopper was in its infancy. It was a noisy, shaky, and still somewhat dangerous way to get around; it required special ninety-octane gas, a blend which was available in only a few locations. Logistics, therefore, were a nightmare, for a fuel truck would need to be dispatched far and wide across the state in advance of the candidate. Nevertheless, Connally embraced the idea enthusiastically, although he seldom rode in it himself.

Johnson raised the matter with Stuart Symington, and Symington, in turn, consulted with Larry Bell, the founder of Bell Helicopter Company. It was determined to be feasible. Thus, on the lawn of the old Hancock Mansion in downtown Austin, a huge mound was molded for the helicopter, which was christened the *Johnson City Windmill*, and this symbol served through the 1948 campaign as a perpetual advertisement for the candidate of the future. Stevenson, in contrast, got around in an ancient dust-colored

Plymouth driven by his loquacious, one-armed nephew. He had no advance scheduling, and simply meandered into local courthouses to shake hands with public officials. This had its own special charm. Not everyone in Texas wanted to be on Johnson's cutting edge.

Immediately after the first primary, Stevenson blundered badly. He flew off to Washington and made the rounds of the foreign policy experts. It was time for him to become cosmopolitan. Texans were affronted on two counts. Stevenson seemed to assume that he was already the senator, even though he still had a primary to win. He inspected office space in the Senate Office Building and consulted real estate agents about buying a house in Washington. Moreover, his trip pointed up his ignorance and inexperience in foreign affairs, making him appear, accurately enough, a provincial figure. The Johnson camp moved quickly to exploit the gaffe, and Stevenson suddenly found himself on the defensive.

Meanwhile, the Johnson strategists moved to embarrass Stevenson on another, rather strange, "issue" of the campaign. Coke Stevenson was by far the more conservative candidate of the two, but Johnson's vociferousness on the Taft-Hartley Act had so alienated the Texas State Federation of Labor that it had endorsed Stevenson. A bizarre crossfire had been carried on throughout the campaign, with Johnson alternately attempting to paint Stevenson as being in league with the Reds, and then trying to show that Stevenson was just as antilabor as he was. When Stevenson went to Washington, he came onto Johnson's turf, and Johnson knew what to do. He impressed Drew Pearson and Jack Anderson into service, knowing that these muckrakers would be more to contend with than the softies of the Austin press corps. Perhaps, Johnson suggested to Pearson, Stevenson should be grilled on his views on Taft-Hartley.

On August 9, Anderson did the grilling.

"A lot of Texans still say they don't know where you stand on the Taft-Hartley Act, Governor," Anderson opened.

"I have already made a statement carried by United Press," Stevenson replied flatly.

"Why do you object to repeating your stand?" Anderson persisted. "Has it changed?"

"All my notes and papers are back in Texas," Stevenson faltered. "I am facing these questions without any material."

"All we ask is your position," Anderson persevered. "It should be fairly simple to say whether you are for or against the Taft-Hartley Act."

"No, I want to repeat my statement word for word, and I might leave out some words."

For this lame performance, Pearson clobbered him in his column, "Washington Merry-Go-Round." "Ex-Governor Coke Stevenson . . . on a recent trip to Washington evaded more issues and dodged more questions than any recent performer in a city noted for question dodging."

Once again in Texas politics it was style rather than substance that mattered. In the great flood of words that gushed out of the candidates on this issue, how it was handled, rather than what was believed, created the overriding impression. Stevenson was coming off as dishonest. He confirmed the suspicion that he had hoodwinked labor into supporting him, and was trying to fool the Texas voters as well. Taft-Hartley, he argued, was a national rather than a state matter, but wasn't the Senate a national body?

Stevenson's mistake was Johnson's big break. The candidate leaped upon it. "You've got to have somebody who will be willing to speak for Texas, not just sit back, smoke his pipe, and do nothing," Johnson said. Even the eternally good-natured Nellie Connally was recruited into a bit of meanness over this issue. She edited a sheet called *Johnson's Journal*, which went to rural mailboxes and whose main purpose was to smear Stevenson with the taint of Communism. As absurd as such an attempt was, it was carried forward with an apparently straight face. The labor leaders supporting Coke Stevenson were "the same Communists who would confiscate the farms of Texas and place Texas farmers under the lash of the Commissar's whip if they were given a free hand." The headlines screamed nonsense: STEVENSON PARDONS RED! COMMUNISTS FAVOR COKE! DON'T LET LABOR RACKETEERS DOMINATE TEXAS! The unions, in this rag, were generally identified as northern or national, two equally evil labels, accentuating sectional prejudices or the separateness of Texas from the nation. Union leaders were "Bigshot Labor Bosses" controlling "Huge Slush Funds." The Communists wanted isolationists elected to the Senate. "That's why the bigshot labor bosses up North are trying to put Stevenson in office," one item read. "Wake up, Texas! Don't let the Reds slip up on you by such cunning plotting."

To imagine Nellie Connally poring over such tripe and gleefully excerpting it is to see her without her makeup. She was reflecting her husband, and he Johnson, and Johnson the contemporary McCarthyite virus. It is little wonder that eight years later, when Johnson and Connally wanted and desperately needed labor support,

labor was distant, believing the two to be dishonorable, untrustworthy opportunists.

Johnson, however, was not shy about confessing his opportunism. Once in a background session with reporters in Austin, he
was challenged about the contradictions in his position: on the one
hand, the redbaiting, and on the other, this apparent humanitari-
anism in relation to blacks and Hispanics. Johnson admitted that
his brief for the minorities did not reflect his true feelings. He
espoused civil rights publicly because he did not feel a Southern
bigot could attain national standing.

As always, Lady Bird Johnson labored gallantly for her
husband's election, but she was tired of these campaigns and had
been for years. This one seemed to go on interminably, and she was
nearing her breaking point. At the end of the campaign, she
overturned a car on the way to a reception and walked away with
a few bruises. Her companion was not so lucky. This episode would
soon become a standard in the candidate's repertoire of heroic Lady
Bird stories. He would tell the story many times later: how she had
put her fellow worker in the hospital, changed clothes, and then
went loyally to the reception and on to a radio broadcast without
ever telling him. She, in turn, added to the tale by telling folks that
as the car rolled over for the second time, the thought passed
through her mind that she should have voted absentee. But the
rumor spread among the press that Lady Bird was deeply unhappy
and had told friends that she would divorce Johnson if he did not
win the election.

On the night before the election, Connally traveled with Johnson
to San Antonio. They had decided the election would turn on the
vote there. For days, Connally had been working on patching up—
or papering over—the feud between the Mavericks and the Kildays.
On August 16 Connally had received a confidential communication.
"It would help if you would get in touch with Jim Kilday and brag
on him, pat him on the back, and let him know that you are counting
on him and his brother, the sheriff, carrying San Antonio. . . . Don't
in any way criticize his friends about the vote we got in San Antonio
in the first primary, but just let bygones be bygones." Connally had
done his work well. Triumphantly, they rode through the barrios
on election day, with Johnson seated between Maverick and
Congressman Kilday.

The night before, Jimmy Knight's meeting with the local bosses
had gone deep into the early hours, with the whiskey flowing freely,
and Connally sitting majestically on the side, the teetotaling man

apart. The planning for the morning went forward. Johnson passed a thousand dollars to Knight. Together, they decided how the money would be dispersed. When Knight handed it to campaign workers or election judges, the amount could be a dollar or two, and it was to be called simple reimbursement to pay for the sandwiches and soda pop. When the candidate himself gave money, it had to be a larger amount. "The price goes down immediately if someone else but the candidate gives it to 'em, but the satisfaction is just as great," Knight would say later, professing stoutly that this was not a payoff but simply an advance against expenses.

This one thousand dollars was the latest installment: money had been pouring into the barrios for two weeks. This was the age of the poll tax, and each precinct leader had his fund to pay the poll tax for his voters. The going rate was a dollar a vote. The system for purchasing the Spanish precincts had taken several weeks to put in place. Men who were bosses in Hispanic businesses were chosen as precinct leaders, and they paid the poll tax of their voting workers. Where the paper ballot was used, the process was planned to begin with the very first voter. He entered the voting booth with a previously marked ballot, put it in the ballot box, and returned to his boss with his unmarked official ballot. Outside, it was marked, given to the next voter, who deposited it and returned with his blank ballot, and so it went throughout the day. At the end of the day, the precinct leader knew with certainty what his vote total was. Elsewhere, in South Texas, the process worked differently. A Latin voter might be given a string with knots tied at the relevant points. The voter held the string to the top of the ballot and let it fall downward next to the names, making his mark by the knots.

But the technology of voting was changing, and new methods had to be devised to meet and defeat it. In the election of 1948, most of the precincts in San Antonio had made the transition to voting machines. The integrity of the new contraption depended upon who watched and who controlled it. All over the west side of the city, election judges and clerks had been paid off, twenty dollars for the chief judge, ten for the clerks. In 1948, that was a considerable sum. These observers simply did not show up. When the polls closed, the doors of the polling place were locked, and the machines were opened. Checking the lists for registered voters who had not voted, the lever was pulled for Johnson on behalf of the absentee. To guard against the half-Mexican, half-Irish mayor of San Antonio, Alfred Callaghan, dropping in on the process, someone had seen to it that he was well supplied with liquor, and he spent election night drunk and passed out in a car.

Throughout the day, Connally and Johnson worked the west side feverishly. They completely reversed the results of the first primary, picking up the 10,000 votes they needed. According to Ruben Mungia, the elder statesman of the west side, at least half of those votes were "suspect."

Historians of Johnson's career have generally focused upon the vote in Jim Wells County, far to the south of San Antonio. But it was the 5,000 or more suspect votes of San Antonio that put victory for Johnson only a handful of votes away.

★

John Connally has denied repeatedly that he knew anything about Box 13 in Jim Wells County, but this is inconceivable. He said he "did not go there," meaning Duval and Jim Wells counties, but one did not have to go to South Texas to influence what happened. In fact, he did go there and was at the center of the theft. Indeed, he was its very linchpin.

That he found himself yet again in a razor-close election astounded Connally. In the special election of 1941, when his side lost to O'Daniel by 1,311 votes, he and Johnson could afford to be "big" about it. Johnson could remain a congressman after the defeat; he was in his early thirties and could look forward to standing for election another day. The election of 1948 was different. For Johnson, defeat meant no congressional seat, a reputation as a two-time loser, the certainty that his political career was over. For Connally, the prospect was that if he were to have any political future at all, he would have to begin all over again, building his own distinct political base out of the Johnson ruins.

Within hours of the polls closing, it was clear that scarcely an eyelash separated the totals of the two contenders. The numbers rolled in steadily to the Texas Election Bureau in Dallas, that semiofficial tabulation service, financed and run by a consortium of Texas news organizations. It had an excellent reputation for accuracy. While the numbers were unofficial—the individual counties would submit their official totals to the state executive committee nine days hence—the Sunday papers reported Stevenson ahead by a few hundred votes. "Anything can happen," wrote the *Dallas Morning News*, but few could dream what really would happen.

Connally stood attorney through the night. With the mistake of 1941 heavily on his mind, when he had reported the returns of their strong counties too early, he instructed their strongholds to slow their vote count and delay reporting. As many as fifty counties were so ordered. Connally had another twenty-five men watching the pro-Stevenson counties for signs of irregularity. Meanwhile, Johnson had been on the phone all night long, checking with his contacts in each county. It gave him an advantage over Stevenson, who had retreated to the quiet remoteness of his Kimble County ranch.

Reporters caught a glimpse of Johnson around 1:00 P.M. He was still in his pajamas, unshaven and disheveled. "My people have advised me to say nothing, and I'm not going to," he said, and turned on his heel. So reporters rushed to Connally, and he was predictably cheerful. "It's tighter than a tick, but I think it's going to be all right," he said. He knew something already that the press didn't, and he had reason for optimism. Stevenson, by contrast, was Mr. Taciturn himself when the press finally encountered him. "I learned long ago as a county attorney not to let anything interfere with sleep," he said dryly.

Around midday on Sunday, with 10,000 votes still out, the bureau had the candidates in a precise numerical tie, dividing to the last digit over 900,000 votes. The state was in for the "long count," that dreaded circumstance where numbers are checked and rechecked, county votes are canvassed and recanvassed, lawyers and judges rush in as challenges and monkey business become rampant, and the final result is not known for days or even weeks.

But toward dusk, the reason for Connally's cheerfulness became apparent. Duval County, the feudal estate of George Parr, fifty miles west of Corpus Christi, across the vast cotton fields of Agua Dulce, had finally reported. It provided a huge plurality for Johnson, nearly 100 to 1. The result was anticipated. One week before the election, Connally had gone to Alice and met with Parr in Parr's office on Main Street. "You've got the vote," Parr said flatly, and they salted the deal with a handshake. The Duval contribution put Johnson slightly ahead.

What the Election Bureau reported—a lead of a few score votes for one candidate or the other—was fast becoming beside the point. A difference of any fewer than a thousand votes meant that the election was a tossup and could be decided only by the officially certified totals of the county executive committee. Those official totals for each county had to be settled by Saturday, September 4, one week after the election, and mailed to the State Executive Committee. Given the closeness, individual tabulators in the counties pored over their votes meticulously, as if they were pharmacists separating pills. Behind the scenes, the telephone lines burned with heated conversation, as the two camps contacted their people in each county. Adjustments to the official tallies trickled into the Election Bureau; a few votes were lost here and there, resulting in no significant change in the overall total. Walter Jenkins kept the totals at the Hancock Mansion, and he felt that his numbers were more accurate than those of the Election Bureau. On Thursday, Stevenson took a heavy hit by losing 118 votes through a recount in Yoakum County in his Panhandle stronghold, and his lead was whittled to 255.

In the midst of this furious recanvass, the real game was taking shape behind the scenes. In a remote corner of the Panhandle, the phone of a county chairman rang. Johnson headquarters was calling. Was there any chance the chairman could recanvass and come up with another couple of hundred votes? It was the file clerk's—or the campaign manager's—nightmare, for the Panhandle chairman was either secretly or overtly a Stevenson man. He immediately called Stevenson at his hotel in Austin.

Simultaneously, a report had come to Stevenson from Jim Wells County, next to Duval, that a fishy recanvass was under way there. He believed that report. If stealing was going to take place anywhere, it would be in the Parr fiefdom.

Parr, the notorious Duke of Duval, controlled five South Texas counties: Duval, Jim Wells, Starr, Zapata, and Webb. Taken together, his "duchy" had the highest illiteracy rate in the state of Texas. The Parr machine had gained its outrageous dimensions over four decades, and it could deliver scandalously lopsided votes, generally a ratio for the candidate of choice of over a hundred to one. Every election year the politicians came courting to ask George Parr for "his vote." Parr's preference had nothing to do with issues, apart from the issue of what a particular candidate could do for the Parrs. Once, a politician who had not been favored with Parr's "vote" had said sardonically to Parr after the election that he appreciated the two votes he had received in Duval County.

"I've always said that woman's suffrage will be the ruination of the country," Parr replied tartly. "My wife and daughter voted for you."

The duchy traced its origins to a contested election in 1911, when George Parr's father, Archer, won forever the affection of the Hispanics by defending his Latin workers in a special election during which three men were slain. By paying funeral expenses and poll taxes, doling out gifts and money, providing jobs at his vast ranch and his racetrack, and giving comfort in crisis, Archer and his scion, George, became the ultimate South Texas *patróns*.

Throughout the years, the bloc votes of the Parr country became the butt of many jokes. In a gubernatorial contest between Ma Ferguson and Dan Moody years before, Archer Parr had supported Ma in the primary, awarding her a vote of 3,000 to 5. But then during the runoff campaign, there was a falling out, and in the second primary the vote was exactly reversed. Coke Stevenson himself had enjoyed these Parr votes in the past. In 1938, when Stevenson ran for lieutenant governor, Parr rewarded Coke with a margin of 2,627 to 26. In the 1942 governor's race, Duval gave Stevenson 2,836 to a total of 77 votes for his five opponents. But, as governor, Stevenson had alienated the blue-eyed Duke by refusing to appoint a man whom Parr wanted as district attorney in Laredo, and during the 1948 campaign Parr had told Stevenson to his face that, while it was nothing personal, he was going to punish him for the Laredo transgression. Stevenson knew perfectly well what that meant, and the shape of it was clear in the early returns. In Duval County it was 4,622 for Johnson and 40 for Stevenson; in Nueces and Jim Wells counties, 5,925 for Johnson and 328 for Stevenson; in Webb, Zapata, and Starr counties, 9,253 for Johnson and 508 for Stevenson.

Hurriedly, Stevenson called a meeting of his top staff. What were they to do? The mood was surly. The election was now in the hands of the political professionals rather than the voters.

"Well, if this is the way Lyndon wants to play—having Jim Wells County recanvassed and recertified after the election—all we have to do is pick up the telephone and our counties can recertify," said an aide angrily. "We'll just fight fire with fire."

A chorus of assent greeted this. Harrison County in East Texas was a sure bet. The offer from there was to add 140 votes to the Stevenson column. The notion moved rapidly toward consensus, until Stevenson himself raised his hand for quiet.

"Gentlemen! Gentlemen! Now wait a minute. I don't play thataway. I do not want any illegal votes counted for me. I don't care what Lyndon and his people do or don't do. We're not going to do it that way." In Stevenson's mind it was more a practical than a moral objection. He did not feel that the Johnson boys would get away with it.

In the days that followed, Johnson made a number of allegations about Stevenson stealing votes, but his charges never carried the weight of real evidence. He howled about a precinct in Kenedy County, south of Corpus, where he had received only eight votes, and he screamed about receiving not a single vote within the vast spread of the King Ranch. Why hadn't anyone called for an investigation of the gold-plated River Oaks section of Houston (the enclave of the fabulously wealthy, where John Connally would live thirty years later), where Stevenson got eight out of every ten votes?

Yet on Thursday, September 2, when he was officially 255 votes behind by the count of the Texas Election Bureau, Johnson curiously proclaimed victory. What did he know?

To their horror, the Stevenson camp noticed that John Connally was not in Austin. Instantly, they suspected what was in fact the case: Connally was in Duval County, there in the thick of it, conspiring with Parr. He had arrived two days before, on Tuesday, and Parr kept him out of sight as if he were a clandestine agent. The Duke had spurned the suggestion that he deal with anyone other than Johnson or Connally, and Johnson could not go to Duval County under the circumstances. Connally went secretly in his stead.

They had to be careful. The Stevenson camp already had an ex-FBI agent poking around, so Parr and Connally met in "odd places," as a Parr aide put it.

With them in the early evening on Tuesday, August 31, in an "odd place," were two Democratic Party officials from Jim Wells County and Luis Salas, the precinct judge for Ballot Box 13, who was a Parr bodyguard and something of a South Texas pistolero. Among his services to Parr, however, the recognition on sight of state politicians did not rank high. He had noticed the surreptitious appearance in Duval of this tall, energetic, forceful man of importance from Austin, and had a simple explanation: Lyndon Johnson had arrived.

"If I can get 200 more votes, I've got it won," Connally said. Salas was impressed that *Johnson* had come to them for help on such a momentous mission.

But Parr had a problem. In Duval he had already used his entire poll tax list to provide the fattest possible margin for Johnson. To go beyond his list, to begin manufacturing names or voting on behalf of dead people, was dangerous. It might even be illegal. But he thought he could find the votes in Jim Wells County.

"We need to win this election," he said in Spanish, turning to Salas. "I want you to add those 200 votes."

For the time being, Salas chose to be difficult. "I don't give a damn if Johnson wins," he snapped.

"Well, for damn sure, you're going to certify what we do," Parr replied.

Salas liked to think of himself as a good party man, the Parr party, so he backed off. He and Parr talked further in Spanish about the details. As he rose to leave, Salas was sure that "Lyndon Johnson" understood that the situation would be taken care of.

Connally had with him Philip Kazen, a political boss from Laredo, who for years had been in league with George Parr. Later that night, in the Adams Building in Alice, a town of 20,000 on the border between Duval and Jim Wells counties, Connally, Kazen, and another man took turns adding new names to the rolls. As vote embezzlers, they were amateurs. They were not too bright in the way they went about the fraud. At the end of the authentic voting list, the votes for Johnson were added in alphabetical order, since the men were proceeding down a list of nonvoters that was ordered alphabetically. Moreover, they wrote the names in the same ink. When they were done, Luis Salas solemnly certified the new total. They did not stop with Box 13. They also added several hundred names to the roll of Box 16, another box in Jim Wells County, so they would have a backup if the 200 new votes from Box 13 were not sufficient. For appearance's sake, they hoped they would not need the Box 16 votes.

Thus it was that Lyndon Johnson two days later could proclaim victory, when the Texas Election Bureau still had him more than a hundred votes behind. Johnson and Connally decided to keep these new votes secretly in their pocket. The "correction" was not to be announced until the last possible moment, when it would be too late for the opposition to respond in kind.

Finally, on Friday, the correction was announced. Stevenson howled bloody murder. Picking up on a Johnson statement the day before to his people to "do their duty," Coke suggested that this was merely a code for stealing. "Almost immediately, last-minute 'gains' for my opponent began to roll in from those counties of South Texas which are dominated by one man. I predict that within the next twenty-four hours further gains for my opponent will be reported by the other counties dominated by this same individual." His prediction was right. The following day, as each county sent off the official tally to the state executive committee, Johnson's majority rose to 162.

★

The convening of the State Executive Committee, whose job was to certify the candidate for the Democratic Party in the fall election, was a week away. The candidates and their strategists jockeyed and plotted and postured, as the justice system began to focus on the election. Connally received a confidential communication that investigators from the U.S. Senate elections subcommittee would soon arrive in Texas. The U.S. attorney general, Tom Clark of Texas (whose son, Ramsey, would later be a member of Lyndon Johnson's presidential cabinet), ordered the Criminal Division into the case.

The *Houston Chronicle* reported that the poll lists and tally sheets of Box 13 in Jim Wells had mysteriously disappeared, and quoted the secretary of the Jim Wells election as saying that after considering the evidence of fraud, the Jim Wells executive committee was unable to determine the "true and correct vote" in Precinct 13. It was fast becoming a case for lawyers and detectives.

On September 10, three days before the State Executive Committee was to convene in Fort Worth, Coke Stevenson marched into Alice. At his elbow were two tough hombres. One was the notorious Frank Hamer, a huge, moon-faced man who was once described as being as talkative as an oyster. Hamer was famous chiefly as the man who finally caught Bonnie and Clyde after a chase lasting 102 days. When he finally approached their car in a thicket, Bonnie had turned her gun on him, and Hamer later said it was like "looking down the Holland Tunnel." But he shot first and didn't much like killing a woman, but then "I remembered the way Bonnie had taken part in the murder of nine peace officers. I remembered how she kicked the body of a highway patrolman at Grapevine and fired a bullet into his body on the ground." Frank Hamer was tough, and the likes of George Parr's goons did not faze him. The other was T. Kellis Dibrell, a swarthy San Antonio attorney who had just resigned as an FBI agent. The ex-governor had come to inspect the poll and tally lists which were kept in the Texas State Bank, the bank owned by George Parr himself. With Hamer leading the way, the party approached the bank. The building had the aura of a fortress, festooned as it was with the large star of Texas carved into its pockmarked limestone facade. Beneath the star and the substantial rectangular windows were carved fair representations of the Indian head and the likeness of George Washington on the current nickel, and the Valkyrie of the dime. The Parr forces were waiting.

Across the street, in front of the feed store, five men with Winchester rifles loitered, and at the bank door itself a dozen pistoleros stood in a half-circle. Hamer halted his gubernatorial party, eyeing the riflemen and then the bank guards. Breaking away, he sauntered across to the riflemen. "Git!" he commanded. The gunmen exchanged languid glances, grumbled something, and then slowly, grudgingly, moved off down the street. Back at the bank door, Hamer was more loquacious. "Fall back!" he hissed. They did, languorously. Stevenson and his men entered the bank.

Inside, the ex-governor demanded of the secretary of the Jim Wells executive committee (who was a bank teller) to see the poll and tally lists. They were produced. Dibrell took them, immediately turning to the end. To his astonishment and delight, he found the last two hundred entries to be in alphabetical order, written in green ink. The first 841 votes were entered in blue or black ink, penned in different handwritings. Dibrell proceeded to take down the last twenty names on the list, before the owlish Parr man snatched the list from him. But Stevenson had what he wanted. In the coming hours the group contacted four "voters" on Dibrell's list and received sworn statements that they had not voted. From a fifth, number 841 on the authentic list, they got a statement that he had voted shortly after 7:00 P.M., as the polls were closing, and yet somehow, 200 more people were supposed to have voted after him. The sixth man listed, Manuel Sanchez, they determined to be dead, thus inspiring the joke that later Lyndon Johnson would tell with such gusto about the child from Jim Wells County who was found in tears shortly after the vote.

"Pedro, why are you crying?" asks the man.

"It is because of my poor dead father, señor."

"But Pedro, your father died a year ago!"

"*Sí*, señor, that's just it. Yesterday, my father came back to vote for Lyndon Johnson, but he no come to see me!"

At one point in the day Stevenson confronted Parr face to face and demanded to see the marked ballots and the poll lists. But Connally had prepped Parr well. The Duke simply laughed, saying he was not an election judge, and he knew nothing of the whereabouts of the ballots. Toward the end of the day Stevenson filed an affidavit in the county courthouse charging widespread fraud in Box 13. His purpose was to force the Jim Wells executive committee to reconvene and to remove the fictitious voters from the rolls.

Back in Austin, meanwhile, Connally was following every move. Stevenson had to be stopped. Led by the fixer, Alvin Wirtz, the Johnson lawyers huddled. By the afternoon, a petition for a temporary restraining order against the Stevenson group was presented to a friendly judge in Austin. It was granted. The Johnson petition charged a conspiracy, complete with secret meetings in private residences and studded with "threats and intimidation" to change the "official" returns of the county, and thereby to reverse the result of the whole election. In other words, the illegal votes were the official votes—and to change the official votes was illegal.

This circular reasoning was blown out with the breath of outrage, as if Johnson were the injured party, but of course the whole business was a delaying tactic. The strategy, to which Connally had become central, was to mire the Jim Wells situation in charge and countercharge, legal maneuver and false issues, while the plenary session of the State Executive Committee convened and certified Johnson as the candidate. A hearing was set for Monday in Alice, to begin at the same hour that the executive committee gathered in Fort Worth.

On Sunday, the *Dallas Morning News* summed up the situation: "The question in Fort Worth is this: even if Stevenson should win his demand for a recount in Jim Wells, and even if the recount turns in his favor, could a revision be sent to Fort Worth in time to turn the tide for Stevenson?" Connally's bet was a resounding No, and he began to lobby in the corridors of the Blackstone Hotel.

★

In Fort Worth there were to be two convocations on successive days, and they were closely tied together. The problems to be solved were broader than simply the issue of Johnson vs. Stevenson. No Democrat had ever won the White House without winning Texas, and this was the year of Strom Thurmond and his Dixiecrat movement, so the problem for the Democratic party nationally was how to enforce the loyalty of conservative Southern Democrats, especially Texas Democrats. Nothing short of the election of Harry Truman in 1948 hung in the balance. On Monday, the State Executive Committee was to meet in the Blackstone Hotel to certify the Senate nominee, and on Tuesday the state Democratic party was to hold its convention in the commodious Will Rogers Auditorium. Since Stevenson's strength lay with the conservative wing of the party—the wing most susceptible to the peculiar attractions of the Dixiecrat movement—the Johnson strategists were intent to advertise the virtue, indeed, the absolute requirement, of party loyalty. They hoped that the Dixiecrats would bolt and thus undermine Stevenson's support. To punish the Dixiecrats was to hurt Stevenson.

For any who participated in the Fort Worth events, the next two days were to become a vivid, indeed lurid, memory. It was old-time politics at its most memorable and its most outrageous, where smoke-filled rooms were crowded with brilliant lawyers, skilled politicians, outright buffoons, and a good many drunks—and the issues that attracted them were of state, national, and, as we now know, historical importance. There would be one more battle like it, eight years later in 1956, before Texas would begin to enter the modern age. But if Connally was later to be good on television, or as a tough horse-trader on the international monetary scene, he was very good now in the back room.

Monday began on a fitting note. Into the lobby of the Blackstone came Creekmore Fath, the chairman of the Travis County Democratic party and the manager of the Truman for President campaign in Texas. Fath was an ardent New Dealer and a true liberal. At the Travis County Democratic convention some days earlier, over which he presided, Fath had taken the dramatic gesture of recognizing a black man to speak, the first time that had ever happened. At once he was denounced by one Joe Hill, a former state senator and the leader of the Texas racists. Hill called Fath a nigger lover and a communist. Now, as Fath came through the hotel lobby, Hill entered from the opposite direction. Surprised, but conciliatory, Fath greeted Hill and asked what he was doing there, whereupon Hill pulled a switchblade knife and lunged at Fath over a gold wicker chair. The two men, one thin as a stick, the other rotund as a ball, wrestled about on the floor before they were separated and Hill was pushed out into Fourth Street. As Fath tried to collect himself, Jerome Sneed, the Austin member of the executive committee and a Johnson supporter, who the day before had told the press that the party machinery was no place to try cases of election fraud, got off the elevator. Still shaken, Fath began to recount the knife attack to Sneed, when Sneed, already overloaded with the excitement of the Johnson-Stevenson contest, slumped and fell to the floor, gripped by a heart attack. The lobby became bedlam, but some kept their heads. Alvin Wirtz rushed onto the scene as the quivering Sneed was attended to, and thrust a proxy document into his hand.

"Jerome," he shouted into Sneed's ear, "your vote is very important! You need to sign this proxy so I can cast your vote for Lyndon!" As others massaged his heart and wiped his brow, Sneed signed, in a manner of speaking, before he was carted away.

Inside the ornate, packed ballroom, upon a raised table, the opposing lawyers took one another's measure. The candidates were not present for the preliminaries. They were closeted in their respective hotel rooms. Connally shuttled in and out of the ballroom as the proceeding got under way.

The Stevenson side was represented by a state senator, Clint Small, and he led off with appropriate outrage. "The issue before this committee is whether or not Precinct 13 in Jim Wells County is to elect a United States senator to serve the next six years," he thundered. "The question is not to throw out votes, but to prevent votes from being thrown in." He waved his Jim Wells affidavits before them: the counted voters who had not voted, the vote of the dead man. The sanctity of the ballot box was the imperative; the stuffing of the ballot box was the crime.

Johnson's case was argued by an Austin attorney, John D. Cofer, one of the select few, along with Connally, who had known five days before it was made public that the Jim Wells vote was 200 votes higher than first reported. The executive committee, Cofer proclaimed, was not a court convened to try election cases. Its sole job was to count votes. "You may not be able to understand the law," he said ironically, "but by Holy Writ, you can count!" Stevenson's affidavits were obtained by duress, he argued, compelled by the most feared lawman in all of Texas. "Stevenson went down there [to Jim Wells County] with a man who had a gun on one hip and said, 'Swear to this!' None of you would try a Negro on the basis of affidavits obtained by a policeman with a gun on his hip." Were they going to take such evidence without cross-examination? Were they going to send Coke Stevenson to the U.S. Senate, based upon a few scraps of paper? "Are you going to let Mr. Small wave an affidavit, and then let me wave one—well, I can wave two for every one you can wave." Then, he did wave one, a statement from one of the Stevenson witnesses, who now claimed that she had been so frightened by the two Stevenson men, Hamer and Dibrell, that she had signed their documents and would have signed anything. Intimidation had been met with counterintimidation.

At last, the tedious county-by-county tabulation got under way, as the candidates pored over the numbers with their accountants as if it were a bankruptcy hearing.

Meanwhile in dusty Alice, the hearing on the Johnson injunction provided a dingy mirror image of the Fort Worth proceeding. The Stevenson lawyer there used different images, speaking of votes fabricated from the whole cloth and submitting that the Johnson's restraining order had no precedent in all judicial history. The Johnson lawyer, in turn, rested his argument on procedure rather than substance, and he went on and on with it, for his real game was to stall for time. Fraud was not denied. The court simply had no jurisdiction over this purely political matter. As the arguments went on interminably, George Parr stood majestically at the back of the courtroom. Earlier in the day he had spoken to a reporter and explained the lopsided Duval vote flatly. Since Stevenson had refused to appoint the Laredo district attorney he wanted, "this is the first time we have had to vote against him." It was a use of the royal *we* that might have made Queen Victoria blush. No doubt Parr nodded approvingly and was unsurprised when in midafternoon the judge ruled in favor of Johnson. Parr was already packed for a trip to Fort Worth, where the following day he would be greeted with the fanfare due a conquering hero.

News of the Alice decision reached Fort Worth as the tabulation approached its climax. That Johnson had won in Alice meant only that he had won a delay, but that was all Connally and the other strategists really wanted. It was inconceivable that the executive committee would suspend its certification until a lengthy legal proceeding could run its course. The judge's decision also meant that Jim Wells County could report no other figure than the inflated one. Now, the official totals gave the election to Johnson by eighty-seven votes. Forevermore he would be "Landslide Lyndon."

The moment of decision had arrived, and the sixty-two members of the State Executive Committee came to it reluctantly. Would they certify Johnson's eighty-seven-vote victory? Many had convinced themselves that there was no moral issue, since vote stealing was rampant on both sides. It made the process easier to swallow if one believed that Stevenson was as big a thief as Johnson. The first five votes all went for Johnson, and then the candidates alternated votes. In the middle of the alphabet Stevenson had a run of eight straight votes, and suddenly it appeared that Johnson was sunk. The room fairly burst with tension.

At the end of the roll call, Johnson appeared to have won the delegate vote by two. But a woman stood and changed her vote from Johnson to an abstention. That tied it at twenty-seven. It looked as if the chairman of the committee would have to break the tie, and he stalled, not wanting to assume that burden, hoping for deliverance. The Johnson forces had already initiated a desperate search for one Charles Gibson of Amarillo, a committee member who unaccountably had not voted and whom they knew to be their man. Finally, Bill Kitrell, Connally's old buddy from wartime Algiers, unearthed Gibson in his hotel room, where he lay drunk. Kitrell wrestled him into a cold shower and then trundled him down to the ballroom. Amid the press and the noise, Gibson could scarcely receive recognition, and ultimately climbed up on a chair to get it.

When he voted for Johnson, the chair upon which he stood was pushed over. Pandemonium broke out, as Johnson threw himself into a series of embraces.

Stevenson was characteristically laconic. He would challenge the certification before the full Democratic party convention the next day, and in the courts, and on and on it would go. But the crucial vote had been taken. To withdraw certification once it had been given was harder than blocking certification, and the tide now ran strongly in favor of the Johnson forces. This had been Connally's idea all along. He knew that the convention had its other problem: to enforce party loyalty in the face of the Dixiecrat challenge. He was in a position to deal, and deal he did. It was a straightforward proposition: the true liberals, the ones likely to worry the most about the morals of this sordid affair, would not raise the Box 13 matter if the Johnson crowd would throw its weight behind the expulsion of the Dixiecrats and replace them with liberals. For Connally and the Johnson people that was an easy deal to accept— in the short run. But the long-term consequence was to sow seeds for a titanic battle between the liberals and the conservatives of the Texas Democratic party eight years later, a battle in which Johnson and Connally again would stand side by side.

That night, the redoubtable Sam Rayburn, in a speech from the pulpit of a nearby church, preached the evangelism of party loyalty. "When you vote the Dixiecrat ticket, you are voting for a Republican administration for the next four years," he raged. He boasted that he was one man in Texas who was still unafraid to speak the name of Franklin Roosevelt. "If we don't march into that convention hall tomorrow with a firm conviction to be loyal to the party, we will be untrue to those who made this country great and who made this country free—untrue to the mountain peaks of American democracy who built this country into the greatest force in history." Even though he was butchering the language, he was butchering the opposition as well. It was a powerful exhortation by a Herculean figure, and it was heard.

The acrimonious atmosphere of the executive committee on Monday now gave way to the brawl of the state convention under Johnson and Connally. Years later Texas would struggle to escape its reputation as a Southern state, but in 1948, there could be no doubt what it was. The Will Rogers Auditorium was awash with Confederate flags as the Dixiecrats, calling themselves Texas Regulars, stormed the place, loudly proclaiming the virtues of Strom Thurmond and segregation. Racist Joe Hill, bespectacled, bow-tied, and roly-poly, his switchblade knife safely in his pocket, was their spokesman. From the podium, he roared his contempt for Truman and his "Commie-crats." He evoked the McCarthy-Nixon hearing far away in Washington, and spoke to the convention of the "escapees from the State Department" in their midst. Boos greeted him. People shouted for him to sit down. With the fighting tenacity of a pit bull, he dared "anyone with the manhood and the guts to come up and make me sit down." The audience squealed with delight. "Surprised to see you up there, Joe!" someone else hurled good-naturedly from the balcony.

"That sounds like one of those colored delegates from Travis County," Hill boomed back. "Those freaks of nature don't bother me. The more you interrupt, the longer you'll have to look at me. . . ."

"Louder, Porky, louder!" And so it went.

As the true liberals watched this display with more amusement than anger, they could think only of the Wobbly song about another Joe Hill:

> I dreamed I saw Joe Hill last night
> Alive as you and me
> But Joe, I said, you're ten years dead
> I never died, said he.
> When working people are out on strike,
> You'll always find Joe Hill.

The opposing forces watched the first test vote closely. It was inconclusive. The real issue was whether a pledge to vote for Truman in the general election was a requirement for participating in the Democratic convention. Connally and his forces were intent that the party loyalty question be settled before the issue of the senatorial nominee, and as the rural delegations began to dominate the big-city delegations forming the core of the Dixiecrat strength, it soon became a purge. Liberals replaced Dixiecrats in the Houston, Fort Worth, and Dallas delegations. As the enemies of Truman were booted out, so the power of Coke Stevenson withered away. A liberal platform followed quickly and passed. It was especially progressive on labor issues, calling for the repeal of restrictive labor legislation without specifically mentioning Taft-Hartley, so as not to embarrass Johnson. In midevening, Johnson emerged from the wings to declare that he had no room in his heart for bitterness. George Parr was brought forward to thunderous applause.

Near midnight, a decision on the senatorial nominee was finally called for. The Dixiecrats had long since departed the hall, taking with them their typewriters and adding machines like huffy children taking home their toys. By voice vote, Lyndon Johnson was declared the official nominee, and only a few nays were heard. As stagehands moved to clean up the debris and delegates shuffled out, Connally tarried on the stage, shepherding through the signing of the certification document by the convention chairman. Once signed, it was dispatched to the Texas secretary of state in Austin, so Johnson could be entered on the official ballot.

The political battle was over, but the legal battle would last another two weeks. In this, Connally had no significant role. On the morning after the convention, Johnson was winging his way to Austin, and Connally was left behind for the postmortem. "My part in the campaign is now over," he declared, weary but smiling. "The job now can be handled by the congressman's lawyers." What he meant was that a legion of the best legal minds in Texas and in Washington (most significantly, the future Supreme Court justice Abe Fortas) would move in to protect the fraud. They would be helped by Harry Truman. He would come to Texas some days later, and in successive campaign stops in Temple, Bonham, and Whitesboro, even as the matter was being considered by the courts, he would declare Lyndon Johnson to be the Democratic party candidate for the Senate. More important than that, Truman would call U.S. Supreme Court Justice Hugo Black from his campaign train outside San Marcos, and urge Black to enter the case and decide for Johnson.

But Connally's job was not quite over. As the convention in Fort Worth broke up, Stevenson's lawyers, including Kellis Dibrell, struck out for East Texas to find the federal judge T. Whittfield Davidson, at his ranch near the Louisiana line. Driving all night, they arrived at Davidson's place near four in the morning. Amid the racket of his hunting dogs, Judge Davidson came to his door in his pajamas and invited the night visitors in. Upon his kitchen table, they laid out a restraining order to enjoin the Texas secretary of state from placing Johnson's name on the official ballot, until the allegations of fraud could be considered in federal court. Their order in hand, the Stevenson lawyers hit the road again and arrived, exhausted and unshaven, at the courthouse in Fort Worth.

As they entered the clerk's office to file the judge's order, there stood John Connally, silent and impassive, aloof and magisterial.

"When I saw John Connally, it convinced me again that someone in the Johnson camp had the ability to listen in on our telephone conversations," Kellis Dibrell said later. "Connally was the mainstay, and I wondered how he knew we were going to be there to file the restraining order. It had taken us hours to drive up to that farmhouse way out in East Texas, and hours to drive back. But we did call in and left word that the judge had signed it, and that we were en route to Fort Worth to file."

Two weeks later, Hugo Black vacated this order on a technical point of procedure, simply ruling that federal courts had no jurisdiction in the matter of a state election, and Johnson's name finally went on the ballot.

Thus, the election of 1948 moved into the history books and into the lore of Texas politics. Who really won? It was a question that was very much alive forty years later, and its answer was about the same as it was on the day it was official.

"Who really won the election?" Creekmore Fath, the Travis County Democratic leader, asked a Johnson campaign manager on the day of the result.

"Well, they were stealing in East Texas," the manager replied. "We were stealing in South Texas. So, God only knows who really won the election, Creek. But today, God was on our side by eighty-seven votes."

★ 9 ★

Oil, Money, and Blood

IN THE MYTHOLOGY OF TEXANS, Olympus is not a snow-covered peak, nor is Zeus some berobed, unapproachable Being, given to grand pronouncements, armed with thunderbolts, bristling with cosmic schemes. Texas icons are more down-to-earth than that. They are the risktakers, the roughnecks who get lucky to a degree scarcely comprehensible to outlanders. They are lucky, not in love or in parentage or in brilliance, but lucky in oil. In the 1930s, 1940s, and 1950s, six were memorialized in this special Texas pantheon. The most famous was H. L. Hunt, the round-faced billionaire who won his first oil well on a bluff in a poker game, whose idols were Douglas MacArthur and Joseph McCarthy, whose racism and anti-Semitism were rivaled only by his passion for nuts, fruits, and exotic elixirs. Hunt had a penchant for women, including, simultaneously, two wives and a mistress, the opera singer Lily Pons. He liked to call the ladies "Honey." When Mrs. Albert Sidney Johnson of Dallas asked him once, "Mr. Hunt, are you rich?" Hunt replied, "Honey, I am plenty rich," and when his secretary was fretting one day, Hunt asked, "Honey, what's worrying you?"

"The same thing that's worrying you, Mr. Hunt," she replied.

"What, Honey?" he asked, and then:

"Money, Honey," she said.

The other Texas immortals were less well known, but equally fascinating.

Hugh Roy Cullen of Houston, whose first job was in a San

Antonio candy store, was said in the early 1950s to have given away more money than any man in the world. Cullen happened to love baseball, the St. Louis Cardinals in particular, and once, when the Cards were mired in the cellar, he sent them a telegram that read, "Every critter here on the ranch is praying for you, down to the last snake." The manager put the wire on the clubhouse bulletin board and his team promptly moved up into third place.

Clint Murchison—big-featured, rugged, short, reclusive—was the quintessential Texas wheeler-dealer from Dallas who traded companies like baseball cards and always bragged about the size of his debt.

Amon Carter, the Fort Worth publisher and serious collector of Western art, was in the late 1930s among the most successful wildcatters in the West Texas Permian Basin.

J. R. "Major" Parten of Madisonville had organized the mammoth "Big Inch" pipeline for West Texas oil in World War II, had introduced Connally to Lyndon Johnson, and supported every liberal Democrat from Franklin Roosevelt onward.

Lastly, there was Sid Richardson of Fort Worth. He was perhaps the least known of this fabulous sextet.

When oil gushed from the Santa Rita rig in 1923—Santa Rita being the patron saint of the hopeless—and the oil boom in the Permian Basin began, Richardson was operating as an independent wildcatter, acquiring drilling rights in the barren ranchland of West Texas, borrowing and begging drilling equipment, hanging out with his rig crews, whose payroll he often could not meet. In the beginning there was no science to oil exploration. It was essentially a blind shoot, and prospecting deals were generally sealed with a handshake. The major oil companies sat back and let the "poor boys" like Richardson undertake the prospecting, lose their money down dry holes and in sour wells, but then bought out any roughneck who struck it rich. In the new oil fields, many greeted poor boys like Richardson skeptically, for you could get a reputation for working "bean jobs," jobs whose pay was strictly room and board. The first-class contractor might never hire you. Still, Richardson had a jolly, easygoing good humor. He could drink hard with his tool pushers and roughnecks, but he was more partial to buttermilk, which he consumed in great quantities and often with a better class of folks, like Baptist ministers. Beneath his casual manner, however, there was a tough shrewdness. Borrowing was the only way to survive, and to survive was to have the chance to strike it rich. Like his future ward, John Connally, Richardson was given to braggadocio about how many millions he owed. Debt was good; it was the measure of the dream; bad deals were made by the comfortable. Debt did not defeat you, but spurred you on to greater effort—and eventually to a streak of luck. Richardson had many lean years before his luck came in. He was doing all right in Wichita Falls until, in 1921, the bubble burst, the price of oil fell from $3.50 a barrel to $1.00 in nine days, and Richardson went flat broke. He built back up until 1930, when newly discovered East Texas oil flooded the market and wiped him out for the second time.

Through the lean years, Richardson's prime source of cash was the Austin publisher Charles Marsh. Marsh and Richardson had a fifty-fifty agreement: Marsh put up the capital for exploration and Richardson put up his know-how, and they would split the profits— if there were any. The arrangement was "buy or sell": if the partners could not agree, one partner would have the right to buy out the other.

Richardson's luck came in 1935 when he acquired the right to drill a test well in land belonging to the Keystone Cattle Company. After he patched together his equipment and secured the backing of Amon Carter as well as Marsh, the well came in at 250 barrels a day. Three hundred and eighty-five wells were to follow in the prodigious Keystone Field, and of those drilled only seventeen were dry holes. The Keystone Field was to enter the rare first rank as a hundred-million-dollar oil field. Throughout his remaining life Richardson was to credit luck above all else in his success. When he was asked about his wealth he would talk about the three-year period before the Keystone strike, when he invested $15 million and could drink every drop of oil he had to show for it. "Luck has helped me every day of my life," Richardson would reply languidly. "I'd rather be lucky than smart, because a lot of smart people ain't eatin' regular." If he wasn't one of the smartest fellows in the world, Richardson felt that at least he was one of the luckiest. "Some people get luck and brains mixed up, and that's when they get in trouble."

By 1940 he had more than 120 producing wells in three West Texas counties, including 33 in the Keystone Field, but he was having to split the take with his partner, Charles Marsh. Marsh's business affairs, however, were complicated by affairs of the heart. In 1931 he abruptly deserted his wife and children for the belle of Marlin, Texas, Alice Glass, and took her East and built her Longlea in the Blue Ridge Mountains of Virginia. He lavished jewels on his mistress and made her into an American countess, only to lose her affections later to Lyndon Johnson. In the nasty divorce that resulted from the Glass affair, Marsh's assets were tied up in court for years, and his partner, Sid Richardson, smelled an opportunity. As the Winkler County fields came in, Richardson went to Marsh, saying he needed $3.7 million to develop the last leases around the Keystone pool. Marsh replied that he couldn't come up with five dollars without permission from the court. Well, then, said Richardson, I'm afraid we'll have to go back to the buy or sell arrangement. It was the full acquisition of Marsh's share that made Richardson a billionaire. "When Sid got the chance," said one observer of this process, "he screwed the guy who brought him into business." By 1951 it was widely believed that Richardson could probably equal the fortune of H. L. Hunt, but Richardson honestly had no way to estimate his worth, for it floated upon his vast oil reserves in the ground. As time went on he diversified his holdings with ranches all over Texas, including one in Wilson County, not far from the modest Connally ranch. He controlled a chain of radio and television stations, a chain of drugstores, and the Texas Hotel in Fort Worth, where Connally and John F. Kennedy were to spend the night before they went to Dallas in November 1963.

In his personal life, at least in his hometown of Fort Worth, Richardson lived simply. Never married, he had bachelor quarters at the Fort Worth Club, that bastion of grace and opulence and male conviviality in downtown Fort Worth, where in his pre-Keystone days his bills went unpaid for years. At the urging of his friend Amon Carter, who was a real connoisseur of Western painting, Richardson became an important collector of Remingtons and Russells. And he bought an island off Corpus Christi called St. Joseph Island, which is twenty-eight miles long and six miles wide and noted for whooping cranes and quicksand. The purchase of "St. Joe" resulted from a friendly ribbing from his rival, Clint Murchison, who owned Matagorda Island just to the north. On Matagorda, Murchison had built a grand home as a retreat for duck hunting and poker. On one of Richardson's visits to Matagorda Island, Murchison turned to him and said, "Why don't you quit sponging off me? Why don't you buy an island of your own?"

"Well, I don't know," Richardson replied. "Are there any islands around here for sale?"

"Why don't you buy St. Joseph Island?"

"How much do they want for it?"

"I don't know," Murchison replied. "But it might have oil on it."

So Richardson went off and bought St. Joseph for a hefty sum, close to a million dollars, only to find that he had to spend another $35,000 to dredge a canal. Then, to build a proper house, he hired and fired three architects, and throughout the process Murchison continued his ribbing.

"How much did you say this house cost you?" Richardson asked Murchison one day, as Richardson's own house was still taking shape.

"About $35,000," Murchison lied.

"Well, I think I'll have to up you a bit. I may have to spend $75,000 on my house." Richardson said this, knowing full well that with his cost overruns, the price of his house would come out around $250,000.

Finally, at the long-awaited housewarming, Murchison approached Richardson wickedly. "How much did you say this all cost, again?" he asked with a grin.

"I'm not going to tell you, you son of a bitch," Richardson exploded. "You're the one who got me into this."

Actually, Murchison and Richardson were best friends. They had grown up together in Athens, Texas, a place sixty miles southeast of Dallas, noted—so its weekly newspaper trumpeted—for "peaches, pears, potatoes, peanuts, pigs, pottery, and poultry." In the frontier town of Wichita Falls in 1919, they became a team, along with other assorted gamblers, fortune hunters, and blueskyers, and they had floated and crashed together with the Wichita Falls bubble. Legend had it that one night Murchison had dragged Richardson out of a poker game to investigate a tip from an oil scout that a supersecret well was about to come in near Burkburnett along the Oklahoma border. In the darkness the pair bluffed the guards to get close enough to smell oil, and the next morning they were over in Oklahoma laying out $50,000 to buy up borderland leases north of the new well. When news of the strike came out a few days later, the Athens boys flipped their leases, selling a fraction of them for $200,000. They went their separate ways into fortune, but into the 1950s, when they were getting to be old men, they continued to talk by telephone almost every morning about 6:00 A.M. Their dialogue had a diffident, jocular quality.

"Richardson, I've decided to get out of debt."

"Murchison, don't do it. The day you get out of debt you'll be dead, and I haven't got time for a funeral."

"Richardson, what's the dope?"

"Murchison, I hear there's a popcorn stand for sale. You want to buy?"

Among the "popcorn stands" that Murchison and Richardson purchased together in later life was the New York Central Railroad. In the shorthand of billionaires, Richardson thought that Murchison had only counted him in for "ten" in the deal, meaning $10 million, when actually it was for "twenty." That discrepancy did not bother Richardson so much as something else. He called Murchison back: "Say, Clint, what was the name of the railroad again?" The deal eventually would redound to John Connally's benefit. In a few years he would become a director of the New York Central, and *he* would have no difficulty in remembering the name.

Richardson and Murchison shared views about the value of indebtedness, and their homilies on its virtues tumbled out of them easily. "Cash makes a man careless." "The only bad deals I've ever made were made when I had money." "If you're honest and you're trying, your creditors will play ball. They know you can do a better job of running your company than they could." It was a lesson John Connally would take to heart, but in a different age it would not serve him nearly as well.

★

Connally stepped into the fabulous world of Sid Richardson in the fall of 1951. For several years, since Johnson's "landslide" victory in 1948, Connally had labored as a front office lawyer with Johnson's old fixer and political adviser, Alvin Wirtz. Among other clients, Wirtz handled the legal business of the Brown and Root concern, which had been Lyndon Johnson's horn of plenty throughout his life. The Wirtz firm, therefore, was a natural place for Connally to be. He was as much a decoration as a practicing lawyer. He was the handsome man up front who brought the flowers and attended the social events; he was visible while others did the tough legal business in the shadows. Herman Brown, however, did not like Connally. When Wirtz died, in October 1951, Connally lost his protector and needed to move on.

Within weeks of Wirtz's death, undoubtedly at the prodding of Lyndon Johnson, Richardson sent his private DC-3 to Austin to pick up Connally and bring him to Fort Worth for a talk. He and Richardson spent a long evening together.

"You're a young man with great promise," Richardson asserted. "I can hire a lot of lawyers. I can hire a lot of accountants, and I can hire a lot of technical brains. But it's extremely difficult to hire common sense. . . ." Common political sense is what he meant. "If you come up here and go to work for me, I won't pay you as much as you'd get elsewhere, but I'll pay you enough to buy bread and beans and get your hair cut, and I'll try to help you make some money." Connally accepted, at a salary of $25,000 a year.

In hiring Connally, Richardson was following the lead of his friend Clint Murchison, who was a Joseph McCarthy Republican by persuasion but who had hired the ardent New Dealer, Gerald Mann, the notorious "little red arrow" from SMU, as his lieutenant. Not long after Richardson hired Connally, a switchboard operator overheard Richardson explaining this two-sided procedure to Dwight Eisenhower. "Murchison is a Republican, but he's got Mann working as his lieutenant," Richardson said. "That's the way we do it in the oil business." With his preference for the shadows and with the importance of politics to his business, Richardson wanted in Connally an attractive emissary, a forceful lobbyist in Washington, and a political entrepreneur. Uncle Sid's relationship with Sam Rayburn and Lyndon Johnson extended back some years, but with issues like jurisdiction over the offshore zone known as the Tidelands and the deregulation of natural gas looming in Washington, his Washington contacts needed constant cultivation.

With Sam Rayburn, money could be both a sore subject and a mysterious one. Young Democrats whose campaigns were in need of support were often struck by the spectacle of Rayburn's safe in his Speaker's office, which was packed with wads of cash. Nobody knew the source of the money, but Rayburn distributed generously to his favorites. At the same time he enjoyed a vaunted reputation for honesty. From magnates like Richardson, the Speaker accepted no gifts and apparently no cash; an attempt to give him a gift could throw Rayburn into a rage. At a dinner for Rayburn in 1949, for example, at which campaign financing was to be discussed, Sid Richardson summoned Rayburn into the men's room, and moments later Rayburn stormed out in a fury. Once outside, the Speaker saw Creekmore Fath, who was then the chairman of finance for the Democrats. "Creekmore," he shouted, "you go in there and talk to him!" When Fath dutifully entered the men's room, Richardson was in a state of shock.

"I don't know what gets into Sam sometimes," Richardson said morosely. He reached in one pocket and pulled out a wad of $5,000, then in the other, and pulled out another $5,000, and pressed the money on Fath.

"How am I going to list this contribution?" Fath protested.

"I don't know. . . . Use the Bass boys," Richardson said dismissively. (The Bass boys were his nephews.)

Thereafter Richardson used more guile in pressing his favors on Rayburn. On one occasion Richardson visited Rayburn's scratchy farm near Bonham in the company of Rayburn's protégé, William Kitrell. Kitrell had been with Connally during the war in Algeria and operated a peanut farm, a peach orchard, and a Dallas clipping service. But he was also known for one of the better Texas rejoinders to Edna Ferber's portrayal of the King Ranch in her novel *Giant*. After Ferber had talked about "the crowd of DC-6s" at the King Ranch, Kitrell had replied, "Two DC-3s, Miss Ferber, do not a DC-6 make." In any event, in Kitrell's company, Richardson was affronted to see the pathetic collection of would-be steers that passed for Rayburn's herd.

"Goddamn it, Sam, what you need is a decent bull!" Richardson said.

"Well, I've got my eye on one bull," Rayburn mumbled.

"Listen, I've got this scrawny little old bull that's no use to me," Richardson said. "Goddamn it, Sam, I want you to have it."

"Don't do it, Sid," Rayburn said.

"Well, I'm going to do it."

Rayburn shrugged.

Richardson, of course, had no such bull at all. He and Kitrell went down the road to a prize livestock dealer, selected the best champion bull on the spread, and Richardson wrote out a check for $20,000. When the bull was delivered to Rayburn's farm it came with a note from Richardson that apologized for this sorry, no-count bull that wasn't worth $50, but it was the best Uncle Sid could do. Rayburn cheerfully rebuilt his herd with the closet champion, and Richardson was to say to Kitrell, "If you ever tell this to Rayburn, I'm going to denut you."

In this world of cash wads and private planes, of gushing wells and private islands, Connally cheerfully took his place. His agreement with Richardson at the outset was that they would try the arrangement and see how it worked. If Richardson didn't like it, Connally would go in the morning. If Connally didn't like it, he could leave in the afternoon. In fact, he would not leave for nine years, and the ethos of the Richardson empire would be equaled in its influence on Connally only by the ethos of Lyndon Johnson. Richardson and Johnson were Connally's role models. They represented the political and the business sides of the same equation. Connally's job with Richardson lasted longer than any other job of his career. He and Nellie settled into a comfortable existence within the small, closed society of the Fort Worth wealthy and worthy, where the big West Texas ranch and oil families—the Carters, the Moncriefs, the Walshes, and the Fortsons—dominated, and where graceful events took place in the Spanish castles and French châteaus overlooking the Trinity River bottom in old Westover, or at the country club. John and Nellie Connally had finally become Establishment. It was all a far cry from the frenzied world of Lyndon Johnson. Connally was narrowing himself into a one-issue oilman, as Lyndon Johnson was beginning to grow as a powerful United States senator.

Richardson had been dabbling at a high level of politics for some time before Connally came on board. Uncle Sid's social views of domestic American life were decidedly medieval, and he was given to talking liberally and passionately about the "niggers." But it was presidential politics that particularly engaged his interest. Three months after Connally joined him, Richardson sailed off to Europe on the *Queen Mary* to see General Eisenhower, to persuade him to run for president on the Democratic ticket and to assure him that if the general did so, he would have plenty of "oil" behind him. To Richardson, party label was not the important thing. Business was, and Harry Truman had turned out to be a disappointment on what really mattered to Texas oilmen in the early 1950s: the colossal issue of the Tidelands, where literally billions of dollars hung in the balance. For many years the oil interests had been trying to shift the oil-rich offshore lands from federal jurisdiction to state jurisdiction. In 1937 the court reaffirmed that the federal government owned the minerals offshore, and this meant that a driller had to pay the hefty federal royalty of 37½ percent on production. Texas claimed it owned the Tidelands, not merely out to the customary distance of three miles, but to 10½ miles, and for its leases it proposed to charge only a 12½ percent royalty. But the Supreme Court had ruled in 1950 that the Texas borderland extended out only 3 miles, as in the other 47 states. Congress had twice passed bills returning the Tidelands to Texas. Twice, President Truman had vetoed them.

So Eisenhower was the man and the solution. Richardson contributed generously to an Eisenhower candidacy, even after Ike decided he was a Republican. The direct contribution to the campaign was reported to be $1 million, but Richardson also paid $200,000 in expenses at the Commodore Hotel in New York which Eisenhower ran up on his return to the United States, as well as the bulk of Ike's expenses in Chicago during the 1952 Republican convention itself. Just before that convention, Connally was intensely involved in behalf of Richardson in trying to persuade Texas Republicans that Eisenhower would be better than Robert A. Taft on the Tidelands question. (Indeed, six months later, with President Eisenhower's help, the Tidelands bill passed after a titanic fight in Congress.)

After Eisenhower was elected, Richardson influenced the president to name the Fort Worth oilman Robert B. Anderson as the new secretary of the navy. This made good business sense, since the navy was the largest purchaser of oil in the world and the navy secretary the man who did the purchasing. Moreover, the Navy Department supervised one of the greatest oil reserves in the world, from Alaska to oil shale in Colorado to Teapot Dome. Richardson was unwittingly establishing a precedent. Eight years later Connally would leave Richardson to assume the navy secretary post, and when he left he was succeeded by yet another Fort Worthian, Fred Korth. It was no coincidence that secretaries of the navy came from a landlocked oil town.

Among the prerequisites of Connally's new job in the Richardson organization was extensive travel with Richardson to his far-flung and always luxurious places of bachelor amusement. One of Richardson's favorite spots was a small roadside hotel in La Jolla, California, called the Hotel Del Charro, that was near a racetrack known as the Del Mar Surf Club. Clint Murchison had built the Hotel Del Charro with capital for construction provided by his own Atlantic Life Insurance Company in Richmond, Virginia. By borrowing close to a million dollars from his own company and paying a standard mortgage, Murchison beat the usury and tax laws. The hotel had only fifty rooms, and it was, from the road, an unimposing sight. Its bungalows, which rented for $100 a day in the early 1950s, were the last word in luxury, however. This was Murchison's store outside of Texas, and he met there with friends and clients and political contacts during the racing season to beat the heat of Dallas and to avoid the notice of places closer to home. It was a "restricted hotel," more of a club than a public accomodation, and its patronage was largely the wheeler-dealers of the oil business, with whom Murchison was most comfortable. Its rules, as laid down by the owner, prohibited pets and Jews. But prominent outsiders occasionally turned up, stars from Hollywood like Liz Taylor and Gregory Peck and titans of science like Edward Teller, but more often, political figures like Richard Nixon, Senator Clinton Anderson, and Senator Joseph McCarthy, of whom Murchison was an ardent supporter. The most prominent guest of all, however, was

FBI director J. Edgar Hoover, and this was noteworthy alone for the fact that, with the proximity of the race track, Mafia figures were also frequently in residence. At the Hotel Del Charro, the FBI and the underworld and the oil business coexisted in a nervous axis of collegiality. When Hoover came, as he did every summer between 1953 and 1959, Murchison picked up his tab. That amounted to about $19,000 of free vacations for the FBI Director over those years.

Hoover might have his hot line to Washington installed in his bungalow, but it was clear who was boss of the Hotel Del Charro. With his curiously small head upon his large, bulking body, it was Sid Richardson. Once when a guest at the Del Charro, an oilman friend of the owners threw a party and had the caviar of chili flown in from Ike's Chili Parlor in Tulsa, Richardson's booming voice blasted an order to Hoover, "God damn it, Hoover, get your ass out of that chair and get me another bowl of chili!" Not every Texan was amused by Richardson's coarse ways. Nearly every day Uncle Sid would put in an early morning call to Mister Sam in Washington, and when Eisenhower's Secretary of Health, Education, and Welfare, Oveta Culp Hobby, was staying in the next room, she found Richardson's language so raw and loud, that she asked to be moved to another room. To those who were transfixed by the sight of the oil magnates around the pool or around the Paddock Bar, the scene brought to mind Edna Ferber's line from *Giant:* "We're rich as son-of-a-stew, but look how homely we are, just plain folks, as Grand-pappy back in 1839. We know about champagne and caviar, but we talk hog and hominy!"

Sid Richardson spent four to six weeks at Hotel Del Charro every summer during the mid-1950s and lived in his customary room by the pool. Uncle Sid was not, however, satisfied with the local cuisine and so he would have fish, steaks, melons, potatoes, and even mesquite charcoal flown in on his DC-3 from Texas. During these extended visits, Connally (billed as a "fine Christian gentleman") would pop in intermittently on the Richardson plane. When he did, the patron in the room next to Richardson's would be abruptly moved out.

Richardson bore a little watching by his staff in these latter years of his life. One morning in August 1955, a busboy at the Del Charro rushed in excitedly to the manager's office with an open envelope which Richardson had forgotten at poolside. Peeking at its contents, the curious manager discovered a letter from Perry Bass, Richardson's nephew, his full partner and heir to the Richardson fortune: "Dear Sid, As you will see, we have a glowing report this month on our sales to the Navy," and the letter proceeded with a month-by-month net breakdown of an ever-rising barrel count of oil sold to the navy in the Eisenhower administration. It was also in this same summer that Richardson, upon his departure from Del Charro, absentmindedly left $5,050 in cash in his room, largely in $50 and $100 bills, which a maid discovered and which the solicitous manager gave to Clint Murchison. Murchison paid the maid a $50 reward.

The proximity of the Del Mar Turf Club was the prime attraction of the Hotel Del Charro for Richardson. In 1954, with Murchison, Richardson purchased the track (with a little judicious muscle from the FBI to move aside the previous ownership), and the magnates announced, with great fanfare, that they were buying the track for charity. The profits of the Turf Club would go to a tax-free charitable foundation called Boys, Inc., whose goals were to "instill virtue in boys and to fight juvenile delinquency."

Connally was made a director of Boys, Inc., a post he held into his governorship of Texas, and he would later testify earnestly to Richardson's deep dedication to helping wayward youth. Among the promises made to Boys, Inc., was the construction of a building for juvenile delinquents in San Diego, but by early 1955, despite dinners and pictures of celebrities in the paper, nothing had been done for the organization, and the local people began to smell a tax dodge. As the grumbles grew louder, Richardson and Murchison hastily ponied up $25,000 to take the heat off, but this did not fool anyone. As the second Eisenhower administration began, a San Diego man wrote to the columnist Drew Pearson, "Isn't it about time the Clint Murchison, Boys, Inc. charity racket was lifted out of the dead end files of the IRS. Everyone in California is sure that the fix is in with the Eisenhower clique. The Murchison-Richardson gimmick is still working for the Del Mar race track, where they have gotten by with a $5 million tax job to date. Perhaps the new administration might want to look at this? Why doesn't the Treasury Department rule on this dodge?"

One reason the Treasury Department wasn't interested could have been that Richardson's own man, Robert B. Anderson, had moved from the Navy Department to the Treasury Department. The sweetheart relationship between the Del Mar track and its charitable operators was to be the subject of lazy investigations by various authorities well into the 1960s. In 1962, three years after Sid Richardson's death, the tax-exempt status of Boys, Inc. was revoked, and it had to pay $720,000 in back taxes.

★

As an embarrassment to John Connally, Boys, Inc., was small potatoes, compared with the full-blown scandal that swept over him in early 1956.

In June of 1954, in the Phillips Petroleum case, the U.S. Supreme Court closed a loophole in the Natural Gas Act of 1938 and imposed federal control over gas prices at the wellhead. Immediately, the oil industry mobilized its considerable forces to lobby for relief. Over $1.5 million was raised in a combined effort by the majors and the most powerful independents to fund a lobbying campaign that was to be unprecedented in its breadth and virulence. The vehicle for this high-pressure campaign was the General Gas Committee, whose steering committee was a fair sample of the oil superpowers. John Connally, representing the Richardson interests, was a charter member, and his Washington savvy, with both Democrats and Republicans, made him the central player in the campaign. (He would later be called its "mastermind.") The other political operative of importance in the group was the brother of the congressional titan from Texarkana, Wright Patman. Elmer Patman, an aggressive and unpleasantly arrogant man, who lived in Austin and knew Connally well, represented Superior Oil of California and its notorious managers, William Keck and his son Howard Keck. The Kecks had the reputation of being among the most ruthless of operators. William Keck was a pioneer in the Texas oil business, who, atop a mule, had made his way to Spindletop, where oil was first discovered in Texas in 1901, and anyone who had been at Spindletop could say that he was present at the creation. Thereafter, in California, Keck had erected a forest of huge, fast oil rigs on a small, 160-acre plot and took oil out of it extravagantly before the authorities moved in on him.

The name Keck Oil Company had to be changed to Superior Oil in the 1920s, after the elder Keck got the nickname of "Kill 'Em Keck" because his tool pushers were notorious slave drivers, and the deaths among his rig crews were so high. "Drag 'im out!" was often heard at Keck wells when a dead man lay on the rig floor. On a Keck rig floor, friendship ceased; the spirit of the company was expressed by a tool pusher to a departing roughneck this way: "Maybe someday you will learn that if you intend to work here, you are either an S.O.B. to the men or you're an S.O.B. to the company."

In January 1956 the campaign of the oil lobby was on the verge of success. Six months earlier, with President Eisenhower's approval, Sam Rayburn had passed a deregulation bill in the House by six votes. But then Lyndon Johnson had had a heart attack, and action in the Senate had to be delayed. With Johnson back on his feet toward the end of 1955, the majority leader declared that the Natural Gas Bill was his top priority when Congress reconvened after the holidays. A classic confrontation shaped up between the oil-producing states and the oil-consuming states—in short, between the North and the South. If deregulation passed and the producers could charge a wellhead price as high as the market would bear, the value of natural gas reserves would multiply exponentially. For the consuming states of the North, however, deregulation would mean an annual hike in their gas bills of an estimated $200 million. Leading the fight for the producers was Lyndon Johnson, and for the consumers the silver-tongued Senator Paul Douglas of Illinois. As the battle drew near, Douglas threatened the unthinkable: if Johnson persisted in this anti-Northern gas legislation, Douglas intended anti-Southern civil rights legislation as an antidote. Indeed, he might just introduce an antilynching amendment to the gas bill itself, in the wake of the lynching in Mississippi of Emmet Till.

Connally took up residence in the Mayflower Hotel, and with Elmer Patman, who also stayed there, commanded the final phase of the campaign. When the bill finally came to the floor late in January, a senator complained, "Never have I seen such intensive, varied, and ingenious types of lobbying—I have been badly overlobbied." An opponent of the bill, Senator Thomas Hennings of Missouri, denounced the oil lobby and warned that it was compromising the American political process. "The concentrated money power of the great oil companies, wielded today to influence the decision of the national government by contributions to both political parties, is a menace to the proper functioning of free government," Hennings exclaimed. One of the crucial undecided votes, Senator Ed Thye of Minnesota, received nine hundred telegrams urging him to support Johnson's bill. Months later the telegrams were proved to be fake, and the tab of $1,500 for their transmission had been paid by the president of Standard Oil, which was represented by Connally's General Gas Committee.

On February 3 the vote was near and passage seemingly assured. Then Senator Francis Case of South Dakota, a supporter of the bill, rose "to make a difficult speech." To a hushed chamber, he announced that a week earlier an envelope containing $2,500 in $100 bills had been left with an associate as a contribution to his forthcoming political campaign. The amount of this thinly veiled bribe was astronomical for the day. The outcry was shrill and instantaneous. Was this a general practice? Were votes in Congress being bought and sold like oil leases? Connally's associate, Elmer Patman, was quickly implicated. The money came from the killer Kecks.

In his hotel room at the Mayflower, Connally blanched and sat paralyzed for a day. Then he quickly left town. The widely held rumor was that Lyndon Johnson had spirited his friend out of Washington for fear that Connally would be questioned and then implicated and indicted in the scandal. The damage was extensive and hard for Johnson to contain.

In the Senate, Johnson made a noisy display of outrage, as he maneuvered to narrow and emasculate the inevitable investigation. What could not be permitted was a broad and tough inquiry into the general practices of campaign contributions by the big interests. He even argued that the flap over the oil lobby was causing his heart to act up again and that his doctor was proposing to put him back on digitalis. Johnson made this plea to Senator Hennings, because Hennings's subcommittee on elections was the appropriate committee to conduct the investigation. "I felt as though I were being cast in the role of his murderer," Hennings would say.

The press understood perfectly what was going on. "The way in which the $2,500 offer to Case was channeled to a perfectly safe 'investigating' committee was a good example of the cooperation between the powers that be on both sides of the aisle," wrote columnist Marquis Childs. Johnson's legislative genius had saved Connally.

In the end, Elmer Patman took the rap. That in itself was a measure of the scandal, for with his connections, Patman too would have been protected, if it had been humanly possible. Patman was fined $2,500 and given a year's suspended jail term. The Keck Superior Oil Company was fined $10,000.

But the scandal did not die. For years to come, it would haunt Connally, and Lyndon Johnson's protection would be needed indefinitely to fend it off.

★

Not many months passed before Connally found himself in a scrape of a different sort. It was more of a war than a scrape, and it would come to be known in future years as the turning point in modern Texas politics. Its roots were in the 1952 Democratic convention, when the tough, effective Governor Allan Shivers broke with the national Democrats over Adlai Stevenson and later endorsed Dwight

Eisenhower. Eisenhower, as we have seen, had come out strongly for the Texas position on the Tidelands, and Governor Shivers, with his "Texas first, last, and always" stance, bolted. But he had headed the Texas delegation at the convention and had promised Sam Rayburn personally that he would support the party's nominee. Therein hung a grudge for Rayburn.

Between the infusion of oil money into the Eisenhower campaign, Shivers's endorsement, and the hard work against Stevenson at the precinct level by men like Connally, Eisenhower carried Texas handily. But even though Connally had worked openly for Eisenhower and Lyndon Johnson had given only weak lip service to the Stevenson campaign, it was Shivers's treason the Speaker would not forgive, for it was treachery to him personally. The drift among conservatives toward being Democrats in the spring and Republicans in the fall had to be stopped, and Shivers had to be crushed for his breach of promise. The stage was set for 1956.

In 1954 there was an intermediate skirmish. Breaking precedent by seeking a third term as governor, Shivers was challenged in the Democratic primaries by Ralph Yarborough, a flowery, old-fashioned former colonel in the U.S. Army, who went by the nickname Raff and who had learned his liberalism in the wheat fields of Oklahoma and in the boom oil fields around Bolger, Texas. For the next twenty years the name Ralph Yarborough was synonymous with Texas liberalism, as he went on to become a United States senator. In 1954, a whiff of scandal hung around the Shivers administration, and Yarborough lost by only 23,000 votes in the first primary. This gave great heart to the liberals in Texas. With labor in the vanguard, they redoubled their organizing efforts. They felt that the moment when they would finally take over the Democratic party of Texas was to come during the precinct meetings across Texas in May of 1956.

As the most powerful man in Texas, Allan Shivers wanted a final *aria di bravura*. As the only Texas governor ever to serve seven years in the job, he was expected to head the Texas delegation to the national Democratic convention in Chicago one last time, despite his defection to Eisenhower in 1952. He wanted to show the party the error of its ways. Sam Rayburn vowed that he was not going to let that happen. His fury against Shivers was unbridled. The moment of confrontation had arrived. In Rayburn's view, if Shivers led the Texas Democrats in 1956, it was the end of party discipline and party loyalty. If a Democratic leader could defect to the Republicans and return unchallenged, the machine would crack up. "I'll have to take that boy's pants before I'm through," Rayburn exclaimed. However, Rayburn himself could not take Shivers on, for he had no statewide organization. He represented only a corner of Texas.

In San Antonio, meanwhile, the liberals cheerfully went forward with their organization. Led by a feisty and quirky political pro named Kathleen Voigt, support among ethnic minorities and urban labor organizations was solid. The statewide organization for Adlai Stevenson was falling into place. Labor stood poised to throw hundreds of its union members into the precinct meetings to challenge the machine and effect the takeover. One day in March, Voigt received a call from Rayburn. "I have wonderful news," he said.

"Good," said Voigt. "I need good news."

"Lyndon is going to run as favorite son!" The favorite son would be, by definition, the head of the Texas delegation.

To Voigt that was no cause for celebration. Lyndon Johnson could not be trusted. If he were a liberal at all, it was in the nineteenth-century agrarian sense, solid on farm subsidies and dams, but weak on modern labor issues and civil rights. To be sure, he had voted against the Southern Manifesto—the prosegregation resolution signed by nineteen senators and eighty-one representatives in 1956—but who could forget or forgive his vote in favor of the hated Taft-Hartley Act? In meetings with labor, Johnson conceded this original sin, but he reminded the unionists that when the bill came onto the Senate floor labor had asked that it be killed: "I took that bill with my own two hands and lifted it right off the floor!" Maybe—but Lyndon Johnson as a favorite son? The liberals were wary. Besides, they thought they could win without him.

In fact, Johnson had not agreed to this campaign at all. Rayburn was playing the sly old fox. He put Johnson forward without his knowing about it, in the expectation that with outside persuasion he could not refuse. But Johnson wanted to avoid a direct confrontation with Shivers. "Allan and I understand each other," Johnson had said once. "We cut each other with the same knife." Johnson vacillated when he learned of Rayburn's ploy. As so many times before in his political career, he wanted to be courted and pressed and flattered and persuaded. Rayburn called a meeting in Washington. Around Rayburn's desk, they gathered: Rayburn, Voigt, and Jake Pickle among them.

"Many think he's a son of a bitch," Voigt said sourly. Her labor constituency would surely balk.

"But he's our son of a bitch," responded a Rooseveltian Pickle. "That makes all the difference in the world."

If Lyndon would agree, who was going to get to run the campaign? Several names came up and were rejected.

"Okay, then I'll get John Connally," Rayburn said finally. They could always count on stalwart John. Rayburn called Sid Richardson to get the oilman's permission.

In 1956 Connally was little known in Texas outside a small circle. He had been a figure of the shadows, one of a number of bright but generally anonymous young men around Johnson. To the liberals and to labor, to the extent he was known at all, Connally was recognized only as an oil and gas lobbyist, one who had been a key player in Lyndon's theft in 1948, who had worked both sides of the street in 1952, who had been in the thick of the recent scandal over the natural gas bill, and one who had never taken a liberal position in his life. He would be a very hard sell indeed to the liberals.

"Lyndon is going ahead with an attempt to either produce some delegates [to the state convention] of his own or to maneuver delegations away from [us]," one labor leader wrote to a friend in mid-April. "For this purpose, he's hired a man named John Connally who is Sid Richardson's right hand man for political affairs and was a 'Democrat for Eisenhower' in '52, a Shivers supporter in '54, and not at all likely to be welcomed by the bulk of the liberal-loyal Democratic leadership over the state. Connally's being in the field for Lyndon has disturbing implications. . . ."

Voigt laid out the deal to her forces: they would get into bed with Johnson for one night. It was like a weekend romance. In return for a seat on the party's executive council and delegates to the national convention, they would have to support Lyndon Johnson on the first ballot as the favorite son of Texas, but on the first ballot only. It was up to labor to decide.

Several weeks later, early one Sunday morning, Connally woke Voigt up. Come to the LBJ Ranch, he said on the telephone. Labor had agreed—"caved in" would have been Voigt's term. It was decision time for Lyndon. Voigt dressed and traveled to the ranch disconsolately. She didn't want to talk to Lyndon Johnson, for it would take time for her to come to terms with this cold political deal. She was as leery as anyone about the probability that Johnson would eventually betray his promise. At the ranch, they piled into a Jeep. Connally sat in back with Voigt and said little. Lady Bird came along. For hours they bounded over the rolling hills of the ranch. Johnson talked endlessly about his steers. Connally offered the occasional rancher's advice. And Voigt was crashingly bored. From time to time Johnson punctuated his tedious cattle talk with a question to Voigt about what organizer she had in such and such a county. This subtext was the play: it was the way Johnson pondered decisions. Finally back at the house, they settled in around the pool, and Johnson began to drink. His talk grew more aggressive and more coarse as he belted down huge blasts of whiskey. The drift of his argument dealt with race. Since he had not signed the Southern Manifesto, Johnson could be sure that Shivers would generate a racist, whispering campaign (which happened). Connally sat on the side, sipping soda pop and remaining noncommittal. Voigt could feel the power play coming. She knew that she and Connally were being used so that Lyndon could come to terms emotionally with what he wanted to do anyway. This time she was going to enjoy it. When the play rolled out before her, it came abruptly. The secretary was summoned. She placed the call to the twelve important newspapers in Texas. Johnson knew all the publishers by their first names. He was going to run. The confrontation with Shivers was on. At stake was the leadership—and the integrity—of the Texas Democratic party. On the following day, April 10, as Johnson made his official statement, Shivers also announced his availability to head the Texas delegation. Johnson won the contest for piety that day. He quoted Psalm 133: "Behold how good and pleasant it is when brothers dwell in unity! It is like the precious oil upon the head."

In the days ahead Voigt and Connally worked closely, if warily, together. At his disposal, Connally had Johnson's 176-member statewide committee, and he worked with local bankers, businessmen, and preachers to pressure local precinct leaders, while Voigt mobilized her numbers, precinct by precinct. The battle against Shivers would be won or lost in the trenches, not on the stump. There would be four rounds: the precinct votes in early May, the state convention in late May, the national convention in August, and a second state convention in September. As the organizing got under way for round one, Connally made promises about turning campaign money over to the liberals, promises which somehow were never realized, but Voigt was not unduly upset. The liberals were doing well, for them, in fund-raising. Once, in an unguarded moment of exuberance, Connally turned to Voigt.

"You operate like I do," he said. "We're termites. If the sun shines on us, we die. We do much better in the shadows."

Johnson, however, was in sunshine as glaring as it had ever

been. Shivers painted himself as the real son of Texas. "Will it be a delegation of Texas free men, unshackled and unpledged, fighting for a Texas viewpoint and for principles of the true Democratic party?" he cried out to a San Antonio audience. "Or will it be a delegation of errand boys, bound body and soul in advance to deliver Texas votes whenever and wherever 'Mr. Sam' decrees?" With nothing to lose, Shivers lashed out viciously. He harped on Johnson's "landslide" of 1948. "George Parr will not be counting the votes at the Texas state convention," Shivers said. Johnson sallied, blaming Shivers for the suicide of the president of a bankrupt insurance company. If suicide was the subject, Shivers replied, what about the suspicious "suicide" of a George Parr associate who had promised to tell the truth about the 1948 election just before he was found swinging by the neck in his jail cell? On the central issue of party loyalty, Johnson had the last word. "I suppose a woman has a right to leave her husband," Johnson said, "but she doesn't have the right to come back four years later and beat him every morning before breakfast."

On May 5 there was, as usual, nothing democratic about the precinct meetings, but it had always been that way in Texas. No one expected fair play. To be elected as a Democratic delegate in the precinct meant nothing if you were "personally offensive" to the delegation leader. This was the unit rule writ large. Democratic gatherings had always been a spectacle of the haves and the have-nots. For now, Johnson and Connally tolerated the liberals. For once, the liberals could stay inside the hall. And Kathleen Voigt was enjoying being where the power rolled. "I've been under the steam-roller and I've been on top of it," she would say. "On top is much more fun." On top she would stay—temporarily. The liberals corralled 1,100 votes; Johnson and Connally had 800, and Shivers had 620. "The voice of the demagogue has been heard throughout the state," Johnson boomed—speaking of Shivers. "The people listened, then voted for the path of moderation. Let demagogues everywhere listen and take notice." It had been, in Johnson's own analysis, a campaign full of hatred and prejudice without equal in modern times.

In their exultation after the bloody battle, the liberals and the Johnson men began to divide up the spoils, or so it seemed. With their plurality at the precinct vote, the liberals, by rights, should have taken over the machinery of the party, but, characteristically, they were split. Since the death of Maury Maverick two years before, they had no unifying figure. Between this vacuum on the left and his natural base in the center, Lyndon Johnson had become the favorite son of Texas. As the liberals cringed, "Love That Lyndon" buttons went into production. "Try this on for size," Connally bubbled to Voigt one day after their precinct victory. "I'll be chairman of the Texas Democratic party. You can be executive secretary." Such a Hatfield-McCoy proposition was absurd, but its mere suggestion hinted at what was coming. Johnson had slain Shivers. Now he was turning on his liberal conspirators in the Shakespearean slaughter. The liberals had made the victory possible, and they expected to share power, but they should have listened more carefully. Johnson and Connally had another notion. In Washington, to a covey of Texans, Johnson aimed at the next target. "Next time we'll knock down the extreme left wing," he said. "We won't allow either the right or the left to carry our buggy off the road."

There was nothing remotely buggylike about the Johnson conveyance now. Connally's preeminent skills as an organizer had won the Shivers battle across the state at the precinct level. Now he winched them into a tighter orbit for the state convention in Dallas two weeks hence. Connally's next assignment was to keep the "red hots" (as he was calling the liberals) divided. The way to conquer the party in this second round was to protect the Shivers crowd in the party ranks, now that Shivers himself was out of the picture.

Several days before the May 22 Dallas convention, Connally called Voigt with a fresh summons to the LBJ Ranch. Come and spend the night, Connally said with menacing urgency. This time Voigt wanted some support. Feisty as she was, and as accustomed to the rough, coarse behavior of primitive politicians, she sensed a bad time ahead. She called Jerry Holleman of the AFL and Fred Schmidt of the CIO and asked them to drive her to the ranch. "I don't know what's wrong," she said, but intuitively she knew something was amiss, something major. "I want you with me." Schmidt also had a certain dread of what lay ahead. Once Johnson had said to him ominously, "One day, you'll be going down the road, happy as a clam, and suddenly you'll find a big tree in front of you, and you'll wonder who put that tree there." At the ranch, with Connally by Johnson's side, they ate great steaks, and the liquor flowed freely. Johnson was excited and overpowering and terrible, as if his favorite son candidacy made his flywheel revolve at a faster, reckless, dangerous rate of speed. His guests watched, awed and frightened, waiting for the mechanism to break loose from its mooring. At one point, later in the evening, when Lady Bird had gone to bed and his secretary, Mary Rather, passed through the room, Johnson grabbed her and threw her roughly onto the couch, and began to smother her with alcoholic kisses.

His demand emerged like a truck from a tunnel. He wanted the liberal forces to vote for him on as many ballots as he desired, till doomsday if need be, until he, their leader, released them. If their commitment to him for only the first ballot were known, his negotiating power at the convention would be compromised. The three leaders listened and declined. They knew they could not sell their constituency on such an open-ended commitment. The demand was repeated, and they again said no—and again—until the rumbles could be heard from deep within Johnson. The silent, scholarly, slender Fred Schmidt seemed to annoy Johnson especially.

"You remind me of the egghead, sitting on the side of the room," he snarled, "making judgments, never saying anything, just making judgments."

At another point he directed a question at Kathleen Voigt and one of the others began to speak up. "Shut up!" Johnson snapped. "You're only her driver."

They protested that their constituencies would never go along with his new demand, and he sneered at their naiveté. "Aw, come off it. Don't give me that crap," he said, and then, reaching for an analogy that came right out of the Hopkins Institute, that Washington whorehouse, favored by politicians, where the booze was expensive and the girls were ripe, "I've been up there where the beer is fifty cents, where you put your hand way up her skirt. . . . Quit kidding me!"

In the midst of this vulgar scene, Connally abruptly got up and left the room. For a time he did not reappear, and Kathleen Voigt decided she also needed some fresh air. On the patio she found him, draped over the wall, vomiting into the bushes. She gave him a glass of water. "When we get into fights like this," Connally sputtered, trying to catch his breath, "it does something to my stomach." Back inside, Johnson was still ranting about those people who eat his steaks and drink his liquor and then insult the Senate majority leader to his face. Lady Bird had been roused from her sleep by the racket and was trying to calm him down with another drink.

The next morning the Brown and Root plane came to the ranch and took the drained party to Dallas. It was the day that the United States detonated its first hydrogen bomb in the atmosphere.

On the eighteenth floor of the Adolphus Hotel, Connally fell into a series of secret meetings with county chairmen, and the fallout was heavy. To the press, he downplayed the significance of the meetings. They were purely organizational. With Shivers defeated and his organizers out of favor, the Johnson forces were merely learning for the first time how to run a state convention. In the lobby and the hallways of the Adolphus, the liberals staged noisy demonstrations, demanding that the disloyal "Shivercrats" be purged, especially in the executive committee of the party. "Throw 'em out! Throw 'em out!" was chanted, as "Love That Lyndon" placards passed through their number. Johnson arrived on the day the convention opened. He wore a white suit and a white bow tie, and he was presented with a white burro with the sign HEADED FOR THE WHITE HOUSE. Meanwhile, at Fair Park Auditorium, the Shivers mascot, a black sheep with the sign STRAY OF 1952, was led across the stage.

Theoretically, there were only two purposes for the convention: to choose the delegation to the national convention and to elect the national committeeman and the national committeewoman. On the man, the liberals and the Johnsonites could agree on Byron Skelton of Temple, for he was a Johnson progressive. But the woman was harder. The liberals were set on having their chief benefactor in Texas, Mrs. Frankie Randolph.

Frankie Randolph was an extraordinary fixture in this burnt-orange landscape. Her father had been a lumber baron in the East Texas town of Camden, and her husband's lineage came from the Randolphs of Virginia. When she was a debutante from one of Houston's first families, her youthful rebellion took the form of dancing in the streets when the Baptists forbade it, and packing a pistol in her purse once when the rules of the cotillion prohibited it. When civil rights demonstrations began, she would have her chauffeur drive her to the poorer neighborhoods of town to join them. A diminutive woman with a husky whiskey voice and deep circles under her eyes, and an inevitable cigarette in her hand, she was a formidable dame. She had never liked Johnson, and he, in turn, knew that he could not buffalo her. He had tried all his weapons on her, and none had worked. (Even later, when he got to the White House, none worked. Once, he called her on a conciliatory note. The White House operator held her on the line until the president came on. "Frankie," he began, and she cut him off. "Nobody calls me that. Certainly not you," she snapped and hung up on him.)

John Connally hated her, and Lyndon Johnson feared her, and together they were determined to deny her the post of committeewoman, even though they had given the liberals to believe that they would acquiesce in her selection. Thus, the liberals cried foul and double cross when Connally maneuvered to have B. A. Bentsen, the wife of the wealthy but bland former congressman from the Valley, Lloyd Bentsen, to be the Johnson candidate. But Lloyd and B. A. Bentsen had been Democrats for Eisenhower. Still worse, a late scandal in the Shivers Administration revealed a land fraud in the Rio Grande Valley where Shivers had made extraordinary profits through tampering with precious water rights in a deal with Lloyd Bentsen's father. The liberal-loyalist faction dug in its heels. Connally thought he had the votes to override them and to install Mrs. Bentsen in any case, but Bentsen herself had no taste for bitter political infighting, especially when it involved Bentsen family business. "We thought [the liberals] just could not be against B. A. Bentsen," Dub Singleton, Connally's man in Houston, was to say. "She was just too pretty, and Lloyd was noncontroversial, so we decided to go with B. A., and we got our fanny beat." B. A. Bentsen withdrew her name when the opposition became mean and vociferous.

Connally and Johnson made one last stab at sidetracking the Randolph nomination. On the morning of the convention's second day, Connally was getting ready for the proceedings, naked and shaving in the bathroom of his hotel room. Dub Singleton was with him, when there was a knock on the door, and, by his vivid recollection, Singleton opened it to find Kathleen Voigt. Singleton shouted to Connally who it was, and Connally shouted back, "Bring her on in." Shocked though he was, Singleton complied, escorting Voigt into the bathroom, where Connally continued to shave, stark naked, while Voigt sat and tried to talk politics. To Singleton, the shock lay in the fact that he had never seen Connally act like Lyndon Johnson. "It would not have shocked me if it had been Johnson," Singleton said later. The irony was that at this moment of degrading Voigt personally, Connally was suggesting that she run for committeewoman against Frankie Randolph, with the support of the Johnson men. If Voigt was too hard to be humiliated by Connally's nakedness—she has consistently denied that this episode ever took place—she was also too cunning to be attracted by his divisive proposal. Hours later, Mrs. Randolph was elected overwhelmingly as the national committeewoman.

On the second day of the state convention, the fruits of Connally's organizational labors soon became apparent. What Johnson had been unable to achieve with his steaks and his booze and his bluster,

Connally achieved with votes at the Fair Park Auditorium. The convention voted to go "all the way with LBJ." The delegation would support Johnson's presidential candidacy as long as he wanted that support. The issue turned to the question of a purge. A liberal put forward a resolution to cleanse the party's executive committee of Shivercrats. His raucous speech resumed the chant of "Throw 'em out." Then Connally stepped forward with a resolution to table. With an earnest tone and a straight face, he pleaded against "political rule by raw, bare power. . . . There are times and places to do things," he said. The time to replace the Shivercrats was in September, when their legal terms expired. Nobly, he embraced a policy of "moderation." The convention passed his tabling resolution three to one.

The achievement was evident. The liberal-labor delegates were bound to the Johnson candidacy and to the delegation leadership under the unit rule. The liberals were blocked from leadership roles through the crucial summer months. When September finally rolled around, they, not the Shivercrats, were the ones to be purged. Lyndon Johnson stood preeminent in Texas. After Connally's organizational victory, Johnson stood before the convention as the grand conciliator.

"I am more interested in converts than I am in culprits," he said with apparent graciousness. "I do not interpret our victory as a mandate to punish and avenge. Let us leave the politics of retribution to small-minded men—to those who are more interested in winning an argument than winning an election."

In Texas political history, the donnybrook of 1956 is regarded as the turning point which established Lyndon Johnson as the unchallenged powerhouse of his state and put him on the road to the presidency. It is also seen as a benchmark in the movement toward a two-party system in Texas. The former, not the latter, is true. For Connally personally, the battle had two consequences. Through his back-room maneuvers and his powerful speechmaking, he became firmly rooted to a wider Texas audience as an implacable foe of the liberals, a fact which was only temporarily blurred by his brief tenure in the Kennedy administration five years later. It also reaffirmed his unique political importance to Johnson, and it deepened further their already extraordinary friendship.

Several days after the bloody state convention in May, both Johnson and Lady Bird wrote letters of thanks to Connally. "Well, we have crossed one more river together," Johnson wrote on May 25, "and I am ready for a long refreshing of the soul at the ranch

[when] I would like to face problems no more serious than whether to plant oats or sudan grass. John, the whole big job of the Convention was right on your shoulders, and I just don't see how you did everything you did. I know that they were pounding at you from all sides—yet you maintained your equilibrium and your patience. I was just as proud of you as I could possibly be. You did your job with astuteness and dignity. Your kind of Democratic Party is the kind I want to will to my children, along with your kind of generalship." To Lady Bird, Connally was positively heroic: "When I saw you stand up against onslaught after onslaught of confused, angry, difficult, and emotional people—my heart went out to you. I think you were enormously strong. I hadn't really figured you would be as reasonable as you were. . . . Do you think you have survived this without any mortal wounds? When I see you, there are a good many things I want to talk over with you. Meanwhile, I think you are handsome on television, convincing and passionate in debate, an able General with your strange assortment of soldiers, and just about my favorite man."

Two months later, in Chicago, Connally gave his first national speech in behalf of Lyndon Johnson, nominating LBJ to be president of the United States. Johnson had "cut through the underbrush of disunity, defeatism, and defection to build the open highway of harmony," Connally told the convention. But then he got caught up in some verbal underbrush himself. Johnson loved the people of the Hill Country of Texas, Connally boomed, and "from that love burns an unquenched flame of trust in their greatness."

★

One final irony remained in the clash of 1956. At the second state convention, in September of that year, a convention which Connally controlled even more tightly than he had the one in May, the purge of the liberal faction was completed. Now that he no longer needed the liberals, Johnson ceased to mask his contempt for them. "I want this convention in the worst way," he snarled to Kathleen Voigt. "Before it's over, your guts are going to be strewn from one end of this hall to the other." To Connally, the purge had an element of personal vendetta. He set out to pay back Mrs. Frankie Randolph, partly because she was a liberal, partly because she was a blue blood, partly because she had beaten him in May. With Connally's iron hand, the Harris County delegation which Randolph headed was disqualified, as were other liberal delegations. The national committeewoman from Texas was locked out of her own party.

Replacing them were handpicked Connally partisans. Afterwards, Johnson felt the heat from Connally's vendetta, and he sent word through an intermediary, the liberal oilman J. R. Parten, that he wanted to bury the hatchet with Mrs. Randolph. Connally talked him out of it. Having asked Parten to set up a conciliatory meal with Randolph, he asked Parten to cancel it after the invitation had been issued.

"You know, John's talked me out of this," Johnson told Parten. "I don't think I want to bury the hatchet with her."

"Well," said the red-faced Parten, "I wish you'd come to that conclusion before you got me into this embarrassing situation."

When, four years later, the Kennedy-Johnson ticket squeaked by in Texas, winning by only 40,000 votes, Major Parten blamed Connally's vendetta against Randolph for the near disaster. Parten thought that the ticket would have carried Texas by a million votes if it had had full liberal support.

"[Connally] was effective in asserting himself as a double for Johnson," Parten told his interviewer. "I thought it was very sad. I thought it was unfair to Lyndon."

"It's almost a variation of that old cliché," suggested the interviewer. "What's good for Connally is bound to be good for Johnson."

Parten, the man who had introduced Lyndon Johnson to John Connally, who knew as well as anyone about the relation between oil, money, and blood, just laughed.

JFK ... from Texas

IN AUGUST 1956, the first contacts between John Connally and John Kennedy took place. Their relationship began on a note of great friendliness, shifted to become bitterly adversarial, then softened into a compromise that served both men, and ended in their appointment in Dallas in November 1963. Connally would come to bask in the reflected glory of John Kennedy and be treated as the true Texas representative to Camelot, a Southern knight more welcome in that stylish assemblage than Lyndon Johnson, who was regarded as an imposter and known, behind his back, as "Colonel Cornpone." Not only did Connally have the wit and the elegance of the Kennedys but it was thought he shared their progressive aspirations for Texas and the nation. That was an illusion, but an illusion preserved outside of Texas. Inside his native state, at least among the politically aware, Connally was well understood.

At the 1956 Democratic convention in Chicago the drama lay in the vice presidential nomination, though Adlai Stevenson's main concern was uniting the party, as the early stirrings of the civil rights revolution were being felt. The old political imperative of "balance" for the national ticket arose as usual, but the balance was like that of a battery, where positive and negative poles somehow come together in a strange electrical field to run a motor. As the vice chairman of the Texas delegation, Connally was the real manager of the delegation, and he had mobilized it behind Senator Albert Gore of Tennessee for the vice presidential nomination. After the first inconclusive ballot, the leader of the Louisiana delegation, Congressman Hale Boggs, came to Connally with the news that a significant shift toward Kennedy was occurring within the Southern bloc. An irony of history was in the making: among the boosters of this Southern shift was Governor Orval Faubus of Arkansas, and Arkansas would be joined by Mississippi, Louisiana, and Alabama, putting a virtually solid South behind Kennedy as well. Connally quickly caucused the Texas delegation and swung it behind Kennedy. At one point in the roll call on the second ballot, Kennedy was within a few votes of the nomination, but then Missouri, Oklahoma, the border states, and a group of Western states shifted to Estes Kefauver, and the Kennedy surge faltered. Kennedy was later to feel that this was a blessing, but he did not forget who had been with him in the struggle.

With Johnson's brief taste of a presidential candidacy and Kennedy's narrow defeat for the vice presidential nomination, both men looked almost immediately to the convention of 1960. They sensed that they were apt to be competitors four years hence, but their relations were civil, if a bit condescending on the part of Johnson. While Johnson returned to his important duties in the Senate, Kennedy campaigned energetically for the Stevenson-Kefauver ticket. In the South, his style fascinated. Hale Boggs was surprised to find that in his own Louisina, Kennedy drew far more enthusiastic crowds than Kefauver.

That year Kennedy also went to San Antonio for a joint campaign appearance with Lyndon Johnson, and both stayed on the outskirts of town. During the visit Kennedy experienced a flareup of his excruciating back pain, that terrible disability which had plagued him ever since the sinking of PT-109 and which had led to his back operation in 1954, the operation that nearly killed him. Kennedy withdrew to his motel bathroom, where he drew a hot bath. Then Johnson arrived, accompanied by an associate from San Antonio, Adrian Spears. After Kennedy let them in he got back into his bath and summoned his visitors into the "inner sanctum," where he often conferred with aides and colleagues. Sensing Kennedy's pain, Lyndon Johnson sat on the edge of the tub and began to ladle hot water onto his back, as they talked politics. This memory would remain vivid for Adrian Spears, when in future years people would gossip about the bitter relations between Kennedy and Johnson. In that moment Kennedy's pain transcended political ambition; it had been only a year since Johnson's heart attack.

In this constellation of pain and tragedy, Connally was to share in his own way during this period. In March of 1958, the family had a shock, when the Connallys' eldest daughter, Kathleen, eloped to Ardmore, Oklahoma, with her high school sweatheart. "K. K.," as she was known, was just sixteen years old, and her boyfriend, Bobby Hale, was eighteen and had yet to finish high school. To John Connally, it was a particular blow, for he had taken great pride in K. K.'s popularity and her good looks; it was often remarked that of his children, K. K. looked most like him. To their friends, the Connallys tried to put the best face on the situation. Bobby Hale was, after all, the son of I. B. Hale, who had been a great football player at T.C.U. in the 1930s and was now prominent in Fort Worth as the chief of security at the Convair plant.

Partly because of the disapproval of both sets of parents, there was trouble in the marriage from the beginning. After a stormy honeymoon, filled with children's lovers' quarrels, they ended up in Tallahassee, Florida, where they took a tiny apartment across the street from the Florida Supreme Court Building and decorated its spare wall with a shotgun and a rifle Bobby had brought from Texas. Bobby took a seventy-dollars-a-week job as a laborer for a boat company. In mid-April, their quarreling reached the point where K. K. left Bobby for several days and holed up in a motel in nearby Thomasville, Georgia. She had found out that she was pregnant. The separation brought both sets of parents to Florida, but by the time they arrived, Bobby and K. K. were back together, and it seemed that nothing could be done.

On the evening of April 27, Bobby and K. K. had a "discussion" about their respective weights, and Bobby was confused when suddenly Kathleen became upset and again walked out. When she did not return during the night, Bobby became frantic and went out to search for her in their various haunts. When he returned to their apartment, Kathleen was sitting on the couch . . . with his loaded shotgun pointed at her head, her finger on the trigger. Bobby fell to his knees in front of her and pleaded with her to put the gun away.

"Bobby, I'm sick in my mind, and I need help. I know *now* that no one can help me."

After a few minutes of pleading, Bobby lunged desperately at the weapon to bat it away, and it went off.

When the police arrived, Bobby Hale was berserk and had to be restrained by three officers from throwing himself off the second-story porch. K. K. died in the ambulance on the way to the hospital.

At the coroner's inquiry the next evening, Nellie Connally wept openly as Bobby Hale told as much of this tragic story as he was able before he became incoherent. John Connally was among the witnesses. Exercising great control, he asserted that K. K. had no history of emotional or psychological distress, and he spoke of their trip to Florida several weeks before. "Obviously, in the light of what happened, we probably were stupid, but as far as we could determine, there were no problems, so we left and went back to Fort Worth," he said. The inquiry concluded that the death was accidental. The Connallys were spirited out a back door of the court house, screened from the hectoring photographers, and they flew back to Texas with the body of their daughter. There, friends, including Lyndon Johnson (who had cancelled an appointment with President Eisenhower), gathered and it was, as Lady Bird Johnson would later describe it, "as painful a time as I can ever remember. John was just like a granite cliff, and Nellie was her sweet, warm loving self. There was a whole lot of us out at their house. Love brought us all. We yearned to make it less painful, and there was no way to do it." To the Connally friends, like Lady Bird, what happened in Tallahassee and how it happened, and indeed, whether the death was suicide or an accident, remained a total mystery. "It's one thing that's always made me be against having guns around the house," Lady Bird would say.

For John Connally, the episode was almost never again mentioned, except late in his life, to describe it as the greatest tragedy of his life, greater than the assassination in Dallas, far greater than his bankruptcy at the end of his career. The haunting quality of the tragedy was Kathleen's last statement: "I know *now* that no one can help me." Inevitably, both John and Nellie Connally must have wondered if there was anything they could or should have done to help.

★

As the election year of 1960 approached, Kennedy and Johnson saw two distinctly different paths to the White House. As a junior senator from Massachusetts with no appreciable record of legislative accomplishment, Kennedy's chance lay at the grass roots. He had to spend several years out in the country, cultivating support among working politicians of the second rank, for Johnson had all the titans behind him. Kennedy had to win enough primaries and then convince the party chieftains that the primaries mattered. And he had to have enough delegates to capture the nomination on the first ballot. Johnson did not think Kennedy could do that. Since he approached the nominating process as if it were akin to passing a bill in the Senate, he felt that the nomination would be bartered and the man with the most powerful supporters would win the prize. In late 1959, with Eisenhower spending more time on the golf course, Johnson had become, arguably, the most powerful man in America. Through nearly a decade of senatorial wars, he had dispensed and was owed more favors than he could ever collect. In Washington, Kennedy was regarded as an upstart, a lightweight, and an absentee by powerbrokers; the senators from the major electoral states all supported Johnson. To his congressional friends, Johnson could validly say, "While Jack Kennedy has been out kissing babies, I've been in the Senate passing bills." He expected they would appreciate that and pull their delegations behind him when the convention rolled around.

But as Kennedy spent enormous amounts of money during the spring primaries and corralled five states uncontested, Johnson became anxious. He wanted to avoid a bloody challenge to Kennedy in the primaries and relied on Hubert Humphrey to cripple the Kennedy candidacy sufficiently for him to move in at a late stage as the unifier. As Kennedy and Humphrey battled on the hustings, Johnson authorized Connally to set up an unofficial campaign headquarters in the Ambassador Hotel in Washington. But Johnson was gripped by ambivalence. He wanted to sew up the nomination, but he did not want to be pricked in the primaries. He wanted a campaign headquarters, but he wanted it to go unnoticed. When a huge sign reading JOHNSON FOR PRESIDENT was hung on the outside of the Ambassador without his permission, Johnson flew into a rage and had it taken down within hours. Thus, Connally's work during the spring consisted largely of heating up the telephone, contacting Johnson's political friends in each state and having them talk to the convention delegates. Johnson himself fretted about this strategy. At times he would talk as if he had the convention locked up, but other times melancholy set in. "If Jack wins West Virginia, the show's over," he told his campaign managers. "If he wins there, he'll take the convention and the nomination."

Connally's resentment grew over the manner in which the Kennedys were throwing money around. In West Virginia he was convinced they had bought the primary vote and that it could be proved. Stories of bagmen skulking about in the night had reached him, but he could not interest anyone in an investigation. When Kennedy trounced Humphrey in West Virginia, it put him comfortably in the lead for the nomination, increasing their worries that Johnson had waited too long to announce. By May the only accomplishment Johnson could boast of was that in the state convention his forces had replaced their old nemesis, Frankie Randolph, with their own national committeewoman from Texas.

As his desperation grew, Johnson and his inner circle became increasingly vicious in their private comments about Kennedy. Adlai Stevenson came to see Johnson on a mission to have the law changed to allow face-to-face debates between presidential candidates, and a stream of anti-Kennedy invective poured out of the majority leader: the polls showed that a Catholic could not be elected; Kennedy's brother Bobby was a snake; his father was a Nazi sympathizer. "I've heard a lot of anti-Kennedy talk from various people," Stevenson would remark later, "but never anything quite as vitriolic as that." But Stevenson told Johnson what he wanted to hear: Stevenson would remain neutral in the nomination fight. To that Johnson replied that he already could count on 500 votes at the convention, and if he couldn't get over the top, he intended to throw his support to Stevenson, for Stevenson was the "only man really qualified in the international arena to lead the country." Stevenson thanked Johnson, but demurred: he was not a candidate in 1960 and he would not be a candidate, no matter how emotional his supporters became in Chicago.

To the very end, Texas pride formed the hot core of Lyndon Johnson's presidential candidacy. Here was the chance for the first Texan president and the first Southern president since Reconstruction. It fired enormous enthusiasm at home. The symbols of the campaign were two-dollar lapel pins and earrings fashioned in the shape of Texas boots and a Stetson hat.

The campaign received generous support from oil interests. Connally went to Houston, where the fat cats had gathered at the old Ramada Inn, and he gave a stemwinder about how much the oil industry had to fear from the nomination, much less the election, of John Kennedy. The twenty-seven-and-a-half-percent oil depletion allowance was a sacred cow, and Connally assured the oilmen that this young, Catholic patrician from Massachusetts had no reverence for it. The oilmen contributed generously. Even H. L. Hunt, with his bizarre trail mix of McCarthyite mossback conservatism and food faddism, threw money into the Johnson campaign. He even assigned a political operative, Robert Notti, to Connally's staff. Notti, however, was not impressed. For once, Connally got poor marks for organization. "The Johnson organization was very, very bad," Notti was to say later. "No one seemed to know what they were supposed to do. They didn't know who had the authority to do what. It was probably the worst-organized campaign group I have ever seen."

But Connally's main problem was his reluctant candidate, and he had to shift tactics. He now had to concentrate on stopping Kennedy. The attacks had to get pointed, personal, and negative. The legitimate themes—that Kennedy was the absentee senator, that he was too young and too inexperienced, too innocent to deal with a Khrushchev—were not enough now. The Johnson campaign was *in extremis;* they had to find something dramatic enough to disqualify Kennedy from the presidency. It could not be women, for Johnson was at least as vulnerable to that charge as Kennedy, and besides, in 1960, philandering disqualified no one. The answer, Connally and Johnson thought, was Kennedy's health. Dwight Eisenhower had had a massive heart attack in office, a crisis that debilitated and nearly killed him, and the question of a candidate's health was of legitimate concern. For years rumors had been floating around about a secret Kennedy illness, and if there were something to these rumors, it could, at the very least, neutralize the issue of Johnson's 1955 heart attack.

In private, Johnson began to salt his talk with innuendo. Kennedy was "a little scrawny guy with rickets," he told Peter Lisagor of the *Chicago Daily News.* "Have you ever seen his ankles?" Lisagor had not. "Well, they're about so round," Johnson said, making a tiny circle with his finger. Meanwhile Connally had with him in the Citizens for Johnson office Mrs. India Edwards, who had formerly headed the Women's Division of the Democratic National Committee and who had a story she thought was relevant. She had heard of a time when Kennedy had been campaigning in the provinces and had stopped for the night at a governor's mansion. Suddenly, in the middle of the night, Kennedy had experienced a desperate medical crisis because he had forgotten pills of some sort, and a state trooper had to rush out to find a doctor and a pharmacist.

At Edwards's prodding, Connally gathered his resources to find out the facts. A partial answer emerged quickly. For many years, indeed going back to the late 1940s, Kennedy had suffered from an adrenal deficiency which had the dread nineteenth-century title Addison's disease. According to the medical encyclopedias, the disease had plaguelike symptoms of milk-white patches on the skin, black freckles over the head and the neck, sharp weight loss, vomiting, and nausea. By its nature, if left untreated, it was fatal, and its manifestation could be adrenal crisis, resulting in a coma of the sort India Edwards heard Kennedy had experienced. An old congressional investigator of Lyndon Johnson's, Don Cook, was put on the case. He reported to Connally through Walter Jenkins that Kennedy had been treated at the Lahey Clinic in Boston during 1948 or 1949 for the condition. Dr. Lewis Hurxthal of the clinic had made repeated trips from Boston to Hyannis Port to administer intravenous saline and other invasive emergency medication. This indicated that the disease had progressed to a point where the patient was in constant danger. On the telephone, Jenkins asked Cook whether Kennedy's medication could lead to complete recovery.

"If a patient stays under medication, he is put in a position of an automobile [driver] who is able to drive only at one speed," Cook replied. "If a patient comes under stress, physical or emotional, it can produce a complete state of exhaustion. I am told that [Kennedy] not only had it, but has it now and is receiving treatment for it."

But what should they do with the information? Cook had a suggestion.

"The public doesn't know anything about this disease," he said. "Someone who is knowledgeable in the field, not connected with Senator Johnson, could make a statement about the disease and its effects and then keep needling the candidates to submit themselves to medical examination."

Cook promised to do further digging. The following day he was back in touch with Johnson headquarters with more details. In the 1940s the treatment for Addison's disease was the implantation of solid pellets of a synthetic hormone-stimulating drug in the thigh and the back. Taken together with saline solutions, the pellets had reduced the mortality rate. But in 1949 cortisone had been discovered; it was the current drug of choice. Cook had been talking to a leading endocrinologist, who had observed Kennedy's campaign appearances at close range. This specialist concluded that Kennedy was taking enormous doses of cortisone. "One of the things that result is what doctors call a psychic problem," Cook reported. "Two of the manifestations are that the patient develops a split personality, and second, very neurotic behavior patterns which include paranoid persecution complexes. It comes about through the retention in the glandular system and in the brain of excessive quantities of water."

Kennedy was beginning to take on such hugely freaklike qualities among the Johnson crowd that it could scarcely be imagined how the poor fellow put one foot in front of another without either drowning in his own drug-induced, self-retained water or being seized with a Goyaesque fit of paranoid schizophrenia. The private eye, Mr. Cook, thought that some "real bird dog" in the press like Drew Pearson ought to be tipped off. This "newshound" needed to be well enough informed so that if Kennedy waffled about his disease the reporter would be ready to follow up.

Connally and Edwards had settled into their Los Angeles convention headquarters when this information came to them. Already they had a press conference scheduled for July 4. It was a political question now. Connally took the initiative.

"Don't you think that it's time we said something about Kennedy's health?" Connally said to Edwards.

"Yes, I do," she replied. "But, John, let me do it because I have no career ahead of me, and you have. You're a young man. It will make a terrible stink. It won't matter to me."

Before the press, as planned, India Edwards did most of the talking. John Kennedy was, she said, the only man "offering himself for president who had been absent eight months in one year because of illness." This referred to the spinal operation Kennedy had undergone in 1954 which resulted in a four-month hospitalization in New York. What Edwards did not know was that the surgery itself rather than Kennedy's spinal condition had been the real threat to his life, for Addison's disease destroys resistance to infection, and, at the time of the operation, it was believed that an Addison's disease sufferer would not withstand such radical surgery. That Kennedy did survive the operation became a small sensation in the field of endocrinology, and his case was written up in an AMA journal. In the article it was stated that the anonymous patient had received the last rites of the Church. For years the Kennedy clan worried that the AMA case history would be connected with JFK and would destroy his political career.

"Doctors have told me that he would not be alive today were it not for cortisone," Edwards told the press in Los Angeles. "It is no disgrace to have Addison's disease. He has it now." She was revealing this fact, she said, because she objected to Kennedy's "verbal muscle-flexing with regard to his youth, as if he has better health than anyone else."

Connally stood on the side, but he did add one note to Edwards's presentation. He would be "delighted" to release Johnson's medical records if all the candidates would do likewise. That Edwards had done most of the talking in the press conference fooled no one. It would always be remembered as Connally's extravaganza. It was the very kind of political hardball with which he had been associated in the past and would often be associated in the future.

The event instantly generated the stink that India Edwards predicted. Kennedy's press secretary, Pierre Salinger, called it "despicable tactics . . . a sure sign of the desperation of the opposition." Ted Sorenson flatly denied that Kennedy was on cortisone. As to whether he might be on something else, Sorenson said, "I don't know that he is on anything—any more than you and I are on." The Kennedy crowd resented the Connally charge, largely because it was so dangerous. It had blown the lid off a cover-up that the Kennedys had tightly guarded for thirteen years. The general impression was that with so medieval a disease as this, the patient would surely die. If that impression took hold, the Kennedy campaign was also going to die.

The response came swiftly. Kennedy's endocrinologist, Dr. Janet Travell, issued a statement asserting blandly that Kennedy's adrenal glands did function and that his resistance to infection was "above average." That scarcely met the thrust of the Connally-Edwards charge. The following day, July 5, Robert Kennedy called a press conference to deny that his brother had Addison's disease *in the classic sense,* and referred the reporters to the book by James McGregor Burns called *John F. Kennedy—A Political Profile,* in which Kennedy's condition was described as a mild form of Addison's. His brother merely had a mild adrenal insufficiency, Bobby Kennedy asserted; it was not dangerous, and it was fully controlled by the wonder drugs of the past decade. Between the doctor's statement and Robert Kennedy's explanation, the press accepted the Kennedy version: an annoying little condition that required a bit of maintenance. No "newshound" or "real bird dog" stepped forward to dig deeper.

Lyndon Johnson scheduled a press conference for later in the day. He could see the ploy had fallen flat. Everywhere the Connally press conference was being criticized as sleazy politics. Senator Mike Mansfield, Johnson's Democratic whip in the Senate, called for an end to this "nefarious technique of questioning a nominee on the basis of sectionalism, religion, maturity, or health. The times call for grown-up thinking on the part of us all." As the smear boomeranged, Johnson had to step forward and disavow the zealotry of his associate and portray himself as statesman and conciliator.

"So far as I am aware, all the candidates are in good health," Johnson told the press. "Senator Kennedy had some difficulty in 1954 that kept him out of the Senate for months. I had some difficulty in 1955 which kept me out for weeks—and I am very glad that both of us were tough enough not to let it get us down." Connally was left holding the bag.

The numbers looked bleak for Johnson, but his campaign managers convinced themselves they still had a chance. Johnson held his IOUs. He could call them in. Operatives like Jake Jacobsen could keep the spirit of Texas patriotism pumped up by bravely distributing the earrings and lapel pins. But as the delegates gathered in Los Angeles, even the most devoted Johnson supporters began to realize they were outmaneuvered. One by one, states from whose leaders Johnson had received promises of support in Washington dropped away to Kennedy. Word of how Johnson and Connally had treated labor in Texas had reached big labor in the industrial North. Johnson was portrayed as a tool of oil and gas interests, and with an oil and gas man as his political manager, it was hard to deny. Meanwhile, Kennedy played the vice presidential possibilities artfully. In the far West, Washington fell to Kennedy. There, Senator Warren Magnuson, who was among Johnson's closest friends in the Senate, was supposed to be in control, but Kennedy had undercut him by dangling the vice presidential nomination in front of the other Washington senator, Henry Jackson. Arizona was counted in the Johnson column initially, but then Connally heard a rumor that a bank loan of $10,000 owed by a leader of the Arizona delegation had been mysteriously and anonymously paid off. This rumor made Connally all the more furious at the way in which he supposed the Kennedy people were spreading their patriarch's money around. Arizona switched to Kennedy at the last minute. Perhaps most bitter of all to the Johnson managers was the spectacle of power failing. Johnson had all the bosses, yet Kennedy had turned that into a liability. The contest had become generational. "We're a young group, and we're going to take over America," said Robert Kennedy, and the younger politicians cheered, while in the wings the Catholic party bosses of the industrial North—Richard Daley of Chicago, Pat Brown of California, Carmine DeSapio of New York, and John Bailey of Connecticut—began to nod approval.

Johnson made one last stab at the nomination. In a series of appearances on the day of the nominating vote, Johnson savaged Kennedy on all fronts. On family wealth: "I haven't had anything given to me. Whatever I have and whatever I hope to get will be because of whatever energy and talents I have." On Joseph Kennedy's supposed appeasement of Hitler: "I never thought Hitler was right. I was never any Chamberlain-umbrella man." On Kennedy's absence during the McCarthy censure debate in 1954 (as Kennedy was near death from his back operation): "When Joe McCarthy was on the march and someone had to stand up and be counted, I was voting liberal. Every Democratic Senator stood up and voted with the leader, that is, all those who were present."

The climax came before the Texas delegation, where Connally sought to orchestrate a face-to-face Johnson-Kennedy debate. Kennedy saw the trap, but the invitation to appear was so public, the interest so intense, that he rose to the challenge cheerfully. When he appeared, he gave a set speech and then sat down to receive his "pistol-whipping," as it was later called. Johnson hurled all the old charges at Kennedy, added a new one, that Kennedy was now the tool of the big-city bosses, and even tried out the religious issue. "I think, Jack, we Protestants proved in West Virginia that we'll vote for a Catholic. What we want is some of the Catholic states to prove they'll vote for a Protestant." With each swipe of the pistol, Connally and his troops roared their approval, but it was the national television audience that mattered, and to television viewers Johnson's attack seemed bad manners toward the party's certain nominee. Kennedy took the beating with a smile and a quip. "I come here today full of admiration for Senator Johnson, full of affection for him, strongly in support of him—for majority leader of the United States Senate." Even Connally had to admire his grace. "We figured if it went well, enough delegates who would be watching would be persuaded," Connally's aide, Jake Jacobsen, was to say. "But it didn't go as well as I had anticipated, although Johnson did a good job. Kennedy also did a good job. It went very friendly and nice. That was our last gasp. It was the end of the road." Kennedy even ended up with a few scattered cheers from the Texas delegation.

★

On the day before their confrontation, Kennedy still had Johnson high on his list of possible running mates. This idea had been promoted by Philip Graham, the publisher of the *Washington Post*, who bridged gracefully the gap between the stylish salons of Georgetown and the corridors of power on Capitol Hill. During the hour before the "debate," Graham had been with Johnson and had been surprised at the deep-seated, personal resentment Johnson exhibited toward Kennedy. With the vice presidential nomination in his mind, Graham had unsuccessfully urged upon Johnson the road of high statesmanship. Now his mission had become more difficult.

Furthermore, the resentment in the Kennedy camp over Connally's medical smear remained intense. As Pierre Salinger would write later, Connally's attack was "beyond the latitude of fair play." Robert Kennedy was determined that Johnson not be considered. That was fine with the Texas crowd: they had their own resentments, particularly the arrogance of the Kennedys and their loose ways with old money. As the majority leader of the Senate, Lyndon Johnson reigned in a major power center. Why would he want to be vice president? Why would he be interested in a secondary role that could only frustrate him? When Johnson came before the Texas delegation the morning after the debate to thank his supporters, the Texans began to pack their bags.

The story of how Lyndon Johnson was persuaded to change his mind has been well told elsewhere: how Sam Rayburn first opposed the idea vehemently and then reversed himself, how Johnson insisted on a personal draft by Kennedy, how Southern governors opposed Johnson's taking the vice presidency (fearing a loss of power in the Senate), how Bobby Kennedy tried to use this Southern opposition to get Johnson to withdraw his name, and how, at last, the far-fetched alliance of Boston and Austin was forged. The critical player in that drama was Sam Rayburn, and the critical moment came in a conversation between Rayburn and Congressman Hale Boggs of Louisiana.

"What do you think about this?" Rayburn grumbled to Boggs.

"Well, do you want Richard Nixon to be president of the United States?" Boggs asked.

"You know I don't want that to happen."

"Well, unless you approve of Lyndon taking the nomination, that's exactly what's going to happen. How can any man turn down being vice president? You wouldn't turn it down."

"Well, that's right," Rayburn conceded. "He's got to do it."

During the critical four hours of July 14, when the nomination of Johnson was sealed, Connally was at Johnson's side most of the time, telephoning and consulting, as he seethed inside. He was passionately opposed to this whole ill-conceived notion. It was bad for Johnson, bad for Texas, bad for the South, bad for the oil industry, and embarrassing to John Connally. For weeks Connally had been spitting out venom about the Kennedys. Now it would be seen as venom from the forked tongue of a chameleon. How could he face the oilmen who had opened their coffers to him after he had terrified them about the Kennedys? What revenge would the Kennedys visit upon him for his charge that Kennedy was diseased?

It was said later that Connally was so furious at Johnson's acquiescence that he hurled his bags out into the hallway of the Biltmore
Hotel, and left the convention early. But that was not like John
Connally. He might smolder inside, but he was not given to public
displays of rage.

A day later, by a pool in Las Vegas, he was still stewing as he
talked with Walter Jenkins and Robert Strauss, but he had attained
a degree of resignation, if not acceptance. That was in contrast to
Strauss, who was still down in the mouth. "Don't be so glum,"
Connally consoled Strauss. "We just got the hell kicked out of us—
and deserved it maybe. We all learned a great deal, and I have a
feeling that we learned some lessons that are going to come in handy
over the years." At that point, the senator from Florida, George
Smathers, wandered by. "You fellows ought to have more sense
than being unhappy about Johnson going on the ticket," Smathers
told them. "Things have a way of working out for Johnson."

★

John Connally suffered through the presidential campaign in the
fall. The negatives in Texas seemed almost insurmountable. The
antagonism toward the Kennedy philosophy was deep and abiding.
The antagonism toward Johnson and Connally personally was nearly
as deep among the Texas liberals, and this undermined what natural
strength they might have imparted to the ticket. Kennedy's Catholicism was as much or more of a handicap in Texas as anywhere in
the nation, given the powerful Baptist ministries of Dallas and Fort
Worth. Due largely to Connally's efforts before the convention, a
deep anxiety in the oil industry over what Kennedy might do to the
oil depletion allowance had taken hold. And many of Johnson's
closest friends and political associates were unforgiving over his
decision to give up a real power base in favor of an empty sinecure.
Herman Brown of the Brown and Root firm never spoke to Johnson
again, so deep was his anger.

As Connally worked for the Democratic ticket, he had to keep
an eye on his own derrick-filled backyard. He was still an oil and
gas man, and in the election of 1960 he may have been that before
he was a Democrat. A pivotal visit for Kennedy to Texas was planned
for the second week of September, early in the national campaign.
What he said about the oil depletion allowance would have a crucial
effect on his chances in Texas. The Texans knew they were not going
to get an endorsement. They only hoped they would not get a rebuke.
After consulting with Connally, the campaign's Houston man, Dub

Singleton, drafted a tepid statement on the oil loophole which he hoped John Kennedy would espouse when he came to Texas. In advance of Kennedy's visit to Houston, Robert Kennedy came to check out the arrangements. When he greeted Bobby at the airport Singleton gave him the statement.

"Now, Bobby, you know this oil and gas issue is very hot in this area," Singleton said. "Here's what we'd like for your brother to say when he comes here."

Robert Kennedy took the piece of paper and read the draft paragraph: "On the matter of the oil and gas industry, I luckily have the advice and counsel of two men who know more about that than any two men in the world, and that's the Speaker of the House, Mr. Rayburn, and my own running mate for vice president, Lyndon Johnson. On any issue involving the oil and gas industry, of course, I'll counsel with them."

Slowly, Kennedy turned his aquatic eyes on Singleton and tore the paper to bits. "We're not going to say anything like that," he said coldly. "We put that son of a bitch on the ticket to carry Texas. If you can't carry Texas, it [the depletion allowance] is your problem." Connally heard about this immediately, and quickly contacted Walter Jenkins at Johnson's office in Washington. Someone had to get to John Kennedy directly, he argued, someone who understood the oil industry and its problems and its political power. He offered himself for the job. "If they [the oil men] think he [Kennedy] is advocating a reduction in the depletion allowance, I'm not kidding when I say we are lost. This oil industry is a really sick industry, and we're not getting enough oil. If they [the Kennedys] make any change, it's going to result in chaos." One misstatement or even a misinterpretation of a vague statement could not only lose Texas for the national ticket, but could even prevent Lyndon Johnson's reelection to the Senate (since Johnson was running, as later Lloyd Bentsen did, for both the Senate and the vice presidency). If Kennedy called for a cut in the allowance, it would create a "tong war" in Texas, more virulent even than the wars over the Tidelands or natural gas deregulation. "As of right now, we have these oil people neutralized," said Connally, the consummate oilman himself. "None of them publicly is against us, and that has certainly taken some doing. If Kennedy comes out for repeal—or anything that can be interpreted that way—there is no power on earth that can save us."

By October, Lyndon Johnson himself was deeply worried about the state of things in Texas. As Bobby Kennedy had underscored it, his first duty to the ticket was to win Texas, but the polls did not look good. On October 18, he sent a "personal and confidential" message to Connally. "I am deeply disturbed about Texas. The Belden poll concerns me a great deal. Won't you give your best thoughts to what should be done—when, where, and how. We just must not win the nation and lose Texas. Imagine how the next administration will look upon us." Walter Jenkins had already emphasized the urgent need for Connally to take things over completely in this close game. "If you could take charge the last month of the campaign, it might well make the difference," he wrote to Connally on October 6. "We have good people, but we haven't got anybody qualified to mastermind it as you can. The Senator is probably not going to run for Vice President but once."

Distinctly secular powers were to save the Kennedy-Johnson ticket in Texas. Kennedy's visit to Houston in mid-September would be remembered more for his appearance before the Baptist ministries than anything he had to say about oil. That appearance was a triumph, defining the role of a modern Catholic leader in a democracy, separating the candidate's beliefs from certain edicts of the Catholic Church on secular matters, reaffirming the absolute separation of church and state in America, doing much to expunge religious bigotry generally, and even applying the lesson of the moment to the sacredness of the Alamo. "Side by side with Bowie and Crockett died Fuentes and McCafferty and Bailey and Badillo and Carey. No one knows whether they were Catholics or not," Kennedy said. "For there was no religious test there."

The second factor that turned the election in Texas was the Kennedy-Nixon debates. Even those had their special moments for Texas. Harry Truman had come to San Antonio on October 11, for example, and had caused a ruckus by saying, characteristically, that any conservative Democrats who planned to vote for Richard Nixon could go to hell. Later in the week, in the presidential debate, Kennedy was asked what he thought of Truman's remark. "Maybe Bess can control him," he replied. "But I can't."

The third factor was Lyndon Johnson's own backhanded contribution. In it he became a harbinger of history, for it concerned an episode of violence in Dallas. In the last days before the election, the presidential race in Texas was a tossup, until Lyndon and Lady Bird decided to have lunch at the Adolphus Hotel on the day that the supporters of Richard Nixon were having a huge rally in the Baker Hotel across the street. As the Johnsons arrived, they were greeted outside the hotel by a mob, consisting largely of snarling

Junior League ladies and other assorted silk-stocking supporters of the ultraconservative congressman from Dallas, Bruce Alger. Alger himself led the mob, carrying a sign reading LBJ SOLD OUT TO YANKEE SOCIALISTS. Elsewhere in the collective nastiness was a sign with the exhortation BEAT JUDAS! As things turned ugly and a bit dangerous, Johnson's political instincts took over. Before the television cameras, the couple waded into the throng, heroically pushing aides and police officers aside. "If the time has come when I can't walk through the lobby of a hotel in Dallas with my lady without a police escort, I want to know about it," Johnson proclaimed nobly. They pawed him. They spat at him. They slammed a placard onto Lady Bird's head. And they elected Kennedy and Johnson in Texas, and, therefore, in the nation.

In the glow of victory, it was, for Johnson, as it had been in the election of 1948 and in the titanic battle with Allan Shivers in 1956: he credited Connally with securing the razor-close victory. Yet again, Connally had added to his reputation as a political mastermind. "For the past twenty years I have counted on you and relied on you more than anyone else," Johnson wrote to Connally on November 14. "It was a deep feeling of comfort to be able to count on you again in these past months of campaigning. Except for you, I know the outcome would have been different, and I wanted to say I am grateful. Give that sweet Nellie my love. Devotedly, Lyndon."

His devotion and gratitude, however, might not have satisfied Connally at this juncture. Connally's great benefactor, Sid Richardson, had died the year before. In the settlement of the estate, Connally had received a handsome sum of money as the coexecutor of the Richardson estate, a sum so large that Connally wanted its generous installments spread over ten years for tax reasons. It was simply time to move on, time to advance his own political fortunes, time to show that he could be a political mastermind in his own behalf. The immediate possibility was Lyndon Johnson's Senate seat. There would have to be a special election in 1961, but before that Governor Price Daniel had to appoint someone until the election could be held a year hence. Connally considered the matter. He was forty-three years old. If he ran and won the following year—a decidedly long shot for so little-known a figure who had never held elective office—the Senate would become his life. He would have to stay at least two terms, or twelve years, before he could expect to command any significant influence in that slow-moving, seniority-honoring deliberative body. All of these considerations were wrong for him: the length of the commitment, the legislative rather than the executive function, the emphasis on age rather than talent. If he decided to quit after two terms, he would be nearly sixty. That would be too late to make a bold turn in a new direction. The Senate had no allure. He took himself out of contention.

Lyndon Johnson had extracted one clear commitment from Kennedy as a condition of accepting the vice presidential nomination: control of all appointments to the administration out of Texas. No doubt the name of John Connally was at the top of his list, for he had said a hundred times that he wanted no man "on his warm side" more than Connally. But a major appointment for Connally was no simple matter. There was no shortage of good people who wanted top jobs in the New Frontier. Indeed, the hallmark of the Kennedy administration was to become its achievement of attracting the best and the brightest in America into public service. Moreover, the men around the president-elect, particularly Bobby Kennedy, were famous for holding grudges, and Connally's supreme labors in the closing days of the campaign in Texas could only partially dilute Kennedy resentment over the Addison's disease episode. Moreover, it was unclear how much or how little influence Lyndon Johnson would be given over major appointments. During the formative days of the New Frontier, he was expressly excluded from the important staffing meetings at Palm Beach, in New York, and in Georgetown. If he did have influence, what job would be right for Connally? What job might he accept? What problems might he encounter in being confirmed? A subcabinet post was the most Connally might reasonably hope for, and for so proud a man not just any subcabinet post would do. At the Defense Department, the secretary-designate, Robert McNamara, had been chosen for his managerial skills, forged at Ford Motor Company, and Kennedy had promised his secretary that he would control the presidential appointments to his department totally. That total control had one exception. The Kennedys insisted that a top job in the Pentagon be given to Paul "Red" Fay, whom President Kennedy knew from PT-boat training in the war, who had worked in Kennedy's 1946 congressional campaign as well as the presidential race, and who had been an usher in Kennedy's wedding. A ruddy-faced, outgoing crony of the president, Fay was assigned the job of undersecretary of the navy, where he could not get into too much trouble. Roswell Gilpatric would later say that the Navy Department was simply "designed around" Fay. With this weak spot in the technocracy, the secretary of the navy himself had to be a strong character. Kennedy wanted Franklin Roosevelt, Jr. Scion of a distinguished line of former secretaries of the navy, not to mention presidents, Roosevelt had served meritoriously in the navy during the war; he was a personal friend of the president-elect, and had campaigned vigorously for Kennedy in the pivotal West Virginia primary. There was also a political agenda. Kennedy wanted to build up Roosevelt as a candidate to challenge Nelson Rockefeller in the 1962 New York governor's race because Rockefeller was considered to be Kennedy's likely opponent in the 1964 presidential race. So set did this appointment seem that Roosevelt had already held a press conference in which he accepted the post after his self-appointment.

But McNamara rejected Roosevelt out of hand. Totally oblivious to political considerations as McNamara and his talent-search team were—to the point of naiveté—Roosevelt presented no executive or business qualification for the navy job, and rumor had it that he was a drunk besides. Kennedy accepted McNamara's decision regretfully.

In late December Sam Rayburn accompanied Johnson to a meeting with Kennedy at Palm Beach. The meeting was largely a courtesy call, meant to deal primarily with congressional relations and, tangentially, to begin to define Johnson's role as vice president. The essential shape of the administration was set. Kennedy was not looking to congressional leaders to help shape it in any event. Nevertheless, whether as a gesture to both Rayburn and Johnson or out of genuine interest, Kennedy opened the question of any appointments the Texans might want to suggest. Johnson said nothing, but Sam Rayburn spoke up.

"There is an able, young lawyer in Texas by the name of John Connally, who you ought to consider," the Speaker said.

"Isn't that the fellow who nominated you against me?" Kennedy said, turning to Johnson with a glint in his eye.

"Yes he is."

"Isn't he the one who ran that campaign against me at the convention?" Kennedy continued, in an oblique reference to the Addison's flap.

"He is," Johnson confessed.

The telephone rang. It was McNamara. He wanted to talk to Kennedy about the secretary of the navy. Having rejected Roosevelt and acquiesced in Red Fay, his talent search had turned up the name of a Fort Worth lawyer named Connally as a possibility for the navy job. McNamara wondered if that wasn't a name that ought to be cleared with the vice president. Kennedy simply handed the phone to a delighted Johnson. Thus, to all outward appearances, Johnson had no role in the Connally appointment. But it would be like him quietly and circuitously to have ensured that Connally's name came to the attention of the Defense Department talent search. It would have been just as characteristic for Johnson to have prompted Rayburn, rather than himself, to speak up in Connally's behalf. McNamara would never have been interested in Connally, however, if the secretary did not think that he had in Connally a strong, effective administrator, especially given the Red Fay situation.

A month later, as Connally's name went before Congress for confirmation, Drew Pearson sharpened his pencil. For years Pearson had been dipping into the exotic world of Texas tycoons and oil politics and had written occasionally about the strong-arm methods of the oil lobby. With the Connally appointment, Pearson was offended at the notion of an oil lobbyist taking the post which was responsible for purchasing most of the government's oil, and which controlled access to the vast naval oil reserves.

"If President Kennedy had switched the appointment of his secretaries of the Army and the Navy a lot of his Senate supporters would be happier," Pearson wrote on January 18. "Connally as Secretary of the Navy not only will buy more oil than any other man in the world, but will be charged with the supervision of one of the greatest oil reserves in the world. He will have to decide whether to lease certain areas to avoid loss from adjacent wells, and if so, which companies to lease to. Inevitably, some will be his old lobbying associates."

Lyndon Johnson heard the column was coming, and personally intervened with his shepherd to the vice presidency, Phil Graham, to have it killed. Pearson lodged a furious protest with Graham, but the column stayed dead and buried.

Pearson did not stop with his column. Taking ammunition from his friend in Austin, Creekmore Fath (whom Lyndon Johnson was specifically blocking for a federal appointment), Pearson formulated a list of tough questions for senators to put to Connally in his confirmation hearing. How much money did Sid Richardson contribute to Eisenhower during the 1952 campaign? How much did Richardson contribute to the Democrats and to Republicans in 1956? Is it necessary to record political contributions in Texas primaries? Have you ever at any time collected political campaign money from members of the Brown and Root firm? Do you know whether Brown and Root is still active in the construction work on American naval bases in Spain? How much money did you raise for Senator Johnson's preconvention campaign in 1960 from oil and gas sources?

Such an interrogation of Connally would have been withering enough. But Pearson also invited congressional scrutiny of Connally's involvement in the Natural Gas Act scandal of 1956. Will you state your own position regarding the Natural Gas Act of 1956? When did you first get to know Elmer Patman? Did you come to know him through your association with Senator Johnson? Was Mr. Patman living in the Mayflower Hotel in January and February 1956, when you were also in residence there? Will you name the senators with whom you were in active contact in promoting the natural gas legislation?

When Connally appeared before the Armed Services Committee of the Senate, the defense was deployed all around the nominee. He came to his hearing escorted by his rivals, Senator Yarborough and William Blakeley, the latter having been appointed by Governor Price Daniel to fill the Senate seat of Lyndon Johnson which Connally had spurned. The day after John F. Kennedy sent forth the word in his inaugural address that the torch had been passed to a new generation, Lyndon Johnson was making sure that the ethos of the old generation was not too closely questioned. Whether due to direct intervention by Johnson, self-censorship, or simple timidity, no senators put Pearson's questions to Connally, and he breezed through his committee examination. He assured the senators that he had no plan to leave his post after one or two years, but to serve as long as it pleased the president. On a more personal note, he asserted that for his appointment as coexecutor of the Sid Richardson estate, "I would earn no fees whatever during my government service. I would not collect any monies due or coming to me, even for past services." This statement had the ring of nobility and, technically, it was correct. Connally did not receive any fees from the Richardson estate during his brief tenure as secretary of the navy. Instead, two days before his confirmation hearing, on January 19 to be exact, he had received a payment of $50,000. That was his payment for 1961. And his payment for 1962, again $50,000, would come on December 27, three weeks before his inauguration as governor of Texas, when the Texas constitution, again technically, would bar him from taking any outside fees. Nevertheless, Connally *was* making a financial sacrifice in becoming secretary of the navy.

Upon being offered the post, he fretted a long time, for he knew that the fees coming to him as the coexecutor of the Richardson estate would be more than $1.2 million. Uncle Sid had been true to his word of putting Connally "in the way to make some money."

But with the offer of the navy post, "I agreed to set a maximum on the amount of fees that I was to receive from the estate," he explained later. "That figure was $750,000, provided it could be paid over a number of years, obviously for tax purposes, so I would not be too hard hit." He had given up $500,000 to take the navy job. As for the $750,000, those monies "are mine. They had already been vested. I was entitled to them as a matter of law. I was entitled to them just as a matter of calculation. No one could take them away from me. No one could make me take less than one-third of the total fees attributable to the administration of the estate. I voluntarily gave them up. . . . I took less, approximately $500,000 less, than I would have been entitled to under the law in order to try to serve my country." If this had a certain whiny tone about it, it was the boy from Floresville talking, the barefoot lad of the mule-plowed furrows, the product of the South Texas tenant farmer, butcher, bus driver, and county clerk, who had schooled himself under carbide lamps, who had grown up to be famous and almost rich, and then, after he had done something he considered noble for his country, was stung at how they wanted to take away from him that which was truly his, that he had honestly earned.

Upon the Senate floor itself, Connally's nomination ran into a patch of stormy weather. The two nonconformists of the Senate, Wayne Morse of Oregon and William Proxmire of Wisconsin, took on the nomination. To Morse, Connally did not pass the harsh test of Caesar's wife: to be above suspicion on a possible conflict of interest. Of the proposition that the administration could only find a qualified secretary of the navy within the ranks of the oil barons, Senator Morse said, "Tell that to the birds, not me." Senator Proxmire carried the debate against the nomination in the Senate. "I certainly do not think [Connally] is going to steal the navy blind," Proxmire exclaimed. "I think everything he will do, he will do in good conscience, but it is going to be done upon the basis of long experience in the oil industry."

"Do I understand the burden of the senator's argument to be that the nominee is not qualified by reason of the experience which he had in the oil industry?" Proxmire was challenged.

"The oilmen of Texas will follow a predictable course, a course designed to benefit the oil industry and resulting in disservice to the public," the senator replied. "It is exactly why we should not have an oilman in charge of the Navy Department." He raised the level of suspicions about Connally's involvement in the 1956 scandal, when the nominee had been a central player in a "very aggressive, militant special interest group." "They know what they want out of government and they go after it," Proxmire said.

But Connally's supporters lined up behind him, and in the absence of hard evidence tying Connally to the 1956 bribe attempt of Senator Francis Case which the confirming committee had failed to develop, Connally was confirmed easily by voice vote. There was one official abstention: Senator Francis Case himself. As the vote neared, Connally sat in the office of Bobby Baker, who was the secretary of the Senate and was, in every sense of the phrase, "Lyndon's boy." Baker was on the Senate floor monitoring the proceedings, while Lyndon Johnson had him on one phone and Connally on the other.

★

Several weeks before the Kennedy administration took office, Nikita Khrushchev gave formal approval for a new route to the eventual Communist domination of the world. Nuclear war could not achieve that objective, nor could local wars, for local wars had the danger of escalation into global wars. There was another way. The triumph of the proletariat could come through "wars of liberation," in which popular uprisings and covert subversion would lead to power. John Kennedy had recognized the vulnerability of American defense policy toward these wars of liberation: "We have been preparing primarily to fight the one kind of war we least want to fight, and are least likely to fight," Kennedy said in the campaign. "We have been driving ourselves into a corner where the only choice is all or nothing at all, world devastation or submission—a choice that necessarily causes us to hesitate on the brink and leaves the initiative in the hands of our enemies."

Connally took over the Navy Department at the moment when the entire defense strategy of the United States, built on the 1950s' assumptions about thermonuclear war, was to undergo a profound reappraisal. In the year he held office, the concept of struggle with the Communist world would shift to flexible response, whereby the United States would have a range of options for conventional, nonnuclear war. It was also a time when the engines of war were experiencing enormous technological advances. Intercontinental nuclear missiles, stored in silos in the plains of the upper Middle West or the deserts of the Southwest, were no longer considered invulnerable. Targeting a missile site halfway around the globe was becoming an exact science, and so the concept of deterrence was shifting to dispersion, to hardening of silos, but most of all, to nuclear missiles in submarines. These submarines were themselves nuclear powered, so that they could stay hidden underwater for long periods of time, not far from the borders of the Soviet Union. The Polaris submarine had not even been on the drawing boards in 1955. On February 2, 1961, at Newport News, Nellie Connally smashed a champagne bottle against the bow of the nation's seventh Polaris, and the 410-foot *Sam Houston* slid into the James River. At the ceremony, President Kennedy called the Polaris "a devastating instrument of incredible destructive power, conceived with but one purpose—to preserve the peace." When the USS *Sam Rayburn* was christened two years later, it would be the twenty-eighth Polaris submarine. During Connally's year at the Navy Department, the small, ever-moving, ever-undetected fleet of Polaris submarines, with several hundred nuclear missiles targeted on Soviet cities, would become the essence of the American "second strike" capability.

At the Navy Department, however, Connally's main job was to be a manager, not a strategic thinker. His responsibility covered close to 800,000 uniformed men and women, another 400,000 civilian employees, 11 shipyards, and an active fleet of nearly 900 ships, including 12 carrier air groups with nearly a thousand aircraft. It was a tight-knit, hidebound outfit that largely ran itself, and if the topside admirals were given the choice, they would prefer the navy do so without civilian intrusion. If the navy secretary was to be more than a figurehead, he had to involve himself in industrial management: scrutinizing the navy's relationship with the military contractors and making more efficient the entire system by which more than a million employees were housed, clothed, and moved from one place to another.

During the intellectual ferment in the Pentagon and the reevaluation of military force structure known as the "McNamara Revolution," Connally stood on the sidelines. While he was ready to implement whatever his superiors decided for his service, he was content to operate as a traditional First Lord of the Admiralty. Within McNamara's culture of cost/benefit analysis and operations researchers, he was an alien, for he was neither a whiz kid, a slide-rule mathematician, nor a policymaker. "He was brought in not knowing who he was, and he did not know who we were, and it became a dialogue of the deaf," Adam Yarmolinsky, McNamara's talent searcher and assistant, was to say. As a result, Connally's dealings with McNamara were formal, if respectful.

There were to be some pleasant surprises. Within a few weeks McNamara's first major decision was to accelerate the Polaris program by ten months, putting Connally at the center of the restructuring of the American strategic missile force. In March 1961 he went before Congress to testify on the program, and he proved a forceful, effective witness on the Hill.

"Now you said you will have, in early 1964, nineteen Polaris submarines—is that right?" asked the powerful Congressman Mendel Rivers.

"That is correct."

"And they will have aboard 304 Polaris missiles. That is enough to destroy the world, isn't it?"

"No," Connally replied. "I don't think that is quite enough to destroy the world."

"That is quite a few missiles, isn't it?" Rivers persisted.

"Three hundred and four are obviously quite a few. In our judgment, that is not enough."

In this emblematic moment, he was performing as the classic advocate for more rather than less. Yet no secretary of the navy could argue against pet navy projects without risking the confidence of his top admirals, and commanding the attention and the confidence of the navy's officers had become Connally's top priority. In early April he gathered some 3,500 naval and marine officers at Washington's Constitution Hall and gave them a rousing pep talk that lasted more than an hour. No navy secretary had ever done that before. As Connally detailed his plans for dealing with waste and inefficiency, he established that he could not be ignored. Actually, he did not have to register his presence with the admirals. McNamara and his talent scouts might have been blissfully unaware of Connally's political connections, but the admirals certainly were not. Before Connally was confirmed, a secret memo went around the fleet: "Bear in mind that the new Secretary of the Navy is closer to the Vice President than his wife."

That Connally had been a decorated naval officer in World War II made him seem one of the club anyway. His actions fortified his words, even to the point of putting him occasionally at odds with the White House. President Kennedy was sensitive to civil rights from his first day in office, and he tended to notice little things that mattered. He noticed that the Coast Guard contingent that marched in his inaugural parade was all white. He ordered a change. And somewhere he had noticed that the stewards who waited so snappily upon naval officers were all black or Filipino, and the president ordered that fixed as well. The complexion of the steward corps, however, involved old navy tradition; it hearkened back as far as anyone could remember and was symbolized by the well-known comment of the faithful steward to old Admiral Bull Halsey himself: "Ah takes care of you, and you takes care of us." The admirals resisted the dilution of their steward corps, while the White House pushed back just as hard. At one point it was suggested that if there were no integration, perhaps the admirals would like to take their mess in a cafeteria, and this unspeakable suggestion caused a near mutiny. Connally at last stepped in and told the White House bluntly to quit messing around with his navy. The matter was quietly dropped.

As the defender of the navy's every wish, Connally was bound to run into trouble sooner rather than later. Early in the administration, McNamara decided that the air force rather than the navy would have primacy over military space missions. Connally grumbled, but McNamara had to cut something from the budget, as millions had been added for the Polaris and space projects. Connally was content to let McNamara make these hard choices, but when he did, Connally bridled. In late May, as a reorganization of the Pentagon power structure was under consideration, a move which would downgrade the service secretaries still further, Connally complained to aides that if McNamara wanted an errand boy, he would have to get someone else.

During this restive time Connally invited the writer Fletcher Knebel to have breakfast with him at the Pentagon. For some months Knebel had been ruminating on the idea for a novel, a novel of suspense and political intrigue about the great "unmentionable" in military circles, but he came to the meeting in the guise of a journalist writing a *Look* magazine article on the New Frontiersmen. He needed to talk to Connally about LBJ. As the steward brought a breakfast fit for the Admiralty's First Lord and his literary guest, Connally fell easily into the role of the storyteller, and Knebel got what he needed for his article. Then the conversation turned to the subject of Knebel's secret fascination. The navy secretary acknowledged the frustrations of his admirals, who bridled under the restraints of civilian leadership and felt muzzled in their political expression. The issue was on everyone's mind. Only a month before, Major General Edwin A. Walker, the commander of the Twenty-fourth Infantry Division in Germany, had been disciplined for indoctrinating his troops in the principles of the John Birch Society.

"I'm worried," Connally said pensively. "Up to 1945, an individual could have some feeling—even in world war—that he had some control over his own existence. But when the atomic bomb exploded over Hiroshima, something happened. People began to feel helpless. Now with hydrogen bombs all over the world, the individual feels even more at a loss to control his own destiny. You can sense the feeling everywhere." The essence of Connally's musing, as Knebel received it, was that the United States might unwittingly be laying the groundwork for a military dictatorship.

Knebel was struck with Connally's foreboding, especially with the sense of helplessness in a high government official. If that were widespread in the Pentagon, it was significant. The novelist appropriated the feelings and instilled them in the thoughts of his fictional president, Jordan Lyman, who became the target of a military coup in the book *Seven Days in May*. President Lyman's adversary in the novel, General Scott, was described as looking remarkably like Connally—or Burt Lancaster. In Connally, the two sides of this dilemma were personified.

Perhaps Knebel was overdramatizing Connally's personal frustrations. Connally had finally come up against the reality of the office he had taken. For all its ruffles and flourishes, the post of a service secretary had been consistently downgraded after World War II, as the power of the secretary of defense was enhanced. The last great navy secretary had been Connally's own boss early in 1942, James Forrestal. Still, as a political credential, the office was a proven attribute. Both Theodore and Franklin Roosevelt had used their Navy Department service to good effect in running for the New York governorship, and they had been only assistant secretaries of the navy.

After only six months in office, Connally began to think about a real political life. To be governor of Texas remained the ultimate dream of most true-blooded Texas politicians, and in this proud son of South Texas, that dream was especially strong. While he had never run for elective office and was little known across the state except as a member of Lyndon's boys' academy, Connally thought that Governor Price Daniel was vulnerable if he decided to run again. The other likely candidates seemed to have no greater qualification for office than he, so he took a poll in the summer of 1961. The bleak result indicated four-percent support. Those who joined the quiet, exploratory campaign at its unpromising inception made up what became known as the 4% Club. To be a member would later become a badge of wisdom and prescience.

Lyndon Johnson was not about to join. He thought Connally's aspirations were absurd and told him so. It was not that Lyndon did not wish his friend well. He simply didn't think Connally could bridge the gap between the Navy Department and the Texas governorship without some modest intermediate step. During this period of exploration, Connally went to the LBJ Ranch with some other political figures for a hunting weekend. Johnson started to rag him in front of Jack Valenti and the others: "Big Mister John Connally— big wheel in Texas politics—He's got *four percent* of the people behind him." Johnson kept after Connally without letup, as they stalked deer, and Connally's pique began to rise. He went home right after the hunt and didn't stay for dinner.

But others saw Connally as a rising star in a dark sky. The Republicans were making significant inroads in Texas politics, as the liberal and conservative factions of the Democratic party remained hopelessly divided. It seemed likely that a Republican from Wichita Falls named John Tower might capture Johnson's Senate seat in November, and atop the Texas Democratic party was a bland and unfocused Daniel, who was threatening to run for an unprecedented fourth term after having imposed an unpopular two-percent sales tax. As a philosophical conservative with the national and international experience that might assuage the liberals, Connally might well unite the Democrats. Among his biggest boosters was Robert Strauss, his old campaign manager when he ran for president of the University of Texas student body, who was now, by his own description, an obscure Jewish lawyer from Dallas. With the Tower scare prodding him, Strauss conceived the idea of a gala party for the secretary of the navy in Dallas, a party to which the business and social establishment would be invited, where the Chamber of Commerce and such local worthies as Stanley Marcus of the Neiman association would be involved, and where the notion of John Connally for governor would be whispered loudly from the stage. It turned into a "hell of a party," as Strauss remembered it fondly. "John, if you don't run, I believe the Republicans are going to win the governorship this time," Strauss remarked to Connally along the way. "Price Daniel is going to get beat by a Republican."

This party began the Dallas love affair with John Connally. It served to change the widespread notion that Connally was a liberal, who was "Lyndon's boy" first, the same Lyndon whom Dallas, above all Texas cities, still held to be an escaped convict for the theft of the 1948 election, and "Jack's boy" second, the same Jack who was a flaming liberal and for whom this upstart, Connally, would simply be holding the state as a prelude to the presidential election of 1964. In short, Connally was running with a bad crowd in Washington. But that didn't necessarily make him a bad person or a bad candidate, if he could leave the Kennedy-Johnson program behind in Washington and bring home the Kennedy style and wit and grace. Then Texas might become a land of knights and maids with its own colors.

Strauss's party did not entirely solve the problem of Connally's low recognition around the state. On November 9, in Austin, however, that liability was addressed effectively, if painfully. Connally had come home to be lionized as a distinguished ex-student of the University of Texas, a singular honor akin to local academy awards, but beforehand he was to review a crack contingent of local Naval Reserve soldiers at the airport. When he stood before one tightly wound soldier, he moved his eyes ritualistically up and down the youth's uniform, and then asked the soldier's name. The trooper heard the words instead to be a command to present arms and thrust his weapon out for inspection as Connally was still looking at his spit-polished shoes. The weapon caught Connally near his left eye, gashing him badly. That night he attended his black-tie dinner looking a bit wan and sporting an eye patch. He would continue to wear it for several weeks. It made a wonderful picture, and the Texas newspapers ran with it for days. It was Connally as the Hathaway man he was later to become. After an overlong time with this unique signature, his friends began to rib him: "Aw c'mon, John. You know that eye healed long ago. Go on and take that patch off!" By December 6, when he formally announced for the governorship after a final meeting of his supporters at Dolphe Briscoe's* ranch, his recognition factor, at least for most of his face, had improved markedly.

His departure from government was met in the White House with sincere regret and there was no resentment over the earliness of his leave-taking. Recognized as an able man who had done a good job, he was simply going on to a larger political calling, and if he succeeded it would be good for John Kennedy in 1964. Indeed, so high was Connally's standing that Robert Kennedy made a last effort to dissuade him from seeking the governorship and instead to assume a higher post in the administration. For many months the president and his advisors had been searching for a man of stature from outside the State Department establishment to become assistant secretary of state for Latin America. Over fifteen people had been approached; no one would take the post, for the odor of the Bay of Pigs still hung over the position. As a result, Latin American

*Dolphe Briscoe was governor of Texas between 1972 and 1978.

policy was in disarray. Connally was tantalized. He had been around Latinos all his life. He knew of President Kennedy's longstanding interest in Latin America, and with his South Texas roots it would be an interesting assignment. In fact, Kennedy had conceived the phrase "Alliance for Progress" while he was on a campaign swing in Texas and on the way to speak at the Alamo. Everything, it seemed, always hearkened back to the Alamo.

"John Connally was my candidate," Robert Kennedy was to say of the Latin America post in 1964—and then he laughed. It was a laugh soaked with the bitterness and the irony and the sheer bad luck of Dallas, as well as with his visceral dislike of Connally as a person. "He wouldn't take it—then he was going to take it—then he wouldn't take it—and the president was going to appoint him."

But fate had a different appointment in mind.

The Assassin

FROM THE BEGINNING of his victorious 1962 campaign through his accession to the governorship in January 1963 and his first bold speeches as the state's chief executive, John Connally epitomized the big man of Texas. He stood in his elegant boots with the wealthy over the poor, the business executive over the working man, white over black and Hispanic, the glamorous over the commonplace. In short, he symbolized Texas royalty over Texas peasantry. He was a taunting, polarizing figure, engendering feelings of intense loyalty and utter contempt, even hate. His first term as governor began in a decisive year of change in America, when political passions were overheated, though they had not yet reached the boiling point, and where hate mail and threats on lives were common. America was in the throes of a racial revolution.

The same year Connally returned to Texas for his political race, another Texan, in many ways his very antithesis, also returned after an extended absence. Lee H. Oswald, as he signed himself, was a small, wiry, homely loner, twenty-four years of age. Like Connally, he, too, considered Fort Worth to be his home, and he had left it with a splash that had made front-page headlines in the *Star Telegram* every bit as large as those used a year later when President Kennedy appointed Fort Worth oilman John Connally secretary of the navy: FORT WORTH MAN TO BECOME A RED TO WRITE A BOOK? . . . FORT WORTH DEFECTOR CONFIRMS RED BELIEFS . . . MY VALUES DIFFERENT, DEFECTOR TOLD MOTHER . . . TURNCOAT HANGS UP ON MOTHER.

The details were lurid and shocking. Oswald had dropped out of high school after his freshman year to join the Marine Corps, the service of just a few good men. His three-year hitch in the corps began with an average qualification as a sharpshooter, proceeded through electronics and radar training, and had concluded with a tour in Atsugi, Japan, on a base from which U-2 aircraft took off for Russia.

Then, reported the Fort Worth paper, the turncoat had read *Das Kapital* as he defended freedom in Japan, had saved all his money—$1,600—to travel to the Soviet Union, and in his last months in the service had thought of nothing but defection. Later, while he languished in the sumptuous Metropole Hotel in Moscow awaiting final word on his citizenship application, he had submitted to an interview by UPI. Why had he defected? He gave three reasons: racial discrimination, the treatment of the underdog, and the hate in his native land.

Lee Harvey Oswald's facade was flamboyant and petulant, but his adventure in Russia began with the pathos of a Dostoevsky tale. He had taken a ship from New Orleans to Great Britain, and then had flown to Helsinki, a point from which he knew the entry into Russia would somehow be easier. Arriving on Soviet soil early in October, he brashly approached his Intourist agent, a stolid woman named Rimma, and blurted out that he wished to apply for Soviet citizenship. In the days that followed, the sympathetic Rimma took him through the necessary gates, helping him with his letter to the Supreme Soviet and, on his twentieth birthday, October 18, 1959, sweetly presenting him with a copy of Dostoevski's *The Idiot*. Three days later, however, Oswald's colossal effort of will was imperiled. In his diary he described his response.

> October 21: Meeting with single official. Balding, stout, black suit, fairly good English, askes what do I want. I say Sovite citizenship. He tells me 'USSR only great in literature and wants me to go back home.' I am stunned. I reiterate. He says he shall check and let me know weather my visa will be extend. (It exipiers today).
> Eve. 6.00. Recive word from police official. I must leave country tonight at 8 P.M. as visa expirs. I am shocked!! My dreams! I retire to my room. I have $100 left. I have waited for 2 year to be accepted. My fondes dreams are shattered because of a petty offial. because of bad planning, I planned to much! 7.00 P.M. I decide to end it. Soak rist in cold water to

numb the pain Than slash my left wrist. Than plaung wrist
into bath tub of hot water. I think 'when Rimma comes at 8 to
find me dead, it will be a great shock. Somewhere a violin
plays, as I watch my life whirl away. I think to myself. 'how
easy to die' and 'a sweet death' (to violins)
about 8.00. Rimma finds my unconscious (bathtub water a
rich, red color) She screams (I remember that . . . Poor
Rimma stays by my side as interrpator far into the night. I
tell her to go home (my mood is bad) but she stays. She is my
friend. She has a strong will. Only at this moment, I notice
she is preety.

Upon his release from the hospital a week later, Oswald again
confronted the daunting face of Soviet bureaucracy, but this time
the strange American was taken more seriously. His passport did
not seem to be enough for them, so Oswald presented his most
prized possession, a laminated card which displayed his honorable
discharge from the Marine Corps. Throughout all that transpired
after his discharge, Oswald defined himself through his Marine
Corps service. The corps had shaped him. It proved his importance.
He flaunted it now with the hope that the Soviets would see how
big a catch he was. Delay was inevitable. Three days later, as he
clattered around his hotel room at the Metropole, he was tormented
with anxiety and loneliness, writing, "Oct 30: I have been in hotel
three days. It seems like three years. I must have some sort of
showdown!"
  The next day he slipped out of the hotel and took a cab to the
American embassy. There he presented himself to a wry and experienced professional named Richard Snyder. Snyder found him to be
a well-dressed, intelligent, and very determined twenty-year-old.
Oswald got right to the point. Slapping his passport down on the
desk, he demanded the right to renounce his American citizenship.
By no means was Snyder unprepared for the situation. Snyder had
processed a renunciation of American citizenship for another
American named Petrulli, who had applied for Soviet citizenship
some weeks earlier. But a month later the Soviets had decided that
they did not want Petrulli, who turned out to be a mental case, and
Snyder had to do a good deal of fudging to reassert American
authority and to annul the renunciation. With Oswald, he was determined to stall as long as he could—although he knew he could not
do so forever, for Oswald was fully within his rights. If Oswald was

in command of his senses, which he certainly appeared to be, the action was, Snyder cautioned him, permanent and irrevocable.

Snyder tried to draw Oswald out, asking him a number of soft questions and stressing the enormous import of what the young man proposed to do. At one point Snyder asked him his reasons.

"I am a Marxist!" Oswald replied histrionically, as if that covered all bases.

"Well, then," replied the comfortable Mr. Snyder, "you're going to be very lonesome in the Soviet Union." Oswald was not amused.

Oswald's speech was aggressive and strident, and he would not be deterred. Finally, Snyder seized upon the bureaucrat's final pretext: the embassy was technically closed that afternoon and for the weekend. The applicant would have to come back in a few days. Oswald stormed out.

Instead of returning the following business week, Oswald wrote the embassy an outraged letter, charging that the consul had denied him his legal right to renounce and that his application for citizenship was now pending before the Supreme Soviet. In a final flourish, which the American consul later recalled to be distinctly "Oswaldish" in its comical pomposity and sonorousness, Oswald wrote, "In the event of [the acceptance of my application to the Supreme Soviet], I shall request my government to lodge a formal protest regarding this incident."

In his interview with Snyder, Oswald had made one threat that could not be ignored. He promised to turn over to the Soviets all the military secrets he had learned in the marines. As a radar operator with a secret clearance, he had access to information about the radar and radio frequencies of all squadrons, all tactical call signs, the relative strength of squadrons, the number and type of aircraft in each, the names of commanding officers, and the authentication code for entering and exiting the Air Defense Identification Zone, as well as radio frequencies and the range of radar both for his squadron and squadrons contiguous to his own. Immediately, Snyder alerted the naval attaché in the embassy, who wired the Navy Department in Washington. As a result, codes, aircraft call signs, and radio and radar frequencies in the scope of Oswald's knowledge were changed. Certain things, however, could not be changed, such as the frequency range of the new height-finding radar, just introduced at enormous cost into the Marine Corps air defense system. In its displeasure, the Navy Department initiated an action against Oswald which would four years later devastate him and for which he would come to blame John Connally.

As he moped around the Metropole Hotel, Oswald's sole link to America and to his past was his older brother, Robert. Robert Oswald had reached Lee by telegram in early November, calling his decision to defect a mistake. On November 26 Lee replied angrily in a long letter, full of cant. "See the segregation. See the unemployed and what automation is. Remember how you were laid off at Convair. . . . I will ask you a question, Robert: what do you support the American government for? What is the ideal you put forward? Do not say 'freedom' because freedom is a word used by all peoples through all of time. Ask me, and I will tell you I fight for *communism*." Toward the end of this harangue, he declared the importance of ideology over blood. He had four parting shots: "1. In the event of war I would kill *any* American who put on a uniform in defense of the American government—any American. 2. In my own mind, I have no attachments of any kind to the U.S. 3. I want to—and I shall—live a normal, happy, and peaceful life here in the Soviet Union *for the rest of my life.* 4. My mother and you are *not* objects of affection, but only examples of workers in the U.S. You should not try to remember me in any way I used to be. . . . I am not all bitterness or hate. I come here only to find freedom. . . . In truth," he said in closing, "I feel I am at last with my own people."

After this farewell from the grandstand, Oswald receded into the proletariat. If he expected to be fussed over, to be made a hero in the Soviet state, he was disappointed. The KGB took no interest in him. He was never questioned about his military service in Japan, nor about new American radars or about U-2 aircraft. He was considered "not very bright" and the local authorities in Minsk, where he was sent to work in a radio factory, were requested to keep an eye on him, lest he turn out to be some sort of "sleeper agent."

Oswald's dream for a "normal, happy, and peaceful life" in Russia was realized for the first nine months of his expatriation. He found the work in the factory easy. His fellow workers treated him warmly, especially as he began to acquire the language. If he was not accorded a hero's status, he was, nevertheless, given special treatment. Assigned an apartment with a splendid view overlooking the Svisloch River, he raked in 1,400 rubles a month, twice the salary of other workers on his level. Seven hundred rubles was a supplement, "to help out," from a mysterious branch of the Red Cross, and Oswald would crow in his diary that this income was the equivalent to that of the director of the radio factory. "It is a Russian's dream," he wrote blissfully in March. The summer brought rapturous walks in the deep pine forests of Byelorussia. He had joined a hunting club at the factory, and with a shotgun on his shoulder (for private ownership of rifles and pistols was forbidden in the Soviet Union) he ventured into the rural regions around Minsk. These trips made a deep impression. The peasants he met and in whose homes he sometimes stayed overnight were frequently close to starvation. Often, out of sympathy, he would leave what game he had shot. He was also fascinated by the radio speakers in peasants' huts, which kept up a constant patter of exhortation day and night and which could not be turned off. At this early stage, however, he merely took note of these exotic aspects of the totalitarian state. Other images cut deeper. In the fall he rhapsodized about the golds and reds of the landscape. "Plums, peaches, appricots and cherries abound in the last Fall weeks," he wrote in his diary. "I am a healthy, brown color and stuffed with fresh fruit."

With the approach of his first Russian winter, Oswald, like the hero of *The Idiot*, developed a melancholy and then a dread of the cold and the darkness. He began to take more notice of the trappings of the Communist state around him. "I am increasingly aware of the presence of Lebizen, the shop party secretary, fat, fortyish, and jovial on the outside. He is a no-nonsense party regular." He began to resent compulsory attendance at boring factory meetings, where the factory doors were locked and no one ever voted No to a formal proposal. He was horrified at the poor quality and the cost of simple necessities like clothes and shoes. While the slogans and exhortations of the state cluttered his mind, the dreary routine of the worker's life began to undercut his operatic dream.

The turning point for Oswald was not political but emotional. In early January, he fell hopelessly in love with a comrade at the factory named Ella, who after a dalliance spurned him. To his diary, he declared that he was "misarable," and a few weeks later he wrote, "I am starting to reconsider my desire about staying. The work is drab. The money I get has no where to be spent. No nightclubs or bowling allys. No place of recreation acept the trade dances. I have had enough." On February 1 he wrote to Richard Snyder that he wanted to go home.

Oswald's overture at this point was exploratory. Ambivalence rather than total disaffection marked his psychology, and he was moving toward negative perceptions of both political systems.

His life took another turn in March when, at a "boring" trade union dance, he met a stubborn blonde pharmacist with a French hairdo named Marina (who had lived the first six years of her life near the Arctic Circle in Murmansk and Archangel). In contrast to Ella, who had snickered at the awkwardness of his marriage proposal, Marina accepted his attentions and in April the two were married. In his diary he declared, "In spite of fact I married Marina to hurt Ella, I found myself in love with Marina."*

Marriage did not change his desire to get out of the Soviet Union, however, and in July 1961 the Oswalds applied for an exit visa, hoping to return to America. The change in Oswald's attitude toward his adopted state was evident in a letter he wrote to Robert just after he returned from a talk with Snyder about going home. "The Russians can be crule and very crude at times. They gave a cross examination to my wife on the first day we came from Moscow. They knew everything, because they spy and read the mails. But we shall continue to try and get out. We shall not retreat. As for your package, we never received it. I suppose they swiped that to, the bastards."

Now that Oswald had asked to go home, the cruelty of the Russians took another form. His "Red Cross" allotment of 700 rubles a month abruptly stopped. Oswald finally saw it for what it was: he had been a paid stooge. He had never told anyone of his supplement and only when he was on his way home to Texas was he able to write about it, and then only to himself. The important thing is the lesson he drew from it.

> Whene I frist went to Russia in the winter of 1959 my funds
> were very limited. So after a certain time, after the Russians
> had assured themselfs that I was really the naive american
> who believed in communism, they arranged for me to recive a
> certain amount of money every month. OK. it came
> technically through the Red Cross as finical help to a Roos
> polical immigrate but it was arranged by the M.V.D.† I told
> myself it was simply because I was hungry and there was
> several inches of snow on the ground in Moscow at that time,
> but it really was *payment* for my denuciation of the U.S. in
> Moscow and a clear promise that for as long as I lived in the
> USSR life would be very good. I didn't realize all this, of
> course for almost two years.
> As soon as I became completely disgusted with the Sovit
> Union and started negotiations with the American Embassy in

---

*This line above all others was to wound Marina when the diary was published several months after Oswald's death.

†The Russian secret police.

Moscow for my return to the U.S. my "Red Cross" allotment
was cut off.
I have never mentioned the fact of these monthly payments to
anyone. I do so in order to stat that I shall never sell myself
intentionly or unintentionly to anyone again.

Soon enough the American government displayed an equivalent
cruelty toward him. Lee Harvey Oswald had achieved one significant thing in his life. He had joined the U.S. Marine Corps, and,
despite the dislike of his mates and two courts-martial (for
possessing an illegal weapon and for fighting), and despite loudly
proclaiming himself to be a Marxist and gaining the barracks
nickname of "Oswaldskovich," he had made it through. His reward
after three years was an honorable discharge. In his billfold he
carried the laminated proof of his achievement as if it were an
executive gold card. It was a credential he would need, and need
desperately, when he returned to America.

In January 1963 Oswald was attempting to control his excitement over the imminent birth of his first child and the prospect of
returning to the United States. On January 5 he wrote to Robert, "I
really do not trust these people, so I shall wait untill I'm in the U.S.
before I become overjoyed." Two weeks later the blow struck. He
received a letter from his mother, Marguerite: the Marine Corps
had changed his discharge from honorable to dishonorable. In fact,
Marguerite Oswald conveyed the news as more catastrophic than it
really was. The downgrading had actually stopped one notch short
of "dishonorable," at "undesirable," but that was bad enough.
Anything less than an honorable military discharge is a curse in
America, especially for a working man, and Oswald knew it instinctively. The news was fresh only to Lee Harvey Oswald. The action
had been taken a year and a half before he learned of it. For two
years his mother had not known where her son was or even if he
were dead or alive, but she had labored bravely with letters to the
Defense Department and the State Department, to Sam Rayburn
and Congressman Jim Wright of Fort Worth, to overturn the Marine
Corps decision or at least to obtain a fair hearing. In her anguish
during his long silence, Marguerite had seized upon the comforting
notion that her son had been hypnotized and drugged by the
Russians before he was carted off to the evil empire. To Mrs. Oswald,
Lee's name had been "dishonored" more by the Marine Corps action
than by her son's apparent defection. In one letter to the navy she
said she hoped the corps "would do something about this awful

thing of a dishonorable discharge, because I have grandchildren. . . . My whole family has served in the service, and Lee served the service for three years. I want his name cleared."

Lee Harvey Oswald was crushed at the news. That he would care at all is noteworthy. Why should a true convert to Communism, one so desperate for political action, one so ready to take up arms against America—in short, the person who was described by the Warren Commission—have a moment of anxiety over what the fascist United States and its most dangerous military force did in his buried military records? The true believer would be amused. But Oswald did care. He cared deeply. At bottom, his military service gave meaning to his life, and it was the *only* thing that did.

He immediately wrote letters to complain of the injustice, and he had a valid case. His discharge had been changed for actions he took not in the Marine Corps but as a private citizen afterwards. It had been changed without a fair hearing, upon the basis of rumors that were largely unsubstantiated and upon statements like his threat to turn over military secrets that were made at a moment of high stress (and which in fact he never carried out). Perhaps more important than the emotional impact were the practical consequences. As he prepared to go home, Oswald knew intuitively that his road in America would be far rougher now.

On January 31, 1962, he wrote to the secretary of the navy. In his schoolboy scrawl, full of his usual misspellings and awkward constructions, now made more awkward by the syntax of the Russian language, he pleaded his case grandly. He began with a reference to the common bond he shared with Secretary Connally. He wished to call the secretary's attention to a case "about which you may have personal knowledge since you are a resident of Fort Worth as am I." The Fort Worth papers, he wrote Connally, had blown his case into "another turncoat sensation" when, in fact, he had come to Russia to reside "for a short time, much in the same way E. Hemingway resided in Paris."

"I have and allways had the full sanction of the U.S. Embassy, Moscow, USSR," he lied, and now that he was returning to the United States, "I shall employ all means to right this gross mistake or injustice to a boni-fied U.S. citizen and ex-serviceman." He asked Connally personally to "repair the damage done to me and my family."

On the same day he wrote to Robert, who was also then living in Fort Worth, for he feared that his letter to Connally would not make it through the Russian censors. He asked Robert to be in touch

with Connally independently to see how this injustice might be recti-
fied.

Connally, of course, had resigned as secretary of the navy the
previous December, six weeks earlier. What the ex-serviceman got
from the ex-navy secretary a month later—on February 23—was the
old bureaucratic brush-off. Connally's response was perfunctory.
He promised to pass the problem on to his successor. Thus, at the
beginning of this painful personal matter, Oswald had been spurned
by a fellow Texan, and he resented it. Connally represented the U.S.
government, and his perfunctory response fortified Oswald's bitterness against the country and now against an individual.

Connally's brush-off was followed by a cascade of subsequent
slights by naval and Marine Corps functionaries. A letter from the
Navy Department told Oswald that the department contemplated
no change in the discharge. On March 22 Oswald appealed for
further review. The department replied that it had no authority and
sent yet another form, referring Oswald to the Navy Discharge
Review Board. Oswald filled out the form in Minsk, but he did not
mail it until he landed in America. This last appeal, before he gave
up, carried the tone of moral outrage: "You have no legal or even
moral right to reverse my honorable discharge." It, too, led nowhere.
It was a classic case of a powerless nonentity mired in an endless,
hopeless battle with an aloof, faceless military establishment, except
that Oswald could now associate one face with his distress.

Finally, in late May 1962, the Oswalds got out of Russia. They
made their way to Rotterdam, where on June 4 they boarded the
Maasdam, a Holland America Line ship, bound for New York.
Aboard ship, Oswald fell into a reflective mood, and on sheets of
Holland America Line stationery, he wrote his thoughts:

> I wonder what would happen if somebody was to stand up
> and say he was utterly opposed not only to governments, but
> to the people, too the entire land and the complete
> foundations of his socially [society].
> Too a person knowing both systems and their factional
> accessories, their can be no mediation between the systems as
> they exist today That person must be opposed to their basic
> foundations and representatives, and yet, it is imature to take
> the attitude which say 'a curse on both your houses.'
> In history, there are many such examples of the members of
> the new order rooted in the idealestical tradition of the old.
> As history has shown time again, the state remains and

grows, whereas true democracy can be practiced only at the local level. While the centralized state, administrative, political, and or supervisual remains, their can be no real democracy, only a loose confederation of communities at a national level without any centralized state what so ever.
The mass of survivors, however, will not beblong too any of these groups. They will not be fanatical enough to join extremest groups and will be too disillusioned too support either the communits or capitalist parties in their respective countries, after the atomic catorahf [catastrophe]. They shall seek an alternative to those systems which have brought true mysery. . . . They would deem it neccary to oppose the old systems but support at the same time their cherished trations.
I intend to put forward just such an allturnative.

The Oswalds arrived in Fort Worth only a few weeks before John Connally won the intense and highly publicized Democratic primary for the gubernatorial nomination. They had no money and almost no possessions, but they did have a six-month-old baby. Lee had virtually no qualifications for employment. Worse than that, the Fort Worth paper had reported the return of the turncoat. Marina spoke no English, and her husband seemed determined to keep it that way. Their isolation and hopelessness might have been even more miserable but for the help of the White Russian émigré community in the Dallas–Fort Worth area. Small but tightly knit and supportive, this community comprised about fifty people who had gravitated to Texas, most of them after the Second World War. Generally they were already expatriates, having arrived in America from such places as Iran and Turkey, to which they had fled from Russia. As a rule, they were fervently anticommunist, just as they were possessed by an enduring fascination for what was going on in Communist Russia. The community had a titular leader, a kind and energetic gentleman in his late fifties named George Bouhe, who had fled Russia across a river into Finland in 1923. Bouhe took an immediate interest in the Oswalds and helped them get settled by providing them with a little cash here and there, ten or twenty dollars, bringing them groceries, and helping Marina find a dentist and a pediatrician. For his pains, he got only insults from Oswald, for Bouhe's charity smacked of the kind of help he was determined never again to accept. Bouhe persisted nonetheless, mainly out of concern for Marina, who seemed to him to be a "lost soul." To

Bouhe, Oswald himself was a simpleton and a boor and, soon enough, a wife abuser. Moreover, from the comparative speed and ease with which the Oswalds had exited Russia, Bouhe came to suspect Oswald of some continuing clandestine relationship with the Soviet state. Still, he persevered because, as a matter of belief, he felt that Communism breeds among the down and out, and he hoped that a greater degree of comfort might assuage Lee Oswald's bitterness.

Part of Bouhe's sympathy and charity went to helping Oswald find work, and here Oswald ran immediately into the problem of his tainted military discharge. He was competing for the lowest rank of employment among the unskilled. "When he went to the Texas Employment Commission in Fort Worth to ask for a job, and they said what can you do—nothing," Bouhe later told the Warren Commission. "Where did you work last—Minsk—. He couldn't progress. He couldn't get any place." Inevitably, it came back to the discharge, for he could fudge his last place of work. "When he was applying for a job, we picked up some application blanks someplace, and you have to say about your military service. And where it says 'Discharged,' I'd ask how? And he would say, 'Put down *honorable.*' "

"That was the extent of your discussion?" counsel of the Warren Commission asked.

"Right. He would freeze up like a clam."

Even though it was easy enough for any prospective employer to check his discharge claim, lying about his marine record worked initially. Oswald's first job, which he got a month after his arrival, was at a Fort Worth welding company as a sheet-metal worker. On his application, he cited sheet-metal work in the Marine Corps as a qualification.

Bouhe confined his role with Oswald to that of an informal social worker. To discuss politics with such an ingrate as Oswald was less than pointless, and Bouhe avoided it studiously. But the old White Russian had noticed Oswald's fixation with his military discharge, had seen how it made Oswald clam up, and how his lying about it launched him into a state of high anxiety. After the assassination, after he read of John Connally's bureaucratic slight, and knowing that Oswald was especially tormented by the bad discharge at the very time when Connally was about to be promoted to the pinnacle of Texas government, Bouhe put the pieces together: "If anybody asked me, did Oswald have any hostility towards anybody in government, I would say Governor Connally."

In early October 1962, a month before election day, Oswald quit his job. He quit on the very day that the candidate Connally came to Dallas to give speeches to a women's group and to the country club set. Apparently he hated the hard, hot, dirtiness of welding. Ironically, the company was sorry to see him go. "I imagine if he had pursued that trade, he might have come out to be a pretty good sheet-metal man," his supervisor told the Warren Commission.

Precisely as this event took place, Marina and the baby took up residence in the home of Alexandra de Mohrenshildt, who was the daughter of another Russian émigré in Dallas, a flamboyant loudmouth named George de Mohrenshildt, who toyed with Oswald in uneven intellectual games and was to exert a very negative influence on him. Thus, Lee Oswald was observed by Alexandra de Mohrenshildt at the very time when he had again put himself on the job market, and she was to see a good deal of Oswald in the ensuing months.

A year and a half later, Alexandra de Mohrenshildt came before the Warren Commission. With this witness, as with others who had known Oswald personally after his repatriation, the commission probed Oswald's comparative attitude toward his eventual victims, looking for some insight that might explain his motive to murder. Alexandra was a good witness, for in the fall of 1962 she had been married to an engineer with liberal politics named Gary Taylor, and she had listened as Oswald and Taylor engaged in political discussion.

"Was President Kennedy ever mentioned in the course of the discussions between your husband and Lee?" counsel asked.

"Never, never," Alexandra replied. "It was the governor of Texas who was mentioned mostly."

"Tell us about that."

"First you are going to have to tell me who the governor was."

"Connally."

"Connally—wasn't that the one that—"

"That had been secretary of the navy."

"That had been secretary of the navy, was it? Well, for some reason, Lee just didn't like him. I don't know why, but he didn't like him."

"Would it refresh your recollection, that the subject of Governor Connally arose in connection with something about Lee's discharge from the marines?" counsel prodded.

"I don't recall. Lee never spoke too much about why he left the marines or anything like that. I don't know. Maybe it was the dishonorable discharge. I don't know. All I know is that it was something he didn't talk about. And there was a reason why he did not like Connally."

"Whatever the reason was, he didn't articulate the reason particularly?"

"No, he just didn't like him."

"But you have the definite impression he had an aversion to Governor Connally?"

"Yes, but he never ever said a word about Kennedy."

"But he did have a definite aversion to Governor Connally as a person?"

"Yes."

"Did he speak of that reasonably frequently in those discussions?"

"No, not really, no. He didn't bring it up frequently."

"But he was definite and affirmative about it, was he?"

"Yes, he didn't like him."

In October, when Alexandra de Mohrenshildt came to know Oswald, and John Connally was in Dallas arguing for the continuation of the poll tax, Oswald had an experience that was becoming routine. The clerk at the Texas Employment Commission identified a good job opening in the photography department of a printing concern in Dallas called Jaggars-Chiles-Stovall. Before Oswald went over for his interview, the company had asked the employment commission clerk about Oswald's last place of employment and was told that he had recently been discharged from the marines. When Oswald entered the Jaggars office he made a good impression. He was presentably dressed and well mannered. Almost immediately the subject of his military career came up, as the potential employer asked about his last place of work.

"The marines," Oswald said brashly.

"Oh, yes—yes," the employer said. "Honorably discharged, of course," he added as a half-question, thinking he was being amusing.

"Oh, yes," Oswald replied with technical truthfulness.

Oswald was again seized with the emotion of rage. Was this going to come up every time? His anxiety that his lies might be found out was intense. Later, the Jaggars-Chiles-Stovall man, John G. Graef, told the Warren Commission that it never occurred to him to check up on whether the applicant was telling the truth about the discharge, though it would have been perfectly easy to do so.

Oswald was to work six months at the Jaggars outfit. But his efficiency began to deteriorate in three months. He did not get along with the other employees, strange loner that he was. His behavior was unpredictable, his attitude unpleasant. Working in the close quarters of a photographic laboratory gave him claustrophobia, and this increased his churlishness. Early in 1963, as his work at Jaggars declined, his thoughts drifted back to Russia, and his memory blocked out the overwhelming negative feelings he had had upon his departure. He began to talk to Marina about reentering the Soviet Union. Wherever he was—Russia with its spies and its drab, boring existence, America with its capitalist moguls and its exploitation— was wrong for him. The system, whatever it was, was to blame. When the actual dismissal took place, in early April, Oswald brought it upon himself by flaunting a Soviet publication at work, once again turning failure into something noble: political martyrdom. On the day that he was fired, Oswald remarked that he hated capitalist exploitation and that the Jaggars firm had reaped a lot more from his labor than they had paid him in wages.

He had seen the end coming. Weeks before his dismissal he had secretly used the Jaggars facilities after hours to forge a new Marine Corps discharge and draft classification document in the name of Alik James Hidell, the name under which he ordered his first weapon, a .39 caliber Smith and Wesson revolver, by mail, as well as his second, a high-powered Italian carbine called a Mannlicher-Carcano.

Three days into his first week of unemployment, on April 10, Lee Harvey Oswald became an assassin. He made an attempt on the life of General Edwin Walker, the reactionary symbol of Dallas, the darling of the Birchers, the one-time candidate for governor of Texas against John Connally. Oswald missed Walker's head by about an inch. He had become a very dangerous man, and in choosing Walker as a target of his murderous frustrations he was turning upon a pure figure of the far right.

Only one person, Marina Oswald, knew about the attempt on General Walker. Her husband had confessed his action to her. In her narrow, isolated world, unable to speak or read English, she knew nothing of American political figures, with the exception of the Kennedys. General Walker might have been a kitchen appliance for all she knew. But when Lee Oswald confided in her, she understood his capability to kill for political reasons, and she was horrified. She saw what form his frustrations and failures were now taking and she, above anyone, appreciated his violent tendencies; she knew the dangerous flash points. Two weeks later, with Oswald still out of work and raging around their dingy apartment, she acted.

On Sunday, April 21, the headline in the *Dallas News* read, NIXON CALLS FOR DECISION TO FORCE REDS OUT OF CUBA. It reported a strident speech which former Vice President Richard Nixon had made the previous day in Washington, excoriating Kennedy for being "defensive" on Castro, demanding a "command decision" to remove the Soviets and calling for a redefinition of the manifest destiny of the Monroe Doctrine into a doctrine of liberation. Oswald laid the paper down and withdrew into an adjacent room. When he reemerged he was dressed in a tie and white shirt. His pistol was shoved into his best gray pants.

"Where are you going?" Marina demanded.

"Nixon is coming to town. I want to go have a look."

"I know what your 'looks' mean," she said coldly, and then, thinking quickly, she inveigled him into following her into the bathroom. Once he was inside, she slipped out and slammed the door, and held it with all her strength. For several minutes he pushed and she held and they shouted at one another, and Marina wept in terror. She pleaded with him not to go, to promise her he would never again go for one of his "looks," and at last, emotionally spent, he agreed and she let him out. In the days after this episode, later known as the "Nixon incident," Oswald became as docile and torporous as a coral snake. Later, the Warren Commission dismissed this event as insignificant.

Actually, Nixon was not in town at all, nor was he coming, and though Marina could not know it, Oswald did. He had said "Nixon" for its shock value: it was Nixon's picture that was on the front page of the Dallas paper, and Nixon wasn't coming to Texas at all, and so the men of the Warren Commission dismissed the incident as having no "probative value."

It was *John Connally* who was coming.

The following day the governor was scheduled to open a conference of space scientists at the Marriott Motor Inn in Dallas, and the conference, held as the American space program gloried in the success of the Mercury shots, was widely advertised. Inside that Sunday paper which Oswald had read and then so ostentatiously laid down before he went to strap on his revolver was a story on Connally's San Jacinto Bay speech the day before. Connally had been at his manly, flag-waving best. In fact, he had waved three flags—that of Texas, that of America, and the bloody shirt of anticommunism. Before the soaring monument on the San Jacinto battlefield south of Houston, he said the spirit of the Texas Revolution made him stand "just a little taller, just a little stiffer to men like Castro and Khrushchev." His speech was full of death imagery. Connally had read from a letter written by the commander of the Alamo, Colonel William B. Travis, a letter well known to Texas schoolchildren: "The enemy has demanded a surrender—I answered the demand with a cannon shot, and our flag still waves proudly from the walls. Victory or Death!" He quoted another letter, this from a fourteen-year-old boy at the tragic massacre at Goliad, that other place sacred to Texans: "They are going to shoot us in the back. Let us turn our faces and die like men." As for the Battle of San Jacinto, it had imparted "renewed hope in 1836 to all people who were under the foot of tyranny or who were threatened by tyranny. It gives equal hope today, when the foot of tyranny stands but ninety miles from our shore."

To Oswald, the sentiments expressed by Connally were no different from those expressed by General Walker or Richard Nixon. All three represented the fascist edges of the despised monolith. In the first line of his grammatically tortured essay, written aboard ship on his return from Russia to the United States, he had wondered about capitalist and even "fasist" elements in America who "allways profess patriotism toward the land and the people, if not the government, although their movements must surely lead to the bitter destruction of all and everything. . . . In these vieled, formless patriotic gestures, their is the obvious 'axe being ground' by the invested interests of the sponsors of there expensive undertaking." In Oswald's jangled kaleidoscope, Connally, Nixon, and Walker were interchangeable parts of the radical right. During this time, Marina Oswald had taken a picture of Oswald, with his revolver on his hip and his rifle coddled in his right arm and held skyward. Turning her fear into mockery, which was her best and only tool to control him, Marina had scrawled across the picture: "Hunter for fascists. . . . Ha. . . . ha. . . . ha." It was the laughter of terror and despair.

Connally was bad blood for Oswald. On October 5, 1962, six months earlier, Connally had swung into Dallas for two highly publicized campaign speeches, and Oswald on the same day was laid off at the welding company. Now Connally turned up in Dallas, exactly two weeks after he lost his job at Jaggars-Chiles-Stovall, and he was having no luck in finding another job. In Oswald's deck of fantasies, paranoias, and delusions, Connally seemed to be the deadly queen of spades. When the queen's face turned up, bad things happened.

If in April Oswald became a hunter of figures on the right, it is hard to imagine President John F. Kennedy becoming a quarry. The political topics which engaged Oswald's passion and his rage now were civil rights, disarmament with the Soviet Union, and Cuba. Upon the first two, Kennedy acted as Oswald would have approved in the year preceding November 22, 1963, and upon the third, Cuba, Kennedy had become a voice of moderation.

In October 1962, when Oswald lost his first job, Kennedy was dealing with the riots at Ole Miss, and with the lurid archsegregationist Ross Barnett. Meanwhile, Oswald's first target, General Walker, who had gone to Ole Miss, was arrested by Kennedy's federal troops for inciting to riot, and upon his release was welcomed back triumphantly to Dallas.

In the spring of 1963, after Oswald took off for New Orleans to find work, Kennedy was grappling with the massive resistance of George Wallace and the police dogs of Bull Connor in Birmingham and was sending in federal troops to protect the blacks there. On June 10, Kennedy gave his famous speech on disarmament at American University. In it, the president was generous about the Russian people, expressing sentiments with which Oswald could agree: "No government or social system is so evil that its people must be considered as lacking in virtue," Kennedy said. "As Americans we find Communism profoundly repugnant as a negation of personal freedom and dignity. But we must still hail the Russian people for their many achievements—in science and space, in economic and industrial growth, in culture and in acts of courage."

At American University, Kennedy took the occasion to announce the opening of high-level talks between Britain, the United States, and the Soviet Union on a limited nuclear test ban treaty. Throughout the summer, the hopeful possibility of an accord dominated the news. On July 20, a draft agreement was concluded, the first effort to bring nuclear weapons under international control in the eighteen years of the nuclear age.

In late July, both Connally and Oswald also made significant and revealing public appearances. On July 19, Connally traveled to Miami for the national governors' conference, and he went with all the high-flown, defiant rhetoric of Colonel Travis at the Alamo. In this case, however, the crumbling walls were the Southern laws of segregation, which were under frontal attack from Kennedy and the civil rights leaders. Of the public accommodation sections of Kennedy's integration plan, Connally said, "They would be laws which in my judgment would strike at the very foundation of one of our most cherished freedoms: the right to own and manage private property." The governor sweetened his speech with praise of moderation and voluntary desegregation, with talk of education and economic opportunity as the solution to racism, with sympathy for the hard-pressed national leadership. But he got himself and his state foursquare in the Southern camp, making the difference between himself and George Wallace and Ross Barnett only a matter of degree, of tone, of emphasis. Interestingly, Lyndon Johnson, who came from the same Texas soil, had now made the leap ahead of his region. Admittedly, it was easier for Johnson—he was a national rather than a regional figure now—and he was supposed to toe the administration's line. But Johnson's words went farther than mere fealty to the boss. In his opening address to the governors' conference, he opened a gap between himself and his constituency in the audience: "Our foremost challenge is to face and dispose of the problem of human rights which has burdened and compromised our society for a hundred years: the problem of inequality of our Negro citizens."

On July 27, a few days after the conference, Lee Harvey Oswald also made a speech. From New Orleans he ventured to Mobile, Alabama, a town whose hardened Dixie attitude toward race was made all the more impenetrable by its romance with Confederate chivalry, and whose powers and leading lights no doubt subscribed to the view their Governor Wallace had expressed to the U.S. Senate Commerce Committee only a few days earlier: that the civil rights movement was led by Communists and directed from Moscow. Oswald had a cousin who was studying to be a Jesuit priest at Spring Hill College. He had invited Oswald to speak to the Jesuit scholastics about his experiences in Russia. This was unquestionably the most dignified moment in the wretched life of Lee Harvey Oswald. He was to be part of a lecture series which included pastors from other faiths as well as other personages who had something significant to say, and he could be sure that the earnest novitiates would treat him with respect and openness. He made a good impression. The audience, including senior priests, found him articulate, engaging, and informative, if somewhat nervous and humorless. Their expectation that they would derive a clearer view of life in the Soviet Union from this recent resident than from official reports seems to have been fulfilled. He engaged their interest immediately with a personal narrative of his time in the Minsk factory and then expressed his central belief: he disliked capitalism because of its exploitation of the poor. He had been disillusioned by Russian Communism because of the gap between Marxist theory and Soviet reality. "Capitalism doesn't work. Communism doesn't work. In the middle is socialism and that doesn't work either," he said.

If Oswald was a crackpot, the scholastics did not perceive it. They took him seriously, plying him with questions afterwards, and Oswald, far from cowed, answered adroitly, succinctly, and without petulance.

"What impressed you most about Russia?," someone asked.

"The care that the state provides everyone," he replied. "If a man gets sick, no matter what his status is, how poor he is, the state will take care of him. . . . If the Negroes in the United States knew it was so good in Russia, they'd want to go there."

That was as abrasive as Oswald got. In the decisive summer of 1963 in Alabama, only a few weeks after Medgar Evers had been assassinated in neighboring Mississippi, and a few weeks before the Birmingham bombing where four small girls were killed, the remark was scarcely revolutionary, but it showed something about Oswald's political passions: the black man and the little man were those with whom he identified. The country was already preparing for the great march on Washington in a few weeks, when Martin Luther King, Jr., would speak of his dream. Southern governors, including Connally, warned of disruptions the march might bring. Kennedy, on the other hand, told a press conference in July that he hoped leaders in government, in business, and in labor would do something about the fundamental problem that had led to the demonstration. To Oswald, Kennedy might, within the limits of the American system, have seemed something of a hero.

Marina Oswald was to say later that her husband never uttered a harsh or angry word against Kennedy; if he had any negative emotion, it was envy. In the year before the assassination, Oswald avidly read William Manchester's flattering biography of Kennedy, *Portrait of a President,* and Kennedy's *Profiles in Courage.* He had become fascinated by the lives of great men, and to Marina he predicted that he would be "prime minister" of America in twenty years. In the spring and summer of 1963, Marina Oswald was pregnant again, as was Mrs. Kennedy, and Marina followed the course of Mrs. Kennedy's term keenly. In April 1963 the Oswalds watched a televised report of the Kennedys in Palm Beach together to see if Mrs. Kennedy was showing signs of her pregnancy. While later testimony suggested Lee Oswald harbored a mild resentment of the Kennedys' wealth, he told Marina that JFK was qualified to be president and deserved to be president. By the summer, Marina would flip through magazines looking for pictures of Kennedy, and when she found one would demand of Lee that he translate the accompanying article, which he did.

The one man who had a revealing political relationship with Oswald was the pompous, supercilious émigré George de Mohrenshildt. Born in Byelorussia, a man twice Oswald's age, a dandy who luxuriated in his manly good looks and physical strength, de Mohrenshildt seemed to be attracted to a relationship with Oswald largely for reasons of self-amusement. To de Mohrenshildt, Oswald was a bauble, who was the most fun when he was confused by de Mohrenshildt's brilliant arguments and awed by the émigré's elegant worldliness. Moreover, de Mohrenshildt fancied himself to be an old-world aristocrat, and he traded shamelessly on the fact that in the high society of New York in the late 1930s he had known Black Jack Bouvier and his six-year-old daughter, Jacqueline. He also fancied himself to be a forward-looking liberal, although when he left Dallas in the spring of 1963, having seen quite a bit of Lee Oswald in the previous six months, he left to take a job with Papa Doc Duvalier in Haiti. The relationship between de Mohrenshildt and Oswald became a sick one as de Mohrenshildt acted out the role of the overbearing surrogate father who secretly despises and ridicules his adopted son. But Oswald had at last found someone to listen to his half-baked opinions and to joust with him.

After the assassination de Mohrenshildt was the best witness on the question of what moved—and did not move—Lee Harvey Oswald, both politically and emotionally. Before the Warren Commission he was defensive and unhelpful, fearful of the consequences for his professional life of his friendship with the assassin, but as time went on de Mohrenshildt was overcome with guilt and remorse for his trifling with Oswald, and in 1977 he committed suicide after proclaiming that he was a moral conspirator in the assassination of Kennedy. In 1978 the House Assassinations Committee discovered a manuscript which de Mohrenshildt was writing to work out his metaphysical responsibility before he took his life. In it the émigré spoke of both Oswald's admiration for Kennedy and his hatred for John Connally. The extent of Oswald's dissatisfaction with the president is contained in his reaction to the lame jokes that de Mohrenshildt would tell him. Had Lee heard the one about what Kennedy said to the businessmen? "The economic situation is so good that if I weren't your president, I would invest in the stock market right now," says the president. "So would we," reply the businessmen, "—if you weren't our president." Oswald laughed heartily. Even better, he liked the one de Mohrenshildt told about Kennedy's terrible nightmare: the president sits bolt upright one night in bed, turns to his wife, and says, "Jackie, honey, I just

dreamt that I was spending *my own money* and not the government's." Oswald laughed heartily at that as well, "but without
resentment," de Mohrenshildt reported.

"Lee actually admired President Kennedy in his own reserved
way," the memoir continues. "One day we discussed Kennedy's
efforts to bring peace to the world and to end the cold war. 'Great!
Great!' exclaimed Lee. 'If he succeeds, he'll be the greatest president
in the history of this country.' Kennedy's efforts to alleviate and to
end segregation were also admired by Lee, who was sincerely and
profoundly committed to a complete integration of the blacks and
saw in it the future of the United States." As he spoke of these warm
sentiments toward Kennedy, he spoke equally of Oswald's torment
over the unfairness of his military discharge downgrade. It explained
Oswald's "hatred of John Connally," de Mohrenshildt wrote.

In all the literature that has been generated by the assassination
of John F. Kennedy nowhere can there be found a single reference
to any personal animosity that Oswald felt toward the president.
Indeed, the reverse is true. To believe that John F. Kennedy, as the
liberal president of the United States and the humane leader of the
free world, was Oswald's prime target, as the Warren Commission
did, one must believe that between the attack on Walker in April
and the killing of Kennedy in November, Oswald's pathology of
violence broadened into a cosmology of direct violent action against
the highest authority, and that somehow he had worked this all out
in his head. The logic of the Warren Commission was that from
April to November, Oswald moved from ire against right-wing
figures to hatred of all figures of authority generally, regardless of
whether they were benign toward the concerns that moved Oswald:
civil liberties, regard for the working man, accommodation with the
Soviet Union.

The night before his own speech in Mobile, Oswald had listened
approvingly with Marina as the president announced the nuclear
test ban treaty. Even on the subject of Cuba, which in New Orleans
Oswald had taken up as the latest cause to draw attention to himself,
the assassin gave Kennedy the benefit of the doubt. To Marina he
remarked that Kennedy was inclined toward a softer attitude
regarding Cuba than many on the American political scene.

In the few months before Kennedy went to Dallas in November,
his statements on Castro were boilerplate. In Florida on November
18, only four days before his death, his rhetoric about Castro was
far from inflammatory. The administration's efforts "to isolate the
virus of Communism" had met with success, Kennedy thought, and

Castro, once a formidable symbol of revolution in the hemisphere, had faded. Kennedy even berated those stale naysayers who continued to complain about Castro and blamed all the hemisphere's problems on Communism or on right-wing generals. "The harsh facts of poverty and social justice will not yield easily to promises or good will," the president said.

Even if one accepts Oswald's concern for Cuba as sincere and deeply felt, is it conceivable that Kennedy's statements on Cuba in the latter part of 1963 could have become the motive for assassination? The Warren Commission thought so. Its members never considered the difference between benign and violent political action, for that moved the question from the familiar turf of politics to the unfamiliar area of emotion and psychology. They were unconcerned to untwist Oswald's "twisted ideological view." By simply labeling it *twisted*, they abrogated their responsibility to explain it.

At issue is Oswald's will to murder, whether, at its core, it was emotional or intellectual. Toward Connally, he seemed to have a simple grudge, a grudge which engaged his emotions and his anger and which was consistent, probably as a secondary consideration, with his overall political instincts. The members of the Warren Commission and later the House Committee on Assassinations may have been reluctant to attempt to untangle Oswald's psychology, but Marina, who knew him best, offered important testimony on that subject.

She testified three times before the Warren Commission. Each time, in greater and more convincing detail, she revealed important episodes she had either forgotten or repressed, as well as providing more convincing explanations of her husband's state of mind. In her first appearance, as the commission's very first witness only six weeks after the assassination, she regretfully acknowledged that she now accepted her husband as the president's murderer. Why had he done it? For good reasons or bad, she replied, her husband wanted to become a memorable figure of history. The commission seized upon this as a simple, comprehensible, and salable motive, and never let go of it. Of Connally, she testified that her husband had promised to vote for him for governor if he had a chance. In her second appearance, in June 1964, she suddenly remembered the "Nixon incident," with her husband shouting at her through the bathroom door, "You always get in my way!" but the commission promptly dismissed the entire matter as insubstantial. Her third appearance took place in Dallas only three weeks before the Warren Commission Report was released, when its conclusions were already set in stone. It was no time to reopen a Pandora's box of motives, but as she was questioned by Congressman Hale Boggs of Louisiana, she said, seemingly out of thin air, "I feel in my own mind that Lee did not have President Kennedy as a prime target when he assassinated him."

"Well, who was it?" Boggs asked, almost languorously.

"I think it was Connally," she replied. "That's my personal opinion—that he perhaps was shooting at Governor Connally, the governor of Texas."

This was not what they wanted to hear, and Senator Richard Russell jumped on her. "You've testified before us before that Lee told you, if he was back in Texas, he would vote for Connally for governor. Why do you think he would shoot him?"

"I feel that the reason that he had Connally in his mind was on account of his discharge from the marines and various letters they exchanged between the Marine Corps and the governor's office, but actually, I didn't think that he had any idea concerning President Kennedy."

"Well, did he ever express any hostility towards Governor Connally?" Boggs asked.

"He never expressed that to me—his displeasure or hatred of Connally," she said, holding her ground, for he seems to have expressed so little of a political nature to her. "I feel that there could have been some connection, due to the fact that Lee was dishonorably discharged from the corps. That's my personal opinion."

Instead of pursuing this new and highly significant tack or calmly attempting to elicit more from her, Boggs and Russell proceeded to browbeat the widow with the inconsistency of this with her prior testimony, and they quickly left the subject altogether. No reference to it whatever appears in their final report because, of course, the final report was already written.

It would be fourteen years before an additional, decisive detail was added to this thorny question of motive. In 1978, Marina Oswald testified before the House Assassinations Committee. Almost offhandedly, assigning no particular significance to it herself and finding that the politicians of the House were no more interested than the Warren Commission had been, she told of how Connally's brush-off letter in February 1962, the origin of the grudge, had arrived at their Minsk apartment in a big, white envelope whose front flaunted the large, smiling face of John Connally, advertising his candidacy for governor of Texas.

Roads Taken and Not Taken

THE ORIGIN OF PRESIDENT JOHN F. KENNEDY's trip to Texas in November 1963 is a subject which has passed through the prism of shame and collective guilt and emerged as a blur. With its terrible result, it appears that nobody really wanted the trip. JFK was irritated to have to make it. John Connally had stalled it and argued against it, and when he could no longer resist it had wanted Dallas eliminated from the itinerary. It was laid on without Lyndon Johnson's counsel, and when the vice president heard about the final arrangements, he resented his exclusion. And Senator Yarborough, the liberal foil to Connally and the fourth player in the political prelude to tragedy, was merely bracing himself against the fierce political winds that were swirling around him.

Even the purpose of the trip remains in dispute. Was Kennedy going primarily to raise money for his 1964 campaign? Was he going to heal a rift between the liberal and conservative factions of the Texas Democratic party represented by Yarborough and Connally? Was he going to shore up a shaky Connally governorship? Did Lyndon Johnson need the presidential trip to bolster his own standing and ensure that he would remain on the ticket the next year? The survivors of Elm Street agree on one thing in speaking later to history: no one was to blame. Nor is there value in applying vague standards of moral or metaphysical guilt for the tragedy, although those standards were liberally applied in its aftermath, especially by the city of Dallas, which was tormented then—and still is—over whether its atmosphere of hostility and even hate for the Kennedys influenced Lee Harvey Oswald in any way.

That said, the presidential trip to Texas was an unmitigated political disaster, even before the presidential motorcade made its fateful left turn from Houston Street into Elm Street. Even if there had been no shooting, it would have reverberated for weeks and probably months as an embarrassment to all involved. It was politics at its least elevating.

By John Connally's account, President Kennedy had been pushing for more than a year and a half to come to Texas, extending back to a time even before Connally became governor. The state of Texas, whose native son was vice president and which had provided the margin of victory in 1960, had contributed virtually nothing to the national Democratic party since his election, and the party labored under a $4 million debt. Kennedy was disgruntled. The flow of "oil" into the tanks of the national party was long overdue. If the president was irritated at having to travel to Texas, his irritation lay in the necessity of the president himself having to unclog the pipes when his vice president or a strong governor should have been able to handle the job without him.

Connally has written that he held off a presidential trip to his state as long as he could, but in any event he was in no position to help or to host until he became governor in January. He has also written that his state recognized its financial obligation to the national party and that it would have discharged it—eventually. But his distance from the national administration and his disagreement with the essence of the Kennedy program indicate that he would have stalled on that responsibility as long as he could.

Through the spring, Connally was preoccupied with getting his first programs through the state legislature, so it wasn't until June that serious planning finally began, with Kennedy again taking the initiative. Early in the month, Kennedy undertook a whirlwind Western swing that included commencement addresses at the Air Force Academy and in San Diego, consultations, and speeches in Honolulu before he returned to Washington for his remarkable address on disarmament on June 10. After his address to the air force cadets he touched down briefly in El Paso, where he was met by Governor Connally and by Vice President Johnson, who had addressed the Naval Academy graduates that same morning. After an open-air motorcade the three repaired to the Cortez Hotel downtown to talk politics. As Connally remembered the meeting, the president got right to the point, even before the governor could take a chair.

"Well, Lyndon," Kennedy said with a twinkle, "do you think we're *ever* going to have that fund-raising affair in Texas?"

"You have the governor here, Mr. President. Maybe *now* you can get a commitment from him."

It was a trap Connally could not wriggle out of. As he would put it later, his string had run out. "Fine, Mr. President, let's start planning your trip," he said with resignation.

The symbolic significance of Texas and Massachusetts was clearly important to both Kennedy and Johnson. They represented the Boston-Austin axis of the administration and much ballyhoo had been made of that at the 1960 convention. It was not long into the conversation before Kennedy gave voice to it again.

"If we don't raise funds in any other state, I want to do so in Massachusetts and in Texas," he said. "If we don't carry any other state next year, I want to carry Texas and Massachusetts."

For Kennedy and Johnson, that was a relatively straightforward sentimental proposition, but it was not so simple for Connally. In a state with two-year terms for the governor, he too faced election the following year, and his chances for reelection did not lie in associating himself with the national administration and its goals. In the culture of Kennedy's America, where grace and elegance and good looks counted for much, Connally had derived considerable mileage from the illusion that he was a Texas version of the Kennedys. But his politics were as conservative as those of most national Republicans in 1952 and 1956, and Texas had just put the Republican John Tower in the Senate. Connally was being asked to spend his political credit for the national liberals, when his constituents loathed the spirit of the Kennedy administration more than the governor himself did.

Moreover, with his election to the governorship, Connally had, at long last, emerged somewhat from the shadow of Lyndon Johnson and was finally becoming something of his own man. He was determined to nurture a clear identity, separate and distinct from both Johnson and Kennedy. Putting himself out for their cause would only improve the fortunes of his archrival in Texas, Senator Ralph Yarborough. Connally detested Yarborough and Yarborough despised Connally, and their mutual contempt extended back to the donnybrook of 1956.

So here in El Paso came the president and the vice president to propose a grand tour of his state, and for Connally the proposal was fraught with political risk. Kennedy plowed on undaunted, apparently insensitive to Connally's problem. He proposed not one political fund-raiser but four, and Connally gulped in disbelief. This was not so much a political incursion as a full-scale invasion. The president thought dinners in Houston, San Antonio, Fort Worth, and Dallas were about right. Whether Kennedy made this suggestion seriously, or simply to test Connally's loyalty, is unclear. He was too good a politician not to understand that four political dinners in one visit would create the unseemly impression of a president come only to milk the wealth of the state. But Kennedy forged ahead. Maybe Lyndon Johnson's birthday, August 27, would provide the right pretext for the political fund-raisers. To the Texans, this too was a lousy idea. Johnson said nothing, his eyes hooded and downcast.

"Well, Mr. President, I would like to think about that," Connally stalled. "You know my feelings for the vice president. His birthday is always a time for celebration, but the very people you want to reach aren't likely to be here. Texas gets mighty hot in August. It's the worst month of the year to have a fund-raising affair—for anybody. People are not interested in politics during the dog days, and I think it would be a serious mistake to come then."

"If you don't like that date, what date do you like?" Kennedy shot back. Connally hedged, but the president would not have it. The easy bantering tone was done. "Let's get on with it," he said in a clipped voice. "We've been talking about this for a year and a half or more. Let's get an agreement about what we're going to do and get together and start making our plans."

No agreement was forged that night in El Paso, only the promise by Connally to come up with a plan. Lyndon Johnson badgered the governor from time to time through the summer. On one call he said again that the president wanted four or five fund-raisers.

"That's a mistake," Connally snapped.

"Well, that is what he wants, and you had better be prepared to do it, or better be prepared to give him a real good reason why you can't do it."

Johnson might have gotten away with that tactic in his congressional office in 1939, but not now.

"All right, I will work out something," Connally replied stiffly, "and be back in touch with you."

In due course, after talking with state legislators and his men in the party, Connally did come up with a plan: one political dinner rather than four, to be held in Austin in the fall. If the president wanted to visit other Texas cities, those stops should be dignified, presidential, and essentially nonpolitical. One fund-raiser, if properly organized, could raise as much money as four anyway, the governor felt, and Austin was the one enclave in Texas where Democrats of all persuasions could come without feeling themselves to be on somebody else's high ground.

The subject languished until the fall, and Connally preferred that it languish indefinitely. In mid-September, however, the White House began to push the governor for a final plan, and a meeting with the president was set for October 3.

★

On September 24 or September 25—the difference is important— Lee Harvey Oswald left New Orleans for Mexico City, where his destination was the Cuban embassy. He wanted to explore the possibility of returning to Russia. His inability to fit into American society had evidently made him forget how the Communist bureaucreats could cruelly buffet him. But in Mexico City, those memories would return in a rush, as the Cuban and Soviet embassies squashed any dream he may have had of a heroic return. They scarcely let him in the front door. Oswald's trip to Mexico was such a blow that it very likely cancels the possibility that, two months later, his impulse to murder had the motive of promoting the Cuban or the Soviet cause.

His preoccupations at home were mundane, not geopolitical. Since August he had ceased to search for gainful employment; at this point, it had become too hard and too embarrassing. That he had been arrested in New Orleans for distributing Fair Play for Cuba Committee pamphlets—in short, for leftist activity—made him even less employable than he had been before. But the root of his job troubles lay in his downgraded military discharge. If that could be corrected, things might be different.

The Warren Commission was to receive persuasive testimony that on his way to Mexico City, Oswald stopped for an afternoon in Austin. He came to see Governor Connally. There he was seen having lunch at Trek's Restaurant before he went to the state capitol, to see again if Connally wouldn't intervene for him over his discharge. Perhaps in person the governor would be more responsive. There is no record of Oswald's visit, no entry in the guest book, but Lee Harvey Oswald evidently did not want to sign the brocaded guest book of John Connally, whom he had vilified as the source of his misery. This time Oswald got his brush-off orally. He was told that the governor did not handle military matters and Oswald was directed to the Selective Service. There he was served by a clerk named Lee Dannelly, who later remembered him well. She remembered him partly because he was so ugly; in fact, he was the ugliest man she had ever seen, but Dannelly had other reasons to remember Oswald. He gave his name as Harvey Oswald, and she searched for it without success in the available files. After he explained the downgrade of his discharge, he said he had been informed that if he lived an "upright" life for two years, he could appeal the status again. The undesirable discharge was making it impossible for him to get a good job, he told her, and it was embarrassing to his family.

This was scarcely a fleeting encounter. Oswald was with the clerk for about thirty minutes. The end result was the same as it had been since he got his first reply from Connally. He was told to write a new address far away, to another agency, about another form, a different procedure, a different board of appeals.

Oswald left Dannelly's office to board the bus for Mexico City, clutching his military records as if they were atomic secrets. He had been unprepared, as always, for the magnificent indifference of the Communists.

★

Before he went to Washington to see President Kennedy, Connally went to Dallas. He was the reluctant captain, ordered by his admiral to do what he considered to be unwise. As a good sailor, he would swallow his pride, go along with the plan because there was no alternative, put the best face on it for the good of Old Glory. A captain, he told his business supporters, could scarcely bar the admiral from boarding his ship. By this stance, he separated himself from the president, without disobeying him. In Dallas he met with the power elite: the chairman of the Dallas Citizens Council, which had controlled Dallas politics for forty years; the president of the Chamber of Commerce; the head of the Mercantile, the oldest bank in Dallas; and executives from the two Dallas newspapers. These were Connally's kind of folks, and in such meetings he was at his best.

Dallas, Texas, as represented by the men in Connally's meeting, was deeply concerned about its image. It wanted to be known as bursting with vitality, a city of limitless opportunity and big dreams, where the myth of Texas wealth was a palpable reality. It was, however, increasingly being portrayed as "a leading center of hate and hysteria" in America. The imagemakers fretted at how people on the outside associated their city with its radical fringe, and yet that fringe, in the past few years, had taken a few memorable actions that were hard to play down, especially the spitting incident against Lyndon Johnson in 1960 (and a similar incident against Adlai Stevenson two weeks after Connally came to Dallas to meet with the business establishment).

If Dallas despised Johnson and Stevenson, it loved John Connally. He was their man on horseback, fitting perfectly Dallas's image of how a leader should look, talk, and act. In turn, Connally liked the way Dallas practiced politics. The city chose its mayor as if it were a pure oligarchy. The businessmen determined the candidate, and the citizens ratified their choice.

Now, at the Adolphus Hotel, Connally virtually apologized to the Dallas leadership for the president's insistence on coming to Texas and to Dallas. Since he could not prevent it altogether, he could at least prevent it from being a liberal love feast.

"I don't intend to default to the liberals," Connally told the group. "I've got to have a nonpolitical body to represent Dallas, and you gentlemen are it by your associations."

Connally was, however, sensitive to the concerns of his listeners about the reputation of Dallas and he worried that some embarrassment would befall the president there. Regardless of the liberal-conservative issue, a discourtesy—an egg or a tomato or a whirling placard (as had struck Lady Bird outside the Baker Hotel)—would reflect badly on Dallas and on the state and be an embarrassment to Connally personally as the president's official host. Connally left the meeting for Washington to argue that Dallas should be reconsidered as a stop in the president's itinerary.

The news of the Dallas visit broke in the Dallas paper on September 26, and others were considerably more fearful of the stop than Connally. Chief among them was Byron Skelton, the courtly national committeeman from northeast Texas. Since May, Skelton had been writing letters to the Texas contingent in the White House about a presidential trip to Texas, alternating enthusiasm and irritation, but he had been excluded from the planning of the trip, and so everything he wrote and said subsequently was dismissed as sour grapes. The Dallas stop worried Skelton, and he worried for the safety of the president. He noted General Edwin Walker's taunts—that President Kennedy was a menace to the free world—which had been prominently reported in the *Dallas Morning News*. As far as he was concerned, the paper had been writing stories for years that were tailor-made to stir up an unbalanced person.

In Washington, Senator William Fulbright of Arkansas was a

grim-faced Cassandra. His distrust and downright fear of Dallas went back to the early 1950s, when his had been the sole vote in the U.S. Senate against appropriations for Senator McCarthy's red-scare campaign, and Dallas had generated a major proportion of the hate mail that followed. The *Dallas Morning News* had made Fulbright its regular whipping boy, especially when he became chairman of the Senate Foreign Relations Committee, charging him with being a "red louse" and unrepresentative of his state. The reactionary Hunts of Dallas had poured a pot of money into unsuccessful campaigns to defeat him. It was a *physically* dangerous place to Fulbright, and he predicted that, given the current environment, Kennedy would suffer some abuse. On October 3, the day before the president met with Connally for the final planning, Fulbright had accompanied Kennedy to Arkansas for the dedication of the Greers Ferry Dam in Heber Springs and for a rousing speech about the rising New South at the state fairgrounds in Little Rock. Repeatedly, along the way, Fulbright returned to the subject of Dallas, warning the president not to go there because it was a very dangerous place.

Despite the warnings and the controversy, the president seemed unconcerned. There was no way he could make a swing of major Texas cities without going to Dallas. That Dallas had voted against him in 1960 hardly made the city unique. As for demonstrations, he had a theory. Generally, the nasty characters in any given American city numbered no more than fifty individuals, and what Dallas could muster would be no nastier than what the fringe might stage anywhere else. When the worrywarts brought up the Johnson episode at the Baker Hotel, Kennedy reminded them that during that same campaign of 1960 he, too, had gone to Dallas and had had one of the more courteous receptions of the entire campaign.

Before Connally saw the president he ventured to Capitol Hill for a meeting with the Texas congressional delegation. It was a breakfast in the Speaker's Room. The governor's task was almost schoolmarmish: he needed to assign to each congressman the number of $100 tickets he had to sell for the Austin political dinner. The congressmen would not have needed those assignments if the governor weren't worried about gathering a full house in Austin, and Connally's level of irritation was high. The situation was further complicated by the fact that Senator Yarborough was being given a testimonial dinner in Austin only five weeks before the president's. Ticket sales to the Yarborough dinner had been brisk. On top of his worries about conservative donors, he now had to worry whether the liberals would be ready to fork out a second $100 so quickly. Chain-smoking and clearly nervous, Connally now said to the congressmen:

"Fellows, the reason I'm here is that I'm meeting with the president in a few hours about his trip to Texas. I don't know what to say. They're going to want me to tell them where and when and how to get money in Texas for the party. Now, I've made a few calls around and, frankly, the people who are supporting John Kennedy in Texas are not the ones with money."

At the table was Congressman Henry Gonzalez of San Antonio, whose relationship with John Kennedy went back to the early fifties, when Gonzalez had been the only Hispanic on the San Antonio city council, and whose cry "Viva Kennedy" to an audience in East Harlem during the campaign of 1960 had started a national wave of adulation for Kennedy among Hispanic Americans. Gonzalez came to this meeting already in a huff. He had heard that San Antonio was slated to get only a few hours on Kennedy's Texas itinerary, when it was the only major Texas city to go for Kennedy in the 1960 election. Moreover, Gonzalez had promoted the naming of a San Antonio high school after Kennedy, and when it was authorized it was the only school in America named after the president. The thought of Dallas and Fort Worth getting nearly a full day rankled Gonzalez considerably.

Furthermore, Congressman Gonzalez knew better than anyone at the meeting of the personal dangers that lurked in Texas for national liberals. As the only true New Frontiersman in the Texas delegation, he was the prime recipient of hate mail from the right, and it came to him by the bale. Three months before, he had been one of only twenty congressmen to vote against further funding for the House Un-American Activities Committee, and shortly afterwards he got a little message from the Minutemen, who among other things held field exercises with machine guns outside San Antonio. He took seriously the Minutemen's message: "You are a traitor. We have the hair trigger on your neck." The warning carried a picture of cross hairs in a telescopic sight, and below it, the words, "In Memoriam, Henry B. Gonzalez."

These considerations aside, Gonzalez simply did not like Connally or anything he stood for. During his campaign for governor, Connally had made the mistake of calling up Gonzalez and referring to him in Spanish as "Papacito Grande," the label for the "Big Boss." Gonzalez prided himself on being a man of the people rather than a big shot who threw his weight around. As he heard Connally poor-mouth the presidential trip now, his blood roiled.

Connally was saying, "I think [the trip] is a mistake. You know the people who are for Kennedy are the people without money. I've checked with businessmen, and they aren't about to contribute to his campaign—"

"Just a minute, Governor," Gonzalez cut in. "Whom did you call in San Antonio?" Gonzalez knew the answer to his question. If Connally had called anyone in his hometown, it would have been the blue-blood banker, Walter MacAllister, or the millionaire builder H. P. "Hap" Zachery, who was a Horatio Alger character like the governor himself. The governor stammered, not about to confess in this crowd.

". . . because I know some people in San Antonio who support the president," Gonzalez pressed, and then delivered his shot. "If you called the ones you've been appointing, Governor, they're all Republicans! I'll get you businessmen. You may not like them, though, because they won't support you!" Immediately an uproar broke out, and the meeting ended in loud, fractious dissension.

When the governor arrived in the Oval Office, President Kennedy greeted him warmly. There was between them a competition of vanities as well as politics, and it was almost sexual. The topic of Connally's good looks had been hotly debated among the Kennedys, and Jack Kennedy had subscribed to Jackie Kennedy's judgment that Connally was "too pretty to be handsome." Now the president pointed to the couch and took his customary place in his rocking chair. The president still had his heart set on four or five fund-raisers. Apparently, Lyndon Johnson had made no effort to dissuade him. Connally was prepared.

"Mr. President, I think that is a mistake," he said emphatically. "We want the money, yes, but we also need to position you in such a way that you're going to benefit politically from it, and it doesn't look like all you're interested in is the money of the state. Frankly, if you come down, and we try to get on five fund-raising events in the principal cities of Texas, people are going to think that all you're interested in is the financial rape of the state."

That was strong language in 1963, and it registered. The president relented. "Well, all right. What do you suggest?"

Connally laid out his plan, which he said was the product of wide discussion among the Texas political community. He added one final suggestion. He hoped Mrs. Kennedy would come with the president to Texas. All the events would include women as well as men, the governor said. "The women want to see her. They've read a great deal about her. They want to see what her hairdo looks like and what her clothes look like. It's important to them."

"I agree with you," Kennedy said. "I'll talk to her about it." Jackie Kennedy was in Greece, resting on Aristotle Onassis's yacht, trying to get her spirit and her strength back after the loss in August of her child Patrick.

That evening, Connally went out to the Elms in northwest Washington to have dinner with the Johnsons, bracing himself. When his meeting with the president was scheduled two weeks before, the White House had specifically requested Connally to keep it confidential from Lyndon Johnson. That had surprised the governor, and he was doubly surprised when Johnson was absent from the Oval Office. At the door, Johnson was visibly irritated.

"I suppose you think I don't have any interest in what happens in Texas?"

"No, Lyndon," Connally replied stiffly. "I know you're extremely interested in what is happening in Texas."

"Why didn't you tell me?" Johnson demanded.

"I assumed you knew I was going to see the president," Connally replied. "After all, it's not my prerogative to say who is in that Oval Office. I assumed if the president wanted you there, you would be there."

Connally was touching a raw nerve, for it was clear enough that Kennedy had not wanted Johnson present. It had been widely noticed that Kennedy acted differently in meetings with Johnson present—seeming deferential, even a bit cowed, as if he were intimidated by Johnson, politically if not physically. Given the bond between Connally and Johnson, Kennedy did not want them to gang up on him.

"You could have told me beforehand what you had in mind," Johnson sulked.

"You knew basically what I had in mind," Connally protested, perhaps too much, thinking of their telephone conversations over the summer. "Anyway, here is what we said . . ." and he related the substance of the Oval Office conversation. Over the twenty-five years of their intimacy, they had been in this situation many times before. Johnson was hurt by Connally's secretiveness, as if they were not supposed to have any secrets between them; at least, Connally should have none. Connally knew what to do. "I'm sorry, Lyndon," he said softly. "I would have talked to you before I went to see the president. Frankly, I assumed you would be there. When I got into the

Oval Office I was rather surprised that you weren't there, but I had no choice but to go ahead and discuss the trip." In time, Johnson settled down, as Connally knew he would.

★

That evening, at about the time Governor Connally, on a cordial note, left the Elms, another social evening in Dallas was drawing to a close. That was the birthday celebration of a Dallas attorney named Carroll Jarnagin, a divorcé and a thirty-seven-year-old plaintiff's lawyer with moderately liberal political views, who had twice unsuccessfully run for the state legislature. Jarnagin was carousing joyfully with a legal client, a woman he liked to describe as an "exotic dancer" whose stage name was Robin Hood. Miss Hood had appeared *en déshabillé* at various lively clubs in Dallas, and toward the end of their evening, over the course of which Jarnagin had consumed a considerable amount of Johnny Walker Red, Robin Hood proposed that they stop by the Carousel Club. She wanted to talk to the owner, a beefy man named Jack Rubenstein, also known as Jack Ruby, about returning to his stage. They arrived at the Carousel around 10:00 P.M. Jarnagin was mellow, but by no means insensate, and the couple took a table not far from the ticket booth at the head of the stairs.

Not long after they were settled Jarnagin noticed a wiry man in his twenties at the ticket booth, about five feet and nine inches in height, and oddly dressed for someone out on the town. He was loudly demanding to see Ruby. The bouncer appeared, and directed the new arrival to the man whom Robin Hood identified for Jarnagin as the owner. Ruby and his visitor took the table next to them, and the following conversation ensued.

Ruby greeted his caller by name, a name Jarnagin later could not recall as he attempted to reconstruct the conversation.

"What are you doing here?" Ruby asked.

"Don't call me by my name," the visitor said testily.

"What name are you using?"

"H. L. Lee."

"What do you want?"

"I need some money. I just got in from New Orleans. I need a place to stay, and a job."

"I noticed you hadn't been around," Ruby said. "What were you doing in New Orleans?"

"There was a street fight, and I got put in jail."

"What charge?"

"Disturbing the peace."

"How did you get back?"

"Hitchhiked. I just got in."

"You have a family, don't you? Can't you stay with them?"

"They're in Irving, and they don't know I'm back. I want to get a place to myself."

"You'll get the money after the job is done."

"What about half now, and half after the job is done?" Lee said.

"No . . . but don't worry, I'll have the money for you after the job is done."

"How much?" Lee asked.

"We've already agreed on that," Ruby said, and then leaned forward to whisper something which Jarnagin did not hear.

"How do I know that you can do the job?" Ruby asked.

"I'm a marine sharpshooter."

"Are you sure that you can do the job without hitting anybody but the governor?"

"I'm sure. I've got the equipment ready."

"Have you tested it? Will you need to practice any?"

"Don't worry about that. I don't need any practice. When will the governor be here?"

"Oh, he'll be here plenty of times during campaigns," Ruby replied.

"Where can I do the job?" Lee asked.

"From the roof of some building."

"No, that's too risky. Too many people around."

"But they'll be watching the parade. They won't notice you."

"Afterwards they would tear me to pieces before I could get away."

"Then do it from here—from a window," Ruby said.

"How would I get in?"

"I'll tell the porter to let you in."

"Won't there be people in the place?"

"I can close the place for the parade and leave word with the porter to let you in."

"What about the porter?"

"I can tell him to leave after letting you in. He won't know anything."

"I don't want any witnesses around."

"You'll be alone."

"How do I get away? There won't be much time afterwards."

"The back door."

"What about the rifle? What do I do if the police run in while I'm running out?"

"Hide the rifle. You just heard the shot and ran in from the parade to see what was going on. In the confusion you can walk out the front door in the crowd."

"No, they might shoot me first," Lee said. "There must be time for me to get out the back way before the police come in. Can you lock the front door after I come in and leave the back door open?"

"That would get me involved. How could I explain that you were in my club with a rifle and the front door locked?"

"You left the front door open, and it was locked from the inside when somebody slipped in, while you were watching the parade. What about the money? When do I get the money?"

"I'll have it here for you."

"But when? I'm not going to have much time after the shooting to get away."

"I'll have the money on me, and I'll run in first and hand it to you and you can run on out the back way."

"I can't wait long. Why can't you leave the money in here?"

"How do I know you'll do the job?"

"How do I know you will show up with the money after the job is done?"

"You can trust me. Besides, you'll have the persuader."

"The rifle? I want to get away from it as soon as it's used."

"You can trust me," Ruby said.

"How about giving me half of the money just before the job is done, and then you can send me the other half later?"

"I can't turn the money loose until the job is done. If there's a slip-up and you don't get him, they'll pick the money up immediately. I couldn't tell them I gave half of it to you in advance. They'd think I double-crossed them. . . . You'll just have to trust me to hand you the money as soon as the job is done. There is no other way . . . Remember, they want the job done just as bad as you want the money. After this is done, they may want to use you again."

"Not that it makes any difference, but what have you got against the governor?" Lee asked.

"He won't work with us on paroles. With a few of the right boys out, we could really open up this state, with a little cooperation from the governor. The boys in Chicago have no place to go, no place to operate. They've clamped the lid down in Chicago. Cuba is closed. Everything is dead. Look at this place—half empty. If we can open up this state, we could pack this place every night. Those boys will spend if they have the money. Remember, we're right next to Mexico. There'd be money for everybody, if we can open up this state."

"How do you know that the governor won't work with you?"

"It's no use. He's been in Washington too long. They're too straight up there. After they've been there awhile they get to thinking like the attorney general. The attorney general. . . . now there's a guy the boys would like to get, but it's no use. He stays in Washington too much."

"A rifle shoots as far in Washington as it does here, doesn't it?" Lee said.

"Forget it. That would bring the heat on everywhere, and the feds would get into everything. No, forget about the attorney general."

"Killing the governor of Texas will put the heat on too, won't it?"

"Not really, they'll think some crackpot or Communist did it, and it will be written off as an unsolved crime."

"That is, if I get away."

"You'll get away. All you have to do is run out the back door."

"What kind of door is there back there? It won't accidentally lock on me, will it?"

"No," Ruby said. "You can get out that way without any trouble. It's a safe way out. I'll show you, but not now."

There was a distraction, and Jarnagin missed some interchanges. Then he heard Lee say, "There's really only one building to do it from, the one that covers Main, Elm, and Commerce."

"Which one is that?" Ruby asked.

"The school book building, close to the triple underpass."

"What's wrong with doing it from here?"

"What if he goes down another street?"

Suddenly, the man called Lee noticed Jarnagin watching him intently. "Who's that?" he said abruptly. "He's from the FBI . . . ," and the conversation terminated. Lee left quickly afterwards.

The following day, October 5, Jarnagin called the Texas Department of Public Safety and related the conversation. He requested that the governor be informed, and he felt his report to the authorities had ended his civic duty.

After the assassination, more than a score of witnesses stepped forward with stories of seeing Ruby and Oswald together in conversation before November 22. For the most part, they were cranks and exhibitionists and self-promoters, and they ranged from places across the country as far away as Los Angeles and Denver. As a professional man, trained in law and in investigation, Jarnagin was the most credible.

The credibility of the Jarnagin account rests upon the following concatenation of events. The first news of President Kennedy's intention to come to Dallas appeared in the *Dallas Morning News* on September 26, a week before Governor Connally went to Washington to finalize the plan. On October 3 Oswald returned from his devastating trip to Mexico City, where he had been spurned by both the Cubans and the Russians in an effort to get a visa to Cuba. Less than two weeks later, on October 15, Oswald gained his employment at the Texas State Book Depository.

After the assassination Jarnagin recognized Lee Harvey Oswald in the newspaper as the man in Ruby's booth, and he sat down, carefully reconstructed the conversation, and mailed it special delivery to J. Edgar Hoover at the FBI. Thereafter he was interviewed by over eighteen investigators from various law enforcement agencies. He never altered his story, and he remains a lawyer in good standing with the Texas bar. Two months after the assassination, in February 1964, Connally's old University of Texas buddy and roommate in naval fighter training, now the district attorney of Dallas, Henry Wade, invited Jarnagin to his home. It would have been Wade's duty to prosecute Oswald for murder, but he had to settle for the prosecution of Jack Ruby. The jury had been empaneled, but evidence had not yet been presented, when Jarnagin went to Wade's house. For four hours they talked. Wade found Jarnagin's story startling, but parts of it did not ring true. The suggestion that organized crime was behind the assassination sounded wrong to Wade. If the syndicate was having problems with paroles for mob figures, it would target the district attorney rather than the governor. It was he, not Connally, who would have been on the "firing line" with the mob.

"I can't put you on the stand without being satisfied that you are telling the truth," Wade told Jarnagin. "We've got a good case here; if they prove we are putting an unreliable witness on the stand, it might hurt us."

The conviction of Jack Ruby was Wade's overriding consideration, not the uncovering of a conspiracy. His best evidence, of course, was the television footage of Ruby killing Oswald. It was hard to get more compelling than that. The conspiracy angle only muddied the waters for him, and he was disinclined to take Jarnagin seriously. Nor was the Warren Commission inclined to take seriously the notion that Governor Connally had been Oswald's target. For the country to have lost its president in the greatest crime of the century, when the chief of state might have been an incidental or accidental target, was an irony too grotesque to contemplate.

Jarnagin himself was later to claim that, like so many others who purportedly had information about a conspiracy, he was physically attacked. Shortly after his interview with Henry Wade, he said he was shot in the leg with a drug pellet, later identified as a concentrated dose of amphetamines, which sent him into the hospital for three months. Jarnagin's interpretation of this attack was that there were powerful forces out there that wanted to prevent the testimony which might validate a relationship between Ruby and Oswald or a conspiracy generally.

History has left us with this: The Warren Commission denied there was a conspiracy, denied that Oswald and Ruby ever knew one another, and denied that the Soviets, the Cubans, or organized crime was behind the assault on Connally and Kennedy. Thirteen years later, in 1978, the House Select Committee on Assassinations supported the Warren Commission in denying that the Cubans, the Soviets, or the mob was involved, *but* it berated the Warren Commission for not pursuing more vigorously the conspiracy angle, and indeed concluded that President Kennedy "was probably assassinated as a result of a conspiracy." It was a conspiracy they were at a loss to describe.

★

On October 21, a dynamo from Wisconsin named Jerry Bruno, known as the best of the advance men, received official notification of the presidential trip to Texas. From Walter Jenkins in Lyndon Johnson's office three days later, Bruno got a proposed schedule and was told that it represented Governor Connally's wishes. As a matter of protocol Connally, as the state's governor, was the official host. More importantly, as a matter of purpose, it was Connally's friends—the hostile, the disenchanted, and the annoyed of Texas—to whom the president wanted to appeal. The White House was determined to be accommodating to the governor.

Almost immediately the trouble began. As word of the itinerary got out, the liberals, who were Kennedy's real friends in Texas, howled in protest. San Antonio, the city of "Viva Kennedy," would get the president for only a few hours. In Dallas, the governor wanted the president to speak at the shiny, modern Trade Mart, the pride of the Dallas commercial establishment. The president was to be spirited efficiently from one swank event to another, seeing little of the general public.

That was as the liberals saw it. Connally saw it differently. It was his constituency, the moderates and the conservatives, whom Kennedy had specifically expressed an interest in seeing. Connally was accommodating him and putting himself out considerably to do so, as he devised a set of basically "nonpolitical" events which would give the president a chance to woo his opponents. Among the big businessmen of corporate Texas, Kennedy's actions in rolling back steel prices the previous year remained an open sore. Then, the president had employed the FBI, the Justice Department, and the threat of wage-price legislation to browbeat the steel industry into forgoing a major price increase. To the corporate world, this was the worst kind of government interference. In the course of the battle, Kennedy had said the unforgivable about businessmen: "My father always told me that all businessmen are sons of bitches, but I never believed him until now." The line reverberated a year later, and Kennedy was still trying to live it down. To Connally, Kennedy had said, "If these business people are silly enough to think I'm going to dismantle the free enterprise system, they're crazy."

Connally was content to let Kennedy try to prove he was not the devil. The Trade Mart speech was to be Kennedy's opportunity to do so.

While Connally and his forces pushed to narrow the president's exposure, Yarborough sought to widen it, and the central irony of that tragic trip to Texas lies in the fact that the compromise itself led to a plan that put the president in harm's way. If either Connally or Yarborough had won totally in their demands, the president and the governor would not have been shot. In roads taken and not taken, the fates were cruel.

The man in the middle was Jerry Bruno. Before he left for Texas, Bruno had met with Johnson's man, Walter Jenkins, with Ken O'Donnell in the White House, and with Yarborough's lieutenant, and was briefed on the feud between the Texas Guelphs and Ghibellines. It all sounded pretty routine to Bruno, who always encountered factions when he advanced political trips. This did not worry him. His experience told him that political competition is always put aside in deference to what is best for the president and the nation. Of Connally, O'Donnell had made only one off-the-cuff remark: "You're dealing with an arrogant guy here," he said, but that was hardly novel either. Bruno arrived in Austin on October

28, scheduled to go to lunch with the governor at the Four Acres the next day.

In their private dinner room, only a few bites into the appetizer, Connally made it manifestly clear that he *and only he* was going to run this show. He presented Bruno with the president's itinerary as a *fait accompli*. "It's going to be my way or no way," Connally announced. "This is it, or he can stay home."

Bruno wasn't prepared for quite this level of high-handedness, and he grew more unsettled as he looked over the schedule Connally gave him. It was not well worked out.

"Well, I want to look over all the sites," Bruno said. "I'll make a report to the White House, and they'll get back to you."

Customary as this procedure was, it unhinged Connally. Leaping out of his chair, the governor strode to a telephone in the corner of the room, picked it up, and in a loud voice demanded to be connected with the White House. When Ken O'Donnell came on the line, Connally went over the itinerary with him in a loud stage voice for Bruno's benefit. After four or five minutes on the phone, Connally hung up and returned to the table.

"It's all confirmed," he said. "This is the itinerary." Bruno wondered why he had come. (In fact, O'Donnell had not confirmed the Connally schedule at all.)

The following day the advance man toured the proposed sites with Cliff Carter, an aide to Lyndon Johnson. At each site he was greeted by a Connally man and a Yarborough man. As the opposing forces tugged in opposite directions, confusion was the result.

San Antonio, Houston, and Austin looked fine to Bruno, but with Dallas and Fort Worth there were problems. Three decisions had to be made, and had they been made differently they would have changed the course of history. One represented a victory for Connally, one a victory for Yarborough, and the third was a loss for both. They are the three Furies of Dallas.

The first had to do with the possibility of an honorary degree being conferred on Kennedy at Texas Christian University in Fort Worth. Connally had broached the idea to the TCU president and he had liked it. It provided a dignified event for Connally's hometown, and it became the raison d'être for the Fort Worth stop. Connally had promised the honor to Kennedy at the White House, and Kennedy was pleased, since the conferring of a degree by a bedrock Protestant university would further bury the fears of the South over a Catholic president. To Bruno at lunch, the event was presented as a done deal. As a scheduling matter, this would work well. The degree ceremony was to be in the midmorning, and then the presidential caravan would motor the thirty miles to Dallas for the president's speech to Dallas businessmen. It was unlikely, under this plan, that there would be time for a motorcade through downtown Dallas, but if there was, it would follow a fairly direct course.

As the planning went forward, Bruno got a call from Connally. He was sorry, but TCU had decided against conferring the degree. The refusal had been presented to Connally as a matter of university regulations and traditions. To follow the normal process, the faculty senate and the student senate would have to approve the degree, and there was not enough time for such deliberations. The elders and the sticklers within the university administration were concerned that a bad precedent might be set if the rules were skirted just for the president of the United States. It might politicize degree granting in the future. Bruno did not buy it. In the first place, Connally had said the logistics were set; the degree had been promised to the president a month before; Connally was supposed to be in total control. What was the real reason?

"Well, he's a Catholic, you know," Connally told Bruno.

What were they to do? There was no reason to go to Fort Worth now. "Let me straighten this thing out," Connally said. "I'll give it some thought." Some time later the governor called back and announced that the Fort Worth Chamber of Commerce would like to give the president a breakfast. One could always count on the local chamber of commerce to pinch hit in the event of a snafu. Bruno's annoyance was rising. For all Connally's puffing about how he *and only he* was in control, how he *and only he* could make a success of the presidential visit, he had thrown things into chaos. Instead of a leisurely sleepover in Houston after a testimonial dinner for Congressman Albert Thomas, the president would now have to fly to Fort Worth near midnight so he could be ready for the hastily pasted-up breakfast. More important, there were now two hours in the late morning that needed to be filled. To kill time, rather than save it, it was decided that Kennedy would *fly* from Fort Worth to Dallas. All the motion to and from airports would consume the dead space in the schedule. From the Dallas airport to the luncheon speech, the motorcade route was redrawn—and lengthened— through Dealey Plaza.

The second Fury watched over the motorcade itself. Connally opposed it vigorously. Having bent the itinerary out of shape, he was now worried that too much was being packed into the president's schedule. Lyndon Johnson's campaigns of 1941 and 1948 came to his mind, and he knew that by overloading schedules you could "work a man to death." If he did not want to advance the cause of Kennedy liberalism in Texas, neither did he want the president to flop. Kennedy should be rested. He should look good, his voice should be strong, and he should exude enthusiasm. A motorcade, Connally knew, was hard work. "It's very tiring. It's exhausting," he argued. "You assume that a person is just riding along, so there shouldn't be any difficulty. But in a motorcade the president is trying even in a fleeting second to make contact with thousands and tens of thousands of people along a parade route. He's looking from one side to another. Even if he catches a human eye for one second, there is a communication. I'm telling you, it's a strain." The governor also feared an embarrassment in Dallas, and the motorcade was an invitation. Connally's negotiator with the White House, Frank Erwin, a corporate lawyer and Democratic committeeman, voiced more specific fears that the supporters of General Edwin Walker would find this a prime opportunity.

To the liberals and to the White House, the elitist quality of the Connally plan was unconscionable. If the president was intent on speaking to Connally's exclusive businessmen's lunch, his exposure to Yarborough's people must be in the streets. Moreover, Kennedy himself was sentimental about the technique of the open motorcade. He attributed part of his success against Richard Nixon in 1960 to his mingling with the people by means of a motorcade. On this point, the liberals won.

The last Fury presided over the decision on the site for Kennedy's luncheon speech in Dallas. Connally had specified the Trade Mart, a boxy commercial complex just off Stemmons Freeway, where the hall for the luncheon was about the right size for the audience Connally was putting together and which, he thought, had the pizazz of the Kennedys themselves. The Dallas establishment was rightly proud of the building, for it projected the kind of energetic image modern Dallas strove for. The alternative was the Women's Building, a venerable, if mundane, mainstay for larger downtown functions, located near the Cotton Bowl at the State Fairgrounds, and not far from Big Tex (the symbol of the Texas ethos, who stands 52 feet tall, wears size 70 boots, and sports a 75-gallon hat). The Secret Service and the White House preferred it. The Women's Building had a larger banquet hall, large enough to accommodate a Jacksonian feast for over 4,000, and this was more in the Kennedy and Yarborough populist style. Moreover, the banquet hall at the fairgrounds undercut one of Connally's most embarrassing propositions: that at each presidential meal there should be a three-tiered head table, where Connally would sit with the president at the highest tier, and Yarborough would occupy a lower station with lesser personages. To Bruno, and to everyone, the thrust of this was obvious. "John Connally wanted to show that Ralph Yarborough had no support from the president," Bruno has said. "This was to be demonstrated in front of the public, in front of the big contributors, and it would be done with the president by Connally's side. The point was to downgrade Yarborough and to humiliate him publicly." But the hall at the Women's Building had too low a ceiling for these striations of importance.

The Secret Service liked the Women's Building for other reasons. If the event were held there, the route of the motorcade would be more direct, continuing straight down Main Street, picking up speed as it entered Dealey Plaza and zipping through the small park at forty to fifty miles an hour. If the Trade Mart were the spot, the motorcade would have to slow nearly to a stop to make a right turn onto Houston Street, and then a left turn at the next street, Elm. It was the deceleration to a crawling speed that concerned the Secret Service, especially since the route of the motorcade was to be published and any nut could quickly determine where he might get a leisurely sighting of the president. The Secret Service had other reservations about the Trade Mart. A series of low-slung catwalks loomed above the lobby through which the president would walk. Bruno took photographs of them, for he was concerned that it might not be possible to secure them totally. When Bruno showed the photographs to the head of the White House detail of the Secret Service, he said, "We'll *never* go there."

On this issue Connally dug in his heels. His mouthpiece, Frank Erwin, warned the White House that if the businessmen Connally had so ticklishly inveigled into attending the lunch had to mix with Yarborough liberals and labor leaders and ethnics, they would boycott. Erwin kept mentioning the "nonpolitical flavor" of the event, as if Connally's choice of an audience wasn't itself political.

Only days before the president's arrival, the struggle over the hall in Dallas had become ugly, so ugly that Connally was threatening to cancel the entire trip. In the minds of the Kennedy people, the main purpose of the trip was to civilize the two factions within the Texas Democratic party, so that Kennedy could have a reasonably united party behind his campaign in 1964. Connally's notion that greed for Texas political money compelled the trip is supported by no one from the Kennedy White House. In Larry O'Brien's opinion, the trip would not have been undertaken at all except for the testimonial dinner for the powerful Congressman Thomas of Houston. Kenneth O'Donnell's attitude was that there was not much the White House was going to get out of the trip, but Texas was a big and important state; the president had to go there, and they should all try to make the best of it. What was proposed for fund-raising in Texas was no different from arrangements already undertaken or contemplated in a number of other presidential trips, as the Democratic party began to gear up for the national election.

In fact, Connally wanted major political rewards for his efforts in behalf of the president. He wanted Kennedy to quash the serious liberal opposition that was developing a challenge to his reelection as governor. As it was shaping up, his prospective opponent was Don Yarborough, who was related to Senator Ralph Yarborough only in a political sense. To Bruno, during the planning for the presidential trip, Connally said more than once, "When is Ken O'Donnell or Larry O'Brien going to get Don Yarborough off my back?"

On November 14, Bruno wrote in his diary, "The feud has become so bitter that I went to the White House to ask Bill Moyers, deputy director of the Peace Corps and close to both Connally and Johnson, to try to settle the dispute for the good of the President and the Party. On this day, Ken O'Donnell decided that there was no way but to go to the Mart."

Bruno was appalled at Connally's warrior attitude. The governor's pose, he felt, was akin to a European baron riding through the peasant fields. Bruno waited in vain for the interests of the president to transcend the local feuding. "With John Connally, it was always what was best for Dallas and Texas," Bruno would say later with some bitterness. "If I heard the phrase 'Dallas business community' once, I heard it a thousand times. His concern was big money. He operated solely on raw power. He was intent to put people in their place." Bruno was becoming so upset at Connally's power play that he was losing his effectiveness. Bill Moyers, former special assistant to President Johnson, moved into the situation, feeling that he could smooth things over, but he soon found out differently. From Texas, he called Bruno in Washington to consult, and they began to snipe at one another over the implacability of Connally.

"Your nose is out of joint because I'm here, and you're not," Moyers charged.

"Connally is not concerned one whit for the president or the country," Bruno fired back. "He's a selfish, greedy, arrogant bastard." Moyers hung up on him.

On November 15, Bruno made this entry in his diary: "The White House announced that the Trade Mart had been approved. I met with O'Donnell and Moyers who said that Connally was unbearable and on the verge of cancelling the trip. They decided they had to let the Governor have his way."

In the decision over the Trade Mart, Connally had won.

★ 13 ★

November 21-22, 1963

ABOARD AIR FORCE ONE, the fresh-faced Congressman Henry Gonzalez settled in beside Olin "Tiger" Teague, the powerful House leader from Central Texas, a veteran of the Normandy invasion who had been elected the year after the war ended and was the most decorated soldier in Congress. There was a lot for this senior and junior Democratic member of the House to be worried about. The glow of the Test Ban Treaty did not blind anyone to the fact that the president's basic relationship with Congress had broken down: for the first time in history not one appropriation bill had been passed through the current session. The administration's problems with so basic a matter as appropriations provided one more justification for the president to come personally to a dinner honoring Albert Thomas, for the Houstonian was a senior member of the House Appropriations Committee. But appropriations weren't the only problem. Kennedy's civil rights program, the centerpiece of his domestic policy, was stalled, and this failure had ensnared other objectives like an elementary education bill, his Medicare proposal, and wide-ranging measures in conservation. To many Texans, Kennedy was all flash and no substance. His own poll showed that only thirty-eight percent of Texas approved of what he was doing as president. If a Kennedy-Johnson ticket was to have any chance whatever against Barry Goldwater in 1964, the state party machinery would have to be strong and unified, and the governor would need to put all the power at his command behind the national ticket.

These were the wider legislative and political concerns, but Gonzalez was now preoccupied with more immediate annoyances. He was still angry over the brevity of Kennedy's stay in San Antonio, and about the spurning of his pet project, the John F. Kennedy High School, which was only a few blocks from Kelly Air Force Base, where the president was scheduled to depart San Antonio. How many John F. Kennedy High Schools were there in Boston? Gonzalez had asked Robert Kennedy only a few days earlier. Gonzalez also hoped for an occasion on this trip to needle the president again about his Vietnam policy. He had been doing so on and off for six months. The air force had decorated his godson, a helicopter cargo master, for over 300 *combat* missions in Vietnam when the official national policy proclaimed America's role to be solely advisory. The godson, whom Gonzalez called simply Miguel, Jr., had been one of fifty-seven American advisers (the official count given by the government) in Vietnam. Miguel, Jr., had requested his godfather to secure a .45 pistol for him the day after he had been exposed to hostile fire during a drop over Vietcong territory, when he had to grab the rifle of his ARVN counterpart to open fire into the jungle. How could the president put boys like his Miguel on the firing line and not give them the means to defend themselves?

"What do you think is going to happen in Dallas?" Teague said, breaking Gonzalez's reverie. Tiger Teague, an old war-horse who was scarcely the type to tremble delicately over nothing, also worried about Dallas. Several nights before in Washington, the editor of the *Dallas Times Herald*, Felix McKnight, had spent the night at Teague's house and had engendered real anxiety in Teague about the safety of the president in Dallas.

"Some embarrassment—that's about all," Gonzalez said distantly. He remembered a function for Wilbur Mills only a few weeks before, when Kennedy had been heckled and had made his hecklers look ridiculous. "Jack be nimble, Jack be quick," he said now.

At that moment the president emerged from his forward compartment, smoking a small, thin cigar, looking pinkishly healthy. In the soft light of the plane, Gonzalez took note again of the startling blueness of the president's eyes. He would never forget them. Jokes about the cigar, whether it was Cuban and all of that, were passed around (Gonzalez had never before seen Kennedy smoke), and there were jokes about a Raymond Moley column in the current issue of

Newsweek, in which the conservative columnist urged Barry Goldwater to hold fast to his hard starboard course so that he could offer a clear alternative to Kennedy and what his administration "is giving us now."

"I saw that," Kennedy said. "I don't think Barry is going to have time for a presidential campaign, though. He's too busy dismantling the federal government."

He might make light of Goldwater, but Kennedy knew he was headed for a state which was likely to prefer Goldwater to him, and he knew that a *Houston Chronicle* poll due out shortly would indicate the extent of the deficit. But he had no deficit in San Antonio, and Gonzalez, one more time, complained about the shortness of his stay there, the only terra firma for Kennedy.

"Yes, yes, Henry," Kennedy said good-naturedly. "You've told me those winning numbers in Bexar County ad nauseam. I've given your area a veteran's hospital. We've made it into a postal distribution center. As I remember, I gave you an hour's lead time on those announcements, so you got pretty good credit there."

Gonzalez was not to be put off, and he pressed until he got a promise. "Okay, Henry, next year, February or March," Kennedy said finally. "I'll come back to San Antonio and stay as long as you want. First, I've got to go to CINCPAC in Honolulu and review the whole Southeast Asia business." The president started back to his compartment. Then, at the door, he turned back to Gonzalez. In the years to come, Gonzalez would keep this fleeting moment frozen in his mind, as his last direct personal touch with the deified president, but also as a fulcrum of history.

"Oh, and by the way, Henry, I've already ordered all the men and all the helicopters to be out of South Vietnam by the end of the year." And he was gone.

Farther back in the plane, the wily, prickly, and altogether suspicious Senator Yarborough was pondering how to make his way through the minefield of the next few days. Connally's strategy to humiliate him (no doubt in cahoots with Johnson) was apparent enough by this time. It was to come at the main political event of the trip, the extravaganza in Austin, when "the long knives of Austin," as they were later dubbed, were to be drawn. If the senior senator from Texas was to be introduced at all, it would be among an anonymous pack of state legislators. Preceding the political dinner, there was to be a reception at the Governor's Mansion, and Yarborough had been ostentatiously left off the list of the invited. While this was a political decision by Connally, Nellie Connally had personalized it. She would not have "that man" in her house. Yarborough stewed. He was a veteran of these personal slights. On the June 5 trip to El Paso with President Kennedy, Yarborough had started up the aisle after the president, when he found his way physically barred until Kennedy was down the ramp and across the tarmac past the line of photographers. Then, in the motorcade going into town, Yarborough listened as Kennedy asked Connally about the percentage of his state budget devoted to education. To Yarborough's astonishment, Connally, this governor who had made education the marrow of his legislative program, replied with the figure of fourteen percent. The senator, too, had concentrated on education in the Senate, with national initiatives which Connally consistently would oppose as too radical—and he knew perfectly well that Texas was thirty-eighth in the country in education and thirty-sixth in public health, but was spending forty-six percent of its budget on education. Kennedy expressed surprise, and Yarborough remained silent.

Yarborough was not a devious man by nature. He cared about protocol and yet it seemed to him that his scramble for respect, despite his unfailing support of the Kennedy program, would never end. He had to fight for his dignity every step of the way. As for the reception at the Governor's Mansion, Yarborough had a Jacksonian view of such occasions: any function with the president made it a presidential party, and the president rather than a mere governor should have an influence over who was invited. Still, his best course now, Yarborough thought, was to keep quiet and let things ride. For months his standing in the polls had been five to ten percentage points ahead of Kennedy's in Texas, and well ahead of Connally's. There were persistent rumors that Lyndon Johnson would be dropped from the ticket in 1964 and, indeed, as Air Force One winged toward Texas, Richard Nixon was telling an audience that Lyndon Johnson was a liability to the Democrats and would be dropped.

Yarborough's determination to keep quiet was ruled by his brain, but when on the plane a pool reporter approached him about the intended discourtesy in Austin, his emotions took over.

"I've had many telephone calls and letters from friends because Mrs. Yarborough and I were not invited to the mansion . . . ," he began casually.

The reporter pressed harder. "How does it feel to be slapped in the face?"

"Well, I'm not surprised. Governor Connally is so terribly uneducated governmentally—how could you expect anything else?"

In Houston, meanwhile, Connally had gone on too long in a speech to the Texas Manufacturers Association in the Sheraton-Lincoln Hotel, and had frantically prevailed upon a friendly oilman to lend him a jet to pop over to San Antonio. With Air Force One already in its final approach, Connally's plane slipped into the pattern just ahead and a relieved governor rushed over to pump a few hands and take his place next to Nellie in the receiving line.

The reception in San Antonio was warm, even tumultuous. With her fragile beauty and her poignancy, Jackie Kennedy was the instant star, as Connally had predicted. The throngs clamored for a glimpse and a shy wave. Taking her first bunch of yellow roses, she glided ethereally alongside her husband through the receiving line, as across the tarmac the crowd beckoned at the chain-link fence. Here, there was no nastiness. Only one placard dotted the crowd:

JOHN CONNALLY
WHY ARE YOU AGAINST EQUAL RIGHTS?
EQUAL URBAN REPRESENTATION?*

From a distance, Henry Gonzalez watched as Kennedy strode to the fence to work the crowd. To his companion he said, in the first of the premonitions, how easy it would be—how easy. Someone had once put a .38 to his stomach and pulled the trigger, and though the gun didn't go off, every time he went into a boisterous crowd in the barrios of San Antonio and the *cascarones*, eggs filled with confetti, were lobbed his way, he was apprehensive. Inevitably, he ducked as if his car were a foxhole. And he remembered the sourness of Wilbur Mills a few days before, when the old congressman had turned to him and snarled, "That damn princeling, silver spoon in his mouth, what the hell does he know about Texas?" How easy it would be.

To the national press, another royal visit of the Kennedys to the outlying provinces was no story at all. They sensed that one purpose of this trip was to heal a political rift, and they smelled an old-fashioned cockfight. Yarborough's comment on the plane had swept through the entire entourage, and now they watched hungrily as the motorcade formed, knowing that the senator was supposed to ride with the vice president. If Connally had been warned never to give Yarborough an inch, Yarborough's friends were telling him not to buckle under to the Connally-Johnson plot to humiliate him. The

---

*The last phrase applied to Connally's opposition to a federal court order to force congressional redistricting.

senator had not understood that he was supposed to ride with Johnson anyway. Larry O'Brien had promised him that he could ride with the most popular local figures at each stop—Albert Thomas in Houston, Henry Gonzalez in San Antonio—and that was fine with him. Now, a Secret Service man, Rufus Youngblood, directed him to the vice president's car. It was a conflict in the White House planning, for Youngblood was acting on Kenneth O'Donnell's orders. Yarborough puffed up in indignation. Here was an ex-colonel in the army being ordered around by a sergeant. He would not have it. He freelanced.

"Henry, can I hitch a ride with you?" he asked, finding Gonzalez near at hand, and he clambered in with the congressman. For a moment there was confusion, a moment long enough for the press gleefully to notice a motorcade with each car packed, except for the vice president's, where a glum Johnson sat alone with his lady. Texas had become the Orient, and Johnson was losing face, and the press at last had something to write about.

The wind was high, gusting to thirty-five miles an hour, as the motorcade took off. For the first time the Connallys experienced Jackie Kennedy's discomfort and ill ease. She was worried about her hair, as was Nellie about hers, but Nellie was used to wind in her hair. If only the bubbletop were affixed—but the president had resisted. It put more distance between him and the people, and made him feel like a laboratory experiment. Now, she asked to swap seats with the governor so she could get more protection from the car's windscreen, and so before the sparse crowds on the outskirts of town, the governor and the First Lady clambered over one another. The president did not like that, just as he would not like it in Dallas the next day when Jackie put on her sunglasses. The crowds wanted to see her as much as him; Connally had told him so. So he insisted she get back into the seat beside him, and the governor back into the jump seat—"where you belong." Nellie would later repeat the quip affectionately when they recounted the day.

Before a crowd of ten thousand at the new School of Aerospace Medicine, only a month before the first Saturn rocket would be launched in the program that would eventually realize Kennedy's goal of an American on the moon before the end of the decade, the president invoked one of his patented stylish touches. He borrowed an image from the Irish writer Frank O'Connor about the boys making their way across the countryside, and "when they came to an orchard wall that seemed too high to climb, too doubtful to try, too difficult to permit their journey to continue, they took off their caps and tossed them over the wall, and then they had no choice but to follow them." So it was with the American space program. This trip was to become a contrast of style. The day before in Dallas, speaking to a convention of soda pop distributors, Johnson had done his earnest best to promote the administration's accomplishments in defense and with the economy, where corporate profits were up thirty percent. There were still gaps, said Johnson, like four million unemployed—and that reminded him of the hillbilly who said about the holes in his roof, "When it shines, they don't leak. When it rains, I can't get on the roof to fix them."

The governor, however, would have reason to be pleased with the president's first day in Texas. San Antonio went well, with larger crowds along the motorcade route than he expected, but, then, that was Kennedy country. Dallas would right the balance. Then they had hopped over to Houston, and there, too, the crowds were large, if somewhat more subdued. Connally was also relishing his torment of Yarborough. Albert Thomas had come to the governor as the first peacemaker, specifically at the request of the president, and asked Connally to back off. Why not have Yarborough introduce the vice president at his testimonial dinner that night, before Connally introduced the president? Connally thought that was a lousy idea, and Thomas dropped it. He still had a few points to score. It remained an open question whether Yarborough would be seated at the head table the next night in Austin, for Connally was still hoping for his three tiers. The warfare was psychological now, and Connally wanted Yarborough in a state of animated suspense a while longer.

At the Rice Hotel in Houston, Connally and Yarborough were, embarrassingly, put on the same floor, as they got ready for the Albert Thomas dinner; guards were posted warily at each door, lest the men emerge by accident at the same time and have to ride down on the same elevator.

The dinner was attended by the "backbone of Houston," and the signs were good. The industrialists and the oilmen listened attentively to the president, were open to his message, appreciated the Kennedy glamor, and applauded enthusiastically. Connally too admired the Kennedy wit and style that night. The president's short speech was "burnished with clever touches," he thought, as when Kennedy praised Thomas as the great champion of the space program and referred to the Saturn rocket which was to lift off soon as "firing the largest payroll—I mean payload—into space," or when the president talked of old men with their dreams and young men with their visions, Thomas being old enough and young enough to have both. In Kennedy, Connally saw himself. He had been told that he brought the same effortless grace and wit to public life in Texas, and he was flattered.

There had been one snafu toward the end of the evening. At the conclusion of the dinner the crush had separated the president and the governor, and before Connally knew it Kennedy had left for the airport without him. Connally was frantic, for he did not want to cause the delay of Air Force One, taking off with a crowd of well-fed but tired and easily irritated politicians. Luckily, he managed to commandeer a squad car, and a wild ride through downtown Houston ensued—lights flashing and sirens blasting, the wrong way up one-way streets, over curbs, through driveways, bumping through gas stations, until the policeman at the wheel finally found the Gulf Freeway and reached speeds close to one hundred miles an hour. Connally loved it.

Finally, when the presidential party had settled for the night in the Texas Hotel in Fort Worth, Connally, after midnight, repaired to the cafeteria for eggs and bacon and milk. This was his hour of the day. An aide gossiped excitedly about the Johnson-Yarborough tiff. "I don't care who rides in which car," Connally said merrily, for, of course, there was no doubt about his own seating arrangements. Upstairs, the Kennedys were settling into their suite, which he and Nellie had decorated for them, appointed with Van Goghs and Monets borrowed from the Connallys' art-loving friends in town. He knew it would be appreciated—and it was, eventually—and it underscored both the Kennedyesque classiness of the Connallys and the classiness of the Texas upper crust.

His opponents had good reason to be buoyed as well. Before the Thomas gala the Kennedys had had dinner alone with the publisher of the *Houston Chronicle*. In deference to the president's visit, the paper delayed the publication of a political poll until Kennedy left town. From the publisher, the president got the news in advance. Goldwater would defeat him in Texas by four percentage points—fifty-two to forty-eight. Connally was running somewhat stronger, looking like a comfortable winner over any potential challenger. But Senator Yarborough was well ahead of them all in Texas. In his frumpy way, the senator had been waiting for his local popularity to register with the president, so it would wash away that tripe which he was sure Connally and Johnson were promoting about him being a drag on the Democratic ticket. On the short ride between Houston and Fort Worth that night, Kennedy remarked to

Yarborough in a tone markedly more warm and inviting than the day before, "Ralph, you're doing very well in Texas."

In fact, in his private conversations, Kennedy was actively rallying to Yarborough's defense. If there was anything that could be done about the rift between the two factions of the Texas Democratic party, only Lyndon Johnson could accomplish it. Only he bridged the two camps. He had associated himself ardently with the progressive thrust of the Kennedy program, and he was Connally's closest friend. That night, in the Rice Hotel, Kennedy and Johnson had their last private chat, and it was stormy. Kennedy criticized the treatment of Yarborough, childish and undignified as it clearly was. While only the two men were present and no record exists of what they said, the result was that Johnson marched fuming from Kennedy's suite. To criticize the treatment of Yarborough put Johnson between two competing loyalties. Connally was running the show, and it is likely that the president turned his Yankee scalpel on the governor in front of Johnson. Then he probably demanded to know why Johnson was so powerless to get the sides together. Did he not realize the importance of unity to their own reelection? The reason for Johnson's powerlessness, of course, was personal rather than political. Only a few months before, Yarborough had publicly called Johnson a "power-mad Texas politician" after the senator seized the notion that Johnson had blocked his appointment to the Senate Appropriations Committee. Johnson had cut off many politicians for saying milder things than this in public. Too many outrages and atrocities had passed between the men over the years. Their antipathy, as Connally put it, was implacable.

As Johnson stormed out of Kennedy's suite, Jackie came from the bedroom to wonder about the fuss. She would later tell William Manchester what had been said.

"He sounded mad," she observed, as she watched Johnson's coattails disappear.

"That's just Lyndon. He's in trouble."

Suddenly, apparently from nowhere, Jackie blurted out her distaste for John Connally. There was something about him that she viscerally disliked. "I can't stand being around him all day," she said. "He is just one of those men—oh, I don't know. I just can't bear him sitting there saying all those great things about himself. And he seems to be needling you all day."

"You mustn't say you dislike him, Jackie," the president replied. "If you say it, you'll begin thinking it, and it will prejudice how you act toward him."

But she did think it, and she wasn't the first woman to feel that way. Many other women had taken a similar instinctive dislike to Connally. His superior air repelled them, making them feel demeaned in his presence. It was all too apparent that they were ornaments to him, there to decorate the room and comfort the men in it. Few accomplished women were ever swept away by him.

In her oral history for the LBJ Library, Jackie Kennedy was to describe her husband's attitude toward Connally on that last night in Houston. "I know he was annoyed with him then. I remember asking that night in Houston what the trouble was. He said that John Connally wanted to show that he was independent and could run on his own. He was making friends with a lot of 'Republican fat cats'—and he wanted to show that he didn't need Lyndon Johnson. Part of the trouble of the trip was [Connally] trying to show that he had his own constituency."

As the morning of November 22 broke, Jackie Kennedy remained the object of everyone's fascination. She alone was making a success out of apparent failure. Without her, the distasteful bickerings of the politicians would have been even more glaring. The other women, Lady Bird and Nellie, fretted about what to wear when they were seen with Jackie. As the Connallys dressed and looked out the window at the workmen across the street, they chatted amiably about how Jackie had seemed to loosen up as the day's campaigning wore on, and by nightfall actually seemed to be enjoying herself. They agreed she would be indispensable in the forthcoming campaign.

Six stories below, on the eighth floor, the president had an early meeting with Lawrence O'Brien. Before them lay the early edition of the *Dallas Morning News*, ablaze with gossip of snubs, slights, and insults among the subalterns. STORM OF POLITICAL CONTROVERSY SWIRLS AROUND KENNEDY VISIT, read the headline. "President Kennedy wound up a day of 'non-political' campaigning in the Lone Star State with almost a hurricane of political controversy swirling around him," began its lead. As yet, neither man had turned the pages to see the scurrilous advertisement inside.

"Christ, I come all the way down here and make a few speeches—and this is what appears on the front page," Kennedy said first in disappointment. "I made one last night and I didn't read anything about it in the papers." Then came the anger. "I don't care if you have to throw Yarborough into the car with Lyndon. But get him in there." O'Brien promised to try to find Senator Yarborough. Stewing, Kennedy sat by the window, his feet propped up on the radiator, as he looked out upon the rain-soaked parking lot where he would soon speak.

"Just look at that platform," he said, gazing down at the naked platform in the middle of the parking lot. "With all these buildings around it, the Secret Service couldn't stop someone who really wanted to get you." It was a premonition that later took its place beside Lincoln's melancholy before a night at the theater, and Martin Luther King's talk of having been to the mountain before a demonstration in Memphis. It was the first of two Kennedy would have on this morning.

Just outside the lobby of the Texas Hotel, O'Brien had the good fortune to run into Yarborough almost immediately, and he made his case forcefully, as Yarborough groused. Perhaps the senator would issue a statement? Perhaps. . . . "You see that press bus over there?" O'Brien cut across him, gesturing across the parking lot. "We've come all the way down here, and you know what every one of those reporters is talking about? They're talking about you and Lyndon." Yarborough grumbled and O'Brien prepared his heavier volleys. He felt Yarborough was "oversensitive." O'Brien did not agree that the senator had been stripped unfairly by Lyndon Johnson of his appropriate patronage powers in the Senate.

"Well, if it means that much . . . ," Yarborough said.

"It does."

"Larry, I would do nothing to hurt the president, you know that," he replied, and the deal was struck. Now, O'Brien's only job was to make sure in Dallas that the promise was kept. He went off and found Johnson shortly afterwards, and told him of Yarborough's reversal.

Soon the president emerged in the lobby. It was drizzling as he strode across the wet parking lot to address a stalwart and enthusiastic gathering. There were no faint hearts in Fort Worth, he began, as behind him Johnson, Connally, and Yarborough stood uneasily side by side at attention. "Where's Jackie?" someone shouted. "Mrs. Kennedy is organizing herself," Kennedy shot back. "It takes her a little longer, but of course she looks better than we do when she does it." The crowd laughed delightedly.

On the way back in, Kennedy came face to face with Yarborough at the elevator. "For Christ sake, cut it out, Ralph," he said saltily. Yarborough was apologetic. The question was closed. But not quite. Moments later, as the president took his seat at the Chamber of Commerce breakfast in the Longhorn Room, he spotted Connally and summoned him over.

"John," said the president, "did you know that Yarborough refused to ride with Lyndon yesterday?"

"Yes, I heard about that last night."

"What's wrong with that fellow?"

Connally did not know.

"By God, he'll ride with Lyndon today—or he'll walk," Kennedy said.

At the breakfast the rituals were soon under way. Upon this occasion the formalities had not been put through Connally's filter of Texas classiness, for just the wrong presents were bestowed upon the Kennedys as mementos of their visit: boots for Jackie and a Stetson for Jack. They took the gifts in good humor. Inevitably, the roar came from the crowd for the president to put on the hat. The president recoiled, but made a wisecrack of it.

"I'll put this on on Monday in my office in the White House. I hope you can be there to see it."

★

In Dallas, Oswald wrapped his weapon in brown paper, and, when his fellow worker picked him up, he put the package in the back seat, mumbling something about curtain rods. It was not Oswald's practice to read the paper in the morning. But he might have seen the story about the luncheon at the Trade Mart in the society pages the day before. Steak was on the menu, and a spokesman for the sponsoring organizations informed the press that the president's steak would be chosen at random. "Obviously, this is done for security reasons," he said cheerfully. "A would-be assassin couldn't be sure of poisoning the president's meal unless he put poison on every steak." Oswald had undoubtedly seen Wednesday's paper with the parade route and the news that the president and the governor would be riding in the second car.

The Kennedys arrived back in their hotel suite after breakfast for what might have been their last few minutes of privacy. Downstairs, Connally met the press to put out a few high-sounding homilies about party unity and to berate them for magnifying the feud between himself and Yarborough. His bland statement had been approved by President Kennedy. In Suite 850, Jackie Kennedy noticed for the first time that they were in the midst of a priceless art collection. Besides the Monet and the Van Gogh, there were a Picasso and a Prendergast, among others.

"They've just stripped their whole museum of all their treasures to brighten up this dingy hotel suite," she said in a compliment that Nellie Connally would have found backhanded. From a catalog which they had not seen the night before in their haste and fatigue, Kennedy found the name of the organizer and called Ruth Carter Johnson, the wife of a newspaper executive, to thank her. He then called for Lyndon Johnson, and the vice president found Kennedy in an ebullient mood. The enthusiasm of the drenched crowd in the parking lot had brightened his spirits. He could go to a thousand Chamber of Commerce functions, and they would mean nothing. But when the people turned out in the rain spontaneously, and cheered, that meant something.

"You can be sure of one thing, Lyndon," Kennedy said buoyantly, "we're going to carry two states next year—Massachusetts and Texas. We're going to carry at least two states!"

"We're going to carry a lot more than those two," Johnson replied, himself buoyed—for, if he had harbored a doubt over whether he would be invited back on the ticket, it was swept away now.

After Johnson left, the dour Kenneth O'Donnell came in to dampen the fun. He had finally been shown the ad inside the *Dallas News*, with its funereal black border; its sarcastic heading of welcome to the president; its sponsorship by H. L. Hunt and Dallas Birchers; and its imprecations, undisguised by its format of twelve rhetorical questions, that Kennedy was secretly in league with American Communists, acquiesced in the Red imprisonment of Cuba, gave succor to the Communist killers in Vietnam, persecuted his conservative critics—and this was no rag handed out by nuts on the street. It was an advertisement accepted by and, implicitly, sanctioned by the management of a major American newspaper. The president handed it to his wife. "Can you imagine a newspaper doing that?" he said in disbelief. "We're headed into nut country now." It put him back into the melancholy of the morning. He was overcome again with dread and premonition.

"Last night would have been a hell of a time to assassinate a president," he said, gazing out of the window. "If anyone wants to shoot a president, it's not a very difficult job. All one has to do is get on a high building with a telescopic rifle, and there is nothing anybody can do."

There had been another piece, which Kennedy did not see. Several days before the president's arrival, A. C. Greene had written a column on the editorial page of the *Dallas Times Herald* entitled "Why Do So Many Hate the Kennedys?" Three factors were listed, and the tone of Greene's editorial came close to legitimizing them.

First, the Kennedys were rich with money that "stinks." "The Kennedy family is new rich and acts it," Greene wrote. "There is a touch of vulgarity in the way the Kennedy tribe lives." This vulgarity, he suggested, was made more obnoxious by their insincere attempt to act like real folks. In their arrogant hearts, "the Kennedys give the impression that ordinary people don't know how to think or act or do for themselves." Second was his religion, and third his civil rights program. The latter was especially infuriating, wrote Greene breezily, because "the President isn't really as sincere in his civil rights pushing as he claims." Next to this discourse was a cartoon of Kennedy shuddering as he stood before a huge smiling elephant marked Dallas, with the title "Profiles in Courage."

If a spark was needed to make some irrational nut burst into action, there were those in Dallas trying hard to provide it. Thursday morning, five thousand cheap handbills were distributed bearing a presidential mug shot, as if it were a post-office "most wanted" poster: WANTED FOR TREASON headlined the sheet. But Oswald needed no jump-start. To a fellow worker who had joined him at the window, Oswald asked with forced naiveté what all the commotion was about, and his comrade told him. Which way was the motorcade coming? Oswald asked. Along Houston Street to Elm. "Oh, I see," he said, and turned languorously back to his work.

Meanwhile, in Fort Worth, Connally finished his press conference, satisfied that he had discharged his duty to the president on the subject of internecine warfare, and he sent word to him through Ken O'Donnell that Yarborough would be allowed, after all, to sit at an unstratified head table during the remaining functions. "If the president wants Yarborough at the head table, that's where Yarborough will sit," Connally said magnanimously.

"Terrific," the president said. "That makes the whole trip worthwhile." As he climbed the ramp to the plane, the clouds receded. His melancholy left him, swept away by the cheers of the street crowd as he rode to the Fort Worth airport for the time-consuming hop to Dallas, swept away by his own usually sunny disposition. The plane rose on its short parabola. Kennedy looked out the window at the improving weather. "Our luck is holding," he said to Connally with a smile. "It looks as if we'll get sunshine."

Kennedy's buoyancy was infectious. When Connally emerged from the plane at Love Field behind the president and felt the sunshine, crisp and brilliant, he was filled with a sense of possibility and pride. The Connallys tarried by the limousine with Jackie Kennedy, her arms filled again with the inevitable roses. She did not find the midday sun and heat very comfortable: the temperature was already in the 80s, the infernal wind was up again, and she was sure she would swelter in her wool suit. As the president pumped hands at the airport fence, his traveling party watched the familiar scene languidly. Congressman Henry Gonzalez, who had felt as if a 250-pound weight had been lifted from his chest when the president left San Antonio safely, joked to his companion about his "steel vest." O'Brien kept a wary eye on Yarborough to make sure he didn't bolt. When Yarborough finally climbed into Johnson's car, the vice president did not acknowledge him but stared glumly forward under his cocked Stetson. Johnson would continue to stew all the way to Elm Street, never turning to Yarborough to say a word, much less a pleasantry, never turning to the sidewalk crowd, whose cheers were not for him. Yarborough put on a plastic smile, for he was enjoying the vice president's discomfort.

On the outskirts of the airport, the motorcade moved swiftly past scattered clusters of people. On a knoll, some distance from the roadway, a lone, disheveled, and sour-faced figure stood by a battered Volkswagen and held up a sign that read, YOU'RE NOTHING BUT A TRAITOR, but Kennedy did not see it. By no means were all the political placards negative. One read, GOLDWATER IN 1864. KENNEDY IN 1964. With the president sitting directly behind the governor, the conversation in the president's limousine was sporadic and "desultory," as Connally would describe it. They eventually came upon another unfortunate sign, which read KENNEDY GO HOME, and this time the president did see it.

"See that sign, John?" he said, leaning forward to Connally.

"I did but I had hoped you didn't," Connally replied, turning as best he could in his balled-up position.

"I see them everywhere I go," Kennedy said, turning back to the crowd. "I bet that's a nice guy."

To Connally, the president seemed to be enjoying himself. At another point, when momentarily the crowds thinned, Kennedy leaned forward again.

"John, how do things look in Texas?"

"That *Houston Chronicle* poll should give us some ideas," Connally replied.

"What's it going to show?" the president asked, knowing full well from the night before what it showed.

"I think it will show that you can carry the state, but it will be a close election."

"Oh?" said the president, showing faint surprise, as Goldwater was ahead by four percentage points. "How will it show you running?"

"I think, Mr. President, it will show me running a little ahead of you."

"That doesn't surprise me," Kennedy said.

As the motorcade entered downtown, the crowds grew to be throngs, and when it turned onto Main Street, pointing down the canyon of sparkling glass and steel and granite, the throngs became a multitude. Connally had never seen anything like it, a quarter-million people packed into a space of a few city blocks. Its size far surpassed what San Antonio, Houston, or Fort Worth had produced. If he had felt before that he and only he could ensure the success of the president's trip, especially in Dallas, Connally was disabused of the idea now. These crowds were not for him. He was a mere passenger, a hanger-on, an appendage. He saw them as "restrained" in their enthusiasm, for this comported with his political expectation, but it was hard not to be swept up in the fantastic reception. Down the straightaway they went, flags fluttering, at a reasonable clip of about thirty miles per hour. At Houston Street, on the east edge of Dealey Plaza, the car slowed nearly to a stop to make its right turn. By the courthouse, Nellie turned to speak to the president in a tone full of excitement, full of pride in Dallas, in Texas, and in her husband for what *he* had just accomplished.

"Well, Mr. President, you can't say that Dallas doesn't love you!" she cried.

"No, you certainly can't," Kennedy replied, with a smile.

In the shadow of the Book Depository, the car made its slow left turn onto Elm and started down the slope into the abyss. As they edged past a large tree, approaching the freeway sign, Connally's mind thrust ahead to the luncheon, only five minutes and an eternity away. The adulation was over.

At the crack of the rifle, he knew instantly what it was. His head turned sharply to the right, but he could not swivel his body that way because of the car's bulkhead, so he swung back swiftly the other way, and then he felt the hammer strike his back. His swivel continued toward the left. His gaze fell on his lap, spattered with his blood. He was hit—badly—fatally, he supposed. His head tilted skyward. "Oh, no! no! no!" he screamed, as he crushed the roses. "My God! They're going to kill us all!" Two, three men were out there, shooting with an automatic weapon, he thought. Nellie's glance riveted on him as she heard him scream. She reached out in horror, pulling him down into her lap. Her awareness grew with the milliseconds. The president was hit, too, she sensed, but he uttered no sound, and he still sat strangely upright, a more distinct target now. He had upon his face, as his widow would later say, a "quizzical look," as if he suffered from a "slight headache." The third shot landed, spraying the passengers with a fine mist. Connally knew what this was. Upon his trouser leg he saw a piece of blue brain, the size of his thumb, and he was a boy again, standing in a field not far from Floresville, with his father and one of the hands, Carlos Estrada, next to a half-slaughtered steer hanging from a neighboring farmer's tree, and he was holding the precious blue brains that were the butcher's delicacy and his reward for unpleasant work. Nellie held him. She now was the only remaining stationary target. The car jerked slower as the driver instinctively hit the brake, contradicting his training. "Get out of line," Connally heard the agent-in-charge shout. "Get us to a hospital quick!" He did not hear Jacqueline cry out for her husband nor hear her scramble over the back seat. He heard only Nellie's comfort. "Be still now," she was saying. "Don't worry, you're going to be all right." She kept saying it over and over, beyond the point under the freeway where he lost consciousness.

"When you see a big man totally defenseless like that, then you do whatever you think you can to help," she was to say. "The only thing I could think to do was to pull him out of the line of fire. Maybe then they wouldn't hurt him any more. . . . We must have been a horrible sight flying down that freeway with those dying men in our arms and going, no telling where. We just saw the crowds flashing by. John said nothing. Once, I saw one little moment when [I thought] maybe he was still alive—and I kept whispering to him, 'Be still. It's going to be all right.' "

But she did not believe it. She thought he was dead.

★

In the parking lot of Parkland Hospital, the limousine screeched to a halt with a jerk that propelled Connally back into blurry consciousness. He knew that he lay across the jump seats and that the president had been hit, hit terribly. He had to get out of the way! With an extraordinary effort of will, he heaved himself out of Nellie's arms and tried to stand. He got nearly upright before the pain overcame him. "Oh, my God, it hurts! It hurts!" he screamed, and collapsed. Men were running and yelling all around the vehicle. An agent shouted to "get the president! Get the president!" In the back seat, Jackie Kennedy cradled her husband's head, covered now with the coat of a Secret Service agent. A figure of stone, immobilized by horror, she would not let go. They pulled at him, reaching over the Connallys, grabbing at the president's body. No, she would not let them have him. Agent Roy Kellerman's coat slipped down to the bridge of the president's nose, revealing the wasted cavity. "You know he's dead. Let me alone," Jackie Kennedy said remotely. "Please, Mrs. Kennedy," the agent said solicitously, then firmly, "Please!" Nellie Connally was overcome with a momentary bitterness. Amid the pandemonium, she seemed to be the only one concerned about her husband. Arms reached over his body toward the back seat, as she pleaded for attention. She knew the man in the back seat was dead. When someone finally reached in and began to lift Connally out and onto a waiting stretcher, it seemed to Nellie as if they were doing so only to clear a path to the president. An orderly had hold of the governor's arms, and the president's pal, Dave Powers, shaking with sobs, grabbed Connally's legs.

The gurney with Connally bolted ahead through the narrow, antiseptic passageway. The governor's body was tense, a good sign, and he roared with pain—his brain was functioning and intact. He was rushed into Trauma Room #2. Even in horror, protocol was observed. The gurney behind was silent, the body limp. It went to Trauma Room #1. Blood covered Connally's head. It was not his blood. Fingers pawed at his clothing. They were having trouble with his pants. "Cut them off!" Connally bellowed, and they did. In the hub of the emergency room, as Secret Service men with tommy guns mingled wildly with doctors dangling the life-saving paraphernalia, Nellie Connally stood, bewildered. She felt utterly alone, wondering if the doctors hadn't all forsaken her husband. She could hear his leonine roar. After what seemed an eternity, someone rushed out and handed her one of her husband's gold cuff links. What did it mean?

Professional hands were at work, as Bill Stinson, the governor's aide, rushed into Trauma Room #2. Dr. Red Duke had his hand under Connally's shirt, pressing hard against his chest.

"How is he?" Stinson said breathlessly.

"He's got a hole in his chest you could pack a baseball into," Duke said.

Stinson moved to the head of the stretcher. Connally was calmer now, almost composed, his eyes shut.

"Governor, can you hear me?" Stinson said softly in the governor's ear.

"Yes, Bill, I can hear you," Connally said without opening his eyes.

"What happened?" the aide asked, smoothing the governor's ruffled hair.

"They shot us both, and I think they killed the president," Connally muttered.

"Where did the shots come from?"

"I don't know—but I think from behind."

"Is there anything I can do for you?"

"Just take care of Nellie," he said.

His pallor was ashen, due to a considerable loss of blood and to his difficulty in breathing, but his pulse was steady and his blood volume was adequate. He did not appear to be in shock. His wounds were terrible. On his right shoulder, in his back, a thumbnail's distance from the crease in the armpit, there was a regular, three-centimeter perforation. At an angle of thirty degrees downward, below the right nipple, there was a ragged five-centimeter wound. This was a "sucking wound," which Dr. Duke closed with his hand, and it, along with the possibility that the bullet had passed through the heart and the great vessels, represented the danger to Connally's life. Here, he enjoyed his first piece of luck. When Nellie had pulled him into her lap and held him, his arm had instinctively fallen across his chest and pressed against the wound, partially holding in his air and permitting him to breathe. The ride from Elm Street to the hospital had taken eight minutes. If it had taken eight more, he would have been dead. Then, there was another wound in his right wrist, and another in the thigh. For the moment, these were considered secondary. In the emergency room, the first impression was that the victim had been hit by two bullets.

An occlusive dressing was slapped on the sucking wound and pressed hard to control the escape of air and aid respiration, for the governor was, as his doctor later put it mildly, "complaining bitterly" about his difficulty in breathing. His lung had collapsed— that much was clear. He was in danger of strangling to death. Expeditiously, an incision was cut between the second and third ribs, and a tube inserted into the lung to reinflate it. The top thoracic and orthopedic surgeons in the hospital arrived, as the patient was prepared for surgery. Both Dr. Robert Shaw and Dr. Charles Gregory were veterans of World War II, and between them they had experience with nearly 1,500 cases of bullet wounds. One story above, the operating "suite" was readied. Dr. Shaw took a minute to explain to Nellie what needed to be done, and she authorized him to do whatever was necessary. As the gurney moved to its next station, Stinson trotted alongside Dr. Duke.

"Is he going to make it?" he asked.

"We won't know until we get him upstairs," the doctor replied grimly.

Upstairs, the gurney came to a stop next to the operating room doors, and as they lifted Connally off his stretcher to take him inside, something dropped from the stretcher to the floor. It was a bullet. A nurse picked it up and dropped it in her pocket. Inside, the governor was conscious enough to answer a few basic questions—when he had last eaten, whether he was on any medication, whether he had any acute allergies—and then, at 1:07 P.M., thirty-two minutes after having been hit, he fell unconscious. He did so, the doctor later wrote, "without excitement."

Once the patient was put under sedation with sodium pentothal, Dr. Shaw proceeded to determine the full extent of the damage. The bullet had shattered ten centimeters of his fifth rib, the length of his middle finger. It had passed along the outer cusp of the rib and had splintered fragments inward, into the body, creating lethal "secondary" missiles. The shards of Connally's own rib, not the bullet, had collapsed the lung, perforating his bronchia. Thus, he was sucking air internally as well as externally. Upon further examination of the right wrist, it was determined that the damage, while great and delicate to repair, would have been considerably greater if the wrist had been struck initially, with the full force of a bullet. The last two similar wrist wounds that Dr. Gregory had attended had resulted in amputation. Hit by a bullet traveling at its full speed, 2,000 feet per second, a wrist would "literally be blown apart." In this case, it was apparent that the bullet had been largely spent, and from the nature of the laceration had probably entered the wrist butt end first while it was tumbling. When Gregory finally turned his attention to the wound in the thigh, he found that it was a remarkably round puncture, stopping in the subcutaneous flesh and not passing into the muscle. Given its size and depth, about that of a pencil eraser, Dr. Gregory concluded that the butt end of a spent bullet had entered, and then dropped out.

The theory soon developed that a single bullet had caused the entire condition: entering his back, passing downward through the outer edge of the fifth rib, tumbling and exiting at the nipple, catching the wrist, then coming to rest in his left thigh.

If Lee Harvey Oswald had hit President Kennedy's brain dead

on, he had missed Governor Connally's heart and great vessels by an inch.

Meanwhile, in an adjacent hallway, a dazed Congressman Henry Gonzalez floated along behind Lyndon Johnson's aide, Cliff Carter, into a small, cramped side chamber of the emergency room. There, Johnson leaned against a doorway, saying nothing, frequently putting a sinus inhaler to his nose for a snort. Lady Bird stood nearby, blanched and quiet. Several other congressmen were present. Agent Kellerman of the Secret Service was shouting into a phone, apparently talking to the military command in Washington and assuring them in bursts of affirmations that he was with the vice president, and that Johnson was unhurt. Gonzalez still had no grasp of the situation. He did not know who had been hit. When he caught a glimpse of the president's limousine on the way into the hospital he had seen the trampled and blood-soaked yellow roses of Texas and his first assumption was that Mrs. Kennedy had been the victim. No one told him now.

Cliff Carter came and went. In the hallway, the head nurse approached him, holding a medium-sized and a small grocery-store bag. The bags contained Connally's clothes. The nurse wanted a signature on a form for their release.

"The governor is not expected to live," she said, bland as broth.

Carter entered the room and handed the two bags to Gonzalez. "Here, Henry, the governor's personal effects . . . you sign for them," and then he was gone again. Gonzalez wandered out into the hallway, glad to have a pretext for leaving and having the vague intention of finding Nellie Connally and giving her the bags. Down the corridor he came to a dead end. To the right was the exit. He looked to the left, and there, completely alone, on a small chair in an empty corridor by the oak-paneled swinging doorway to Trauma Room #1, sat Jackie Kennedy. To Gonzalez, muddled about what had happened, she looked like a frightened rabbit. She gazed at her hands, arranged in her lap, still sheathed with pink gloves that were caked with blood. Gonzalez went to her. Putting a comforting hand gently on her shoulder, he said, "Mrs. Kennedy, can I get you a glass of water?"

She looked up and nodded. Down the hall he found two nurses who were locked in gossip and laughing raucously. Gonzales asked for water. The nurse snapped that she did not have any handy. Gonzales *ordered* the water, and it was grudgingly provided. "And this is no time for laughing," he scolded, as he turned back to the First Lady.

As he stood by Mrs. Kennedy, the door opened, and inside the room Gonzalez saw Mrs. Kennedy's press secretary, Pamela Turnure, and the president's secretary, Evelyn Kennedy. Turnure smoked a cigarette. Between them was a body, covered with a sheet. The soles of the feet were the only flesh in view. "No, it can't be. No, not here, it can't be," Gonzalez muttered to himself. Now he knew. Curiously, his Spanish tradition flashed before him—a line from Adolfo Béquer's *Rimas:* "How lonely are the dead. . . ." Distantly, he heard Mrs. Kennedy ask him for a cigarette. Fighting with himself, he took a few steps into the awful room to get a cigarette from Turnure.

On the floor above, Nellie's friends were finding her. The congressman from Houston, Jack Brooks, evoked a Texas version of the stiff upper lip. "Oh, he'll be out deer hunting at the age of ninety," he said cheerfully, not appreciating how poor a joke this was. Lady Bird Johnson had gone to Nellie. Of the two women she now must comfort, Lady Bird knew that both had recently experienced wrenching tragedies: Nellie with the suicide of Kathleen three years earlier, Jackie with the death of two-day-old Patrick three months before. In Nellie's face, Lady Bird perceived a tough determination.

As they fell into a long embrace, Lady Bird said, "Too much has happened. He's *got* to get well."

"He is, Bird. He's going to be all right," Nellie replied bravely. To many, later, the bravery of Nellie Connally in those first eight minutes was unsurpassed. It would be remembered that from the moment her husband was hit, she had pulled him into her lap, leaving herself exposed and stationary for whatever other bullets might fly at the car.

To go to Mrs. Kennedy was inexpressibly more difficult. What could one say? Jackie Kennedy and Lady Bird Johnson had maintained a courteous distance. They came from different cultures, different traditions; their men were very different, and they almost spoke different languages. Despite the correct and even occasionally warm feelings between them that accompanied official duties, they had each allowed their true feelings to pop through privately. Once Lady Bird had remarked patronizingly that Jackie Kennedy, unsophisticated as she was as a political woman, was a "girl born to wear white gloves." In turn, Jackie had once snapped, about Lady Bird's unquestioning loyalty to her husband, that Mrs. Johnson would walk naked down Constitution Avenue if Lyndon asked her to. Now, in Dallas, all that was far from their minds. Lady Bird found Jackie composed "as a shadow."

"Jackie, I wish to God there was something I could do," she said.

No comfort was possible between Nellie and Jackie. In the pandemonium, as the doctors worked furiously on the governor and the casket was ordered for the president, the two women found themselves seated briefly together in the hallway, two women in nearly identical pink wool suits, identically blood-spattered, one only inches yet worlds luckier than the other. After some moments of silence Mrs. Kennedy finally turned to Mrs. Connally, moving herself to inquire after the governor's condition.

"He'll be all right," Nellie replied stiffly. There was nothing she had to say or ask or offer in return. Determined and hardened, Nellie Connally was clinging to life.

At 1:35, almost exactly an hour after the monumental insults to his body, Connally went into surgery. He had, of course, no comprehension of what was transpiring on the floor below: a priest insisting upon time-consuming formal pronouncements to the Almighty, a coroner standing upon the rules and threatening to block the removal of the president's body, nurses insisting on the signing of endless forms, a youthful justice of the peace browbeaten by presidential assistants and shoved aside by gun-toting Secret Service men, an oak casket too heavy to be lifted by ordinary men, a press corps behind barriers clamoring for snippets of information, a country without a president, a blood-spattered widow, and his closest friend, Lyndon Johnson, seized with terror, thinking the assassination was the precursor to a Soviet nuclear attack. As Connally was under anesthesia, Johnson commandeered a police cruiser for the drive from the hospital to Love Field. The new president lay down on the floor in the back and ordered an officer to lie on top of him.

Even with the body of the president gone, terror still reigned at Parkland Hospital. How and why the shots were fired remained a giant mystery. Lee Harvey Oswald was still blithely riding Dallas city buses and easily hailing taxicabs as Connally went under the knife. Who had fired the shots? How many assassins were there? Was it an organized attack from abroad or a conspiracy from within? These questions were unanswerable, and that heightened the uncertainty and the terror. All that could be done at Parkland was to secure the place and make certain that no more gunmen reached the governor of Texas.

To Bill Stinson, the governor's aide and the highest state official present at Parkland, his immediate duty was clear, even if his emotions were muddled. Should the governor die, there would need to be a transfer of power. Should more gunmen from this conspiratorial vanguard appear, the National Guard might have to be called out. Who would do it? How was it to be done? Stinson seized and secured a line to Austin and kept it open before he rushed to the operating room and demanded to be present during the governor's surgery. The chief surgeon began to object.

"You will not operate unless I'm present," Stinson ordered, and pushed by him. "I am the senior state official here, and if power shifts, I need to know immediately."

Beyond Stinson's aggressive official posture, his dominant thought was about his friend and boss and mentor. He adored Connally. "My God, I may lose this dear man," he thought, and struggled to control himself. Clothed in surgical gown now, Stinson stood out of the way as the doctors opened Connally up. As the chest wound was exposed, Dr. Red Duke said in astonishment, "I've never seen *anything* like this."

★

Across the airwaves of Air Force One, known as Angel, where prominent figures were known in code, the radio traffic crackled with the terrible news. Volunteer was administered the oath of office, before Angel took off at 2:47 P.M. Wayside, with a planeload of cabinet members on their way to Tokyo, had read the wire reports from Crown, and ordered the plane to turn back to Honolulu. Watchman worried with Witness over whether a helicopter could even lift Lancer's heavy casket and take it to Bethesda. Dagger informed Crown that Volunteer would come immediately there and that Victoria and Venus would then proceed to Valley. Warrior talked with Winner about arrangements for the press upon arrival, when Volunteer would have a short statement. Then, blowing it all, Tiger told Tanker that *President* Johnson would deplane in the front of the aircraft upon arrival at Andrews.

Aboard Air Force One, the new president settled low in his seat, brows knit and eyes hooded, voice low, a man overwhelmed, grieving, and desperately concerned about the precarious life of his closest friend. There were a thousand affairs of state to attend to, and a few affairs of the heart, and toward the end of the flight to Washington he turned to the latter. He had to reach Mrs. Rose

Kennedy. From the far distance of miles and culture, she was finally there on the line with this man who had replaced her slain son.

"I wish to God that there was something that we could do," Johnson blurted out, in evident anguish.

"Thank you very much," Rose Kennedy replied, curtly. "That's very nice. I know you loved Jack, and he loved you."

Lady Bird was also on the line, ever the standard of grace through these awful hours. "We're thankful that the nation had your son as long as we did," she said.

"Thank you, Lady Bird," Rose Kennedy warmed. "Thank you, Mr. President."

The Connallys remained uppermost in their minds. Surgery on the governor's chest was completed at 3:20 P.M., and somewhere over the middle South, Lyndon and Lady Bird watched a snowy television, as Dr. Robert Shaw came before the television cameras. Moments later, Angel was calling Parkland, and finally the plane was connected with Nellie Connally.

"We just heard some reassuring news over the TV," Lady Bird said. "We're up here in the plane. But the surgeon, speaking about John, was so reassuring. How about it?"

"The report was true," Nellie replied. "The surgeon who just finished said that John is going to be all right—unless something unforeseen happens."

Lyndon was there too. "Nellie, can you hear me?" he called down to her. "I love you. I know that everything's going to be all right—isn't it?"

"Yes," Nellie said, strong-voiced now. "Everything's going to be all right."

"God bless you, darling," he said.

"Same to you."

"Give John a hug and a kiss for me," said the president.

"Good luck," Nellie replied, and she was gone. Actually, she had known for over an hour that her husband was likely to survive. Twenty minutes into the operation the doctor told Stinson that the bullet had missed the great vessels and the governor would live. He left and found Nellie, desolate and weeping, in the hallway. Kneeling in front of her in his surgical gown, taking both of her hands in his, he said, "He'll make it," and she collapsed on his shoulder, "Thank God," she said.

Concern for the Connallys stabilized Lyndon Johnson in the coming hours. For Lady Bird, the Connallys represented more than the very closest friends they had. This catastrophe had happened in her state, and as a result her husband had acceded to an office he could never have attained on his own. His detractors were bound to cast this accidental elevation as some dark, medieval tale of regicide (as indeed it would be so cast in the play *MacBird*). Johnson called for Lady Bird's car at the White House and ordered her home. Her wise and irrepressible press secretary, Liz Carpenter, went with her.

"It's a terrible thing to say, but the salvation of Texas is that the governor was hit," Liz said.

"Don't think I haven't thought of that," Lady Bird replied, and then, gazing out into the miasma of a Washington night, "I only wish it could have been me."

At the White House Johnson ordered a television. Apart from the brief glimpses of television he had seen on Air Force One, he had no perspective on the day's events wider than his own confined experience. Now, the romantic images of the handsome, athletic, well-born, graceful, martyred president flooded the screen— Kennedy and his small children vacationing at Hyannis Port, Kennedy at his inaugural, and Robert Frost, squinting against the cold January light, huddled against the biting cold, speaking of the dawn of a new Augustan age with power and poetry, where young ambition was eager to be tried . . . and Kennedy himself talking of the torch being passed to a new generation . . . Kennedy . . . Kennedy . . . Kennedy. "Let's turn that off," Johnson snapped. "I can't take this." His actions were aimless. He read some wire copy and took no calls except one from his comforting ranch partner in Stonewall, Texas. He tried several times to get through to Connally's hospital room, but Bill Stinson was turning away all calls, and in any event the governor was still unconscious. One of the last things Johnson did before he retired for the night was to talk again to Nellie Connally.

★

The following day, Saturday, the pattern continued. As Johnson vigorously seized the reins of the presidency and began the transition of power, he found time to make repeated calls to Parkland. He spoke always to Nellie, because Stinson and the doctors forbade any direct calls to the governor, who lay groggily in a semicomatose state. He flickered awake enough to notice for the first time that his arm was battened to a brace in traction above him. Until then, he had not known that his wrist and his thigh had been hit. In this twilight, he asked after Kennedy, and Nellie told him. "I knew—I knew," he mumbled miserably. By this time, some twenty members of his family had gathered at Parkland Hospital. Texas Rangers, armed and nervous, guarded his door. They had reason to be nervous. Only later did it come out that Jack Ruby had mingled with the press on Friday at the hospital, merely a half-hour after the shootings on Elm Street.

On Sunday, Connally's first full day of consciousness, Oswald was shot and brought to Parkland. Ironically, Connally's aide, Bill Stinson, took charge of the emergency room as Oswald was brought in, and secured it with state patrolmen. In the course of the procedure, a reporter from the *Dallas Times Herald* was discovered hiding under a sheet beneath a gurney, and he was shooed out. Stinson watched as they worked to keep the wretched killer alive. Compared to the gaping cavity in Connally's chest, Oswald had only a small perforation in his belly, but the eyes in his misshapen, sallow face never flickered open. Stinson watched, hoping for a deathbed confession, but it never came.

What had been let loose in America? No one was sure.

★ 14 ★

Governor for Life

In MID-DECEMBER 1963 CONNALLY was wheeled out of the hospital, looking gaunt and wasted, with deep circles under his eyes and his arm and leg still in long casts. For many weeks he had scant energy and little interest in the affairs of state. Later in December he made his first, widely noticed appearance in public, as Chancellor Ludwig Ehrhard, the German chancellor, came to visit the new president at his Blanco County ranch. As the first of nineteen guns blasted out a noisy salute for the foreign dignitary, the governor flinched. In mid-February the press thought he looked tired and distracted at an air base ceremony, as he constantly rubbed the back of his immobilized right hand. He had been told that his cast would have to stay on for another six weeks, and after that he would need to wear his arm in a sling.

Connally had become a national hero. His friend Lyndon was in the White House. Texas lay at his feet. And yet, he came to appreciate only slowly that all this had considerable political advantage. His priorities before Dallas had been set by the political realities of the Texas governorship. It was an office severely constrained by law. After Reconstruction it had been deliberately gutted, with the transfer of many executive powers to a score of governing boards and commissions. Since the governor's term was short—two years— he had to serve several terms before he could appoint enough board members to do his bidding. This created a feeling of constantly shifting sand beneath the governor. A favorite story about this concerns the Texas judge who is told that a legislative committee had just voted to eliminate his bench.

"Who testified against me?" he snorts.

"A banker named Jones," is the answer. "He's usurious," says the judge. "He cheats little ol' ladies out of their life savings. Who else?" His friend goes down the list of the committee members who voted against him, and the judge denounces each as a blackguard and a scoundrel. Finally, the friend roars with laughter and confesses that he was only kidding. The legislative committee had actually voted to retain his bench.

"Now why did you go and make me say those things about the finest group of men I know?" moans the judge.

In addition to the problem of the independent boards, the powerful secondary positions in the state administration were elective, and so the governor could not even control the major players in his administration, for they were beholden to the people rather than to him. As for the legislature in Texas, it is usually wild and untamed, and in any event it is the province of the lieutenant governor rather than the governor. But Connally was now in a position to transcend these limitations. For all he knew, his unprecedented power might be transitory. What could he do with this new stature? What vision of Texas might he now project? What grand programs had suddenly become possible?

The social ills of Texas were daunting in 1963. For all its fabulous oil wealth, it was thirty-third in the nation in per capita income, forty-fourth in adult literacy, and last in per capita expenditure for child welfare services. It had the largest pool of poor in the entire United States. Its educational system was near the bottom. In its racial attitudes, the state of Texas was only slightly more advanced than Alabama, Mississippi, and South Carolina. Only two percent of blacks actually attended school with whites. With blacks and Latinos making up more than a fourth of the state's population, the pattern of discrimination was deeply ingrained and all-pervasive, and it affected every aspect of social and economic life. With Connally's predecessors, Allan Shivers and Price Daniel, the political establishment had fought hard for segregation. Shivers had resorted to unspeakable demagoguery in 1956 when the town of Mansfield erupted in violence over a desegregation order in Texas. He had dusted off the antebellum doctrine of interposition, and had pushed a referendum vote to determine the people's attitude toward segregation, getting the result he wanted: four to one for segregation. Daniel had then boasted to the voters that he had signed the

Southern Manifesto when he was a U.S. Senator (the document of Southern resistance that Lyndon Johnson had refused to sign), and had called a special session of the legislature in 1957 to pass the so-called referendum law, a law which prohibited school boards from abolishing the segregated system unless the voters in that school district specifically voted to do so. As a result, from 1957 to 1962 virtually no desegregation of public schools took place in Texas. As Connally took over, the outgoing Texas attorney general declared Daniel's referendum law unconstitutional, and Connally's incoming attorney general, Waggoner Carr, affirmed his agreement with his predecessor. Only with this change in official policy and with pressure from desegregation suits in federal court did the snail's pace of desegregation resume in Texas. But it got no support or encouragement from Connally.

The problems of racism and poverty and illiteracy were confounding, but there was also opportunity. The state was amassing an unprecedented treasury surplus, partly from the oil industry, whose benefits made state income taxes unnecessary in Texas, partly from Price Daniel's unpopular two-percent sales tax, which Connally had attacked in the campaign and now benefited from. With a hero's luster and an emperor's lucre, he faced possibilities as big as the Texas sky.

Shortly after his election in 1962, on a plane trip from Texas to Washington, Connally had found himself next to Walt W. Rostow, then a top policy planner at the State Department, and as Connally leafed through a thick folder of reading material, Rostow was naturally curious about what Connally's goals as governor would be. "I want to do something really big as governor," Connally said dreamily. "There are only three possible areas: race, welfare, and education. I've decided, if I'm going to unite the state, that education is the thing to choose. I'm going to be an education governor." His first message to the legislature in 1963 bore out this ambition, as he painted a dismal picture. The brain power of the state was drifting elsewhere: eighty-six percent of the honor graduates of the university at Austin went to graduate school elsewhere; faculty salaries at the university were forty-sixth in the nation, lower than those at such less-than-eminent institutions as Chico State College in California; salaries at Texas Tech and Texas A&M were lower than those at a more-than-obscure institution like Bemedji State College; New York produced five times as many PhDs yearly as did Texas. In his call for a new day and a new era, Connally proposed several supercommissions for the study of the problem. In mid-July

1963, his Governor's Committee on Education Beyond High School recommended that $100 million be spent on teaching salaries, libraries, research, and new doctoral programs.

This accent on higher education squared with the Kennedy-esque image that Connally wanted to project in Camelot South. He would be the governor of ideas and of the space age. Smart industry, particularly the defense contractors, followed the intellectuals, and he invited the state to consider the clean, growing businesses that surrounded MIT, Cal Tech, and Johns Hopkins. Texas needed to get into the competition, but it would only do so if it dramatically improved its universities. With all this talk of big new investment in Texas, the business community, which had helped Connally get elected, leaped behind this new program. Big labor, which had cautiously and begrudgingly supported Connally in 1962, also supported the program initially.

Cutting across this image as a man of the future was Connally's position on race. Four days after his blue-ribbon commission on higher education presented its report, Connally had gone on state-wide television to denounce President Kennedy's proposed Civil Rights Act. What he was to say had been the subject of heated debate within his inner circle. The speech itself was made over the stren-uous objections of his closest advisers. The public accommodations section of the civil rights bill was the source of Connally's annoy-ance. He had made a survey of theaters, restaurants, and motels across the state and had concluded that Texas was doing swimmingly well in desegregating its public accommodations voluntarily. While the backward dominions of South Carolina, Alabama, and Mississippi might need the federal lash to open their public places, Texas did not. His aide, Larry Temple, argued force-fully against the speech, afraid that the governor would associate himself with the racism of George Wallace, but Connally cut him off.

"We don't need a law to tell us how we ought to do things, because we're doing them already," he said. The sanctity of private property was involved, as well as the interference of the federal government in state affairs.

Moreover, Connally was well satisfied with the pace of school desegregation. It was a matter of tone and emphasis. The "passionate" and the "extreme elements," as he was given to calling the civil rights activists, might stress the two-percent figure of black children in the same classrooms with whites, but he chose to look on the bright side. He chose his words of rebuttal carefully: Fifty-three percent of Negro schoolchildren in Texas now live in school districts which have programs of desegregation actually in progress." He also chose to ignore what the "extreme elements" could say: that those programs were a "classroom-a-year"; that Austin, the most progressive Texas community, nearly ten years after the Supreme Court decision, had advanced integration only to the fourth grade; that civil rights legislation existed to deal with recalcitrant resisters and outright racists, not to applaud reasonable citizens; that East Texas, where the vast majority of black Texans lived, was no more integrated than the most backward parishes of Louisiana; that Connally's own home city of Fort Worth, the fourth largest city in Texas, remained totally segregated, a symbol of total resistance; and that at Texas colleges integration consisted of only a handful of students per institution. Nonetheless, Connally pointed out to the television audience that 16 of 21 public senior colleges and universities and 26 of 33 public junior colleges were "desegregated" and that he was proud of "reasonable, responsible" Texans for this kind of "dramatic progress."

Implicit in Connally's July 19 speech was his concept of leadership: "It is my responsibility to reflect the sentiments and the convictions of ten million citizens. . . . To do less, I would fail in my obligations to be the spokesman, the advocate of our people." The people, as he perceived them, were against the interference of the federal government in their affairs. The "success" of Texas in its civil rights progress had come because "we have avoided the cold, arbitrary tool of government edict." Some might characterize the Supreme Court ruling in *Brown v. Board of Education* as a cold, arbitrary edict, and it was certainly true that Texas was avoiding it, even to the point of passing legislation to put state resources behind frustrating federal desegregation suits. But Connally was resorting to the standard codes of governors across the South at this time of massive resistance.

Nowhere was this more evident than in his opposition to the public accommodations section of the act: "I fear that these provisions could carry potential danger to the people of this state that is far greater than any now envisioned. They would be laws which could strike at the very foundation of one of our most cherished freedoms . . . the right to own and manage private property, a right as dear to a member of any minority group as to any other Texan."

Three days after Connally's speech, Lyndon Johnson received a staff memorandum which cited the Texas statutes reinforcing segregation in public facilities: statutes requiring railway and streetcar companies to provide separate coaches or compartments for blacks and whites (the violation of which could result in a $1,000 fine); statutes requiring train depots to have separate facilities; statutes requiring white passengers to sit in the front of public buses and blacks in the rear; statutes requiring coal mines to have separate washing facilities for black and white miners; and the most general grant of power, Article 1015b, a statute granting city councils the power to segregate black and white neighborhoods. The memo to Johnson concluded tartly:

> Clearly the Legislature of Texas has taken a number of steps to continue the absolute freedom of the use of private property, in the interest of separating the races. It has long asserted its power to regulate theatres, movie houses, and other places of amusement, treating them as public houses of amusement. . . . It seems curious that, in the light of such a history, the Governor should now be talking of the right of property ownership in absolute terms, and expressing his opposition to a proposed law which would regulate the use of private property in the interest of equal treatment for all citizens.

Moreover, Connally's pronouncements had placed Johnson in an awkward position. On August 5, Hobart Taylor, Jr., the son of a black millionaire in Houston and the vice chairman of President Kennedy's Equal Employment Opportunity Committee, wrote to the vice president, "I am very much disturbed about the reaction among Negroes in Texas to John Connally's speech with regard to public accommodations. Moreover, I have been personally placed in an embarrassing position. I have received several calls about this, and I would like your advice as to how to respond."

The pretext for Connally's July 19 speech on civil rights was to speak to Texans before he attended a national governors' conference in Miami Beach. At that conclave, Governor Nelson Rockefeller would attempt to pass a resolution favoring a broad national policy of civil rights, and Lyndon Johnson, attending as a presidential surrogate, would challenge the nation "to face and dispose of" the problem that had haunted it for a hundred years. Connally's aide, Larry Temple, had been concerned that the governor would join George Wallace, Ross Barnett, and Orval Faubus in the public mind, but Connally carefully allied himself with the border states' governors in parlimentary maneuvering to forestall consideration of Rockefeller's resolution for at least a year. Connally meant to position Texas as a moderate, border state. At a strictly Southern governors' conference one month later, in White Sulphur Springs, West Virginia, he distanced himself further from Wallace and Barnett.

When these delicate maneuvers were over, Temple was well pleased. After Connally's speech, a state poll indicated close to ninety-percent approval, and Connally's popularity soared. To Temple, the speech had an unforeseen benefit. It cut "the umbilical cord" that had linked John Connally to John Kennedy and Lyndon Johnson. Temple recalled, "By making this statement, which was contrary—very strongly contrary—to what President Kennedy wanted, and strongly contrary to what Lyndon Johnson's view was, [Connally] demonstrated finally for everyone that he was his own man. That independence was a very valid, good result."

That umbilical cord would, however, prove a lot tougher than Temple realized. The ties between Johnson and Connally remained strong. But as Johnson became more focused on the civil rights situation his compassion did not convey itself to Connally. Lady Bird was to say that the difference between her husband and John Connally was that Lyndon felt he could "make a difference" if he threw his "whole stake" into the fray, while John was more of a "consolidator." At this juncture Connally was protective of his stake and did not want to risk it.

Only a few weeks after he succeeded to the presidency, Lyndon Johnson summoned to his office a man with whom he had frequently clashed over the politics of race. To the liberal labor lawyer, Joseph Rauh, Jr., Johnson announced that the highest goal of his immediate presidency, his gift and his obligation to the legacy of John F. Kennedy, was to pass Kennedy's sweeping civil rights bill through Congress. The president asked for Rauh's help and for his cooperation. And then, in an extraordinary moment for Lyndon Johnson or for any president, he said, "If I've done anything wrong in the past, anything that offended you, I'm sorry." They talked about Texas. The U.S. Civil Rights Commission was about to release a state-by-state survey of the human rights situation in the South, and the Texas figures were abysmal. Rauh worried that with Connally as governor, there was scant hope that the figures would improve. Knowing Johnson to be the quintessential political animal, Rauh remarked that the poor Texas record on civil rights threatened Johnson's reelection chances a year hence.

"Draft me a memo to John Connally, will you, Joe, and tell me what I ought to say," Johnson replied. "And mark it Eyes Only."

★

In 1964, with Texas at his feet, Connally's mind was not running to grand social schemes. No sooner had he returned to a semblance of good health than he had to contemplate a reelection campaign. He greeted the prospect with a groan. Before the president's fateful trip to Texas the previous November, Connally had tried and failed to get the Kennedy White House to command the firebrand liberal Don Yarborough not to contest Connally's governorship in 1964, for Yarborough had come within 25,000 votes of Connally in 1962. Under usual circumstances, Yarborough, who, beyond his forensic talents, looked much like the Hollywood music man Robert Preston, would be an even tougher opponent in 1964. But now, with Connally's heroic proportions, when the sympathy vote alone could win him a second term, there seemed to be no point in Yarborough persisting in a second race. But persist he did, despite considerable pressure on him not to run.

In February, Connally's closest friend, and a close friend of Lyndon Johnson as well, Congressman Joe Kilgore, was determined to challenge Senator Ralph Yarborough for the Democratic senatorial nomination in May. Kilgore had no friends and political associates closer than Johnson and Connally; he had been one of the bright young men who had traveled all over the state in 1941, at Connally's direction, to campaign for Lyndon Johnson for senator. And he had been Connally's roommate in college. Kilgore had turned sharply conservative once he got into Congress, however, and this had created tension in his relationship with Johnson. In early 1964, as Johnson began to think about his grand design, he realized his friend Kilgore would be certain to oppose his sweeping social program in the Senate, whereas his longtime adversary Senator Yarborough would be sure to support it. For Connally, no such conflict existed with Kilgore, so when Kilgore came to Connally he received his blessings. But, as a friend, Connally warned Kilgore: If you are going to cross Lyndon Johnson, watch out.

Over this conflict of loyalty and ideology, Connally and Johnson fell into fierce disagreement. The governor deeply resented anyone, even the president of the United States, telling a man he ought not to run for public office. "I'm entitled to one Texas vote in the Senate," Johnson snorted in reply. (The other Texas vote was the roly-poly Republican John Tower.) At the last minute before the filing deadline, Johnson put out the word: "I'm going to support Ralph Yarborough. I'm not going to be *against* anyone else, but I'm going to be for Ralph, because he will support my campaign and my issues."

This word was accepted graciously by Allan Shivers and Lloyd Bentsen, who were also considering running against Yarborough, and they promptly withdrew. But Kilgore wanted the Senate seat more, and his bitterness was great. Connally tried to help—and to help himself in the process. If the president was going to block Kilgore's run for the Senate, why couldn't he block Don Yarborough's run for governor? Suddenly, amid the ruins of Kilgore's candidacy, Connally tried to barter his way into an uncontested election. The fury that Connally felt toward Johnson at this moment became as intense as it had ever been. Kilgore withdrew in anger only ten hours before the filing deadline, and Don Yarborough filed for the governor's race. For weeks Connally's bitterness lasted, and it was evident to all, as numerous reports of the rift appeared in the press.

As usual, time healed Connally's sense of betrayal. He had a simple credo about politics: fight hard and rough, but when the battle is over, forget and dismiss. His overwhelming natural advantage in the governor's race asserted itself soon enough, and as he pulled comfortably ahead his anger with Johnson dissipated. He campaigned little. For him to show up at the opening game of the Houston minor league baseball team, the Colt .45s, and throw out the first ball lame-winged, was worth a hundred stump speeches. To look elegant for more formal occasions he had a London tailor make a suit which had a sling for his injured arm sewn into the material itself.

The major Texas papers doted upon him: "John Connally personifies confidence. Defeat is not in his make-up," the *Houston Chronicle* purred. "Retreat is not in his vocabulary. Skillfully, he directs this confidence where it belongs: in Texas and her people. In his mind, Texas has everything in her favor—charm, vigor, a reservoir of intelligence, a colorful history, courage for the present, a sense of destiny, abundant natural resources and proud people who are united to make this state the envy of the other 49." In short, John Connally was the personification of Texas, as establishment Texas wanted to see itself.

Nevertheless, Don Yarborough campaigned vigorously, passionately, effectively. As the May primary neared, it seemed as if he was gaining, until Connally did a simple thing to put the race beyond reach. During a speech in South Texas, he suddenly took his arm out of his magical sling, and at that point Yarborough knew the campaign was dead. "That kills us," he told his campaign staff. "That's it. I can't do it." To the sardonic, it seemed as if Connally had used his black arm sling to support his arm long after the limb had healed. But for an audience actually to see his arm emerge from its protective sheath was an epiphany.

After Connally swamped Yarborough two to one there was talk of Oswald's gift to Connally of a "silver bullet." For years to come this talk would hover in the political debate.

"He ain't never done nothin' but get shot in Dallas," the Texas comptroller, Bob Bullock, was to say eight years later. "He needs to come back here and get himself shot once every six months." In this black humor the silver bullet had become an irresistible political device, powerful in its political velocity, devastating upon impact. For Connally, it was always there if he ever got into real political trouble, and it was something of a decoration which appealed to his magnificent vanity.

"He's terrible bad vain, y'know," Bullock whispered.

★

Connally's vanity was to be stroked in a different fashion in early 1964. In late February he went to Laredo for the boisterous annual George Washington celebration, where in this most Mexican of American cities, he was to be honored signally as Mr. South Texas. Among the Hispanics of the Rio Grande Valley, who revered John Kennedy alongside Jesus, Connally had ascended to Kennedy's right hand after Dallas, and in Laredo, they wrapped his arm and sling in a Mexican blanket as if it were a colorful ecclesiastical vestment. In the Cadillac Bar in Nuevo Laredo that evening Connally, Nellie, and the children were having dinner, when a lively, fun-loving, attractive coed from the University of Texas approached their table to introduce herself. Eighteen years old and a freshman, she had learned her pluck and her forwardness from her lineage as the rebellious daughter of a prominent political family in one of the larger Texas cities. To introduce herself to the governor came naturally, even though she had done it on a dare from her date. Connally greeted her warmly, took her hand with his left hand, and introduced her to his wife and family. They chatted amiably about the governor's association with her grandfather, who had been a longtime conservative Republican mayor. Connally held onto the girl's hand for an embarrassingly long time, until she grew somewhat flustered and tried to pry herself away. Several days later, back in Austin, the governor called the girl's sorority house and invited her to his office on the pretext of getting to know her better and talk a little more about her family. Flattered, she went, and she talked to him in his conference room as any attractive, nervous eighteen-year-old might talk to a forty-seven-year-old handsome and charismatic celebrity.

Thereafter, through the spring of his recuperation and the hour of his primary triumph, Connally called her frequently. To the giggling girls at her sorority house he identified himself importantly as "Duke." When messages were left at the sorority house that Duke had called yet again, the curiosity of the giddy sisters was aroused. Toward the end of the spring semester he threw himself at her on one of her office visits, enfolding her in his arms and kissing her, no doubt in the manner of a child-adoring Rhett Butler. It was not until the fall that the affair was consummated in a motel. The dalliance lasted only a few nights, for after a wild college party the girl eloped to Mexico with a young man she scarcely knew, in what one might be tempted to interpret as a Tolstoyan tale of remorse and resurrection. To Connally, the affair was a momentary, unimportant assignation, and over the years it was simply the best-known episode in what became an affectionately regarded reputation for occasional philandering. There was something about politics and women, as the Texas politician John White would put it, that just naturally went together. To the girl, it was scarcely her last or only fling with a prominent politician, for after a long time she could talk about a stable. But she would remember her affair with Connally more vividly than he. In 1968 her rebellion took a turn to the political left, although she kept it within socially acceptable bounds. And she developed literary pretensions, deciding that she wanted to be a novelist. She was taken in by the Austin literati, particularly by a group of newsmen, who were by nature a lusty and sometimes raunchy lot and gathered occasionally as a club calling itself the Mad Dog, Inc.

In this appealing party girl they saw the promise of a Texas Fanny Hill, and they guided her toward overripe prose which they hoped might result in a moneymaking pornographic novel. She wanted to call the novel *Consequence of Favor*, but they persuaded her that *Sweet Pussy* might be a bit more commercial. In her writing she suffered from an inclination toward Victorian prudishness; when she wrote about her affair with Connally, along the lines of ". . . and the dawn light streamed through the shades and the Governor desired me again," they egged her on to something more graphic. In the end, after the obligatory fleshy scenes, she settled on a compromise between the commercial and the honest, as the heroine of her book contemplated past transgressions with regret.

> He stood up and went to her and put his hands on her arms. She started to draw away, but it felt good for him to touch her in a friendly way, and she stood still. A vision of Nicholas and the Governor flashed to her, the way they had complicated her life, their selfish, insouciant demands on her time and her body, the manner in which they had jeopardized their own friendship by both sleeping with her, their faulty and aggressively thoughtless masculinity and contempt for weak things, their hatred of opposition to what they thought was right and proper in government and society, their powerful insolence and pride, their detachment from and indifference to life as it welled up all wrong and askew around them. Stanley put his arms around her, and she crumpled against his shoulder. . . .

In 1968, during a time when she was marching in the Austin streets as the most fashionably dressed of the antiwar protesters, she went to Washington, where upon a whim or as part of the "research" for her novel, she tried to call President Johnson several times. She was staying with a friend in Georgetown who had a Chinese houseboy, but the boy spoke no English. Several weeks later she would hear back in Texas that Johnson had tried, at the height of his Vietnam decision making, to call her back three times, and that he was curious to know more about this girl who kept calling him, but the president apparently had been unable to penetrate the understanding of the Chinese houseboy. "They were all such hustlers in those days," said a ripe and much-traveled femme fatale recently, draped upon a soft couch in her elegant, book-lined living room, off her bedroom with its oversized nude portrait of Sal Mineo. She spoke of moments twenty years before with coy fondness rather than remorse, as if their memory made her feel young again and rebellious and slightly naughty in a dangerous, old-fashioned sort of way.

★

On November 20, 1964, only a few days after both Connally and Lyndon Johnson had been reelected in landslides, Johnson was in San Marcos, Texas, where he made a sentimental, little-noticed speech at the local state college. He had come to attend the inauguration of a new president at Southwest Texas State Teachers College, where Johnson had worked his way to a college degree as a student and part-time janitor. The president was full of good humor and good stories that day. He spoke of a recent toast he had given at a small dinner given by his secretary of state, Dean Rusk, where there were at the table four Rhodes scholars and three graduates of Harvard, two from Yale, one from Princeton, and only one from San Marcos State. "I have traveled a long way from this college to the office I now occupy," he said, turning serious. "In few times—yes, in few nations, in man's journey, has it been possible for any man to travel such a road."

In this meaningful setting, he talked of poverty in the shimmering adobe-caliche soil where the living was harsh and where want and hunger were no strangers, and he moved his audience. Here, his speechmaking did not have the saccharine, piteous quality it sometimes had, in other settings, at other times. And he chose this time and place to proclaim his goal for a Great Society in America. Its ultimate test would be the quality of men and women it produced and the quality of life it imparted to all of its people, and Johnson dedicated himself to assuaging the lot of the one-fifth of the American people who were still ill fed, ill clad, and ill housed. He also announced that San Marcos was to be the first Job Corps training site in the Southwest, and it was clear to all that he intended to watch over this fond site personally. The aura of history hovered over the speech. He reminded his audience of how important the work of New Deal public service programs had been, when one-third of the nation was sunk in poverty, and how important the few pennies they provided had been, not only to himself but to other Texas leaders. "The great leadership that is now being given this state by your governor, one of the ablest chief executives and one of the soundest leaders that we have known, was made possible when he came from Floresville without a dollar in his pocket and he got an NYA job at seventeen cents an hour."

The announcement of the Job Corps site at San Marcos came as a surprise, and it was interpreted as a sign of the president's impatience at how slowly his War on Poverty was taking hold. The hostilities had been declared by Congress in the late summer. Millions in public monies were to be deployed by Johnson's commander in Washington, Sargent Shriver, where Shriver, not local leaders, divined what need was greatest and where the money could do the most good. All over the nation, governors and mayors bridled. The process was brought into high relief in Texas because Johnson wanted Texas to be the model for the nation. San Marcos was to be the prototype for the Job Corps. But his friend the governor was restless.

In April 1965 Johnson returned to dedicate the San Marcos site, which was at Camp Gary, an abandoned helicopter base. This time, Governor Connally was present, and again Johnson referred to Connally's humble beginnings in another "job corps," the NYA, which Johnson had headed from 1935 to 1937 in Texas, when Connally was one of its enrollees. "I remember that it was about thirty years ago that I had Governor Connally and a good many other people on this platform in the job corps of that day," the president said. "Governor Connally talks about not having to borrow money to pay his income taxes these days. He did not have to borrow it then either. But he's always been a modest man. I can give testimony, even if it is not eloquent, that he's come a long way from that $25 a month to $25,000 a year." Then, with an expansive gesture to the several hundred uniformed Job Corps students, he added, "So you fellows, you have got something to shoot for here."

Connally was by no means opposed, in theory or generally in practice, to the Great Society. In fact, it might be argued that the concept for the national preschool program called Head Start had its genesis in Texas, in the Connally administration. The governor had backed a preschool language program for Mexican-American children at the outset of his governorship, and by mid-1965, between the state and federal Head Start programs, Texas had more enrollees than any other state in the Union—over 71,000 children. Some 282 grants and projects, totaling $25 million, had been approved by August 1965. Approval came quickly from Connally when local and state officials were in control. Control was the point. At the very center of the War on Poverty concept was the desire to avoid the layers of local bureaucracy and the inclinations toward the pork barrel which had always scuttled giveaway programs in the past. States, therefore, had limited influence over the substance and the location of the major programs, but in the initial Economic Opportunity Act of 1964 governors were given the right to veto. The power was seldom exercised across America. On May 5, 1965, Connally became the first governor to use the power, and he used it in a particularly controversial way by canceling an eleven-county Neighborhood Youth Corps project that was sponsored by the Texas Farmers Union and was particularly dear to Texas liberals.

There was consternation in Washington. Shriver passed the news to the president with regret, and the president let Senator Ralph Yarborough do the running for him. Governor Connally was trying "to frustrate the purposes of the War on Poverty," Yarborough proclaimed to the U.S. Senate, and in the Senate Labor Committee he led a campaign to remove the gubernatorial veto altogether from the original legislation. It was a campaign to which President Johnson gave his quiet but full blessing, and when it succeeded, giving Sargent Shriver the power to override any governor's veto, Senator Yarborough gloated, "It was the crippling actions of a few governors who caused this veto power to be taken away from the governors of all fifty states, most of whom did not misuse this power. A few governors have used veto power to cut wages down on projects, to purge people they did not like from serving on local boards, and in one extreme case, to veto absolutely an eleven-county rural antipoverty project said to be the best planned rural antipoverty project in America. It was such irresponsible action that forced me to devote much time to aid in eliminating the governors' unrestricted veto power over poverty projects, which has now been done." Yarborough's counterattack on Connally did much to deepen Connally's reputation as backward on social issues.

Yet the issue was one of simple turf, more than political philosophy, and it was a national issue. In the first year of Johnson's War on Poverty, Sargent Shriver had limited access to the president, so great were the complaints from provincial officeholders. In Texas, the antipathy toward federal control ran deep. The notion that a Washington bureaucrat, housed in some faceless gray building on M Street, would know better about the needs of the people in San Marcos, Texas, than the people of San Marcos themselves was abhorrent. With his concept of reflective leadership, Connally mirrored the antipathy glintingly. Still, Johnson wanted a true war on poverty, and he wanted his commander to treat the situation as if he were invading an occupied Europe. In Texas, the president wanted a textbook victory.

Sargent Shriver found himself in the middle on the Texas battlefield. He saw Johnson and Connally as "two heavyweight sluggers" who were after the same prize, two "ambitious, political animals who came out of the same jungle . . . lions out of the same bush . . . who had the same emotions, the same aggressiveness, the same showboating, the same strengths and weaknesses." If Johnson was serene in his broad vision of a different future, and if Connally seemed rooted in the present and past, the difference, to Shriver, lay in the fact that Johnson had achieved the ultimate prize of the presidency, and Connally had not. The struggle over his program in Texas was no more complicated than power. It was personal rather than ideological. And it was sure to come to a head, probably over the San Marcos situation.

It happened on one of Connally's trips to Washington. He began his mission with a convivial evening at the White House, but the following day he stormed into the Office of Economic Opportunity with several advisers. Shriver met with the delegation in his conference room, and the meeting had the air of a Cold War summit meeting. In a way, Connally and Shriver suffered from the same penumbral problem: Shriver would always be seen as a Kennedy, Connally as a glossy Johnson, and this very inability to emerge from the shadows of their respective benefactors imparted a special edge to this confrontation. It was how they saw each other. To Connally, Shriver was a bleeding-heart liberal who had been elected to nothing and had been appointed as a sop to the Kennedy legacy. To Shriver, Connally was a tough provincial, surrounded by cronies who could only turn his program into a pork barrel. It was an uneasy meeting.

Connally laid out his position succinctly: he thought this control of community action programs where only one-third of the boards were public officials was absurd. (By statute, the other thirds were composed of private agencies and certifiable poor people.) What made sense, Connally thought, was for the programs to be run exclusively through the governor's office. Shriver listened patiently, for he had heard the argument before. In frustration, Connally reached slowly for an aide's file.

"It has been brought to my attention that one of the people you have installed in charge of the community action program in Waco* is a former convict, an actual felon," Connally said. "That shows me that you people don't know what you're doing up here. You don't know enough to keep a guy like that off the board. If that ever got out, it would embarrass me, embarrass you, and embarrass the president."

So this is his trump card, Shriver thought, and he responded on a level where Connally was ill at ease. "Well, Governor, I've known about that situation for six months," Shriver said. "Frankly, it has caused me a serious moral problem. I've thought a lot about it. You're right. That man is a convicted felon. He served nine years in the penitentiary. He came out and moved to Waco, where he's been a model citizen for fourteen years. The business community finds him acceptable. He was made the leader of that community

*The midsize Texas city where this situation occurred was not Waco but has been changed for obvious reasons.

action program upon the recommendation of the city. Now I've faced this question: if I throw this man out because he is a convict, I would have to cite the reason. I would drag up his past, a past that he's paid for. I would humiliate him, ruin his life, a life which he has reconstituted. He would probably have to leave Waco, and resign from his present job. I've thought about it a lot, Governor. I think that firing that man would be morally irresponsible."

Connally grunted. Shriver was beyond help. The governor packed up his files and left.

The next day, the *Washington Star* ran a story with the headline CONNALLY THREATENS TO QUIT POVERTY WAR. By the *Star* account, the governor had grown so upset at not having more authority over the poverty program in Texas that he threatened to close Camp Gary in San Marcos, which, by this time, had become one of the largest Job Corps installations in the nation and was known to be Johnson's favorite battleground in the War on Poverty. The article was sprinkled with the inevitable quotations from Senator Yarborough in the Senate debate the previous August, and even a statement by the Texas Farmers Union after Connally had vetoed their prized, eleven-county Neighborhood Youth Corps project, referring to "Connally's disregard for the purposes of the war on poverty and his attempt to substitute his own political reasoning in place of laws written by Congress." The newspaper savored the possibility of a personal rift between Johnson and Connally.

As soon as the *Star* story was published, Marvin Watson, Johnson's chief of staff, called Connally, undoubtedly at the instigation of the president. Watson took an unusual step in recording their talk surreptitiously and planting a transcript of it on the president's desk shortly afterwards. It was not unusual for the White House to record conversations, but almost never were conversations with the president's closest personal friends recorded. That it was done here shows the degree of suspicion that the issue over San Marcos had introduced into the Connally-Johnson relationship. Connally's fury over the *Star* story was evident when he came on the line. He had made no threat, to Shriver, to the *Star* reporter, or to anyone else, to close down Camp Gary. He was proud of the camp, had worked diligently to get such corporations as Texas Instruments involved, and that very day had said nothing but nice things about OEO in a press conference with the Texas press.

"You've got to remember that most of the people down here dislike the poverty program," he told Watson as the tape rolled. "Most of these reporters, every one of them thinks this program is a big boondog. Everyone of them wanted me to pick a fight this morning. I did not do it. I did not utter a critical word. I spent all my time bragging about what we have done," and then, as if he knew he was being recorded, he said, "Tell the president the [Star] story does not reflect what transpired. It's distorted. It does not reflect my personal attitudes."

Watson—and Johnson—were assuaged.

Still, Connally's apparent indifference toward the social concerns of his mentor became the butt of political satire, a pastime which is rich and time-honored in Texas. Connally was providing good raw material for this sort of fun, not only with his horror at paying youth corps workers the "enormous salary" of $1.25 an hour, a full quarter above the minimum wage, but also his penchant for superboards over regular boards, his proposal that the governor's term be lengthened to four years, and his self-appointment as an "education governor" as he opposed a hike in teachers' salaries. During this period, for example, the North Dallas Democratic Women held their annual bash and staged a musical comedy called *Political Paranoia II*. In its final skit, called "Caesar's Circus," Connallius Caesar was brought forward to be questioned in what was announced as "Jolly John's Legislative Quiz." As he strode to his throne, he averted his eyes from a starving schoolteacher who happened by in tatters, a tin cup in hand. The *Texas Observer* was to capture the parody:

"Governor, there are many poor families in Texas," the Lady began. "How do you plan to alleviate this problem?"

"The society ladies of Texas do a marvelous job on holidays by giving poor families baskets of grapefruit and broken tricycles," replied Connallius.

"This is a basic question in economics," said the Lady. "If a boy in Texas makes a dollar and twenty-five cents an hour, and he works two hours, how much does he make?"

Connallius (after a long, thoughtful pause): "He makes too much. Certainly more than his mother and father. A dollar and twenty-five cents would ruin the economy of the state of Texas!"

"Governor, the public-school teachers are grossly underpaid. What do you say about that?"

"That depends on whether I'm running for office or have already been elected."

"What do you feel the length of the governor's term should be?"

"As long as I am governor—," said Connallius Caesar, "oh, I'd say maybe ten or maybe fifteen years or so."

"Our colleges are forty-fifth in the nation," the Lady persisted. "What do you intend to do about it?"

"Why, I think I can solve the problem by appointing a super-board, maybe a supersuper committee to watch the superboard."

"Thank you, Governor."

It was a measure of Connally's self-assurance that he loved these affairs, attended them whenever he could, laughed heartily, and when it came his time to speak, dished out better than he got. This was in sharp contrast to the oversensitive and insecure Lyndon Johnson, who grew silent and glum when he was parodied. "Bird! I'm leaving!" he would snap at his wife, and would storm out of unpleasantly hot roasts. Connally welcomed the heat.

★

To Connally, the right way to combat poverty was not to make war on it but to outsmart it. As he groused with Johnson in 1965 and 1966 about Great Society measures which trespassed upon state privilege, he set out his own program for Arcadia in Texas. "What are we going to do?" he asked himself rhetorically about his pool of black and Hispanic poor—the largest in the nation. "We're going to give 'em education. Once they get that, they're going to be in a position to become productive taxpaying citizens of this state. That is a good investment." In his first legislature as governor, he had constructed the bureaucratic framework for this push forward. In his second, the pivotal legislature of 1965, he meant to make his vision into a reality.

It was to be the zenith of his governorship.

"A new Texas has been imposed upon the face of the old," he said in his inaugural address in late January. "It is a Texas which bursts with vitality: growing, exploring, seeking its place in the sun. It demands a great deal, but it yields much in return."

After the speech he threw the governor's mansion open to the people of Texas, an act that there was seen as more Pappy O'Daniel than Andrew Jackson. Connally was rightly proud to show off what Nellie had accomplished in refurbishing the Greek Revival mansion, which had become like a middle-aged woman in need of resuscitation and whose plumbing needed an overhaul. The governor was particularly proud of the color and style his wife had brought to the mansion's gardens, where Nellie, no doubt, had been influenced by the horticulture of Lady Bird Johnson.

The day after his second inaugural address, he went before the legislature to detail his "space-age" program. He proposed to

restructure the entire system of higher education into three tiers
and, over time, to advance faculty salaries ten percent above the
national average. He was going to deemphasize physical construction and focus upon the quality of education. "Brains not bricks"
was his motto. To the noisy demand of public-school teachers that
they get a hefty raise of forty-five dollars a month, the Governor
acquiesced, but spread increases over a ten-year period as a
cautionary note about the budget. Because this increase was expensive, he did not shrink from suggesting the possibility of new taxes
(and two years later, he would demand a whopping tax increase). In
his farm boy's dream to become the governor of the intellectuals
and of the cultivated, he suddenly broke from his recitation of cold
figures and dry programs and, startlingly, launched into . . . poetry!
It was as if suddenly he had been transported back to 1936, and this
was the Atheneum Society, and the premium was on the voice that
could declaim most penetratingly through the huge oak doors of the
Law Building. If public-school teachers should be paid more, then
local school districts should pay a greater share of the increase, and
that reminded him of the New England poet, Sam Walter Foss. The
governor broke sonorously into verse:

> Oh, ship ahoy! Rang out the cry
> Oh, give us water or we die.
> A voice came o'er the waters far
> Just drop your bucket where you are!

In this vernacular place, Connally's poetic display was thrilling,
and he was cheered mightily. He was onto a good thing. If poetry
was good politics, so be it. He concluded with James Russell Lowell,
and the place went wild.

> Life is a leaf of paper white
> Where on each one of us may write
> His word or two, and then comes night
> . . . .
> Greatly begin! Though thou have time
> But for a line, be that sublime,—
> Not failure, but low aim, is crime.

As the ghosts of Ma and Farmer Jim Ferguson stirred, the
reporters rushed to the governor's aides to learn more of the governor's hitherto unknown interest in verse. Coleridge, Browning, and
Keats, they were told, engaged Connally's idle moments, but Tennyson's "Locksley Hall" was his special favorite.

If, in Tennyson's "Locksley," a young man's fancy lightly turns to thoughts of love in the spring, in the spring of 1965 Connally's thoughts turned heavily to thoughts of an international exposition in San Antonio and of a permanent Institute of Texan Cultures. The concept for a "Fair of the Americas," later called HemisFair, had been percolating for six years, as San Antonio businessmen had recruited first Congressman Henry Gonzalez and then Senator Ralph Yarborough in the effort. Taking their inspiration from the Seattle World's Fair of 1964, the business establishment argued that a world's fair in San Antonio would bring millions of dollars into Texas, while the more culturally minded argued that there was no place in Texas where the unique story of Texas was dramatized for a modern audience. Governor Connally embraced the idea with the excitement of a grade-school boy at his first science fair. With the legislature, he threw his weight behind a bill to appropriate $4.5 million for the HemisFair building. Not long after the bill was passed, he promised to ask the next legislature for more money, bringing the total state contribution to $10 million.

Here was a project that went to the heart of what Connally wanted to accomplish as governor. He had, for some time, argued that the people of Texas did not appreciate the richness and uniqueness of their history, nor was the diversity of their culture accepted. In an era of racial tension, and as supposedly the very embodiment of the Texas establishment, he spoke openly and positively of the twenty-six strains that contributed to the Texas "bloodline" and of how diversity was the essence of what Texas was. About tourism in Texas, he lamented, albeit diplomatically, that the Neiman-Marcus store in Dallas was the number one tourist attraction in Texas. His talk about HemisFair had the feel of a deprived child before whom, suddenly, great treasures had been spread. "HemisFair is something that excites me so much that really my words tumble over each other in trying to explain it," he said. "Texans know so little about their own state, notwithstanding that we are extremely proud of it. . . . This will trace the cultural growth of Texas from the earliest prehistoric discoveries up to the age of space . . . and beyond. I hope we can project what Texas has been, what Texas is, what Texas will be. It should be something that will be of compelling interest to all of the people of this state, of this nation, and frankly, of the world." He wanted not a moment of concentration, but a lasting, living testament from pictographs to cowboys, conquistadors to astronauts.

For the boosters of the idea, enlisting Connally was a stroke of genius. He became its commissioner general and set out to South

America as a diplomat from Texas to persuade Panama, Venezuela, and Brazil to contribute exhibits to the Fair. When the HemisFair opened three years later as the only international exposition of 1968 in the United States, it was a grand success. But the Institute of Texan Cultures, which survived as a permanent museum, serves as the most lasting legacy of the Connally governorship.

By May of 1965 Connally was the consummate man of power: confident, domineering, aloof, nearly untouchable. He had supplanted a hostile Speaker of the Texas house by appointing him to the nirvana of the Texas Railroad Commission* and installed a twenty-six-year-old protégé called Ben Barnes in his place. With his political godson handling things in the legislature, Connally was comfortable, for he was free to concentrate on what interested him, like higher education, and leave the rest to Barnes. When he focused, he was shrewd and effective. Unlike Lyndon Johnson, he did not enjoy the lapel-grabbing and the cajoling and the false flattery of a legislature. "Individually, they're all great," Connally would say later of state legislators. "I traveled the state. I was in their districts. I bragged on them. I worked with them. But as soon as the legislature convenes, they all come to Austin, where they're surrounded by lobbyists. They're constantly told how important and strong they are, and how valuable their service is. I suppose anybody in public office has more than their share of vanity—but you haven't seen anything until you've seen the combined arrogance and vanity of a legislature." A cosmopolitan now, he was distressed by the parochial fixations of legislators, and he shrank from them. His distress hardened into contempt with time, as he came to view the powerful legislators as "experts in extortion."

At last, the oars of state government were beginning to work together. He had been in office long enough that his appointments to the various independent governing boards and commissions were making a difference, and this in turn strengthened his power. With a few exceptions, his appointments had been excellent, men and women of stature rather than the old political hacks, and this brought new vigor to the commission system. He sweated over his appointments. "If you want to talk about real infighting," he said once, "try making an appointment to the Board of Cosmetology." Discarding traditional Texas xenophobia, he pushed through the legislature a resolution to appoint distinguished out-of-state members to the governing boards of state universities. While he was

*The Texas Railroad Commission regulates oil production.

hostile to Lyndon Johnson's national civil rights program, he began to appoint more blacks and Hispanics to state positions than all the governors of Texas before him combined—in fact, three times as many: by 1966, 3,300 Mexican-Americans held positions in state government, and the Latinos returned the favor by according him eighty percent of their vote. Legislators rebuked him for appointing a black to the prison board and formed a delegation to protest. Connally told them that if they vetoed his choice, a minister from Fort Worth, he'd appoint another black and then another and another. They skulked away, and his original choice was confirmed overwhelmingly. Even more controversial was his appointment of the first black as a Texas highway patrolman. This was more than mere window dressing, but there was a lot of that, too. Connally seemed to rise to the carnivals of governance. From the Watermelon Thump in Luling to the Black-Eyed Pea Jamboree in Athens, Buccaneer Days in Corpus Christi, the Rattlesnake Roundup in Sweetwater, and the Turkey Trot in Cuero, Connally made good royalty, and he looked very good on a horse. Not always did the ceremonial side of life appeal to him, however. Once, friendly Tigua Indians from El Paso smeared war paint on his face, and Connally turned away in manifest revulsion.

Inevitably, confidence in power turned into arrogance. In the summer of 1966, in light of Connally's disparaging remarks about $1.25 as the wage for poverty program workers, and inspired by the labor activities of Cesar Chavez in California, organizers in the Rio Grande Valley conceived of a march of 490 miles, to dramatize the plight of the migrant worker in Texas. The march would culminate in a big rally in the capital on Labor Day, where they would demand to meet with the governor and demand of him that he call a special session of the legislature to enact a $1.25-an-hour minimum wage for Texas. On July 4 a ragtag group of migrant workers, ministers, and labor organizers set out from Rio Grande City in the heat and the dust. The marchers had heartrending tales of exploitation and grinding poverty to tell, tales of backbreaking work, seven days a week, at wages as low as forty cents an hour. South Texas was the bottom of the social tree for the nation; the migrant labor force left their homes in April, fanned out over the nation, and did not return until October. Their stories, writ large, pointed to the outrage of 167,000 migrant laborers in Texas who made less than $1,000 a year. "*Viva la Huelga!*" they shouted about their strike, which so far had had spotty results. "*Abajo con el miedo!*" they said of the fear under which they had lived for generations.

Connally did his best to ignore the little band as it meandered north through Corpus Christi to Floresville, but as it drew nearer to the capital it received increased press attention. Senator Yarborough gave it encouragement from Washington by stressing his efforts to enact a federal minimum wage of $1.60 an hour, and a telegram from the senator was read to the desiccated and bedraggled crowd in the town square of Floresville. When they reached San Antonio, they slogged through a driving rain into the San Fernando Cathedral, where a service for them was held, and with Senator Yarborough in attendance, the archbishop blessed the congregation by endorsing the minimum wage demand and spoke of the suffering and of the docility of Mexican Americans. "*Viva el campesino!*" Yarborough shouted buoyantly, and the cathedral was filled with cheers. In Austin, Connally concluded the march could no longer be ignored.

Five miles outside the neat and quaint old German town of New Braunfels, as the group trudged northward, suddenly a shiny Lincoln Continental screeched to a halt and out stepped the immaculate governor, with Speaker Barnes and the Texas attorney general, Waggoner Carr, in tow. In their astonishment, it took some minutes for the weary leaders of the march to recover, as Connally strode into their midst, shaking hands, introducing his companions, and saying the most complimentary things about the dignity and the order of the march, as well as how much he sympathized with the lot of farm workers.

"Governor, the Latins love and respect you," said Father Antonio Gonzales of Houston, one of the march leaders.

"I know that. I appreciate that," Connally replied. "They feel I have a sense of compassion about them and their problems. And I do, and I'm going to continue to have." The conclave was in danger of becoming a love fest. In their speeches, the organizers had been making customary demands of a 1960s street action, including a face-to-face meeting with the governor, and now that they unexpectedly had him in such a situation, they did not know quite what to say. "You don't need a march to come and see me, Father," Connally said deflatingly. His office was always open to all the citizens of Texas, he said, and he had been available to see their representatives at any time in the past month since their march began. With the marchers looking slightly hangdog, the governor pointed to his adult education program for Mexican-Americans, to his Head Start triumphs, to the schools for migrant workers which he had started and now had over 20,000 students in them. "We have attempted to do everything we know how to do," he said as shouts of "Viva! Viva!" rolled over him and trucks roared by. "And we will continue to try to upgrade the quality of education."

If he had left it on this note of civilized exchange, the moment might have fulfilled Connally's intention to upstage and to undercut the coming rally in Austin, but he seemed driven to overpower them, even to rebuke them for sins that they had not committed. Even though the march had been a model of decorum, Connally abruptly cast it in the mold of uncontrolled civil rights marches elsewhere in the South which had led to violence, bloodshed, riots, and the destruction of property. "As governor, I'm aware of the fact that things can get out of hand in marches, as they have elsewhere in the United States, and that's the last thing we want in Texas." For a people whose problem was docile forbearance, Connally was reaching far off the point and offending as he did so, and yet he pressed further in a gratuitous slight. Of his absence on Labor Day, he said, "I did not want my absence to be interpreted as a lack of interest in the problems of Texas—but if I did not have a previous engagement, I *still* would not have met with you. . . . I do not feel that as governor, I should lend the dignity, the prestige of [my] office to dramatize any particular march."

He seemed oblivious to the fact that nothing could be quite as dramatic as this, as from the fringes of the sweaty crowd shouts of "*Viva la Huelga!*" and "A dollar-twenty-five!" rained down.

"I've come to ask for your help for a minimum wage in Texas," George Nelson, a labor leader, said plaintively. "Will you do that?"

"You want me to call a special session?"

"Yes, we do."

"The answer to that is no. I will not. This problem did not recently originate, nor is it going to be readily solved in the next few months. I've had many requests for special sessions from many different groups, all of whom have real problems. I tell you categorically today that I will not call a special session for this purpose, because I don't think the urgency of it is of such a character that it [is] compelling. So the answer to that is no."

"I think it's very urgent," Nelson persisted. "People in the Rio Grande Valley don't have enough to eat and don't have decent houses to live in. I say, it's extremely urgent."

"I'm sure there are people who have substandard housing—all over this state, all over this nation, all over this world," Connally replied. "There's never been a time in the history of this country when government was more aware of it or attempting to do more about it than we're doing right today. . . . Those of you who are men of reason and intelligence will not expect the impossible of anybody."

"We're not expecting the impossible, Governor," Nelson snapped back. "We're just expecting the possible, a minimum wage of $1.25, which is only reasonable. . . ."

The confrontation loitered on a while longer, before the governor retreated to his limousine and drove off in a cloud of dust. For a day, it seemed as if the wind had gone out of the march. But as the marchers entered Austin and swelled to thousands, and as news of Connally's patronizing highhandedness got out, the episode of New Braunfels boomeranged. It became a symbol of the indifference of the political establishment and a rallying point. Connally's stock among the Latins of his state plummeted.

The showdown at New Braunfels would be remembered for years. The image of Connally, with his limousine, his cool high fashion, and his paladins by his side, chastising the dusty and the hot, the brown and the poor under the August sun, was a lasting one. It came to be considered, even among his closest advisers like George Christian, one of the worst mistakes of his governorship. Christian, away in Washington at the White House, would lament immodestly that if he had still been in Austin, it would never have happened. But Connally could not bear the thought of these hordes surrounding his house, chanting, singing, brandishing their signs and slogans, happy in their work, as now the house of his friend, Lyndon Johnson, was constantly surrounded in Washington over Vietnam. Connally had conveyed the impression that such lowly people as these were not invited to his mansion—how dare they presume to come? The episode magnified as time passed, and it came to overshadow the real, positive things that Connally had accomplished.

In the succeeding months, the situation in the Rio Grande Valley grew more tense and more polarized, as the strike against melon growers widened and became more dangerous. Less than a year later, Connally dispatched the hated Texas Rangers, long the symbol of oppression for Chicano laborers, to the Valley. Predictably, their bruising excesses, reminiscent of Central American justice, became Connally's. Once loved and even deified, Connally was suddenly hated by a substantial portion of the Latin community. Rumor spread that he whipped his own wetbacks on his Floresville ranch. While that was a boilerplate rumor, oft used by Mexican Americans about the powerful white politicians to discredit them, it was a measure of Connally's downfall. In June of 1967, the U.S. Civil Rights Commission took an interest in the Valley situation, and even the FBI was deployed, as if the Rio Grande Valley had joined the Birminghams, the Selmas, the Plaquemine Parishes as a last redoubt of massive resistance to minority justice in the South.

★

There remained about Connally an air of heroic poignancy.

Through his years as governor after November 22, 1963, an annual ritual developed for him every fall, when the anniversary of the Kennedy assassination rolled around, and he would again address himself to the mystery of why Kennedy had died and he himself had lived, and what deep changes the emotional scars of the event had caused in his character and in his view of life. The connection to the Dallas murders, Oswald's as well as Kennedy's, cropped up more frequently than once a year. When Jack Ruby was tried and his defense lawyer, Melvin Belli, made uncomplimentary statements about Texas and Texans, Connally took it upon himself to distinguish Ruby and Oswald from other Texans, as he chastised Belli for his intemperate remarks. When it became fashionable to talk about the sickness of Dallas, Connally was among the leaders who debunked the notion, and Dallas, sunk as it was in guilt, self-doubt, and self-analysis, loved Connally all the more for his support and comfort.

All the figures who survived the Dallas motorcade were intensely aware that the history of Dallas was being written during the period that followed, and they viewed the process nervously. Of particular concern was the "authorized" version of the assassination, with which the Kennedys had blessed and cursed the writer William Manchester. Manchester had written a praiseworthy biography of John F. Kennedy before the president's death, and was openly admiring. "He was brighter than I was, braver, better-read, handsomer, wittier, and more incisive," Manchester was to say. "The only thing I could do better was write."

When the Kennedys laid their hands upon him, Manchester was flattered and he got to work. Connally had seen Manchester in his gubernatorial office, and the author had taken an instant dislike to Connally, viewing him as vainglorious and given to fascistic impulses.

Only Lyndon Johnson (and Marina Oswald) among the principals had refused to see Manchester. Johnson's attitude was bound up with political considerations. Robert Kennedy had won his senatorial seat in 1964, and Johnson was gripped by paranoia over the possibility that Kennedy would challenge him for the Democratic nomination in 1968. How Manchester portrayed Johnson's actions before and after the Dallas assassination could engender even more personal antagonism and bitterness between the two potential contenders, further complicate their relationship, and actually have a bearing on Kennedy's decision to challenge or not to challenge Johnson. To talk to Manchester was a no-win proposition for Johnson; it was simply too dangerous.

A bizarre situation ensued, in which the author was invited first to submit a list of written questions to the White House and then to come to the White House for a kind of rehearsal with Johnson's aide, Jack Valenti, of what Johnson's answers might be if he were present. When Manchester's questions arrived, they were put in memo form for Valenti with recommendations like "vague response," "no comment," "legal question," "we have no information." Even though he perceived the stonewall, Manchester went for his interview with Valenti, if only because not to do so would be a dereliction of duty. In the company of a second Johnson aide, Valenti and Manchester plowed through Manchester's questions one by one. Many of them addressed ambiguous recollections on the part of some participants or discrepancies which only Lyndon Johnson could clear up for the accuracy of the historical record. Valenti and Manchester were not, however, the only parties to their conversation. At curious moments in the interview the buzzer on Valenti's phone rang. He would pick up the phone, listen, hang up, and excuse himself on some pretext. Upon his return some minutes later Valenti would say to Manchester, "By the way, on the question you asked back there about" such and such, and he would elaborate or change the previous answer.

"Why the president of the United States would have nothing better to do than eavesdrop on my conversation with Valenti, I can only guess," Manchester was to say many years later. He never got his interview with Johnson directly.

In early 1966, Senator Kennedy took a major step toward the direct confrontation Johnson feared. As the U.S. Senate fell into an acrimonious debate over a $12.3 billion appropriation for the Vietnam War, Kennedy broke formally with the administration he had briefly served. He proposed the unthinkable: that the Vietcong participate in a negotiated settlement. Kennedy invoked his experience in the 1962 Cuban missile crisis as the basis for his Vietnam position against inflexibility toward the enemy. Now, the Vietnam doves finally had their presidential candidate. From Texas, Connally tried to bolster Johnson's spirits. Two days after Kennedy's declaration, Connally was on the phone to the White House conveying the news from down home that the Senate doves had changed no one's mind and that everybody assumed the wicked Kennedy was orchestrating the entire campaign against the president. On the issue of war appropriations, Connally urged Johnson to remember the parents of the 200,000 men in Vietnam, and said, "The real gut issue is: Are you going to support these troops with the necessary military equipment and strong foreign policy?" Why shouldn't Senator Richard Russell answer Kennedy? Connally asked. Russell, after all, had also been a participant in the 1962 Cuban missile crisis and he supported the president's policy. But mainly, Connally wanted to enter the debate with Kennedy. He was coming to Washington in a few weeks to address the National Petroleum Council. Now, he wanted Johnson's permission to make the statement that the people should support its responsible officers, particularly the president of the United States as he made foreign policy, and that he did not understand a situation in which a congressional committee had the right to make military decisions. It would not be the only time he sought permission from the White House to argue a point in public. Johnson happily approved of Connally's speech and urged him further to challenge any congressional voice which would attempt to circumscribe the power of the commander in chief as he prosecutes a war.

It was not enough, however, for Connally simply to take an isolated shot at Senator Kennedy, for in the run for the presidential nomination two years hence, the mobilization of Johnson's support in the political trenches would be critical, and that was where Connally was at his best. Both Johnson and Connally worried about holding the Democratic party machinery intact for 1968. Even in Texas, where the disaffection over Johnson's war was rising as everywhere else, they had to worry about Bobby Kennedy undermining the Connally-Johnson hold over the party.

An event in March of 1966 advanced the worry, when a federal court decision struck down the antiquated poll tax in Texas, and a new voter registration period was ordered. With no poll tax, more than 100,000 new voters were going to be registered, and they were predominantly black, Hispanic, and liberal; in short, they were Kennedy supporters. Here Johnson found himself caught between his Great Society programs, the plum of which was the 1965 Voting Rights Act, and his desire to shut Bobby Kennedy out of the presidential race. This time, ideology had to take precedence, and the FBI was ordered into Texas to ensure fairness and noninterference with voter registration. Connally was furious and, in private, his fury was directed at Johnson personally. "You can't tell that dumb son of a bitch anything!" he snapped to an aide, and when Johnson called, Connally said loudly, "Tell the son of a bitch I don't *want* to talk to him." In public, Connally lit into Johnson's attorney general, Nicholas Katzenbach, for the FBI action and attacked him daily for several weeks. Again the issue was turf rather than ideology. It was not that Connally favored the poll tax; on the contrary, he had proposed its repeal to the 1965 Texas legislature. But he resented federal intrusion on Texas soil, as if Texas were incapable or unwilling to enforce the voting laws. At an off-the-record news conference in March, Connally proclaimed that the relationship between himself and the president had become strained. "Eastern liberals," he said, "are giving the president bad advice." Johnson, in turn, had begun to blame the liberals for everything, including Connally's truculence. "Knee-jerk liberals" were "crackpots" and "troublemakers" were turning good "progressive" politicians like John Connally to the right. To his resident historian, Eric Goldman, Johnson fumed about the liberals who had "hacked away and hacked away, criticizing everything [Connally] did, until he had to move to the right to get some support."

There was an element of a charade to all this. It was good politics for Connally to make a public spectacle of "fussing" with the federal government, for it solidified the governor's support among the Texas conservatives, and thereby solidified Johnson's support, before the state Democratic party convention in May. That was the convention which would elect the apparatchiks who would be in place in the early part of the 1968 political season when the challenge of Senator Kennedy to Lyndon Johnson would sort itself out. Of this game of mirrors, the liberal curmudgeon of San Antonio, Maury Maverick, Jr., would say, "[Johnson] can go to these conservatives and give them favors, but he also knows he can pick up a stick and hit 'em across the snout just like you hit a pig." Connally was Johnson's stick. Once Connally secured the slate of party organizers he wanted, his "rift" with Johnson faded into the prairie sunset.

Bearing upon this elemental struggle between Johnson and Robert Kennedy was a quiet, literary drama that was playing itself out in the summer and fall of 1966 in the far-flung places of Hyannis Port; New York; London; Middletown, Connecticut; and a cottage in the Maine woods. Manchester's book on the Dallas tragedy was being

readied, if that is the word, for publication. With painful inevitability, the author was becoming estranged from the very Kennedys
who had sanctioned his exclusive account. As *Look* magazine paid
an enormous price for the serialization rights, Jackie Kennedy
became anxious about the confidences she had shared with Manchester. Wild rumors began to fly about what was in the book,
including the totally false report that the lovemaking between Jack
and Jackie was described. The rumor to which Connally and Johnson
paid attention appeared in *Time* magazine four months before
publication. The book "paints an almost unrelieved portrait of
Johnson as an unfeeling and boorish man"; it "is flawed by the fact
that its partisan portrayal of Lyndon Johnson is so hostile that it
almost demeans the office [of the presidency] itself." Since the
Kennedys had initiated the book and conditioned its publication
upon their approval, the Texans naturally assumed that Bobby
Kennedy was the evil deus ex machina in the vilification of Johnson.
They believed the rumor that a Bobby Kennedy for President
campaign would be launched with the book's publication.

Actually, the reverse of what they believed was true. The most
difficult side of the revision process for William Manchester applied
to the *political* changes that the Kennedys and executives at
Harper & Row were demanding to soften and even to romanticize
the portrait of Johnson. The Kennedys, in fact, were trying to protect
Johnson rather than to get him, even if their motivation, too, was
political. Bobby Kennedy and his closest political advisers felt that
a negative portrait of Johnson in such an emotionally charged area
would be viewed as unpatriotic. In a Kennedy-authorized book, such
a portrait would hurt rather than help Bobby Kennedy's presidential chances. Thus, when Manchester wrote the taut, if tart, line that,
to Lyndon Johnson, "the shortest distance between two points was
a tunnel," or when he quoted a JFK remark accurately that "the
three most overrated things in the world are the State of Texas, the
FBI, and the political wizardry of Lyndon Baines Johnson," or when
he stated correctly that LBJ had been bored as vice president, his
own editor considered these "slurs" on the president and the presidency. With the backing of the Kennedy clan, he tried to get the
references excised. Worse than that, when Manchester wrote
accurately of the tension and harsh words between Johnson and
Bobby Kennedy at Johnson's first cabinet meeting as president,
heavy pressure was brought to bear on Manchester to portray the
meeting as harmonious, and, thus, overtly to falsify history. Connally
and Johnson knew nothing of all this. Instead, they could imagine

Bobby spending late hours crafting smearing lines and wicked scenes with his literary tool, Manchester.

In December the White House got hold of the galleys of the complete book and put Johnson's confidential aide, Jake Jacobsen, to work on culling through the manuscript for the controversial passages, on finding inaccuracies, if he could, and on formulating answers to the uncomplimentary passages from the Johnsonian point of view. It was too late for all this, of course, since Johnson had little standing to complain after he had refused to see Manchester. Some within the Johnson circle continued to grouse about Johnson's stupidity at not seeing the author. "I *still* think you should talk to him [Manchester] before his next book," James Rowe wrote on December 15. "As I said before 1964, he is the kind of man you could easily charm despite his Bobby Kennedy connections. When you don't talk to him, he is terribly and unfairly rough on you. He is the kind of man you can handle easily." Rowe was not above lending credence to the twisted rumor that Johnson himself had been circulating. "[Theodore] White confirms your observation that Manchester has been in and out of mental hospitals. The last time he was in a mental hospital he thought he was John Fitzgerald Kennedy.* He is now convinced he has written a masterpiece for all ages, and no one, including the Kennedys, should be permitted to stop him." *The Death of a President* is a masterpiece. The irony was that the Kennedys were trying first to bowdlerize the text and then to block its publication by court action, as they were joined by the Johnsonites who were trying to discredit it in public and private.

Only John Connally had the standing and the freedom to criticize in a way that would not be too overtly self-serving. (Although he did not know it, one of the political revisions that Manchester accepted was the deletion of some uncomplimentary comments that Jackie Kennedy had made about him before the Dallas motorcade.) As the first installment of the book appeared in *Look*, Connally called a press conference on January 11, 1967. Carefully coordinating his effort with the White House, the governor denounced Manchester scathingly. His own words revealed his ignorance of the literary and the historical process. He was speaking out now, he said angrily, in the name of "unmanaged history." Because of the deep emotional scars which he and Nellie felt should be borne in silence, he had

---

*In fact, a year and a half into the writing, when Manchester was driving himself too hard, writing fifteen hours a day, he did teeter on the edge of a breakdown and admitted himself to a Connecticut hospital for ten days with nervous exhaustion.

refrained from presenting "the facts," but now he had changed his mind. The Manchester book, he said, was "filled with editorial comment based on unfounded rumor, distortion and inconsistency"; it was "a shocking, transparent attempt to dictate history through a captive voice"; it was an "astonishing propaganda instrument cleverly woven to reflect favorably on those [the Kennedys] who gave it birth, while rudely discrediting others [Lyndon Johnson and John Connally] involved"; it was a "recitation of recollections and observations collected and reflected through the prism of prejudice." Connally was on weak ground, but he did not seem to know it. To the extent that anybody outside a small group in Texas paid any attention to this, it helped Manchester and his book.

The following day, at the opening of business in the newly convened Texas senate, a resolution was put forward to commend Governor Connally's statement and to "condemn the publication of distortions, rumors and inconsistencies" of irresponsible writers. Among the fifteen Texas senators who voted for the resolution was the sponsor, D. B. Hardeman, who later went on to a new calling as an aide to Speaker Sam Rayburn. Among the six senators who voted against the resolution was Senator Barbara Jordan, who would later help John Connally escape going to jail. A day later, in an ebullient mood, Connally called presidential press secretary George Christian to pass the news to Johnson that the public reaction to his public blast against Manchester had been "highly favorable," and to identify the villains in the Texas senate who had voted against the resolution. Christian put this in a memo to the president: "[Connally] said it is the consensus of everyone he talks with and from every report he gets that you should remain silent on the controversy. He has the definite feeling that you have gained from a 'gentlemanly attitude' toward the whole thing."

Connally's promise to break his silence, to set the record straight as it were, so that "legitimate historians" might reach "objective judgments," was a mission which he found more difficult to accomplish than he imagined. Enlisting his friend Robert Strauss in the project, they tried their hand at the "objective facts" of the Dallas tragedy without "editorial comment" through the "prism of prejudice." The result appeared in *Life* magazine on the fourth anniversary of the assassination. Its thrust was that J. F. Kennedy had come to Texas not to heal a split between him and Yarborough, but to bolster the president's own sinking popularity and to pillage the state for political contributions. In the process of putting this article together, Connally made a curious appeal to the White House.

He wanted back the *original* of the letter Lee Harvey Oswald had sent him on January 20, 1962, asking Connally as the secretary of the navy to redress the outrage of Oswald's devalued military discharge. Connally's attempt to retrieve this bizarre piece of mail came out only twenty years later, in 1987, and it was widely assumed that Connally had simply wanted it for its financial value. The reason was deeper and more interesting than that. He and Oswald had a macabre relationship in history which the original letter represented. Connally admitted the possibility, if only to his subconscious, that his innocent but coldly bureaucratic response to Oswald had planted the seed of epic tragedy. That letter should, by rights, be in his own estate, he felt. George Christian became his intermediary, but despite this high-level interest, Connally's request was turned down by the National Archives, which held all the original and now extremely valuable documents of the Warren Commission.

"Should we do this for Governor Connally?" a memo to the archivist of the United States read. "To do so might cause requests from other people such as Marina and Marguerite Oswald for free copies of other letters written by Oswald to the Government." The archivist said flatly, No.

★

As the legislature convened in 1967, Connally had become the lone star of Texas. He was Texas, and Texas was John Connally. For over three years, since the assassination had swept away his frustration with the job and removed the uncertainty of his political future, he had had virtually everything he asked for. He stood alongside Allan Shivers as the most effective and powerful Texas governor in this century. He had had the good fortune to be governor at a time when a Texan was in the White House, and that bond was good for Texas. He represented the passage of Texas into the modern age, and he advanced that passage, so that his state was associated as much with its technological instruments and its space capsules and its glistening skyscrapers as with its roughnecks and oil derricks. He came of age in politics as television came of age. In his personal deportment and his elegant diction, in his concern for Texas brains as well as its brawn, in his moderate, if uninspired, stance on race when other Southern governors spewed racist venom, in the energy he brought to the ossified machinery of state government, in the international, cosmopolitan air that HemisFair brought to his stewardship, and in his general good humor, he represented a better present and a better future for his state. His goal, for his own people, was to change their reputation from "blustering braggadocio" to a new concept for the Texan: proud of his past, humble in his present, with faith in his future. Texans felt good about themselves when he was governor. While his critics wrote sniping editorials about him as the Emperor of Texas until 1970 as if this were a fearful prospect, and denounced him as the voice only of business and the well-to-do as if this were a curse, a good many Texans, perhaps most of them, would have been quite content to appoint him governor for life.

For one who had become larger than life and who had come to think of himself as larger than life, it had become difficult to continue working on the humdrum business of governance. Connally became increasingly distant and inaccessible, and this drove some to extraordinary measures to gain an audience. The representative from Angleton, Neil Caldwell, for example, was keen on the issue of industrial safety and had a bill working its way through committee. Though Connally seemed to favor the bill, the governor would not see the legislator, for Caldwell was "off the ranch." But Caldwell was a sculptor when he was not a lawyer, and he decided that he was prepared to "sink to any level" to advance the cause of industrial safety. Taking the most flattering pictures of Connally from various angles, he began to work at night in a studio at the university on sculpting a bust of the governor. When the bigger-than-life, white hydrostone piece was complete, Caldwell showed it to Speaker Barnes, who, though no connoisseur in such matters, liked the work, and it was decided to have a major presentation in the House Chamber. Caldwell was made the head of the delegation to bring the governor to the House Chamber for the ceremony. As the sack fell away and the house members burst into prolonged applause, Connally gazed upon his likeness pensively and silently for quite a long time, walking slowly around it. When he finally spoke, genuinely touched, he spoke of art and beauty. Caldwell's access improved after that, and his industrial safety bill breezed through. Not long afterwards, the legislator took some relatives to meet the governor and Connally greeted them warmly, speaking mostly about the bust, which now occupied a prominent place behind his desk.

"But you know, Neil, I think you could have moved my hairline back just a bit," said the governor.

15

The Catalyst

IN THE EARLY SPRING OF 1967 Connally and Lyndon Johnson had their first discussions about their respective futures. Connally was tired. He was suffering for the first time in his life from a mild case of ulcers. His energy had never really returned completely after the Dallas assassination, and now, after the reckoning of his fiftieth birthday, he had to acknowledge that he would never be quite the same. To his closest observers, he was visibly slowed. Bravely, Nellie tried to make a joke of the lingering effects of Dallas, telling friends that the only vestige of the event was the fact that her husband couldn't turn his right wrist over to accept change at the checkout counter, but she was always there to pick up the coins when he dropped them. That was for public consumption, but she had not wanted him to run again for governor in 1966. She had pushed hard, and lost. Now, she had a better case. No one had ever won a fourth term as governor of Texas. Even with his total command of the legislature, concentrating more power in the governor's office than it had had at any time since Reconstruction, Connally was bored and frustrated. Publicly, he exaggerated the constitutional limitations of the job, even as he had superseded them. People were telling him that Texans wanted him to be governor forever. But to Edward Harte, the supportive publisher of the *Corpus Christi Caller Times*, he confessed that he had lost his "optimism." This was conveyed to Johnson that spring. Connally probably would not run again. Later, after he made his own decision about reelection, Johnson asserted that Connally's attitude had "really tied down" Johnson's own decision to resign. In short, Connally was the catalyst for Johnson's withdrawal from the presidency.

To the outside world, while his friend in the White House grew more and more mired in the swamp of Vietnam, Connally continued to project himself as Big Tex himself, the very picture of Texas manliness. On July 19, he flew off to East Africa for an extended safari and stayed away six weeks. It was the most public of vacations. He went as a guest of ABC, which wanted to film the safari of celebrities for its series "The American Sportsman," and Connally went in the company of other leading men who were also symbols of American macho: the tough private dick of the small screen, David Janssen, and the veteran of "Cheyenne" and "Kodiak," Clint Walker. Bing Crosby was along to croon in the wilderness and Phil Harris to tell the jokes. The party of hunters and assorted spear carriers amounted to over a hundred people. There may have been four-course meals with china and silver under the African sky, but the images coming back to Texas were perfect: Texas had a governor who was a *real* man. This was no jackleg operation of amateurs; it bore no relation to shooting Texas deer from someone's Lincoln Continental convertible. They were going after big game that was fast and dangerous: Thomson's gazelle and lion, cape buffalo and warthog, sable and elephant.

It was the time of the annual migration of wildebeest and zebra across the golden expanse of the Serengeti plains, and they camped first not far from this bountiful spectacle in northern Tanzania. From there, the expedition was to move 600 miles southeast to Selous, the largest game reserve in the world. As the party packed up to fly in small planes, Connally announced that he was going to drive, and he enlisted Clint Walker to go with him in a Land Rover. For two days they bounced and lurched across the plains past Mount Kilimanjaro, through herds of game and past Masai warriors. Connally was in heaven, the trip reminding him of the one he had taken as a young navy lieutenant from Algiers, searching for a Texas buddy, never found, posted somewhere in the Atlas mountains. In Walker, who was taller and arguably even more handsome and manly, he had a fitting companion. At Arusha, they laid over at the New Safari Hotel, where the ghost of Ernest Hemingway stalked the halls. Selous was to be the climax of the trip. First, they went in search of leopard, the most elusive and most dangerous of African game, constructing blinds and baiting more than a dozen trees. Once a huge leopard stood before them in a tree, but the cameras were not present, so they held their fire. Then toward the end of the safari, in the crowning moment, they went for elephant. When a

9,000-pound bull loomed, Connally raised his .458 Magnum and caught it as he had been instructed. "It was one of the finest kills we've ever had," the ABC producer said exultantly. "He caught it with a fantastic brain shot."

While Connally was away, talk among the liberals was mounting on how the Vietnam policy of Lyndon Johnson might be turned around. They had concluded that Johnson himself was the central problem. To the left, the president's emotional obsession with "winning" in Vietnam had become pathological, and he seemed to associate this victory with some strange concept of American honor, whose protection was somehow worth the carnage and whose pursuit demanded an interminable American presence. Lyndon Johnson, as the herald of honor, honor of any kind, put his detractors into paroxysms of blinding, blithering rage. It became fashionable to use the parlance of psychiatrists: the president had become verifiably, clinically, certifiably mad. With his obsessions, his delusions, his fixations, the troop strength in Southeast Asia had topped 500,000. The count of American bodies was averaging 300 per week. This was having profound consequences. Civility had long since disappeared from political debate, of which, in early 1967, the staging of the play *MacBird*, which made Johnson into the real assassin of his predecessor, was symptomatic, as was the filthy-speech movement on the campuses. Johnson's talk of honor amid carnage was doing much to unhinge the values of the young and to undermine respect and deference toward elders and toward authority.

Not only outsiders spoke of Johnson dementia. Within Johnson's own staff at the White House, there was growing concern about the president's wide mood swings. Doubts within the closest circle around the president extended back to 1966, when Johnson had lashed out at those who worried about the wholesale slaughter of draftees and called them "nervous Nellies." As Johnson swung from high to low and back, his behavior seemed to insiders to fit the classic description of the manic-depressive. His demands for loyalty (with its inevitable corollary of paranoia about disloyalty) reached unprecedented levels, to the point where the staff judged their worth in terms of whether they were in or out with the president.

"I realized in my personal relationship with [the president] that I was in danger just like everyone around him of capitulating to what you might call the Valenti syndrome, which was to judge myself as a person by [Johnson's] judgment—in accordance with his judgment of me," Harry McPherson, Johnson's chief speechwriter in 1967 and 1968, said. "When I was in favor, I was on top of the world. When I was out of favor, I was in the dumps. That struck me as ridiculous. I made a number of efforts to pull back from an intense relationship with him. It has saved my sanity and judgment so far as it has been saved."

Bill Moyers was another who was disturbed by Johnson's psychological and emotional state, and his worries were fortified by his growing disagreement with the Vietnam policy. Moyers left the White House in December 1966, leaving in bitterness and leaving bitterness behind him. "I thought I could make him more like me," Moyers said valiantly. "But I've found in the last several months that I'm becoming more like him; so I got out." Safely gone from the government and settled into a new life in journalism, Moyers wrote to McPherson about their service to Johnson during a time when, Moyers thought, the most turbulent clash of elemental forces in American society since the 1850s was occurring:

"Perhaps in time, it will be said that a lesser, simpler man might have been crushed in the awful sweep of things we have experienced in the last five years. His would have been perplexing years even in a halcyon era, for as Creon said to Oedipus, 'Natures such as this torment themselves.' I will always remember him with a curious admixture of affection and awe, concern and chagrin, respect and remorse. No man ever did more for me, and for all the troubles between us, he was the most fascinating man I ever met." Moyers could talk of Johnson as an "erratic wheel" upon which steady hands were needed, and McPherson echoed this clinical view, talking of Johnson's need for a "balance wheel." Borrowing a phrase from a psychiatrist friend, McPherson called Johnson a "clean-tube man" who cleaned his "tubes" by blowing out his fears and rages regularly, but that did not make for a very tranquil or happy machine shop at the White House.

John Connally alone escaped the dangers of ardor and the torment of ambivalence. The distance of Texas and the stature of the governorship liberated him, and he was not given to doubts about the administration's policy in Vietnam. He was a hawk with a hawk's predatory instincts. This put him in a unique position once again with Johnson, to advise him and to compel him to listen, to defend him against the din of criticism. Connally's influence derived from his agreement with the Johnson cause and from his total loyalty. He was *fidus Achates* to an embattled, buffeted, and fairly exiled Aeneas.

In August, as Connally took aim on the bull elephant in Africa, the liberals debated whether to take aim on Johnson. The issue was tough: Johnson represented power itself, and to many on the left, a challenge to him was hopeless, even though his approval rating among the American people had plummeted to thirty-six percent. Some, like liberal attorney Joseph Rauh, argued that the Vietnam plank at the next Democratic convention should be the focus of their effort. On September 22 the dilemma was debated at Hickory Hill. Robert Kennedy, seated upon the couch, peace beads around his neck, listened intently as Arthur Schlesinger, Jr., argued the case for the plank strategy. Allard Lowenstein argued for Robert Kennedy as the peace candidate and the champion to challenge Johnson. The arguments went on back and forth for hours, until Kennedy himself finally spoke up.

"You're a historian, Arthur," he said, turning to Schlesinger. "When was the last time millions of people rallied behind a plank?"

As Kennedy uttered the line, Hurricane Beulah blasted the Texas coast and the Rio Grande Valley, isolating vast regions, causing massive flooding, bursting dams. Just back from Africa, Connally had no time to ease himself back into work. Senator Yarborough rose on the Senate floor to welcome Connally back to Texas politics as usual. The senator's needling had the aim and timing of a critic who instinctively knows how to infuriate and never passes up the chance. Before Connally had gone off to Africa, Yarborough had charged the governor with being "unfeeling" at a time when agricultural workers were on strike in the Valley, and he got the usual counterblast.

A few days later Yarborough announced that he was considering running for governor in 1968, a post he, as a true Texan, had long coveted as the highest prize in politics (higher than U.S. Senator, maybe higher than president), but, said Yarborough, he would run *only* if Connally went for a fourth term. He castigated Connally for delaying in declaring the Valley a disaster area. The governor "silly-sallies [*sic*] and dilly-dallies around," said the senator sonorously. Connally's composure disintegrated, and his rage reached new heights: playing political games with human tragedy was beyond the pale. The governor had had enough. His disgust took an old-fashioned, even Shakespearean, tone. Yarborough's criticism was "the foulest distortion of the facts," said the governor, and Yarborough was "a very despicable man." Lyndon Johnson rallied to Connally's defense as they toured the devastated areas of the Valley together, and afterwards, on September 28, they repaired to the Johnson Ranch to discuss whether the joys of high office were worth this outrageous fortune.

To the few staff members present, such as the White House appointments secretary and future congressman James R. Jones, this was no ordinary social visit between Johnson and Connally. This was a *decision* weekend. They would not wait for the soft light of dusk to pile into Johnson's white convertible and scour the fields for deer with a cassette of "Mrs. Robinson" playing and agents in the trailing car fixing the drinks as required. Instead, Connally and Johnson and Lady Bird were out early in the morning, back only for lunch, and then out again for the afternoon. The governor was firm: he was not running again, period. Moreover, he was definite that Johnson should not run again either. They both had done their public duty. They should retire gracefully. To Lady Bird, Connally's message was music. She remembered conversations as far back as 1964 when her husband had agreed to only one term as president. Only two months before, on July 31, they had had a long conversation again about Johnson "coming off the mountain." Only three weeks before, on September 7, immediately after Connally had returned from Africa, he had been at the ranch and listened as Lady Bird said that she could not face another campaign. She, too, was tired, and she worried about her husband's health, especially his heart. "If we ever get sick," she said mordantly, "I want to be sick on our own time." But this was in the nature of a determined hope, a fervent wish, rather than a decision, and personal hope was not entirely compelling—nor would the lady's wishes necessarily win out. John Connally, on the other hand, spoke to the hard political reality: Johnson should leave and announce his decision as soon as possible, preferably even at the Democratic dinner only nine days away.

Connally's advice was sincere, and his concern for his friend genuine, but his position on September 28 was not without consequences for himself. If Johnson were to withdraw now, the immediate beneficiary would be Robert Kennedy. With every anti-Vietnam statement by Kennedy in 1967, the paranoid Johnson saw the launch of the Kennedy presidential campaign. On the other hand, announcing a withdrawal early would give a conservative contender the time to mount a challenge to Kennedy. To all in the Texas political circles it was abundantly clear that Connally considered himself at least as well qualified to be president as Lyndon Johnson, and probably more so. He was the heir apparent. Hopes and determinations and decisions floated about in the murky twilight. Longings went unexpressed. Connally's sense of decorum, if nothing else, left him silent about his own ambitions.

This was a time of illusion in the tortuous course of the Vietnam War, and Johnson's generals were upbeat about the overall military situation. They had divined "the light at the end of the tunnel." Only two days after he and Connally had their long ride through the fields, Johnson made a speech in San Antonio, where he promised to stop all the bombing if talks between the sides could commence immediately with reasonable hope for conclusive results, and if the North Vietnamese would promise not to take military advantage of the situation. This became known as the "San Antonio formula" in the White House, and it was operative until the Tet Offensive in January shattered the illusion. Vietnam remained the central consideration in Johnson's thinking about whether he would run again. He could argue it both ways. If he achieved a stunning military victory or a surprising diplomatic breakthrough, he could either leave in triumph or stay to complete his cherished Great Society program. If there were a terrible military defeat, or if the diplomatic stalemate continued, he could leave to give some other president a chance to solve it, but to do so would give the impression of retreat and even cowardice. Within the small coterie of people who knew what Johnson was pondering, a circle which numbered no more than five or six, all except John Connally were technicians who simply stood ready to implement whatever the president decided. Only Connally had the stature to tell the president what he *should* do.

In October, Johnson dispatched his press secretary, George Christian, to Austin to discuss again with Connally this most sensitive of all subjects. More as a profession of loyalty to the Democratic party than as a serious element in his thinking, Connally had told Johnson that if his presence on the Democratic ticket in 1968 as governor, or even as a senatorial candidate against Republican John Tower, were an absolute requirement of Johnson's running—and winning—again, he might consider it. Given the evident passion of Connally's determination not to run, it was an offer the president could not possibly accept. Nevertheless, Connally's absence from the ticket would substantially weaken the chances of the Democrats in Texas. Now Christian sanctioned the obvious by saying that such a sacrifice by the governor was not necessary: Connally was free to make his decision, regardless of Johnson's course of action. With Christian, the topic of timing arose again. If the president was going to withdraw, Connally thought a dignified, nonpolitical occasion was appropriate. The State of the Union message in mid-January was the obvious choice. Still, Connally pushed for Johnson to find an earlier moment, preferably in December. For an hour and a half Connally and Christian thrashed the problem through, getting down to the tone and even the actual words that Johnson might use. Once again Connally was the clarifying force. Christian was neutral. He was a mere messenger in Austin. If he knew the president's personal predilections, he knew Johnson's bent for letting a decision loiter along until it absolutely had to be made. And while he knew Lady Bird was pushing for a withdrawal declaration, he knew equally well that she would ultimately have little influence on the final decision. It was Connally who mattered.

There was another element in the mix which could easily tilt the decision the other way. Events could force another campaign, and reveal an underlying personal reality: Lyndon Johnson, the epitome of power politics, would never give up power voluntarily. When the president talked about ending the term in 1969, no one in his inner circle dismissed the remark as insincere. They just didn't believe he could bring himself to do it. Only a few days after Johnson and Connally's long outing at the ranch, Secretary of State Dean Rusk, Secretary of Defense Robert McNamara, CIA Director Richard Helms, and National Security Adviser Walt Rostow sat down in the Oval Office and, seemingly out of nowhere, Johnson suggested that he would not run again. Silence fell over the group, as the advisers sat quietly in shock. "Well, now, Mr. President," McNamara finally said at this apparent bad joke, "you don't want to get cute."

On November 10, Connally went before the doting press of Austin. "I have reluctantly concluded," he told them, "that after the strain of what will have been eight years of vigorous public service, I no longer can be assured in my own heart that I could bring to the office for another two years the enthusiasm, the resilience, the patience that my conscience would demand and the state would deserve." The confession of physical fatigue, of flagging interest, the implicit recognition of his growing imperial distance and his peevishness, had a disarming allure in Texas. The *Dallas Morning News* paid tribute to its hero. The decision was based on "the man's innate honesty. He is tired. He feels increasingly frustrated, which makes it difficult for the Governor to govern. To carry on, without the zeal of desire, is hard. The zeal to lead and to fight may be less, but not the love of the state that nurtured him." Next to the editorial was a romantic cartoon of a vacant governor's chair against a backdrop of the flag of Texas and large footprints walking away. "Big Chair to Fill" was the heading.

Speculations about Connally's motives were rife. A week before, in El Paso, he had joined Johnson for a meeting with the president of Mexico and for the dedication of a memorial to American-Mexican friendship. At the occasion, the customary receptions were reversed. Johnson was wildly cheered, but when the president turned proudly to his friend and introduced him, boos and catcalls filled the hall.

Perhaps, the press speculated, this had finally compelled Connally's decision. From the distance of the White House, Johnson followed Connally's announcement intently. To Robert McNamara, the president expressed surprise and relief that the reporters did not connect Connally's decision to his own situation.

Through November, Allard Lowenstein continued his relentless search for a challenger to Johnson. He had run through the obvious choices: Robert Kennedy, though tantalized, continued to demur. Other doves in the Senate—George McGovern, Frank Church, Lee Metcalf—had said no. Lowenstein was into a second rank of assorted long shots, symbolic candidates, and flamboyant outsiders: Congressman Don Edwards of California, Major General James Gavin, even Canadian-born John Kenneth Galbraith, who was disqualified legally from the presidency. Somewhere between Metcalf and McGovern, in his now alphabetical search, Lowenstein came upon the name of Eugene McCarthy. McCarthy was a north-woods version of John Connally: tall, silver-haired, rural in his roots, athletic, fifty-one years of age, and bored with high office. Yet he had at least two qualities Connally lacked: he was cynical, with a wickedly mordant wit, and he had a vibrant Catholicism which could engender sincere moral indignation. On November 30, McCarthy announced. In doing so, he threw the concept of honor back in Lyndon Johnson's teeth. "There comes a time when the honorable man simply has to raise the flag," McCarthy said.

In his announcement, with considerably more wit than Connally could muster, McCarthy denied that he was merely a stalking horse for Robert Kennedy. In promising to enter five or six primaries, McCarthy confessed that he wouldn't mind if his effort eventually resulted in the nomination of Robert Kennedy instead of Lyndon Johnson. Wasn't that being a stalking horse? he was asked. McCarthy denied it and reminded his audience of the 1948 Kentucky Derby, when two horses from Calumet Farms, Citation and Coaltown, ran for the roses, in similar devil's-red silk, and Coaltown was supposed to be the stalking horse, he said, but the stablemates were neck and neck at the three-sixteenths pole, and Coaltown never quit. The political press listened to this image in puzzlement and realized that a new phenomenon had entered the presidential sweep-stakes.

But Connally went considerably beyond characterizing McCarthy as a mere Kennedy stand-in. The next day, in New York, where he laid over on the way to Paris, he took up a new dual role, the public defender of Lyndon Johnson and the protector of the right flank of the Democratic party. "I don't think he'll make many converts," the governor said blithely. "He's acting primarily as a catalyst for the dissidents. It can't do anything but result in greater dissension in the party. If any senator gives the prestige of his office and the force of his personality to coalescing the dissent in the Democratic party, it's going to hurt to that extent." Connally doubted that McCarthy had anything new to say about Vietnam; otherwise he would have revealed it in his announcement.

But this was New York, not Texas, and Connally's placing of party discipline above the right of debate and free speech did not wash up north. He was instantly challenged by John Burns, the New York State chairman of the Democrats: "Rather than attack Senator Kennedy and Senator McCarthy, the governor should appreciate that in New York there is a substantial number of people, including many Democrats, who are not in full agreement with the administration's Vietnam policy. . . . If we fully face up to the issue and have an intelligent discussion over Vietnam, we will be able to keep many voters within the Democratic party." Without quite appreciating it, Connally was fortifying, for a *national* audience, the impression that he was "Lyndon's boy, John." What was needed, as Burns suggested, was a wide-ranging and spirited debate about a failed policy, out of which new ideas and new initiatives might come. The situation was far too complicated, far too desperate, to be controlled by simple loyalty to the leader. On the level of intellectual debate, it was Connally, not McCarthy, who had nothing new to add. And the impression he left now would put the presidency—and the vice presidency—just out of his reach, now and in the future, as a Democrat or as a Republican.

★

After his meeting with Connally in October, Christian returned to the White House and prepared the first draft of a Johnson withdrawal statement. Toward Christmas, a few new members were added to the small circle who knew what was under consideration. In October, Johnson asked General William Westmoreland what the effect would be on troop morale in Vietnam if he withdrew, as if he believed that the troops there possessed an intense affection for him. The troops would be shocked, Westmoreland replied, but the war effort would not be hurt. In other events—the devaluation of the British pound and the possible adverse effects on the dollar— Johnson found reasons through December not to follow Connally's advice for an early announcement. If part of him wanted to withdraw, the political animal in him would always find epic events that prevented him from doing so. Still, in mid-December, Johnson took another step toward the Pedernales. He recruited his former assistant, Horace Busby, to redraft the initial Connally-Christian statement. The president took Busby for a four-day trip around the world in mid-December—to Rome, Australia, and Vietnam—and laid out the assignment. After New Year's Day, the Connallys came to the LBJ Ranch for the traditional gathering of the two families. The weather was gray and bleak, fit only, as Lady Bird would say, for people to "sit by the fire and tell tales." After dinner, the four, Lyndon and John, Nellie and Lady Bird, retreated to the president's bedroom and discussed the inevitable question for three hours.

"You ought to run only if you look forward to being president again, only if you want to do it," Connally said at one point. "You ought not to run just to keep someone else from being president." This last was superficially a reference to Robert Kennedy, but it applied equally to Connally himself. Nellie floated in with sweet emotion. "You'll probably find, after you've made the decision—if you decide not to run—that there is an ephemeral period when you feel as if everything has stopped. You are sad. You almost feel like you're dead. Then, when time passes, there is a great wave of relief."

As Lady Bird watched them tiptoe on this "hot griddle," she found no "cool oasis." She thought her husband was talking himself out of it. In Lyndon, there was "no definite time for an acceptable exit." Still, the president was in a reflective mood. He was feeling his age and his fatigue. He spoke of his uncertain health and his history of heart problems. The fact that his father had died of heart failure at the age of sixty-four took on the air of mystical inevitability; if he chose to run again, he would be sixty-four in the last year of his term. To the Johnsons, the personal serenity of the Connallys was evident. Johnson felt younger around Connally, and while it had served him in his early career, Connally felt older around Johnson. Connally was only a vigorous fifty-one, and yet to Johnson it seemed as if the men were the same age, facing withdrawal together at the end of their careers. The State of the Union message arose again as a possible time, but Johnson had an argument against that, an argument more forcefully stated now. His withdrawal would undermine everything else he said in the speech, everything he hoped to accomplish before he left office.

Toward the end of the conversation Connally cut through the morass. "The only way to answer all of these arguments is to die in office," he said with an uncharacteristic touch of morbid irritation.

On January 15, two days before the State of the Union speech, Johnson was in his usual grumpy, chaotic frame of mind. It was always that way with his State of the Union speeches. The staff expected the president to be unbearable. Should the speech be programmatic or philosophical? Should it be tough or conciliatory on the war? Especially, should this be the last year of his presidency, or should he grasp four more years? Questions of tone and emphasis created havoc. Harry McPherson, who was drafting the speech, found it the worst experience of his White House years. Johnson had seized upon a metaphor and fell in love with it: "When a ship plows through waters, it makes waves." To McPherson, the metaphor was dangerous. At some point, a different aquatic image was considered, in which the Johnson philosophy was to be regarded as a river and the Johnson programs were as the logs carried downstream, but McPherson was finding that in the inevitable compression for television, the river level kept falling, and he was left only with logs, logs stuck in the mud of a dry riverbed, going nowhere.

McPherson could not know, of course, what was really tormenting Johnson. The central person in the drafting of the president's withdrawal statement was Horace Busby, and he labored secretly and separately on the second floor of the White House. Even as Busby submitted his draft on January 15, he attached a discussion of the advisability of using it and, therefore, contributed to Johnson's ambivalence. To Busby, the danger was that the president would appear self-pitying in a way that would undermine the "essential dignity and even nobility of the announcement." Announcing early would avoid the pitfall of 1952, when Estes Kefauver had seemed to drive Truman from office after the Tennessee senator won the New Hampshire primary. The forum and the timing were good, Busby thought. But, inevitably, came the doubt: "In 1958, you had to go to the UN to keep the world from regarding Eisenhower as a lame-duck, impotent President. I think it is possible that making yourself a lame duck might have unforeseeable serious consequences abroad without offsetting gains at home. I would not belabor that view, however, because on a decision like this, I earnestly believe every man—including Presidents—must step to his own drum. If you do what is right for your own self, it will be right in the history books. I think all who care about you know what is right for you to do now."

In the larger scheme of things, lofty though it sounded, that was not very helpful advice. On the night of the speech, only one major figure pressed for Johnson to make his move, and that was John Connally. At 5:10 P.M. he called George Christian and urged again that Johnson "go" with the statement that night, as if he knew instinctively that Johnson would need a slight shove at the last minute. Christian summarized Connally's reasons in a brief memo and sent it into the Oval Office. Beyond the previous reasons that Connally had given—the nonpolitical, dignified setting, the huge television audience, etc.—the politics of the announcement were underscored. "The longer you wait, the more difficult it becomes . . . Delay in announcing helps Bobby, who is already free to operate while others are not." Johnson carried the memo around with him fretfully in the several hours before he left for Capitol Hill. He confided to his appointments secretary, James Jones, what he was considering, but Jones found it idle chatter. He accepted the conventional wisdom that Lyndon Johnson could never give up power. Politicians, Jones knew, were always threatening to quit and never could. Moreover, Johnson tilted the arguments against a move now. His legislative programs would be diluted; before he withdrew, the committee process should run its course on his initiatives; and so on. In any event, he told Jones, he would not decide until the last moment. To Jones, that meant he would not decide at all. Lady Bird, meanwhile, had retrieved the statement she had written all the way back in 1964 about only one full term, and the words sounded good to her. By 6:30 Johnson had his words, and he showed Lady Bird the memo in which Connally urged him to go. She felt she could not push. John held more sway than she, she knew. Off they went to the Hill.

Somewhere toward the end of the long, tediously programmatic speech, the TelePrompTer failed, and Johnson had to read from the typescript on the lectern. Lady Bird watched, wondering as he approached the closing passage whether he would reach into his breast pocket. Her body tensed.

"Would he end with the statement? Did I want him to? Would I be relieved if he did or if he didn't?" she later recalled wondering.

He didn't, and the next morning the press was generally sour about the president's endless laundry list. When Johnson spoke of his great ship stirring and troubling the waters, the feeling was that the time had come to put this ship into mothballs.

★

In the days after this flop of a speech Johnson instructed his staff to update his withdrawal speech weekly. The magical moment when the time was just right continued to elude him. Of course, in the wake of the Tet Offensive it could not be right, and that took care of February. Meanwhile Connally positively luxuriated in his status as a lame duck; he did not feel crippled in the least. The outpourings of affection from his state were many and flowery. When major jobs in Washington became vacant—secretary of defense in November 1967, even chief justice of the Supreme Court in the spring of 1968—Connally's name was always on the short list of contenders. Telegrams poured into the White House from Texas and elsewhere urging the president to exercise provincial and brotherly loyalty. Sometimes the advocacy came from the most unlikely quarters. "I just heard on the news that Chief Justice Warren has resigned," Rev. Billy Graham wrote. "If this news report proves to be correct, it is my prayer that you will give serious consideration to balancing the Court with a strong conservative as Chief Justice. I am convinced that many of the problems that have plagued America in the last few years are a direct result of some of the extreme rulings of the Court, especially in the field of criminality. I believe that our mutual friend, Governor John Connally, would make an ideal and popular choice. He might not be popular with the extreme liberals and radicals who are already fighting you anyway. But he would make a great chief justice." Johnson would have loved to have Connally, as George Christian put it, "on his warm side," but to Connally that might have been altogether too warm, and nothing ever came of the idea.

On his fifty-first birthday, February 17, 1968, his friends and supporters threw a huge gala for Connally in Austin. They rented Gregory Gymnasium on the UT campus and draped it in Texas amber, and the candlelight from the tables sparkled on the sequins of the ladies' gowns. The usual cast of Connally boosters lined up to pay tribute to their prince and potentate: Robert Strauss, Jake Pickle, and Larry Temple. They were joined by Admiral David MacDonald, whom Connally had served in World War II and who served Connally when the latter was secretary of the navy. At 9:30 Lyndon Johnson entered quietly and secretly through the basement—the president was growing accustomed to clandestine entrances. Outside, over two hundred disappointed demonstrators hoped for the president to run their gauntlet, but the Secret Service had outsmarted them again. Noisy and passionate, they sported their messages: "Wrong Time, Wrong Place, Wrong War," "No Escalation Without Representation," "Rich Man's War, Poor Man's Fight." Loud arguments broke out over the ill-treatment of their favorite victims: the indictment of Benjamin Spock, the arrest of H. Rap Brown, the sentencing of Le Roi Jones. As Johnson slipped into the hall, this display was reduced to distant murmuring. But he could easily imagine the scene, for it took place almost every day now outside his house in Washington.

The demonstrators, especially their bad manners, their attire, and their hygiene, dominated the remarks of the notables inside. Frank Erwin, the chairman of the university's Board of Regents, told the dinner guests that he was disturbed when "a bunch of dirty nothins can disrupt the working of a great university in the name of academic freedom," and Connally himself, in his closing remarks, reassured his friends that the protestors were only a small minority of the student body. "They do not reflect the maturity, the stability, or desirability of the other 29,000," he said. Lyndon Johnson tried to make light of the matter in his remarks, but his tone was bitter-sweet. "As I came in rather hurriedly, I was looking at these well-dressed demonstrators, and I knew I was at the right place," said the president. "I knew it was a gathering either for John Connally or for Lyndon Johnson."

Johnson paid warm tribute to his friend briefly and elegantly. As he reminded the audience that he had given Connally his first job, the NYA job at the university, at the princely wage of twelve dollars a month, he spoke of their thirty-year friendship, when Connally was "almost" a brother to him, and said, "There's no man on this earth that I would rather have by my side than John Connally."

Shortly after 10 o'clock Johnson slipped away in the dark to his plane. There he greeted his old political operative, Cecil Burney, who had been summoned from Corpus Christi and now awaited the Boss's instructions. On the trip back to Washington Burney was given the old Johnson treatment as he was "invited" to open the Johnson for President campaign. Events were moving quickly. Only a few hours after the arrival of Air Force One at Andrews Air Force Base from the South, another plane bearing Army Chief of Staff Earle Wheeler landed from the West. Wheeler came with the request to the president, developed in coordination with General William Westmoreland in Saigon, for yet another 206,000 troops, over and above the 535,000 already there. This figure, the generals agreed, would "ensure victory" by taking advantage of the Allied "opportunity" created by the Tet Offensive.

As Connally gloried in the final days of his governorship, the month of March became the turning point of the Johnson presidency. It was the time when Johnson gave up two dreams: winning in Vietnam and winning another term easily as president. At a White House breakfast only hours after the president arrived back in Washington from the Connally testimonial, General Wheeler made his formal presentation for the additional troops and unwittingly initiated a thoroughgoing reevaluation of the entire Vietnam policy. Instead of convincing the advisers that the new troops would ensure victory, the request was widely viewed as general panic in the military high command. The result was that in thirty days Administration policy changed from hopes for victory to longings for decent disengagement. On March 31 the troop authorization would be scaled back to one-twelfth of the original figure and bombing would be curtailed by eighty percent, limited to the panhandle of North Vietnam.

Meanwhile, on March 12, Eugene McCarthy made his surprising showing in New Hampshire, losing to Johnson by a scant few hundred votes. Since Johnson was not on the official ballot and his votes had come as write-ins, McCarthy took the delegates. Robert Kennedy entered the race four days later. On March 27, the political-master–cum–Postmaster General, Lawrence O'Brien, wrote Johnson a memorandum expressing fears about the Chicago convention and the November election if the present Vietnam policy continued. To his surprise, O'Brien found himself a part of a quiet uprising within the cabinet, made up of the "political" members, plus Vice President Humphrey. Because total loyalty to the president was the paramount imperative of the administration, the cabinet members had kept their misgivings to themselves until now. Suddenly they were talking about what they could do together to alter Johnson's disastrous course. O'Brien expected that some joint action, some joint dissenting statement by five or six cabinet members against their own administration's policy, was certain to happen unless Johnson stepped down. Had such a cabinet revolt taken place, it would have been unprecedented in American history.

On March 28 O'Brien flew off to Wisconsin, where the next presidential primary was to take place on April 2. In Milwaukee he orchestrated an enthusiastic pro-Johnson rally, made up largely of postal employees and, as at some party rally behind the Iron Curtain, the functionaries cheered their paymaster thunderously. Afterwards O'Brien had someone drive him past the McCarthy headquarters, where youthful workers, seized passionately with their cause, labored past midnight, and then past the Johnson headquarters, which was dark. The next day, March 29, Johnson reached O'Brien, breathlessly excited about the reports of the Milwaukee rally he had seen on television.

"I don't think you should be too enthusiastic about it," O'Brien said deflatingly.

"Well, what do you think will happen?" asked the crestfallen Johnson.

"I don't think it looks good for you."

"Can you be more definite?"

"Yes. I think you're going to be badly defeated."

"How bad?"

"Sixty-forty. Maybe two to one."

"You were there only one day!" Johnson protested.

"That's true, but that's my sense of the situation. Frankly, Mr. President, your supporters are very depressed. I don't know if they would tell you that, but there it is."

Of the three pulls being exercised on the president at this moment—the romantic urge to return to the bluebonnets of Texas, the reappraisal of his Vietnam policy, and the prospect of an unprecedented political defeat—the last was the most compelling. This was the factor Connally had hoped the president would not have to face: withdrawing much sooner would have prevented it. Now Johnson was inevitably going to be coupled with Harry Truman and his forced decision not to seek another term for president in 1952. As the weekend of March 31 approached, Harry Truman was much on Johnson's mind. Johnson asked Jim Jones when Truman had finally announced his retreat. The answer was March 31. As with the death of his father from a heart attack at the age of sixty-four, historical parallel again took on a powerful, almost immutable quality. This was truly the last chance.

Johnson came into the weekend of March 31 a frustrated man. The world seemed topsy-turvy. His victories, as he viewed them, were constantly being portrayed as defeats. To have contained the Tet Offensive and to have ruptured the heart of the North Vietnamese and Vietcong infrastructure was, to the American people and, more especially, to the American press, not a victory but a defeat. To have won in New Hampshire on a write-in effort was being treated as a setback. Astute politician that he was, he knew that these perceptions were important. The course of the Vietnam War, whether its goal was victory or disengagement, did not demand the president's departure from office. Indeed, when Johnson reversed the direction of the Vietnam policy that weekend, the success of the new course was more assured if he stayed than if he left. Nor was Johnson unduly impressed with O'Brien's bleak prediction of certain defeat in Wisconsin. On the very weekend of his speech he had received a poll from the Oliver Quayle group indicating that, regardless of the results in Wisconsin, he would prevail eventually if he ran. He would be nominated and he would be reelected, the poll concluded, although the process might lacerate the nation. Johnson's choice was deeper than simply the question of whether to run or not to run. To seek renomination, to win reelection, would necessarily involve profound compromise for his war policy. The fatigue of the nation would have to be accommodated. The dovish elements of the party would have to be assuaged. Thus, to run would be to lose control of the war. Johnson himself would say to Texan Bill Stinson, "I know I can win, but I couldn't serve." But if he withdrew there would be ten more months for him to follow his own instincts on the war without reference to the public clamor. When he said he didn't want political considerations to distract him from concentrating on the war, it meant in part that he would be free of public opinion.

As a political matter, Johnson had probably already waited too long to withdraw. Only the liberals, those doves with their fluttering wings and fibrillating hearts, opposed him. It was too late for a solid moderate or conservative Democrat to organize a viable candidacy, one who would stay the Johnson course toward an "honorable" solution in Vietnam and who would protect the Johnson legacy on the domestic front. To withdraw would mean either Kennedy or Nixon as his successor; both represented offensive prospects. Actually, between the two, Kennedy was the more offensive prospect. Nixon at least could be expected to pick up "Lyndon's burden."

Over the weekend of March 30, as upstairs in the White House Horace Busby labored anew on a withdrawal peroration, this was precisely what Johnson's closest political advisers, Jim Jones and Marvin Watson, argued. *Events* had overtaken Johnson. He must run again. To withdraw was to turn the party apparatus over to Robert Kennedy, to drown the Johnson legacy, to undermine the chance of an honorable disengagement from Vietnam. The advisers appealed foursquare to Johnson's vanity. Johnson listened, but this time he was not flattered. One by one, Connally's arguments of the fall and winter came forward with conviction. The president had no duty to appoint his successor. If the American people wanted Robert Kennedy, they would have him. He would pursue his new Vietnam direction free of partisan concerns until his time was up. It was a genuinely noble moment for Lyndon Johnson.

★

On the night of March 31 Governor Connally was chairing a meeting of his Commission on Fine Arts when word was passed to him about the president's announcement. He professed great shock and displeasure: "I'm stunned! I'm stunned!" he boomed to the press in Austin, as in Washington the president's press secretary confirmed that Connally had been one of the few people with whom the president had consulted secretly for months on this question. Within minutes after the president was back at the White House, Connally called him. "I told him, 'I'm sorry for the nation,' " Connally said later. "I'm sure he felt a sense of relief for himself and his family." Inevitably, Connally was asked about his own plans now, and he issued the usual disclaimers: "This doesn't make me anything but sad," he said.

Connally's sadness had a personal element. Johnson had waited far too long for Connally to have any hope or expectation for a presidential bid of his own. Perhaps, if Johnson had heeded Connally's advice to withdraw in the fall, it might have been different. But Connally did not appreciate how much the tarnish of Lyndon Johnson had rubbed off on him in the public mind. If through the fall and winter he hoped that he might fill the vacuum which Johnson might leave, in fact it was never in the cards. The audience even of his Commission of Fine Arts in Austin might have groaned and felt sad at the news that night, but elsewhere, broadly and deeply through America, there was exultation. The country would not be ready for a big Texan again for a very long time. In Kansas City, a city deep in the American heartland, James Reston, a columnist for the *New York Times*, was giving a trade speech to a convention of establishment Middle Western newspaper executives when the news was passed to him. After confirming it with his office, Reston announced the item to his audience. To Reston's astonishment, the seemingly comfortable, reasonably conservative hinterland crowd rose up as one and cheered and clapped continuously and riotously for five minutes.

16

A Pyrrhic Defeat

WITHIN TEXAS, after Johnson's declaration of March 31, local pride asserted itself immediately, not so much to mourn Johnson as to praise Connally. The governor's popularity was unprecedented in Texas history. In two of his six years his approval rating had exceeded eighty percent, and now it stood, after all the bruising battles, at a handsome sixty-two percent. "I cannot think of any other man who is better qualified than John Connally to succeed Lyndon Johnson," a Fort Worth Democratic leader said to resounding approval. To many Texans, particularly those who were concerned with fine art, John Connally would be a far more graceful symbol of Texas in the White House than Johnson.

Immediately, Connally was put forward as a favorite son candidate for president. Two things needed to be accomplished immediately. A holding action had to get under way to preserve the Johnson forces intact until another leader could step forward. As important, emotionally anyway, was the need to prevent Bobby Kennedy from consolidating his strength. Only two days after Johnson's withdrawal, Connally's man, Frank Erwin, said of Robert Kennedy, "I remain convinced that Bobby Kennedy's cold ruthlessness, demonstrated opportunism, and his overriding personal ambition render him totally unfit to hold any high office." No one in Texas thought to wonder how many presidential candidates would be left if ruthlessness, opportunism, and ambition disqualified them from high office. At another point, Erwin said that "unity at the price of having Bobby Kennedy as president is too high a price for unity."

For several days Connally vacillated. Events were moving so fast it was hard to keep up. On April 4, Martin Luther King, Jr., was murdered, and the black sections of major American cities erupted in rage and rebellion. Texas cities escaped as Connally called for calm, but whether by a slip of the tongue or in a rare revelation of an essentially racist sensibility, the governor uttered one of the most provocative statements of any leader in America. As smoke and flame leapt above mean streets throughout the country, as 110 American cities experienced riots, Connally said of King, "Much of what Martin Luther King said and much of what he did, many of us could violently disagree with, but none of us should have wished him this kind of fate. . . . He contributed much to the chaos and the strife and the confusion and the uncertainty of this country, but whatever his actions, he deserved not the fate of assassination." It was an astonishing statement, especially from a victim of an assassination attempt himself. Had Connally died in Dallas and had some opponent uttered a similar veiled suggestion that Oswald's act was understandable and even partly justified, Connally's supporters would have howled for revenge. It was a remark that blacks neither forgot nor forgave. Barbara Jordan was incredulous and deeply hurt at Connally's gross insensitivity.

The uproar (which was quietly underreported in Texas) was instantaneous, and Connally tried to wriggle out of it. He protested that he had been misquoted. "What I really said was, 'However much people may think he contributed to chaos and confusion, he did not deserve this fate.'" The television tape of the statement showed, to the contrary, that the original words, revealing the original instinct, had been accurate.

As so often in politics, one extraordinary gaffe limited possibilities. Connally had long since lost the affection of blacks and Hispanics. This remark turned ideological opposition into wrath. Henceforth the choice of Connally for any national ticket would have to be made against the reality that there would be wholesale defection by the minorities.

The remark did something else to Connally's fortunes. It might have been natural for the intimates of Lyndon Johnson, especially those from Texas and the Southwest, to shift their allegiance to Connally after the president's withdrawal. Many of them, after all, had come to Johnson through Connally, and secretly admired Connally more. Universally, Connally's skill and ability were regarded as equal to Johnson's, if not greater. Robert Strauss, the Democratic boss and Connally's friend going back to the University of Texas, had never wavered in his admiration. "John Connally is a macro-man," he would say. "I have never known a man with more leadership abilities. He has that rare ability that all great men have of retaining vast amounts of useful information and with total recall. He has the absolute ability to shuck off worthless information. The son of a bitch is the best at selling the merchandise once he has the tools."

The King remark highlighted a nagging worry that Johnson intimates had harbored about Connally: he was visibly uncomfortable around poor people and had very little to say to them. This had been widely noticed. James R. Jones, Johnson's chief of staff, during this period had said to his fiancée, partly in admiration, partly in sadness, that Connally had "an incredible skill to get to the heart of a memo or an article or an issue. He has the aura of the presidency about him, but he is really uncomfortable around poor people, and it seems to remind him distastefully of his roots, whereas Johnson basks in the afterglow of speaking with the poor and enjoying it. [Connally's] is a major flaw for a Democrat."

On April 7, Connally walked through a gauntlet of hostile civil rights activists at the Driskill Hotel in Austin to announce that he would accept the Texas nomination for the presidency. He spoke of the need for reason and stability in troubled times; he disavowed any real ambition for winning the nomination itself; he denied he was trying to block Bobby Kennedy or anyone else; and while he was not supporting Hubert Humphrey, he expressed the hope that the vice president would run. It was a tacit recognition by the favorite son himself that the nation was not yet ready for John Connally.

Connally's praise of Humphrey was a curious position for him, because he did not respect Humphrey. To Connally, the vice president was simply too scattered mentally, too disorganized politically, and too liberal philosophically. Humphrey, after all, was the author of Medicare and the Peace Corps. Since 1949 he had been for federal aid to education and, since 1956, for a nuclear test ban treaty. This was the same Humphrey whom Lyndon Johnson had disinvited from National Security Council meetings in 1965 because he openly argued for a bombing halt and cut across the president in front of his generals. (As a consequence, Humphrey was kept out of the war council for fifteen months.) That Humphrey should now emerge as the champion of the South, with Connally, who had passionately opposed these measures, as his herald, was irony itself. Humphrey, like Adlai Stevenson and Harry Truman before him, was scarcely Connally's idea of a knight on a white horse.

Still, he was putting Humphrey in his debt in the weeks after March 31. At a Democratic governors' conference in St. Louis in mid-April, Connally took the lead to protect the right flank for Humphrey. The national press began to treat him as the kingmaker as well as the departing king's chief defender. On April 21 he appeared on "Meet the Press." In general his performance was uninspired. He tried to be conciliatory through most of the program and to disguise his distaste for Bobby Kennedy,* but toward the end of the program, Connally's antipathy finally peeked through. Why had the governor refused to say he would support Bobby Kennedy if Kennedy were nominated? he was asked. Kennedy was "entitled to the same degree of support from me and from other party officials throughout the country as he was willing to give President Johnson, just before Kennedy announced his candidacy opposing the president," Connally replied. "Mr. Kennedy said he would withhold judgment, and that is the position I take with respect to him."

During the spring of 1968, in one of those curious convergences of fate which marked Connally's career, another governor emerged into the national spotlight and occupied a prominent role for the Republican party. Ronald Reagan had ridden into office from the extreme right with the same good looks and theatrical delivery as Connally. Governor Reagan did not suffer, however, from a mentor's shadow. He was something altogether new: a political performer from the world of entertainment who was adept at promoting simple formulas for complex problems. Reagan always promised a happy ending. Like Connally, he hailed from small-town, rural America; unlike Connally, he romanticized his roots. In his 1965 autobiography, whose title, *Where's the Rest of Me?*, became more apt as the country got to know him better, he would write sentimentally about his upbringing in Illinois: "There were woods and mysteries, life and death among small creatures, hunting and fishing. There were the days when I learned the true riches of rags." That was a line John Connally could never have written. When Reagan took the

---

*When Robert Kennedy was attorney general he treated Johnson in a number of ways with an attitude he was later to reveal in his posthumous autobiography. He regarded Johnson not as a political animal but as an animal per se, and as a habitual teller of unnecessary lies.

lectern to raise money for the Republicans in this watershed year—and he was to raise over $1.5 million—he could deliver lines with a pacing and a stage presence that Connally could envy: "Sometimes I think the reason Bobby Kennedy's so concerned about poverty is that he never had any when he was a kid." . . . "We really can't blame President Johnson alone for the mess we're in. A mess like that takes teamwork." Reagan and Connally were to have something else in common, but Connally didn't know it yet. For twenty years Reagan had been a loyal Democrat, an ardent supporter of the New Deal and the Fair Deal, and a founding member of Americans for Democratic Action (ADA). It was only the Red scare in Hollywood during the McCarthy era in the early 1950s that revealed to Reagan the "seamy side of liberalism" and turned him sharply to the right. But Reagan's "conversion" had long since receded in memory.

Some months before, in October 1967, Connally and Reagan had come forward as the dominant figures of their respective parties at a national governors' conference. Already there was talk of a Reagan presidential candidacy. With his amiable good humor, Reagan deftly denied the rumor, for Governor Rockefeller of New York was also at the conference, and he was supposed to be a leading candidate for the Republican nomination. "I have a carry-over from my previous occupation," Reagan said, nodding toward Rockefeller. "I never take the other fellow's lines." The governors' conference was held aboard a navy battleship, the USS *Independence*, as it steamed from New York to the Virgin Islands. The farther south this political battleship went, the hotter became the political climate over the central question of the time—Vietnam. Connally was inevitably the champion of the Johnson Vietnam policy, and he wanted the governors to reaffirm a resolution of total support for President Johnson on Vietnam. They had given that endorsement in 1965 and 1966. Connally's resolution would urge the president to "persist and persevere" in Vietnam.

The approach of the political season, however, made the Republicans uncomfortable embracing a Democratic president, and they looked for a way out. Several days out to sea, a radiogram from Marvin Watson in the White House to former Texas governor Price Daniel (who was now acting as the president's liaison with the governors) was mistakenly delivered to Governor Reagan, and Reagan blithely opened it. In general, it was a rehash of past governors' conference actions on Vietnam, but toward the end it suggested that Daniel confront one Republican governor who appeared to be wavering in his support and to challenge another who claimed that

Johnson had made partisan political use of the governors' support in the past. The contents of the memo might be shared with Governor Connally, the radiogram suggested.

Reagan gleefully called a press conference and waved the telegram before the press. Here was a prime example of White House manipulation to create support for its Vietnam policies. Connally was furious, both angry at Reagan for his breach of decorum and embarrassed to be shown, on paper, as the tool of the White House. "Every man has to live with his own set of ethics and morality," he snorted. "I don't read other people's mail or messages." The Watson radiogram gave the Republicans the excuse they wanted for parting with Johnson without openly challenging his war policy.

Connally needed half the votes of the Republicans to pass his resolution and he pressed forward, intent to force a roll call vote and thereby embarrass any Republican who would go on record against the nation's leader. Reagan was the first to speak for the Republicans. The Connally resolution, he began in his honeyed voice, was "one more step in what some of us recognize as the introduction of partisan politics into the governors' conference." Connally was instantly on his feet, demanding to be recognized on a point of "personal privilege." Genuine anger was in his voice. For a moment there was bedlam as many voices spoke at once. Startled at the force of Connally's anger, Reagan tried to back off. "No words of mine were intended to reflect on Governor Connally," he said. "I had even hoped that these few days at sea might produce a budding friendship."

Connally would have none of it. "There was no thought in my mind to inject partisan politics into this discussion," he fumed, glaring at Reagan over his half-glasses, and he personalized the point in classic Texas fashion. "I consider it a personal affront for you to assume that I do this for partisan political reasons." Reagan sank deeper into his chair, and Connally blasted forward as if he were speaking now to the Sons of San Jacinto. "The commitments of this nation are not partisan commitments. The blood being spilled is not partisan blood. When we see riots, marches, draft card burners, insurrections all about, it's time to stand up." It was "pseudo-intellectuals" and "clergymen and that type" who always dissented from wars throughout American history, Connally said. It was not important what the approval or disapproval of his resolution did to the "man in power." But it was important what it did to the country. If this was pure demagoguery, it was effective—to a point. The assemblage rose and cheered him for some minutes—and then tabled his resolution. As the governors did so, 55,000 "pseudo-intellectuals, clergymen, and that type" gathered in Washington to demand that America get out of Vietnam.

That had been in October 1967. On March 30, 1968, the night before Johnson announced he would not run again, Connally was again the instrument of both attack and defense in relation to the Vietnam policy. In Indianapolis, where Robert Kennedy would soon stand before the voters in the Democratic primary, Connally suggested that one candidate had come "very close to treason" during the campaign. Kennedy had proposed a deal, Connally said. If Johnson would gather a distinguished panel together—with Kennedy himself as a charter member—and agree to accept their recommendations on Vietnam, Kennedy would withdraw from the presidential race. "Never in the history of the United States has such an arrogant demand been thrown on the desk of the president," Connally thundered. His roar was a howl in the wind. The country had ceased to be concerned with slights and discourtesies to its president. The mood was shifting profoundly, and on May 7, Kennedy went on to win in Indiana with 42 percent against 27 percent for McCarthy. In the District of Columbia, on the same day as the Indiana primary, Kennedy beat Humphrey 62 percent to 37 percent. Connally could rage, but he was associated with a president the country had turned against and with a policy that had failed.

During the summer, Vietnam was joined by another issue closer and more threatening to Connally personally. This was the unit rule, whereby the head of a convention delegation controlled that delegation totally, once its majority will was declared. The real fight was always before the political delegation was chosen, when ideological differences and personal antipathies clashed and a bruised and bloodied victor always emerged in complete control. Connally was comfortable with such a system, for he was generally victorious under it. The big boots of John Connally, which could flatten you in the dust, had become legend.

By 1968, however, the consciousness of America had been dramatically raised about subtle forms of discrimination and the unit rule lay exposed as an undemocratic, palpably racist way of doing things, for it left political debate to a competition between regional blocs, and the minorities were just that: in the minority and, therefore, unrepresented. Kennedy and McCarthy, of course, were against the unit rule, but so was Hubert Humphrey even though it would work to his advantage as the front runner. Connally thought he had maneuvered successfully to preserve the unit rule for the Texas delegation, but the issue was not dead, as he would discover at the convention.

In early June, bolstered by the candidacies of Kennedy and McCarthy, Texas liberals were preparing a stiff challenge to Connally for control of the Texas delegation, but Robert Kennedy's assassination on June 5 left them in disarray, and on June 11, at the state convention, the Connally forces seized the moment and won easily on the unit rule. Connally then proceeded to handpick the 104 members who would make up the Texas delegation to Chicago.

By late June, Humphrey appeared to be heading for the nomination and speculation was rife over who his vice presidential choice would be. As George Wallace daily became a more formidable force, more moderate elements in the South began to push for an acceptable Southerner on the ticket. Connally took his place at the top of that list. It made eminent sense. He would balance Humphrey regionally and ideologically. His choice would assuage the die-hard Wallace supporters in the South and ensure that the Democrats would take Texas in November. In this year of political assassination, here was the heroic survivor of Dallas, forever joined in blood with the Kennedys. Blood was more powerful than program. Also there was his relation to Johnson, and Johnson still controlled the machinery of the party. He was still feared, if no longer respected. The president's hopes and expectations remained the great unknown. He stood magisterially on the side, watching the process unfold, still able to hand out rewards and punishments, still with considerable room for maneuver if the process was not to his liking. Already, the strains between Johnson and Humphrey were evident. Choosing Connally as his running mate was one way that Humphrey might please Johnson and enlist his support.

The eyes of the Humphrey camp were also on Ted Kennedy, and into July, Humphrey's aides whispered and dreamed and hoped that Teddy would emerge from his grief in time for the convention. A Harris poll suggested that Kennedy would instantly add five million votes to the Democratic ticket. Party professionals lined up to speak of the strength Kennedy would impart. Mayor Daley thought that the convention would draft Teddy Kennedy and said he hoped it would. Kennedy stayed in seclusion with family at Hyannis Port for six weeks after his brother's assassination, sailing off Cape Cod on his rented yawl, *The Mira,* and pondering the responsibility of being father to his brothers' children as well as his own, fifteen in all, with one still on the way. On July 23 he came back to Washington. Driven from the airport by aides, Kennedy pulled up at the Senate Office Building and was unable to get out of the car. "I just can't go in there and face them," he mumbled desolately, and they quickly spirited him away to the airport again.

On the same day, Connally was attending the national governors' conference in Cincinnati. The press regarded him as the best barometer of what was happening behind the scenes and listened attentively to his every word. At one point, almost offhandedly, he was asked about Edward Kennedy. His response was astonishing. He questioned whether Kennedy even had the ability to be president, leaving inferences about his youth at thirty-six years and his inexperience, as well as his current isolation and paralysis. If tough was Connally's reputation, this was tough—and gratuitously cruel, for it was obvious to everyone that Edward Kennedy was in no shape to be a candidate for anything. Also, Connally doubted this talk about Kennedy strengthening the ticket: "Many politicians and the press have created the illusion, incorrectly I think, that [Humphrey] might need a liberal on the ticket, someone with views that might appeal to liberals." Connally doubted this. Someone "of more moderate views" than Humphrey would be a better choice, he thought.

The next day at the White House, George Reedy in the president's press office reported to Johnson a conversation with the *U.S. News and World Report* White House reporter: "[He] suspected that John Connally had knocked down the Ted Kennedy Vice Presidential candidacy at your instructions. I told him . . . that I could not imagine your doing such a thing when you had announced your determination to stay out of the campaign. I also pointed out that this was not a very logical way of knocking down the Kennedy candidacy. He seemed satisfied. . . . I doubt he will pursue it further."

The inquiry reflected the growing feeling in the press: for the hardball season, Connally was Johnson in not-so-effective disguise. Two days later Kennedy took his name out of consideration. "This year is just not possible for me," he said.

★

In the first three weeks of August, events marched swiftly toward the appointment in Chicago. It was as if certain things had become more important than the choice of the nominee: the nature of the Democratic platform, particularly its Vietnam plank; the complexion of the individual state delegations, especially the white Southern delegations; and the treatment of Lyndon Johnson, particularly on his birthday, August 27. On all three questions Connally was the man to watch. He was the keeper of the Johnson legacy and the guardian of Texas pride. It was his job to ensure that due tribute was paid to Johnson's accomplishments, that the president's foreign policy was not dismissed or humiliated in the platform, that the old Johnson-Connally way of doing business, now generalized into the Johnson-Connally-Daley axis, was preserved. He had tools: a solid 104 delegates behind him in a state the Democrats had to win in November, a vice presidential candidacy that had to be treated gingerly and respectfully, and the threat, if things did not go his way, to put the name of Lyndon Johnson in nomination.

On August 6 the numbers indicated that Humphrey could win the nomination on the first ballot only if the favorite sons released their delegates. This arithmetic strengthened Connally's position further. Of the eight favorite son candidates, five were from the Southern states, and of these Texas was by far the most significant. A few weeks before, Richard Nixon had chosen Spiro Agnew as his running mate, largely because the Southern bloc had demanded it. A similar situation was now unfolding with the Democrats, with leading Southerners predicting that the South would be lost if Humphrey did not put a Southerner on the ticket. The South spoke from strength, and Connally was its strong man.

There was quicksand beneath Connally, however, and it was the unit rule. On August 9, Senator Yarborough announced for Eugene McCarthy and in doing so demanded Connally abandon this vestige of political bossism. McCarthy himself came to Houston around this time to speak to a group called Texan Democrats for an Open Convention, for this group had announced that it would challenge the Connally delegation as "nonrepresentative" of the black and Hispanic communities. Yarborough then took charge of a rump delegation which would go to Chicago and demand to supplant the Connally delegation. A few days later, on August 13, a McCarthy spokesman in Texas called the Texas delegation a "handpicked clique of cronies, dedicated to misusing the votes of 11 million Texans, for the benefit of the governor's vice presidential ambitions."

Meanwhile, the platform hearings got under way. On August 15, at a speech in Madison Square Garden before 19,000 ardent followers, McCarthy announced his proposal for the Vietnam plank. "We cannot continue to be prisoners of those who would not settle this war," McCarthy said. "The time has come to make a realistic attempt to break the impasse at the Paris negotiations."

In Worcester, Massachusetts, Edward Kennedy came out of

isolation. Vietnam, he declared, had become a bottomless pit, and he put forward a new plan to get out: an unconditional end to the bombing of North Vietnam, a negotiated withdrawal of all U.S. and North Vietnamese troops from South Vietnam, reconciliation between the Saigon Government and the NLF, and a general lowering of the violence in the countryside of South Vietnam. McCarthy immediately altered his plank and embraced the Kennedy position.

From his retreat at the LBJ Ranch, Johnson watched. He was rightly concerned about the impression the convention debate would convey to Moscow, to Hanoi, and to the negotiators in Paris. He could not control the stump rhetoric of his detractors, but he could still control the language of the foreign policy plank. The wording of the plank itself, rather than the hot air of the deliberations, was what the foreign enemies would notice. It must show that policy was still in LBJ's hands and that a Democratic successor would continue the spirit of the Johnson policy, so the Communists should negotiate now in Paris rather than wait for a new president.

As for a draft, Johnson was noncommittal with his staff only a few days before the convention opened. On August 16, Texas Congressman Tiger Teague laid out the scenario for a Johnson draft: "Unless Humphrey makes it on the first ballot, I'm confident Johnson will get it. If the convention goes into a deadlock, Humphrey will nominate Johnson, and he will win by acclamation." Elliott Roosevelt, a national committeeman from California, textured the scene, saying, "I've noted that the national committee keeps advising us that the whole day of August 27 will be turned over to a eulogy of President Johnson and they aren't scheduling the vote on the nominee until after the 27th. I anticipate that a spontaneous draft will arise from the floor demanding the renomination of President Johnson. They'll beg their delegates to go for the president. I'm convinced that the president was sincere in his March declaration, but faced with the possibility for reuniting the party and that he is the only solidifying force, he will place the country and the party above himself."

If there was to be a "spontaneous" draft from the floor, it was obvious which delegation would generate it.

Johnson may have been noncommittal about a draft, but he never wavered about the celebration planned for August 27. Desperately, passionately, he wanted to go to Chicago for the birthday party of his life, whatever the consequences. Strongest among those who wanted to accommodate him was Mayor Daley, who had reserved the legendary Stockyards Inn for the night and had commissioned a birthday cake fit for a Texan, and who along the way was telling Connally, "If Lyndon Johnson wants the nomination, he's got my delegation." The president made his desire to go to Chicago abundantly clear to his appointments secretary, Jim Jones, and to his aide, Larry Temple, even though he was professing the opposite to his press secretary, George Christian. To Christian, Johnson kept on the high road: "I just don't think I ought to go to that darned thing. I'd just be the focal point of something," he said. "I'm not the candidate. I don't know who the candidate's going to be. I don't want to get in the middle of it. Frankly, George, I'd rather be somewhere else. If I go [August 27], they'll accuse me of trying to upstage the nominee. If I go on that day, I'll get right in the middle of a fight." Christian dutifully conveyed this to the press on background, and, as usual, the press did not believe him—not on an event that appealed so directly to Johnson's vanity. Moreover, if Johnson did not go, he would be the first Democratic president since Roosevelt in 1944 not to attend his party's convention.

On August 18, Connally made the familiar trek to the LBJ Ranch for a long session on convention strategy. Larry Temple joined them for dinner. Temple was one of the handpicked Texas delegates, as was Marvin Watson, who was slated to be LBJ's man in charge in Chicago. Watson would be assisted in Chicago by another Johnson and Connally associate, the smooth Jake Jacobsen. Since Johnson remained the leader of the party, he controlled the machinery, and the ranch was to be the machine's nerve center. Johnson was intent that the line of communication between the ranch and the convention be disguised, so both he and Connally could deny they were talking frequently, or at all. The main channel would be from Connally to Watson to Temple or Jim Jones at the ranch. Later, Jones would describe his role as Charlie McCarthy to Edgar Bergen, sitting on Johnson's knee, and conveying the presidential orders to Connally and others, even though the parties on the other end of the line could probably hear the ventriloquist's real voice booming in the background.

Vietnam remained Johnson's preoccupation. He did not want the Vietnam plank to "kick him in the teeth." The day after the strategy session with Connally, Johnson traveled to Detroit to appear before the VFW. It was a forum which traditionally encouraged presidents to passionate saber-rattling and flag-waving, and at this important moment, just before the most wide-ranging, serious political discussion of Vietnam policy in four years was to get under way, Johnson succeeded only in cementing himself as an immovable object. He sprinkled his speech with the cattleman's language against "cutting and running," with the usual warning against being "hoodwinked" by the enemy, and with more talk of honor, honor, and honorable terms. He had even directed his speechwriter, Harry Middleton, to include a passage which invited the protesters to go to Vietnam and share the foxholes and see what the young soldiers were going through. Middleton thought that was a lousy thing to say, and he didn't include it in the speech. Johnson would later thank Middleton for his insubordination. The speech caused little stir, for at this stage it seemed entirely predictable. Only Lester Maddox of Georgia and Richard Nixon praised it enthusiastically. But John Connally went off to Chicago with Johnson's Detroit speech as his text. As he did, the heaviest fighting since the beginning of the lull in June broke out in South Vietnam. In the week of the convention, 308 American soldiers would die and another 1,134 would be wounded.

★

Connally had planned to ride ceremoniously and boisterously to Chicago with his delegation aboard a train scheduled to leave on the Friday before the convention's plenary session opened. A more urgent mission pressed upon him now. Surrounded by threat and counterthreat, he flew early to Chicago with guns blazing: he might not support Humphrey if the vice president persisted in making weak statements about Vietnam; he and his delegation might bolt the convention if the unit rule were scrapped; the challenge to the fair representation within his delegation boiled down to no more than the fact that "the liberals got beat, are unhappy about it, and think they have a right to complain." Connally arrived in style, settled himself with fanfare in his suite in the Conrad Hilton, and took charge of his white Thunderbird Landau with its special Illinois license plate, No. 61 (which was a measure of his importance at the convention). In style, in substance, in symbol, Connally instantly became a lightning rod.

Joseph Rauh, the dandy of the Establishment liberals, was coordinating the rules and credentials fights for McCarthy, and he acidly took note of Connally's arrival. With his bow ties, his gravelly voice with its rich Rooseveltian rhythms, his unwavering New Deal liberalism, Rauh despised this big, bragging, glad-handing oilman-politician, and classed him together with the segregationist Southern politicians he had fought all his life. By his deft legal arguments,

Rauh, more than anyone, had been responsible for the seating of the Mississippi Freedom Democratic delegation at the 1964 convention, and in that fight he had heard a story about Connally that was, to Rauh, emblematic and unforgettable. Connally and the governor of Georgia, Carl Sanders, had gone to see LBJ in 1964 in protest over the plan to seat the black delegation from Mississippi. Since Johnson was moving quickly in the civil rights front, he looked hard at the two governors and said in surprise, "Do you really want me to seat a lily-white delegation from Mississippi?"

"If those buggers walk onto the floor," Connally snapped back, "Southern delegates will walk off."

That was the Connally of 1964, but to Rauh, the Connally of 1968 was no different. Indeed, the Texan might have been even a bit more menacing, because he was more powerful. Now, echoing Connally's threat in reverse, Rauh set two conditions which would cancel his support of Hubert Humphrey: he would not support the party's candidate if the platform proclaimed Johnson to have been right in "his disastrous cause in Vietnam," and specifically he would not support Humphrey if Humphrey chose Connally as his running mate.* He had voted Democratic all his life, Rauh explained to the *Chicago Tribune*, and he expected to do so again in 1968. "I don't think either John Connally or a pro-Vietnam plank will be supported by this party," he said. Nevertheless, to Rauh, Connally was only the most effective segregationist in their midst, not the most lurid. Lester Maddox had the latter distinction, and thus, for strictly tactical reasons, the McCarthy forces focused their challenge on the Georgia rather than the Texas delegation. With Georgia, they had Maddox as the villain and the debonaire Julian Bond as the matinée idol, and this provided a far better focus for a challenge than Connally as the villain, Ralph Yarborough as the hero, and Lyndon Johnson as the wirepuller in the wings.

Nevertheless, the challenge to the Texas delegation went forward in the Credentials Committee on the day Connally arrived in Chicago. The San Antonio curmudgeon Maury Maverick, Jr.,

---

*Predictably, Rauh's attack made him "personally offensive" to Connally, and the antipathy caused a snafu in the Humphrey campaign that fall. Humphrey flew into Fort Worth with Rauh on the plane, as a show of reconciliation, and Rauh bounded off the plane to pump Connally's hand effusively. He thought he was doing a good thing. A short time later Rauh had to be secretly spirited out of Texas on a pretext, so infuriated was Connally at his presence. After the platform fight, in which Rauh had baited Connally mercilessly, Connally promised that he would support Nixon if Rauh ever set foot in Texas.

showed the flag for the Texas liberals. "This regular delegation, controlled by Governor Connally, is broadly representative only of people who will vote for the Republican candidate for president," Maverick told the committee. "Our liberal delegation is broadly representative of the people who carry Texas for the Democrats. Don't shun these people or you won't carry Texas." The insurgents demanded 50 of the 104 seats in the delegation, claiming that they represented 48 percent of those who voted in the last six Democratic primaries. On the regular delegation there was one elected black delegate and there were five other blacks whom Connally had chosen. In the parlance of the time, these five were called "Connally Toms," and Connally was alternately charged with "oppression," "boss rule," and "political blackmail."

At this moment the vice president put forward his ideas, but they were neither sincere nor positive nor worthy of a great leader. He had wanted to break with administration policy as far back as April, when he drew up a position which reflected his personal feelings on the war. Johnson had bullied him out of it.

"If you break with me over Vietnam, you'll never carry Texas. I'll make sure of that," Johnson threatened.

At this stage, Humphrey's ideas were important more for what they were not than for what they were. His plank would not condemn Johnson past policy; it would not favor a coalition government with the Communists; it would not advocate a unilateral American withdrawal. Humphrey would accept almost anything else if he could reach an accommodation with the doves. In fact, the Humphrey forces were on the verge of that accommodation. They had taken the language almost verbatim out of Teddy Kennedy's Worcester speech and inserted it in a proposed draft. This was to be the long-awaited and, for Humphrey, politically necessary break with Johnson. Senator Fred Harris of Oklahoma had the job of selling the language to the various factions, principally to the conservative Democrats, particularly to John Connally.

Harris went to see Connally shortly after the governor arrived in Chicago. It was the first time they had ever met. Harris expected to find a flexible politician, one who was impressive and strong-willed and loyal to Johnson, to be sure, but one who would listen to the interest of Humphrey and the party. Instead, Connally surprised Harris with the fervor of his conservative convictions. He came off as an ideologue of the right, to whom the storm over unit rule and the challenge to the Southern delegations and the Vietnam peace initiatives were all part of the same liberal weakness.

Humphrey, Connally told Harris, was caving in to the longhairs, the feminists, and the crazies; the governor's attitude was that they should not be given an inch. Nevertheless, for this brief moment, Connally promised not to fight the Humphrey plank. The vice president would be crazy to recommend it, but if that's what he wanted to do, Connally would not openly fight him.

Immediately after the meeting, he was on the phone to Johnson, who perceived a sinister collapse by Humphrey to the weaklings of the left. Charles S. Murphy, a former undersecretary of agriculture and an old Johnson operative, was dispatched to Chicago as the president's emissary to the Platform Committee. Murphy consulted constantly by phone with Johnson as the drafting process went forward, conveying back to the committee what was acceptable, what was unacceptable, and what the president would openly disassociate himself from. Murphy's presence suffocated the negotiations between Humphrey and the doves.

On the same day, half a world away, Soviet tanks rolled into Czechoslovakia to provide "fraternal assistance" to the Czech people. The images of Czech citizens taunting Russian soldiers, marching through the streets with the bloodstained national flag, throwing pathetic rocks, and even destroying a few tanks riveted the free world. In Chicago, the invasion provided a shock. The premise of the McCarthy, Kennedy, and McGovern camps on the Vietnam plank was that the Communists were reasonable—you could deal with them—on Vietnam and a wider range of East-West issues. Now it was undeniable that the hard-liners were in charge in Moscow. Some commentators assumed the invasion to be a boon for Richard Nixon. Senator Yarborough thought it presented a new reason to nominate Lyndon Johnson.

The following day, August 22, Connally rose to address the Platform Committee at the height of the debate over the Vietnam plank. It was a climactic moment, since the Czech invasion had put everything in flux and the committee appreciated that Connally spoke for others besides himself. Before the invasion, the doves could have counted on perhaps 40 votes out of 110 in the committee. Now, a number of those were reconsidering. "I have seen at first hand the ravages of war, the waste, the terror, the tragedy," Connally said. "I yield to no man in my desire for peace." But he was troubled: "It is cruel and evil to promote hope of peace without tangible assurance of achieving such a peace. These are strong words, I know, but these are times for strong words. The cause of peace should not be used as a vehicle for potential favor or fortune. The cause of peace is not the personal property of any politician or political party."

Connally took up the dovish proposals one by one, his voice shaking with passion and outrage. He was at his best: angry, impressive, impossible to dismiss or mock, and well rehearsed. He transported the leaderless majority as, with echoes of Johnson's Detroit speech, he knocked down the conciliatory proposals. "These proposals sound attractive, especially when used in conjunction with casualty lists and Treasury expenses of the war. . . . But how do they measure up against the cold hard truth of reality?" They were, he said, the course of appeasement and surrender. "They have a fatal flaw. They are predicated on the assumption that the enemies of freedom want peace. What sign, what signals do we have that such is the case? History tells us that such is not the case. Tyranny begets tyranny. We need only look at the tragic events in Czechoslovakia for confirmation of this fact."

This was the political trenches, where Connally was superb. The committee gasped as he turned directly on Senator McCarthy by name, shattering a standard taboo. He scoffed at McCarthy's apparent indifference to the Czech invasion: "Senator McCarthy's reaction to the Russian invasion is, in my personal judgment, a deplorable circumstance, a very regrettable one, particularly when the people of the world view him as a leading contender of the Democratic party. Beyond any question, utterances such as these can do nothing but hinder the negotiations which we have had under way for several months in Paris with North Vietnam." He called upon the committee not to denounce American past actions, but to denounce Communist aggression in South Vietnam, Czechoslovakia, and anywhere else in the world, to write a plank which "supports the determined fight of this administration to preserve not only our own freedom, but to help provide the opportunity for freedom for peoples everywhere."

The excited committee burst into cheers and extended applause when Connally finished. It had been a brilliant, bravura performance. A masterpiece of polarization, the speech became an outlet for venting the frustrations and the hostilities of the majority. Senator William Benton of Connecticut grabbed the microphone. "I think you have caught the spirit of the majority of the committee," he shouted over the din. "I think you will get the plank you want!"

The effect was immediate, not only on the Platform Committee itself but on Hubert Humphrey. Before the convention, the vice president had waffled, sounding conciliatory one moment and tough the next, and it had caused great tension between him and President Johnson. Before Connally rose to speak to the Platform Committee Johnson had said coldly to Humphrey, "You are stretching the patriotism of men like John Connally to the limit." But now Connally had made it politically possible for Humphrey to resume his place as an advocate of the administration's Vietnam policy. Humphrey had to be either for the president or against him. There was no longer any middle ground. Connally's speech to the Platform Committee represented the collapse of the compromise plank and the rebels squealed with pain. Speaking for the Kennedy contingent, Pierre Salinger charged that Connally had "grossly distorted" the views of the doves and that his speech was "the old type of McCarthyism." Salinger continued, "I think Connally is a bad guy. Anybody can adopt him if they want to."

Humphrey was in Connally's debt. Not long after Connally's speech Humphrey told the press, "North Vietnam is not going to get a better deal out of me." In case Humphrey missed the point, Connally added, "Humphrey cannot disavow the fact that he is and has been a part of the Johnson administration. That is his strength. Ninety percent of his delegates are Johnson delegates."

Connally had won the big battle for Johnson on the Vietnam plank, but the battle over the unit rule was not going so well. Humphrey's aide, Bill Connell, an adoptive Texan himself, had tried to reassure Connally. The governor was not to worry. The rule would not be scrapped at this convention, and the solid Connally delegation would be seated as it was. But as Connell soothed Connally, Humphrey was dispatching a letter to the Credentials Committee calling for action "at this convention" to scrap the rule. John Connally exploded at this apparent treachery.

A Connally incensed and double-crossed was a sight to behold. He stomped. He blustered. And he was dangerous. First, he threatened to walk out of the convention with his delegation. He would not abide by a convention decision to abolish the rule, for that would be an "unconscionable breach of faith." He was reconsidering his favorite son candidacy and might withdraw it altogether to nominate "another great Texan." The warning "Johnson is coming! Johnson is coming!" began to be uttered with foreboding in the hallways. It was no performance this time. In the three days before the convention opened Connally was seriously working to undermine the Humphrey nomination.

His chief ally was Mayor Richard Daley, another staunch defender of the unit rule. Daley, too, was withholding his delegation's support for Humphrey because he considered the vice president to be a lousy candidate. "If we're going to have another Lyndon Johnson, let's draft the real thing," Daley was saying, and if he couldn't have Johnson, he wanted Teddy Kennedy. With Humphrey's support soft, Connally began to suggest that Johnson might be renominated regardless of what the convention did on the unit rule.

Behind the surface politics, the fate of the unit rule was directly linked to John Connally's future in the Democratic party. His hope for the vice presidency rested solely on his leadership of a solid South, where every delegate could be controlled by a handful of Southern governors who were Connally friends. When he talked of the rule as the essence of democracy and spoke of its history going back to 1846, he was arguing for its retention not only in 1968 but, even more importantly for him personally, in 1972. Under a series of reasonable scenarios, 1972 was to be his year to run for president. If he were nominated now as vice president with a weak and compromising candidate like Humphrey (who was then running some fifteen percent behind Richard Nixon in the polls), he would be perfectly poised for 1972. Equally, if Humphrey spurned him for a non-Southerner—and lost—Connally could march into the nomination in four years as the leader of the decisive region. All that could happen only if he could count on the old certainties of power politics. Beneath him, however, the sands were shifting.

The dream of a Johnson nomination remained the repository of all Connally's annoyances—over Humphrey's vacillations, his weakness on the unit rule, his bent toward a compromise on Vietnam, his partial acquiescence in the challenge to the Texas delegation. After a raucous session of the Texas delegation on August 23, Connally told the press in the hallways, "There is a growing sentiment to make that nomination, period," and around the Conrad Hilton the prospect of a Johnson nomination became known as Connally's "blackjack." The Rules Committee, however, could not be beaten into submission. Hours after Connally's statement, it passed a "freedom of conscience" resolution, meaning that delegations could retain or scrap the unit rule as they wished at this convention. The South was now bound by will and inclination, but no longer by law. The resolution was a repulse to Connally, but not yet a total defeat.

It was not until the talk of a Johnson nomination got serious that Humphrey's agents, Larry O'Brien and Fred Harris, stirred themselves to meet with Connally. Their delay in paying homage made Connally smolder the more and heightened the tension.

Moreover, Harris was then being prominently mentioned as a potential running mate for Humphrey. He was being considered because he was young and vigorous and dovish, and the Humphrey camp was preoccupied, even obsessed, with youth. (Harris's opponents in the Humphrey staff reminded the candidate that not only were the young against the war, they had dropped out of the political process altogether.) Therefore, Connally viewed Harris suspiciously as a rival. To O'Brien and Harris, forthrightly, even bombastically, the governor made it clear that he would tolerate no smear on Lyndon Johnson. Also, Humphrey should know that if this challenge to the Texas delegation persisted with Humphrey's acquiescence, he would indeed renominate Lyndon Johnson. O'Brien listened, but he was not impressed. Connally was an extremely important figure at the convention, to be sure, but he was not likely to disrupt the convention by doing something stupid that in the end would cause him to lose face. In short, the threat to nominate Johnson was a bluff, O'Brien felt. Nevertheless, the message was passed to Humphrey that he should attempt to mollify Connally personally, and the vice president reached Connally by phone soon after. Humphrey backtracked and apologized, saying he favored the abolition of the unit rule, but not at this convention, and that he supported the seating of the Texas delegation "as is," and then Connally let him have it: the vice president had royally messed up the situation. He, Connally, might blast the vice president publicly on the unit rule later in the afternoon. No, he was not ready to release his delegates and drop his favorite son candidacy.

"You do what you want to, and I'll do what I want to," he said cryptically.

This was quickly reported to Johnson at the ranch. Jim Jones, the president's Charlie McCarthy, was giving Johnson almost minute-by-minute accounts, culled from the Johnson operatives—Connally, Jake Jacobsen, and Marvin Watson:

1:10 p.m., August 24:

♦ Jake Jacobsen says the 600 vote Southern delegates are holding well.

♦ Jake thinks Connally may issue a statement later today blasting VP over the unit rule.

♦ Jake says no one is in charge of the convention. There is a real vacuum.

♦ Jake says this Convention is going to draft the President if there is the slightest indication the draft will be accepted.

2:55 p.m., August 24:

♦ Governor Connally reported that [he has heard] Mayor Daley is supposed to announce for Vice President tomorrow.

♦ Connally says he sure hopes someone could get to Daley and get him to withhold his endorsement until Monday or Tuesday. That would give the Southern states time to show their strength to Humphrey.

The rages of John Connally were getting so much attention that they led very late that night to one of the more bizarre twists of the entire convention. In the McCarthy camp sat the brilliant, peripatetic Richard Goodwin, whose roots were in the Kennedy administration, who had stayed on as a speechwriter in the Johnson White House until his opposition to Vietnam had made him an apostate. He had been active in finding a challenger to Johnson and had been with McCarthy through the snows of New Hampshire until Bobby Kennedy had announced, but had returned to McCarthy after Kennedy was murdered. Now, in Chicago, he operated as an ambassador without portfolio. In Connally's unhappiness, Goodwin perceived the glimmer of an opportunity, and at 3:00 A.M. Sunday morning he awoke Robert Strauss, whose room was next to Connally's and who was well known as the conduit to Connally himself. Goodwin professed to be in Senator McCarthy's room, and he had a matter of the greatest importance which he wanted to discuss with the governor on behalf of McCarthy. Could the governor come to Goodwin's room when he woke up? Strauss relayed the message at a decent hour, and Connally was both insulted and intrigued. If Goodwin wanted to talk, he could come to the governor's room, as protocol dictated. Goodwin arrived full of charm and guile, and proceeded for the next three hours to fascinate Connally and Strauss, regaling them with stories of traveling through the small towns of New Hampshire, he with his typewriter on his lap, McCarthy with a midday bottle of whiskey. As he got closer to his purpose he talked of what Connally and McCarthy had in common, of how Connally had promoted McCarthy over Humphrey for the vice presidential nomination in 1964, of how on domestic issues they shared many beliefs and were kindred spirits.* Then came the proposition, as cold a deal as the Devil had ever imagined. If Connally would denounce Humphrey and endorse McCarthy, he would be chosen as McCarthy's vice presidential running mate. Together they would win the nomination, and then, after a glorious victory in November, they would split the patronage. To Connally would go a set number of cabinet and Supreme Court appointments. When Connally recovered from his astonishment, he turned the deal down and Goodwin left. Moments later, Strauss and Connally emerged from the bedroom to greet their wives in the sitting room. Connally reached over and kissed Helen Strauss on the cheek.

"Helen," he said sweetly, "your husband just turned down the chance to be chief justice of the Supreme Court."

Not many minutes after this, at the LBJ Ranch, Jim Jones typed a memo to the president about developments in Chicago.

10:50 a.m., August 25, 1968:

♦ Goodwin came and said the McCarthy people wanted Connally's help and in return would be willing to get a watered-down Vietnam plank and also let the Southerners choose whomever they want for Vice President. Connally's comment was that these men of so-called high moral principle are certainly willing to compromise.

In fact, Eugene McCarthy had known nothing of the Goodwin initiative, and considered it absurd when he did hear of it, if for no other reason than that he knew John Connally never had had the power to compel his Texas delegation to go directly against the wishes of Lyndon Johnson.

★

At the International Amphitheater in Chicago, the delegates, finally free of the taunts and solicitations of the street, streamed into the garrisoned convention, past the barbed wire atop the Cyclone fence around the parking lot, through cordons of helmeted police, past the security agents carefully inspecting credentials, into the false

*If McCarthy shared some beliefs on domestic policy with Connally, he had also opposed the fondest of Texas causes: he had voted to restrict the oil depletion allowance; he was against Texas methods of dealing with migrant workers; he was for a long time the sole voice against the Tidelands proposal and had voted against the Natural Gas Bill of 1956, for which Connally had lobbied so vigorously as an employee of Sid Richardson.

air of celebration. The playwright Arthur Miller was one of them—
he was a McCarthy man from Connecticut—and from the moment
of entering the hall he felt a "tingling sense of aggressive hostility."
A sense of foreboding came from the almost tyrannical control
exercised by Johnson's operatives. Marvin Watson had been in
Chicago for two weeks, dispensing the real power: what delegations
would be seated where on the convention floor, which candidates
would get their headquarters where, who would get convenient hotel
rooms and how many, who would get blocks of gallery passes, who
would have convenient banks of telephone lines. Even the likely
nominee was shut out from the arrangements. "I found it ironic
when the McCarthy camp began complaining that they were being
discriminated against, being frozen out in favor of Humphrey,
because we were receiving exactly the same treatment," Lawrence
O'Brien would write later. "The Johnson people had everything tied
up."

Connally took charge of the Texas delegation, which was
predictably located near the Illinois delegation, and right under the
podium where the diminutive Carl Albert of Texas, the Speaker of
the House and the chairman of the convention, would not have to
stand on tiptoe to see him. Texas and Illinois, Connally and Daley,
had all the power, it seemed, to bend the convention to their will.
But from the opening of the real business Monday night, that power
began to slip from their grasp. The first item of importance was the
unit rule, that "hoary relic of old machine politics," as it was being
called in the press. Connally and Texas had been the loudest
supporters of the hoary relic, and now, in less than a half-hour and
by voice vote and with boos and catcalls for Texas, the unit rule
was scrapped. Then came the first roll call on a procedural matter,
and Connally boomed defiantly, "Mr. Chairman, Texas, voting under
the unit rule, casts 104 votes no," and the boos grew louder.

After midnight, the challenge to the legitimacy of Connally's
delegation finally came to the floor. There was more at stake than
Connally's situation, for this would be the first test of Humphrey's
strength and would be interpreted as a measure of his control.
Everything that involved Texas could be decoded to reveal the
convention's attitude toward Lyndon Johnson. The presentation ran
along predictable lines. Robert Strauss, soon to be the national
committeeman from Texas, gave a rousing finale in defense of
Connally. Pointing to Connally's accomplishments in education and
in mental health, Strauss dared the opposition to deny that the
distinguished governor of Texas had brought more blacks and

Hispanics into state government than any governor in the history of the state. This was a "vicious and unwarranted attack upon our state, its leadership, and its citizens," Strauss exclaimed.

At the LBJ Ranch, the Johnsons watched the battle on television excitedly. "I couldn't possibly go to bed until John Connally had won that fight," Lady Bird exultantly wrote in her *White House Diary*. When the vote came, a vote from which the Texas delegation was excluded, New York and California voted against Connally's Texans, which was a vote for Yarborough's rump delegation. Even Virginia, liberated now from the unit rule, split its vote down the middle, heralding the demise of the once solid South. But as the vote progressed, the shape of the Humphrey deal with the liberals became clear: to dislodge Lester Maddox's Georgians and to seat Connally's Texans. The final vote was 1,365 to 955 in Connally's favor, but the liberals and the doves were credited with marshaling more support than had been expected. Humphrey was in control, but barely. Connally sought to downplay the liberal showing. "This vote didn't reflect the merits of the case," he told the press.

The catcalls for Texas and for Connally personally had affected the governor more than he let on. By Tuesday, members of the Texas delegation were being booed in their hotel and in the streets when they moved about in a group. The liberals, the doves, the street clowns were his enemy now, not Humphrey, and no further purpose was served by being hostile to the vice president. That antagonism in the preconvention days had accomplished its goal: Humphrey had collapsed totally to Lyndon Johnson on the Vietnam plank, the Texas challenge had been turned aside with Humphrey's help, and the South had had time to "show its strength" to Humphrey. Since Sunday, when Humphrey had made his strong statement on Vietnam and Connally had chewed him out over the unit rule, communication between the two had improved markedly. Connally showed it by paying a visit to the Humphrey headquarters on Monday, slapping the Humphrey aide and fellow Texan Bill Connell on the back and saying, "We've been playing games. Let's forget this nonsense. We're with you." On Tuesday morning Connally dropped his favorite son candidacy and released his delegates to Humphrey. It created a domino effect in the South, and by the afternoon, when the Vietnam plank would come to the floor that evening, Humphrey had a lock on the nomination.

Tuesday, August 27, was supposed to be Lyndon Johnson Day. Yet Lady Bird woke up with a sense of emptiness, as if this were really the end, an end to be marked by silence, by absence, and by disengagement. She had all but given up hope for Lyndon's "valedictory speech" at the convention. Though there was a wistfulness in her mood, she had the breadth to be fascinated by the Chicago extravaganza and secretly wished she could be there incognito to witness "one of the spectacles of our time." Nellie, who was there, only wished she could be home at Picosa, the Connallys' beloved Texas ranch. "The world is in convulsions all around us—our Party, our Country, our whole world," Lady Bird wrote in her *Diary*. "Lyndon is plowing right on, working as he can every day on those things he can control and assaulting those things vigorously that he has even little hope of controlling." The DRAFT LBJ posters, printed by the thousands, would stay locked in the basement of the Chicago amphitheater and the LBJ birthday cake would molder at the stockyards, as the Johnsons flew off to Austin for a quiet private birthday party with their daughter Luci. Briefly, Johnson met with the press along the way. For some reason, he felt compelled to tell one of those unnecessary lies: "I am not talking to the convention. I am not sending any emissaries. I don't have anyone reporting to me other than Cronkite." Still, he held out the remote possibility that he might fly to Chicago later in the day. When Jesse Unruh, the boss of the California delegation, heard about Johnson's chat with the press, he contemplated the prospect of Johnson's arrival with malicious glee and remarked to John Burns, the head of the New York delegation, "I understand the Great Cowboy may come tonight. Well, we're waiting for him."

Across town in Chicago, Johnson was being celebrated at an "un-Birthday Party" organized by the Mobilization Committee to End the War in Vietnam. Calling its dark comedy a "freakout for the biggest freak of all," it was a tribute to Johnson's historical career "all the way from the first election he stole in Texas to the new anti-personnel weapons his Administration has developed for use in Vietnam and the ghettoes." The feast meant to depict "the grubby reality of a Texas politician." With strobe lights bouncing off mirrors, a rock band calling itself the "Holocaust No Dance Band" blasted out such numbers as "The Master of Hate" and dedicated it to Johnson.

> Suicide is an evil thing
> But at times it is good
> If you've been where the master lives
> I think you surely should.

The party, said its organizers, was designed to "put a little joy into a week of terror," and upon the walls of the hall used for the occasion were pictures of Vietnamese civilians in varying poses of butchery, as well as ghetto youth in combat with cops. William Burroughs, Jean Genet, and Dick Gregory imparted the nimbus of high art to the affair. Calling the Chicago police "mad dogs," Genet found it "perfectly natural that these dogs wanted to bite and even eat hippies, students, and journalists."

The street theater moved inexorably toward its bloody climax on this night of the Vietnam debate, when the police and the Illinois National Guard would lose control in Grant Park and send scores of victims, including twenty-one journalists, to the hospital. If Connally was disgusted and offended by all this, he was also, like Lady Bird, utterly transfixed by it. That night, after the convention debate, safe from the odor of tear gas and Mace, he would stay up late into the predawn hours watching the television reports on the happenings across the street from his hotel. "The spectacle of such a thing happening in America fascinated me," he said, honestly awed.

Still, to Connally, what was happening on the floor of the convention held the greater fascination. In a surprisingly subdued and even civilized debate, the Johnson plank moved inexorably toward victory. When the vote came the next afternoon, it passed 1,567 to 1,041. To the reporters, Connally put his own spin on the vote, asserting that it was a "vote of confidence" for President Johnson and would make a Democratic victory in the fall easier. Johnson himself had made a personal appeal to the Texas delegation that its vote on the plank be unanimous, and it was.

Immediately, Eugene McCarthy considered withdrawing his name from nomination, for he would not have been able to run for president on that platform in any event. But his supporters would not let him. The Chorus was feeling the weight and the grandeur of its own tragedy. "My people wanted a showdown," McCarthy would say later. "They wanted death. They had to lose publicly." And so the nomination went forward. John Kenneth Galbraith would be one of the seconders for the McCarthy nomination. "McCarthy has shown that resort to violence first destroys those who employ it," Galbraith told the convention. "His campaign has shown that this may not yet be the age of John Milton, but he has shown that it is not the age of John Wayne or even of John Connally." Members of the California and New York delegations leaped up and shouted, "Screw Connally." Reporters rushed to Connally for his reaction. "Where I come from," he said, "it sure helps to have that Galbraith agin ya." With each passing reference, Connally was getting more firmly rooted as a symbol of the wild and bull-headed West.

After the vote on the Vietnam plank, a new and bizarre possibility for the humiliation of Johnson arose, and, again, the Johnson crowd at the convention had to work hard to sidetrack it. Bitterness was intense over the Vietnam plank, as much over the method by which the party had now, by inference, accepted official and moral responsibility for Johnson's war as over the substance of the plank itself. William vanden Heuvel, a delegate from New York, let it be known that he intended to place Johnson's name in nomination later in the evening, because Johnson "is the only one who can run on the Vietnam plank they have given us." The use of a Johnson nomination threat had been turned on its head. "Why take the dummy when you can get the ventriloquist?" Richard Goodwin said wickedly. Connally had attempted to use the threat to undercut Humprey before the convention, and now vanden Heuvel was about to use it to embarrass Humphrey and humiliate Johnson out of political spite.

When the press got wind of this and reported it on television, Lyndon Johnson was immediately on the phone to the convention floor, where he reached Jake Jacobsen and gave him the assignment of heading off the nomination. So it had come to that: a presidential nomination as a tool of scorn and contempt. Jacobsen collared vanden Heuvel behind the curtain of the stage and talked to him for more than an hour. The presidency, not the president, would be hurt by such a move, Jacobsen argued. Reluctantly, vanden Heuvel relented, and he credited the "urbane Jake Jacobsen" with dissuading him.

That trap avoided, the Humphrey nomination went forward according to script—or almost. The vote itself was interminable. It began at 8:30 P.M. but it would not end until just before midnight, when Pennsylvania put him over the top. Parliamentary and procedural motions constantly interrupted the roll call, and it was in the course of one of those eddies that Senator Abraham Ribicoff took the microphone to deplore "Gestapo tactics in the streets of Chicago," turning Mayor Daley purple with rage and with profanity, and thus providing a lasting image for the convention.

During this endless vote, Humphrey repaired to a small prenomination victory celebration at the Conrad Hilton, trying his best to be the happy warrior once again as the virulence of the real war on the street outside began to subside. The victory party had more the cast of a wake than a celebration. Calling upon his old joy and enthusiasm at this climactic moment of his political life, he went about his rounds, while the reporters hounded him sourly about the streets and about the boorishness of Richard Daley. Humphrey had rejected the suggestion that he make a postnomination pilgrimage to Grant Park with his children to talk with the demonstrators. Still, his business day was far from over. He had yet to deal with the Southern bloc. A meeting after the nomination had been requested respectfully several days before by Buford Ellington, the governor of Tennessee, and Humphrey had a pretty good notion of what the thrust of it would be. As the Southern governors arrived, it was clear who was their leader and spokesman. The men sat down around a semicircular table and Connally commandeered the seat at the head, to the left of Humphrey, a spot fitting for the second in command. The South and the border states had been central to Humphrey's nomination, he opened, and these states would be essential and decisive to his election; indeed, the South represented the margin of victory. They had come to underscore the importance of this and to say that Humphrey's running mate should be someone who would run strongly in their section. Given the fact that George Wallace was going to run a third-party campaign, a Southern running mate was all the more important. Others around the table reemphasized Connally's points. To Humphrey and his aides, it was clear that Connally was going to be their candidate. Lawrence O'Brien, now Humphrey's campaign coordinator, was there, and he suddenly spoke up jarringly. On the contrary, he thought the running mate ought to be someone with ties to the Kennedys, who would be strong with ethnic, Catholic, and blue-collar voters—not necessarily someone with an elective office background. Humphrey and his aide, Ted Van Dyk, exchanged glances. O'Brien was describing himself! They had not realized that O'Brien had developed such grandiose ambitions. After his veiled announcement of availability, O'Brien abruptly got up and left the room, never to return. There were some mumbles and grumbles as the Southerners struggled to regain their initiative. It was headed for a forceful summing up by Connally, when Humphrey cut in:

"Well, fellows, I want you to know I've made my choice. He's not a Southerner, but he's someone you're going to like—*Ed Muskie.*"

Stunned silence fell over the room. Ed Muskie? Of Maine? Maine, with its population of less than a million? With its four electoral votes? Humphrey aide Ted Van Dyk was as shocked as the Southerners, but he was thrilled. He knew Humphrey was not a good "operational politician"; the vice president was a compromiser by nature, especially in tough back-room negotiations. He was sure that Connally on the ticket would lose more votes in the North than he could ever produce in the South, and he also knew that Muskie was still not decided upon, by any means, as the running mate. But this was a masterstroke. As he looked at the stricken faces of the Southerners, Van Dyk had to contain the smile that wanted to appear.

His power play in shambles, his face ashen, Connally struggled to get hold of himself.

"Well, Mr. Vice President, it's clear that you've—you've got your mind set on someone other than a Southerner. I'd like to throw another name into the equation. He's strong on national defense. He's a Northeasterner who hasn't held elective office, but I served with him in the Defense Department and I know he'll be strong in the South—*Cyrus Vance.*"

This time it was Humphrey who was stunned, but only momentarily. Later, Vance would be amused to learn that for a lost moment in history, he of Yale and Establishment New York had been the Southern candidate for vice president.

"Thanks, fellows," Humphrey replied. "I'll take that under advisement. You'll learn of my choice tomorrow." They were dismissed awkwardly.

At last, Connally knew definitely what he had suspected for days: that he had never been under serious consideration as running mate. He had been used by Johnson and by Humphrey for their own purposes, and now he was discarded. Humphrey's need was to find a running mate who could be reasonable and thoughtful, who could reach out to the antiwar elements of the party who were Humphrey's natural allies, and eventually, together, turn away from the Johnson war policy. To Humphrey, the son of the Farmer-Labor Coalition of Minnesota who had entered national politics as a passionate reformer and civil rights activist, "an Alamo guy" like John Connally came from almost a foreign country, if not a different planet.

Thus, for Connally, the unpleasant experience of the 1968 convention was nearly over, but for the cheers for others. The next night, when Humphrey gave his acceptance speech, he was interrupted seventy-five times with applause, and thrice with boos. The boos came when the name Lyndon Johnson was mentioned. Ever since the days when he was a hard-pressed naval officer aboard ship near the Philippines in 1944, Connally had longed to be with Lyndon Johnson for the old-fashioned political fights. But there had been nothing good and old-fashioned about this. Chicago in 1968 soured him. It was their last fight together. It had been glaringly public, and the epithets thrown at Connally were labels that a broad national audience had not heard before—not about him, anyway. The labels, Connally knew, would stick. The riots and head-bashings in the streets imparted a wider context to the quarrels between ambitious men. The electorate was engaged emotionally in what went on at this convention as Connally had never seen it before. The back room where he had been so adept had suddenly come into the living rooms of the American people, and they had not liked what they saw. He had come off as a villain and a throwback, as his party tilted toward its progressive wing and as his real support began to consider finally going over officially to the Republican side. He smoldered as he returned to Austin, angry still at members of his own party and at some Johnson intimates who had abandoned and even double-crossed Lyndon. He was, to use his pet phrase, "personally offended" as he had never been in his political life.

Since 1939, he had bridled under the curse of being Lyndon's boy, and now, abruptly, Lyndon was gone, gone and disgraced. But his taint remained, at least within the Democratic party. "There were two Americas in Chicago," Arthur Miller would write later. "One was passionately loyal to the present, whatever the present happened to be. The other is in love with what is not yet." For Connally, the present had shifted beneath his feet. Within the castle of the Democratic party, he was a knight-errant once again.

17

Turning

THE MAJESTY THAT MARKS the transition of power in the United States began on January 20, 1969, with coffee and sweet rolls and chitchat in the Red Room of the White House. Promptly at 10:30 A.M., Richard Nixon, soon to be the thirty-seventh president of the United States, arrived at the North Portico. There he was met by Lyndon Johnson, and together they strode nobly through the gathering of congressmen and assorted well-wishers to receive their very different congratulations. Johnson soon withdrew to his office for the last time; he was still president for another few hours, and there was unfinished business. The night before he had assigned his chief of staff, Jim Jones, to fill every vacant board and commission with Democrats and have the appointments ready to be signed and sent to Capitol Hill. As Johnson signed, Nixon chatted amiably, glancing at his watch occasionally, wondering where the president was. He suspected Johnson was enjoying administering this last dose of the Johnson treatment. In time, Johnson emerged, and the president and the president-elect climbed into the black limousine for the ride to the Capitol. Behind them, Everett Dirksen, the Republican leader of the Senate, and Jones clambered onto the jump seats. As the limousine pulled away, workers in the Oval Office began to pack up Johnson mementos and to take down the curtains.

The sky was leaden, but the rain would hold off until nightfall. That would give the new president the chance, with passing clemency, to consecrate his presidency to the cause of peace and to the hope for harmony between the races, and even to quote a little Shakespeare. It would be *Julius Caesar,* act 1, scene 2, where Cassius says to Brutus, "The fault, dear Brutus, is not in our stars, but in ourselves. . . ." If Nixon and Johnson on this day were meant to be Cassius and Brutus, recognizing the frailties of man in the course of history, they did not dwell upon the theme. Yet it was a humbling invocation, and even Lyndon Johnson himself, who seemed to cast a giant shadow on any event he attended, receded now into the shadow, the shadow of the quadrennial pageant of the inauguration. As the limousine made its way down Pennsylvania Avenue, the security precautions were elaborate. This inauguration marked the midpoint in a war that was to be the most divisive of the twentieth century. In those vast numbers of Americans who opposed the Vietnam adventure, this transition of power meant not change but continuity. At no other time in American history was there such a feeling of one American emperor passing power to another. To many of those in the streets Vietnam I and Vietnam II rode down the parade route together in the car. A wedge of motorcycle policemen guided the black limousine and secret servicemen rode on the running boards, as in the alleys near the National Theater, a few pathetic, youthful dissenters, filled with passion and a sense of their own moral righteousness, readied their beer cans and rocks.

The leaders talked not about peace or war, about opportunities lost and possibilities to realize, but about Texas. Nixon was obsessed with the state. He talked incessantly about it—and nothing else— on the entire route to his investiture as president. His election had turned on five key states, Illinois, California, Ohio, Missouri, and Texas, and he had won all but Texas. For much of his political life Nixon had distrusted and hated Texas Democrats and suffered at their hands. In 1960, when he lost the state to Kennedy and Johnson by only 45,000 votes, he ascribed the loss to theft. This time he had even given his aide, H. R. Haldeman, the specific assignment of finding out where the stealing was likely to take place and what, if anything, they might do about it. The answer, of course, was that nothing could be done, but in September Nixon had had every reason to believe that at last he would win the Lone Star State handily.

Two weeks after the debacle in Chicago, Humphrey had gone to Houston and stumbled awkwardly over Vietnam. Connally avoided the occasion, refusing an invitation to attend, for he was still smarting over Humphrey's weakness in Chicago and his treachery over the unit rule. Into October, Lyndon Johnson remained estranged from Humphrey and was doing nothing in Texas for the campaign. With no one bringing it together, the Texas Democratic party gave in to its natural tendencies. It remained hopelessly divided, and it was essentially idle in the national campaign. Together, the Yarborough and Connally factions of the party had raised only about $150,000 for the Humphrey-Muskie ticket, a pathetic flow from the hot wells of Texas political oil. It was one-tenth of what had been raised in 1964. By his lack of enthusiasm for the national ticket, if not by overt deed, Connally discouraged his big money boys from contributing to the Humphrey campaign. Many helped Nixon instead.

Only a month before the election, Nixon was still confident that he had Texas easily and, given past indignities and outrages, the prospect warmed him. Then, for no apparent reason, a hurricane developed in the Democratic camp, and the Texas Democrats woke up. During the drive to the Capitol for Nixon's inauguration, Johnson did not enlighten the president-elect about what had happened. It was this. On October 8, Robert Strauss, who was in charge of the Humphrey campaign in Texas, had received a call from the White House. "The Boss wants you up here in the morning," Johnson's chief of staff, Jim Jones, announced curtly. Strauss protested that the following day was his wife's fiftieth birthday. Parties were planned and he would come in a few days. Jones said, "Fine," and hung up. Ten minutes later the phone rang again. With greater significance, Jones said, "The *Boss* wants you up here in the morning. He says, bring Helen and tell her to bring a nice dress." Annoyed, but thoroughly intimidated, Strauss was in Washington the next morning, at the White House, at 7:00 A.M., in the president's bedroom, where by his own account Johnson "kicked hell" out of him for the way he was running the campaign in Texas.

"I'll handle Yarborough, and goddamn it, you tell Connally to do the following things," Johnson barked, ticking off the specifics. "You're runnin' those stupid goddamn ads in the newspapers . . . paid for by Robert Strauss, et cetera, et cetera . . . just to get your name in the newspaper. Save your fuckin' money and spend it in getting out the vote, particularly in the Valley, in the last week. You know how to run a campaign in Texas, and you and Connally go down there and run the goddamn thing. We can't be embarrassed by having this son of a bitch Nixon carry the state." Later in the day, the Strausses went to tea at the White House with Lady Bird and to a state dinner for Prime Minister Keith Holyoake of New Zealand that night, where Helen Strauss was seated next to a gracious Lyndon Johnson, who made not a single mention of the imposition or Mrs. Strauss's birthday nor offered an apology for the mugging in the bedroom.

Two weeks later, in a surprising spectacle of unity, Connally and Yarborough came together with Humphrey for the candidate's second, considerably more successful, trip to Texas. Yarborough gushed to the press in Fort Worth about how the party had never been so united and about his epic struggle with Connally. He was ever the army colonel. "We've never had all-out war," he said. "We've just had skirmish operations to test each other's flanks and borders." For his part, Connally was also buoyant, speaking of Humphrey as a miracle worker who brought the factions together, but Connally was angered when he was asked if his support for Humphrey was real or a sham. "If I don't mean what I do, I don't do it," he said tartly.

It was a strange and transitory moment but it was enough to bring the liberals and conservatives together and by the last week of the Humphrey campaign, with Robert Strauss working hard and spending freely in the Valley, the election was a tossup. On November 3, Humphrey returned to Texas for the last time. Fifty-eight thousand people filled the Astrodome for a tremendous rally, the largest crowd of Humphrey's political life. The occasion was graced by President Johnson himself, and the entire party establishment, left and right, was on the podium—except the incumbent Democratic governor. He had some other, more pressing, engagement. As the bands played and the flags fluttered and the balloons floated and the speeches went on and on, Ted Van Dyk, the Humphrey aide, raced up to Robert Strauss with a flash that had just come across on the AP wire. Connally was going to endorse Richard Nixon! Strauss snatched the wire copy and took off at a run across the vast floor of the arena, his frumpy figure disappearing into the cavernous corridor. Ten minutes later he returned, breathless. There was nothing to it, he told Van Dyk. He had talked to Connally. There was nothing to it—then.

Up to the morning of his inauguration, Nixon had only a glimmering of what might have happened, and he could not get Johnson to provide any specifics. That Johnson and Connally, with so little money and at the last minute, could mobilize their forces so impressively fascinated Nixon. He would have loved to be the beneficiary of such skill. Johnson was going home, but Connally was very much alive. He intrigued the new president. There seemed to be little future in the Democratic party for its old-line Southern conservatives, and party politics in the South were changing fundamentally with the success of Nixon's "Southern strategy." Connally's battle in Chicago had ended in defeat and humiliation, the kind where bitterness lingered. Nixon perceived the possibility of a recruitment. He filed away the thought.

In the spring of 1969 the thought came out of the file. The president tapped Roy Ash, CEO of Litton Industries, to conduct a major study of government reorganization and accorded it the highest presidential stature. The president's accent was on efficiency in management, and he was sure that the overstuffed and bloated bureaucracy needed to be streamlined. Ash picked his own commissioners from within business—except one. H. R. Haldeman, now President Nixon's chief of staff, suggested that Ash consider former Governor John Connally, who had just left office and had joined the Houston law firm of Vinson and Elkins.

Boring and bureaucratic though it might appear, the Ash Commission had to do with power: who had it, who needed more and who needed less, and how it was to be exercised. John Connally was fifty-two years old. He had been out of Washington for seven years. The Republicans were united and consolidating their gains, while the Democrats were shattered and increasingly dominated by their fringe. Ever attentive to his future, Connally realized that he might be sixty, or even sixty-four, years old before the Democrats regained the presidency. Moreover, he was convinced that the Kennedy clique in the party would always stand in his way, if he reached for the ultimate rung of power as a Democrat.

On the Ash Commission, Connally would be working the handles of power. Within the Washington Beltway, he could take a harder look at the Republicans without making any commitments. Moreover, a job in Washington would keep him visible. Once during this period he went overboard to achieve this goal. At a White House party, his formal attire was described by *Washington Post* gossip columnist Maxine Cheshire as "midnight blue cowboy": "His Tex Ritter tuxedo was two tones of azure and delphinium with piping around the double-breasted jacket and four mother-of-pearl buttons. His shirt was two different tones of blue and so was his large bow tie."

Connally's qualities were quickly apparent to the other members of the commission. Among the cautious business executives, he became the voice for the bold stroke and the big thought. His contempt for "incremental thinking" was absolute. The result was that he pushed the commission toward a proposal for three "super-cabinet" positions to deal with economic and social matters, but by its very boldness gave it no chance whatever to pass successfully through Congress. Cabinet members were also suspicious because the commission was addressing their fiefdoms. So, from the beginning Ash was in great need of political savvy, and Connally had it. Together they developed a kind of dog and pony show for the cabinet and the congressional committees, where Ash laid out the dry facts and then Connally covered them with a sweet coating of political unction. Word of Connally's forcefulness began to spread through the Nixon administration and to the president himself. Since Litton Industries was based in Los Angeles, Ash tried always to schedule his commission's meetings with Nixon when the president came to San Clemente. The president's schedule was looser there. Upon these occasions a pattern developed where, after commission meetings, Connally and Nixon would retreat alone just for political kibitzing.

To the Republicans in Texas in 1970, there was no sense whatever that Connally might be thinking of becoming one of them. On the contrary, the governor was as intimidating as ever: attacking, wounding, winning. At last Connally had found the candidate to defeat Ralph Yarborough. He was Lloyd Bentsen, the wealthy and handsome, if somewhat cold, Dane from the Rio Grande Valley. Bentsen had been in Congress in the early 1950s, but had left to make a fortune in cattle and insurance. He had been on the Connally team since the gubernatorial race in 1962 and in 1964, until Lyndon Johnson discouraged it, had considered running against Yarborough. Bentsen had been part of the inner circle who had urged Connally to run for an unprecedented fourth term as governor. At a conclave for political discussion and bird hunting at Picosa, Bentsen had stood up and said, "John, you're a leader. You've got all the qualities, and you've been successful. If you retire and come back to the ranch, you'll never have as many cattle as Bob Kleberg [the owner of the King Ranch], . . . and if you decide to practice law, I doubt that you'll reach the heights that you have reached in political life. You're a person who attracts people. . . ." Connally thanked him and rejected his advice, but he made a mental note of Bentsen's support. In 1970 he returned the favor, encouraging Bentsen to take on Yarborough and offering, in effect, to mastermind the campaign. Before Bentsen agreed he asked Connally if he himself did not want to make the race. Connally said both he and Yarborough had instinctively shied away from a final, classic showdown lest it have the final result of Sherlock Holmes and Dr. Moriarty.

Starting with a two percent rating, Bentsen took the race on, with the power of the Connally machine behind him. At first he found himself oft-confused with Dwight Eisenhower's portly secretary of agriculture, Ezra Taft Benson—"Have you ever heard of a popular secretary of agriculture?" Bentsen would say in a rare flash of humor. It was a campaign which, even for Texas, was memorable for its meanness. Bentsen painted Yarborough as an "ultraliberal," as a peacenik and an integrationist who was in favor of busing, and who even supported the Supreme Court in its decisions on school prayer. He ran TV ads which showed peace marchers flaunting the Vietcong flag and implied that old Raff was right in there with the rabble. It worked, and after eighteen years the symbol of Texas liberalism was brought down.

It was not over for Bentsen and Connally, however. In the general election Bentsen faced a two-term congressman from Houston named George Bush. Bush might even have been considered the favorite, with a resurgent Republican party behind him after the victory of John Tower. But Bush had counted on facing Yarborough, and he was put off balance by Bentsen, a man with whom he agreed on virtually every major question except party label. In a bland campaign, Bentsen prevailed by 200,000 votes. His victory came largely on the strength of organization—Connally's organization—and with the support of rural Texans. It was the confluence of fates that made this Texas triangle memorable. Connally was the rainmaker. Bentsen owed his national stature entirely to Connally, and in an ironic way, so too would George Bush. When Bush and Bentsen opposed one another on the presidential level in 1988, Connally had long since descended into bankruptcy and humiliation.

After the election of 1970, the Nixon presidency took stock. What were to be its priorities in the coming two years, and how should the Nixon team change? The chief of staff, H. R. Haldeman, asked the senior White House staff to address these questions, and the answers were carefully considered by Nixon himself. The political adviser, Lyn Nofziger, was one of the memo writers. Among his points was the thought that the cabinet was essentially a bland collection of men, with no one who was exciting to the public. It was time, wrote Nofziger, to bring someone with star quality into the administration, perhaps one who could be built up as a possible successor to President Nixon. Moreover, the administration might consider bringing a distinguished Democrat into the cabinet, the way Kennedy and Johnson had the Republicans Douglas Dillon as their treasury secretary and Henry Cabot Lodge, Nixon's own vice presidential running mate in 1960, as their ambassador to Saigon.

(Nofziger might have added that Roosevelt had the Republican Henry Stimson as his secretary of state, although upon joining the Roosevelt administration Stimson was immediately read out of the Republican party.) Nofziger's memo interested President Nixon keenly, but for another reason. As a student of Disraeli, Nixon was taken with Disraeli's phrase about "exhausted volcanoes" as the phrase was applied to second-term statesmen. A new face with new force could invigorate him during his second term. Treasury was the logical spot for the bright political star. Nixon was bored with economics, but he knew they decided elections. He determined to push out the bland banker, David Kennedy.

On the afternoon of November 19 the Ash Commission met with the president for the last time, to present its final recommendations. As Roy Ash rose to give the presentation of his commission's findings, he got entangled in the complexity of the bureaucratic reorganization that his group was proposing. Nixon listened glumly to the seemingly interminable confusion over the relationship between the proposed supercabinet posts and their field level offices, and on and on. To Nixon, the main attraction of this grim exercise was the opportunity, with these supercabinet posts, to reduce the size of his cabinet, or put another way, to reduce the number of cabinet officers who had direct access to his office and could tug directly on his sleeve.

Then John Connally rose and bailed Ash out. Lucidly and engagingly, he reexplained the recommendations and registered the key points before he moved to the turf that really engaged Nixon's interest—the political merits of the recommendations. Win or lose on the reorganization in Congress, the administration, by making these proposals, would appear forceful and forward-looking, with an accent on change, while its opponents would have to argue for the status quo. That was simply good politics. This led to a spirited discussion, as the two political pros made a connection. Later, Nixon would say that in five minutes Connally had convinced him to go ahead with the complex reorganization plan.

That night, at a White House dinner for the commission members and their wives, Nixon turned to Ash and asked pointedly about Connally's overall performance on the commission. Ash was expansive. Connally had rescued him from hostile politicians (or uninterested presidents) more than once, and he gave Connally high marks for pushing the normally cautious businessmen in the group toward the bold strokes. After dinner Nixon asked Connally if he wouldn't stay over and come to see him in the morning. What happened the following day became legend. Connally told Nixon he would consider only two jobs—secretary of state and secretary of the treasury. While the president took that under advisement, he invited Connally onto the Foreign Intelligence Advisory Board, a post which entitled him to top-level CIA briefings. It was not a bad day's work for Connally. In his precise, perfectionist's script, H. R. Haldeman wrote himself a note: "Convinced [David Kennedy] has to go. Need someone [Arthur] Burns will respect. . . . Need leadership at Treasury. Find a way to get Connally somehow."

Within the White House there was far from unanimous jubilation as Connally's name started to float around. Indeed, on November 1, a few days before the election, Peter Flanigan, an assistant to the president for economic matters, had received a sharp letter from Peter O'Donnell, the chairman of the Texas Republican party, complaining bitterly about Connally's access to the White House through the Ash Commission, while the governor was simultaneously stumping Texas for Lloyd Bentsen. This White House access was dangerously undermining George Bush, O'Donnell complained. Flanigan, who was a personal friend of Bush, passed the O'Donnell letter on to H. R. Haldeman with the cryptic notation: "Connally is an implacable enemy of the Republican Party in Texas, and, therefore, attractive as he may be to the President, we should avoid using him again." On November 30, when Connally's appointment to the Foreign Intelligence Advisory Board was announced, the senior senator from Texas, John Tower, and George Bush were instantly in touch with the White House to express their "extreme" distress over the appointment. Tower was sure that *he* was the next target of another Connally surrogate, Connally's own youthful alter ego, Ben Barnes, who was still riding high as the lieutenant governor of Texas. Moreover, only a few weeks before, John Ehrlichman had expressly promised Tower that Connally would not get a major appointment in the administration. Bush had a more immediate concern. He was out of work, and he wanted a job. As a defeated senatorial candidate, he hoped and fully expected to get a major job in the administration. Yet the administration seemed to be paying more attention to the very Democrat who had put him on the job market. What gives? Bush was justified in asking.

The allure of bringing Big John Connally into the cabinet had taken hold of Nixon, however. Here was the exciting figure, the tentative Democrat, and, if circumstances changed—who knew?— perhaps the dominant man of vision who could be his successor. Spiro Agnew had been chosen as vice president for cold political reasons, but he was scarcely the man of breadth and range to carry on the Nixon legacy. Tower would have to be assuaged, and Bush would get a good job, but getting Connally—well, that was something else again.

On December 4, Nixon decided to offer Connally the Treasury job, and he gave Haldeman the task of cementing the deal. In his careful, obsessive way, Haldeman spent two days in drafting his "talking points" for the call to Texas.

- ♦ P feels you're only man in Dem party that cld be P.
- ♦ We have to have someone in Cab who *is* capable of being P.
- ♦ Overall has sympatico feeling for you.
- ♦ Feels urgently you are deep needed in this position and *another* posit in future.
- ♦ Needs you as advisor & counselor to change Treas. system, but really wants you as *counselor-advisor-friend.*
- ♦ Wants you cause thinks you're best man in country as adviser in national and int affairs.
- ♦ P does *not* want to use you politically. Don't give up Dem reg.
- ♦ I hope & pray you won't turn him down. P has fought lonely fite. If you come in, you will be closest confidante [*sic*].

When Haldeman finished his rehearsals and made the call, he took notes on the reaction.

- ♦ C made clear he wanted more than just Treasury.
- ♦ Just secy of anything wldn't appeal.
- ♦ Problem of personal finances. Real prob of divesting. Will try like hell. Will have to make extensive adjustments.
- ♦ One concern, probly not a prob: flack within Rep party.
- ♦ Press wld waylay C at every corner.

The following day, Haldeman wrote that the deal was done, and two days later, that "I've never seen the President so pleased—from the personal standpoint." Nixon's self-congratulations over the Connally coup would go on for weeks. There was a touching, schoolboy quality to this courtship: the lonely, homely, rejected, and embattled boy who asks the glamorous leader of another school for help and even to be his close friend, and, to everyone's astonishment, the star agrees. From the beginning, the emotional side of the Connally-Nixon relationship was noticed. It has been referred to as "the president falling in love," and there is no doubt Connally himself sensed the special glow. Instinctively, Connally knew how to use Nixon's longing. His chief technique became flattery. The legend surrounding this relationship began in the first days, as Connally began his education to take over Treasury. Haldeman called to say that he would send over several briefers on economic matters from the White House. Connally replied tartly that he would call Haldeman to tell him when—and if—he needed to be briefed, and when *he* would go to see the *president* to get his briefing. Perhaps from his first dealings with Lyndon Johnson in 1939 Connally knew how to start a relationship off on the right foot. With Johnson, his problem had been to establish respect as an equal. With Nixon, it was to instill awe as a superior.

Before the Connally appointment could be announced, George Bush had to be serviced, and the White House scrambled to find a decent job for him. In fact, pleasing Bush was one of Connally's demands to the White House, for he knew that Texas Republicans would be furious if he upstaged George. On December 7, when Haldeman wrote the note "Connally set," the next note read: "Have to do something for Bush right away." Since no job immediately sprang to mind, Bush was assured that he would come to the White House as a top presidential adviser on something or other, until another fitting job opened up. Timing was a factor. Connally was pushing for his announcement to come sooner rather than later, preferably in the charitable Christmas season, because he was afraid that, with more time, the press would "cut him up." Unexpectedly, Daniel Patrick Moynihan reconsidered his acceptance of the UN ambassador post and, with a sigh of relief, the White House offered it to Bush. Bush's appointment was announced on December 11, Connally's on December 14. While George Bush was to maintain a smoldering, visceral dislike of Connally, one that lasted well into the 1980s, it was Connally to whom he, like Lloyd Bentsen, owed his elevation in 1970 to national stature.

Editorials in the press greeted the announcement of Connally's appointment with disappointment and dismay, reacting only to his suitability on the basis of his meager economic background, not to the hidden but more powerful currents for his tapping. Still, the White House listened carefully to the Washington gossip. Lyn Nofziger slipped over to the bar at the National Press Club and came back to write what the reporters were really saying.

There is no way to minimize to the press the political aspects of the Connally announcement. That is all [the reporters] want to talk about. Any statements that this was an effort by the President to "bring us together" or to present a united front in the battle against unemployment or inflation was met with derision.

The general feeling is that the appointment was an astute political move. However, some liberal reporters say that the benefits are only short term. They believe that in the long run, the damage they think was done to the Party structure will hurt us as much or more with the Republicans than the appointment will help us with conservative Democrats. . . .

There is general respect for Connally as a tough politician and as an able administrator. But his decision to take the Treasury position has many of them puzzled. One of their questions is: "Where does Johnson fit into the picture?"

My feeling is that there is little we can do on a crash basis to convince anyone that this was not primarily a political appointment. It is going to take constant iteration by word and action that Governor Connally is a part of the team and was picked for reasons other than political if we are to get this viewpoint across.

Connally himself undertook the education of John Connally. He pored over briefing books on the vast and complicated and diverse regions of the Treasury with an energy that was kinetic. He put in eighteen-hour days, which included grueling sessions with the staff where they would ask him tough and far-reaching questions about economic policy, as if they were congressmen or reporters, and he would answer and then listen to their critique of his answer. Chief among his teachers during this period was William McChesney Martin, who had been chairman of the Federal Reserve Board for nineteen years and whose reputation as a gentleman and as a "hard money" man was widespread in Washington. They would engage in two-hour tutorials. As Connally's crash course advanced, Martin implanted in the secretary-designate's mind the difficult notion—difficult politically—that the United States would inevitably have to devalue the dollar.

"The United States doesn't have the capacity to keep its balance of payments in order and doesn't have the capacity to keep inflation under control. So we're a double failure," Martin told Connally. "But if you do [devalue], for God's sake, don't brag about it."

By January 7 his mastery was such that in a four-hour off-the-record discussion with the top bankers in Wall Street he gave a forceful defense of Nixon administration economic and fiscal policy. Several weeks later he was introduced to the Federal Reserve family. Afterwards, the scholarly and avuncular Fed chairman, Arthur Burns, wrote to Nixon that Connally had given a "rousing" address on revenue sharing, governmental reorganization, and, in particular, "your great courage in presenting these programs to the American people. The more I see of Connally, the more I like him. I think that he will prove a great asset to you and that he and I will be able to work together very effectively."

On the day he met with the New York bankers, three weeks before his confirmation hearings before the Senate Finance Committee, Connally also had a conversation with John Ehrlichman in the White House about possible problems with his confirmation. This conversation might have been Connally's first unwitting contact with the underworld of the Nixon administration, for Ehrlichman was secretly recording the conversation. The FBI and the IRS, not to mention the congressional committees, were conducting their routine background checks, and the White House had its own expert, John Dean, on the case, but as a friend. With Connally's background of high-level business, legal, and governmental involvement, the challenge to find skeletons was daunting.

The authorities were sniffing around Connally's association with Nate Rogers, the magnate of Texas spectacles, who owned the largest optical company in Texas, called Texas State Optical, and who was very active politically. Rogers operated in the old tradition of lobbying around the statehouse: cash-only contributions, and he contributed heavily to the campaigns of state legislators, especially those in whose districts he had branches of his optical company. Thus he protected his interests by political indebtedness, even though he was altogether anathema to the independent optometrists of the state. Rogers had been appointed by Connally to the State Optometry Board. Ehrlichman now told Connally that he had heard Connally had taken a "substantial contribution" from Rogers in 1967. Since Rogers dealt only in cash, Connally could plausibly deny the contribution. So Ehrlichman moved to possible problems with the IRS.

"The Internal Revenue feels that you're going to have to undergo audits on your last ten taxpaying years," Ehrlichman said. "Dean suggests, and I think he's right, that the proper posture for you is to request those audits before you go up for confirmation."

"Right."

"So I mentioned this to the president. He agreed, but he wanted me to check with you and see if that's agreeable with you. If it is, they can give you very fast service—like a three-day audit."

"Hell, yes, it's agreeable," Connally said exuberantly. "They've checked me every damn year."

"I know they have," Ehrlichman replied. "But you're going to run weak in this problem of having heavy deductions related to your ranch expenses for more than five years running. You're going to run into that hobby provision."*

"Yep."

"So Dean wanted you to be alert to that, but if you'll make the request for audits, they will give you very rapid service. And you can make that direct to our man over there, Roger Barth, if you want to."

"Would I normally make it through him or through the district director?"

"I honestly don't know," Ehrlichman said. "The head of the whole auditing operation in the IRS headquarters in Washington is a fellow who has assured the rapid service."

"What's his name?" Connally asked.

"I can't tell you that, but our man is Barth."

"At the White House?"

"No, in IRS. He's the assistant to the commissioner. He's the only really loyal guy we know we've got over there. And he can give you some suggestions on that."

When the time finally came, the confirmation hearing before the Senate Finance Committee seemed at first like a stroll to the clubhouse. His adversary of the past, John Tower, escorted Connally to the hearing, where the chairman, Russell Long of Louisiana, was in a jolly mood. Scanning Connally's financial records, Long complimented Connally as a successful man—by Louisiana standards—and underscored the financial sacrifice Connally and his wife would incur in tax liability by liquidating assets. Connally agreed that it was not in his financial interest to take the job, for the sacrifice—by Floresville standards—was great. But after hours of conversation with the president he had been convinced that he could make

*The "hobby-loss" provision of federal tax law disallowed tax deductions for farm or ranch expenses unless the ranch turned a profit for two out of five years.

a contribution. "I suppose I was vain enough to believe it and silly enough to try it," he said amiably.

On the problems of postwar reconstruction, the balance of payments, trade practices, and new taxation, Connally was more than conversant. But it was the air of commonality that made the hearing fly along. Senator Long told of how Lyndon Johnson, "when you were his administrative assistant," used to stick pamphlets in his pocket and say, "Read this," and Long would read it when he had the time. Now he wanted to stick a pamphlet in Connally's pocket about the outrageous practices of America's trading partners, for Long was upset about the way they were cheating America. Connally responded with what was to become his standard technique in coming months, by saying he couldn't agree more, and jollied Long along by recalling the advice a wise man had given him as a boy: "You can tell a fellow to go to hell, but you can't make him go." Long would relate to that, for to him our trading partners were going to act the same way, no matter whether they had the approval of the United States or not, and that reminded him of the bartender who came back and asked the bar's owner if it was okay to let old Joe Smith have a beer on credit. "Has he had the beer yet?" asked the proprietor.

The answer was yes.

"Then give him credit."

There was, however, to be a blip in this chummy conviviality. A few days later, in a front-page story, the *New York Times* revealed that over an eleven-year period, including Connally's six-year tenure as governor of Texas, the Richardson Foundation of Fort Worth had paid Connally $450,000 ($750,000 turned out to be the real figure) as coexecutor of the Richardson estate after Sid Richardson's death in 1959. Connally had gone to extraordinary lengths to conceal the payments, the *Times* asserted, and the payments were per se illegal, for they violated the provision of the Texas constitution which barred its governors from accepting outside compensation while in office. In the belief that it was onto a juicy story of graft, the press leaped in. The *Washington Post* called for a delay in confirmation until the matter was thoroughly aired.

The Finance Committee met again on February 2, and Connally demanded to make a second public appearance before the committee in order to explain. He was at his best as the disappointed and outraged victim of yellow journalism. The arrangement for the executor's fees had been made long before he ever thought about running for governor, he explained, three years before, in fact. The deferred payments were simply a way of getting what was due to him over time rather than in one lump. As to his "concealment" of the arrangement, he had not "bragged" about the payments, to be sure, but everybody knew of his association with the Richardson estate.

One by one, the senators came to his defense. Chairman Long wondered how many members of Congress still received side income from precongressional legal work. If they were disqualified from their office for that, the halls of Congress might be empty. "If there is any question of ethics here, the problem lies with professional journalism," Senator Robert Griffin of Michigan said. "It seems as though any responsible journalist would have put in the first or second paragraph at least that his story referred to compensation paid for services performed prior to [his] service as governor. It would be very difficult to straighten this out in the minds of many people who were misled by the headline yesterday. . . . If this is all there is to it, the *New York Times* owes you an apology." Once again, John Connally had jumped nimbly through a loophole. By a vote of thirteen to none, the Finance Committee recommended confirmation, and on February 9 it became official with an overwhelming vote before the full Senate.

In the East Room of the White House two days later, a collection of administration officials, congressional dignitaries, and Connally partisans gathered for Connally's swearing-in. In the crowd was Senator Fred Harris of Oklahoma, who had opposed Connally's confirmation and who, as a populist, remembered his surprise at the inflexibility of Connally's ideological conservatism during the 1968 Democratic convention, when briefly they had seemed to be rivals for the vice presidential nomination. Harris came with his young aide, Fred Gipson, from Seminole, Oklahoma, who, too, was ill disposed toward Connally. With the customary circumstance, Nixon and Connally entered the room, as Harris and Gipson took in the spectacle from the back of the room and whispered to one another. Nixon was the shorter man, and he had those oddly forward-hunching shoulders and that face of lumps and mounds. To Harris, it was a face put together by a committee. Connally, by contrast, was perfectly elegant and graceful and full of easy humor. Nixon began the presentation with stumbles and mumbles and the totally forgettable "historical" first that this was the first Texan ever to be secretary of the Treasury.

"Now, if you were a stranger, and you came into this room,"

Harris whispered to Gipson, "which man would you say was the president?"

Connally took the podium. "Mr. President, will you permit me one big sigh," he said, and the audience burst into laughter.

"This is a lot easier forum than the Senate of the United States," Nixon interjected, explaining Connally's joke, in case anyone had missed it.

"I finally made it," Connally said to more titters. "Today, I go on the payroll."

In the back of the room, Gipson turned to Senator Harris.

"If I were president of the United States, I wouldn't appoint that guy to a job any higher than prosecuting attorney in Pocatello, Idaho," he whispered. "And then I'd be afraid he'd try to run the government from there."

★ 18 ★

A Most Unusual Finance Minister

SEVERAL WEEKS AFTER Connally was confirmed, Richard Nixon turned to the mirror and considered his image. Why was it that the country did not know and appreciate Nixon the man, as opposed to the president and his process and his policies? Why was his staff not collecting the little human anecdotes about him and feeding them quietly to the press? He was not, the president concluded, being effectively merchandised. This line of concern had been inspired by Connally, for the new secretary and Nellie had spent a combined birthday weekend at Camp David in late February, and there Connally had discoursed upon a few human touches in the president. It was as if the president's men were listening to something utterly new. Of course, the president heard about it. On March 1 the president wrote to his chief of staff, H. R. Haldeman.

"Over the past two years, I can think of at least one hundred incidents like the ones Connally noticed at the birthday party at Camp David," the president wrote. "The fact that none of them were noticed, or if they were noticed, no system was in place to see that a subtle way of getting them to public attention would be found. This indicates a fatal flaw in what we have been doing." He directed Haldeman to have his top advisers "search their memories as well as their files and records to see what they could come up with in the line of actions by RN which reflect the man rather than his process or policies. . . . Of course, I imagine that most of the personal files will be rather dry and pragmatic, emphasizing 'what was decided' rather than the warmth and color [of the President], which is far more important to the average person." That the president could disembody himself in this way—speaking of RN as if he were some creature with whom he had only a vague acquaintance—was obviously at the heart of his problem over authenticity.

Haldeman got right to work. To colorize the president would take the total concentration of the staff. He organized a dinner at Blair House to which fifteen of the president's top advisers were invited, including Henry Kissinger, the national security adviser, and George Shultz, the director of OMB, as well as John Ehrlichman, Charles Colson, Ronald Ziegler, William Safire, and other presidential counselors. The featured speaker was to be John Connally, since by the president's own directive, Connally, new as he was, seemed to notice the human side of President Nixon more keenly than anyone else. For the Nixon White House, even a dinner like this where the president's men were supposed to let their hair down and talk honestly about their boss behind closed doors could not be left to spontaneity. On the morning of the dinner the political tough guy, Charles Colson, wrote a "talking points" memo to Haldeman on how the dinner was meant to go:

1. Explain *purpose of the dinner*—to get a better understanding of our most serious public relations problem, i.e., Richard Nixon as a man.

2. The General Problem—all of us try to sell a program. Programs don't sell the President. The President must be sold as a man and a leader.

3. Illustrations of the Problem—President's desire for "color" press arising out of recent events.

4. Some examples of the President's characteristics, which we all know but the public doesn't: warm personal side, lack of conceit, courage, long view of things, toughness, dedication, intellect.

5. Finally, a *Comparison with Truman*—he was elected in 1948 not because of what he did, but because of his personal characteristics with which people identified.

In his introduction of Connally, Haldeman should state the problem, Colson recommended, and then "Governor Connally will give his evangelical pitch." Upbeat conversation was sure to follow.

By coincidence, on the morning of the big image meeting, the "style" section of the *Washington Post* reported a black-tie dinner to honor John Mitchell the weekend before, where the attorney general, in his toast, had said, "We've got to change the Nixon image. People do not see the president for what he really is or what he is really doing." John Connally felt the same way, Mitchell told the guests: "He called a lot of Republican senators together the other day and told them they are not selling the president to the country." John Ehrlichman had been stewing about the *Post* story all day. "It almost made this meeting impossible," he grumbled as he entered Blair House. "It did the president no favors." Then he settled into the conference to discuss the very problem Mitchell had defined.

When the men gathered behind closed doors the first order of business was how to keep the doors airtight. The bunker mentality had not yet flowered into full bloom in the Nixon administration, but there was an acute sense of being watched day and night by a hostile press. At the outset Connally allowed that if the substance of the meeting or the meeting itself got out, "it could be self-destructive."

"Somebody's going to know about this meeting," one staffer said gloomily. "I think this is a meeting to welcome Secretary Connally to the White House."

"Why do they have to know about it?" Connally said with annoyance.

"Somebody may see people walking out of here together."

"A George Shultz farewell dinner is a great idea," Safire said ominously.

"This is just a gathering of the White House staff to get to know Secretary Connally better," Haldeman said. That benign little cover-up in place, the men got down to business.

When Connally rose to give his impressions after four weeks with the administration, he talked for more than twenty minutes. He spoke in a way that only an outsider who was above Haldeman's iron-willed, emasculating rule could speak. If he was an outsider, he had also become the best insider they had, for he knew the opposition intimately; technically, he was still part of it. But the thrust of his observations was how to get Richard Nixon reelected the following year. From the outset, it was clear that he had burned his bridges to the Democrats long since. He was a thoroughgoing Nixon man now. More than that, Haldeman put him on the level of the vice president. In an "action memo" around this same time, Haldeman had written, "We need to constantly reexamine the role of the Vice President and his maximum usefulness, developing ideas as to what are the best uses of his assets; especially ways to utilize him as our Big Gun and Connally as our Number two big gun."

At Blair House, Connally was blunt and incisive. The problem of the administration was threefold as he saw it: Nixon was a "hell of a lot better president" than he was getting credit for; he was doing things for which "he's not only getting no credit, but no attention"; and the administration was forcing issues like revenue sharing and the environment that could not be forced and which did not catch the public's imagination. Revenue sharing—the proposal to fund social programs by matching federal and state resources—had about as much sex appeal, Connally said, as a cup of coffee. Moreover, with such a program, "you put yourself in the hands of men in public office, and that's always a fatal mistake." No one laughed. The public official, Connally instructed them, "is always going to look out for himself. If he thinks you're going to get him in a little trouble, he'll desert you damn quick to look after himself." The staff should step back from their daily work and consider their overall goals. The chief goal was reelection. Forget about the war, he told them. By 1972 the war should be "in excellent shape," but they should stop thinking that the end of the war would be the end of their problem. He would take bets that there would not be a billion dollars' difference in the wartime and the peacetime budgets.

This was all fine, but Nixon the man was the subject. When he came to that, he enthralled them. When they thought of Nixon, what image came to them? he asked, and then gave them ten seconds for an image, any image, to form. What about past presidents? "Truman had something going for him. It wasn't always good. He had a certain human trait that people understood and believed and related to—that gave him support. When he denounced the music critics after they panned his daughter's piano playing, the average person in the nation could understand that human reaction—a man getting mad, because they panned his daughter's music playing. . . . When he called Drew Pearson a son of a bitch for lying about him, people could understand that anger. When Truman defended Harry Vaughan,* who I always thought of as a good Chicago bartender, people understood basic loyalty. . . . Johnson had much the same

---

*Major General Harry Vaughan was President Truman's much-investigated military aide who, besides his assorted indiscretions and corruptions, was known for his unforgettable lines. Asked in 1946 if an important meeting on a coal crisis had concluded, Vaughan replied: "I assume it has. The president is in the swimming pool by himself. The world may be going to hell, but the president has got to keep clean."

thing, but he threw it away, because he tried to be something he wasn't. He tried to change his personality."

What image did Richard Nixon have? His answer was—none, none at all, zilch. Part of the reason was the press, he said, playing to their worst antagonism, because the press, especially the reporters and editors, was totally against them, and there was nothing they could do about that. More important, the White House was talking too much about program and never about the human side of Nixon: "If you gave the average person the choice, what would they like to hear—about revenue sharing, taxation, government reorganization, or what Tricia's boyfriend is like? What do you think they would pick?" Finally, a few nervous titters sprang from the stiff crowd.

Having asked them to form an image of Nixon in their minds, now, he challenged them differently. If they were asked to write on a blackboard the qualities they would want in a president, what would they write?

> I would write that I'd want a man who was intelligent, and he [Nixon] sure as hell is. I'd want a man who was studious, and he is. I'd want somebody who has guts, and he does—great courage. I'd like somebody who had a little bit of a mean streak in him—a little streak of ruthlessness, because no *kind* man ought to be president of the United States. A *kind* man can't make the tough decisions that have to be made in the interest of this country. This man *does* have that much meanness and ruthlessness in him, and, thank God he does. I'd want a man with compassion—who had concern for other people—not kindness in a collective sense, but kindness to individuals, and that's not inconsistent with being mean or ruthless. You [can] be mean and ruthless to the mass but not to individuals. These are all things I would list, and this man Nixon has every one of them! He is the most misunderstood man I know in public life. He gets less credit for doing more things than any man I know.

And so if the President's men would only talk in public about Nixon the man rather than Nixon's program, they would sell the president "solid as a cake of ice."

If Connally was talking about Nixon, he was talking more about himself. All the noble qualities of the perfect president which he had enumerated—intelligence, studiousness, guts, ruthlessness—he had himself. As he knew well, he had other qualities in addition that

Nixon sorely lacked: charisma and manliness, charm and elegance, good looks and supreme confidence. Yet, this performance before the White House staff—he would be asked to give it before the cabinet as well—showed why Nixon was so drawn to Connally. From the earliest days of their association, when Nixon was asked about himself, he would say, "Talk to Connally. He understands me." To talk to Connally about Nixon was to receive a romanticized view which helped Connally with Nixon as much as it helped Nixon with his listener. Nixon liked that. It infused him with Connally glamor and Connally certification. It invigorated him amid the other, lesser "exhausted volcanoes" around him. If he could not emulate a Kennedy style and elegance, he could, at least, aspire to a Texas toughness—and coarseness. As Henry Kissinger would later state it, "Connally's swaggering self-assurance was Nixon's Walter Mitty image of himself." Peter Petersen, the president's economic adviser and later his secretary of commerce, was to state the matter drolly. He had formulated an axiom called "Petersen's Principle of Interlocking Neuroses." Generally, he applied his principle to good marriages, but now he was ready to apply it to the Nixon-Connally relationship. It went: "The rocks in my head fit the holes in yours." On March 8 at Blair House, Nixon was using Connally to infuse the administration with Connally's romantic view. Almost instantly, Connally became Richard Nixon's greatest salesman.

★

In his first ten days in office, Connally testified seven times before Congress. Quickly he conveyed to the gray eminences around him like Herbert Stein and Paul McCracken at the Council of Economic Advisers, Pete Petersen, the economic adviser to Nixon, and Arthur Burns at the Fed that he was taking charge. He was not many days into his new job before his enthusiasm and his purposefulness began to carry these normally cautious and entrenched titans of economic wisdom along with him toward a bolder and more comprehensive approach to inflation, the worsening balance of payments deficit, and six-percent unemployment. This air of command was in itself noteworthy. When his appointment was first announced, the Republican governor of Massachusetts, Francis Sargent, had asked, "Can he add?" and Connally himself was later to confess that he knew virtually nothing about high finance when he accepted the job. In the quadriad meetings of the four major advisers on economic policy—the chairman of the Federal Reserve, the director of OMB, the chairman of the Council of Economic Advisers, and the Treasury secretary—people joked that now with Connally three members would be speaking Greek and one Latin.

There was an element of truth to this. Unlike the other three, Connally understood that economics was political economics. Notwithstanding the fact that the people were generally bored with economic matters and did not understand their underlying dynamics, economics determined the outcome of elections. If inflation, unemployment, the deficit, and foreign trade continued on their current trends, Richard Nixon would be in bad shape in 1972. It had happened before; indeed, it had happened in 1960, when the high unemployment had, at least in Nixon's mind, cost him the presidency the first time around. When Connally came into their midst, the top economists realized that here was a man who clearly had the ear of the president, who was obviously smart and dynamic, and who, regardless of whether he could appreciate their esoteric economic models, could formulate and sell economic solutions in a way they could not.

At the outset Connally reinforced his leadership by paying attention to the little things that matter in Washington. Not many days after his confirmation he summoned H. R. Haldeman to the Treasury and made the crew-cut chief of staff wait over thirty minutes in the anteroom before, humbled sufficiently, he was called into the presence of the secretary. News of this naked assertion of power spread fast through the department. If Connally gained the admiration of the top Treasury officials for the move, he gained their gratitude by asking them all to stay. This was an unusual move in Washington, especially for a political character like Connally, who might have been expected to surround himself with a Texas cadre. As he asked them to stay, so he demanded they sharpen up their appearance and project an air of confidence. It became apocryphal that, early on, he threatened to fire his undersecretary for monetary affairs, the imposing, six-foot-eight-inch Paul Volcker, if Volcker didn't replace his hangdog, baggy suits. To the civil servants at Treasury, there was a feeling that, at last, they had moved into the big leagues. Finally they had a secretary who knew how Washington worked, who would not be intimidated by the White House, who knew how to put a legislative campaign together, who knew what was important to congressmen and how to frame an issue for them. By the quickness of his mind, the shrewdness of his political sense, and the force of his personality, many at Treasury were sure that they were in the presence of a future president.

Other Connally touches were noticed. Before he joined the

administration, the quadriad meetings were held over breakfast at
the Cosmos Club near Dupont Circle in Washington, because that
was Paul McCracken's club, and since McCracken had been in
Washington during the Eisenhower administration, he was supposed
to know his way around. When Connally took over, these meetings
instantly shifted to the Treasury secretary's dining room. There was
another reason for these economists to take Connally seriously from
the start. He had hinted that he would like to abolish the Council
of Economic Advisers altogether. Lastly, he made one thing *perfectly
clear* in both a Nixonian and a Johnsonian sense: he would tolerate
all "human frailties" but one, disloyalty to John Connally.

Behind the dismal figures on inflation and unemployment after
the recession of 1970 was the overarching situation of America
withdrawing from the longest, costliest war in its history. For seven
years the economy had been on a superheated war footing, creating
high employment and enormous energy in the defense industry. In
early 1971 disengagement was under way. The economy was the
first to feel the effects. At his confirmation hearing Connally had
been asked if full employment and zero inflation were possible
without a shooting war, when 500,000 young men were coming back
into the work force and the defense industry would necessarily be
cutting back. Predictably, he fell back on a definition of terms. The
current six-percent unemployment was clearly not acceptable, but
four percent might be. Four percent inflation would be worrisome;
a two-percent rate was tolerable.

One of the first issues to come to the desk of the new secretary
was a baldly political move by congressional Democrats to grant
President Nixon the authority to impose wage and price controls in
an economic emergency. So abhorrent was this tampering with the
free enterprise system to principled Republicans that the Democrats
were sure Nixon would never use the authority; if the economic
indicators worsened, the Democrats would then flagellate the president with questions of why he was not invoking Democrat-given
authority. The Treasury staff came to Connally with a draft statement denouncing the Democratic measure as a cynical political
move. On one of his first Saturdays at Treasury, dressed casually
but nattily as always, Connally read the draft quickly and then
leaned back in his wing chair.

"Why are we doing this?" he asked quizzically. "You know, I
learned one thing as governor. If the legislature wants to give you
a new power—you take it. Put it in the corner like an old shotgun.
You never know when you might need it. Besides, we might want

to use this." The staff went away, confused and a bit crestfallen. Six months later the administration reached for the shotgun.

Within a week of his confirmation, Connally was put in charge of the most pressing problem of postwar reorganization. The defense giant the Lockheed Corporation was collapsing and had come to the government for help to avoid bankruptcy. With sales of over $2.5 billion and a work force of 72,000, Lockheed was the nation's largest defense contractor. But it was staggered by the huge cutbacks in defense and aerospace contracts and cursed with overruns on current contracts like the gigantic C-5A military transport plane. The largest setback, however, came in its civilian rather than its military division. The project was the widebody L-1011 airbus, known as the TriStar, which was meant to compete with the DC-10 and the European A-300 airbus for intermediate-range, large-capacity flights. The engines for the L-1011 were made by Rolls-Royce, Ltd., of Great Britain. In December 1970, to the astonishment of many, including Lockheed, that venerable old bastion of upper-class snobbery went belly up. When one looked behind its symbol of the flying lady, Rolls-Royce was a luxury Britain could no longer afford. Like Lockheed, it was a company which, as John Kenneth Galbraith would inelegantly tell Congress, had "gone soft sucking on the public teat." The question was: Would the administration allow Lockheed to collapse as well?

For Connally, the situation posed interesting philosophical and personal questions. He came into office vowing to be an "activist" secretary of the treasury. His impulse was to be a fixer, not a bystander, even if to be a bystander in the face of poor economic performance was the correct course for a conservative. Lockheed had caused its own problems. It was a badly managed company which had not planned for the inevitable downturn after the war and after Americans landed on the moon. It was continuously plagued with cost overruns and had been forced by the government to absorb a $480 million loss because of miscalculation. Moreover, in the L-1011, it was arguably making a bad, uncompetitive plane.

The precedent of a bailout bothered Congress. If Lockheed were helped, where would the demands stop with other badly managed, incompetent companies? The year before, Congress had rejected a similar plea from the ailing Penn Central Railroad. Under bankruptcy, Penn Central's reorganization had jettisoned its tired management, streamlined its operations, and improved its service. Lastly, Lockheed's civilian and military divisions were entirely separate. Ninety percent of its business was defense and aerospace, and most of its facilities were actually owned by the government. Indeed, the very buildings where the L-1011s were manufactured were government-owned. Even if the corporation were to go under, the national defense was not threatened, because its weapons division was fully shielded and protected. To the true believers in free enterprise, of which Connally noisily proclaimed himself to be one, Lockheed should be left to save itself or sink in the swamp of its own mismanagement. In America, that was what bankruptcy laws were for.

Ever the conservative fixer, Connally argued for a bailout. For an administration that wanted full employment, the loss of 30,000 Lockheed jobs at one bite was intolerable. The effect of a Lockheed bankruptcy might ripple geometrically through the economy. "Would not a bailout set a precedent?" Connally was asked on May 6. He denied it. The government had done this kind of thing before, he argued, particularly with the Reconstruction Finance Corporation in the 1930s, with a so-called V-loan to Douglas Aircraft when it merged with McDonnell in 1967, and with the loan guarantees to savings institutions across America. That he would invoke these parallels was revealing. They were Rooseveltian and Johnsonian solutions, radical depression or wartime remedies for flagging industry. But now America was suing for peace in Vietnam and the economy was reasonably sturdy. Moreover, the cited loans were never made in the astronomical figures that a Lockheed bailout would require, nor just to one company, nor for the purpose only of making that company competitive with other American businesses.

On June 7, Connally went before the Senate Banking Committee to propose a $250 million loan guarantee to Lockheed. By the time of his testimony, the survival of Lockheed depended on the guarantee. After the collapse of Rolls-Royce, the consortium of banks which were funding the production of the TriStar had announced that they would no loan any more money unless the U.S. government guaranteed the loans. The British government, in turn, promised to support Rolls-Royce, but only if Lockheed guaranteed to buy its engines from Britain and not switch to an American manufacturer, like General Electric or Pratt & Whitney. Some protectionist congressmen were pressing hard for a switch to an American engine as a condition of congressional approval. The American government was being effectively boxed in.

Into this complicated situation, Connally stepped bombastically. By guaranteeing the loan, the government would recoup its existing investment, save itself a huge tax loss, and protect tens of thousands of Lockheed stockholders; it would keep the company alive for several years, protect 30,000 jobs and a billion dollars in payroll, permit Lockheed to generate cash flow, and produce more than 200 needed aircraft for the airline industry. "This does not mean necessarily that Lockheed is ultimately going to survive," he testified. "I am not here to say that this loan is absolutely going to insure the continued existence of the Lockheed Corporation."

"What bothers me about this is that Lockheed's bailout . . . is not a subsidy," Senator William Proxmire of Wisconsin challenged him. "It is the beginning of a welfare program for large corporations. In welfare you make a payment, and there is no return. In this case the government gives the guarantee and there is no requirement on the part of Lockheed to perform!"

"What do we care whether they perform?" Connally shot back.

Proxmire was to be the most spirited adversary for Connally on the committee. An ascetic independent, known for his sharp tongue and his budget knife, the senator had denounced Connally's nomination as secretary of the navy eleven years before, had questioned Connally's qualifications to be secretary of the treasury, and confessed now that Connally was scarcely his favorite candidate for "Democrat of the Year." To Proxmire, the notion of bailouts, especially in peacetime, was abhorrent as a matter of principle. The purpose of the bankruptcy laws was to get rid of incompetent management, and they were good laws. If, in traumatic bankruptcy, stockholders took a bath, they deserved it, as far as Proxmire was concerned. That was the nature of owning stock: you were rewarded when things went well and punished if they didn't. Bailing a corporation out kept the free enterprise system from operating as it should. "You have to do it on a selective basis, and the selection is necessarily going to be based on political influence," he was to say. "It will, therefore, be corrupt."

"If the Congress approves the Lockheed loan guarantee, why wouldn't firms run to the administration and to Congress whenever they got into financial trouble?" Proxmire asked Connally. "Why wouldn't this be a precedent for all of them to do it?"

"I say this not too facetiously," Connally snapped back. "I think it *will* set a precedent—for all the companies that employ in excess of 75,000 people, that have 35,000 subcontractors 71 percent of which have less than 500 employees, that are the largest defense contractors in America."

"So it is only for the big boys," Proxmire said, underscoring the obvious. "You see, what concerns me especially is that you are removing something that is far more important in the long run than anything you can do for Lockheed. That is the very direct, painful price that business has to pay if it does fail. Once that [pain] is out of the picture, an important part of the discipline of the American economic system disappears. If they get in trouble, and if they are big enough, they know they're going to be bailed out by a government loan guarantee. You lose the vitality and strength and discipline of our system, don't you?"

"I don't think so, Senator," Connally replied. "As a matter of fact, we have a pretty regulated society. We sometimes kid ourselves that it is a free enterprise system, but it is not all that free. Much of it lives under regulation. Much of it lives under subsidy. The government takes many actions to encourage various businesses of all kinds for various social purposes. So I don't think it is all that much of a departure from what we have known in the past." Spoken like a true Democrat.

The colloquy between Connally and Proxmire continued hotly into the next day. Occasionally it inspired a rare flash of anger from Connally, as when Proxmire suggested that Lockheed had a "sweetheart deal" with the government and that the government had a political stake in keeping Lockheed afloat. Did not Lockheed do ninety percent of its business with the government? Now, the company was in trouble in the ten-percent-civilian side of its house, and the government was about to save it there as well. Still, in his grilling, Proxmire developed a begrudging admiration for the forcefulness and straightforwardness of the witness: "After listening to you, I am convinced if Lockheed had had the good judgment to have you represent their case to the banks as you have represented it to this committee, they would have had no trouble getting a loan *without a guarantee*. . . . If the TriStar program is as sound as you think it is, wouldn't the banks have a natural incentive to loan Lockheed the additional $250 million to protect their investment?"

"If they were convinced that it would be a success beyond any doubt, they might well make the loan," Connally replied. "I don't know how a banker thinks. I have always been a borrower, not a banker." Neither Proxmire nor Connally could foretell how famous Connally was later to become as a borrower.

"I suggest when you come back," Proxmire said tartly, "you come back not as a cleanup man with a bat, but a cleanup man with a broom."

While Connally's performance was impressive, the Banking

Committee was far from convinced. The following day Undersecretary of Defense David Packard came before the committee. Packard had entered government from the pinnacle of the Hewlett-Packard Corporation, and he had been trying to straighten out the Lockheed mess for a year. From his first words, it was clear that he resented Connally's interference in the Lockheed case, and he set out to undercut Connally's testimony. Packard made his obligatory nod to administration desires in the case, but with an enthusiasm that John Kenneth Galbraith was shortly to describe as akin to what one might show toward tertiary syphilis or terminal leprosy.* Packard said flatly that, as a former high-level corporate manager, he was not for government bailouts, and in this case he was not even sure it would help. A bailout of Lockheed would have no impact whatever on national defense, he testified, for he had arranged matters in the past year, particularly the C-5A contract, so that in the event of a Lockheed bankruptcy, defense contracts would not be touched. Moreover, he shuddered at the thought that the Lockheed bailout would set a precedent, for that would be "dangerous," and he besought Congress to make a large mental note that this would not be done again. To that, Senator Proxmire observed that the distinguished undersecretary was sophisticated about business and defense but naive about the "politics of precedents." Toward the end of his testimony, Packard was asked how this colossal mess had come about, and he replied with an anecdote from his early days in business. A banker had once told him, "You know, there are more companies that fail from indigestion than fail from starvation."

Dr. Arthur Burns, the chairman of the Federal Reserve, followed Packard, and he, too, undercut Connally and the administration. Guarantees were a last resort, Burns testified, to be given only when there was a reasonable assurance of repayment and when there was no other way to prevent serious damage to the economy. When Proxmire pointed out that Connally had assured the committee a few days before that the damage of a Lockheed bankruptcy to the overall economy would be slight, Burns's reply was succinct: "If the effect on the economy would not be serious, the loan should not be guaranteed."

Surely the most entertaining, if not the most incisive, witness

---

*"I am not absolutely certain, speaking medically, that there is such a disease as terminal leprosy," said the poet-economist to the committee. "But it was needed for the meter."

to appear before the committee was John Kenneth Galbraith, the wit of Cambridge. From any principled position, Galbraith asserted, the bailout was wrong. A principled conservative should be against it for its tampering with the essence of the free enterprise system.* A principled liberal should be against it: fairness dictated that if a corporate giant was to be bailed out for mismanagement and miscalculation, the small Wisconsin farmer or the Fort Worth retailer should have similar rights.† Even a principled socialist should oppose it: Lockheed's cost overruns were socialized, but not its profits, so this was "socialism not for society, but for a private corporation and its creditors. It is not old-fashioned socialism for the poor, but new-fashioned socialism for the rich," Galbraith said. Since Connally was coming from none of these three principled positions—which defined his value to Richard Nixon—Galbraith had a word for him.

"I have said on other occasions, a point I don't make with great solemnity, that the Lockheed loan has only one real justification. That is to rescue not Lockheed, but [to rescue] my old friend, the secretary of the treasury," Galbraith said dryly. "I have sympathy for him. As the new boy in town—and a Democrat in a Republican Administration—he has need to prove himself with the president. But surely he could be helped out in some slightly less expensive way." While he was too gracious to associate his "old friend" with it directly, Galbraith also laid out the definition of another kind of American conservative: the one who avows the most passionate commitment to free enterprise, to risk, and to the market, and then "rushes with obscene haste to the government whenever a dollar is to be lost or made."

In midsummer, the Lockheed bailout squeaked through Congress, passing the House by only three votes and the Senate by

*Alan Greenspan, the conservative future chairman of the Federal Reserve, testified against it, and Senator Barry Goldwater voted against it. Indeed, Goldwater's negative vote underscored the deep principle of conservatism that the senator felt was involved. He was personally close to Daniel J. Haughton, the chairman of Lockheed, and, as an amateur pilot, he had flown nearly every experimental Lockheed plane that had been produced by Lockheed's famous secret "skunk works" in Los Angeles. The L-1011 plant was physically located in his own son's congressional district. Despite all this, Goldwater voted no to the bailout and even refused to make a "live pair" vote with the incapacitated Senator Karl Mundt of South Dakota, who was for the measure but could not make it to the Senate floor. Goldwater would not contribute in any way to the possible victory of his Republican administration.

†Leonard Woodcock, then president of the United Auto Workers, testified against it.

a single vote. Connally and Richard Nixon were active in the last-minute lobbying, and the measure passed only after the Treasury lobbyist, Jim Smith, had miscounted the testy Senator Margaret Chase of Maine and liberal Democrat Lee Metcalf of Montana in the opposition.

★

The Lockheed matter was a tangible, immediate, circumscribed situation which in the spring and early summer of 1971 the new treasury secretary could tackle and win for the administration. While it presented subtle questions of political and economic philosophy to professional economists, it was a practical political matter to Connally. "I can play it round or I can play it flat," he often said. "Just tell me how to play it." If the administration wanted a Lockheed bailout, fine; he would set out to secure it.

There were, however, far wider and more complicated economic problems that faced the country in 1971, and these required a deeper understanding of economic forces. Indeed, they required a sense of economic history. The "almighty dollar" was falling from grace. It had been steadily declining for a number of years in relation to other major world currencies like the yen and the mark. If, since World War II, the United States had grown stronger economically, other industrial countries had grown stronger faster—and, in great measure, because of American largesse. Germany and Japan, in particular, had drawn equal to the United States in economic health, and they, of course, had started virtually from scratch in 1945.

And yet, the international monetary system in 1971 was still rooted in a structure devised in 1944 at Bretton Woods, New Hampshire, to deal with the post–World War II recovery, and which brought the International Monetary Fund (IMF) into existence. Gold and the dollar were at the center of the Bretton Woods system, in which member countries of the IMF could exchange their weaker currencies for the hard currencies of the West and in which dollars could be converted into gold, valued at thirty-five dollars an ounce, through the "gold window." As industrial countries other than the United States came into their own in the 1960s, the U.S. balance of payments worsened, and the trade deficit widened. Because the U.S. had made itself the center of a fixed exchange rate system—in the interest of international monetary stability—other currencies were "pegged" to the dollar. Their pegs could move up or down according to the purchasing power of their money, but the dollar was to remain static. American presidents traditionally were loath to tamper with the system, fearing international panic—even though it was clearly outmoded and no longer met the reality of the modern world. John Kennedy, for example, was continuously badgered by his magnate father, Joe, about the deficit. "What really matters is the strength of the currency," President Kennedy said once. "It is not the *force de frappe* which makes France a factor. Britain has nuclear weapons, but the pound is weak. So everybody pushes it around. Why are people so nice to Spain today? Not because Spain has nuclear weapons, but because of all those lovely gold reserves."

The problem in 1971 was that all those lovely gold reserves in America were becoming perilously low. Because the dollar was weakening relative to other currencies, because the dollar was increasingly overvalued as other hard currencies were undervalued, the U.S. found itself in a position where it was essentially pricing itself out of the world markets. Since World War II, the U.S. had maintained the noble, charitable, passive posture as the mudsill of global finance. It could no longer afford to do so. Foreign goods were outcompeting American goods. As Connally assumed the Treasury job, he viewed this as an ultranationalist: Western Europe and Japan were flooding American markets with underpriced goods, while at the same time they were raising barriers against American penetration into their own markets. It grated upon him that with its currency as the key world numeraire, the U.S. was constrained from making the monetary adjustments of every other industrial nation. Dollars were flooding out of the country. Dollar holdings in foreign central banks escalated. In 1966, foreign banks held $15 billion. By the end of 1970, as Connally took over on the heels of the 1970 recession, the figure had risen to nearly $24 billion. Only seven months later, on July 30, 1971, foreign holdings leaped another $12 billion to $36.2 billion. At the Victorian rate of $35 an ounce, American gold stocks amounted to only $12 billion, one-third of what could be claimed if there were a run on American gold. If European countries came for their ingots, there was going to be a sorry spectacle at Fort Knox.

With this elementary arithmetic running against the United States, the political pressures to look inward had been increasing for some time. If America could not be the world's policeman in Vietnam, neither could it be the world's *pro bono* banker. Connally was a good representative of this nationalist sentiment. He could amuse the pipe-smoking economists with his coarse barnyard talk about what he intended to do to the masculine parts of the Belgian

1. Student body president, University of Texas, 1938.

2. Idanell Brill, Sweetheart of Texas, 1938.

3. Pappy O'Daniel and his Light Crust Dough Boys, July 1938.

4. John ("Cactus Jack") Nance Garner arrives for the Neutrality Congress, September 20, 1939.

5. Congressman Richard M. Kleberg.

6. Congressman Martin Dies.

7. Congressman Lyndon Johnson, thinking victory was in hand in 1941.

8. Sam Rayburn with the leaders of the "Little Congress," February 1941.

9. The USS *Essex*.

10. Calculatin' Coke Stevenson.

11. The *Johnson City Windmill*.

12. The campaign of 1948: sometimes thirteen speeches a day.

13. Lyndon's boy, John: at the 1956 Democratic Convention.

14. Uncle Sid with his attorney (*left*) and the Senate majority leader.

15. Two pals contemplate a legacy: at the dedication of the Sam Rayburn Library, Bonham, Texas, October 1957.

16. The secretary of the Navy-designate examines a model of a Polaris submarine with the outgoing Navy secretary, William B. Franke.

17. Dame Frankie Randolph objects!

18. John, Golfrey, Merrill, and Wayne Connally await the early returns in the 1962 governor's race.

19. With his mother, Lela Wright Connally.

20. Opponent Don Yarborough, the "music man" of the liberals in 1962 and 1964.

21. Official candidate's portrait, May 1962.

22. The persona of Texas: Fort Worth, 1963.

23. Houston airport, evening, November 21.

24. Ralph Yarborough, Connally, and LBJ behind the president, Fort Worth, morning, November 22.

25. Dallas.

26. The limousine and the grassy knoll.

27. "I feel fine . . . a bit weak . . . but fine": leaving an Austin hospital, December 15, 1963.

28. Yellow roses for the president's grave, February 28, 1964.

29. Hubert Humphrey between the Texans, LBJ Ranch, November 1964.

30. Showdown at New Braunfels: with House Speaker Ben Barnes and Rev. Antonio Gonzales, representing the Rio Grande Valley farm workers, September 1, 1966.

31. "Stunned and shocked" at LBJ's decision not to run again, March 31, 1968.

32. Triumph over the "rump" delegation, Democratic National Convention, Chicago, 1968.

33. Turning: Nixon announces a big catch after the surprise resignation of Secretary of the Treasury David Kennedy.

34. The president and his favorite cabinet member in the Rose Garden.

35. Special envoy, with Prime Minister Indira Gandhi of India, July 5, 1972.

36. A skeptical George Bush, chairman of the Republican National Committee, listens to the new convert, May 1973.

37. Prosecutors John A. Sale (*front*) and James L. Quarles III.

38. At U.S. District Court, Washington, April 1, 1975, led by defense attorney, Edward Bennett Williams.

39. Judge Hart listens as Edward Bennett Williams lays $10,000 in cash before the accuser, Jake Jacobsen.

Character witnesses:

40. Barbara Jordan. **41.** Rev. Billy Graham. **42.** Robert Strauss.

43. A standing ovation in the Texas Legislature for the acquitted, May 23, 1975.

44. Rebuilding the GOP after the Ford defeat, December 1976: with Nelson Rockefeller, Ford, and Ronald Reagan.

45. Last campaign: February 1979.

46. As Texans saw them.

47. The auction,
Houston, January 1988

48. Bereft and
bankrupt.

ambassador if His Excellency came in to demand gold for his Eurodollars, but his frat-house talk might not be enough.

By instinct and by nature, Connally was for a bold plan, but he did not have the faintest idea of what that bold plan might be when he took over at Treasury. The plan was left to a group within Treasury known as the Volcker Group. It met regularly under the aegis of Paul Volcker to discuss the worsening inflation and the worsening international financial situation. For the first two years of the Nixon presidency, the administration had adopted a position of "benign neglect" toward monetary reform. In the spring of 1971, Volcker kept his own counsel about his views. Within the Volcker Group, he presided like a giant, inscrutable guru: The master asked questions but gave no answers. He was caught between the need for action and the traditional caution of the Treasury establishment. Moreover, his grounding taught him to revere the venerable Bretton Woods regime. However, Connally's arrival galvanized both Volcker and the group into action. Within the Volcker Group itself, Volcker remained uncommitted, because to reveal his thoughts there was the same as revealing them to the world. But not many weeks after Connally took over, Volcker drafted a memo in which he "anticipated" a devaluation of the dollar. How it was to be done—and when—he did not know or predict, but it was surely coming. Apprehensive about putting his potentially explosive thoughts on paper, he showed his draft memo to Connally, and the secretary in turn showed it to a few more people, including Richard Nixon.

Through the spring, the situation worsened, and there was a self-perpetuating quality to the downturn. The mere publication of the payments deficit in the second quarter stimulated a further flight of short-term capital. By May the outflow of hundreds of millions of dollars to Europe in response to the higher interest rates there was rapidly moving the U.S. toward a crisis. Speculation in the international money markets that a dollar devaluation was coming began to be a factor.

As time passed, Connally grew in confidence, and not a moment too soon. In early May, Germany and the Netherlands let their currencies float. Austria and Switzerland revalued. This threatened American gold reserves further—in the economists' term, America was "bleeding gold"—and Volcker began to lean toward suspending the convertibility of surplus Eurodollars into gold. If the gold window were closed, the result would be unclear. To Volcker, it would have to accompany action to reassure the Allies—certainly some kind of incomes policy and perhaps mandatory wage and price controls.

In late May, Connally traveled to Munich to make a speech before a convention of international bankers. It was his first major foray into the international banking scene, and his arrival was much anticipated. Within that cosmopolitan circle of elegant, somber, and faultlessly cautious men, men who were used to considering the world economic order amid velvet curtains and priceless art and upon gilded tables, Connally came as an amusing curiosity. They expected a backslapping, tub-thumping rube from the hinterland of America. At first they were disabused. For Connally came early, spent more time with the central bankers than previous American finance ministers had done, and sat silently and decorously through the initial deliberations. On the day of his speech he suffered from a cold, and to Volcker, who watched the speech, Connally's feverishness heightened the abrasiveness of his delivery. Volcker, of course, knew what to expect, for he had drafted the key passages. One section, however, was Connally's alone. It included lines about how the U.S. would never devalue nor would it ever raise the price of gold.

"But we may have to!" Volcker protested before they left for Europe.

"I don't care," Connally replied. "It's a good thing to say."

The overall theme of the speech was mutual cooperation and accommodation. Within that context, however, he insisted that Europe accept a greater share of defending the free world, that it liberalize its trade policies and ease its exchange restrictions. He assured the bankers that the administration was committed to the integrity of the dollar as the world's key currency. And then he put out his categorical denials:

"We are not going to devalue."

"We are not going to change the price of gold."

Both in tone and in substance the speech went over poorly. It fed Connally's cowboy image abroad.

A month later, Connally would add to his list of negatives. On June 28 Nixon called his chief economic advisers to Camp David to discuss the sluggish economy. Despite the bland reassurances that Connally had been putting out—that he was not unduly concerned about the outflow of short-term capital, that he contemplated no change in American gold and foreign exchange policies, that the U.S. was winning the struggle against rising prices and controlling inflation, and on and on—there was internally an air of crisis. Something had to be done. When Connally came off the mountain he went before the White House press on June 29, first, to be officially designated by the administration as the chief economic spokesman, and, second, to declare what President Nixon was *not* going to do:

"He is not going to institute a Wage-Price Board."

"He is not going to impose mandatory wage and price controls."

"He is not going to ask the Congress for a tax reduction."

"He is not going to engage in further spending."

These became known within the administration as the "Four Nos." Put together with the Munich speech, they amounted to "Six Nos." They were all false.

In fact, an elaborate charade was under way. In the spring, Nixon and Connally alone had agreed that they had to deal dramatically and comprehensively with the ill health of the economy. It was simply good politics. Economics was political economics. The criticism of the administration over the economy was becoming increasingly shrill. Movement in Congress was active toward legislation to force the president's hand. Nixon needed to take the initiative, with an eye toward his reelection campaign in 1972. When Connally returned from Camp David to enunciate his two plus four nos, it represented a temporary defeat for him. Nixon had simply decided to do nothing—yet.

On July 15, however, congressional leaders came to the White House to be briefed on Nixon's triumphant trip to China, and instead they hounded the president about the economy. They would not settle for further exhortations to patience. After they left, Connally turned to the president and said, "If we don't propose a responsible new program, Congress will have an irresponsible one on your desk within a month."

Finally, it was time to act. Nixon ordered Connally to propose a plan. It arrived on the president's desk on August 6, and even Nixon was surprised at its sweeping nature. In the shorthand of government, it was a "total war on all economic fronts," not only closing the gold window and altering, perhaps forever, the international monetary system, but also imposing the very mandatory wage and price controls that had long been anathema. "I'm not sure this program will work," Connally told the president. "But I'm sure that anything less will *not* work." As to timing, the secretary urged the president to "sit and simmer" a bit longer, even if things got a little worse. They should wait for an event that would make this grand initiative seem all the better, all the more justified.

Nixon did not have to sit and simmer long. Following its demand for $282 million in gold on May 11 to repay a debt to the IMF, France returned on August 9 with the demand for $191 million in gold for its surplus dollars. Two days later, Great Britain, contemplating its future entry into the Common Market, demanded $3 billion—all its dollar reserves. If Britain's demand were honored, the gold stock at Fort Knox would drop below its statutory bottom of $10 billion, and a run on American gold was sure to follow. Connally had gone off to Picosa for his summer vacation. It lasted one day.

With an air of total secrecy and with an awareness of their actions' historical significance, the principals flew off to Camp David. At 3:00 P.M. on Friday, August 13, the quadriad meeting was expanded beyond its normal members of Connally, Shultz, McCracken, and Burns to include speechwriter William Safire, Herbert Stein of the Council of Economic Advisers, Paul Volcker, and Pete Petersen of the Council of International Economic Policy. (Conspicuous by their absence were Secretary of State William Rogers and Henry Kissinger, who was in Paris engaged in secret negotiations on Vietnam.) Volcker underscored the reason for the intense secrecy, knowing what might be coming: secrecy was necessary lest there be an international panic. If there was a leak, millions of dollars might be made by speculators. Haldeman leaned over and whispered, "Exactly how?" and that seemed to break the ice.

When the meeting opened the president turned to Connally, and he put forward the plan. To the participants in the second tier, like Herbert Stein, there was a clear feeling that the decision had already been made. The president and Connally were not inviting argument. Rather, they were seeking help to work out the mechanics. Connally laid out the principal aspects: a ninety-day freeze on wages and prices, an end to convertibility, an investment tax credit, and a ten-percent surcharge on foreign imports. From the beginning, the politicians, Connally and Nixon, constituted a majority of two. In the plan, there was philosophical pain for all the professional economists, but they were divided. Their pain lay in different parts of the economic orthodoxy. For months, Arthur Burns had been publicly advocating a form of incomes policy called a wage and price review board, but he was against closing the gold window. His incomes board was the "soft" option at Camp David, but Connally, even though he had repeatedly been saying in public that Burns's proposal was too radical, wanted the harder option of the freeze. Shultz and Stein, cautious products of the Chicago School of Economics as they were, were keen about closing the gold window, but found any form of wage and price control philosophically abhorrent. As the sole detractor of the gold window closing, Burns found himself isolated. He was offended by Connally's aggressive approach, which he likened to the confrontational posture of the 1930s. Volcker, meanwhile, wanted the gold decision and felt it had to be coupled with an aggressive antiinflationary program to reassure the Allies, but he opposed the ten-percent surcharge as too aggressive and too protectionist. It was not needed to achieve the realignment, he felt.

"What's our immediate problem?" Connally asked this divided assemblage. "We're meeting here because we're in trouble overseas. The British came in today to ask us to cover $3 billion—all their dollar reserves. Anybody can topple us—any time they want. We have left ourselves completely exposed. There is no political risk [to what is proposed]."

"Yes, this is widely expected," Burns countered. "But all the other countries know we've never acted against them [unilaterally]. The good will . . ."

"We'll go broke getting their good will," Connally cut across Burns.

"I hate to do this, to close the gold window," Volcker put in. "All my life I've defended exchange rates, but I think it's needed."

"So the other countries don't like it," Connally said. "So what?"

"But don't let's close the window and sit," Volcker said. "Let's get other governments to negotiate new rates."

Connally would not hear of it. He did not want to discuss their actions after the shock. "Why do we have to be reasonable?" he asked. Then he thought of Canada's recent unilateral decision to float. "Canada wasn't."

"They can retaliate," Burns insisted.

"Let 'em," Connally said. "What can they do?"

"They're powerful. They're proud, just as we are," Burns said. But he was losing. His influence with Nixon had been declining for months in direct proportion to the soaring of Connally's influence. Volcker brought up the negative feeling about the gold standard in the business community.

"There is a certain public sentiment about the 'Cross of Gold,' " he said, invoking William Jennings Bryan.

"Bryan ran four times and lost," Nixon said dryly.

"We don't have a chance unless we do it," Connally said. "Our assets are going out in the bushel basket. You're in the hands of the 'moneychangers.' "

Referring to the moneychangers was good stump rhetoric, but

Burns was unimpressed. "May I speak up for the moneychangers?" he asked. "The central bankers are important to you. . . ." But he had lost, and the assemblage split up into smaller groups to work out the details.

As they came off the mountain, the summiteers could not be sure what was going to happen. They were preoccupied with the launching of the attack rather than its aftershock. Connally had specifically avoided a discussion of the consequences, perhaps because he did not want to limit his negotiating position. This was no time for the olive branch. Nixon made his speech to the nation on Sunday night, so as to announce his action before the money markets opened and to preempt the chance that the moneychangers might make an instant fortune in speculation. As he did so, Paul Volcker was on his way to London, then on to Paris and Bonn, on a mission to assuage the European central bankers and to try to moderate a wild oscillation as the dollar floated. Although they returned to Washington in high spirits, the economists had no grasp of how the freeze on wages and prices would work, how it was to be enforced, what its effect would be in its ninety-day life or thereafter, or whether a nasty black market would come into existence. The action was to institute no bureaucracy for enforcement, and so it was left to the high-mindedness of the businessman.

Herbert Stein of the Council of Economic Advisers was among the most troubled. While he had concurred in the gold decision, he was passionately but quietly against wage and price controls for deep reasons of principle. Since it had been clear that the decision had already been made when he arrived at Camp David, there had been no point in fighting about it, as Burns had. Still, as Stein worked on the details of this objectionable action, a quotation from *Macbeth* occurred to him: "I am in blood / Stept in so far that, should I wade no more, / Returning were as tedious as go o'er." After Nixon made his speech, Stein's son called his father. "Ideologically, you should fall on your sword," he said, "but existentially it's great!"

The morning after, Connally was offered to the press as the administration's existentialist, and later Nixon would describe the performance as "brilliant." If that was true, its brilliance lay in turning a dismal defeat into a triumph. The Camp David actions were, at last, the official acknowledgment of the dollar's weakness. They marked a historic end to America's preeminence in the world economy. They were leading inevitably to a major devaluation, an eventuality which Volcker would say was a time for sackcloth and ashes. The normal "spin" at a time like this was for leaders to speak of discipline and belt-tightening, or even perhaps to berate the excesses and self-indulgence of the people, as Jimmy Carter was to do eight years later—to his great regret.

Not John Connally. Having been responsible for the basic decision, Connally now had to sell it. For several hours at the Treasury he held forth. Sharp, incisive, and unrepentant, he projected none of the uncertainties that the economists felt. In the back of his mind, no doubt, was the warning of his tutor, William McChesney Martin, about devaluation: "If you're going to do it, for God's sake, don't brag about it." He expected business to follow the spirit and the letter of the new policy. He would not speculate on the reaction of the international markets or the stock market or what would happen after the freeze. He denied that the action constituted devaluation. He covered up the fact that the British demand for gold had prompted the decision. This was John Connally talking tough, and if anybody was missing that point, he held up an editorial from the London *Times* on Monday morning, with its headline THE UNITED STATES GETS TOUGH, AT LAST. Laughs greeted his assertion about the international community that "there's no question that [the action] shook them up!" and the question as to whether he had had to lay his job on the line to get the new policy. Implicit was the recognition that once again Connally had been the catalyst for a historical event. He also got a jolly response when he was asked about his erstwhile "Four Nos" on June 29, and whether the actions now did not create for him a "credibility gap." He replied, "Of the four items I laid down, we are not doing three of them. I did say we were not going to ask for any tax reduction. I will eat those words, but I will say this; I will have to eat a lot fewer than a lot of other folks I know." Challenged over whether he had not misled the press in June, he put forward unabashedly the principle that a politician should be able to say one thing while he planned the opposite. There had been the absolute necessity for denying plausibly the actions they intended.

"The American people would think they had a dolt for a president, if they thought he would take a position and never change it," he said brazenly. "If we had talked about the imposition of a wage-price freeze [in advance], what do you think would have happened? Everybody in this country would have raised their prices, increased wages. It would have been a counterproductive move of major proportions. We could not announce to the world that we were going to suspend the convertibility of the dollar at some future time. We could not talk about that. We could not leak it. We could not hint it. If we had, it would have been disastrous in the markets of the world. Billions—tens of billions—of dollars would have changed hands. Because an administration changes its policies or enunciates a new one where it contains elements, both on the international and domestic front, that require absolute secrecy, I think it's basically unfair [for the press] to say, 'Well, you misled us!' "

Out of nowhere, amid this weighty discussion of macroeconomics, someone piped up, "Mr. Secretary, if it were offered to you, sir, would you accept the Republican vice presidency?"

"Doesn't someone want to put an end to this press conference?" Connally asked, in mock exasperation.

Nixon was listening, and he was exhilarated. With one dramatic stroke, Camp David had taken its place in economic matters next to the opening of China in foreign affairs. The stock markets soared on Wall Street. Politically, thanks to Connally, Nixon appeared suddenly as the unlikely champion of the little man against the killing inflation and against the price gougers. They—he and Connally—had set a course now, and the economy was sure to move to greater health, just in time for the 1972 campaign.

Connally as his vice president? It was worth thinking about.

★

The historical significance of the August 15 bombshell was recognized instantly, and its reverberations would be felt and remembered seventeen years later. The cosmopolitans were the most affronted, for they saw the destruction and final collapse of the Bretton Woods regime not so much as a tragedy of substance but a tragedy of style. They had worked diligently since 1944 to establish an atmosphere of openness and of cooperation and of negotiation among the major trading partners of the free world. This secret, nationalist, unilateral surprise shattered that long-nurtured ethos. Eugene Rostow, who had been undersecretary of state for economic policy between 1966 and 1969, called the Camp David decisions a retreat to autocratic rule, a violent action, and shock therapy. Sixteen years later Rostow still felt it was the "crime of crimes." Nixon had wrecked a system, fashioned in the crucible of World War II, which had worked well for a quarter-century. To Rostow, the United States was still paying for Camp David into the late 1980s, as the international community struggled to find the stability that gold had once provided: "The Nixon-Connally actions killed that system. It eliminated restraints. It shattered discipline worldwide on wage rates and deficits. It translated monetary matters to a political level. We're under no discipline now to keep our budget balanced. That's why international interest rates rose, because there is such uncertainty about exchange rates. It was one of the most costly mistakes from an economic view ever made."

The experiment with wage and price controls was also to take a beating, as it was viewed in hindsight, but it was a more benign thrashing. The freeze was regarded merely as an interlude which did nothing permanent to affect the underlying inflationary pressures. Those pressures were themselves not as oppressive or uncontrolled as Connally had made them out to be. When the overall figures came in for 1971 and early 1972, they showed no substantial difference from the precontrols period, despite this tinkering with basic market forces. The real headaches came in the period after ninety days, when the Nixon administration tried to withdraw gracefully from its adventure—and found it not so easy to do so. People had grown comfortable with this taste of socialism. To Herbert Stein, who focused his attention on the postfreeze thaw, the Connally freeze was "merely a sin." It did no lasting damage to the economy. To be sure, the fixed prices of oil, which had their root in the 1971 measures, led directly to the oil crisis of 1973–74, when the American people would suffer from the Arab oil embargo and high prices and long lines at the pump. But John Connally had been out of office for nearly a year and a half when those chickens came home. No one cared or remembered to charge him with responsibility for that. In 1974, milk rather than oil was his problem. The freeze on prices also brought into existence a vast new area of competition in Brazilian soybeans for American agriculture. But the country survived these crises, as Stein would point out. Had nothing been done on August 15, the United States might have simply "oozed along" for a while and eventually might have imposed more stringent and damaging controls.

If the 1971 wage and price controls were merely a sin, they were a sin that some Nixon economists were determined never to repeat. When Nixon did repeat them in a milder form in 1973, at the urging only of Connally and Roy Ash and over the strong, unified objections of the professional economists, George Shultz resigned as secretary of the treasury. Then, Stein would warn Nixon that, like Heraclitus, the president could not step over the same river twice. You can if the river is frozen, Nixon responded, Connallyesque. By all accounts, this second freeze was an unrelieved disaster.

The Camp David decision had come about largely because of Connally. He had pushed for the bold, comprehensive plan since

February. His collusion with Nixon had given the president the confidence to cut across the economists and to make the political considerations of an economic decision paramount. He had appealed to Nixon's nationalist instincts and had schemed to exclude the internationalists. August 15 marked the official end of the "Marshall Plan psychology" in postwar economic history.

The Great Jawbone

EXTENDING BACK TO THE DAYS of heated debate in the Atheneum Society at the University of Texas, when he could address the question "Is there such a thing as a virtuous woman?" and argue either side forcefully, Connally was famous for his jawbone. Large and well shaped as it was, at significant moments his chin had a way of protruding like an exclamation point or forming a pout in an expression of outrage or accentuating his stubbornness and belligerence. It did much to command the attention both of his audience and, later, of caricaturists. In the months that followed the shattering August 15 decisions, Connally's chin would become the perfect symbol of his process. "Jawboning" to economists has its specific technical applications, but in general it refers to the process of persuasion, moral or otherwise, by high officials on economic matters, when institutions or established regulations do not suffice. Very often it is needed, this jawboning, when normal procedures have failed. On August 15, Nixon and Connally had produced a spectacular. Now they had to deal with its consequences.

Having been excluded from the Camp David weekend itself, the foreign policy experts crept back into the situation quickly, for the foreign policy implications of the New Economic Policy were profound. Before August, Secretary of State William Rogers had confessed himself to be "bored stiff" by economic problems. Henry Kissinger, still the national security adviser, felt himself equally on weak ground and recruited a Yale professor to give him a crash course in the "rudiments." "Even in my most meglomaniacal moments," Kissinger would write later, "I did not believe that I would be remembered for my contributions to the reform of the international monetary system." And Pete Petersen, the head of the White House Office on International Economic Policy, had been alternately bypassed and flattened by Connally, who would tolerate no White House staff intrusion upon his Treasury Department terrain. After August 15, they all had to be involved—and quickly.

Within the alliance of America's main trading partners, a period of intense uncertainty and high anxiety followed, as the international monetary system drifted into a protracted crisis. The trading partners consulted warily, seeking to position themselves before the real negotiations began. On September 16, in London, in the comfortable setting of the music room at Lancaster House, Connally enunciated the United States position before an audience of European and Japanese finance ministers. In this transition to a new system, the U.S. would be satisfied with a $13 billion annual improvement in its balance of payments and a favorable trade balance of $7 billion. These were conservative figures, he declared, not negotiating figures. The heft of that goal staggered the ministers, and they listened glumly. They felt that if only the United States would raise the price of gold and accept a devaluation of the dollar, the world monetary crisis would ease. Connally greeted that suggestion stonily. He wanted to reduce the role of gold in a new system, if not eliminate it altogether. Moreover, toward the end of the month he contributed to the anxiety by suggesting that IMF, the centerpiece of the Bretton Woods regime and temple to the Third World, might have outlived its usefulness.

As the prime negotiator for the United States, Connally's chief weapon after Camp David was the ten-percent surcharge on imports. The Japanese were already whimpering about it in mid-September, since thirty percent of all Japanese imports went to the United States. But the yen was undervalued, trading at 9 percent above its pre-August parity, and Connally was intent to hold their feet to the fire. The surcharge was a club, and technically it was also an illegal weapon. In late September the international body called the General Agreement on Trade and Tariffs (GATT) questioned the legitimacy of the surcharge, but the matter languished.

A curious reversal of roles was under way during this transitional period. The economists applauded Connally's brazenness now and were glad to have him crusading on their side. The diplomats, however, grew increasingly nervous. They did not relish this conflict within the alliance and the inevitable confrontations that would follow. The substance of what Connally wanted was fair enough—to realign the major currencies of the world in accordance with their real purchasing power—but Connally's bellicose manner was an affront and could not go on too long before it ruptured a delicate balance. "Many were shocked by the new American assertiveness," Kissinger was later to write. "As time went on, I began to suspect that Connally was sufficiently Texan to relish a good scrap for its own sake." Connally was now openly taking the position in cabinet meetings that the longer the U.S. could keep the surcharge on, the stronger would be its negotiating position. Kissinger disagreed. This confrontational stance had to end, for it inevitably would inspire countermeasures from abroad, and eventually it would instigate a form of economic warfare. Arthur Burns, who was doing his best to undercut Connally, had given Kissinger a glimpse of the retaliatory countermeasures some trading partners were planning. Moreover, Kissinger worried that Connally's hostility would encourage anti-American political forces abroad. "Connally saw no reason to treat foreigners with any tenderness," Kissinger wrote. "He believed that in the final analysis, countries yield only to pressure; he had no faith in consultations except from a position of superior strength. . . . Such language had not been heard since the formation of our alliance. It shook the crockery of our bureaucracy almost as much as it did the comfortable assumptions of our Allies that the doctrine of consultation gave them a veto over unilateral American actions." To Kissinger, Connally was far from a subtle force on the international scene. He was a man who understood a frontal assault but not an indirect maneuver. Kissinger ascribed Connally's self-confidence to his roots as a Texas self-made man, but even so Connally took Kissinger's breath away once when he said to the Harvard diplomat, "You will be measured in this town by the enemies you destroy. The bigger they are, the bigger you will be."

Others were still sharper about Connally's shredding of the diplomatic fabric. George W. Ball, who had been undersecretary of state for economic affairs under Kennedy and then number two man in the State Department under Johnson, was particularly offended by Connally's bad manners. Ball and Connally went way back. In fact, as a young navy lieutenant, Connally had worked briefly for Ball in the Lend-Lease administration in 1942, after Congressman Lyndon Johnson had pressed his "able young" assistant upon the office. Ball had formed an early impression of Connally then. He had given the young Texan an office with a telephone. The telephone had been a mistake, for young Connally was constantly on it to the Texas network, and Ball got little significant work out of him in the months he was in Lend-Lease. Then, early in the Johnson administration, when he was undersecretary of state, Ball had had an unforgettable interchange with President Johnson about Connally.

"George, you know John Connally pretty well, don't you?," the president asked.

"Not well, but I know him," Ball replied, wondering what was coming, knowing Johnson's penchant for withering gossip. "After all, you sent him down to work with us in Lend-Lease during the war. Of course, we saw one another when he was secretary of the navy."

"Well, that John's an interesting fellow. He's got a lot going for him," Johnson said. "You know, he'll go far—almost to the top. But he lacks one thing, and that could destroy him someday." Ball thought to interrupt, but he knew Johnson was into one of his teasing gossips, and so he stayed silent. "He's sure as hell impressive. He can walk into a room, and everyone knows he's there. He knows how to press the flesh, and where the bodies are buried. He's a good politician. . . . It's too bad he lacks just one thing."

Ball was unable to restrain himself. "What's that?" he asked, but the president was not quite ready to tell him.

"He's an awful quick study. You give him a memo or a brief, and he can get right up and make a powerful speech about it. Sometimes he can be real eloquent. Too bad he lacks just one thing, or he could go clear to the top."

Ball could stand it no longer. "What is that one thing, Mr. President?" he insisted.

"John Connally doesn't have even the tiniest trace of compassion," Johnson said. "He can leave more dead bodies in the field with less remorse than any politician I ever knew. That'll keep him from the top."

Johnson paused. The game was over. He was deadly serious now. "You know, George, I can use raw power—I can use raw power as well as anyone. You've seen me do it. But the difference between John and me is, he *loves* it. I *hate* it!" Ball discounted this last line, but he never forgot the interchange.

And he remembered it especially now, as he saw Connally bully his way across the field of international finance and watched the bodies fly. "Language of such arrogance," Ball wrote, "had not been used by an American cabinet minister since Secretary of State Richard Olney in the Cleveland administration had sent a note to the British government in a dispute over Venezuela, pronouncing the U.S. 'sovereign' in the whole Western Hemisphere, and insisting that 'its fiat is law upon the subjects to which it confines its inter-position,' because 'its infinite resources render it master of the situation and practically invulnerable as against all other powers.' Unhappily, Nixon chose to play Cleveland to Connally's Olney, reinforcing the Texan's self-righteousness with similar statements of his own."

Not everyone regarded Connally's behavior as arrogant or self-righteous. The currency of the United States was in desperate shape, and the international system institutionalized its distress. After years of neglect, a major "correction" was absolutely necessary. If conflict and confrontation marked this transitional period, what else could be expected? For years Western Europe and especially Japan had enjoyed a sweetheart relationship with the United States. Paul Volcker was one who cheered Connally on and scoffed at the criti-cism by the nervous Nellies in the State Department. If the matter was left to them, he felt, they would settle for a three-percent realignment and that would be the end of it. He wanted fifteen percent.

Six weeks after the August shock, the International Monetary Fund and the World Bank, the two great institutional achievements of Bretton Woods, held their joint annual meeting in Washington. Several days before, Connally requested a meeting with Pierre Paul Schweitzer, the director of the IMF, as a gesture of mollification. Connally and Schweitzer had an awkward relationship. The first time they met, Connally had come to the IMF, where Schweitzer had laid on an elegant European feast, replete with fine wines and after-lunch liqueurs which, of course, only the Frenchman consumed. As a consequence, Schweitzer, who had been a heroic leader of the French Resistance during World War II and still walked with a limp from Nazi torture, had grown foggy as Connally grew impatient. Connally eventually stormed out. Having gotten off on the wrong foot, Schweitzer remained unpopular with Connally— and vice versa, since Connally had taken the gratuitous step of inviting Schweitzer to his Treasury office to watch President Nixon's speech on closing the gold window. Through September, relations between Schweitzer and the administration worsened, as Schweitzer publicly pressed the U.S. to make a "contribution" to solving the international monetary crisis by raising the price of gold. (A year later Schweitzer was fired as director of the IMF, and rumor had it that Connally had been instrumental.) Now, at their lunch preceding the IMF convention, Schweitzer urged Connally to restore fixed exchange rates quickly and for the United States to devalue the dollar.

The next day Connally went before the IMF and proposed a deal. If countries would make "tangible" progress in dismantling specific trade barriers, if they would let their currencies float freely, the ten-percent surcharge would come off. The latter was a reference to the phony floating that had gone on since August 15, where countries had tried to give the appearance of floating, while they really intervened and controlled the process quietly in the background. The economists were calling these "dirty floats," and Connally wanted to purify the waters. Again, his message got a chilly reception. A Japanese minister said a "free float" would clearly not work; the French, affronted as they were by Connally's disparagement of gold, said the secretary's speech was nothing new. The industrial nations of the Free World remained at a monetary and trade impasse.

In later October and early November, Connally used the inauguration of Nguyen Van Thieu in South Vietnam as a pretext to travel to the Orient. It was unclear whether he would go to Japan and make a serious effort to break the deadlock, or whether this extended trip, which included beach time with Nellie in Bali, was an escape from the intense pressures in Washington to negotiate. On November 9 he arrived in Tokyo with fanfare, as his hosts greeted him with considerable trepidation. A month before—pondering the $3 billion trade deficit with Japan—the United States had issued an unqualified ultimatum to the Japanese to limit their exports of synthetic textiles. Japan had lost a bit of face by accommodating the Americans. So Connally's reputation had preceded him. The Japanese expected him to arrive in boots, with a pearl-handled pistol, and a bullet belt full of demands. But some shrewd diplomatic hand had apparently conveyed a timeworn verity about Japanese life to Connally: you might win a battle or two with bluster, but you will surely lose the war that way. Thus a totally surprising John Connally presented himself. He was bland and deferential and solicitous. In a kind of sashimi Western, he let the Japanese do the blustering and the complaining and the shooting from the hip. Since in addition to the $3 billion trade surplus with the U.S. they sat on foreign exchange reserves of $14 billion and an economic growth rate of six percent, their demands for substantial concessions from Connally sounded a bit hollow. He let the point register with silence. When he spoke, he spoke of history. Over the past quarter-century, when the United States had all the wealth, she shared her prosperity and she helped rebuild Japan. "Now we need help, and we are going to some of our friends," he said. It was presumptuous of him to tell Japan to do anything, but if they wanted to help, some possible steps they might want to consider—if they thought well of it—were revaluating the yen, or lifting trade tariffs, or contributing to the cost of Asian defense. Of course, he was pressed on the hated surcharge, which had brought the Japanese economy to the brink of recession. He responded with gentle sarcasm. The surcharge was not the only restriction upon the movement of goods around the world. Take a recent Japanese tariff of $135 a head on the import of American feeder cattle. "That's roughly equivalent to the total value of the animals," Connally said. "I would be happy if many countries of the world would limit their tariffs to ten percent."

It was a subtle and stylized ritual, and Connally played it brilliantly. He prepared to leave with no promises from the Japanese, because he had asked for none. Before he left he visited Eisaku Sato at the prime minister's home. There, Sato questioned Connally closely about a transcendent fascination, the events of Dallas on November 22, 1963. The prime minister extended to Connally his heartfelt condolences for the governor's injury. After his departure, the Japanese saw their duty clearly, and they expressed their admiration for Connally. One senior official in the Finance Ministry compared Connally's performance to the ancient samurai ritual of *ei nuki*, where two brave samurai take their positions opposite one another on a tatami mat, with their swords in their scabbards, on their left sides. At a signal, each warrior gets one cut, and the retainers wait to see who falls over dead.

"We played *ei nuki* with Connally," the senior minister told a reporter for the *New York Times*, "and we fell over."

As Connally was meeting with the Japanese, Henry Kissinger began to assert his influence in the White House. As far as Kissinger was concerned, the Connally-induced tension in the alliance had gone too far. If the lack of an agreement persisted much longer, Kissinger feared a generalized recession in Western Europe as well as Japan, a downturn that would rightly be blamed on American actions, and, in turn, might do serious damage to the carefully nourished comity of the alliance. Connally continued to refuse to put forward a plan for monetary reform, for he said he had not yet "squeezed the maximum out of the situation." Kissinger finally persuaded Nixon that the president's indulgence of Connally, indeed, his encouragement of him, was becoming counterproductive. With Connally playing the samurai far away in Japan, Kissinger opened an initiative to President Georges Pompidou of France. A meeting between Nixon and Pompidou was proposed for a month hence. Kissinger began to work on the indirect maneuver as a counterpoint to Connally's frontal assault.

With Connally on the way home, Nixon wrote to Kissinger on November 12, "Before Connally returns, it might be well for you to go over and have a talk with Volcker . . . to get him programmed for some of the problems we will have to discuss with Connally when he returns. It is important that Volcker not set up a cabal against the White House as we make these very important decisions."

France was as tough as Japan to corral into an accommodation, largely because the French had an obsession about gold. For decades French citizens had been hoarding it, and as a result French politicians always insisted upon it as the standard of value. De Gaulle had once said about gold, "It has no nationality and it is universally and eternally held as the inalterable and fiduciary value, par excellence." If Nixon and Pompidou, who was a Gaullist, could come to an agreement, the other nations would fall into place, and if Kissinger could set it up, Connally would have to fall into place as well. The battle for the heart and mind of Richard Nixon now became a battle between Kissinger and Connally. If Connally argued that Nixon's reelection depended upon economic success, very well, Kissinger would argue that the president's reelection depended upon forthcoming summit meetings with Mao and Brezhnev, and those foreign spectaculars could only take place after cordial meetings with Allied heads of state. With Connally instigating all this tension, the foreign heads of state were scarcely feeling cordial. Meanwhile, Kissinger's French opening was successful. The meeting between Pompidou and Nixon was scheduled for December 13 in the Azores.

As Kissinger flanked, Connally saw that his "credit" for the eventual solution of the monetary crisis was in jeopardy. If Kissinger settled the conflict, Connally would be credited only for the dislocation. Personally, Connally was prepared to keep the surcharge in effect for another whole year, but Kissinger was plotting with Arthur Burns to undercut him. With the Azores meeting set, the momentum was toward a settlement. Connally had one last chance to assert his authority. The Group of Ten, the organization of the free world's major trading partners, was scheduled to meet in Rome on November 30. If Connally achieved nothing there, he would concede the field to Kissinger.

The Rome conclave was to be an extraordinary, memorable one.

To Paul Volcker, it was the most remarkable international meeting he had ever attended. Held in the Accademia dei Lupi, an elegant Renaissance palace with formal Italian gardens, high ceilings, and poor air circulation, it provided Connally with his turn to be chairman of the group. The advocacy of the United States position, therefore, shifted technically to Volcker. On the first day Connally stalled for time. As chairman, he allowed a German central banker to drone on for several hours, reading an eighty-page statement, and on his grand perch the secretary of the Treasury fell asleep. When the German banker finished, Connally woke up and moved that the meeting go into executive session, a move which excluded the central bankers altogether. Behind closed doors, the atmosphere among the finance ministers was acrid with threat and counter-threat. The Common Market, and especially Great Britain, pressed a hard line, and the United States answered in kind. The U.S. "proposal" was the same old thing. It put the onus on nine of the Group of Ten to accomplish an eleven-percent realignment, while big number ten did virtually nothing. As usual, the U.S. refused to consider a devaluation of the dollar, raising the price of gold, removing the ten-percent surcharge, or eliminating the investment tax credit that favored American companies. Particularly galling to the French was the American refusal to consider a return to gold as a hinge for the dollar. Pierre Paul Schweitzer's phrase about an American "contribution" to a settlement became the general refrain, led by the French finance minister, Valery Giscard d'Estaing. The European line was that no movement was possible until the U.S. considered devaluation. At the end of the first day, a French delegate referred to the Connally behavior as "a new form of diplomacy—diplomacy by twist." The Italian minister threatened for the first time that if there was no agreement soon, Europe should consider a "regional monetary system." Still, for unclear reasons, Connally told the press that in executive session the ministers had finally gotten down to "nuts and bolts."

"Were any of these nuts and bolts made of gold?" someone asked coyly.

The next day the finance ministers came quickly to a seminal moment. In his gruff, raw New York accent, Volcker finally played his wild card. Giscard was expatiating once again on the need for an American contribution, when Volcker spoke up:

"Hypothetically—just for the purposes of discussion—how would you respond to an offer by the United States to devalue, say, ten or fifteen percent?"

Even though he was chairman, Connally waded in. "What would the gentleman's reply be, if *I* suggested ten percent?"

The shock was profound. Silence fell over the Accademia as finance ministers whispered to their retainers for close to an hour. For three and a half months Connally had scorned the suggestion of an American devaluation. Suddenly, here he was proposing a whopping devaluation, far in excess of what the European ministers wanted or expected. Volcker was among the surprised. Why had Connally suggested ten percent? he wondered. That narrowed their negotiating position. Fifteen percent would have been a better starting point.

At length, the British chancellor of the exchequer, Tony Barber, broke the silence. "We could never agree to such a devaluation," he said.

"I'm astounded," Connally replied. "What would you have in mind?"

"Five percent."

"Under no circumstances could we agree," Connally replied. "It's not enough," and he fell into a lecture about the U.S. Congress. Only Congress had the authority to change the price of gold, and President Nixon would never recommend to Congress any such change without assurances about sharing the burden of military defense and about trade.

"We did not know this was a matter of serious concern," a European minister said disingenuously.

Connally was to say later that President Nixon had given him "almost unlimited authority" to negotiate the realignment, and this confidence put Connally in an advantageous position vis-à-vis the other ministers. None of *them* had the authority to propose anything without consulting with their home governments. "Just go ahead and do what you think you have to," the president had told Connally in September. And Connally had done it. An avoidance syndrome had afflicted the government for several years and now Connally had moved to shatter it. From total refusal to consider devaluation, he shifted the issue to massive devaluation.

Actually, Connally was operating in his own interest. He could not go home empty-handed, for Kissinger was bound to exploit a Connally failure. In the irresolvable conflict between international finance and international relations, the matter was reduced, as usual, to a question of power and of personality. Connally saw that Rome had to be a triumph for him. Kissinger, however, was intent on taking credit regardless. Later, writing to his own recipe,

Kissinger said, "The Group of Ten met in Rome without major results, as planned. The stage was set for the decisive meeting in the Azores." That was not as Connally saw it. Back in the United States, he reported a stunning development to the president. In a December 6 memo, the secretary wrote of a "precise" agreement reached in Rome that had coupled trade questions to an overall solution to the monetary crisis. "I believe this is a *breakthrough*, and it is important to follow it up."

On December 13, in the "islands of the hawk," as the Azores were known, the presidents arrived for the decisive meeting. A fundamental axiom of foreign affairs was at work in the gray Azores: when two heads of state meet, the overwhelming push is for a successful conclusion. The presidents' respective retinues would have a bearing on how the meetings were to proceed, and on who between Connally and Kissinger was to be ascendant. Pompidou was accompanied by Valery Giscard d'Estaing, and the two men did not get along. Indeed, they were from opposing political parties and in this case it meant something. Pompidou, the Gaullist, did not want Giscard, the Republican, to get credit for anything. Therefore, Giscard was excluded from the presidential meetings. Perforce, this required that Connally be excluded on the American side. But even in his enforced isolation, Connally projected a muscular, menacing presence. Like the old tradition in this Portuguese island, he was the fighting bull to whose horns is attached a long, sturdy rope, before the animal is released upon the expansive beaches, there to be held back by the crowd as the strapping young men taunt him. Connally, who did not stand for accommodation, was being held back, but his presence could not be ignored, and Nixon might choose to release him. "Connally was not eager to be perceived as having moved to compromise," Kissinger was to say later. "[Connally] was willing to *have* a negotiation, but he preferred to keep himself in reserve for a deadlock."

Meanwhile, Kissinger took over the direct negotiations with Pompidou. Although he felt himself on shaky ground in these matters of high finance, he was not ready to concede the negotiations to anyone else. He considered himself to be the highest ranking official present who was *for* a successful agreement (thus ignoring the presence of Secretary of State William Rogers). Connally was forced to stay behind with Volcker, housed in a rudimentary military barracks where they had to employ the wife of an American sergeant to type, uncertainly, their monetary and trade position papers. Kissinger, meanwhile, helicoptered off to Pompidou's grand villa.

Looking out over the lush meadows of this Portuguese outpost, where Columbus had stopped in 1493 on his way home from the New World, it was not lost on Kissinger that from this point in the mid-Atlantic, Portuguese explorers, "inspired by faith and sustained by greed," had launched their spectacular journeys.

Regardless of their competitiveness, it was clear where Connally and Kissinger each stood with the president, and now they worked well together. The Azores conference proceeded upon multiple levels. Secretary of State William Rogers and French Foreign Minister Maurice Schumann were present, but their talks were a sideshow to the central discussions. With Volcker at his side, Connally defined the basic United States position, both on monetary and trade matters, since the two areas were now combined for the first time as a result of Connally's breakthrough in Rome. Kissinger then took this basic position to Pompidou. As Pompidou was by profession a banker and a financial expert, Kissinger felt himself very much at a disadvantage, and felt that to engage in technical negotiation with such an imposing opposite number would be "suicidal." Moreover, Connally was closeted with Giscard, and they could talk detail. As Connally later described it, these technical discussions were "intricate, complex, and intensive," while Giscard himself was "sophisticated, determined, smart, skilled, and tough." The two finance ministers were negotiating not only the new parity between the franc and the dollar, but also their hopes for parities with every other important currency, particularly the mark and the yen. Historical as well as economic sensitivities complicated the process. The French wanted the franc to stay just a little ahead of the German mark, and nobody in Europe wanted to drop the barriers to the Japanese. "It's a merry-go-round," Connally would say after the first full day. "Each country is a problem. We're all a problem to each other. The real problem is, When do you sit down and say: I'll do this if you'll do that?"

A Texas reporter was present, and he wanted to put the process into horse-trading terms: "In our own terms in Texas, Mr. Secretary, how does the horse look, and are you about to make a trade?"

Connally chuckled at this warm breeze from home. "The horse is at least sound," he said, presumably talking about the dollar and not about himself. "We've determined he's not winded. He's got good teeth. He's not overaged. So far as we can tell, he's of sound limb." The rest of the press shook their heads in puzzlement.

Undoubtedly, Connally longed to be present at Kissinger's sessions with Pompidou, and more than once he manifested his annoyance with Kissinger's ignorance of financial affairs. A technical discussion turned out to be unnecessary, however. Pompidou was ready to make a French contribution to a settlement. He agreed to an overall nine-percent realignment—combining an upward revaluation of the franc and a devaluation of the dollar—and Nixon agreed to stand by the accommodation and argue forcefully for it with other countries. The United States accepted curtailments on the free floating of major currencies, as France acquiesced in the departure from gold as a standard.

From the Azores, the American contingent flew home in high spirits and with high expectations. Nixon and Kissinger prepared to fly to Key Biscayne, as Connally called for a meeting of the Group of Ten three days hence. But before the principals went their separate ways, they gathered at the White House for a bipartisan meeting with the top leaders of Congress. As usual, Nixon turned to Connally, his great salesman, to brief the congressional leaders.

"The Europeans have a way of whipsawing you," Connally began. "They say they can't go ahead [with an agreement] unless the Common Market agrees, but then any one of them can make sure the Common Market won't agree. Frankly, we used the Congress as a bargaining lever."

"We scared them with you," Nixon said.

"We think that having broken ground with the French, we might get a resolution of this problem this week," Connally continued.

"Will you need congressional action next week?" asked the Speaker of the House, Texan Carl Albert.

"No, afterwards," Nixon replied.

"Don't take away our bargaining lever!" Connally pleaded.

"Pompidou said to the president that he wanted a change in the price of gold," Kissinger contributed. "The president implied he couldn't put before Congress that recommendation prior to seeing the whole package."

"I said, 'The Congress won't buy a pig in a poke,' " Nixon said.

"That was a helluva translating problem," Kissinger chortled.

"We trust us more than we trust them," Connally said. "Each of them hides behind their commitment to the Common Market. It's extremely difficult to get all your coons up one tree."

"That would be hard to translate, too," Nixon said. Then he turned serious. "It's hard to avoid comparisons. Everybody wants to know who 'won.' If one side completely whips the other, nobody wins. That is not the way it works. After it was over, I said to

Pompidou, 'You have really taken us,' and he said 'No, it is unconditional surrender for us.' Actually, it is a good deal for us."

"We need Pompidou to keep the others in line," Kissinger added. "He has an election next year, and he can't look like he gave in too much. But he got more theory than practice."

"The price of gold to a Frenchman is 'practice,' even though it is 'theory' to us," the president said. "The French peasants hoard gold at no interest. When they see the price of gold go up, even if it is not convertible, it sounds good."

"That sockful of gold feels heavier to the French peasant right now," Republican senatorial leader Hugh Scott observed.

"Right," Nixon said. "That is why we can't claim triumph—just a good deal all around. You noted the story that John Connally was being too tough. He *had* to be—or he wouldn't have gotten anything."

"It was largely due to the effort of Dr. Burns and Paul Volcker," Connally said graciously.

"We didn't have to make a deal, you know," Nixon continued. "We hoped first we could have made a deal with Canada and then maybe Japan. We had to give Pompidou a reason for him to deal. The French had no incentive, unaffected as they are by the surcharge, but this was the only way he could get us to raise the price of gold."

"The French categorically agreed to help us with nation after nation, not alone on trade but in the basic realignment of currencies," Connally said. "But we have to be careful. What we get now is all we will get for a long time."

"That's why we can't settle for too little," Nixon said.

"Will this be complicated legislation?" Gerald Ford asked.

"No," Nixon replied.

"You cannot come to Congress with a vague figure," the powerful Wilbur Mills said. "You need a set figure, for the price of gold is sacrosanct with some people. I was speaking at New York University about needing to change the price of gold, and a man who was in the class of 1912 came up and threatened to hit me!"

"Our present thinking is to make the deal and then ask the Congress to approve the deal," Nixon said.

"It would be a grave matter with the president speaking for the country and the country not agreeing," Connally said.

"The reaction has been good in Congress, maybe too good," said Senate Majority Leader Mike Mansfield. "I would hate to remove your bargaining lever. You want opposition?"

There was laughter.

"No!" the president yelped.

"It wouldn't hurt if a few people expressed a wait-and-see attitude," Connally said.

"All we want you to say today is this," Nixon said. "Express confidence in the secretary of the treasury as he negotiates with the Group of Ten. This will mean action early in the session, up or down, like a treaty. Congress can't go and add a lot of—codicils."

"Reservations?" Mansfield helped.

"That's the word," Nixon continued. "When we make this deal, we can't be second-guessed."

"The markets would go wild," Connally said.

"Our understanding with Pompidou is specific," Nixon continued. "We won't give out the numbers, and neither will the French. This is a good deal from our standpoint. Frankly, it is so much in our interest, it would be overwhelmingly supported. Would you characterize it that way, John?"

"Absolutely," Connally replied. "Of course, if Congress wants, we could get the IMF to do it [change the price of gold] first and then have it ratified by Congress. But we could do that only if Congress understood clearly that we are not circumventing them."

"That would be easier," Mills said.

"The quicker the better," Nixon said.

"Gold is emotional," offered another Texas powerhouse, Wright Patman. "Anything that generates pressure would be good."

"We are not going to take the IMF route, unless we get trade," Connally said.

"But we have broken the logjam, and the solution is now certain," Nixon said.

The meeting began to break up, but Connally wanted a last word. "One caution. Don't give away the idea of handling this through the IMF," he warned.

"What do you want us to say?" Carl Albert asked. "I would like us to be on all fours on this."

" 'Impressed and encouraged' are good words to use," Wright Patman suggested.

From Washington, Nixon and Kissinger withdrew to Key Biscayne and left the stage to Connally. On December 16, only three days after the Azores conference, the finance ministers convened at the Smithsonian Institution. In the Azores, Connally had warned that the Group of Ten could not keep meeting month after month with no agreement. Uncertainty itself was becoming the central concern. If the nations simply could not agree, they should agree formally to disagree. With France now carrying the case for settlement to the Common Market, there was hope. At the Smithsonian, Connally was the pivotal figure. An agreement was his to accomplish or to lose. As the ministers gathered, the U.S. Treasury announced another huge deficit in the balance of payments for the third quarter—$3.1 billion—equivalent to the deficit for all of 1970. This distress strengthened Connally's hand. The French-American proposal was laid out, and Connally waited nervously for a response, as the finance ministers consulted interminably with their home governments. In a diverse group of industrial nations, the secretary did not underestimate the complexity of what he wanted to achieve. A few days earlier, to the congressional leaders at the White House, he had reduced the diversity and the complexity of nations to this homily: "You cannot compare rabbits and horses, just because they both have four feet." Parities and trade policy went to the central nervous system of each country. At last, late on Friday evening, December 17, Karl Schiller, the German finance minister, and a dejected Giscard came to Connally.

"We have failed to reach an accord among the Six," Schiller said about the Common Market countries. "You are going to have to work it out."

As he would later narrate it for the author Martin Mayer, Connally fell into a frantic series of one-on-one talks with the respective finance ministers. He began with Schiller.

"You'll devalue fourteen percent," he said to the German.

"What are the French going to do?"

"They will stay at the price of gold."

"The Italians?"

"The same."

"The Japanese?" That was the sticking point. The Japanese were not budging, falling back into the ritual of *ei nuki* not only with Connally but with nine separate samurai. Connally had asked that the yen be revalued upward by twenty-five percent, but had hinted that he would accept nineteen percent. Now he came in under that.

"Seventeen percent," he said to Schiller. "But whatever happens, we'll insist they revalue three percent more than you do."

Within the European community this began to turn the screw. All-night meetings took place, and the international wire buzzed with the deliberations. The process was noteworthy as the first time the principal industrialized nations had sat down to negotiate the relative parities of their currencies not only toward the dollar, but toward each other. It was a case of each currency impinging upon another, and that made the technical wrangling complicated and difficult. In the end stage, the most difficult negotiations took place between neighbors. "Where neighbors touched neighbors," Connally would say, reaching for an image he no doubt borrowed from a baronial finance minister from the Low Countries, "that is where the cheese became really binding."

The next morning a few minor adjustments had to be made, but an agreement was at hand—except for the Japanese. Minister of Finance Mikio Mizuta had ceased to talk to Connally directly, for the American demands, even in the range of an eighteen percent "upward cut" of the yen, would represent the greatest economic shock to Japan in twenty-five years. Instead, Mizuta had sent his assistant. A half-hour before the ministers were to reconvene for the Saturday morning session Connally was summoned out of the room to see Mizuta's retainer and to hear bad news: the minister could not accept seventeen percent. Connally went into a slow boil. Turning his back on the underling, he promised to announce that there was an agreement except for the intransigence of the Japanese.

"You don't understand," the official said. "In 1930, the finance minister revalued the yen by seventeen percent, starting a depression, many unemployed, and he committed suicide. Can't you give my minister some other number?"

This historical superstition made a powerful argument for both sides. The recession of 1930 led directly to the rise of the military clique in Imperial Japan. Actually, the unhappy finance minister in question had been assassinated. "Sixteen point nine," Connally snapped.

"Okay."

By the afternoon, the agreement was reached. The price of gold was raised from $35 to $38 an ounce, affecting a devaluation of the dollar by 8.57 percent. The official American devaluation, including congressional certification, would await a successful conclusion of trade negotiations with the Common Market and Japan. The ten-percent surcharge was dropped immediately. President Nixon rushed back from Key Biscayne to make the announcement of the accord personally. With Connally by his side, the president surrendered to extravagance. This was, he said earnestly, "the most significant monetary agreement in the history of the world."

But in the succeeding months it became clear that the heart of the United States was not in the agreement, and it was not forcefully defended, as Nixon and Connally had promised. Inevitably the Europeans and the Japanese lost faith in it. Why should they defend the exchange rates that had been established at the red castle of the

Smithsonian if the United States was not prepared to do so? The monetary situation remained unstable. Technically, as an exercise of political skill, it was a considerable accomplishment to get the industrial nations of the world to agree on a matter as complicated as this. But Connally's achievement was transitory. The Smithsonian Agreement was merely a signpost, a way station toward a situation of free floating that Connally's successor, a real economist named George Shultz who had strongly held convictions about monetary policy, was to bring about in 1973. The stature of the Smithsonian Agreement as the most significant monetary agreement in the history of the world was fleeting, even in Nixon's mind. He did not mention it in his memoirs. As for the first devaluation of the dollar since the early 1930s, Nixon would never brag about that.

★ 20 ★

Unholy Trinity

A MONTH BEFORE THE Smithsonian Agreement was concluded, Lyndon Johnson returned to Washington for only the third time since the end of his presidency. He had come primarily to give the Arthur K. Solomon Lecture at the New York University Business School, but stopped in Washington to see old friends.

That night there was a small party at the home of Willard Deason, whom Johnson had put in charge of the Interstate Commerce Commission during his presidency. Deason went back to LBJ's college days at Southwest Texas State Teachers College in San Marcos, had been with Johnson through early political campaigns, and had been with Connally and the KVET crowd after the war. Connally, who had gotten back from his Oriental trip only that morning, was present at the gathering as well, still flushed with exhilaration over his talks with the Japanese. The evening was warm and jovial. Johnson and Connally fell into rancher's talk, for the president was having some problems with his cattle, and he deferred to Connally as the expert on all matters of livestock. In due course, the conversation shifted to the exotic area of international monetary affairs, as Johnson asked Connally to explain what was going on. "What is a floating dollar anyway?" Johnson asked, and Connally swung into an erudite lecture on international finance. To Johnson's close friends and longtime associates, the moment was emblematic, and a hush fell over the room. LBJ sat crumpled in the corner, silent and attentive, a listener for once. He had become a twilight figure, and at last he ceased to dominate and overpower. By shifting his loyalties shockingly to Richard Nixon, Connally had finally escaped the straitjacket of being Lyndon's boy.

Johnson never quite got over his mystification at Connally's decision to join the Nixon administration. He was annoyed that John had not consulted him and was annoyed still more the way "that son of a bitch" Nixon had informed him of Connally's appointment. The previous December, Nixon had called, and they had exchanged pleasantries before Nixon, in that sneaky, gloating way that Johnson detested, had said, by the by, that he wanted to introduce his new secretary of the treasury, "an old friend of yours," and had passed the phone to Connally. After he hung up, Johnson sat down and wrote a letter to Connally. It was perhaps the only letter in the memory of Johnson's closest associates of which no copy was made, and which was sealed and marked "confidential" by the ex-president. A few days later Johnson expressed his attitude to Liz Carpenter: "I should have spent more time with that boy," he said sadly. "His problem is he likes those oak-paneled rooms too much."

If the party at Deason's was symptomatic of Connally's elevated station within the Johnson crowd, in part elevated because he had escaped it, his stature within the Nixon crowd, especially after the Smithsonian Agreement, was equally exalted. At the beginning of 1972, the promise of Nixon's initial invitation—to be much more than merely secretary of the treasury, but to be a "counselor, confidant, and friend"—had been realized. On February 1, Haldeman wrote an "action memo" which directed the special treatment Connally was to receive. Haldeman ordered Alexander Butterfield, who was the keeper of perquisites at the White House, to give Connally first use of the weekend retreat at Camp David and always to have a helicopter at Connally's disposal: "You should take the initiative—keep pressing him—give him the highest priority over all other cabinet and over all staff." Ehrlichman was to "watch this situation like a hawk. Go over and sit down with Connally and get his judgment. If Connally is not for a matter, the president won't do it."

If Connally's attentions flattered Nixon, if together they had now achieved historic things, if Connally was the president's best salesman and his choice to be the next president, Connally garnered the affections of the president as well for something he had *not* done. Unlike most of the Nixon crowd, Connally never belittled the president behind his back.

Through the winter and spring of 1972 Connally went about his duties at Treasury with increasing impatience. He was, as his friend and colleague George Christian was to put it, a man who always had his eye on the clock. An old axiom of his professional life was beginning to assert itself. Once he mastered a job, he began to lose interest in it. After the Camp David decision and the Smithsonian Agreement, the emphasis shifted to managing these new improvements to the engine of the economy. That was the province of technicians, not leaders.

The boards which occupied Connally's time sounded almost Communistic: the Wage and Price Board, Phase II, Cost of Living Council; and, inevitably, as in Communism, the various entities fouled their lines with one another. Increasingly, the public was becoming dissatisfied. A Harris poll in late January 1972 showed that only twenty-nine percent of the American people gave the administration a positive rating on "keeping the controls effective" and stopping rising costs (sixty-six percent gave a negative rating). Connally was being forced into constant jawboning with industry representatives. Essentially his job was to scare the corporate executives into keeping their prices down. In an "eyes only" memo, Charles Colson urged Connally to call in the heads of the ten largest supermarkets and browbeat them into dropping the price of hamburger by five cents. "Supermarkets have been terrified that the federal government might, at some point, move in and crack down on them on a variety of issues," Colson wrote Connally on February 25. "Knowing how you are in handling people, I suspect that they would happily swallow a nickel a pound on hamburger to avoid incurring your wrath." While Connally knew the uses of wrath, this was not his idea of how the economy would work, nor how he wanted to spend much of his own time. Colson could feel Connally's lack of concentration. On March 1, in a memo marked "Personal/ Eyes Only," Colson wrote to OMB Director George Shultz about his inability to get Connally focused on the deteriorating public confidence in the administration's economic policy. "Yesterday [Connally] told me that he felt there was a long way to go to the election, that we shouldn't worry. I have a number of ideas, but I'm stymied if I can't get Connally concerned," Colson wrote. "What I fear is that we will let the situation drift to the point that we will need to do something very dramatic to turn public attitude, and there are not very many dramatic weapons left in our arsenal."

As Connally's impatience with such distractions grew, he began to spend more and more time in Texas. His beloved Picosa Ranch drew him away from his increasingly disagreeable duties and from his sometimes claustrophobic relationship with Nixon. To the president, these powerful Texas politicians with their big boots and big spreads were a matter of evident curiosity. If he had never been welcome at the LBJ Ranch, he had something still better at the Picosa Ranch. Connally eventually invited the Nixons to pay a visit on April 30. When the time came, the presidential helicopter came in low over the lush folds of Wilson County and over the verdant expanses of coastal Bermuda grass, before it set down near a horse fence not far from the big house. There with a ranch wagon to meet the president and the First Lady was Connally, dressed in Western shirt and bolo tie—and Nellie in a long blue floral dress which blew in the prairie wind. At the portico of the fieldstone house, leathery cowboys lined up with the Mexican house staff to greet the president, before the guests were ushered into the impressive hallway whose marble floor once graced the Japanese embassy in London.

Later that evening more than two hundred guests, including former Texas Governor Allan Shivers and Richard Kleberg, the owner of the King Ranch, gathered on the expansive lawn in a festive mood. A wreath of chrysanthemums floated cheerily in the pool, and a mariachi band warmed the guests under the huge Spanish oak. At a pit which Connally and his hands had dug, roasting ears boiled in pots on a grate. Tenderloin steaks, big as rifle stocks, flew on the grill. Connally and Nixon emerged, dressed nattily for the occasion. Connally sported a black-and-white-checked jacket with country pleats in the back, a black tie, and boots. Nixon was in two tones of California powder blue, and the ladies were in long cotton dresses—Nellie in a flouncy blue, Pat in prim calico red.

"This is big country, and it produces big men," Nixon observed. It was not true, said the president, gazing out over the fields, that in Texas you could look farther and see less than any place on earth. "As a matter of fact, you can see a great deal," he allowed. "Now I feel I've seen what Texas is supposed to be."

Before they ate, Connally took Nixon down by the long fence, where, on cue, several ranch hands galloped up on palominos and proceeded to give the president a demonstration of steer roping and cattle cutting. Afterwards they trotted up to the president for some small talk about life as a Connally cowboy.

Just after nine, Connally called for the attention of his guests, a group which he said included many—"I can't say all"—of his dearest friends. He couldn't say all, he said, reaching for a laugh, because there were a few members of the press present, and besides, he was a little vain, and he wouldn't want the president to think that all his friends could be assembled under a roof as small as forty by sixty feet. He had learned in politics that you always "fish with live bait," and so after an elegant appreciation he asked the president to say a few words, for he knew—vicariously—that the ivory towers of the White House were not so high, nor its walls so thick, that applause could not penetrate and lure its occupant out. Nixon, in response, was equally appreciative. He said that Connally was capable of holding any job in the United States. He was only glad that the governor was not then seeking the Democratic nomination for president. When the questions came, they centered on Vietnam. The subject was also on Nixon's mind. Kissinger was in Paris, preparing to meet Le Duc Tho in a final, climactic showdown, and that morning he and Kissinger had talked by phone. At Picosa, Nixon was asked why he didn't order strikes on the dams and dikes of North Vietnam. Surely they were legitimate military targets. Such strikes were not needed, the president replied, not yet anyway, and besides, they might cause unacceptable civilian casualties. But the North Vietnamese ran a very great risk, if they continued their offensive in South Vietnam. Nixon knew his answer would reach Paris by the morning.

When the festivities began to wind down, the president withdrew to Connally's study to dictate a memorandum to Kissinger. At Connally's Sam Houston desk, surrounded by guns and flags and a miniature covered wagon, the ambience came through in the dictation. "If they get a delay as a result of their talk with you," Nixon wrote Kissinger, "we shall lose the best chance we will ever have to give them a very damaging blow where it hurts, not just now, but particularly for the future. Forget the domestic scene. Now is the best time to hit them. Every day we delay reduces support for such strong action. . . . You shall tell them that they have violated all understandings. They stepped up the war. They refused to negotiate seriously. As a result, the President has had enough, and now, you have only one message to give them: Settle or Else!"

When he woke up in the morning Nixon threw open the blinds to gaze out upon Connally's expanse, and called for his breakfast. He was brought eggs and country sausage instead of his normal wheat germ, and he decided that he might change his diet from the "drab and uninteresting foods" he was used to at the White House.

Meanwhile, on May 2, the secret talks in Paris between Henry Kissinger and Le Duc Tho quickly broke down. Kissinger wired home that the administration should prepare to consider "crucial choices." With the collapse of negotiations, there was also distressing news from Vietnam itself. Garrisons on the outskirts of Hué had fallen, and the old imperial city itself was once again in jeopardy. Negotiations had ended because the North Vietnamese could smell total victory. If Hué fell there was no telling what would be next. The time had arrived at last when the full force of American military power should be unleashed. Nixon was no longer constrained to his use of force by hopes for a negotiated settlement. To the contrary, he felt that successful negotiations were now only possible with a crushing military blow. The United States had to show, Nixon felt, that victory was not close for the enemy, but still very far away.

The options were awesome, and Nixon and Kissinger sailed off along the Potomac aboard the presidential yacht *Sequoia* to consider them. Nixon favored a two-day B-52 strike on Hanoi and Haiphong, the consequences of which were likely to be the cancellation of a scheduled summit meeting with Brezhnev—a meeting Nixon had been eagerly anticipating. But Kissinger worried that a "one shot" strategy, no matter how devastating the shot was, would not "meet our needs." He preferred some more protracted military escalation. In this he was supported by General Creighton Abrams, who was now the commander in Vietnam. Abrams wanted B-52 strikes up and down the length of South Vietnam. As the discussion went forward, Nixon raised his ante to a three-day strike against the major North Vietnamese cities. Kissinger countered with the option of blockading North Vietnam and mining the Haiphong harbor. This was a considerably more aggressive step than the B-52 strikes, for it could widen the war dangerously. It could lead directly to a U.S.-Soviet confrontation. Were American ships in the blockade prepared to stop and board Soviet ships bringing arms to North Vietnam?

For a day the president temporized. The sticking point lay more in his indecision over the Moscow summit than over the military action. Nixon tilted toward canceling the summit himself, to preempt the Soviets. For Nixon it was a matter of showdowns, and he ordered Kissinger and Haldeman to consult with Connally, who was the master of showdowns. Later, Kissinger would write of Nixon's propensity in times of crisis and decision to turn to a very small group of advisers who, the president was sure, already agreed with his basic inclinations. If he expected Connally to sanction the three-day strike and the cancellation of the Moscow summit, he was to be roundly surprised. One can only speculate what Connally might have done at this moment had he been president.

This much is clear, however. At his private lunch table at the Department of the Treasury, Connally was given to terrorizing his subcabinet with talk of holocaust and humiliation. He sometimes proposed that the United States employ nuclear weapons from the stem of North Vietnam to the stern of South Vietnam, to win the war. Those present were not sure whether this hair-raising bellicosity was entirely sincere, but it was serious enough to deeply trouble Paul Volcker, for example, about the prospect of Connally as a national leader. Volcker admired Connally for much of what the secretary had accomplished at Treasury, but the talk at the table left Volcker with the gut feeling that Connally was given to dangerous excess.

On May 4, one day before Nixon wanted to order the B-52 strikes, Haldeman and Kissinger settled into the sofa in Connally's office at Treasury. In his notes, Haldeman described this meeting as a "cold turkey briefing on the summit situation and to get [Connally's] judgment" on the proper response to the collapse of the Paris talks. Haldeman was concerned about something else, however. Connally had already let it be known that he wanted to resign, and Haldeman needed to convey to him that the secretary could not leave then, not in a crisis over the war and in the midst of a major confrontation with the Soviets. If Connally left in an international crisis, "we'll get a big bang against us," Haldeman wrote, undoubtedly acting as the president's mouthpiece. "Dems on the warpath, with Soviet support." By bringing Connally into the center of this decision, the president could hold onto him a little longer. In Kissinger's mind, by contrast, the purpose of the meeting was to consult "the best political brain" in the administration about the domestic political consequences of the various actions. At last, in this crisis atmosphere, the tensions between Kissinger and Connally faded away.

Kissinger laid out the plan, Haldeman spoke up to disagree with its component of canceling the summit peremptorily, and then Connally took over. Haldeman was right, Connally advised. The president should not cancel the summit. There was no domestic political gain from that, since the president would be criticized for imperiling Soviet relations regardless. Leave the dilemma to the Soviets, and make it difficult for them. He was not sure they would cancel in any case. Kissinger instantly and uncharacteristically was persuaded. In a flash, he saw clearly that his advocacy of a preemptive cancellation had been a mistake. Later he wrote that "Connally's strong stand gave me an opportunity to rectify my mistake."

As for the military course—that was the heart of the matter to Connally. It must be clear to the Soviets that "we are *not* going to be defeated or surrender. . . .

"We can't lose the war," Connally said. "We'll lose the country if we lose the war. We won't lose the country if we lose the summit."

The military course had to be decisive. The president had to have the "guts" and the "leadership" to meet the situation without fear of what the Soviets would do. The confrontation would be safer, in fact, if it was bold rather than tentative. The question was simple: What would the most effective military action be? Kissinger and Haldeman walked away gratefully. Connally had defined the issue with startling clarity. As Kissinger would say later, in government the answers can never be better than the questions. Haldeman was also happy. Connally had agreed to stay in office several weeks longer if the summit was canceled. "If it's on, you can go before that," he told Connally.

By nightfall Nixon had agreed to the mining of Haiphong harbor with no action on the summit. On May 8, before he announced the decision to the nation, the president convened his cabinet. "We have crossed the Rubicon," the president said. "This has to work." With the mining there was a definite, precise goal—to deny the enemy the resources to wage a "nakedly aggressive" war. Then, in a phrase Connally might have resented, the president said, "Instead of the foolish, gradual escalation of LBJ, this is cleaner and more defensible."

The summit was not canceled. Nixon and Kissinger flew to Moscow on May 20.

★

Four days earlier, John Connally resigned. He did so one day after Governor George Wallace was gunned down in a Maryland shopping center. It was immediately assumed by many, including his closest friends, that the assassination attempt and Connally's resignation were linked. Since the Secret Service was an arm of the Treasury Department, since the secretary had himself been wounded by an assassin after a breakdown of security in Dallas nine years before, his resignation was akin to the good naval officer who steps down as an implicit acceptance of responsibility, just as he might have expected a high official to resign after he and Kennedy had been victims of negligence. This was one area of his department that Connally could not allow, for personal reasons, to fail. The Wallace assault was an unbearable replay of Dallas, his friends decided. His old friend Tex McCrary gave voice to these suspicions in a letter he wrote Connally on the day of the news: "I had felt that nothing could either surprise or shock me anymore, not even the shooting of George Wallace. . . . I knew Huey Long well, and I always did sense the inexorable parallel. But your resignation did both surprise and shock and *dismay* me. Of course, the Wallace tragedy did hit you harder than any man alive, including Teddy Kennedy; and for Nellie, it must have been a brutal jolt, a replay in slow motion of an insane instant in America's history of pistol passion. . . . [Nevertheless] I do not suggest that you were, for even one nightmare moment, activated by fear of personal peril."

At his last cabinet meeting, on May 16, Connally denied to his colleagues that his resignation was linked to the Wallace assassination. The decision had been made months ago—in January, in fact—and his arrangement with Nixon had always stipulated a limited time. It was easy for a man to adopt an air of indispensability, he told the cabinet, but, despite unfinished business, it was time for him to move on. Still, pistol smoke lingered over the decision, and his colleagues sensed that Connally was deeply affected by the event in Laurel.

Nixon was graceful in his farewell. He told the story of sitting next to Anthony Barber, the British chancellor of the exchequer, at a dinner in Bermuda only a few days after the Smithsonian Agreement.

"Without John Connally, you wouldn't have had an agreement," Barber had told Nixon.

"Never has one cabinet member done more for his country in a year and a half," Nixon said appreciatively. In his response, Connally expressed his pride at having served "the greatest administration in history."

He planned to go back to Texas and did not intend to do much until September. That is what he had told the cabinet the last time. The promise lasted a few days. When Nixon returned from Moscow, Connally was with the president only a day later in Key Biscayne. He had come to collect his reward for service above and beyond the duties of a normal Treasury secretary. But before they got down to business there was the inevitable political shoptalk. Connally had heard that Teddy Kennedy, belatedly, wanted the Democratic nomination, but he had waited too long.

"McGovern and his people have the bit in their mouths, and they're running with it," Connally said.

Nixon thought Kennedy had enormous "residual" appeal, but Connally was skeptical.

"Whatever you do," he told the president, "keep the door open for Democrats and Independents. If McGovern is nominated, you'll see an unprecedented defection."

"Don't worry," Nixon replied. "I learned something in 1960. The door will not only be open—I've been weaving a welcome mat." The mat had the initials JBC as its centerpiece.

Connally's reward was an eighteen-nation tour of the world as the president's personal emissary. Air Force Two was provided to underscore Connally's near-presidential stature, and since such a trip preempted both Agnew and Kissinger, old jealousies flared up again. The trip was an expensive gift. Ostensibly, Connally was briefing world leaders from Buenos Aires to Sydney on Nixon's China opening, but the real purpose was to build up Connally's stature as an international statesman, with an eye toward his assumption of the presidency in the Bicentennial year of 1976.

Speculation was rife in the press. The *Christian Science Monitor* suggested the possibilities. After his return Connally rather than Henry Kissinger would replace William Rogers as secretary of state in the second Nixon administration, since there were no more challenges for Kissinger's "Metternichian skill," or, more intriguingly, Nixon would tap Connally as his running mate for the November election and then a year or two later, the president would apply the poker rule of "get out when ahead," leaving the presidency to Connally.

As Connally took off on his grand tour, five burglars were apprehended in the Watergate office of the Democratic party leader, Lawrence O'Brien. When Connally returned to Washington over two weeks later, the Watergate cover-up was in place.

This conjunction of facts would enable Connally to argue, for years to come, that he had nothing to do with Watergate. He was out of the government and even out of the country when the attempted burglary took place. But it was more complicated than that. The break-in in itself was part of a wider master plan of political intelligence and political warfare in 1972. And John Connally had been central to its thinking and had participated in its planning. Indeed, even when he was half a world away, he was never far from Richard Nixon's mind. On June 23, 1972, the day of the conversations that were later characterized as the "smoking gun," Nixon was plotting with H. R. Haldeman about how to use national security as an excuse to block an investigation of laundered money found in the possession of the Watergate burglars, when a call came through from Charles Colson. Nixon ordered Colson to track Connally down. When Colson finally reached him in Canberra, Connally was in high spirits and he talked with Nixon by phone for half an hour. He was having a wonderful time and, given what was going on, he was glad to be "down under" rather than in Washington. He was worried about the bugging but quipped buoyantly:

"McGovern did it."

★

John Connally had departed his post at Treasury at the top of his game. The Washington press had adored him. The senior economists admired him. To Richard Nixon, he had become a right arm. After the eighteen-nation trip, he had become as close to being a head of state as is possible without actually being one, and his international stock as a tough American statesman was sound. Nixon had promised that a new assignment for him would be announced when the ex-secretary returned from abroad, and the press speculated about what might be grand and dignified enough for him now. Perhaps he would be sent to Paris to take over negotiations with the North Vietnamese, when and if those negotiations got back on track. Either secretary of state or secretary of defense in a second Nixon administration seemed a distinct possibility.

In June of 1972, John Connally stood upon an Olympian peak. At that moment of his life all things seemed possible. Six months before, Richard Nixon had told him explicitly that he was his choice to be the next president. "I believed that John Connally was the only man in either party who clearly had the potential to be a great president," Nixon would write later. "He had the necessary 'fire in the belly,' the energy to win, and the vision to lead." What the right path was to make this happen was merely a tactical question. They had discussed the vice presidency. Agnew not only lacked broad vision, but he was bridling at his lack of respect in the administration. With severe financial problems and with attractive offers coming his way from private business, Agnew would be easy enough to persuade to leave. As the Republican convention drew nearer, Nixon discussed with Haldeman the possibility of getting Agnew to step aside before the convention. This notion was also put to John Mitchell, who was now in charge of the Committee to Reelect the President (known by the acronym CREEP). Mitchell was decidedly negative. Agnew had a strong constituency among conservative Republicans, a constituency Nixon should be careful not to alienate.

With Connally still a Democrat, the move could boomerang with Nixon's staunchest partisans. Connally himself was not sure that the vice presidency was his best course and told Nixon so. Thus, the idea went aglimmering as on June 12, five days before the Watergate break-in and fifteen months before Agnew was ignominiously driven from office, Nixon asked Agnew to stay on. Had Nixon decided to tough through a Connally appointment at this moment, Connally, of course, would have succeeded to the presidency two years later.

Meanwhile, some top Democrats still harbored the faint hope that Connally would return to the fold. Robert Strauss, then the treasurer of the Democratic party, saw the outlines of a Democratic debacle in the distance. If McGovern was a disaster, the Democratic party would be in shambles. Amid the ruins, Strauss intended to run for chairman of the party, and he would have the job of putting the party back together. To Strauss, a man who believed in coalition government, Connally's service in a Republican administration had by no means tarnished his credentials in the Democratic party, and the two had remained close friends throughout Connally's Treasury stint. "I think you will be the next president of the United States as a Democrat," Strauss said pointedly to Connally as they pondered 1976, even before 1972 had played itself out. "The country is going to be ready for a Southerner or a Southwesterner."

In early August Connally's new assignment was announced. He would head a political organization called Democrats for Nixon. It was a shocking move that left many aghast. Democrats for Nixon was nothing more than a paper creation under John Mitchell's Committee to Reelect the President. Its goal was to make a virtue out of partisan disloyalty. Despite the misgivings about the Democratic challenger, Senator George McGovern, and the despair over the apparent ascendancy of the left wing of the Democratic party, this Nixon-Connally conspiracy was unforgivable, and it infuriated many Democrats who had wavered in their opinion of John Connally. Robert Strauss knew it to be a disastrous, profound mistake instantly, but of course he was not consulted. By this single act Connally demeaned himself as a statesman and read himself out of the Democratic party officially, definitely, irredeemably.

This questionable endeavor was set up in spare offices in the Madison Hotel in Washington, where, in an uncarpeted waiting room, a red, white, and blue couch was the only decent furniture. The early recruits made an odd lot. George Christian, Lyndon Johnson's and John Connally's former press aide, became the press spokesman. Leonard Marks, the director of Johnson's U.S. Information Agency, joined, as did the smooth Jake Jacobsen, who had been Johnson's confidential assistant from 1965 through 1967. Jacobsen, in fact, had been a founding member of the group and had corralled from Connally the promise to join the effort early on. Jacobsen's law office was right across the street from the Madison, so he was within Connally's easy reach, and Jacobsen's position as a lobbyist for the milk industry helped lubricate an early $25,000 contribution to Democrats for Nixon. A grab bag of celebrities came aboard: athletes Sam Huff and Mickey Mantle; entertainers Frank Sinatra, Sammy Davis, Jr., and Charlton Heston; presidential scions James and Elliott Roosevelt; industrialists like Robert Six of Continental Airlines and Henry Ford II. (Six, it turned out, had given $45,000 to Ronald Reagan's campaign in 1970, Frank Sinatra had given Reagan $25,000, and Henry Ford had contributed $16,000 to Eisenhower's campaign in 1956.) Other recruits included Frank Fitzsimmons, the president of the Teamsters; mayors Louie Welsh of Houston and Frank Rizzo of Philadelphia; and six former governors from the South besides Connally: Marvin Griffin of Georgia, Farris Bryant of Florida, Mills Godwin and William Tuck of Virginia, Allan Shivers of Texas, and the lurid segregationist John Bell Williams of Mississippi. As the columnist Clayton Frichey said of those governors at the time, they all had one thing in common: no future with the Democratic party. Richard Nixon was disappointed when he saw the list.

With $180,000 borrowed from CREEP, the Democrats for Nixon campaign began on August 16 with full-page ads in major American newspapers. They were a prototype of what is now called an "attack ad." McGovern would "hacksaw our defense budget"; the Democratic candidate supported "busing of school children as a national policy"; he would withdraw from Vietnam without getting the release of the American POWs; he believed in "tax increases and welfare schemes that are unfair and unworkable." It was not so much what was being said as who was saying it. Connally had become the instant curiosity of the 1972 campaign. Every television interview show wanted him, and sixty-second spots on defense, welfare, "confidence," and leadership featured Connally. He was a twentieth-century technological mugwump, with his mug all over the television and his wump still technically in the Democratic party. He was constantly asked if all this presaged a switch in party affiliation and a Nixon-backed Connally for President campaign in 1976. Upon the former, he conceded that a party switch was possible if the Democratic party couldn't be "rescued" from McGovern. On the latter, he disclaimed any interest in being president. If all the television exposure appealed to his vanity, his mission displayed his mean streak. The dignity and the accomplishment of his previous sixteen months were quickly swept away and forgotten in this mean-spirited sideshow. As Connally reduced himself to a Nixon hatchet man, McGovern began to say on the campaign trail that Democrats for Nixon consisted merely of "John Connally and his billionaire friends." He would add, "I don't mind being called radical by that crowd."

It did not, however, diminish him with Richard Nixon, for this was true Nixonian politics and even had the imprint of historical precedent. Nixon liked to think of Connally's effort as akin to Democrats for Eisenhower in 1952 (of which Connally was also one). Connally was totally casting his fate with Nixon's. If Connally were to succeed Nixon, it would take a popular second Nixon term to pull it off. A party switch this late in a political career would be viewed skeptically. Lifelong Republicans were sure to be profoundly suspicious, but a popular, outgoing president might be able to overcome the antagonism. In 1972, on the field of the main chance, that did not seem to Connally to be a bad bet.

Moreover, Nixon relished the thought of clandestine recruitment among the opposition. This was juicy political espionage. Just after the Democrats nominated McGovern and several weeks before the official announcement of Democrats for Nixon, the president wrote Connally several "eyes only" memoranda about the president's own efforts to attract big names from the opposition. He had been talking to ex-Senator George Smathers of Florida, and Smathers was prepared to defect—but only after his son, Bruce, won the Democratic nomination for a seat in the Florida legislature. Smathers had told the president that Senators Warren Magnuson of Washington, Russell Long of Louisiana, Robert Byrd and Jennings Randolph of West Virginia, Herman Talmadge of Georgia, and Joseph Montoya of New Mexico were all unhappy with the McGovern nomination and were looking for a way to avoid endorsing the Democratic candidate. Wrote Nixon, "I told him [Smathers] that our desire was to get, if possible, endorsements from leading Democrats in the House and Senate, but, lacking that, if we could get neutrality with them, taking the position that they would concentrate their efforts on the House and Senate races and would stay neutral with regard to the presidential race—this would be very helpful."

Nixon's dalliance in espionage did not stop at mere senators. On July 24 he had called Lyndon Johnson at the LBJ Ranch. Before the Johnson call, Connally had told Nixon how upset President Johnson was about his ill treatment at the Democratic convention in Miami, where Johnson had been snubbed, ignored, and otherwise mistreated as a nonpresident and a nonperson. This had hurt the prickly Johnson, for he remembered well, in his tally-sheet view of political life, how many favors he had dispensed to McGovern over the years. The Johnson daughters, Lynda Bird and Luci, were particularly livid, as were their husbands (one of whom was Chuck Robb, the future governor and senator from Virginia), and the girls were threatening to oppose McGovern publicly. Within his own family, Johnson was having to conciliate and console his own offspring. Outraged wires and letters poured into the ranch from Johnson loyalists and Johnson responded with a bland form letter about how good the Democratic party had been to him for forty years, and how he would support Democrats at all levels this year, but a vote was a matter of conscience and he would not presume to criticize any Democrat who decided to vote for the Republican candidate this year. During their telephone call, "He [Johnson] went on to say that he had agreed with most of the positions I had taken during my tenure in office," Nixon wrote to Connally, "and that he found himself in sharp disagreement with the nominee of his party. He said that he did not want to do anything that would make my job harder and would therefore not discourage any of his friends who wanted to join you in the Democrats for Nixon organization. He said, as a matter of fact, he had a very difficult problem with his own family, particularly his two daughters and sons-in-law, all of whom had expressed a desire to oppose McGovern. Naturally, he said that he felt that he had to keep them from doing that because it would be broadly misinterpreted."

Several days after this July 24 memo, Connally visited LBJ at the ranch and personally explained his involvement in Democrats for Nixon. "I'm a free man," Connally told Johnson. "I do what I have to do."

With Democrats for Nixon, Connally and Nixon went further than simple efforts to recruit defectors from the Democratic enemy. They used classic methods of espionage in other areas of the political war. Their goal was more than political victory; it was nothing short of the annihilation of the opposition. Together they set out to penetrate the enemy high command. As the Watergate Committee and the House Impeachment Committee would later reveal, there was a master plan of political intelligence whose central target was Lawrence O'Brien. As chairman of the Democratic party, O'Brien was considered the greatest threat to Nixon's reelection, for as the weak-kneed Watergate figure Jeb Stuart Magruder was to say, "We had hoped that information might discredit [O'Brien]." John Ehrlichman said it more pointedly. The Republicans had hoped to send O'Brien to jail before the election. It was the search for disparaging information that led to the break-in at O'Brien's office on May 28, 1972, and the more historic reentry on June 17, when the burglars were caught.

The failure of the burglaries did not deter the Nixon crowd, however. There was a parallel and, in some ways, more insidious campaign under way against O'Brien, one to which Connally is linked incontrovertibly. John Ehrlichman had learned that an IRS investigation of Howard Hughes had turned up a connection between Hughes and O'Brien, and its report indicated that O'Brien may have derived substantial unreported income from his Hughes dealings. Ehrlichman exhibited intense interest in this connection, and because of his pressure, which was conveyed through the White House man at IRS, Roger Barth, and support from the then secretary of the treasury, George Shultz, an IRS interview of O'Brien was conducted in August 1972. Connally was directly a party to the IRS harassment of O'Brien. He urged Nixon to have the IRS put the heat on O'Brien immediately for its potential practical benefit, and this is confirmed by an August 9, 1972, memo from Nixon to Haldeman.

The important factor is urgency. Connally strongly urged that in addition to following through on the $150,000 that was paid to O'Brien and Associates . . . we should follow through on [O'Brien's 1968] returns. . . . O'Brien at that time, of course, was making a great deal out of the fact that he was an unpaid National Chairman. Connally believes that following up there may bring us some pay dirt. The point here is that Connally's very strong conviction is that dropping something on O'Brien will have far more effect now than at a later time and will keep all of our Democratic opponents a little loose. The longer we let it go, the more possibility the charge will be made that it was a last minute smear. I consider it of the highest priority—to ride the IRS on this matter. . . . What is most important is that the IRS audit of O'Brien begins . . . tomorrow. This means that today, the call must be made by the IRS to O'Brien, so that the stage can be set for a subpoena in the event that O'Brien does not show up voluntarily. Don't let him delay.

Then, with Connally as the promoter and Nixon as the initiator, the IRS engaged in patently political harassment by advancing a full-blown audit of O'Brien well before the election and continuing it long after it was clear that O'Brien was absolutely innocent. This misuse of the IRS was to become a central count in the second article of impeachment against Richard Nixon two years later. But Connally's role as an accessory to the abuse of power did not come out.

In the coming month Connally's name had a way of popping up during cover-up sessions between Nixon, Haldeman, and John Dean. In the White House conversation of September 15, the three were trying to think of instances where the Democrats had "bugged" the Republicans, as if they could deflect the entire Watergate investigation by merely showing the public that in American politics "everybody bugs everybody else." Their minds turned naturally to LBJ, and Nixon proclaimed indignantly that Johnson had used the FBI to wiretap his very own campaign plane in the last two weeks of the 1968 presidential campaign. "Goddamnedest thing you ever saw," said Nixon. Why shouldn't they leak that to the press?

"The difficulty with using it is that it reflects on Johnson," Nixon said sullenly, answering his own question.

"Right," Dean answered.

"He ordered it. If it weren't for that, I'd use it," said the president. He was thinking out loud now. "Is there any way we can use it without reflecting on Johnson? Could we say that the Democratic National Committee did it? No, the FBI did the bugging, though."

"That's the problem," said Haldeman.

"Is it going to reflect on Johnson or Humphrey?" Dean asked naively.

"Johnson. Humphrey didn't do it," Haldeman said.

"Humphrey didn't do it?" Dean repeated.

"Oh, hell, no," Nixon said.

"He was bugging Humphrey too!" Haldeman said, and laughed.

"Oh, goddamn," said Nixon.

Haldeman laughed louder at the absurdity. "I'll tell you who to call. I want you to ask John Connally. Whatever he thinks—maybe we ought to just let that one fly." Haldeman scrawled a note to himself.

Later in the scheming, Dean turned the conversation to an immediate palpable threat both to the cover-up and possibly even to the president's reelection campaign. That scourge of the bankers and inveterate populist Wright Patman of Texarkana, who was the chairman of the House Banking and Currency Committee, was making noises about using his committee to investigate the fact that $3,200 in new, consecutively numbered bills, found in the possession of the Watergate burglars when they were apprehended, had been traced through a Florida bank to a Minnesota donor and that the money had been illegally laundered through Mexico. If Patman got his sanction to conduct a full-fledged investigation before the election, to issue subpoenas and call witnesses, there was no telling what might come out. That threat truly could open a "can of worms," as Dean said. "Whether we will be successful in turning that off or not, I don't know," John Dean said, but he had a plan. Such a congressional investigation would jeopardize the civil rights of the Watergate burglars in their forthcoming trial, and the political forces should be mustered to make that case to the appropriate congressmen. "One suggestion was that Connally is close to Patman. If anybody can talk turkey to Patman, Connally might be able to." After all, Patman had served in the Texas state legislature with Lyndon Johnson's father. Nixon was skeptical. "Connally can't be sent up there," said the president protectively. But Nixon thought it wasn't a bad thing to run the matter by Connally. He might have some ideas. So, with Haldeman's and Nixon's approval, Dean called Connally. In his book *Blind Ambition,* Dean reconstructed the conversation after he observed that, of all the presidential cabinet members he had run background checks on before they were appointed, only Connally had "dodged" his standard conflict of interest clearance.

> "Governor, this is John Dean, over at the White House."
> "Oh, yeah, John," Connally replied warmly. "What can I do for you?"
> "Well, I was talking to Bob Haldeman, and he suggested I might call you about these Patman hearings. We need to find something to help us reason with the congressman from Texas about how these hearings are not a good idea, here before the election."
> "Well, yes," Connally replied. "I believe I can think of something. I understand from the grapevine down in Texas that Patman might have a couple of weak spots, and one of them is he might have some campaign contributions he would not want exposed. Now, I believe I heard the congressman received some contributions from an oil lobbyist up here. I don't believe Mr. Patman has reported them either."

"That's interesting," Dean said. "Do you have any idea how we might establish that for the record?"

"No, John, I don't believe I can help you there. Why don't you just check into that and see what you come up with?"

"I will, Governor. Thank you."

Fortunately for Nixon—and for Connally—Patman's committee voted twenty to fifteen on October 3 against giving Patman his subpoena power before the election, and the Nixon operation took heart that they would be able to sidetrack, or at least emasculate, congressional investigations of the entire Watergate affair.

The peak of the Democrats for Nixon effort came on October 20, two weeks before the election, when Connally gave a half-hour address on national television. He had an ethereal look to him that night. The powder blue of his suit against his pancaked face and his silver hair made him look like one of those ideological actors who roll out of Hollywood every four years to declaim someone else's white-hot message. The set was a library with a simple imitation Colonial desk, oak panels, books in perfect order, and a large globe to which Connally strode occasionally to impart interest and diversion from his severe talking head. He heralded the splendid achievements of Richard Nixon, "the youngest elder statesman of our era"—the China opening, the Moscow summit, the troop withdrawals from Vietnam—before he settled into the memorable thread of his speech. John Kennedy was invoked: "Sometimes party loyalty asks too much," and Franklin Roosevelt, Harry Truman, and Lyndon Johnson followed. The achievements of these four Democratic presidents and one Republican, Dwight Eisenhower, had laid the groundwork for the accomplishments of Richard Nixon. Nixon was the culmination, the realization, the fulfillment of Democratic party dreams.

It was the first major attempt by the Republican party to appropriate the heroes of the Democrats, and the art of it would be much advanced later under Ronald Reagan. But it started here with Connally. Predictably, it infuriated the real Democrats who were sure of their philosophical moorings, as it shook and tantalized those who were Democrats in name only. As a sheer effort of polarization, it was a masterpiece. "President Nixon has kept us on that wise course," Connally said. "George McGovern has demonstrated that he will not."

★

Three months later, on a cold, rainy January day, they brought Lyndon Johnson home for the last time to be laid to rest on the banks of the Pedernales. Rev. Billy Graham officiated. In his wonderful, heavy German accent, the Catholic priest from down the road, old Father Wunibald Schneider, spoke of this "forthright man . . . this stalwart president . . . who had the patriotism of George Washington." Anita Bryant belted out "The Battle Hymn of the Republic," including the line about his "terrible swift sword." As the mourners shivered, Connally stepped forward to deliver his eulogy. His mentor, his friend, his benefactor was dead. Johnson had done more for him than any other man, and he, in turn, had done more for Johnson than any other, and the two would, for better or worse, always be coupled. In the mist against the tawny hues of the bleak landscape, Connally's silver-toned voice washed over the assemblage. He spoke his lines gracefully, with the precision of one trained in declamation and diligent in rehearsal, as if all that stage training and hard work had been preparation for this moment. In the exactness of his diction, in the lilt of his elegant phrases, in the correctness of his pacing, in the handsomeness of his face, he displayed his difference from Johnson. Johnson spoke plainly all his life, Connally said. "The wellspring of his thought and words and deeds was always the fundamental character of the plain people he loved, and whose dreams and aspirations he tried so hard to bring to reality." If that was his difference from Johnson, Connally also spoke of Johnson's roots which were also his own. Here was their common ground; this was the glue that held them together over a lifetime of anger and argument and love. Connally spoke of the Hill Country, but his thoughts applied equally to the loamy ground of Floresville. "The Hill Country of 1908 was not much different from the frontier his father and mother had known. The comforts and amenities were few. The educational opportunities were determined by the quality of a gentle teacher or handful of teachers, and man's fortunes were dictated by the amount of rain or the heat of the sun or the coldness of the north wind. Yet a child's dreams could be as wide as the sky and his future as green as winter oats, because this, after all, was America."

At the end, Connally addressed the tragedy of Lyndon Johnson. It had begun with a tragedy in Dallas in which he had been a player, and by which his own life had been profoundly affected. But it was the possibility that grew out of tragedy that he defined. "It is fashionable to refer to Lyndon Johnson as a tragic president," he said. "But I believe history will describe his presidency as tragic only in the sense that it began through tragedy. . . ." That oblique reference to Dallas was sufficient. It had made Lyndon Johnson president, and assured that John Connally never would be president. If Connally had escaped Kennedy's hideous fate, Lyndon Johnson's fate would escape him as well. It was Connally's good fortune to be only wounded in Dallas; it was his bad fortune that in Lyndon Johnson the country derived a distinct, if partly unfair, image of what a Texan president would be.

★

Three months after Lyndon Johnson died—and a few hours after he informed a sad but understanding Lady Bird—Connally switched his allegiance officially to the Republican party. It was, he told a Houston press conference, his true philosophical home. The Republicans best expressed the broad views of most Americans, whatever their official party affiliation. The move had been expected for months, even by Lady Bird, who thanked him now for waiting a decent interval after Lyndon Johnson's death. There had been other reasons for delay. Connally was waiting for Nixon to get on top of Watergate. He might have hoped that the president's widening problems would simply wither away, but the clock had caught up to him. If he were to have a chance at the Republican nomination in 1976, he had to begin to pay his dues to his new party, and as Watergate problems grew more confounding, at least Connally could not be charged this time with opportunism unless he was betting that Nixon, emerging unscathed, would remember who had rallied to his side when things looked very bad. The jokes which greeted the Connally switch bespoke the high risk of it. Frank Mankiewicz, the wry Washington politico who had been McGovern's campaign director in 1972, wagged his wicked tongue at Connally. "Connally's switch raises the intelligence level of *both* parties," he said. Elsewhere, the gag circulated that this was the only known instance in recorded history of a rat swimming *toward* a sinking ship. In Texas the irrepressible Liz Carpenter told a Democratic fund-raiser, "It's a good thing John Connally wasn't at the Alamo. He'd be organizing Texans for Santa Anna now." At another point, the joke would be turned around: "If there had been a back door at the Alamo and John Connally had been there, he would have run for governor of Mexico." Among Republicans, pleasure at the conversion ran along predictable lines. But no one was ready, just yet, to concede the 1976 Republican nomination to the newcomer. "There are other people who have been struggling in the vineyards of the Republican party for a long time," said Spiro Agnew. "They may have some desire for the nomination themselves." With mounting financial problems of his own and the knowledge that he had become the target of a Baltimore grand jury on a charge of fraud and corruption, Agnew did not mention himself.

A few days after his party switch, Connally agreed to return to Washington as a part-time counselor to President Nixon. His duties were left undefined, for Nixon wanted Connally's specific role to emerge as events unfolded. The Ervin Committee hearings on Watergate were set to begin in ten days. This time, Nixon would need far more than salesmanship. The Ervin Committee represented a titanic clash between the legislative and the executive branches of government. Yet, for titanic clashes, no one surpassed John Connally in experience. It was May of 1973. The taping system in the Oval Office had not been revealed—and Connally could reasonably believe that Nixon was being unfairly savaged in the press and had considerable powers of survival still to employ. It was a matter of mobilizing the full power of the presidency for the political war that was coming. As early as March 1973, Connally had urged a wavering and ambivalent Nixon to make someone "walk the plank." First, he began to push for the removal of Haldeman and Ehrlichman, and later for the firing of Ronald Ziegler. The Nixon staff was bloated and tainted. The president had too many compromised underlings, and they were compromising him.

As the summer of 1973 proceeded, however, the damaging evidence accumulated and Connally began to retreat rather than to step forward. On his visits to Washington, he secluded himself in a suite at the Mayflower Hotel and almost never showed up at the White House office that had been assigned him. Then came Alexander Butterfield's revelation on July 16 of the White House taping system. It was at this point that Connally indelibly associated himself with the Watergate stonewall. When Butterfield made his devastating revelation, Nixon was indisposed, ill with viral pneumonia that had been brought on by exhaustion, and committed to a bed at the Bethesda Naval Hospital. Connally tried urgently to get through to Nixon. When at first he had difficulty, he reached the defrocked H. R. Haldeman in California instead. "Please, Bob, use your influence to convince the president to burn those tapes," Connally said. "Tell him to do it right. Have Ziegler assemble the White House press corps in the Rose Garden, pile up all the tapes, set a match to them, and let them film the bonfire. Say they must be destroyed now that their existence has been made public." (Haldeman was to learn later that Connally did succeed in reaching Nixon directly with his advice.) Connally never attempted to hide the stance he took in this matter. Indeed, he seemed to revel in it, for it underscored his "toughness," and he often bragged about it openly from lecture platforms in the months and years to come. He did not, however, define his real motivation for wanting so desperately for Nixon to destroy the tapes. Like Rockefeller and Kissinger and Patrick Buchanan, who also urged destruction, Connally knew full well that he was personally recorded all through the tape archive in compromising ways that he did not *ever* want to be made public.

As a practical matter, if Nixon were inclined to follow Connally's advice, he had, realistically, two days in which to do it. Senator Howard Baker of the Watergate Committee had signaled to the White House on the Saturday before Butterfield's public revelation on Monday that the tape system was known to the committee. Upon Butterfield's public testimony, Senator Sam Ervin wrote immediately to Nixon asking for committee access to relevant tapes. At Nixon's bedside at Bethesda Naval Hospital, the debate with the exhausted and ailing president went on interminably. Alexander Haig flip-flopped, arguing for and then against destruction as the winds of the discussion shifted. At one point, Nixon wondered if all the tapes couldn't just be stored under his White House bed, until he was informed that, so many tapes were there, he would have to sleep eleven feet above the floor. Leonard Garment, one of Nixon's Watergate lawyers, argued forcefully against destruction. To him, the whole notion was absurd. For one thing, the sheer magnitude of the tape archive made the physical logistics of destruction complicated. Where would it be done? Who would carry the boxes? And, most important, who would throw the match? Those who played any part in the destruction of evidence, except Richard Nixon himself, who was above *that* law, would instantly become conspirators in a major crime. As to Nixon's own situation, destruction would certainly generate a serious impeachment effort by responsible parties in Congress, even though a formal request for the tapes from Congress or the special prosecutor had not yet been sent. In short, Connally's advice to destroy, selfishly motivated as it was, was absurd logistically, criminal to its perpetrators, mortally wounding to the Nixon presidency.

On July 18, the special prosecutor, Archibald Cox, officially requested nine presidential conversations. Cox stopped short of an official subpoena on the president in this first "request," so as to give the president an opportunity for voluntary compliance. With each passing hour, however, the special prosecutor's office grew increasingly more anxious that the very thing Connally was proposing might happen. Consequently, two days after his initial request, Cox followed with a second letter to the White House, urging that the tape *evidence* be kept intact and that access to it be limited and carefully controlled. Cox's second letter put the White House on notice. On the day of this second letter, Nixon was released from the hospital. If there was a moment for Connally's bonfire, this was it. Cox's "request" did not as yet have the full force of the law, and Cox himself was technically, arguably, a member of the administration. The request could still be rejected under the rubric of executive privilege and national security at less political and legal cost than it could be later. Generated as they had been by the president as his private, confidential work product, the tapes themselves could be destroyed upon the argument, as John Connally's own lawyer, Edward Bennett Williams, was later to express it, that "Nixon had no obligation to make or keep the tapes and could have argued that his motive in destroying them was to prevent secret exchanges with other heads of government from being compromised." To Connally, Nixon had to have the "guts" to do it now. But Nixon delayed, and Connally chafed. If he was not going to be listened to and if his advice was not heeded, why did he hold this post as presidential counselor? Connally wondered.

On July 25, the White House counsel replied to Cox's second letter that the special prosecutor should not worry: the tapes were under Nixon's "sole personal control" in "secure condition" with access "carefully documented." The following day the president informed the special prosecutor of his refusal to turn over the tapes either to the special prosecutor or to the Ervin Committee. The president was prepared to fight it out legally. The same day the special prosecutor responded with an official subpoena. Now, the legal and political cost of destroying the tapes multiplied exponentially. Once the tapes were under official subpoena, their destruction was a clear obstruction of justice. It would flout the president's oath to see that the "laws were faithfully executed." To do otherwise would be a high crime or misdemeanor, and impeachment resolutions in the Congress were sure to follow.

On the day that the president decided upon a formal legal battle, John Connally resigned his post as a counselor to the president. He had held the position for only sixty-nine days. What Connally understood intuitively, if not consciously, was that the coming investigation would challenge at its very root the political ethos in which he had flourished for thirty-four years. With the Ervin hearings and the special prosecutor's office, the net was going to be cast wide rather than narrow. Watergate would, soon enough, come to stand for far more than a criminal break-in and its cover-up. Connally might help President Nixon to frustrate investigations into the break-in and the cover-up for a while, but the danger to Connally personally was in the Watergate-related matters: investigations into campaign financing, especially the loose practices of the milk lobby and the influence peddling of the ITT Corporation, into misuse of the IRS, and even into White House political dirty tricks. Before the Ervin Committee lay a miasma of broad political corruption and abuse of power. As the summer of 1973 proceeded, it was most definitely not in Connally's personal interest to be a visible Nixon man, taunting and daring the investigators. So he receded into the Texas landscape.

One last triumph awaited Connally before darkness descended.

Through September 1973, as the Ervin Committee hearings paused to shift gears to "Watergate-related matters," and the focus turned to the legal activities of the special prosecutor, a quiet drama was being played out in Baltimore. There, the U.S. attorney was concluding a major investigation and moving closer to a criminal indictment of the vice president of the United States. The case against Spiro Agnew, a politician who had presented himself to the American people as the paragon of clean politics, was a simple one of graft and personal corruption. Since 1962, when he was the county executive of Baltimore County, Agnew had been receiving kickbacks in the form of cash payments from state contractors. The most shocking of many damaging charges against him was that he had accepted the round sum of $10,000 in the basement of the White House itself. There was something magical about the figure, it seemed. Two months later, the first report of a political kickback in exactly the same amount to John Connally would surface.

On October 10, Spiro Agnew resigned. At long last, President Nixon had his opportunity to choose John Connally as his vice president and as his heir apparent, and to fulfill the long-delayed desires of them both.

Connally holed up in the Mayflower Hotel, relaxed and cool, preparing for power. At his side was his aide, Mickey Gardner, who had handled Connally's Washington affairs since the spring of 1972, and who now set out to organize a smooth transition. At Connally's bidding, Gardner made calls to several individuals whom Connally wanted on his vice presidential staff. Among those contacted was Sam Hoskinson, who had been the national security officer in charge of Connally's eighteen-nation tour a year before. "Are you prepared to join the staff of the new vice president?" Gardner asked Hoskinson significantly. On October 10, Connally as the new vice president was a done deal. Word was passed to Congress.

On October 11 a firestorm of opposition against Connally burst into flame and spread quickly. It erupted in every important segment among the Democrats and the Republicans, in the press, and even within the White House itself. The intensity of its heat showed what Connally had become on the American political scene. He was an incendiary. Flames broke out as if from spontaneous combustion. Among congressional Democrats the fire raged uncontrolled. They were determined to kill the nomination of this defector, whatever the cost. Senator Daniel Inouye sent a message to Nixon through the president's congressional liaison, Bryce Harlow, that "it would be a major error to recommend John Connally—not because he is unqualified, but because many of his colleagues on the Democratic side would be determined to destroy Connally and would engage in indeterminable harm [to] his personal interests." In short, the Democrats stood ready to go beyond destroying the Connally nomination, to destroying Connally himself. Senate Democrats caucused and discussed widening the legislative rules for considering presidential appointments, so that they could look into every conceivable business or legal deal of the nominee. At best, the rules change was intended to protract the confirmation of Connally indefinitely. Connally's friend Russell Long of Louisiana tried to control his rampaging Democratic colleagues and found them turning on him. Long wrote Nixon about this a few days later: "It was clear to me that the purpose was to drag the confirmation process out indefinitely, and to see if something bad could not be found against Mr. Connally. When I opposed efforts to unite the Democrats against your nomination, I recognized that Common Cause, the ADA, and other liberal-oriented organizations would be urging that I be replaced as Chairman of the Finance Committee . . . because I would not bow to the will of the majority of the Democratic Caucus." Senator James Buckley, the conservative Republican from New York, warned that there were rampaging Republicans as well as Democrats. "There will be a disposition to probe maliciously and extensively into the special interest affiliation of John Connally," Buckley told the White House. "This would be disastrous if the process were pursued for a long time." Skepticism was great that Connally's record could withstand close scrutiny. The terms "skeletons and scars" were widely invoked. He was too political, too divisive, too partisan (one way or another), too difficult to confirm, too easy for Democrats "in good conscience" to vote against. With his skeletons and scars, he would provide the Democrats with the chance for another "big show."

Even within the White House itself there were grave doubts about the wisdom of a Connally nomination. There, the imagery changed from fire to blood. Blood was already in the water. Nixon had been badly wounded by the Ervin Committee hearings, and the special prosecutor's office was nearing indictments of parties beyond the Watergate burglars. Nixon was being warned that if he defied a Supreme Court order on the tapes, impeachment resolutions would flow from *responsible* quarters. A Connally nomination would put more blood into the water when the Congress was already falling into a feeding frenzy. On October 11, Nixon's speechwriter, the gentle and thoughtful Ray Price, wrote a five-page memo to the president. "Quite obviously, the choice you make this time will be critical to the Administration's prospects for recovery from Watergate," Price wrote. He set before the president two criteria of particular importance in the current atmosphere. The nomination should be a unifying and a healing event, and the nominee's confirmation had to be assured. The administration simply could not afford another defeat. On these two grounds, Connally would be a disaster, Price wrote. He was bitterly divisive among the Republicans, and his nomination would be an open invitation to the Democrats "to play the crassest sort of politics and, by so doing, cripple if not topple the Presidency. . . . They'd comb every inch of his past, and I can't believe that in thirty years of acquiring millions while in Texas politics as a protégé of Lyndon Johnson, there isn't something that could be unearthed and that would be unearthed in the Watergate climate and that would provide a pretext for every member of the House or Senate who wanted to vote No on political grounds— to vote No on ethical grounds."

One major figure of Congress disagreed, standing stolidly against this antagonism toward Connally. That was Gerald Ford. He put Connally forward as his first choice. To Ford, Connally was clearly the best qualified for the job.

Nixon and Connally had talked for a year and a half about being a team. They had mused together about a total realignment of party politics, creating a reconstituted Whig party in America, which would include everyone on the political spectrum except the liberal Democrats, and in which Connally and Nixon would become the modern-day equivalents of Henry Clay and Daniel Webster. Now, regretfully, Richard Nixon concluded that his fondest dream was not possible. Instead of calling Connally directly with the bad news, for Nixon never liked to confront anyone personally with disappointment, the president had Alexander Haig do it.

Good news was different. When Gerald Ford was called in, his good news was qualified. "I want to make one thing clear," Nixon told Ford. "I'm supporting John Connally for the nomination in 1976." That was fine with Ford. He would accept the role of caretaker president gladly, for he had already made plans to retire from public life.

At the news of Gerald Ford's nomination, disappointment in Texas was profound. Connally was the big loser, a man whose bright future had suddenly turned—at best—uncertain. "If he does have further political aspirations, he must chart a new course," wrote Robert Baskin, the senior political analyst of the *Dallas Morning News*, "and the difficulties in finding that course are all too apparent."

Ahead on the new course was a criminal prosecution for corruption.

21

The Accuser

JAKE JACOBSEN, WAS, BY NATURE, a fastidious man. Clothes had interested him from his youth when, as Manny (short for Emanuel) Jacobson, he grew up on the boardwalk of Atlantic City as the son of a hard-pressed Jewish apartment super and a Catholic mother. Later, when John Connally or Lyndon Johnson would seek his advice about their dress or how to impress certain audiences, Jake would recommend Louis Roth suits, for he had a rackful himself and thought they imparted a dignified, sculptured look to powerful men. He was always immaculately groomed himself, never a hair out of place, never a spot of dirt beneath his buffed nails. Jacobsen, like Connally, considered himself to be a handsome man, and he was. There was something vaguely Oriental in his face. Perhaps it was the pointed quality of his thick black eyebrows, which rose to inverted Vs above his large doe eyes, or the intense blackness of them against the white of his hair, suggesting the careful preparations of a Kabuki dancer.

A soldier in the Army Air Force during World War II, he had come to Texas for navigation school in San Marcos, the town where Lyndon Johnson went to college, and there he met his future wife, Florene. She was a small-town Catholic girl from Nacogdoches in East Texas, lovely and flighty, exuding that sweet and sometimes empty-headed vulnerability that Yankees often associate with a peculiar flower known as the Southern belle. After he finished a military tour in China during the war, where he flew "over the hump" and collected enough missions to be awarded the Distinguished Flying Cross, they were married and he entered the University of Texas Law School, determined as a Yankee and as a half Jew–half Catholic to make it in the bedrock of hard, conservative, segregationist Texas.

Jacobsen did well at UT. He graduated tenth in his class, and was invited onto the Texas Supreme Court for a year as a briefing clerk. A year later he was hired by the then state attorney general, Price Daniel. In the attorney general's office Jacobsen was considered bright and attractive, a quick study who was eager to take on big challenges. He was thrown in with other young comers, particularly Joe Greenhill, who was several years older than Jacobsen, and who years later became the chief justice of the Texas Supreme Court. As he arrived in the attorney general's office, the epic battle over Lyndon Johnson's "victory" in the 1948 election was under way, but Daniel was friendly with both Coke Stevenson and Johnson and was determined to keep his office out of the fray. With Greenhill, young Jacobsen went to work on *Sweatt v. Painter,* a temporary landmark on the road to equal rights, supplanted five years later by *Brown v. Board of Education.* Heman Sweatt was a black who had applied to the University of Texas Law School during Jacobsen's first year as a student there. Denied entry solely because of his color, he was told to apply to a law school for Negroes which was to be established the next year, but which would have no permanent faculty, no library, and no accreditation. Sweatt brought suit against the law school, charging that he was being denied the equal protection of the Fourteenth Amendment, challenging the "separate but equal" doctrine of *Plessy v. Ferguson,* and demanding to be admitted.

The attorney general's office represented the law school and Jacobsen was required to defend with all his skill a continuation of Southern segregation and the concept of "separate but equal." It was the first of a number of personal compromises that would later become codified into a philosophy of public service, which submerged personal belief and scruples beneath loyalty and expediency. Jacobsen was a genuine liberal and was personally offended by the conservatism and racism of the Texas establishment, but he stood ready to support segregation with all his energy if that was his boss's position. With Greenhill, Jacobsen won a string of victories in the lower courts over Sweatt's attorney, Thurgood Marshall, and Sweatt's supporters like the CIO, which was represented by Arthur J. Goldberg and the American Jewish Congress. The U.S. Supreme Court agreed to hear the case, and Jacobsen traveled to Washington to argue it, a heady experience for a young lawyer in his late twenties. In Washington, Jacobsen and the state of Texas lost, as the Supreme Court reversed the decision of the lower courts. In his decision, Chief Justice Fred Vinson spoke of the greatness of the UT Law School and its contrast to the Negro school, and wrote, "It is difficult to believe that one who had a free choice between these law schools could consider the question close." But the court decided narrowly, simply demanding that Sweatt be admitted to UT and refusing to address the broader question of the validity of the "separate but equal" doctrine.

On that trip north to the Supreme Court, Jacobsen continued home to New Jersey, where he was confronted by his elder brother, Howard. Howard was horrified that Jake had taken up against liberals and labor, Jews and blacks. Jake's defense was:

"Howard, I've got to do what I've got to do to make a living. I live in Texas now, not New Jersey."

The reality of living in Texas soon reasserted itself for Jake Jacobsen. Daniel ran for the U.S. Senate in 1952 and won, but Jacobsen was ready to strike out on his own. Like Connally, who now had joined Sid Richardson in Fort Worth for the same reason, Jake was ready to make some money. His intelligence, his immaculate presence, and his experience in state government suggested that he should move easily into one of the well-established Austin law firms. As he made the rounds, however, he was turned away. In due course he concluded that his Jewish heritage was the problem. Greenhill suggested, naively to be sure, that if Jacobsen changed the spelling of his name, that might help. He had been christened Jacobson, so he changed the *o* to an *e* as if to suggest he was of Scandinavian rather than Jewish descent. Of course, this changed nothing, and Jake reluctantly gave up the quest and joined Price Daniel's senatorial staff in Washington. His experience of rejection in Austin instilled in Jacobsen competing impulses. He was embittered against the Texas establishment (of which John Connally was to become the epitome), just as he admired many of its stalwart members. He longed to be in the club that had rejected him.

In Washington, Jacobsen worked with Horace Busby, whom Daniel had brought to Washington as his administrative assistant. But Busby grew more and more fatigued with the frenetic life of a Capitol Hill assistant and had increasing difficulty in showing up at the office. As a result, Jacobsen took over as Daniel's chief aide and began to acquire a reputation as a man of influence. His opposite number in Johnson's office was Walter Jenkins. Jacobsen was a man of exact detail, but also of consummate discretion. His preference was always to recede into the background, into the wings and shadows. Uncomfortable with the press, he avoided reporters assiduously and almost always directed their inquiries elsewhere.

Price Daniel adored Jacobsen. Jacobsen was one person who had the patience to wait as Daniel mumbled and tried tortuously to formulate a thought. "Daniel used to say that a lot of people lost a good thought he had because they interrupted him," Jacobsen said later. "Most people couldn't sit there and wait for him to get finished. Hell, it'd make you so nervous, you'd die. But I'm a patient man. I could listen." Daniel was also dependent on Jacobsen because he could make decisions. In 1956 Daniel moved from the Senate to the Texas governorship, and Jacobsen moved with him. In the governor's mansion, Daniel's inability to grapple with hard choices forced Jacobsen to be more assertive. "Daniel was the most indecisive man I have ever known," Jacobsen recalled. "If an issue came up, and he thought that by leaving it on his desk it would solve itself, it stayed on his desk. He wouldn't make a decision to save his life. He wouldn't delegate anything either. He wouldn't tell me to do something. Problems would just sit there. It was going to drive me crazy, so gradually, when something came up, I'd make a decision. He never said not to. He knew I was doing it. Finally, I was doing most everything that needed doing in the governor's office. I was actively the governor."

As de facto governor, Jacobsen made several personal decisions that would come back to haunt him in his titanic struggle for survival with John Connally years later. One of these was the appointment of a press secretary for the governor. Since Jake was inept with the press himself, he searched for a gubernatorial press spokesman who would be suited to Daniel's halting, phlegmatic nature. Jacobsen found the answer in George Christian, an unassertive, jovial wire service reporter from Austin.

Connally and Jacobsen had met for the first time when Jacobsen worked in the attorney general's office, but their acquaintance grew more important to both when Jake was the point man for Daniel in both the U.S. Senate and the governor's office. As required of any Texas governor, Daniel was a relentless booster for Texas oil interests. When a powerful independent oilman like Sid Richardson wanted something done, Connally went to see Jacobsen. Jacobsen's most vivid memory of this early relationship, however, was Daniel's inauguration as governor, to which Connally came with a charismatic evangelist named Billy Graham. To Jacobsen, Connally and

Rev. Billy Graham were cut from the same cloth. Both were tall, handsome, and dynamic, and it was clear that they got along well. Even then, Jacobsen saw a touch of the hypocrite in Connally's half of that friendship. It was not based upon religious devotion, as Graham might have supposed, but upon Sid Richardson's interest in Graham. John Connally was meant to be the perfect reflection of his boss's interests.

"John's role in those days was to keep the fences mended for Sid Richardson with all state officials; I was one of them," Jacobsen was to say. "I was a comer, a bright young fellow with a career ahead of him. John knew who I was and wanted and needed to know me, and, of course, I wanted to know him too. He was Price's friend, so I made myself available. I let him know I wanted to be helpful wherever I could be. John is a very personable man. He made friends with me." Jacobsen spoke of this friendship hesitantly, as a former groupie might speak of a fading rock star. He could talk in significant tones of how the men had mutual respect for one another for being good at what they did, but the two never had dinner together, never socialized, much less partied together, and they had different inclinations as private men.

Their careers intersected frequently over twenty-five years, however. Jacobsen was the secretary of the Democratic party convention where Johnson and Connally wrested control of the party from the Shivers forces in 1956. In 1960 he was in Los Angeles when Connally drew attention to John Kennedy's Addison's disease, and Johnson was nominated vice president. In 1962 Connally ran for governor, and Jacobsen managed Daniel's faltering campaign against him. After Connally won the primary he called on Jacobsen.

"Jake, will you help me in the general election?" Connally asked.

"Well, I didn't help much in the primary," Jacobsen replied dryly.

"No. I sent several people to see you, and you ran them off," Connally said. "You are a loyal Daniel man, and you stayed a Daniel man. And I respect you for that. . . ."

"Price made me what I am, John. I was nothing, and he brought me along."

"I know, Jake. Listen, if he doesn't mind, I'd like you to give me some guidance. You know state government. You know where the bodies are buried. . . ."

Jacobsen was flattered, and after checking with Daniel he readily agreed. But if Connally had asked him into the club Jacobsen still remained in the outer circle. Connally's closest advisers kept their distance, considering Jacobsen a Johnny-come-lately and not really their type. His pleasant and deferential style invited courteous distance rather than intimacy. He drank sparingly, only an occasional highball from time to time; he was not a carouser, but was stolid and dutiful to his often ailing wife. He was also regarded as a man of impeccable taste and Connally was keenly interested in his advice about his personal appearance. In a conversation in Seguin, shortly after Jacobsen joined the Connally campaign, Connally plied Jake with questions about the way he should dress before different audiences, whether he should comb his hair differently or cut it shorter, when to be faintly Western in his presentation, and when to be buttoned-down and mainstream American. Jacobsen felt that in 1962 Connally still displayed his bucolic Floresville roots and gravitated toward inexpensive suits and dizzying geometric ties.

In the first year of Connally's governorship, Jacobsen's contacts with the new governor were fleeting, and when they did meet the subject was clothes or furnishings rather than politics. Connally had also taken an interest in the appearance of the governor's mansion, and Jacobsen's taste in furnishings was as highly regarded as his taste in clothes. Jake had suffered through the Daniel governorship, when Daniel refused to spend "three dimes" on the governor's mansion and kept threadbare, dreary furniture about. Once, when Governor Daniel ascended the stairs of the mansion, plaster from the ceiling fell on his head. Now Jacobsen was happy to advise. The result was pleasing. With Nellie, Connally turned the mansion into a cheerful, inviting place with a splendid, relandscaped garden and a charming but dignified governor's office, with Sam Houston's impressive oak desk at its centerpiece. What neither Jacobsen nor Connally could know was the significance of Jacobsen's role in fanning Connally's passion for expensive things.

In November of 1963, Jacobsen was in his fifth year of private law practice. He had left Daniel's staff before Daniel began his second term as governor. It was time for him to cash in on his decade of public service, for his own sake and particularly for Florene's. Still shut out from Austin's closed legal fraternity, he had gone into practice for himself, and he was doing well. One of his first clients in 1958 was KTBC, the Johnsons' radio and television station, which he had agreed to represent for a modest retainer after Lyndon Johnson, over a Mexican dinner, had prevailed upon him to do so. Other clients flocked to him rapidly, for his contacts in state government were extensive. He proved himself a capable lawyer and lobbyist. By 1963 he was making over $150,000 a year, not too shabby in the 1960s for a small law office. And he was enjoying himself.

Though excluded from the inner circle of the Austin legal establishment, he remained a part of the political coterie of Austin, whose members planned the first presidential visit to the Texas capital. The dinner in Austin on the night of November 22 was to be the *pièce de résistance* of Kennedy's Texas swing. Among the organizers, the liberals like Jacobsen felt they had to put on the best show of the visit, since the animosity toward Kennedy in Texas remained high. Bill Moyers advanced the dinner. John Connally personally strong-armed blocs of Democrats to buy tickets to it, and Jake Jacobsen arranged the feast. Of those who know how to stage a lucrative, lavish, classy political banquet, Jake Jacobsen was among the best. He knew whom to call and how to raise wads of money. He threw himself into the job. It was to have been the cap of a glorious day for the president.

Ten days after Lee Harvey Oswald did his work, Jacobsen, accompanied by Cliff Carter, called on Connally at Parkland Hospital. By this time the governor was strong enough to sit up in bed, but he remained in evident pain from his terrible wounds. Nellie stood by his bed, a cheerful presence as always, as Jacobsen chatted amiably. Ashen and drawn, swathed in bandages, Connally tried to be graceful, saying he thought he would make a complete recovery. The doctors were predicting that he would even regain full use of his shattered arm. Sorry as he felt for the wounded man, Jacobsen went away heartened by the prognosis and filled with optimism for Connally's future.

★

Jacobsen's professional stock continued to rise through 1964, but he was tormented by a personal problem of long standing. For ten years, his wife, Florene, had been sinking into a deeper and deeper dependence on sedatives. She had been in and out of treatment centers. She changed doctors like purses. She would acquire pills wherever she could, and Jacobsen would come upon them, squirreled away in the most surprising places in their commodious limestone house in the old, respected Austin neighborhood of Tarrytown. For Jake, the political years with Daniel had been the worst of times. The hours were long and the pay modest, and Florene, a small-town Catholic girl, felt socially uncomfortable in Austin. She imagined countless social slights from the wives of Jake's professional associates and severed more than one friendship over them.

To Florene Jacobsen, life was made up of perpetual minor crises. Things were better now, as Jake was making significant money in the law firm, and Florene had money to acquire a sumptuous wardrobe and expensive china which rarely came out of its closet. If money made Florene happy, Jacobsen set out to make it. It was for her that he altered his career. Beyond his burgeoning law practice, he fell into a business association which seemed to promise a comfortable retirement for himself and his wife.

In San Angelo, Jacobsen had represented a client named Ray Cowan in an antitrust suit. The state had charged Cowan and others with collusion to rig state bids over school buses. The charge was valid, but Jacobsen had skillfully handled the defense and had managed to get Cowan off. In the process, the two became friends, and in due course Cowan proposed that they form a business partnership. Jacobsen was good with banks, and Cowan already had his bus business. The partnership seemed destined to succeed. That Jacobsen was entering into a relationship with a man whom he knew to be capable of criminal fraud did not seem to faze him. In short order, the partnership began to acquire assets. The bus business went international, opening a plant in El Salvador and producing buses for sale throughout Central America. Using the bus plant as collateral, the partners borrowed money to acquire controlling interests in four banks and three savings and loan associations. With these assets, Jacobsen was suddenly a millionaire—on paper— and the paper was handled by Cowan. Cowan paid the interest on the loans and reduced the principal from time to time. Jacobsen signed the notes when the partnership needed to borrow money for an acquisition. Cowan supplied him with periodic financial reports, but Jacobsen did not bother to examine the books.

Over Thanksgiving, in 1964, Jacobsen's phone rang. It was the president calling, with a summons to the LBJ Ranch, one of those flattering high honors that few men can resist. The president sent a helicopter, which set Jacobsen down far out in the fields of horsemint, Texas thistles and purple nightshade, where LBJ and Lady Bird were hunting deer from their white Lincoln Continental convertible. Come to Washington, the president ordered. I want you to handle my personal business, as well as sensitive governmental business.

For Jake, it was not an easy decision. He had turned down LBJ years before, when he was asked to join Johnson's Senate staff. The cut in salary now would be on the order of two-thirds. Florene would be miserable. His business assets would have to go into a trust and be handled by Cowan. He was also in the middle of contesting an IRS demand that he pony up $50,000 in back taxes. Pay it! Johnson commanded, speaking as the ultimate tax commissar.

Still, the chance to work in the White House in a position of confidence might be worth the sacrifice and worries. He told the president he would accept, but only for a fixed period of two years. In May of 1965, he assumed his duties, taking up residence on the second floor of the White House in an office next to Lawrence O'Brien. Jake became a Texan amid the Kennedy holdovers. Once again, Jacobsen had been hired largely for his discretion. He was entering a tight orbit where secretiveness was a prime requirement: into the most private business of the Johnson family and into the very most private side of the president's life. It was not a position for a gossipy or an egocentric person, nor for one burdened with high principle over presidential skulduggery, personal or financial.

Within a short time there developed between Jacobsen and Johnson an easy intimacy. Jake's job was to be part fixer, part confidant, part court jester, part personal valet. Some White House staffers saw him as Johnson's "baby-sitter," there to deal with Johnson's tantrums as well as to keep the president from hurting himself. Jacobsen handled sensitive assignments when the president feared gossip or leaks or scandal, and Jake was known as the only one on the staff who kept a recording device in his desk. His responsibilities ranged from the grand to the trivial, for he had the substance to deal with distinguished scientists, just as he had the finesse to handle a nasty firing or a disgruntled congressman, and the savvy to trade for a piece of land in the Hill Country.

The many sides of Johnson's personality came into Jacobsen's view. He saw the president's charity: once, Johnson was driving the back roads near the ranch when he passed a cramped shack, housing a family of eight. He turned to Jacobsen in the backseat and told him to contact the Johnson architect in Austin and have him design an addition to the shack—"But don't tell anyone about it." On another occasion, when Jacobsen accompanied Johnson to the simple Catholic church down the road in Stonewall, Johnson started to complain impressively about the bare, hard benches and the heavily accented Teutonic message of old Father Wunibald Schneider. Then he was seized by a thought.

"Jake," he said, "I'm going to give you an assignment. You're going to donate kneelers to the church." Jacobsen chortled and went off and did it, and thereafter Jacobsen's kneelers became a big joke for the president, oft told to ranch visitors.

Jacobsen also saw the president's thin-skinned defensiveness. After the assassination the air remained heavy with scandalous rumor and hurtful jokes, one of the sickest being:

"Well I guess ole Lyndon won't be goin' deer huntin' this year," says one fellow to the other.

"Oh, why is that?" says the other.

"Because Oswald won't give him back his rifle!"

It was a pall that wouldn't go away, and when William Manchester prepared to publish his account of the Kennedy assassination, an account authorized by the Kennedy family, Johnson had Jacobsen read the book and provide him with a chapter by chapter synopsis.

He also felt the president's cruel testing and crudeness: "Here comes ole Jake," the president might say as Jacobsen wandered into the president's bedroom in the morning. "Where were you last night, Jake? Out screwing all night?" It was a common presidential taunt, and Jacobsen felt privately that the president was really talking about himself. Jake had an answer for that one. "Mr. President," he said, "if I got a woman and screwed her, she would damn sure be an FBI plant, and you would know in the morning how many times we screwed, how many times she grunted, what I said to her, and what she said to me, because you'd have a damn transcript of it on your desk in the morning. I ain't gonna do that, Mr. President. I ain't gonna give you that opportunity." For Johnson, that made a good joke, but for Jacobsen to talk this way required an awkward posturing that ill suited him.

If Jacobsen knew Johnson's vulgarity, he also knew his sensitivity. A pattern developed in which Jacobsen became the only aide whom Johnson took to the ranch when he retreated to Texas, and whenever they went to Texas the president made sure that Florene was also on the plane.

Jacobsen was well aware of it when the president played fast and loose with money. Asked once whether Jacobsen had ever directly arranged for money to be given to the president, Jacobsen would not answer directly. "It was a common practice," he said. "It was done. Nobody thought anything bad about it. I wasn't going to publicize it. I wasn't going to a newspaper and say, 'I just gave President Johnson $50,000.' But it was done. It was very common. I felt nothing about it." And he related this to the bribe that, later, he was charged with giving to John Connally, and he broadened the point to all of old Texas politics. "In the era of old Texas politics, John Connally knew about payoffs. President Johnson knew about them. Governor Preston Smith knew about them. Governor Daniel knew about them. These are old, old Texas politicians. They all knew about [payoffs]. There wasn't anybody who didn't know about them. If you were raised in politics, you saw this, and you didn't think anything about it. And you did it. Does that answer your question?"

Since he was considered the best-dressed man in the White House, Jacobsen in due time came to look after the president's personal appearance. He recommended certain suits and shoes and arranged for tailors and cobblers to come to the White House to outfit Johnson. He even became the utility makeup man for routine public appearances, applying pancake to the folds of Johnson's face and the dark circles beneath his eyes, circles which became deeper and darker in 1966 and 1967 as the news from Vietnam grew steadily worse. Because he could help with the president's grooming as well as with other, more substantial tasks, Jacobsen was taken along on several state visits abroad: the Far Eastern trip in October 1966 and to Punta del Este in April 1967. On the former, in New Zealand, Jacobsen was in a caravan several cars behind the president's when suddenly he heard the president's voice booming over the loudspeaker from the presidential limousine. "Jake Jacobsen . . . report immediately . . . and bring your tools." They were headed for a reception at the prime minister's house, and Jacobsen grabbed his makeup kit and trotted up to the president's car to make his boss presentable.

To Jacobsen, Lyndon Johnson was a singularly ugly man, but his face was etched with character, so, true to his craft in amateur theater, he did not want to put too much makeup on it. As it became known that he performed these personal functions for the president, Jacobsen developed an acute sensitivity about being considered a slave and a flunky. As he saw it, he was there to serve as the president required. There was about his service a distinct selflessness and independence that transcended what people felt about him. He was unengaged emotionally and he was incapable of being demeaned by Johnson.

"Everything is fine, Mr. President," he said once, trying to quiet some passing storm.

"How can you say that, Jake?" Johnson raged. "Look at this paper and see what they're saying about me."

"Well, you don't see the name Jacobsen in those papers, do you? It just says Johnson, J-o-h-n-s-o-n. They're not talking about me."

Jacobsen's day generally began in the president's bedroom, his suite of rooms separate from Lady Bird's, where two or three aides would arrive as the president awoke and began to concentrate his mind on the events of the day. Jacobsen handled the night reading for the president, getting the *Congressional Record* delivered to his apartment on Washington Circle the night before, and arriving in the morning with it neatly clipped and marked. It was during these bedroom warmups that Jacobsen occasionally encountered John Connally. Jake knew well that it did not pay to criticize Connally before the president. The president himself might complain about his old friend, and did frequently, especially about Connally's resistance in Texas to the Great Society programs: "Aw, that son of a bitch has forgotten his roots. He got rich, and he can't remember what he did down in Floresville." It was a constant refrain for the president, but if an innocent bystander took up the refrain, Jacobsen was ready to duck. Johnson could criticize Connally, but no one else was allowed to. Jacobsen knew that Johnson's affection for Connally had actually been enhanced by an admiration for Connally's abilities with money. "Johnson always respected a person who could make money," Jacobsen said once, and no doubt he felt that this precept had something to do with Johnson's attitude toward him as well.

As far as he was concerned, Jacobsen had his own, not insignificant influence on the president and the president's policies. "If you give me the right to see somebody every morning before they go to work, I want to tell you I'm going to have some influence," he would remark. "You give me access to all the conversation, and I'm going to exert a sway, whether I do it by raising my eyebrows or by looking down. Whether I want it or not, I have it. You can't just sit there like a snake."

Because Jacobsen was so discreet and correct, one often had to determine what he was feeling by observing his eyebrows, which, dark, thick, and arched, in high contrast to his whitening hair, were the most expressive features of his face.

Jacobsen had promised the president two years, and he kept his word—to the day. The promise of a set time at presidential service is a vow frequently enunciated and rarely honored. That was especially true for Lyndon Johnson's people. But Jacobsen's personal circumstances demanded that he leave Washington when he said he would. His resignation occasioned a certain admiration, and even envy, among other White House aides, who wondered how Jacobsen could turn aside Johnson's forceful pressure to stay. Jacobsen's departure was not as graceful as it seemed to be, however. Johnson took Jake to Punta del Este the month before he left, and that appeared to be a reward. In fact, Johnson and Jacobsen were having a falling out. Jake found himself caught up in Johnson's afternoon horse-trading, those sessions where Johnson often kibitzed with his Texas cronies over a piece of land here or there or some other deal, in a testing game to see who could hornswoggle the other. Jacobsen had often protected the president from embarrassing deals growing out of these sessions. Now, Jacobsen himself was importuned by Johnson over the savings and loan association in Fredricksburg, not far from the LBJ Ranch. Jacobsen owned the controlling interest in it, and Johnson now demanded a share. Jacobsen refused flatly. To have Lyndon Johnson as a business partner could only spell trouble. Johnson was furious. Didn't Jacobsen owe him this? Such pressure by a sitting president is clearly illegal, and Jacobsen's willingness to testify about it during the trial of John Connally eight years later would cause a stir.

★

Jake Jacobsen left the White House with one major client already signed up for his private law practice. It was the Associated Milk Producers, Incorporated, or AMPI. AMPI had a grandiose reputation in the political world as one of the most prodigiously generous of all campaign contributors nationwide. For years it had been a touchstone for liberal Democratic candidates. In the 1950s and 1960s, the organization contributed as much as one-third of the campaign budget for Minnesota senators Hubert Humphrey and Walter Mondale. The group paid fantastic fees for speakers at their conventions. When ex-Senator Harold Hughes of Iowa was offered $5,000 to speak at an AMPI banquet in the 1960s, his astonished response was: "The hell you say! When is the next plane?" Congressman Wilbur Mills, chairman of the Ways and Means Committee, had been a particular favorite for obvious reasons. The Ways and Means Committee held decisive sway over government price supports for dairy products, and to the dairy industry price supports were a matter of life and death.

Based in San Antonio, AMPI was a one-issue organization, with one question to all political candidates: How do you stand on the dairy price support? In general, due to their basic credo, Democrats believed in a decent wage for the average farmer, even if that meant artificial support, large government surpluses, and a higher price in the grocery store. Conversely, the Republicans worried more about government tinkering with the natural supply and demand mechanism of the marketplace. The parity level for milk products referred to the percentage of support the government would guarantee, so that the price of a hundredweight of milk would be the equivalent to the price of other products on the market. If a bushel of wheat in 1900 could buy a pair of overalls, for example, then today, at parity, that bushel should still be able to buy the overalls. By statute, the parity level could be no higher than ninety percent nor lower than seventy-five percent, and the exact percentage was left to the discretion of the secretary of agriculture. If the parity level was too high, it excessively stimulated the production of milk, overloaded government surplus warehouses, and raised the cost of milk to the consumer. If parity was too low, individual farmers suffered unfairly. The difference in a few percentage points of parity level meant literally millions of dollars lost or gained to dairy farmers.

AMPI had a simple philosophy about all of this. It needed to influence every political figure it could, in any way possible. The certain way to power and influence was money, a lot of it. Political contributions were the avenue to influence, and AMPI had convinced its membership of more than 40,000 that a personal contribution of $100 a year, earmarked for political lobbying, was an excellent investment. To gather and then distribute this money, AMPI established a political arm with the important name of Trust for Agricultural Political Education, or TAPE. The proceeds from members' contributions amounted to a huge political war chest, and its appropriation was left to a few somewhat unsophisticated managers at the top of the organization. They decided what campaigns to support. The contributions were transformed into cash, and an AMPI functionary, a diminutive, sad-eyed figure named Bob Lilly, moved around the country with a heavy satchel, dumping wads of cash on candidates who thought correctly about price supports. In the late 1960s and early 1970s, AMPI was contributing generously to the campaigns of nearly half the sitting U.S. Senate and a quarter of the U.S. House of Representatives.

Jake Jacobsen had dealt frequently with the milk producers when he was in the White House, for they were always "hanging around." President Johnson considered the Texas-based cooperative to be home folks, and they did not have to plead their case strenuously with him, nor for that matter with Governor Connally in Texas. Both Johnson and Connally were far more than gentleman farmers in their own extensive ranch operations. As private citizens, they understood full well the rising cost of seed, fertilizer, and feed to the farmer, and their tilt was toward the man at the feedlot rather than the housewife at the checkout counter. As president, Johnson issued tariff restrictions on foreign dairy products, even before he received recommendations from the tariff commission.

In late 1967 AMPI showed its thanks. It agreed to pay the cost of printing a book of Johnson's most memorable statements to the Ninetieth Congress, complete with color pictures of the president. It was like a vanity press without the tab. The tab in this case was $104,521, and it was paid by a corporate AMPI check. So certain of its clout was AMPI that it even took a tax deduction for its charitable act. (The IRS eventually got onto that. By the time the IRS investigation of this deduction got under way, in 1972, John Connally was secretary of the treasury, and Jacobsen, as the AMPI lobbyist, had a good working relationship with him. Jake called Connally about the difficulty. As it happened, the old Johnson and Connally associate, Robert Phinney, was the district IRS director for Texas. Phinney argued against referring the tax problem to Justice.*

In Jacobsen, AMPI had a perfect lobbyist, a man who was bedroom-close to the sitting president, who had superb contacts throughout Texas state government, most especially with the governor, and who had an excellent entrée into the banking world. Jacobsen in turn had found the perfect client: the group put him on a retainer, and before the relationship was severed he had made over $350,000 from the cooperative.

Jacobsen took up his duties with the milk producers enthusiastically. AMPI put him to work in raising money all over the country at local membership meetings. He loved the work. AMPI had a sleek Sabre jet, and it spirited Jacobsen into the byways of the American heartland, where he stood, elegant and manicured, before wide-eyed leathery farmers and delivered his message: They were in a regulated industry. They depended totally upon the whims of elected officials. "If you want to get consideration from anybody, you're damn sure not going to get it just because you're a farmer. You can write a letter, and you'll get an answer, but these people get lots of letters, letters from people they don't know and frankly don't care much about. But they pay attention to those they know. How do they get to know you? When they need a crowd at an airport, you provide it." But Jake's real message was not crowds, but money. Jacobsen salted his talks with anecdotes from his days in the White House, the kind of insider gossip that left his weather-beaten

*Eventually the deduction was not allowed, and the AMPI did not contest this decision.

audiences impressed and fascinated, and they emptied their coverall pockets for the cause. It produced, in Jacobsen's words, a "political slush fund that just wouldn't quit." AMPI had more money for political purposes than any organization he had ever seen.

In early 1969 Jacobsen and Connally, now both private citizens and still loyal Democrats, met for the first time about the future of the milk industry. That estate had dramatically improved in the late 1960s, as independent dairy cooperatives across the nation banded together into three major cooperatives, of which AMPI was the most powerful and politically effective. The ultimate goal of the milk producers was to form one massive dairy cooperative for the nation. Jacobsen had been with AMPI for nearly two years, and now he sought Connally out to discuss the formation of the political arm for AMPI, TAPE. The idea was not new; it was an adaptation of a concept used for years by big labor. (Labor's political arm was known as COPE.) Jacobsen wanted to know whether Connally approved of TAPE and whether he felt there was any legal bar to its formation. Connally did approve and found no legal impediment.

When Richard Nixon moved into the White House in January 1969, AMPI realized that it had lost its political leverage in Washington. It had no friends in the new administration and potentially many enemies, for it had vigorously supported the presidential candidacy of Hubert Humphrey. It was only a matter of a few months after Nixon became president that AMPI made its first overtures to the new administration. It did so in characteristic fashion. Jacobsen had opened a law office in Washington with Milton Semer, an attorney who had served with him for a year in the Johnson White House. At Jacobsen's direction, in April 1969 Semer contacted the new U.S. attorney general, John Mitchell, with the message that his client, the Associated Milk Producers, wished to make a contribution to Nixon's reelection campaign in 1972. Mitchell referred Semer to Herbert Kalmbach, the impassive, blue-eyed fundraiser who would become one of the first major witnesses before the Senate Watergate Committee in 1973. Kalmbach had taken charge of over a million dollars in surplus funds from the 1968 Nixon campaign and had been designated the chief fund-raiser for the president's reelection.

Semer, Jacobsen, and AMPI started a process with Kalmbach which eventually would send Kalmbach to jail for 18 months and result in the conviction of 21 corporate executives and substantial fines for 17 corporations. Kalmbach was bold. In his second meeting with Semer, he recommended a contribution of $100,000 in cash.

This was to start what Kalmbach later came to call his "100 Club," a select, gold-plated group whose members were entitled to make special requests. In the next three years, Kalmbach would travel the country, strong-arming corporate executives like George Steinbrenner, J. Paul Getty, and Leonard Firestone into making huge contributions to Nixon's reelection. Before he resigned on April 7, 1972, the day a new, tougher campaign financing law went into effect, Kalmbach had raised close to $9 million.

On the day before Semer met with Kalmbach for the second time, in July 1969, he met with Jacobsen and AMPI executives in Dallas, and they discussed their quid pro quo for any contribution. They wanted four things. First and foremost, they wanted the administration to commit itself to the maximum ninety percent parity under the law. After that, they wanted the president to meet with AMPI officials for a photo session. They wanted Nixon to speak at their annual convention the following year, and they wanted a regular channel into the White House to voice their concerns. (This last AMPI demand did not register firmly with Kalmbach, but it would become important later.) In the discussion with Semer, Kalmbach got the impression that the organization's generosity could exceed $100,000, so he set AMPI's goal at $250,000 before the end of 1969. On his ledger sheet, Kalmbach noted in his Watergate shorthand: "Semer: 100–250."

In 1969 there was nothing illegal per se about contributing $100,000 to a presidential campaign. The issues rather were whether it was a corporate contribution, what was to be the manner in which the contribution was to be reported, if it was, and, if the money was in cash, how it was to be accounted for. Under the Corrupt Practices Act of 1925, which was still the law governing political contributions, a corporation was specifically barred from making a contribution over $5,000. Was the AMPI "100" a corporate contribution or simply the accumulation of its individual members' donations of $100 a head? Kalmbach did not ask; in the end, he did not care. He did care about the manner of the contribution: he wanted it in cash and he made that very clear. He was reporting to H. R. Haldeman in the White House, and Haldeman was pressing him to keep the cash supply for political missions high. In due course, it would become clear why Haldeman wanted so much cash on hand.

In fairness to Jacobsen and Semer, Kalmbach's insistence on cash and his disinterest in reporting the contribution made them uncomfortable. More than once in July, Semer inquired tactfully if it would not be better to make the contribution with a corporate check. But there was no mistaking Kalmbach's desires.

On August 2, 1969, Semer flew out to California and proceeded to Kalmbach's home in Newport Beach, where he opened a little valise and passed the money, arranged in packets, in crisp $100 bills, just like in the movies.

★

The year 1969 was, for Jake Jacobsen, a bullish year, perhaps the peak of his personal fortunes. Besides the milk producers, he was acquiring other large corporate clients like American Airlines. He and Cowan were expanding their banking interests. He was confident and bold, and luxuriating in being a distinguished former assistant to the president of the United States.

But in 1970 his storm clouds appeared. Jacobsen began to get calls from bankers who complained that his partner, Cowan, was not reducing the notes on their loans. When Jacobsen confronted him, Cowan said he was having a few problems, but he was working them out. The calls from banks grew more persistent, and finally one day Cowan confessed to Jacobsen one searing shocker: that the original note, pledging South American companies to buy buses from the Jacobsen-Cowan concern in El Salvador, had been *worthless*. "Those guys in Central America just signed those notes as a favor to me," Cowan said breezily, "so I'd have something to pledge at the banks." By his own account, Jacobsen was thunderstruck. It was upon that original pledge that their entire partnership had been based, for they had used the South American business as collateral to buy other properties, including interests in various banks. In short, the whole business, from buses to banks, was based upon worthless paper.

Later, when he was in trouble, Jacobsen sought to portray himself as the innocent victim of Cowan's perfidy. He adopted an unvarnished devil-made-me-do-it defense. Cowan had induced him to sign a number of documents, including loan applications in their savings and loan associations, when Cowan was basing the approval of the loans upon fraudulent documentation. Before the slew of investigators that would soon descend upon him, Jacobsen could admit stupidity and even negligence, but he denied criminal intent. He protested that he should have thought before he signed, that he should have looked deeper into Cowan's dealings, but he was preoccupied with his law practice, Florene worried him to death, and so on. But he was not so distant from his partner's chicanery as he protested.

In early 1971 Jacobsen could still declare his net worth to be something more than $3 million, but his problems were compounding and his anxiety was rising. A twilight period ensued when he remained in league with the slippery Cowan, as they together tried to extricate themselves with a series of shady deals. Using their power as directors of their three savings and loan associations, they approved loans in a number of land and real estate deals in which they had secret business interests, misapplied the proceeds from the loans to their own benefit, and knowingly used phony appraisals to inflate the value of their properties. But the tricks were not working, and their three savings and loans began to founder. Within a few months, the authorities began to consider Jacobsen and Cowan's criminal liability for the impending default of their S&Ls. In a letter to the Justice Department, the general counsel of the Federal Home Loan Bank Board recommended prosecution: "An examination revealed that as of July 1, 1971, largely as a result of the criminal conduct of [Jacobsen and Cowan], Lubbock Savings and Loan, First Savings of San Angelo, and Community Savings and Loan in Fredricksburg faced imminent prospect of receivership because of indicated losses totalling in excess of $5.5 million."

This was deep water. Furthermore, the full crookedness of his partner was beginning to dawn on Jacobsen, as he discovered that Cowan had been cooking the books for years and had even stolen from the partnership during Jacobsen's two years in the White House, while Jacobsen's assets languished in a blind trust. Jacobsen rushed to El Salvador to confront the crooked businessmen who had signed the original worthless note, and initiated legal proceedings against them. Wildly, he surveyed his other holdings, including land holdings and an Austin apartment house, and he tried to sell what he could to pay his creditors. The heat of the prosecutors began to get intense. "It's hard to explain the nervousness and the apprehension," Jacobsen would say in describing his state of mind at this time. "You've got to hire a lawyer. Suddenly, you're a potential defendant in a criminal action. You're called in to sign documents. The district attorney calls you before the judge. It was a feeling I didn't like. It just tears you up inside. I became distressed, extremely distressed." He began appearing before grand juries elsewhere about other assets—in Wichita Falls, in Abilene. He began to get sued. When he paid one creditor, it was fraud upon the others, and he was sued again for that.

A loan Jacobsen had approved at the San Angelo S&L—and then personally received the benefits from in the form of a check for $93,000—became his main legal problem. On March 13, 1972, after having been interviewed by the FBI, he was hauled before a grand jury in Wichita Falls convened to consider possible embezzlement charges against himself and Cowan. There, Jacobsen committed his first perjury. Twice he denied that he had ever been on the loan committee of his bank. It was an extraordinary lie, for bank records clearly showed that he had been on the committee for nine months before the loan on the questionable land deal had been approved, and that he had signed a number of other loan memoranda.

With the perjury charge added to the charges of misapplication and embezzlement, Jacobsen now stood to go to jail for thirty-five years. But it would be another two years before he would appreciate the scope of his jeopardy.

Through his tortuous slide in 1971 and 1972, Jake Jacobsen had one valued friend. That was John Connally, and Connally had been a sympathetic ear and occasionally a helping hand. In September 1971 Jacobsen was under great pressure from the Federal Home Loan Bank Board to get out of the savings and loan business. The board was trying to get him to sell, perhaps to avoid criminal prosecution, but Jacobsen considered the board's proposal for selling to be based upon an unfair formula. So he went to Connally and prevailed upon the secretary of the treasury to call the chairman of the Home Loan Board, the former senator from Kentucky, Thruston Morton. This Connally did, twice, on September 23, 1971.

Matters private and professional, legal and shady, had gotten hopelessly intertwined between Jacobsen and Connally. The day after Connally made the calls to Morton on Jacobsen's behalf, Jacobsen came in to see Connally in his office. Why had he come? Connally would later suppose publicly that perhaps Jacobsen had come simply to find out what Morton had said about his banking problems. But Jacobsen would testify that on September 24, 1971, he had given Connally a $5,000 gratuity from the milk producers, $5,000 in $100 bills, whose wrappers Connally had taken into his private bathroom and flushed down the toilet. Call it a gratuity or a bribe or a token gift to the sultan. Whatever it was, the charge alone was enough to ruin the career of John Connally. For this was now the era of Watergate. The ethics of American political life were undergoing a sea change, and Connally and Jacobsen would become both examples and victims of that change.

If Connally was grateful that day for a gift from Jacobsen, it went unrecorded, but Jacobsen's doting affection for Connally for his efforts did not. On April 28, 1972, Jacobsen expressed his thanks to Connally in writing: "It occurred to me that I had never really written to express my gratitude to you and doing so is emotionally difficult for me when we are talking. In all my life I have never had anyone in high position treat me as kindly as you have. I know there is no possible way for me to express to you my real gratitude although I know you must feel it when I am talking with you.

"The purpose of this letter is to tell you how deeply grateful I am to you and to express the hope that in some small way I can merit your kindness and friendship."

Three years later Jake Jacobsen took the stand as John Connally's chief accuser in Connally's trial for bribery and conspiracy. Connally's defense lawyer, the formidable Edward Bennett Williams, handed Jake his letter of April 1972 and had him read it aloud, as Connally listened impassively at the defense table. Jacobsen shriveled inside as he read, but he acknowledged to himself that in 1972 those sentiments were entirely sincere.

22

The Crime

NOT MANY DAYS AFTER John Connally became secretary of the treasury on February 11, 1971, Jake Jacobsen had a good idea about how to be a thoughtful friend. He found a copy of Connally's favorite picture of himself from the governorship days—a smiling, full-faced portrait with the star of Texas in the background—went to a local photography outfit, and had hundreds of prints made at his own expense. Connally could well have afforded to make the pictures himself, Jake knew, but the governor's circumstance had changed. Connally had more power and was making less money. It was part of Jake's lobbyist's code that politicians should not have to spend their own money on trifles like pictures to sign and give away to their official visitors. Furthermore, as a good lobbyist, he knew instinctively how to identify those little things that would please the powerful man and make him grateful and sympathetic. Later, Jacobsen had one regret: he wished he had kept to the practice of spending his own money on gifts for politicians, rather than the money of his corporate clients.

This was Jacobsen's first meeting with Connally as treasury secretary, but it was scarcely to be his last. In the three and a half months that followed, Jacobsen and Connally got together regularly, ten times in all for a total of more than seven hours, and they exchanged numerous phone calls. That was more time than Connally spent with any other person outside of government, twice as much time in fact. What did they talk about? Clothes, Texas politics, and birds, Jacobsen would later say. Birds? Boehm birds, the ceramic collector's items that were often the gifts of presidents to visiting heads of state, which Jake could get from a jewelry shop in Atlantic City at cost for the secretary and which Connally collected as handsome decoration for the mantelpiece and the dinner table at the Picosa Ranch. Soon enough, when they exhausted the subject of birds, their conversation turned to milk.

In his first weeks as the secretary of the treasury, Connally had thrown himself into his new job with all his energy and force. He worked madly seven days a week, eighteen hours a day to master the job, reading the official reports and documents of his department's divisions late into the night. Nevertheless, he seemed always to find time for Jake when he came to town, and a month after Connally took office Jacobsen had good reason to take up residence in Washington for a few weeks. The time approached again for the secretary of agriculture to reset the parity level. It stood at a mere 79 percent, only four percentage points above the legal minimum, and the dissension in the farm belt, especially among the dairy farmers, was loud. AMPI and other farm lobbies had geared up their annual campaign to get the parity level higher, and their lobbyists fanned out over Congress. Wilbur Mills was their congressional champion. As chairman of the Ways and Means Committee, he had been pestering the director of the Office of Management and Budget, the future Reagan secretary of state, George Shultz. Eighty-seven members of Congress had written or wired Secretary of Agriculture Clifford Hardin to increase parity to its legal maximum of 90 percent. Mainly, congressional support came from the liberal Democrats like Edward Kennedy, George McGovern, and Hubert Humphrey, but other moderates and Republicans were advocating a raise at least to 85 percent.

The economic experts resisted. Given Nixon's economic philosophy, there was no case for raising the price support. It would be inflationary; it would raise dairy surpluses markedly; and it would cost the taxpayers at least $100 million in surplus storage costs and higher milk prices. But the issue was highly charged politically and the administration brought in that old master of political spitball, Charles Colson, to evaluate the political considerations. In an "eyes only" memorandum to John Ehrlichman on March 10, Colson conceded that the economic arguments were too compelling to permit a higher parity pleasing to the milk producers. His concern was to protect AMPI's pledge of $2 million to the Nixon reelection campaign. So he searched for other measures besides the parity level that the administration could use to assuage the dairymen: "The leaders of the dairy industry can 'sell' to the farmers no increase in parity, if they can say that the importation of milk substitutes like cheese will be controlled." For once, Colson was being naive.

In that first meeting with Connally on March 4, when Jacobsen had presented his glossy photographs, Jake had inevitably raised the issue of the forthcoming price support decision and had found Connally responsive.

"I don't believe Nixon understands the situation very well," Connally remarked.

"Would you be kind enough to explain it to him?" Jacobsen said with his unfailing politeness. "I'm in no position to do that."

"Why sure, Jake," Connally replied offhandedly. "I'll bring it up the first chance I get."

He found the chance the next day. In Connally, the milk producers had their only real entrée into the administration, and Jacobsen was their only way to Connally. "John Connally was assigned to me," Jacobsen would tell me. "He was my only contact." But Connally's support was genuine. He believed that a higher price support was fair, for his instincts were still those of a Democrat and of a rancher. Jacobsen did not have to push hard, and he reported the ease of his sales job back to the milk producers.

Again, on March 11, Connally saw Nixon, and again they discussed the milk support. But Connally was losing the argument to the Republican economists, and on the following day, March 12, Secretary Hardin announced that the administration would hold the line at 79 percent of parity. "The long-term well-being of the dairymen requires that prices be kept at levels which will permit the overwhelming proportion of milk to clear through commercial markets," Hardin's statement read. "Dairymen know from past experience that they do not benefit when dairy production substantially exceeds demand and excessive surpluses pile up in Government warehouses."

The milk industry was shattered. Immediately AMPI's executives and lobbyists met in an emergency session at the Madison Hotel in Washington. Congressmen and senators were divided up, and a plan for congressional pressure upon the administration to reverse its decision went into effect. Even ex-President Johnson was contacted in the hope that he would pressure key congressional Democrats. But John Connally was their chief hope.

Within a few days there was considerable activity in Congress to override the administration's decision and on March 19, Jacobsen rushed in to see Secretary Connally. This time their meeting was uncharacteristically brief and devoid of pleasantries. It lasted only fifteen minutes.

"Mr. Secretary, we are not trying to undercut the administration," Jake said after expressing the profound disappointment of his client. "We are not trying to create problems for you, but we do not think we have been treated fairly. We do not have any recourse except to try to get congressional relief. Beyond any question, we are going to be successful."

If there was a bit of posturing in Jacobsen's representation of his congressional clout, he had a more useful tool. It was AMPI's pledge of $2 million to the Nixon reelection campaign a year before. Now Jake conveyed a clear message: if the administration did not reverse its parity decision, the pledge would be terminated. Connally promised to see what he could do. This was a dark and thinly veiled threat, but Jacobsen presented a positive inducement: not simply meeting the original pledge but fattening it. How Jake presented this prospect of even more money is not clear, nor is it clear whether he was offering money to Connally personally for his assistance. What is clear is what happened next. After his meeting with Connally, Jacobsen rushed to the Madison Hotel and met with his AMPI managers. Present at that meeting was Bob Lilly, the compliant AMPI bagman. Lilly later testified that money, not votes, was the chief subject of the conversation after Jake's meeting with Connally, and Connally's susceptibility to monetary persuasion was the focus.

"Isn't it true," a Congressional interrogator would ask, "that at the [March 19 meeting at the Madison Hotel] it was decided upon the suggestion of Jake Jacobsen, that perhaps another one quarter-million dollars would be committed in order to secure Mr. Connally's assistance?"

"Yes," Lilly replied. "Mr. Jacobsen stated that certainly when Mr. Connally entered into this, certainly some new money would have to be committed. Somewhere between $500,000 and $1 million was discussed. Jacobsen indicated that $250,000 would be a fair figure to commit as new money." Connally was emerging as an expensive friend, but not nearly as expensive as the losses to the industry of a 79 percent parity level.

Later, the Watergate interrogator came back to this point with Lilly, just to be sure it was clear.

"There is no doubt in your mind that Mr. Jacobsen was of the opinion, perhaps as a result of his meeting with Mr. Connally, that in order to secure Mr. Connally's assistance in obtaining a favorable decision by the administration in regard to milk price supports, new money should be committed by AMPI?"

"That is true," Lilly replied.

As Jacobsen and Connally were meeting on March 19, so were the chief economic advisors to President Nixon, Ehrlichman and Shultz, meeting with Secretary Hardin. From that meeting, the recommendation was to hang tight and hold the line at 79 percent parity when President Nixon met with the milk producers four days hence. The administration should wait several weeks to see if the Democrats really could move a bill for a higher support through Congress. To these committed Republicans, that made honest, down-to-earth sense.

There were two levels to the unfolding story. One was the above-board conflict over votes and economic philosophy; the other was the sub rosa, often unspoken consideration of money and campaigns. Connally was the key figure in the latter, more important under-world. On March 20 he had a nine-minute telephone conversation with Nixon about the milk situation. Connally was getting a good feeling that the screw was turning. He was speaking not only with people inside the administration but with the congressional leader-ship as well. Since he was the only Democrat in the cabinet, it was natural that the Speaker of the House, Carl Albert, who was leading the charge for a mandatory parity bill, had called him and that Wilbur Mills had called twice. Connally knew full well how impor-tant it was to Mills that AMPI get a good deal from the administra-tion.

Within hours, Connally climbed into his silver limousine and headed for the airport. By chance, two taxiloads of AMPI officials were headed for the airport at the same time, and on the bridge over Fourteenth Street they passed Connally's Mercedes, waved, and tried to get the secretary's attention. The AMPI officials arrived at the Page Terminal first, where their Sabre jet and, coincidentally, Connally's plane were parked. Moments later Connally strode into the terminal. He greeted the delegation warmly, and then pulled Bob Lilly to one side.

"The decision is in the bag," the secretary said with an air of confidentiality, and then strode on to his waiting plane. There was no doubt in Lilly's mind what the secretary meant, for Connally was their champion within the administration, virtually their only supporter. This word from the inside had an immediate effect on the AMPI executives, beyond their jubilation at Page Terminal. Since Jacobsen had threatened the loss of all pledges to the Republicans, it was important to act positively now that the decision appeared to be in the process of being reversed. One of the first things Bob Lilly did on Monday, March 22, was to draw AMPI checks totaling $10,000 as a contribution to the Republican party campaign committee, which was holding a fund-raiser in Washington two days hence. It was a small item in the scheme of things, but it sent the right message.

The meeting between Nixon and the dairy producers was scheduled to begin at 10:30 the following morning, March 23. Fourteen minutes before that meeting, Connally was on the phone to the president. After the characteristic banter in which Nixon reached and overreached in making comparisons between his own actions and those of the ancient Greeks and Romans, Connally made his last-minute pitch for the president to please the milk producers by announcing that he would reverse Secretary Hardin's decision. Nixon was not ready to do that just yet. Hardin remained opposed for sound economic reasons. More important, if the gift to the producers was going to be made, their gift to the campaign needed to be reconfirmed. The $2 million pledge went unstated, but it was well understood. On whether to tell them outright in a few minutes that 85 percent of parity was theirs, Nixon said to Connally, "I want to be sure I don't cross the bridge today."

The dairy producers waited apprehensively in the Cabinet Room, and what happened next became the occasion for Alexander Butterfield, the Nixon aide who managed the secret White House taping system, to write an idolatrous memo to the presidential file:

> Then all of a sudden, BOOM . . . the President was announced and standing among those at the south end of the room. He looked tan, healthy and relaxed. The dairymen were noticeably surprised, for they expected a somber man. The President smiled broadly and without a pause began walking around the Cabinet table shaking hands, laughing, joking, and saying something to identify himself with each home state. By the time he took his seat, the prevailing mood was one of complete informality.
> He demonstrated warmth, gratitude, sincerity, understanding and just plain humanness—and in so doing he moved a large group of somewhat uncertain and apprehensive visitors to express themselves similarly. No one could have been with

me and gone away with the thought that RN is an isolated man. We have a President who listens, who cares.

It was precisely this kind of fawning from the president's inner circle to which John Connally presented a refreshing antidote.

In their presentation, the milk producers were earnest and sincere. The AMPI director argued that a 79 percent parity amounted to a loss for the farmer of a half-billion dollars, whereas 85 percent parity was a gain of $40 million, with no attendant cost to the government. Nixon toyed with them.

"Raising the thing to 85 percent doesn't bother me a bit," he said, lifting hopes. "But how is it going to look a year from now?" dashing them. "What is it going to do in terms of encouraging overproduction?" The producers protested that they could voluntarily control production. Nixon smothered them with homilies. "Show me a country that loses its rural heartland, and it almost always follows that the country loses its character," he said in an apparent awareness that over 600,000 dairymen had gone out of business in the preceding ten years. "The new frontier is now in the center of the country, not on either coast." Such platitudes were not what the producers wanted to hear. As the discussion got heated and the issue was joined, Nixon tried to break the tension with his special brand of humor. "The room is not tapped," he said as the tape rolled beneath the table. "Forgot to do that." Nervous laughter rippled across the room. The president remained noncommittal on the central issue. At the end of the meeting Nixon passed around cuff links, as if they were consolations. Apologizing that the trinkets with the presidential seal looked more expensive than they really were, he said, "You know the old story. Kings and emperors give only gifts of gold. Well, these are not gold, but only presidents can give them." The cuff links did not have his name on them, the jovial president said, so they could be worn at any political function. It was Nixon's only allusion to the fact that the milk producers played both sides of the political street.

In the hours that followed the forces positioned themselves in advance of the truly important meeting toward the end of the day, when Nixon was to meet with Connally and the agricultural experts to decide the parity question. The milk producers waited nervously in the Madison Hotel. Jake Jacobsen called Connally with one last pep talk. Nixon in turn talked to Colson, who would be handling the reassurances about the $2 million pledge. Secretary Hardin spoke with the AMPI director, trying to reassure him about how well the talk with the president had gone.

When the meeting convened in the Oval Office, Connally moved effectively into his role as the leading man. Nixon wanted to hear the political case, not the economic case, and only Connally could express it forcefully. The meeting was the pure essence of power politics. Connally began with the pitiful state of the American farmers; the farmers were nearly beyond help, and yet in this matter their case had merit. "I would not recommend that you do this, Mr. President, if it didn't have merit to it," Connally said. When he turned to AMPI, he spoke with the authority of inside knowledge. "These dairymen are organized, they're adamant, they're militant." Sometimes they resorted to strong-arm tactics, especially with their checkoff system, which produced their slush fund, but "there's no point in denying to the farmer what's the practice for the laborer. I wouldn't judge it on a moral basis." As a tactical matter, it was important not to appear to be forced into the decision either by the producers or by Congress, Connally contended. If 85 percent was inevitable anyway, the president should get credit for it rather than someone else.

"You don't want to be in a position where people think they forced you into doing something for them," Connally instructed them as if they were his pupils. "If you do something for them this year, they think you're doing it because you're their friend. If you wait till next year, I don't care what you do for them—they're going to say, 'Well, we put enough pressure on them this year, they had to do it.' And you get no credit for it. It's still going to cost you an enormous amount of money next year, and you get no political advantage out of it."

"We have a damn near insoluble problem," Nixon said with mock agony in a remark for the ears of the economists in the room.

Connally pressed on with the politics. The liberals in Congress were going to pass a mandatory parity bill, and were going to dare Nixon to veto it. They were scheming about how to use the parity issue to cut Nixon up. "They've got it all figured out," Connally said, ". . . just exactly how many electoral votes it will cost you if you veto an 85 percent bill. They say it will cost you Missouri, Wisconsin, South Dakota for sure. A veto will probably cost you Ohio, Kentucky, and Iowa." And what if he allowed Congress to pass such a bill and then signed it? "If you do that, you've cost yourself the money, and you've lost your political advantage. You're definitely worse off."

The economists listened quietly, for they were definitely out of their league. Within ten minutes Connally had turned the issue. His arguments, especially those which tied the very reelection of the president to the issue, were overwhelming, unassailable by an earnest agronomist like Hardin or a scholarly economist like Shultz. This was the very kind of situation where Connally's value to Nixon was inestimable, and a prime example of why Nixon was coming to admire Connally's leadership ability. As Nixon watched the Connally performance, he began to realize how he could use Connally in other situations, not just Treasury matters, where he expected stiff opposition for a political decision by other administration experts.

"All you experts sitting around—this is one of those situations where you have to make a political judgment," Nixon said finally. "My political judgment is that Congress is going to pass it. I could not veto it, not because they're milkers, but because they're farmers. It would be just turning down the whole damn middle America— where we need support. Under the circumstances, I think the best thing to do is just relax and enjoy it." With that allusion to rape, one could say that at least in this case the victim was assured a substantial cash reward.

Connally knew the experts had to be assuaged, so he threw them a bone. Secretary Hardin, after all, would publicly have to reverse himself. If anyone noticed, it could be embarrassing. Trade for two years, Connally suggested. Tell the dairymen that if they get 85 percent this year, they cannot come back next year and ask for more. That was a political notion which sounded downright economic in its good sense. The others seized on the idea. It made them feel better, and the discussion shifted to mechanics.

"Let's not trade through agriculture until some other conversations are had," Connally said mysteriously. The economists may not have known what he was talking about, but Nixon and Ehrlichman knew.

"You're now thinking of the political offer?" Nixon said. It was as close as the $2 million offer got to an overt mention.

If there was capital in campaign contributions to be made by this decision, there was political capital on the Hill that could be made as well. Who should inform the leaders of Congress?

"Let's have it done by somebody who can get something out of it," Nixon suggested. Revenue sharing was now atop his legislative agenda. "George [Shultz] and John [Ehrlichman] are going to have to deal with Wilbur Mills and Carl Albert on revenue sharing and these other programs. I think it should be George and John. What do you think?"

"That would be great," Ehrlichman said eagerly.

Again Connally could offer inside political information. "I was told that you could almost name your price with Wilbur, if you did this—short of all-out support for revenue sharing."

They talked on—moving onto a tangent of hog and cattle prices. Connally had some standing in that area as well, for he was the only genuine rancher in the crowd. "Cattle prices would shock you," he said with authority. "Just remember when you talk about food prices, and you bleed for the consumer—food prices in the United States are cheaper than they've ever been in the history of this nation. In terms of the hours it takes to feed a family, it's sixteen percent. That's the lowest in the history of the world."

"He's my favorite secretary," Nixon said sweetly, and they all laughed, knowing it was true. And they laughed when Ehrlichman said jovially, "Better get a glass of milk. . . . Drink it while it's cheap."

★

In the twenty-five minutes with Nixon, facing the stiff opposition of every professional agriculturist and economist in the room, John Connally had carried the ball and scored. That was what Nixon had wanted. Connally was dominant, articulate, combative, and persuasive. Without him, the strict economic arguments would surely have prevailed; they had to prevail. He emerged as the sole champion of the milk industry in the administration, and he had won the fight single-handedly. When Connally became the target of a criminal investigation two years later, this conversation in the Oval Office emerged as a central piece of evidence. It had laid the groundwork for the profound gratitude of the milk producers, a gratitude they were anxious to make manifest and real. When Connally faced a grand jury before the tape of the conversation was available, he claimed that the decision about raising parity to 85 percent had not been finalized in the Oval Office. He learned about the president's final decision in the newspapers, he testified. After the tape was played to him deeper into the investigation, he still maintained that the decision was not final, because the dairymen might have balked at the two-year deal. Such tortured disputation strains the mind. Once again, it was John Connally being too clever by half.

It was not until the Connally trial was over that three minutes of conversation between Connally and Nixon, alone, immediately after the meeting came to light, as well as a note from H. R. Haldeman. With this new evidence, the unholy nature of this cold political deal is unmistakably clear. In effect, John Connally became the administration's enforcer for the $2 million pledge.

As the participants rose to leave, after Ehrlichman had delivered his little joke about a glass of milk, Connally turned to Nixon.

"May I have two minutes with you on another matter?" he said to the president.

"Sure, sure, sure. Sit down. Absolutely."

The others filed out. When they were gone, Connally turned to Nixon. It was not another matter at all, of course, but the same matter with its hidden element finally spoken openly.

"It's on my honor to make sure that there's a very substantial amount of oil in Texas that will be at your discretion," he said. Oil? Was this a bribe or a gratuity to the president—Texas oil in return for his milk decision?

"Fine," Nixon said without hesitation.

"Unless you, unless you . . ."

"Fine," Nixon said more affirmatively.

"Unless you want somebody else to do it. . . ."

"No," said the president.

Perhaps it was really not oil that was being offered, but *oil* was simply a code for Texas money, the Texas money of the milk producers, the very money in campaign contributions that had underpinned the entire discussion of the last half-hour. What the president said next seemed to clear up the matter.

"This is a cold political deal," Nixon said. "They're very tough political operators."

"And they've got it," Connally said of the oil and the clout of AMPI.

"They've got it," Nixon agreed.

"Mr. President, I really think you made the right decision," Connally said.

If there was any doubt over whether a decision had been made then and there, there could be none now. Connally was cementing the decision with this little coda to the main meeting.

"Sorry to bug you about it," Connally said.

"I'm glad you did," Nixon replied.

H. R. Haldeman had joined them, and he escorted Connally out of the president's office. Two minutes later Haldeman, the most meticulous of note takers, wrote upon his yellow pad, where he kept abreast of presidential actions, "Connally is going for more money."

Not long after the wheels of the money machine began to turn, Connally called Jake Jacobsen, and Jacobsen in turn called the AMPI officials across town at the Madison Hotel. They were closeted with a battery of lobbyists, going over the list of congressmen and senators who had been approached and had promised legislative pressure. When Connally contended later in the legal proceedings that he was not especially unique as a target for the milk people, and that they were all over Washington like "locusts," he was right until this moment. Jake reached David Parr, an AMPI official from Arkansas (who later was sentenced to a year in prison as part of a conspiracy to contribute to campaigns illegally). Parr then burst into the smoky room of lobbyists and AMPI executives.

"It's all been taken care of!" he exclaimed. "We don't have to do anything more with Congress."

Their problem was different now. Within minutes the real enforcer, Charles Colson, was talking to an AMPI official, and he probably made clear what the administration expected of the dairymen now. The steps were logical enough. The AMPI officials rushed to their plane at National Airport and flew to Louisville. There, at 4:00 A.M., they met with an official from their sister dairy cooperative called Dairymen, Inc., or DI. As the *Daily News* might put it: AMPI TO DI: $300,000, PLEASE. The DI official was horrified, for DI had nothing like that amount lying around. But the AMPI men stressed how important an instant showing of support to the Republicans was. There was to be a Republican fund-raising dinner only hours away, and it would look good if all three major dairy cooperatives bought blocks of tickets. Reluctantly, DI, in the coming few hours, managed to pony up $25,000 in the form of five checks, and these were flown separately to Washington.

After the fund-raiser that night, the head of AMPI greeted Nixon's personal lawyer and fund-raiser, Herbert Kalmbach, in the lobby of the Madison Hotel, and they repaired to Kalmbach's room. After pleasantries, the AMPI head, Harold Nelson, reaffirmed AMPI's pledge of $2 million to the Nixon campaign. This was the word the Nixon group was waiting for. Now the official announcement of the 85 percent parity decision could go forward. Kalmbach reported the reaffirmation to John Ehrlichman in the White House the following morning, and Ehrlichman in turn passed the word that Hardin could announce his reversal to the press. At the Department of Agriculture the announcement was cryptic, not the sort of thing that might indicate the great drama that lay behind it:

"Secretary Hardin today announced an upward adjustment of the support price for manufacturing milk. . . ." In the release, the high cost of feed, double its recent level, was cited as the ostensible reason for the secretary's reevaluation. And Hardin himself would baldly state in a legal, sworn affidavit that the rise in the support price was based entirely on a reconsideration of the evidence, the cost of feed, and all that.

In dairy circles there was jubilation. The Nixon announcement meant a $700 million hike in revenue to the dairy farmer. If John Connally was the White House hero of the tale, Jake Jacobsen was the hero in-house. He was the man who had gotten the job done. His professional standing soared, not simply within AMPI but with the other dairy cooperatives and dairymen generally.

Five days after Hardin's announcement, on March 30, Connally and Jacobsen spent more than an hour together, and two weeks after that, on April 16, they met for another thirty minutes. At both sessions they congratulated each other on their joint accomplishment with the milk support. Jacobsen was effusive in expressing his gratitude, and Connally was touchingly sympathetic when the conversation turned to Jacobsen's financial difficulties in Texas. There was a lot to gossip about.

On April 28, Jacobsen dropped in to Connally's office at Treasury once again. How it was that the subject came up Jacobsen could never remember precisely. Early in the conversation Connally had expounded upon his job, how challenging, how interesting it was, and, of course, the foreign travel it involved. He mentioned with high anticipation the forthcoming trips: to Europe, to Asia, to the Middle East, and how in the ancient worlds of Persia and Turkistan he and Nellie hoped to buy carpets for the living room of the Picosa Ranch. While this registered on Jake, and he listened politely, he was anxious to turn the discussion back to dairy issues, such as the import quota on foreign chocolate and ice cream. Abruptly, by Jake's recollection, Connally said:

"The dairy people have raised a lot of money for a lot of people. Why don't you see if you can't raise a little of that money for me?"

Jake did not hesitate. "Why, of course, I'll do that, John. If it will help you and the family, of course I will."*

Jake has said that there was nothing unusual or untoward about the request. It fit easily into a pattern of operating that had been common ever since he had been in politics, and certainly during the years with Lyndon Johnson. Wilbur Mills came to mind. There was no telling how much money the milk people had given to Mills, and not for as good a cause as this. Mills was just going out, getting

---

*At trial, Connally denied that this exchange took place.

drunk, and screwing that Fanne Fox woman. Connally was going on trips with his wife, buying things for their lovely ranch. That was not unreasonable; it was even laudable. If the milk people didn't want to do it, they had the option to say no. Jake felt nothing about it; certainly he felt no twinge of conscience. This was Texas pol talk, and both understood the language. "I didn't feel as if by doing this John would do one thing for me that he wouldn't have done if I didn't give him a dime," Jake would say. It was just a gift, a simple gift, not unlike the treasures that used to pour into his house annually at Christmastime, when he had been important in government. It was something like a tribute to the sultan.

Jake put his mind to what amount of money would be appropriate. He didn't want the amount to be too small, for that would look as if the milk people were not appreciative. He didn't want the amount to be too large, because that would make it look as if they had purchased the price support decision. The amount of $10,000 seemed about right. Later that day Jake called Bob Lilly in San Antonio. There was no varnish to the request, nor did there need to be any explanation for Lilly about why it was needed. Jake wanted $10,000 for John Connally. "Connally has delivered for us," Jake said. "Now we're going to have to deliver to him. You think you can come across with ten?"

Lilly took the request to his managers, the two top executives of AMPI, and again there was no hesitation about the request. Their discussion centered simply on how to do it—by avoiding a tax consequence or creating a money trail. They settled upon a dummy account that would be for unspecified "repairs" as the best way, and Lilly was sent out to borrow the money from the Citizens National Bank as if some problem with the air conditioning had unexpectedly arisen.

How beautifully AMPI and Jacobsen were set up to do political business was clear. Jacobsen owned the controlling interest in the Citizens National Bank and could make virtually anything happen with the bank that he demanded. He had insisted that AMPI keep their corporate account and their political account for TAPE with his bank. Between January 1970 and September 1971, AMPI maintained balances of over $1 million at Citizens, and during one three-month period their accounts on hand soared to $5 million. At the end of 1970 Jake had requested AMPI to make a deposit of $200,000 so that the end-of-year deposits would look good on the books (the amount was withdrawn after the first of the year). With such good credit, an AMPI request for a loan of a mere ten grand was a snap decision for any loan officer.

On May 4, Lilly borrowed the money at Citizens in a few minutes and delivered it to Jacobsen at his law office. The money came in $100 bills. This concerned Jacobsen, for, as he would later tell the Senate Watergate Committee, "a lot of politicians do not like to take $100 bills."

On May 8, Jake called Connally. He was ready to bring to Washington what they had talked about. By Jake's memory, Connally said, "Fine."

At 11:20 A.M. on May 13, Jake opened his Box 865 at the Citizens Bank, got the money, and then flew to Washington, checking into his suite at the Madison Hotel. There he split the money into two packets of $5,000 each and put the envelopes in his breast pocket. Later Jake would be questioned as to why he had split the $10,000 in half, and he would reply, "To get more credit." The following day, May 14, he arrived for his appointment with the secretary promptly at 11:15 A.M. They spent an hour together. For both, this was a session where their professional and private lives mixed. For Jake, the Sharpstown scandal in Texas, which had involved fraud and embezzlement in a number of savings and loans, was widening and beginning to suck him in. His own savings and loans had exchanged countless bad paper loans with the collapsing Sharpstown Bank, and Jacobsen's personal problem was to contain the damage within his own financial empire—if he could. Connally, as treasury secretary, might be able to help.

By Jake's account, toward the end of the conversation he reached into his pocket for one of the envelopes and gave it to Connally. "This is part of what we talked about," he said. "There's more where this came from."

Then, Jake has said, Connally arose and went to the small bathroom adjacent to his commodious office and closed the door. Jake heard the toilet flush. When Connally emerged, with nothing in his hands, he expressed his appreciation and Jake went away, feeling good. Out on the street he crossed Pennsylvania Avenue to the American Security Bank. There he rented a safe deposit box, number 546, and put the remaining $5,000 in it. Between Box 865 in Austin and Box 546 in Washington, a money trail, so beloved by prosecutors and investigative reporters, had begun—with one difference. What goes in and out of a safe deposit box, as well as its value, is a private matter, about which no records are kept.

Four months later Jake Jacobsen retraced his steps. He needed more credit. He had seen Connally in the interim, for lunch at their customary corner booth at the Montpelier Room of the Madison Hotel. That had been on June 25, but nothing of importance had transpired.

On September 23, Jacobsen visited Connally again in his office. They talked primarily about Jake's problems with the Home Loan Bank Board, whose pressure upon Jake to get out of the savings and loan business was becoming intense. Toward the end of their forty-five-minute meeting, primarily about that, Jacobsen later testified that he asked, by the by, if the secretary was ready for the rest of the money, and Connally said he was. After Jake left, Connally made two phone calls to Thruston Morton, the chairman of the Federal Home Loan Bank Board, to plead Jacobsen's case.

The morning of September 24 was unusually busy for the secretary of the treasury. It began at 9:00 A.M. with a thirty-minute presentation to the president and the cabinet about the convocation of the 114-nation International Monetary Fund in Washington on the forthcoming weekend. After the cabinet meeting, Connally and the chairman of the Federal Reserve Board, Dr. Arthur Burns, were closeted alone with the president for an hour. As Connally, Nixon, and Burns got down to business, Jake went to his safe deposit box across the street and emptied it of its contents.

At 10:35 A.M. Connally strode brusquely into his office, where Jake waited. It was as if Jake had a toothache and the dentist had promised to try to work him in. In twenty-five minutes the secretary was due to testify before the Senate Foreign Relations Committee about the IMF matter. Later, at his criminal trial, Connally would make much of the importance of the historical moment. Delegations from 114 nations were coming to town, and his testimony before the Senate was crucial. He was feuding with Arthur Burns, and he was preoccupied with the value of the American dollar. He was pressed for time. His aides waited in the wings, intent on conferring with the boss on last-minute questions that the senators might have, to organize his briefing books and documents and his opening statement for this important appearance. But he always had time for old Jake even though this time there was no chitchat. By Jake's version, Connally took Jacobsen's envelope, went to the bathroom, flushed the toilet, and came out to say thanks and sorry that he was so pressed.

★

In October 1973 it had been over a year since Jake Jacobsen had seen John Connally. After Connally left the Nixon administration to run Democrats for Nixon, their lives had intersected only briefly, when Jake helped to set up the Connally offices in the Madison Hotel and had served as a treasurer of sorts for the strange paper organization. (Connally had put the word out in the office that Jacobsen was not to handle the money that came in the form of contributions to the organization.) After Nixon's reelection they had drifted apart, as Connally joined the prestigious Houston law firm Vinson and Elkins, and Jacobsen, after his bankruptcy, was doing what he could to keep from going to jail over his chicanery in the banking business.

Around this time, on the outskirts of San Antonio, something happened that was to affect both Connally and Jacobsen profoundly for the next decade. As in most classic confrontations involving a skilled accuser and an accused in a high place, the conflict between Connally and Jacobsen had its origins in their friendship of twenty-five years. It was to be a case of friends turned adversaries, and, eventually, mortal enemies. The process began with the AMPI bagman, Bob Lilly. One afternoon Lilly, in a state of high anxiety, called John White, the Texas commissioner of agriculture. Would White drive to San Antonio immediately and meet him at the Howard Johnson motel on the north edge of town? He was in desperate trouble, he said. White agreed and set off south. For years the commissioner had been dealing with the dairy producers and knew them well, both for their single-mindedness and for their generosity with political contributions. He had benefited himself. To White, Lilly was an intense, diminutive, and rather amusing fellow who had always been a good Democrat. Lilly had once entertained White with the story of going on Democratic party business all the way to the northern reaches of Alaska to have a meeting with a group of Eskimos. In a fit of gratitude to Lilly for coming all that way, the Eskimo leader offered his highest gift in return: the use of one of his greasy wives for a night. The thought of nervous, uptight Bob Lilly from Texas in such an unsanitary situation had for White the hilarity of a *New Yorker* cartoon.

Lilly was not joking now. He was extremely upset and scared. In San Antonio, over coffee, he blurted out that he had come under investigation for illegal AMPI campaign contributions and he had been offered immunity from prosecution for his testimony. It was an old game. The prosecutors were casting about for bigger game than Lilly. White had been around for a long time, and he had seen a lot as an old intimate of Sam Rayburn. Now his response was definite. Lilly had to tell the truth. If he didn't, they would nail him for perjury and he would go to jail—as simple as that.

"If I do testify truthfully it will hurt a lot of people," Lilly protested, and he named them, holding back the biggest name. White repeated his advice. "But . . . but it will hurt *John Connally!"* he added. White told him he had no choice.

Within hours of when Lilly began singing to the prosecutors, Jacobsen heard the devastating news. In his present dire circumstances with the San Angelo investigation, this was not news that Jake needed. Immediately he tried to reach Connally, and finally succeeded the next day, October 24. When Connally picked up the phone Jake relayed the bad news that Lilly had mentioned a $10,000 gift to Connally. By Jake's account, there was a pause.

"But you never gave me any money," Connally said.

Jake says Connally drifted. His words, Jake felt, were not for Jake, but for anybody else who might be on the line, and who might have been put there by Jake himself. That was okay. Jake was ready to go along with it.

"That's right, I didn't," he replied.

Abruptly, Connally launched into an oration. He was being hounded by prosecutors. They were just trying to rope him into this Watergate mess. All kinds of wild charges were being hurled at him. There was some trumped-up matter about a land deal in Florida. It was persecution, plain and simple; ambitious prosecutors were out fishing. Jake listened quietly to Connally's telephone speech, somewhat impressed at its extemporaneous force and lucidity. He also understood that he was hearing what their defense was going to be. It was to be a total denial. Jake didn't give, and John didn't take. At the end of their conversation they made an arrangement to meet at his hotel in Austin in a few days, when Connally was coming to Austin to attend the annual distinguished ex-student dinner at the University of Texas, an occasion at which he was to be the master of ceremonies.

Beyond his duties that night as the master of ceremonies before a doting audience at the meeting of the Ex-Student Association, he was preoccupied with the major speeches that faced him in the following week. He was scheduled to speak before a banquet of the New York Navy League and then he was to fly to London to appear on the same podium in Prince Albert Hall with Prime Minister Edward Heath of Britain and President Valery Giscard d'Estaing of

France; Walter Cronkite was to host one of these "this is your life" affairs. Now at 9:00 A.M., on Friday, October 26, with Nellie in the next room, he had to deal with the fawning Jake Jacobsen on the grubby details of Bob Lilly's testimony to the prosecutors.

Nevertheless, Connally did not undervalue the meeting, and he did not hurry the conversation. He seemed to perceive the potential damage. How could they possibly explain away the $10,000? Jake was pliant, as always. He was willing at this point to do nearly anything, anything that would work, so that he could protect Connally from being sucked into a scandal. This is a point Jacobsen would stress over and over in retrospect. In the early stages of the investigation, he was prepared to put himself at great personal risk to shield Connally, even to the limits of perjury and its consequence of jail.

Jacobsen later told the authorities that they discussed two possibilities. Jake might simply deny that he ever received $10,000 from Lilly. But that would put Jake into a direct collision with Lilly and the other AMPI officials who had approved the gratuity. That was a real disadvantage. Jacobsen said that Connally suggested another possibility. Why not replace the $10,000 or "whatever you need" in Jacobsen's lock box? This had a better chance of working. As Jake remembered it, Connally suggested they could just say the money had been in Jake's safe deposit box all the time: "What you can do is say that you offered it to me for political purposes, for me to give to other candidates, and I turned it down because I was a Democrat in a Republican administration. I didn't want to be giving money to Democrats since I was in a Republican administration, or to Republicans since I was a Democrat."

That sounded plausible to Jake in this Era of Plausible Denial, but what could he say was the reason he held the money so long— for two full years?

"You say, you kept it and offered it to me again as a contribution to the Democrats for Nixon from the dairy producers," Jake quoted Connally as saying. Their lunch together at the Madison Hotel on June 25, 1972, could be the time the "offer" was made. "We will say I turned it down then because of the internal and external problems of the dairy co-op."

In June of 1972 AMPI was having tax problems, and stories of being loose with political contributions had begun to appear in the press. As for the year or more after June 1972 that Jacobsen had ostensibly held the money, "You could say the Watergate matter started to heat up a little bit, and you didn't want to be returning the money during the Watergate business. You were just going to hold it until the Watergate matter quieted down, and then you intended to give it back."*

Their session at the Sheraton Crest lasted an hour. "Oh, we were clever as hell, we thought," Jake would say years later. "We were just going to pin 'em down. We were a couple of amateurs, fooling around in an area where we had no business." With his powerful personality and that confident air that projected invulnerability to the outside world and imparted to himself the feeling that he could get away with anything, Connally could have swept the weaker Jacobsen along with him. Jacobsen says he promised that he would stick to the lie, no matter what, and that Connally seemed satisfied. If it had been a friendship of equals, based upon mutual respect as Jacobsen imagined it, it ceased to be anything like that, given the immediate dangers for Jacobsen.

Those dangers were apparent instantly. Within three hours of their Sheraton Crest session, Jake learned that he had been subpoenaed to appear before a federal grand jury. Frantically, he attempted to reach Connally, but the governor was out rehearsing his gags with the other distinguished ex-students of the University of Texas, and Jacobsen was not invited. On Sunday, Connally finally returned Jake's call.

"Something has happened that has kind of speeded up the matter we talked about at the Sheraton Crest," Jake remembered prefacing his news of the grand jury subpoena. "Something has to be done about getting this matter straightened out, and getting the thing done. It has to be done quickly. We've got to do it right now." He meant the replacement of the $10,000 in his safe deposit box. The transfer had to be a fact before he appeared before the grand jury.

"Why don't you come to my office tomorrow, and we'll see what we can do about it?" Jake says Connally replied. "Charter a plane and come see me in my office in the morning."

When Jake arrived at Vinson and Elkins in Houston the next morning he was ushered into Connally's office by Connally's pert and plump and loyal secretary, who liked to joke about herself as the "happy hooker." As a shrewd lawyer, Jake was on his guard, for he sensed that their interests were diverging. He was relieved when Connally greeted him heartily and talked frankly about their problem in a way that suggested to the suspicious Jake that their

*At trial, Connally contested this conspiratorial conversation.

conversation was not being recorded. "I could tell he was appreciative of what I was doing," Jacobsen has said. "I certainly wasn't helping myself. There wasn't anything good about it for me." As Connally humored Jacobsen, he had to worry about folding yet another layer onto the cover story. Why were they meeting now? There was a bank merger which Connally could not complete. Perhaps Jake was in Houston to collaborate on that. Why couldn't he have simply called Jake? Well, he was worried about Jacobsen in his state of high anxiety over his mounting legal problems and wanted to eyeball him personally. But he had seen Jacobsen only three days before. . . .

"You sit still a minute," he said now.

Ten minutes later, by Jake's memory, Connally reentered his office with a cigar box. When he opened it, a single rubber glove lay upon packets of money. Carefully, meticulously, Connally put on the rubber glove finger by finger and began to flip through the supposedly old bills. Did Jake want to count them? Jake demurred. He would take Connally's word for it. He took the money and left abruptly. Two hours later, back in Austin, he went to his safe deposit box, number 865, signing in as the rules required, and thereby creating a corroborating record for the prosecutors later.

Where Connally might have gotten $10,000 in old bills in a few hours later became a source of much speculation. To the authorities, the chief suspect was a millionaire rancher in Denton, Texas, named Rex Cauble. In 1973 Cauble was already a lurid figure on the Texas landscape but he was to get even more lurid later. He counted in the ranks of the Texas superrich, having built an empire called Cauble Enterprises with a combination of quarter horses, oil, banking, and fancy Western wear named after his famed quarter horse stud Cutter Bill. His acquaintance with John Connally extended back eleven years, when Connally returned to Texas to run for governor and Cauble was dazzled by this fresh star in the Texas firmament. The rancher dispatched $15,000 to the Connally campaign, but this was too much, and Connally called him to request that the amount be cut by one-third and at the same time to ask if Cauble would become one of the campaign coordinators. When Connally won the race he awarded his benefactor with the chairmanship of the Texas Aeronautics Commission at the time when the brassy upstart Southwest Airlines was elbowing its way into the market-place and finding in Cauble its champion. Upon the wall in Cauble's office in Denton there was a picture of Connally with the inscription—it was written a few years after Connally's legal troubles—"As long as I have known Rex Cauble he has been a doer. . . . He has taken the word 'citizenship' seriously, ready to respond to the needs of his fellow man or his community."

One can only imagine the smile that must have crossed Cauble's face when he read the inscription. On the morning of October 29, 1973, Cauble walked into the Western National Bank of Denton, which he owned, and wrote out a customer's draft for $7,500 in cash. Shortly thereafter the plane of Cauble Enterprises took off for Houston as, in Austin, Jacobsen prepared to board a charter plane for the same destination.*

More of a concern than getting the money could have been that someone had to go over each bill and determine that it was old enough to have been in circulation two years before. As would soon become clear, later crystal clear in the Connally trial, ensuring that $20 bills are old enough requires inside knowledge. But as Jacobsen remembered, Connally told him that he had at least gone through Cauble's money and taken out the bills with his own signature on them as secretary of the treasury.

On November 2, Jake went before the grand jury. He had a bad feeling about his testimony from the start. It was not so much his lies that unsettled him, for he had lied before. Rather, it was the demeanor of the prosecutor, Jon Sale, toward his testimony. To Jake, Sale seemed disinterested and cavalier. He was sardonic and downright contemptuous of what Jake was saying. "It seemed as if he knew what I was saying wasn't true," Jake recalled. "Maybe it was in my imagination." He was coming up against the universal problem of the occasional liar.

"What did you do with that money?" Sale asked.

"I took it and put it in my safe deposit box," Jake replied. "I left it there and talked to Secretary Connally about whether or not he wanted to give money to somebody or what he wanted to do with it, and he said he didn't have anybody he wanted to give any money to, so he didn't use it."

"Then what did you do with it?"

"Well, I kept it."

"Where is it now?"

"It is in my safe deposit box."

---

*Two years later, when the Watergate special prosecutor's office showed Cauble a copy of his bank draft and asked him to explain it, he professed that he had overheard a female friend complain that in her lifetime she would never own a Lincoln Continental, and so, as a gesture, he had taken the money out of his Denton bank in cash that morning just to buy her a Mark IV as a surprise.

"Did you tell Mr. Lilly that Secretary Connally had no use for it?"

"No, I haven't told Mr. Lilly that yet. I kept it and then along came Democrats for Nixon, and I thought he might use it then. But he didn't use it then [either]."

"Are you saying that on the second occasion you asked Secretary Connally if he wanted the money?"

"Yes."

"And again he said no?"

"That is right."

"Then what did you do?"

"I just left it in my safe deposit box and forgot about it, frankly, for a little while."

"Did it ever occur to you that Mr. Lilly's intention was that this money go to Secretary Connally, not to your safe deposit box?"

"Certainly, that was Mr. Lilly's intention."

"Without any formal meaning to this word, isn't this a form of stealing Mr. Lilly's money or deceiving him?"

"No, I am going to return it to Mr. Lilly."

"This was 1971 when he gave you the money."

"Well, the reason I waited so long was that this Watergate thing came along, and I thought I just wouldn't want to be returning money during this, but now that I am mixed up in it anyway, I might as well go on."

"As far as you know, when did the Watergate thing come along?"

"Well, just shortly after the campaign."

"Shortly after the campaign? What do you mean by that?"

"Well, I don't know for sure."

"When you say the Watergate thing, what did you mean?"

"I meant the publicity about giving of money and withholding of money, and all of the Watergate-related activity."

"That would have been at least a year after you got the money, if not more—anywhere from a year to two years after you got the money."

"I haven't had it two years."

"You got the money in the spring of 1971, correct? The $10,000 that you have acknowledged receiving, you received in or about May 1971, right?"

"Yes, I think that is true."

"Nothing connected with Watergate came about until the spring of 1972 at the earliest, isn't that right?"

"That is true, but in the meantime the Democrats for Nixon

came along, and I held it during that period, thinking maybe Secretary Connally could use it."

"To this day, you have not told Mr. Lilly that you have kept the money in your own safe deposit box."

"Aren't you supposed to pay taxes on money like that in a bank?" a grand juror piped up.

"What was your view as to whether or not this was income to you, Mr. Jacobsen?" the prosecutor said, rephrasing the question.

"I assumed I was just a trustee, that it wasn't my money."

The day after this grand jury appearance Jacobsen testified before the Senate Watergate Committee and dispensed the same lie. The following week he gave a deposition under oath in a suit Ralph Nader had brought, charging illegal campaign contributions by the dairy cooperatives, and again he lied. Thus, Jacobsen now had three instances of perjury on the record. All these perjuries he says were committed to protect his friend, John Connally.

When he returned to Austin, Jake was summoned to the office of Connally's intimate friend and former gubernatorial assistant, Larry Temple. Temple had with him Marvin Collie, a lawyer in Connally's Vinson and Elkins firm. By training, Collie was a tax attorney rather than a criminal lawyer, and he fancied himself a fast friend of Connally's within the firm, to the point of sycophancy. His presence at this session was his own doing, rather than authorized by Vinson and Elkins, and it shows that at this stage, with such freelance help, Connally was not taking his jeopardy too seriously.

Jacobsen maintains that around this time he was offered a deal. If Jake would stick to his story, his addicted wife, Florene, would be taken care of for life no matter what happened, no matter how long Jake might have to go to jail. This contention has some credibility. He was under enormous pressure, and Florene was his mortal vulnerability. "If there is one thing in my life that has made me take wrong decisions, it was my wife's illness," Jake would say. "That was the reason I got in with that crook Cowan, and it was the deciding factor in how I dealt with this. John Connally had told me that if I would stick to my story he would see that Florene would be taken care of, and I would be taken care of. I gave serious thought to that, but in the end I couldn't make myself do it. My wife had already gotten to the point where she was saying I was a crook. I knew I had to be around, or she would have gone to pieces." He also thought that if he maintained the story he would stay out of jail. It would be some months and another perjury or two, however, before Jacobsen abandoned the lie.

When Jacobsen called him on November 12, Connally was back home from Europe. Sounding a bit more upbeat about his testimony than he felt, Jake said it had gone pretty well. "I didn't have much trouble with what I told them," Jake said bravely, "and I hope yours goes well too." Their fortunes were now tied together. If Connally did well, corroborating Jake forcefully and plausibly, they might both slip through.

In fact, on November 14, before the grand jury, Connally fell on his face. He said a number of things which later could be proven to be false, especially after Jacobsen turned state's evidence. Connally would be called before the grand jury a second time in six months, and then he would be forced to contradict himself. At first his denials were nearly total, even to this extent:

"Mr. Connally, did Mr. Jacobsen tell you the source of the $10,000?"

"No, he did not."

"He didn't tell you it had come from AMPI or the dairy industry?"

"No."

Five months later Connally would try to correct this mistake, but it was too late.

Before the second grand jury, in April 1974, he said, "My best recollection is that he said that the milk producers were going to start making some political contributions in 1971, and that they would be contributing to candidates in both parties and that there was $10,000 available then to be given to any committee or candidate or campaign that I would designate."

"So it is correct to say that when he first mentioned the $10,000 he did mention the source of the money."

"Yes. I don't recall that he mentioned anything in particular. As I recall, he did say milk producers."

In his November grand jury appearance, he obfuscated his dealings with Jacobsen, which would later rebound harshly against him. (In italics are the statements for which, seven months later, he was indicted for perjury.)

"Did you express any surprise or did you think it odd when he offered to make available to you this $10,000 cash political contribution in the spring or summer of 1971?" the prosecutor asked.

"No, not odd, because the posture in which he put it—Jake and I have been good friends for a number of years, and he obviously would not do anything—he didn't offer it to me; he said, 'The money is available for a committee or candidate of your designation, if you will make one,' " Connally replied. "And I said, 'Well, I don't want to do that.' And I have already explained that to you, but it wasn't odd at all, simply because he was as familiar with the fact that, as I was, that I was here and he was trying in some way to befriend the people that I felt should be befriended.

"And I just simply said, 'I don't want to participate.' "

"When have you last discussed this matter with Mr. Jacobsen?"

"Oh, gosh, a long time ago. I don't recall."

"Have you discussed it with him recently, within the last three or four weeks?"

"No."

"Have you had any conversations with him the last three or four weeks?"

"No, I have been gone for a little over two weeks now, and I had one conversation with him about two and a half weeks ago, I guess, or three weeks ago, in which I asked him to check into a bank application for me, *but that is the only contact I have had with him.*"

"Where was that conversation?"

"In Houston."

"In person?"

"Yes."

"What was the occasion of his visit to Houston?"

"Well, I am not sure I know precisely, but part of it was for this purpose."

"Would you give us a little more of the surrounding circumstances?"

"Well, only that one of the people that we normally represent in my law firm had filed an application for a bank charter in an area where they owned a lot of real estate. It was a national bank charter. Frankly, in the firm, we don't handle bank charters and yet, they wanted us to look after it, and I didn't want to look after it. I didn't want to participate in it, so I asked him if he would do so, and that is the last conversation I have had with him."

"Do you know if that was prior to or following his appearance before this grand jury?"

"No, I don't know. I don't know when he appeared."

"Were you aware he has appeared before this grand jury?"

"I understand now he has but I have not talked to him since then."

"Did you discuss this $10,000 cash sum with him during that conversation?"

"No, I don't recall that we did."

"I suggest that given the somewhat peculiar nature of this transaction, that is $10,000 cash, that Mr. Jacobsen received from the dairy interests, that his making it available to you, that it is a subject matter which I would think you would recall had you discussed it with him that recently?"

"Well, I think that is probably right. *We have discussed this whole dairy thing, but I don't recall we did it on that occasion and in our discussions, we have simply treated it just like we treat anything else, we are both going to tell the truth about it, and that is all there is to it."*

"When was the last occasion on which you did discuss, as you describe it, this whole dairy thing with Mr. Jacobsen?"

"We really haven't—I am just trying to think if there was any definitive discussion of it. *I don't recall having any major discussions with him since last fall."*

Two phases of a case against Connally were taking shape. The first phase was the gratuity itself: whether, in fact, Jacobsen had offered $10,000 (or more) to Connally, and whether Connally had accepted it. Only two witnesses could answer those questions, John Connally and Jake Jacobsen. In November of 1973, before every duly constituted panel, under oath and not under oath, their stories to the authorities squared precisely in their denial that Connally had taken the gift. The second phase was whether there had been a cover-up, in which Connally and Jacobsen (along with several confederates) had conspired to mislead the grand jury and the Senate Select Committee. In this second phase, the evidence was far stronger than simply the word of the two potential co-conspirators. In the cover-up there were records to test. More important to the layman than the lawyer perhaps, there was a logical link between the two phases of the case: if the gratuity had not been accepted, there was nothing to cover up—no stories needed to be concocted, no facts needed to be obfuscated, no new money needed to be exchanged, no surreptitious entries into safe deposit boxes needed to be accomplished. But criminal investigations and criminal charges are not held together with logical propositions. The rules of law can be restrictive.

The central piece of evidence was the $10,000 itself which, according to Jacobsen's grand jury testimony, had lain untouched in his safe deposit box for two and one-half years, a time in which he went bankrupt and desperately needed every nickel he could lay his hands on. It was money, Jacobsen said, he had forgotten about.

One of the lawyers in the special prosecutor's office had tried a case in New York with similar elements, in which the prosecutors had determined by the bills themselves when the money had actually gone into circulation. For this reason, Jacobsen had been asked in the grand jury if he would permit the FBI to inventory the contents of his Box 865 in Austin. Knowing he had no option of refusal, Jake agreed. The date for the inventory was set for November 27.

On November 24, a Saturday, Jake got a call from George Christian, the PR man and Connally associate whom Jacobsen knew from the old Price Daniel days, who announced that the governor was in town and wanted to see Jake the next day. For everything Jake and John now did together there had to be some plausible explanation; they knew by then that later they might be asked for the reasons why they met. For this meeting, the rationale was developed that negative stories were appearing in the press about Connally's appearance before the grand jury and in executive session with the lawyers of the Senate Select Committee, and he wanted to discuss with Christian and Jacobsen what to do. On the stand one and one-half years later Connally submitted the following explanation: "The purpose of the discussion at Mr. Christian's house was to try to get some judgment as to what I ought to do. My own personal feeling was that if I were called to reappear before the Ervin Committee, my own desire was that I appear in a public meeting, which frankly I felt would be televised. That's the type of forum that I thought I should appear in and not any more executive sessions or meetings with the staff."

The boldness of that formulation notwithstanding, Jake remembers nothing of the Ervin Committee or of executive sessions or of press relations ever arose in the session at Christian's house. The situation was becoming more and more complicated by the minute. Jake Jacobsen knew perfectly well why he was being summoned, and Christian should have known, if nothing else, that of the three only he had not yet been called before the grand jury. It was in Christian's interest not to get sucked into a conspiracy now.

Jacobsen arrived at the Christian home punctually at 9:30. Even though he had been associated on and off with Christian for years, he now stepped across the Christians' threshold for the first time. Christian's wife let him in and gave him a cup of coffee, and then she left for a tennis game. Minutes later Connally arrived. He carried with him a briefcase. Why the briefcase? The item would later trouble the staunchest of Connally supporters.

Certain facts about this parley are undeniable. It lasted a little over half an hour, and Jake had very little to say. Almost immediately after Christian ushered Connally into his living room he made himself scarce, as if by prior plan, going upstairs to dress his four-year-old son and then take the child to the kitchen to give him an apparently heaping bowl of cereal (for it would take the boy a half-hour to eat it). He did not return to Connally and Jacobsen until a few minutes before both rose to leave. What about the grand discussion about Connally's demand for a public hearing before the Ervin Committee? Jacobsen would guffaw years later when he heard that such an explanation had been earnestly offered. "That's a bunch of crap that George walked out because his little boy needed his help," he would say. "He did walk out. I remember that, but John probably told him to. I don't think for one minute that George would think to walk out on his own. He would do whatever John told him. If John had wanted him there, that little boy would have had to fend for himself."

Jake was nervous and Connally seemed equally so. Pleasantries were attempted, but they were forced and artificial. Jake knew he was there for one purpose, and he had brought the old $10,000 with him. In short order, in Jake's version, Connally said again that he had told Jake earlier on the telephone that there were "Shultz bills" in the first batch of $10,000 which he had given Jake in Houston. It had been one of those ultimate moments of terror. He had thought to remove the bills with his own signature on them, but not those with his successor's. Connally could scarcely have been offered a bribe of money with his unknown successor's signature on it. Before long, Jake remembered Connally opening his briefcase, taking out a bundle wrapped in a newspaper, and handing it to Jake. Jake, ever casual with cash, reached in his back pocket and handed Connally an envelope with the old money. It was over as fast as Christian's lad could take two spoonfuls of Wheaties in the kitchen.

Again, where would Connally get a second batch of $10,000 in cash? Again, the authorities suspected that the trusty Rex Cauble had galloped to the rescue. Connally had called him and Cauble had flown immediately to the Picosa Ranch on November 23, two days before the meeting with Jacobsen at George Christian's house. The purpose of this visit, Cauble later told the prosecutors, was to provide some advice to Connally about which of his fine Arabian horses should be gelded. To the prosecutors it was a concatenation of events that was simply too revealing to be coincidental.*

As Jake recalls, he then had two problems. First, he had promised the Watergate prosecutors that he would not go to his safe deposit box until the FBI had inventoried its contents. That was scheduled for three days hence. How was the money Connally had just given him to get into his box without leaving a trace?

"You just have to do it, because the money has got to be old enough to bear out the story," Jake remembered Connally saying coldly.

"I'll do the best I can," Jake replied.

Jacobsen's other problem was that the trustee in his bankruptcy case had inventoried both his safe deposit boxes at the Citizens National Bank to determine his full assets and had found both to be empty. Box 865 had only a few entries on its signature card, so it could not be used. But he had another box, number 998, and it had a number of entries. It afforded a greater degree of plausibility for the absence of any money when the bankruptcy trustee had taken a look, and the presence of $10,000 when the FBI looked in. What if the FBI questioned the bankruptcy trustee? Jake knew he was getting himself farther and farther out on a limb with every move.

The next day, Monday, Jake went to the Citizens Bank after it had closed. There, a comedy ensued that later would make Jacobsen feel like a chastened seven-year-old, and made him wonder how ridiculous his protection of John Connally was going to get. Since

---

*Rex Cauble was never called as a witness in the Connally trial, for he stoutly denied that he had ever given Connally the two batches of $10,000, and for protection he retained the prominent Washington attorney William Hundley, who had defended John Mitchell in the Watergate case and Tongsun Park in the "Koreagate" scandal. Cauble was interviewed in the special prosecutor's office five days before the Connally trial, and after his denials it was decided that this hostile witness could not be useful.

In 1982 Cauble was convicted of ten counts of racketeering in connection with the smuggling of 108 tons of marijuana into Texas. It was the largest drug smuggling case in Texas history. Before this came to light he had been a loud advocate for antidrug campaigns because his own son was an addict. Indeed, John Connally had appointed him to be a Special Texas Ranger, a private distinction for law enforcement enthusiasts. Cauble was also an honored member of the Texas Narcotics Officers Association, a group for which he threw glittering parties in his architect-designed horse barn in Denton. Before Cauble was sentenced to ten concurrent terms of five years as a racketeer, John Connally appeared as a character witness.

"I do not believe Rex Cauble is guilty of the charges brought against him," Connally told the judge and jury. "Somehow the case went awry. Somehow this case never portrayed this man . . . as a man of inordinate pride and self-esteem who would sacrifice anything for his loyalty to his friends."

his bankruptcy, he was no longer an officer of the bank, so Jacobsen enlisted his former law partner, Joe Long, who was the chairman of the board of the bank, to help him make an entry into the vault without a trace. Bank employees had begun to go home as Long lifted the master key from an empty desk. As the two men approached the vault, they were presented with a discouraging sight: the vault was cluttered with equipment of the tellers who had closed down for the day, a warren of cash drawers and carts of records. The two men looked at each other despairingly and plunged fearlessly forward, clambering over the carts to Box 998—two grown men in business suits looking very undignified indeed. Of course, they were caught. A scowling secretary appeared at this moment with the president of the bank, and the secretary asked disapprovingly if the mountain climbers had signed in. As she stood by, Jacobsen and Long climbed back out, and Long signed in for his box. That done, they went back again and accomplished their mission, but two more witnesses had been generated.

The following day, November 27, 1973, Jake Jacobsen went to the Citizens Bank again and met the FBI agents at the appointed time. He watched as they opened Box 998, and when the cash came into view he heaved a sigh.

"I'm glad it's still there," he said.

23

The Trial

With the turn of the new year, the focus of the Watergate scandal had shifted to the courts. The special prosecutor's office had survived the Saturday night massacre on October 20, 1973, and was now fully operational and spinning its web.

One of the three prosecutors in the campaign contributions section of the office was Charles Ruff, a soft-spoken, ascetic man who had been struck down with a strange viral disease in Africa when he was young and was confined to a wheelchair. Like a number of men in the office, Ruff was a product of the Southern District of New York, that tough federal judicial district that includes Manhattan, with all its Mafia and racketeering cases. But Ruff had also had a year of Texas experience, which had made Jake Jacobsen a familiar figure to him and something of a symbol of the general corruption of Texas banking.

He saw Jacobsen as one of many borderline characters who populated Texas savings and loan associations and used them as their own private purses. What Jacobsen and Cowan were doing with their savings banks in San Angelo and elsewhere, with their high-risk loans and phony real estate appraisals, was simple enough to Ruff: they were raping the banks. If Ruff had no personal animus toward Jacobsen, he had no sympathy for him either. To Ruff, Jake was simply weak, a man who had lived in the horrendous shadow of LBJ and had profited by it, largely by being the strawman for LBJ in a number of questionable deals. With Jake's ever-present presidential cuff links and his "silver fingernails" and his Uriah Heepish manner, Ruff considered him to be a character out of a Texas pulp novel.

By early February 1974 the boat was pulling out for Jake Jacobsen. On February 6 he was indicted in the San Angelo case on charges of misapplication and perjury that carried a possible jail sentence of thirty-five years. On a parallel track, the FBI had now conducted its inventory of the money in Jacobsen's safe deposit box and, possibly to the shock of Connally, that money, too, was found to have bills which could not have been in circulation in May 1971. Thus, on the face of it, Jacobsen had perjured himself when he testified to the grand jury that for over two and a half years, from May 1971 to November 1973, he had not touched the $10,000 he got from Lilly to gratify what he characterized as Connally's request. So on February 21, in Washington, only two weeks after his San Angelo indictment, Jacobsen was indicted again for perjury, this time in the milk case. In the latter indictment it was stated that he had gotten the $10,000 from AMPI to bribe a public official, but the public official was not named. The press had its suspicions, however. In reporting the Jacobsen indictment, CBS said that John Connally's name had been brought into the investigation, and Connally responded with a dignified denial:

"Jake Jacobsen did come to me—Jake had been an old friend and still is—and said that the milk producers were getting ready to make contributions to candidates and committees, and that there was $10,000 available to be given as I designated. So I said, just leave me out. I'm going to wait, and I don't know what I'm going to do in terms of political activities, but at least at the present, I don't want any part of it."

The prosecutors had Jacobsen dead to rights, and he knew it. His own attorney was telling him that in the San Angelo case he would surely be convicted on at least some of the major charges, and in the milk case he had testified under oath to a story that was not logically possible. That was known as perjury. What was he to do? In his own mind, Jake felt his problems in the milk case, especially his perjuries, had all resulted from a noble attempt to shield John Connally. His whole career as an assistant to powerful men had given him the secretive, protective instincts of the loyalist. But now, with the sudden change in the political ethos that Watergate had wrought, those instincts might put him in jail for the rest of his life. What was the price of loyalty to be now? From her drugged stupor, his own wife, Florene, lashed out at him and called him a crook. Jake knew that she would never survive his incarceration.

To his friends, Jacobsen fretted about what to do. He had only two things to trade: what he said was the real story about his transactions with Connally and the real story about his illegal deals for Lyndon Johnson when he was president. He had little confidence that his confidant's knowledge of Johnson's chicanery in office would help him now. Johnson had been dead for a year. Sordid tales of presidential criminality were only of historical, not legal, interest. It would do him little good to confide to the prosecutors about how Lyndon Johnson had tried to strong-arm him into making the president a partner in a small, rural Texas bank.

Perhaps the most scandalous and potentially the most useful information was what the bagman Bob Lilly had already told the prosecutors in confidence, which Jacobsen might be able to corroborate. Lyndon Johnson, then the president of the United States, had, through his aide Cliff Carter, solicited and received gratuities from the milk producers far in excess of the amounts with which John Connally was being charged. On two separate occasions, the dates of which were provided to the prosecutors, Cliff Carter had requested cash payments of $15,000 for the sitting president. For these "requests," Jacobsen was always the messenger. "Cliff wants to talk to you" was Jake's standard line, and Lilly knew what the subject was to be without asking. Furthermore, in his second interview with the Watergate special prosecutors (on November 2, 1973, ten months after LBJ's death), Lilly blurted out that not long before he left the White House, President Johnson had demanded $250,000 from the milk producers as thanks for all his support as president. The money, Johnson said, was to be used to organize his staff after he left office, and he even suggested that the membership of AMPI might be levied an additional few dollars per head to raise the money. In the parlance of AMPI, this became a "commitment" to Johnson.

But Jake decided it just wouldn't work. In the Watergate climate it was Nixon, not Johnson, who was the target of interest. To a friend, Jake remarked about Johnson, "They could get Johnson on a dozen things if they wanted to, but nobody will be interested. It's chickenshit stuff." Furthermore, Jacobsen was beginning to see the inevitability of turning against John Connally. If he turned on both Johnson and Connally simultaneously, people would merely say, "This man will turn on anybody, including the dead."

A new prosecutor, Frank Tuerkheimer, took charge of the case at this point. Even though, like Ruff, he was a graduate of the tough-guy school of prosecutors in the Southern District of New York, Tuerkheimer had the mild manners, the thoughtfulness, and the decency of the law professor he was. A tall, dark, earnest man of thirty-five, with a nest of unruly hair, he had grown up in the Bronx as the son of a German butcher, and had spoken his parents' native tongue in the home. Within the prosecutor's office he was considered the perfect choice for the milk fund case because, eventually, it was to be tried before Judge George Hart, who was not impressed by theatrical, flamboyant characters in his courtroom. Hart was a Nixon appointee, an irascible old Republican, who had already demonstrated his distaste for the whole panoply of Watergate cases. Before Judge Hart, Tuerkheimer's civility seemed to have the best chance of success.

The problem of the prosecutors was obvious: the credibility of Jake Jacobsen. On the primary charge—that Jacobsen had tendered a bribe to Connally—there were only two witnesses. It was, therefore, a classic case of one man's word against another's. Left at that, Jacobsen—the perjurer, the embezzler, the thief—had no chance of persuading a jury that he, rather than the noble John Connally, was telling the truth. But in the subsequent "obstruction period," linked logically as it was to the passing of the gratuity, there was hard documentation, and it demonstrated a consciousness of guilt on the bribery charges.

The special prosecutor's office addressed itself to the basics. Was there a case against John Connally? Was it worth the energy of the office to try to make the case? The special prosecutor himself was not involved in the discussion of these questions, for Texan Leon Jaworski had disqualified himself from the milk fund investigation almost immediately after he became the special prosecutor because his law firm in Houston had brought a lawsuit against AMPI. As the investigation proceeded, Jaworski had even better reasons for disqualifying himself. He knew Jake Jacobsen well from the days when Jake was the assistant attorney general of Texas, in the early 1950s. He also knew John Connally, somewhat more casually. When Connally was governor of Texas he had appointed Jaworski to be chairman of the Governor's Committee on Public Education, and that was enough to compromise Jaworski in the case. Nevertheless, his disqualification was not total. To his deputy, Henry Ruth, Jr., and to Ruff and Tuerkheimer, Jaworski advised caution; Connally was still considered a strong contender for the Republican nomination in 1976. By Jaworski's own account, "I did not want him tarnished by news reporters that he was under investigation, until the matter was completed and a decision had been made as to whether the investigation should be closed or action be taken." To one other than Henry Ruth it might have retarded or even sidetracked the Connally investigation.

On April 11, Connally made his second visit to the grand jury. This time there was no hiding his appearance. The day before, Jack Anderson put the situation starkly in his column: "A crack FBI squad has dug up evidence that Connally pocketed $10,000 from the Associated Milk Producers, Inc., and hastily returned the cash after the dairy lobby came under investigation." The *Washington Post*, the *Washington Star-News*, and the wires echoed this news in separate stories.

The prosecutors, however, needed Jacobsen. Nine days after Connally's testimony the prosecutor began to deal. Jacobsen's attorney asked a high price. The entire San Angelo fraud matter must be dropped. Potential charges against Jacobsen on any other banking misbehavior must be foreclosed. Any charges that might arise out of his solicitation of the bribe money for Connally from Bob Lilly must be dropped. Even the threat of permanent revocation of Jacobsen's law license, if he pleaded guilty to a felony, was to be defused.

During the first weeks of May the prosecutors considered the proposition. With the corroborating evidence from the obstruction period, they were convinced that they could make a strong case against Connally if they had Jacobsen's testimony. What would they gain and what would they risk by agreeing to a plea? To dispose of such serious charges against Jacobsen was no trivial matter. Yet the country was at a critical juncture. At the root of Watergate was the question of whether public officials, especially the highest officials in the land, were above the law. In value to society, it was far more important to proceed with a strong case against Connally than to put a marginal character like Jake Jacobsen behind bars. The special prosecutor's office was not seized with a grand philosophy—they were under pressure and taking one case at a time—but in the choice of whether to dismiss the charges against Jacobsen in order to prosecute Connally lay the balance of the greater good to society. It was unstated, but implicit.

The ethics of the state of Texas were also under severe scrutiny at this same time. The entire upper slice of Texas political leadership was crashing down in the Sharpstown scandal. "Sharpstown" had come to represent the corrupt symbiosis between Texas politicians and lobbying interests, and between 1971 and 1975 the scandal had tainted the governor, the lieutenant governor, the Speaker of the House, and many other state legislators. Jake Jacobsen's practices and associations in his banking business epitomized what the Sharpstown business was about. Now in the emerging case of *United States v. John Connally*, Watergate joined Sharpstown; the nation joined Texas.

On May 21 the office of the special prosecutor officially concluded its arrangement with Jacobsen. It bargained away all of Jake's Texas charges in return for a plea of guilty to one count of offering a gratuity to a public official. By so pleading, Jacobsen was punishable by two years in prison and a $10,000 fine. The arrangement required him to give testimony in "matters where he may have relevant information."

In the weeks that followed, Jake took up residence in the special prosecutor's office. He told his revised story over and over and over again. Every detail, especially those details that could be tested against records and against the testimony of Lilly and Connally, was explored. Jake approached his ordeal without enthusiasm. He had no interest in seeing his erstwhile friend go to jail. He was interested only in staying out of jail himself. Furthermore, Tuerkheimer was not his type: he thought the professor was something of a "horse's ass." That Tuerkheimer rode a bicycle to work in the morning, rather than something chrome-plated and leather-appointed, became as noteworthy to Jacobsen, in a negative sense, as Jacobsen's silver fingernails were noteworthy to the New York prosecutors.

The consequence of these sessions came on July 29, 1974. The day the second of three impeachment articles against Richard Nixon passed the House Judiciary Committee, and eleven days before the president resigned, John Connally was indicted.

★

In the seven months before Connally came to trial, Texas rallied to his defense. There was a feeling that the federal constabulary was conspiring to disgrace one of the state's proudest figures and, by implication, the state of Texas itself. Indeed, it was Connally's dignity in adversity that his fellow Texans most admired. All manner of bitter rationalizations were adopted: the indictment was the work of sour Democrats, still angry over the party switch and intent to deny Connally the nomination of the Republicans. Liberal Kennedy Democrats, said to reign in the special prosecutor's office, were out to humiliate Connally. The plea bargain of Jake Jacobsen was an abuse of judicial power. Connally could not possibly get a fair trial before a black jury in Washington, D.C. On and on the arguments went.

As he waited, Connally adopted the role of the victim. He was sensitive about not wanting to embarrass his friends in Houston by associating with them, and such sensitivity made it into the social pages of Texas newspapers. His friends reacted by inviting his association all the more. (Not all of them: Senator Lloyd Bentsen, still harboring presidential ambitions, distanced himself.) Three months before his trial began, the Houston Chamber of Commerce unanimously elected Connally its vice chairman, implying that Connally remained good for business. The Houston Rotary Club, the largest in America, invited him to speak, and Connally delivered his stock theme of "faith in America." The poignancy of that message was not lost on the audience and they gave him two standing ovations. When he went to social functions in Houston where he might encounter Jaworski, his friends made sure that the men stayed on separate sides of the room.

Instinctively, Connally knew the value of props. A *Wall Street Journal* reporter came to interview him before the trial, and she found him in a contemplative pose, reading the self-defense of Clarence Darrow in his 1912 jury bribery case. Darrow was tried in Los Angeles, far from his Chicago home, just as Connally was being tried far from Texas. Connally read his visitor a passage: "I'm a stranger in a strange land," Darrow had told his jury, "but here have gathered around me as good, loyal, and faithful friends as any man could have on earth. If you convict me, there will be people to applaud the act. But if in your judgment and your wisdom, you believe me innocent, I know that from thousands will come thanks to this jury for saving my liberty and my name." As Connally finished reading, he smiled.

"You know, Darrow got off," he said. "I console myself with the thought that character is born of adversity."

In November the prosecution and defense lawyers came together in the chambers of Judge Hart to argue a critical legal point. The Connally indictment fell into two distinct areas: bribery and obstruction of justice. There was a loose parallel between the Watergate cover-up and the situation that faced the court in the Connally trial. Richard Nixon had been brought down by his acts in covering up the Watergate break-in, but Connally's estimable defense attorney, Edward Bennett Williams, argued that in the Connally case the bribe was the substantive charge, while the cover-up charges were secondary. Therefore, Williams contended the two sections should be severed, lest the prosecutors rely unfairly on the cover-up and perjury charges in an attempt to prove the more substantial bribery counts.

All the parties understood the background of this maneuver. The prosecution's case was strongest on the cover-up. That was where the documentation and the corrobation lay—the money trail, the furtive meetings between Jacobsen and Connally, the provably false testimony, the consciousness of guilt. In the bribery counts, it was a classic case of whom one believed, Connally or Jacobsen. The grand jury had believed Jacobsen, because it had indicted Connally. An open trial was a different proposition, however.

It was a thorny problem. Judge Hart put the question starkly to the prosecutor. How would the prosecution be hurt if the sections of the case were severed? Perhaps the prosecutor answered too honestly, and Williams rephrased the prosecutor's answer to suit his own needs: "Your Honor, stripped down to its essence, his answer is that the prosecution would lose the prejudice that comes from having the jury know that the defendant was indicted when he laid his defense before the grand jury."

Williams was asking for two trials. He knew he could win the first trial on style alone, when the jury judged Jacobsen's word against Connally's. He doubted seriously that, when he won the first, he would ever have to defend Connally in a second trial.

In effect, the entire case now turned on the judge's discretion. What bothered Judge Hart was the fact that Connally's grand jury appearance had itself added a second crime to the charges: the crime of perjury. "I must admit that, where the defendant has appeared before the grand jury and has been indicted for perjury in addition to the substantive offense, the possibility of this working against the defendant in an unfair manner has always worried me a great deal, not only in this case but in some other cases," he said to the opposing attorneys in chambers. He bought the Williams argument, and many would say later that Williams won the case for Connally four months before the trial. It was a question of place and time. The prosecutors from the Southern District of New York grumbled that if this were Manhattan and Connally were a Mafia don, the link between the charges would never have been cut.

Within the special prosecutor's office, the lawyers analyzed the strengths and weaknesses of their case, which now had to be tried on such narrow ground. Their strengths fell into two areas, as they saw it: first, the areas where Connally was contradicted by other witnesses and by Connally himself, and second, the areas, especially the cover-up phase, where the "logic of fact" supported Jacobsen's version of the events. The weaknesses of the case boiled down to one haunting question and to the credibility of Jake Jacobsen. The haunting question was this: Why would John Connally, this man of such evident accomplishment, this personage made of presidential timber, risk his career and his reputation for a mere $10,000?

In a memorandum, Tuerkheimer and his assistants expressed their belief that the answer was threefold:

First, it is very unlikely that Connally in 1971 felt he was risking anything in dealing with Jacobsen whom he had known and worked closely with for almost one quarter of a century.

Second, since Jacobsen was dealing with Lilly, a mere professional acquaintance who was much further removed from Jacobsen than Jacobsen was from Connally, it was Jacobsen who is taking the real risk. It is inconceivable that Jacobsen should in his April 28 conversation with Lilly distort the truth in favor of criminality by asking for money for Connally personally when it was supposed to be for political candidates. As a practical matter, therefore, the person who was actually taking the risk at the time was Jacobsen. It is unlikely that he would do so unless he meant what he said when he took it.

Third, the argument that Connally would not violate the law for a mere $10,000 is weakened by the narrow factual issues of the case. . . . Just five weeks before Jacobsen received the money in May of 1971, AMPI had reaffirmed its $2 million commitment to the Administration. . . . It would be almost an insult to Connally to give him a mere $10,000 for *contributions* when AMPI was talking in terms of $2 million. Unlikely as it is that Connally would violate the law for a mere $10,000, it is equally unlikely that AMPI would lawfully deal in such small sums with him.

In short, Jake was taking the risk. The spirit of the gift was personal thanks, not politics. And in the context of the $2 million commitment and high-cost politics, the sum of $10,000 was sweet to a person even of Connally's means, but an insult as a campaign contribution.

When the trial finally opened on April Fool's Day, the scene at the United States Courthouse off Judiciary Square had become familiar to Washingtonians. Connally was the fourth Nixon cabinet member to be tried by Watergate prosecutors, but as the Washington press pointed out that morning, a presidential cabinet member had not been tried for bribery since Albert Fall was convicted of the crime during the Teapot Dome scandal in the 1920s. Dressed in a pinstriped suit and sporting a homburg that appeared slightly too small, Connally looked thinner than Washington, with its short attention span, remembered, for he had shaved fifteen pounds off his weight, like an overweight boxer getting ready for a title bout. A serious and determined Edward Bennett Williams led the path through the crowd. To the swarm of the press, Connally arrived like Tarquinius Superbus, exuding a pride and serenity that inspired some to write again of his "effortless superiority." With him were Nellie and his son, John, and also Thomas "Tommy the Cork" Corcoran, the ex-aide to Franklin Roosevelt, as if the defendant wanted to display the high level of his friendships.

In the courtroom Williams approached the selection of the jury as a longstanding, comfortable bachelor might approach his dinner meal. He had no fancy recipe, no exotic ingredients suggested by sociologists or poll takers. He wanted to cook this case in a way that had worked well for him for decades and had made him the most successful defense lawyer in America. He simply followed his gut instincts. His client had had a distinguished career in government, and so Williams wanted jury members who respected the institutions of government, who, if possible, had themselves benefited from government service, and who had a high opinion of American leaders. While he bridled at the prevalence of black juries in the capital city that was eighty percent black, and even remarked that whites, not blacks, were the minority in need of affirmative action in Washington, he sought to turn his jury pool to his advantage. His client had been the intimate of Lyndon Johnson for more than thirty-five years, and Johnson had done more for civil rights than any president since Lincoln. Because Williams knew who his character witnesses were going to be, he wanted jury members who were faithful, even soulful, churchgoers. In general, the defense hoped for a jury composed of middle-class blacks, with as many government bureaucrats among them as possible. What it did not want were young dudes who might remember Johnson's Vietnam more than his civil rights, who had no steady jobs, who had lost faith in government and its leaders over the war and Watergate, or who found the Church and its evangelists quaint and amusing. Williams got essentially what he wanted. Two of the twelve jurors were white, although one of them was to become ill and was replaced with an alternate, who was black. They were split evenly in sex and presented a reasonable mix of government servants and blue-collar types. The surviving white was Dennis O'Toole, a PhD historian of American Colonial history, who worked as an educator at the National Portrait Gallery and who was immediately chosen by the others as the foreman.

Behind the scenes, the lawyers on each side sparred with one another before Judge Hart on a series of motions which had a profound effect on the outcome. These sessions largely took place in Hart's chambers and, taken together, they further limited and narrowed the evidence that could be presented in the trial. Judge Hart was able to dispose of several issues summarily. The venue of the trial, for example, was a predictable issue. Williams wanted Connally tried in Texas—San Antonio was his choice—because of the inconvenience and expense to all his Texas witnesses and because of the atmosphere of Washington itself, infected as it was by the virus of Watergate. Judge Hart responded that Watergate had infected every nook and corner of the country equally, and he was hard put to say that the contagion was any worse in the capital city. Williams then shifted the argument to the problem of leaks in Washington, where, according to him, the FBI and the special prosecutor's office were supplying the press with juicy items. The columns and articles, however, had simply reported the state of the investigation when Connally made his second appearance before the grand jury, and that scarcely amounted to taking aim, except in that truth has its consequences. So Williams zeroed in on the record of the Watergate special prosecutor's office itself and tried to make a liability out of its extraordinary success record.

Then there was the question of the three minutes at the end of the March 23, 1971, meeting in the Oval Office, when Connally had asked to see Nixon alone "on another matter" and, when alone, had said to the president, "There's a very substantial allocation of oil in Texas that will be at your discretion." Williams argued that this conversation was inadmissible, for it was irrelevant to the charges, it was confusing in its meaning, and it was unintelligible in its words. Tuerkheimer disagreed forcefully. Connally was cementing the quid pro quo of the Nixon decision, he argued. In return for the rise in parity, either the president himself personally, or at least his campaign, was going to get—what? "It would seem to me to be a question for the jury to determine whether the reference to oil means money," Judge Hart remarked, obviously somewhat miffed at Connally's big-shouldered boasting to Nixon.

Tuerkheimer was becoming irritated at the judge's denseness, for in his mind the importance of the tape was clear. Moreover, he had played the three minutes for Connally in the special prosecutor's office and felt that Connally stonewalled in his responses to it. "When we played the tape for him, he still took the position that the decision wasn't final," Tuerkheimer said. "I think that the last segment here makes clear beyond any doubt that as far as he knew this was the final decision. [Connally] cemented it with the president. That is inconsistent with the position he has taken in the past, and it deals with an element of the crime."

Actually, it dealt with two elements of the crime. It showed the parity decision as a higher-parity-for-campaign-contributions deal, whose cementing was substantially to benefit both the Nixon campaign and Connally personally, and it undercut Connally's veracity when he argued to the grand jury that the decision was not final. In short, Tuerkheimer said, it undermined Connally's credibility.

Hart, however, remained befuddled and annoyed. The codes and the riddles of the Nixon men lacked precision for the jurist. They were too open to varying interpretations. He ruled that the November 23 meeting could not be introduced and the prosecution lost a piece of valuable evidence which went to the heart of the case and was revealing about the Nixon-Connally relationship.

As this became a case that was going to be decided more on style than substance, the contrast between the prosecution and the defense tables could not have been more stark. At the prosecution table sat four grim, dogged young men; the "color" commentators of the press promptly dubbed them "the undertakers" and staked five dollars among themselves to reward the reporter who noticed the first trace of a smile upon the humorless inquisitors. The opening argument for the prosecution was handled not by Frank Tuerkheimer, but by his assistant, Jon A. Sale. Like Tuerkheimer, Sale had gained his experience under Robert Morgenthau, in the New York City prosecutor's office, and his academic training at NYU. Younger than Tuerkheimer by four years, at a youthful thirty-one, he appeared more facile than his colleague and, therefore, an even more glaring contrast to Edward Bennett Williams of the defense, who was nearly twice his age.

In yeoman fashion, Sale laid out his case, with the facts and the dates and the testimony that would be heard. His purpose in his opening statement, he said, was akin to showing the jury the cover of a jigsaw-puzzle box, and he hoped that this glimpse at how the puzzle would finally fit together would assist them. The cash was the key: "This cash, unlike most cashes, left a trail of footprints right from Mr. Lilly to Mr. Connally."

When Edward Bennett Williams rose to address the jury for the first time, he carried with him, beyond his prodigious talents and vaunted reputation, the weight of symbolism. He stressed that this was not a Watergate case, and his very presence seemed to underscore the point. Here was an attorney who had represented the Democratic National Committee against the Republican Committee to Reelect the President over the Watergate break-in itself and had won. Moreover, he had a prominent place on Nixon's enemies list. Nixon had seethed on tape about Williams's lawyering for the Democrats and about how he and his men were going to "fix that son of a bitch" after the 1972 election. There was, however, no ideological consistency to the big-name clients whom Williams had defended in the past and upon whom he had built his reputation: the *Washington Post;* Frank Costello, the Mafia don; Tony Boyle and Jimmy Hoffa, the labor racketeers; Senator Joseph McCarthy; Adam Clayton Powell; Robert Vesco; Bobby Baker. He was the ultimate gun for hire, and by this stage of his career he was a cannon. But in his first appearance before the jury, this was not immediately clear. He was not eloquent in the classical sense, nor did he have a honeyed voice. He did not possess a commanding physical presence. A bit overweight, with a pudgy, Irish cop's face and, in Texas writer Larry King's words, a potato for a nose, his power lay in preparation, consistency, succinctness, and, in the beginning, politeness. He was not out to win the jury over in his prelude. He meant to grow on them.

Williams began with a homey analogy: "As the old mountaineer said about his pancakes, no matter how thin I make them, there are always two sides to them." His side of the pancake took shape soon enough. The accuser was a criminal who had cut a sweet deal for himself and had slithered out of thirty-eight years' worth of criminal charges in return for the denunciation of his old friend and benefactor. In asking for $10,000 from AMPI for Connally, Jacobsen was really asking for money for himself, for he was confident that Connally would turn down the offer, and he could then pocket the money. Jacobsen had "embezzled" the money, Williams argued. "He had converted the money to his own use. . . . He began to scheme as to how he could extricate himself from his trouble." The phrases tumbled out of Williams like grenades as he sought to prejudice the jury against Jacobsen's testimony before he ever appeared before them. Williams was riding the line of permissible courtroom behavior and the judge reproached him at the bench, out of hearing of the jury, for taking "full advantage," instructing Williams "to simmer down a bit." But the seed of prejudice had been planted.

By the third day of the trial, after expert witnesses had explained the meaning of parity and price supports in the commodity world, the proceeding moved to its first critical juncture. Some minutes before Jake Jacobsen took the stand, Merrill Connally, looking very much the part of the urban cowboy, sought to buck up his brother's spirits.

"John," he said, "now don't lose your composure when that man starts testifying."

"Don't worry," Connally chortled stagily. "I've known so many lying sons of bitches that one more won't crater me."

In physical appearance, Jake Jacobsen did nothing to disabuse the jury of the notions that Williams had planted. Dressed in a conservative brown suit, he had a sallow and drawn visage and his large eyes and black, arching eyebrows imparted a look of surprise, like "an astonished lizard," Larry King would write. These reptilian descriptions fit with the impressions of Dennis O'Toole, the foreman of the jury and the Colonial historian. To him, Jake appeared "a little sleazy and slippery, like a man who had gotten rich recently as he scrambled up the greasy pole of Texas politics." There was more beneath these first impressions than the thoughts Williams had sought to nurture. Something in Jacobsen seemed to epitomize the country's attitude toward Texas. Jake was nouveau riche and tacky Texas incarnate.

For Jake, the three days on the stand were the culmination of a Chinese torture. He simply wanted to fulfill his bargain and be done with it, slink away and forget it, if he could. As Tuerkheimer guided him, he moved through his testimony in a soft voice, without emphasis and without evident interest in whether his testimony was convincing. He had no stake in whether the jury believed him or in whether Connally went to jail, so he told his story matter-of-factly, certain that what he said was supported by his recollections and by such documents as existed. He longed only for liberation.

Dennis O'Toole and the other jurors listened intently to what Jacobsen had to say. It was by no means inconceivable that the impressive, well-tailored, statuesque grandee at the defense table had taken a grubby little bribe from Jacobsen. O'Toole had read books about Lyndon Johnson and his world. He understood that within the Johnson crowd gifts for political favors were scarcely a rare occurrence. Still, he kept his mind open for the cross-examination of Jacobsen and the appearance of Connally himself on the stand.

On the sixth day of the trial Williams loomed before Jacobsen for the first time. At first Jake did not find his interrogation intimidating, and he thought his coaching by the prosecutors would be adequate to the ordeal ahead. As the questioning unfolded, the surprises came from Williams's total command of the material, not only of the milk fund details, but also the details of Jake's other legal difficulties. Meticulously, wrenchingly, Williams took Jacobsen over the details of his San Angelo and Lubbock and Amarillo indictments, over his various perjuries and felony charges, over his loan misapplications and phony appraisals. It was the cumulative effect of it that was convincing, the sheer weight of his apparent misdeeds. When, at long last, toward the end of the first day of cross-examination, Williams finally got around to the milk case, he focused again on Jacobsen's perjuries and indictments. Suddenly Jake felt very much alone. His coaching had not prepared him for this. Why had the prosecutors not shown that all his stories to the authorities had been fabricated to protect John Connally? When Williams reviewed his banking indictments, why had the prosecutors not objected and placed the blame upon his crooked partner, Ray Cowan? Why did they not protest that indictments were not convictions, and that he was presumed innocent of these charges? As Williams pressed on, Jacobsen began to shine from perspiration. He drank water frequently. He was parched, not only from his grilling but also from the antihistamine he was taking for a cold. He licked his dry lips, and this contributed even more to his sinister aspect in the eyes of those already prejudiced against him.

Before the court resumed for the second day of Jacobsen's cross-examination, the lawyers convened as usual with Judge Hart. The judge was annoyed that Williams was taking so long on the details of the peripheral Texas cases and found them "a little tedious."

"I'm sorry you think it's tedious," Williams replied, having none of it. "I have to do my job."

"I agree. You run your case, but I think we ought to do it within reasonable limits. This is too important a case in so many ways, particularly that the public feel this is a fair trial."

"I don't care what the public feels, and I don't care what newspapermen feel," Williams snapped petulantly. "I am not interested in this at all, and I don't care whether they think it's tedious or not." In Williams's mind, this lengthy and indeed tedious recitation of Jacobsen's incidental crimes was the raw material for his final summation to the jury.

Tedium was not to be the problem when the court's session began minutes later, for the cross-examination of Jacobsen moved toward its climax. Having battered the witness with his ancillary misdeeds, Williams now choreographed the spectacle of a crooked bagman at work. The testimony was somewhat confusing for the jury, because it centered on the cover-up phase of the case, and the jury was to consider that period only as evidence of a consciousness of guilt.

Williams homed in on the transaction in Houston when Connally had given Jacobsen $10,000 to put in his safe deposit box to trick the FBI into thinking that the cash had languished there for two and one-half years. Williams was fascinated by the cigar box and the rubber glove or gloves. Was the glove light beige or yellow? Jake could not recall. It could have been white. Where was the glove?

"The rubber glove may have been on top of the money, or it may have been on the side of the money or something," Jake stammered uncertainly and then pulled himself together. "I believe the rubber glove or gloves was on the side of the money."

"Was it one glove or two?" Williams asked.

The logic of it suggested there were two, Jake said. "You couldn't hardly handle money with one glove." (So logic rather than truth was now compelling his testimony, Williams would later argue in his summation. Could you believe a witness who testified largely from logic?)

"The logic was, you couldn't hardly, as you put it, handle money with one glove," Williams repeated sardonically. "Was the cigar box one that holds fifty cigars or holds twenty-five cigars?"

"I don't recall," said fastidious Jake. "I don't know the difference between cigar boxes. I am not a cigar smoker."

Now, Williams spread $10,000 out on the table before his witness. What the attorney asked the witness about the stacks of cash, set in neat piles of twenties, fifties, and hundreds, was irrelevant. Few in the room had ever seen that much cash in one place; that the sight had been routine to the bagman in the witness stand made him all the more exotic. Williams instructed Jacobsen to count the money, asking him to identify the first George Shultz bill he came to. To see him handling the money had the prurience of an Xrated movie, but it was great theater and pretty good lawyering besides.

Perhaps Tuerkheimer could have done something to rehabilitate his star witness in his redirect, but it was hard to think what that might have been. Whether the prosecutor was constrained by the rules of the court or felt the situation to be hopeless, he did not try very hard. He asked a few random questions—and then the witness was excused, to retreat in disgrace and humiliation, to be snubbed by his old Texas friends as a pariah and a snitch, a man who could not be comfortable in Texas even thirteen years after his testimony. In his bitterness more than a decade later, he would say that he put himself in the hands of idiots.

★

Connally's accuser lay shattered, but John Connally himself still had to survive an interrogation on the witness stand. And he needed to do far more than just survive if he was to have any future as a political figure. Vindication was not enough. He had to show that the charges were scurrilous and malicious, that they had been brought for the most sinister of political reasons. It would have to be forgotten that the indictment had not been returned by the special prosecutor's office until the entire investigative file of the case had been evaluated by the Criminal Division of Gerald Ford's Department of Justice. That Criminal Division had insisted that Connally be charged and tried.

Before the courtroom would be treated to the Connally testimony, there was a succession of apparently minor witnesses. Connally's secretaries, fierce loyalists both, denied that Connally had ever left his office in Houston once he closeted himself with Jacobsen that day in October, much less did he come back with a cigar box and rubber gloves. Bob Lilly, the AMPI bagman, breathless from a severe heart condition and with an oxygen pack by his side, testified to Jacobsen's money requisitions. George Christian testified that the meeting at his house in November had been to discuss Connally's public relations problems rather than to pass a second batch of $10,000. And Connally's friend Larry Temple confessed, without damage, that indeed he had "debriefed" Jacobsen after his grand jury testimony and before Connally's. Then there was an endless, mind-numbing procession of Federal Reserve Bank experts who spoke ad nauseam about how money in their bank was put into circulation by serial number rather than by the administration of any given secretary of the treasury. Taken together, the point of this testimony was to support Jacobsen's construction of the facts in the cover-up phase. But the procession of the Federal Reserve witnesses was worse than counterproductive, for their testimony not only bored but annoyed the jurors with its apparent irrelevance. The historian and jury foreman, Dennis O'Toole, simply edited all this testimony out of his mind as clutter. The only question to him was whom to believe, Jacobsen or Connally, about the initial gratuity. The rest were nonissues.

On April 15, John Connally finally took the stand. Erect, forceful, beautiful to look at, his presence was electric. Larry King wrote that he seemed like a two-million-dollar shipment of silver. His mouth, which some regarded as vaguely feminine, displayed no mirth, no cynicism now. He did not overstate his accomplishments. Rather, they were salted into his testimony sparingly, as if to show the burdens under which men of great stature operate. He told of how Jacobsen had come to him in 1971, ashamed of his impending bankruptcy, and of how he had sought to comfort old Jake by saying sensitively, "Now, Jake, that's not so bad. My daddy went broke." He spoke of being on the staff of General Eisenhower in Algiers, an assertion that went unchallenged, since no one thought to question whether the junior lieutenant had ever laid eyes on Ike in the eight months he had been far down the hill from the grand Hotel St. Georges in the modest Lend-Lease office.

The May 1971 meeting with Jacobsen (when Connally allegedly got his first gratuity) arose and the witness spoke of how preoccupied he was with the momentous Lockheed bailout. The September 1971 meeting (when Connally allegedly got the second installment) arose and the importance of the witness on the world scene was again evident. After meeting with the president and the Federal Reserve chairman, Arthur Burns, "I went to my office where I met a number of members of my staff, gathered up all my papers, briefing books, and my testimony [for the Senate Foreign Relations Committee]. I talked with [the staff] about last-minute questions and answers, issues which might be raised [by Senators]. Representatives from 114 nations around the world were coming in that weekend, and so we were appearing before the Senate. It was a rather important [testimony] in terms of trying to outline what our monetary policy was going to be." It seemed implausible that in such historic circumstances this distinguished public servant would have the time or the interest or the need to collect a bribe from a bagman.

"Did you ever ask Mr. Jacobsen for any money or anything of value?"

"I did not."

"Did any such conversation ever take place wherein you asked him for something of value by reason of your aid in the dairy support program?"

"No such conversation ever took place."

"Did such a conversation take place in your Treasury Department office or outside your office?"

"Not there. Not in the Treasury. Not anywhere. No such conversation ever took place. I never asked him anything at any time."

He was a dream witness: coherent, succinct, immensely impressive. His denial was total and it was spoken unhesitatingly, as if from the heart. To the jury foreman, Dr. O'Toole, the task had been made reasonably simple. The jury had been instructed about the standard of guilt beyond a reasonable doubt, about the need for the state to prove its case. As Dr. O'Toole understood his duty, he was not to determine what really happened in Connally's office between the secretary and Jacobsen, but only to judge the specific evidence presented to him and to decide if the state had established its charges beyond a reasonable doubt. The difference was between real truth and legal truth. The jury would be instructed to receive the testimony of a convicted felon and perjurer with extreme caution, just as it should consider seriously testimony about the good character of the defendant. Indeed, Judge Hart would instruct the jury that testimony of good character could, *in itself*, create a reasonable doubt about the validity of the charges against the defendant. To the lawyers in the audience, who came to observe the case for the sheer sport of seeing an epic battle, the absence of at least some substantive, corroborating piece of evidence like a discarded cigar box or rubber glove was glaring. With no surprises, Connally was unshakable upon the stand under cross-examination. He was the distant, splendid, icy figure he had been throughout his career.

Even if the verdict now seemed certain, the show was not over. Criminal guilt or innocence ceased to be the issue. Vindication, exoneration, absolution were now at stake. Could it be shown that John Connally had been wronged, terribly wronged, by this unfair, even malicious, proceeding? That would be determined by the two final stages: Connally's character witnesses and the summation of Edward Bennett Williams.

It is sometimes said that in the end John Connally, the prototype male chauvinist, was saved by two women. This is not quite true. As a criminal defendant, he was saved by the constraints and the peculiarities of the law, by brilliant lawyering, and by the absence of any eyewitness to the bribery other than Jake Jacobsen. As a politician who longed for a future in high electoral politics, if he was "saved" in any sense, it was by one woman and one preacher. In this is irony. If he cared little for women, he felt nothing at all about religion.

The parade of stars who came to pay tribute to Connally began with Robert McNamara, for whom Connally had worked when he was secretary of the navy. For this witness, as with the six who followed, the rules of the court were strict. How long and how well had the witness known the defendant? What was his reputation for honesty and integrity? After McNamara came Lady Bird Johnson, calling herself Claudia Taylor Johnson. Some of those closest to the president's widow thought it cruel to ask Lady Bird to testify, for what if Connally were found guilty? Once she was asked, though, they knew it was impossible that she would decline, especially since her son-in-law, Charles Robb, was in Edward Bennett Williams's law firm. Her halting, slightly confused, evidently embarrassed demeanor showed her ambivalence. In what she said, rather than in her mere presence, she was not a good witness.

"Some folks don't like him, but I don't think any of them doubt his integrity," she told the court.

Dean Rusk, James Rowe, Jr., and Robert Strauss followed. None of them carried much weight, for they were power figures of political Washington, and their support was predictable and unpersuasive. Then, one William Franklin Graham, Jr., was called. When Billy Graham rose to his feet and strode to the witness stand, as if it were a pulpit, one could feel electricity in the courtroom. To Dr. O'Toole, who did not count himself a man of religion, the preacher positively "radiated energy." When Graham sat across from Connally, it was easy to see why the two men had been attracted to one another. Before the jury and the assemblage there were now in the dock two shipments of silver that seemed to have come from the same mine.

"What is your work at the present time, sir?" Williams asked.

"I am an evangelist, preaching the gospel of Jesus Christ all over the world," Graham replied, and across his left shoulder Dr. O'Toole heard a soft, gentle "Amen!" float by from a black female juror behind him.

Connally and Graham had first met in the office of a mutual friend—Sid Richardson went unnamed—when the minister was reading the Bible and the friend said he wanted his lawyer to hear the reading. Since then, Connally had spoken from the platform of two Graham crusades, and they had played golf together often. Connally's reputation was unassailable "in my judgment," Graham said, and the way he used the word seemed to confer almost divine sanction.

After him, to the astonishment of most, the familiar, hulking figure of Barbara Jordan came forward. The brilliance of this coup was instantly evident. She was probably the most famous black woman in America in 1975. Her eloquence and her grace at the impeachment hearings against Richard Nixon on the House Judiciary Committee had been the high point of that drama. She represented the central city of Houston, to which all on the jury except Dr. O'Toole could feel a kinship. Her deep, slow, Pentecostal voice, which enunciated sentences with the precision of an opera singer, was magnetic.

Why was Barbara Jordan there? In 1964, as governor, Connally had vetoed her nomination to the State Committee of the Democratic party. When she became the first black in the Texas state legislature in seventy-one years, Connally totally ignored her. He had opposed the restructuring of the congressional district that carved a congressional niche for central Houston and which would make her the first black woman in Congress from the South. He had positioned himself against the "libs" and the blacks and the labor groups that were her constituency. He had appeared on statewide television to denounce John F. Kennedy's civil rights bill, had fought hard against the whole concept of equal public accommodations during the Johnson presidency, and had consistently opposed such Johnson Great Society programs as Medicare. In 1968, Connally's remark at hearing of Martin Luther King's murder that "those who live by the sword must die by the sword" had brought tears to her eyes and she was deeply wounded. Later that year, when she heard that Connally would be the favorite son candidate for president from Texas, she remarked: "Why, that son of a bitch. How does he think he can be anyone's favorite anything?" In short, John Connally was the antithesis of everything Barbara Jordan stood for.

The deeper truth was that Jordan was a trader. She had long since discarded ideological or racial petulance in favor of accommodation. If she couldn't beat the Texas establishment, she was determined to join it. Once, to a labor stalwart in the Houston Democratic party, she had said churlishly, "Liberals like to lose." Robert Strauss, the old persuader and arm-twister, had asked her to testify for Connally, and her immediate answer was a resounding no. He asked her to think about it—going on intuition. This request seemed to throw Jordan into a frenzy of self-examination. She had come to fear being thought of as "knee-jerk," and if she testified she anticipated the scorn of liberals but dismissed it as something she could live with. If she could live with the scorn of liberals, she longed for "conservative and business types" not just to tolerate Barbara Jordan but to support her. The Martin Luther King remarks became an example of Connally's honesty. In the end, she ennobled for herself her decision to testify: her appearance for Connally would ensure fairness.

Twelve years later, as Jordan was ensconced as a distinguished faculty member at the LBJ School of Public Affairs in Austin, people still asked with what was she threatened, overtly or by implication, to testify, or what had been offered as an inducement. Some found significance in the fact that at the 1976 Democratic Convention, with Robert Strauss still national chairman, Jordan was the surprising choice as keynote speaker.

Her lofty explanations did not convince. Her testimony in court was as concise as it was pivotal. Its background went untranslated. "As far as I know from my association with him, he has a very good reputation for honesty," she told the court.

Not everyone was as taken with this testimony as the jury. Indeed, what struck a few learned observers who knew the background of John Connally in Texas was the cynicism of it. Larry King was disgusted by the groveling of Barbara Jordan and, even more, by the sacrilege of Billy Graham. From his own experience in Texas politics under the "old rules"—rules so loose where cash was involved as to be no rules at all—King felt that Connally was probably guilty, but he had reveled in the contrast of Jacobsen beside Connally as a "rat beside a show horse." Had he been a juror, however (the "thirteenth juror," as he called himself in his *Atlantic* article), he confessed that because of the awkward prosecution and lack of hard evidence, he would have voted for acquittal. But Jordan and Graham engaged his passion as nothing else. About Jordan, he felt she had displayed the ultimate corruption of a black who had made it and then had betrayed her own people. However, he reserved a special contempt for Billy Graham.

"Graham had sucked up to powerful men all his life until he himself became powerful," King would say. "Both of them stood there with their golf-course tan, and Graham with his lacquered hair that looked like a football helmet." The exploitation of religion for this purpose was to King the ultimate fraud, for he had watched Connally closely enough for fifteen years to know that the ex-governor had never gotten down on his knees to pray for anyone, much less a transcendental God. "They were two members of the same club, with one in trouble. Graham was using Jesus to get a thief off the hook."

On the phone, King vented his rage to John Henry Faulk, the treasure of Texas humor who for forty years had fashioned the folklore and the foibles of his state into thigh-slapping routines and had begun to render them in one-man shows across Texas and the nation. King's scathing comments inspired John Henry, who was always on the lookout for good material, and as the Connally trial drew to a close, he found an occasion to turn the situation to his wicked caprice. In 1975 Faulk lived in Madisonville, Texas, where J. R. Parten, the liberal oilman, also lived. Around this time Parten's wife had died, and there was a gathering of mourners at his home, to which luminaries from across the state were drawn. At the reception Faulk encountered Ralph Yarborough, and he pulled the former senator aside, knowing that Yarborough's dislike for Connally had reached stratospheric levels of paranoia. (Throughout his political life Yarborough laid his troubles on Lyndon Johnson and John Connally, with some justification.)

"Senator," said Faulk, "I ran into a piece of information the other day. I wish I could tell you about it, but it's privileged. I believe it's the most shocking thing I ever heard in my life—having to do with John Connally's trial and what's really going on up there in Washington."

"What? About Connally? What is it?" Yarborough snorted alertly. John Henry suddenly saw him as an old bass coming up for a fly.

"I heard a secretly made tape. It's privileged, because it's lawyer-client. I think it's illegal for me even to have heard it. My God, it was shocking."

"Well, damn it, Johnnie, what is it?"

"Senator, you wouldn't want to be privy to something like this, would you?"

"Nothing you could tell me would surprise me about that damn Connally. You know that."

"God, I wish I could tell about this, because it's a just—well, unbelievable—Barbara Jordan, Billy Graham, Mrs. Johnson. Why, Senator, the way that Connally talked about them is unbelievable! Conversations taped between Edward Bennett Williams and John Connally. But I can't reveal this. It would be—dishonorable. You wouldn't want me to do something *dishonorable*."

"No, no, of course not, Johnnie. I respect you for your . . ."

"Senator, if you will promise. . . . Really, the public should know about this. . . ." Faulk began to wonder about being so mean to the old man, playing on his mistrust and dislike like this, but he was into it now, and he couldn't stop himself. "It all started when Williams asked Connally if he knew what a character witness was. Now, Senator, did you know that John Connally, a graduate of the University of Texas Law School, had no idea what a character witness was? 'What the hell is a character witness?' he asks Williams. 'Well, that's someone who would testify to your sterling character, someone who is prominent.' 'Hell, anybody that knows me . . . I wouldn't be able to get anybody like that.' "

"That's right!" Yarborough squealed gleefully. "Goddamn it, he knew that, didn't he!"

"So Connally says to Bennett Williams, 'What are you looking for?' and old Williams says, 'Do you know any American citizen, universally respected and recognized, who would testify in your behalf?'

" 'Well, Bird owes me an awful lot. I believe I could get Bird Johnson to do it.'

" 'Now that's it!' Williams says. 'She's just the kind of person I'm talking about . . . a beloved figure. Do you know a black?'

" 'Hell, you can forget about it, if we've got to have a nigger. No way on earth I could get someone like that. . . . Wait a minute. I know this big old budding nigger woman from down in Houston— Barbara Jordan. She's a congressman.' "

"My God, he said that?" Yarborough said in a shocked whisper. "We've got to get that tape!"

"Yes, he said that," Faulk plunged on. "He said, 'She is just corrupt enough to do it.' 'Now what about a minister of the gospel?' Williams asked. Now, Senator, John Connally said, 'You joking? An ordained minister that would vouch for my integrity? Oh, come on. I don't know any preachers in the first place. . . . Wait a minute! . . . I know a son of a bitch who would do it, sure as hell. . . . I know Billy Graham. . . . For the right price, I believe he is corrupt enough to do it!' And Williams says, 'Listen, John, couldn't we get him to testify that he had prayed with you?' 'You're really joking now,' Connally says. 'The jury wouldn't buy that!' "

Yarborough clenched his fist. "Goddamn it, Johnnie, we've got to get this," he said between gritted teeth. "We've got to get this tape! The public needs to know!"

"Senator, don't you scare me, your talking like that," Faulk said, genuinely frightened by Yarborough's intensity and his total belief, but too fearful now to confess the fiction. Thankfully, they were interrupted at this point, and Faulk felt a deliverance. In the years afterwards, John Henry Faulk never had the nerve to tell Yarborough that he'd made it all up.

★

In the years since Connally's trial, the summation of Edward Bennett Williams has sometimes been invoked in law schools as a classic of defense. Particularly admired was his reduction of the accuser to the dark precincts of a slug's existence, while the defendant was elevated to near-divine proportions. The jury foreman, Dr. Dennis O'Toole, did not see it that way. He listened intently to the summation of the prosecution, where he found that the earnest Mr. Turkheimer was confounded by the sheer complexity of his circumstantial evidence. Next came Williams, and O'Toole was won over by his earthy straightforwardness.

At the outset of his closing argument, Williams laid out again the financial desperation of Jacobsen in 1971, but now he tied it to the bribe money for Connally. As Jacobsen was getting money from AMPI for Connally, so his loans were coming due almost every week. When he was getting money from Bob Lilly, it was a "bonanza" at a time when Jacobsen desperately needed it. The week he got $10,000 from AMPI, he borrowed $100,000 from the National Bank of Commerce in Dallas. On the very day he got his last bribe money from Lilly, Jake made a $5,000 payment on a loan to a bank in Fredricksburg, Texas. Though Williams had denounced the state's case as circumstantial, he now employed a construction of the facts that was even more circumstantial and which could not be examined or challenged. He left the jury to ponder whether what he was now saying wasn't at least as plausible as what the state had laid out in the past two weeks.

"The house was crumbling. His financial empire was done. The sheriff was practically at the door in 1971," Williams thundered, as he lumbered before the jury, stopping occasionally to engage their gaze. "In constant default on his indebtedness, all those very months when he says he was taking money from Mr. Lilly for Mr. Connally, Jacobsen was a desperate man. He was embattled and beleaguered."

Its cleverness lay in its simple plausibility, and it was irresistible. It made the case so clear, so understandable that one had to wonder suddenly why the trial had lasted two weeks, why the preceding investigation had gone on for more than a year, and why the jury should now spend more than a minute or two to dispose of it. It also made Jacobsen into the complete villain, and a very imaginative one. Of course, it ignored the frequent meetings between Jacobsen and Connally after Lilly began to talk. It ignored the fact that Jacobsen's indebtedness amounted to $8 million, and that a mere $10,000 could do nothing to affect such an astronomical fix. "Williams did a heck of a job on me," Jacobsen would say sadly years later.

"In short, members of the jury," Williams said, "the man who was brought here, the man upon whom the prosecution asks you to predicate a verdict of guilty beyond a reasonable doubt, is a man whom they have charged with swindling and fraud, a man they have charged with perjury, a self-confessed habitual liar, and I suggest to you a proven embezzler. They put him on the stand. He takes the same oath that he says he has defiled a hundred times. . . . Corroboration? There is no corroboration for Jake Jacobsen except what he architectured to cover up his embezzlements."

This was the refrain to which Williams returned again and again. He spoke of the prosecutors' efforts to protect Jacobsen's law license as a reward for testifying and made it into a kind of personal insult to Williams himself. "I say, for shame," he said in lowered, guttural tones. "I blush in embarrassment at that man practicing law. I blush in embarrassment that the prosecution would be concerned that a man who was an avowed perjurer, an alleged defrauder and a swindler, stay in the practice of law."

Of Connally, Williams changed his tone to dignified understatement. "Is he some captain of crime? Some scoundrel to be caught? Don't you know that once we introduced character witnesses, the state then could bring out anything it had to show his past was stained?" And then he turned, glowering at the prosecutors in the pure theater of the adversarial process. "Don't you know they examined every record and bank account he has, trying to find loose money? You didn't hear anything from them of John Connally having money stashed in safety deposit boxes, did you? No, they found no irregularities. . . . The prosecution's case is in a shambles."

And then he softened, regarding now his client. "For you, members of the jury, this case is three weeks old. For this defendant, it is more than a year old. A year of accusations, humiliations, anguish, assaults on his integrity. Three weeks from now, this case may have faded from your recollections. You'll have gone on to other things. The prosecution will go on to other matters. The court will go on to other cases. But what you do in that jury room will place an indelible mark on John B. Connally for the rest of his life. Nothing in a life of glory and tragedy will be as final as your verdict."

In the jury room at long last, the jury took an immediate straw poll. The vote was nine to three for acquittal. They proceeded into the evidence, asking at one point for the whole of Jacobsen's testimony. Even though his level of education far outstripped that of his fellow jurors, Dr. O'Toole determined to stay in the background. He did not want to direct the discussion as if it were a seminar; he only wanted to insure that the issues were fully talked out. In the absence of hard evidence on the bribery charges, they were all operating almost on instinct. In due course, they seemed to be moving reasonably smoothly toward their verdict. Two or three members of the jury were doing most of the talking. Then, just as their deliberations appeared to be in their final stage, a juror who had been silent during virtually the entire deliberation abruptly switched his vote from acquittal to conviction. There was something about John Connally that had come to offend him deeply as he had thought more about it. He had decided that this big-time, slick politician was indeed a crook, just as he had been charged. He clung doggedly to his position, as others argued with him.

Outside in the hallway, Connally sat quietly as his fate was under discussion. Whatever the truth, he now called upon his enormous inner strength, and it showed in his deportment. Well-wishers came by, Democrats first—they knew that in his heart he was still one of them—and then several Republican senators, for the word had spread that the case looked good for the defendant. For some considerable time Connally fell into conversation with a client of Vinson and Elkins, his law firm, which formed an elegant distraction and underscored his serenity and his acceptance of the process. It was widely noticed and reported that for a time Connally read the Bible. As it happened, it was the only book other than law books which was within reach, and Williams had intrigued him by invoking the Book of Daniel in his summation, as the "first recorded cross-examination in history." It is also the book where the phrase "the writing on the wall" originates.

In the jury room the panel was wearing down its recalcitrant holdout. At last he threw up his hands in defeat. "All right, then," he said in soft capitulation. Of such mundane sentiments are important verdicts often forged. As Clarence Darrow might have said, Connally's liberty and his name were safe—but not entirely.

★ 24 ★

Rehabilitation

AT THE HOUSTON AIRPORT on April 18, 1975, it may not have been quite like the reception the Oilers would receive if they were to defeat the Patriots in a dream North-South Super Bowl, but there was something of the same feeling. The stage band from Kashmere High School had turned out, as well as over fifty lawyers from Vinson and Elkins, along with the chairman of the Houston Chamber of Commerce and other assorted cheerleaders. Nellie's mother, Katie Brill, was there, accorded the status of Queen Mother, and Nellie hugged her fervently, trying not to crush the yellow roses against her brown and white print dress. HAPPINESS IS JOHN AND NELLIE CONNALLY HOME, read one sign. HAPPY DAYS ARE HERE AGAIN, read another Rooseveltian adaptation for Texas's new Mr. Republican. The band fell into "When Johnny Comes Marching Home Again," as the two hundred devotees belted out the "hurrahs."

For Connally himself this was a moment for earnest reflection on the American judicial system. He had been able to afford the best legal talent in the nation, but now his mind turned, however briefly, to those who did not have his resources. At some time in the future, somewhere down the road, when the right moment presented itself and the stars were in their proper alignment, he wanted to devote time to the criminal problems of the indigent, he told his friends. Someone wondered if he wouldn't perhaps like to serve as a court-appointed attorney for an indigent defendant. If the spectacle of John Connally pleading the case of a criminal suspect before night court for no fee seemed far-fetched, it went to the tenderness of this moment that the governor would not even rule that out.

At his brief airport press conference, Connally touched on other legal issues his trial had raised: the possible abuse of the plea bargaining process and the invasion of privacy that a major criminal trial necessarily involved. He spoke not in bitterness, for his mind, he told the tearful and exultant crowd, never ran to bitterness— certainly not when he could savor victory rather than defeat.

"A trial is like love or war," he mused. "You don't know what it's all about until you've been through it."

Nellie tugged on his sleeve. "Let's go home," she said.

For a year and a half, Connally had lived with this cloud over his head, but for Texans, particularly the Connally faithful, the talk of clouds had always been meteorological nonsense. The storm had drifted down from the North like acid rain; it was Watergate, or it was the criminal justice system, or it was Jake Jacobsen, but now their hero had triumphed over these pernicious forces, and he could resume being the first citizen of Texas. He had, after all, been certified "innocent." As always, there was a huge gulf between the way Texas viewed him and the way the nation viewed him. In Texas, the talk about Connally as presidential timber began almost immediately after the verdict. In late June a colloquy between Connally and a *Houston Chronicle* reporter epitomized the Texas boosterism, and it demonstrated how Connally could misread what had really happened to him. It was almost as if the interchange was a well-rehearsed vaudeville act, with the reporter as the straight man:

"Governor, it's been said that the only cure for presidentitis is an injection of embalming fluid. What do you think?"

"I agree, but every rule has its exceptions."

"You?"

"I don't have presidentitis at all."

"You don't want to be president?"

"Not really. As candidly as I can say it, if I can help achieve certain objectives for the country, I'd rather not be president."

"Rather not?"

"It seems to me that whatever fun or pleasure once attended that office is gone now. It's gotten to the point where some people are saying the president should pay plane fare for his wife when she flies with him. A member of Congress proposes a bill that would prohibit the president from giving any foreign chief of state any gift worth more than fifty dollars. Ridiculous! Some people have used the last three years to try to tear down the presidency. A group of freshman congressmen meets with President Ford, and afterwards one comes out bragging that he didn't stand up for the president!

"Now I'm not saying I'd never take the job under any circumstances, but the truth is, I'd rather not. I'm fifty-eight years old. Why would I want to be surrounded by all that trouble and turmoil? I've seen the job, and, for me, much of the mystique is gone. At best, it is a profoundly difficult job, and now we're in a time when everybody seems to be trying to make it more difficult."

It was quintessential Connally, proud, unrepentant, swaggering: the office had ceased to interest him. The truth, however, was that the presidency remained the last, maddeningly elusive goal of his life. Time was running out for him. Even the adulation of his home state did not deceive him into thinking that a run for the presidency only a year after his acquittal in a Watergate trial wouldn't take a miracle. That meant that 1980 was his last chance. Then he would be a Septemberish sixty-three years old.

Distant as it now seemed, a presidential bid had one compelling possibility beyond the mere acquisition of the office. Connally wanted a public spectacle of vindication. He wanted the American people to prove to him that they really believed a man innocent until proven guilty. The electorate had to show that his indictment and his trial were now irrelevant politically. He would stand before them as a victim of an unjust, capricious prosecution. Did they believe in their system or didn't they? As far as he was concerned, his slate had been wiped clean. The people must show that they felt the same way. It was a matter of principle.

In July the rehabilitation of John Connally began in earnest. At the Hyatt Regency in Houston his friends threw a "Salute to John Connally." This was no ordinary testimonial, no routine affectionate roast. It was a fund-raiser, Texas style, for which nearly 4,000 Republicans and conservative Democrats paid up to $1,000 a plate, to get Connally back into political action. The guests were the sort who had limousines collect them at the steps of their private jets, and the coverage in the social pages of the Houston papers dwelt upon the silvery presidential appearance of Connally, the jewels of the ladies, including Nellie's pearl and diamond necklace, and the frenzied crush of the press. Texas was toasting "Big John," and they never toasted anyone, before or since, in quite the same way.

When his turn came to speak, Connally presented himself to this audience of the rich and successful as their prince and savior. "I do not believe we must march inexorably to a point in our history when half of the American people will be working to support the other half," he told them. And then, unwittingly, he defined the contradiction of his career: "If I am wrong in the opinions I express, history will soon forget that I passed this way. But if I am sufficiently accurate in what I believe to be best for this nation, then it is my hope and prayer that I can contribute in some small way to the preservation of this country and this economic and political system as we know it."

This was a fantasy. If history was going to remember him, it was not going to be for his ideas, whether they were right or wrong, but for his style and the force of his personality, for his intimacy with two presidents and his Watergate trial and Dallas. It had become a hallmark of a Connally speech that people would go away mesmerized, not unlike the feeling after a Billy Graham sermon, but if they were asked later what he had said, they could not remember. It was how he said it, whatever it was, that mattered. Still, this was how he saw himself—or wanted to be seen—a man of understanding and vision, a man who had been wronged by his nation, who was now going to show that he was still the figure of ability who had been indispensable to Lyndon Johnson, who had survived an assassin's bullets, who could help Richard Nixon become a presidential leader, and whose nation now needed him desperately.

The next morning, when the counting was over, $400,000 had been raised, and it went to found an organization called Vital Issues of America (VIA). VIA was supposed to be nonpartisan and nonpolitical, and the organizers promptly applied for tax-exempt status as an educational think tank. In its application to the Texas secretary of state the organization defined its goal as simply to "promote the social welfare of the Nation." Its purpose was to identify those issues that concerned the board of VIA. Half of that board was comprised of partners in Connally's law firm, Vinson and Elkins. VIA was, of course, immediately suspected of being what it really was: a dignified vehicle on which Connally could ride his way back into national politics and leave the storm of Watergate behind him. As if to deny the obvious, the charter of VIA tangentially addressed the issue of Connally promotion. VIA would have no "power to influence selection, nomination, or election of an individual to public office."

In the immediate wake of his corruption trial, Connally had to start on the edge of American society to find audiences willing to listen to his thoughts about America and the world. Rather than highbrow foreign policy groups or distinguished economic councils, he found himself adorning stockholders' meetings and animal-breeding associations and dispensing an upbeat message of the positive-thinking, you-can-be-a-success-too variety. Even at such soft gatherings as these, he was occasionally clipped. In August, in the suburbs of Dallas, at the shiny new business tower of a jewelry concern, the Zale Corporation, he had been brought in as a star to address the employees. The usual question period began auspiciously, as if Connally had drafted the questions he would like to be asked at this stage of his career.

"Can we trust the Russians' friendliness?" a woman asked.

"I don't trust them as far as you can throw a chimney by the smoke," Connally replied in a pet phrase—to a few mild titters. "They're coming on very hard with submarines."

Then a younger, slightly unkempt man in the front row stood. "What do you believe is the greatest threat to America—Russian submarines or corrupt government officials?" he asked.

The laughter began slowly, with a few giggles, then became general before it swelled to a great, throbbing wave that reverberated around the room for several minutes. Connally stood with a genuine blush and waited for this expensive fun to subside.

"Abuse by government officials . . . ," he began, faltered, began again. "From the military standpoint, the Russians are a far greater threat," he said. His statement was undoubtedly true. "We're all human. We've had corruption at all levels of government because we're all human. People lose their equilibrium, their sense of values. . . . There's a little larceny in the hearts of us all."

Connally's VIA ended up holding four symposiums—in Atlanta, Washington, Los Angeles, and Houston. The Houston symposium on energy was basically proindustry, and came out with recommendations along the lines of previous Connally positions. His drift on oil had been oft stated: "I can defend the major oil companies," he told a group of Republicans in March. "They've put up the risk capital, explored, found, developed, refined, transported, and retailed at the pump fuel cheaper than any other civilization in the world." As always, Congress was the whipping horse. "They're taking a short-range, shortsighted, very selfish political view, saying they're going to take care of these bloated oil companies and give people cheap gasoline. That's cheap demagoguery of the worst kind."

The chief draw at the Houston symposium was former Secretary of Defense and Energy James Schlesinger, and he gave voice to the subtext of the conference—and the entire VIA enterprise: "We need John Connally back in Washington."

One rather bizarre offshoot of VIA emerged in May 1976, when Connally unveiled his Citizen's Alliance for Mediterranean Freedom. Its purpose was somehow to reverse the gains the Italian Communists had made three months earlier when the Moro government toppled. Quite how Connally and his alliance proposed to do this remained vague, although the fact that the alliance planned to work through ethnic, veteran, and labor organizations gave it the feel of a CIA front. It had been reported in February that the CIA had spent $6 million to support the non-Communist parties in Italy. Because, on April 2, President Gerald Ford had appointed Connally to his Foreign Intelligence Advisory Board and thereby treated him to top-level classified briefings at the CIA, his alliance became that much more suspect. Nevertheless, this exotic new interest gave Connally the chance to speak on international matters.

Wasn't his Alliance for Mediterranean Freedom meddling in the affairs of a foreign country? he was asked. It probably was meddling, Connally replied. "I don't think we should be criticized for doing just that. We meddled in Italy thirty years ago." He just didn't want Italians to be "beguiled by the unfulfilled promises of Communism."

After its four symposiums and its Italian dalliance, VIA evaporated, but it brought Connally a year of speeches on important subjects from sometimes lofty and always well-paying platforms, as well as travels around the country to establish academic and political contacts, all for future reference. He also attended Republican party functions and by the spring of 1976 emerged as the most successful fund-raiser for the party. His passionate partisanship was an overt attempt to win over the skeptics in the party. Paying his dues to his new party in this fashion won many converts, but not everyone was snowed. Many Republicans who watched him wither the Democrats could not forget that only a few years before they were being shriveled by the same broadside.* If one was ready to forgive the party switch and to forget the milk trial, there was still about Connally the air of an opportunist and a dangerous gambler. His convictions, it appeared to many, were always in line with the main chance. Lowell Weicker, the liberal Republican

---

*In his first race for the Texas governorship, Connally's opponent in the general election had been a tough oilman from Breckenridge, Jack Cox, who was a former Democrat turned Republican. Before an AFL-CIO meeting on July 20, 1962, Connally had said, "The majority of you and I are Democrats. There are those who do not consider that important . . . those who shed their party affiliation as quickly as you shuck your coat under the hot Texas sun. You've seen one of them this morning. One thing is for sure. I am not and never will be a turncoat!"

senator from Connecticut, for example, called him "a great political mercenary" and would have been quite happy to hand him back to the Texas Democrats.

By the spring of 1976 the effort at reclaiming his reputation had been so successful that Connally was being prominently mentioned as a vice presidential running mate for Gerald Ford, even though through the early Republican primaries Connally maintained a strict neutrality between Ford and Ronald Reagan. In part, the brilliance of his rising star derived from the general haze of the Republican sky. Once again, he was perceived as a leader towering over dwarfs, a leader in a metaphysical sense. A Republican party activist named Earle Mayfield, Jr., of Dallas, gave unsolicited advice to President Ford that Rockefeller resign early—since he had said that he definitely would not serve as vice president in a second Ford administration—and that John Connally should replace him:

"Connally should be appointed Vice President as soon as Governor Rockefeller resigns. The quicker Connally is appointed, the quicker he will be confirmed. There are several Southern Democratic Senators who will vote to confirm Connally *NOW*. But the closer the confirmation is to the election, these Senators will have to vote against his confirmation. Connally's name on the Republican ticket will: 1.Insure that Texas will go Republican. 2. Probably defeat Lloyd Bentsen. 3. Insure that the Wallace people will flock to the Ford-Connally ticket."

On March 31, Connally was bold enough to invite twenty-two Republican chairmen and vice chairmen to the Picosa Ranch, ostensibly to discuss Republican strategy in the election year. For several days he turned on charm and conjured up magic, plying the guests with drinks and man-sized homegrown steaks, and impressing them with his immediate recall of the gain rates of individual Santa Gertrudis steers in his herd. He wowed them with the virtues of coastal Bermuda grass in this harsh, parched climate. Then he stood before them, in cowboy boots, string tie, and Western-cut jacket one night and expounded on the dismal state of the Republican party. From Picosa, he derived tremendous strength, and it showed in his deportment. For years his friends and his political associates had been amazed at how the ranch could transform him. Get him there, dog-tired, they would say, and within three days he'd be ready to take on the world. Get others there, and in hours they would be ready to give him the world. Before the Republican chairmen, he was enormously impressive standing in front of his fieldstone hearth, and his fine Western art, and the tusks of his African safari, and the grillwork that ornately encircled his initials and seemed to be branding his listeners.

"We just can't talk about being Republicans and get elected," he told them. "We represent twenty-one percent of the people, and unless we appeal to those who call themselves independents and Democrats, we're not going to get elected to anything. It's not enough for you to sit in smoke-filled rooms and plan a little strategy. It's hard work that wins elections." The implication: The Republicans needed someone who could appeal to Democrats and independents, as well as fat-cat Republicans. "Things have changed in the United States, and we, least of all in the Republican party, want to be advocates of the status quo." Inference: The Republicans needed an activist rather than a passive conservative at their head. "America gave more, and we produce more, than any society ever created in the world. Yet it is so grossly misunderstood that we assume success to be its own advocate. It is not. Success today is viewed almost as a strain of greed." In other words, the people wanted a self-confident, manly symbol of American success. "If the United States is not the leader of the free world, then it has no leader. No one can assume the mantle of leadership, not even a combination of countries. . . . I'm an optimist, but I think you have to get out and lay it on the line to the people. I think that's what they want, and I don't think either party has been doing it."

The chairmen listened, transfixed. It was as if they had been looking for leadership all along, but only now, in this unlikely grassland of South Texas, had they finally found it. For this moment, before reality reasserted itself, they were ready to follow him anywhere. The chairman from Vermont, Walter Kennedy, also known as "Peanut," was a case in point: "I was invited down to discuss Republican strategy, but I would have gladly come down just to discuss the vice presidential nomination of John Connally. He was probably too good for politics."

In April the contest between Ford and Ronald Reagan for the Republican nomination was becoming intense, narrow, and rancorous, but fate finally dealt Connally a good hand. The Texas primary on May 1 was shaping up as the decisive vote of the season. Since Connally remained the most popular politician in the state, with both the Republicans and Democrats, the rivals came courting, and this, in turn, advanced Connally's dignity and his power within the party. When Gerald Ford appointed Connally to the Foreign Intelligence Advisory Board, the president hoped to get something important in return, and the Connallys dined with the Fords at the

White House on the night of Connally's swearing-in. Scarcely the grateful and ingratiating guest Ford hoped for, Connally proceeded to tell the president that he had no chance whatever to win Texas. Reagan was too popular and too well-organized in his state. "It would have been nice if Connally had endorsed me then and there," Ford was to write wistfully, "but I didn't ask him to do that, and he didn't volunteer."

In the coming days Connally's analysis of the Texas situation seemed to be correct. As Ronald Reagan made several swings through the state, he was one outside politician who looked just right when they handed him a ten-gallon Stetson in Fort Worth and asked him to put it on. His mouth went with his hat. "We should tell Panama's tinhorn dictator just what he can do with his demands for sovereignty over the Canal Zone," Reagan said to much ambient noise. He needled Ford outrageously by suggesting that the administration had plans to recognize North Vietnam. For the most part, his emotional pleas found a receptive hearing.

President Ford, the optimist, had discarded Connally's pessimistic estimate of the Texas situation and thought he had a chance to win. He, too, made several forays through the state before primary day. They were not successful. Laboring under his reputation for malapropisms and pratfalls, Ford tried to be Tex-Mex in San Antonio when confronting a tamale for the first time, but no one told him about removing the inedible husk first. The result was every politician's nightmare. At a number of stops along the way, Ford was asked about Connally's silence, and the president, controlling his disappointment, replied that the governor "for his own good reasons" had withheld an endorsement of either candidate. It was appropriate, said Ford with a straight face, that he go head-to-head with his opponent on the merits. Connally's prediction of disaster was more than borne out. Reagan trounced the president and took all ninety-six Texas delegates to the convention. In the succeeding days Ford also lost Alabama, Georgia, Indiana, and Nebraska, and Reagan inched ahead in the delegate count.

Connally stood aloof, presenting himself in early June on the "Meet the Press" show as the "unifier" of the party. He was hoping vaguely for chaos and deadlock in which the party would turn to him for the top spot, but, more realistically, he was positioning himself to be the running mate of either Ford or Reagan. By early summer the GOP convention chairman, Robert Dole, tilted toward Connally for the vice presidential choice. Rogers Morton, Ford's campaign manager, was pushing hard for Connally within the White

House, and even crusty Barry Goldwater, a man not easily given to trifling infatuation, said of him, "John Connally knows more about American business, American foreign policy, American defense— and how to get it across to the people—than any man in America, including the president."

In the final primaries in June, even though he lost California to Reagan, Ford reversed his fortunes by winning New Jersey and taking most of Ohio's delegates. Once again, he moved ahead in the overall count and was well positioned to capture the remaining 400 uncommitted delegates.

Then, on July 26, Reagan did an extraordinary thing. He announced that the liberal senator from Pennsylvania, Richard Schweiker, a man with whom he had virtually nothing in common except blind ambition, would be his vice presidential running mate. Schweiker was politically at odds with Reagan on all the fundamental issues; he had assured Ford of his support several months before; and Pennsylvania was already in the Ford column. The couple was so odd, and the deal so cold, that it gave the word "balance" a bad name. Connally was among the very first to leap upon the gaffe. Less than an hour after the news was on the wire, Connally was on the phone to President Ford. "You are unmistakably the better choice, not only for the party but for the country," he said earnestly. It happened that Connally was going to be in Washington the following day, and he offered to make time in his schedule to endorse the president publicly. Ford accepted. When, at the entrance to the West Wing of the White House, Connally made his "unequivocal" commitment the next afternoon and promised his every resource and all his ability to Ford in the fall election, the first question to him was predictable.

"How about getting on the ticket?" the reporter asked.

"That subject was not discussed today," Connally replied. "I do not know what the president proposes with respect to his running mate. He has not told me. He has not hinted who it might be. I have not asked him, nor will I ask."

As Ford's chances for the nomination brightened, a Connally movement for the second spot on the ticket took shape in Congress. When Ford asked the Republican leaders, Senator Hugh Scott and Congressman John Rhodes, to solicit recommendations from the fold, Connally's name came back at the top. Led by Congressmen Hansen Moore of Louisiana and James Collins of Dallas, along with the Arizona senators, Goldwater and Paul Fannin, twenty-eight House Republicans signed a letter recommending Connally.

Moreover, the Chicago insurance magnate W. Clement Stone (who had given $2 million to the Nixon reelection effort in 1972) had been asked to poll the choices of major Republican contributors, and his response came back on August 7, with Connally leading the other contenders, Vice President Rockefeller, Senator Charles Percy, Secretary of Commerce Elliot Richardson, and Secretary of the Treasury William Simon. The Stone memorandum to the president read:

> John Connally is well qualified to be elected President, and if necessary to assume the Presidency. He has charisma and is a very convincing influential speaker and can effectively answer negative comments of opponents in a manner that brings positive results. But in the minds of some individuals the so-called "milk scandal," that he is a "wheeler and dealer" and that he had the good sense as a matter of principle to change from a democrat to a republican will affect some voters unfavorably, but I believe his positive activities during the campaign will offset these negatives. He could be most helpful in winning for the Ford-Connally team in many states including Texas and some of the southern states.

When the talk of Connally as Ford's choice began to get serious, the hostile forces surfaced vengefully and began to attack the idea. The blocking action began in early August with the governor of Ford's own state, William G. Millikin. Ford sent word immediately for Millikin to desist. Then two members of the House Impeachment Committee, William Cohen of Maine and Tom Railsback of Illinois, publicly came out against Connally. "The justification for Ford's pardon of Nixon was to put Watergate behind us," Cohen said. "If you put Connally on the ticket, it seems to me you bring it back." Despite the customary nod to the fact that the Impeachment Committee had failed to draft an article of impeachment against Nixon on the milk scandal and that Connally had been found not guilty in his trial, the criticism of these members, who had been privy to all the evidence, carried weight. Railsback asked for an appointment with Ford to present to him portions of the House Judiciary Committee evidence against Connally.

Ford tried to dampen these members' public statements. Such comments are "not helpful for the party," Ford said, and they should have been conveyed privately. So the negative comments came privately. With his apologies, the independent-minded Republican from California, Congressman Paul McCloskey, sent the White

House different negative information on Connally. Before his conservation subcommittee four years before, testimony was taken to the effect that as secretary of the treasury, Connally had intervened with the Justice Department to block a suit against Armco Steel, which was being charged with flushing 1,500 pounds of cyanide and other toxic chemicals into the nearly flammable Houston ship channel. Armco's corporate officers had contributed $14,000 to Nixon's reelection campaign, and after the Justice Department suit Armco's president, C. William Verity (later to be President Ronald Reagan's secretary of commerce), had written in protest to Nixon personally. After Connally stepped in as Nixon's instrument, the Justice Department proceeded to vacate its own judgment against Armco, allowing it to continue to spew its poisons into the public waterway. To the Houston Rotary Club shortly afterwards, Verity chortled, "I pray every night for John Connally. If I could have another son, his name would be John Connally. At last there is reality in Washington, and it changes the entire outlook for the steel industry—and most gratefully, for Armco." Congressman McCloskey found this to be a classic example of illegal political influence, the very method of operation which characterized the ethos of Watergate. The episode cast no credit on Connally, McCloskey wrote to the president.

But the most persistent and effective Connally opponent in Congress was a sixteen-year veteran named Paul Findley, a moderate Republican from rural Illinois who was prominent on the International Relations Committee, and who had been the prime mover in an impeachment effort against Spiro Agnew (before Agnew resigned voluntarily). Findley represented the solid moderate center of the Republican party, from which Ford himself came and which the president could not afford to alienate. On July 23, Findley had written to Ford that Connally would be a "disaster" as a running mate because of his association in the public mind with Watergate. "The Democrats have already made Watergate one of their prime campaign issues. Putting Connally on the ticket would be like pouring gasoline on the fire," Findley wrote. "By contrast, your reputation for openness and honesty is beyond question. . . . Our candidate for Vice President must, like Caesar's wife, be above suspicion, too. The Republican party has dozens of capable men and women whose integrity, like yours, remained intact throughout the Watergate era—indeed, some whose integrity shone like a beacon in the darkness." To Findley, Connally was part of the darkness rather than the light. The congressman did not stop there. He wrote his sentiments to all the Republican members of Congress, and the matter was brought to a quiet boil.

The situation was getting out of hand, and it was beyond Ford's ability to control it. Connally, in turn, reacted angrily. After the Cohen-Railsback statements, reporters collared him in Cleveland before a speech and asked for his reaction. "I'm not going to stand by, vice presidential prospects or not, and let Mr. Railsback or Mr. Cohen besmirch me any longer," he fumed—and then he went a little overboard. "I wasn't, in any way, involved in Watergate, and if they implied that I was, they are guilty of the grossest kind of misconduct." Several days later his anger had become rage. On the ABC show "Issues and Answers," he was asked about the Railsback, Findley, and Cohen remarks, and he picked up on the initials R, F, and C, and said they stood for "Republicans for Cannibalism." He was seeing his prize go aglimmering, and he tried to turn the issue around. It was "highly questionable," he said, whether he would accept the vice presidential nomination if Ford offered it to him.

At the Mayo Clinic in Rochester, Minnesota, where his wife was undergoing radical brain surgery, Congressman Paul Findley considered this performance and decided, even in his anguish over his wife, to dictate a second letter to Ford infusing his views with an even greater urgency and poignancy. His passion about Connally stemmed from the fact that he was also a member of the Agriculture Committee and for years had been importuned by the lobbyists of the milk producers in the most brazen way. In one of his early terms in the House, the milk producers had given his campaign a substantial contribution, and within days of his election, to Findley's shock, they came calling to announce what they now expected of their boy. It was the last contribution Findley was ever to get from the milk producers.

Since he knew personally how the milk lobby operated, the fact that Connally had been so close to them created a piece of baggage that smelled and was bound to smell more in a presidential campaign. Marking this second letter "Personal and Confidential," Findley broadened his opposition to Connally from the vice presidential possibility to any position whatever in Ford's campaign or his administration. The congressman focused the president's attention on an ugly little episode from the Watergate sideshow known as Nixon Dirty Tricks.

Connally's Democrats for Nixon had circulated an anti-McGovern letter to the Greek-American community in an attempt to sour the Greek-Americans against Nixon's opponent in 1972.

Shortly after his nomination McGovern had given a statement to Elias Demetracopoulos, a prominent Greek exile journalist who was regarded as a serious and distinguished voice for human rights and democracy in Greece. In the statement, McGovern promised to cut off all American aid to the junta if he were elected, and the candidate's position was made public. This elicited a letter to McGovern from the mayor of Savannah, John P. Rousakis, a Democrat for Nixon, who professed to be appalled by McGovern's position and at the candidate's irresponsibility in relying on an "obscure Greek Communist journalist."* Democrats for Nixon got ahold of this letter, with its slander of Demetracopoulos, and circulated it widely in the Greek-American community in the United States. It is inconceivable that within that hollow shell of an organization called Democrats for Nixon, Connally did not know about it. The Watergate Committee had seen this as a prime example of political black propaganda. Findley now saw it as one more disqualification for John Connally.

"Either in raising money from the milk industry or permitting the dissemination of slanderous material by his committee," Findley wrote Ford from the Mayo Clinic, "[Connally] has shown questionable judgment as a campaign leader and a spokesman for the President of the United States. I believe that should he be placed at the helm of your campaign, the attack on Connally would become so intense that you would have no alternative but to make another change in your campaign leadership before the November election."

On August 1 Connally was being treated in the press as Ford's likely choice. Ten tumultuous days later he was slipping down the list. On August 9 Ford said publicly that he was looking for a "middle-of-the-road" Republican as his running mate, and this implied someone safe and unflamboyant, one who would be unlikely to upstage the bland president. Nevertheless, the Texan survived a White House interview on his health and finances and remained in the group of six names that Ford took to the convention.

As his nomination began to look certain, Ford had to be concerned with mending his fences with Reagan, for he knew that he had no chance of winning in November without a unified party.

---

*The slur on Demetracopoulos would continue to rattle around in Connally's closet long after 1976. It continued to crop up periodically in Evans-Novak and Jack Anderson columns into 1980, as an ugly skeleton. Mayor Rousakis also was to have his problems. In 1984 it came out that for ten years he had been involved in a wide range of public and private corruption, from extortion to selling appointments to prostitution.

The two adversaries met in Kansas City around midnight, after the convention vote. Among the first questions discussed was Ford's vice presidential choice. Since Reagan had made it known weeks before that he was not interested in the slot himself, Ford now threw out his six names. Reagan favored Robert Dole.

While this seemed to make Dole the instant front runner, it was not conclusive, and it was not until 3:15 A.M. that the president gathered with his top advisers to make the choice. Elliot Richardson was eliminated first as anathema to the Reaganites, and William Simon next as too inflexibly conservative. And then it came to Connally. In Ford's mind, Watergate was less of a negative factor than it was in the minds of his advisers, but the president knew that in the public mind, Connally's acquittal had not erased the doubt. Vice President Rockefeller spoke up enthusiastically for Connally, for he and Connally had met several weeks before, and after Rockefeller had questioned Connally sharply he came away a believer. But Ford's pollster, Robert Teeter, was also present. He had taken soundings. "Teeter's polls showed that [Connally's] wheeler-dealer image just wouldn't fade away," Ford would write later. "Too much polarization, we concluded, and he was off the list." In such anticlimactic moves are men's destinies decided.

Connally was not even at the Kansas City convention while his fate was being decided. He had made his appearance there a few days earlier, his first address to a national Republican convention, as one of the newer members, and this speech was a flop. The press ignored it, and the delegates on the floor milled about and socialized. On the day that Ford chose Robert Dole, Connally was already in New York. There he addressed the national convention of the Veterans of Foreign Wars, a comfortable, more attentive safe haven altogether, and the veterans cheered his ringing condemnation of Communist tyrants, his calls for a stronger defense, his support of liberty. But he got his biggest hand when he reverted to football imagery, for it seemed as if he was speaking about himself: "I don't know how long we will be number one in the free world. I do know that I never want to be number two." They stood and applauded at that, but a few breaths later, when, ponderously, he invoked the Athenians and told of how they had wanted comfort and security more than they wanted freedom, and how in the end they lost their comfort and their security and their freedom all in a bunch, the audience was unmoved. It would, however, prove a fateful statement for John Connally personally, ten years later.

Supernova

THE POLITICAL SEASON OF 1976 could be only mildly disappointing to John Connally. He had achieved far more than he might have dreamed possible in reestablishing himself as a star in the political firmament. Gerald Ford's narrow defeat by Jimmy Carter could be laid to two factors: first, Ford's blandness and his bumbling, and second, to the mean, hatchet-man performance of his running mate, Robert Dole. In the wake of defeat, Republican professionals were saying that Carter's victory was merely "tactical," rather than "strategic." If Ford had chosen Connally, Connally would surely have avoided such remarkable Dole gaffes as his assertion that Democrats (rather than Hitler, or the Archduke Ferdinand, or the Communist Chinese, or Ho Chi Minh) had dragged America into every war of the twentieth century. In Texas and elsewhere in the South Connally probably would have provided the margin of victory to the GOP. In short, Connally was now the logical leader to pick up the fallen GOP banner.

There was another theory that gained currency, especially in the several years to follow when the Carter presidency began to falter. It was that if Connally had not switched parties in 1973 he might well have been the presidential nominee on the *Democratic* ticket in 1976, instead of Carter. The Democrats necessarily had to turn to a Southern moderate or conservative candidate after the McGovern debacle of 1972. Only because there was no dominant Democrat in the field, so the theory ran, had the obscure Jimmy

Carter emerged as the standard bearer. Between Carter and Connally there would have been no contest. Connally himself upon occasion had wistfully embraced this view. Between American political parties is a continental divide, and Connally was to remark to friends that in retrospect, crossing that divide was the worst mistake of his life.

But if he loved politics, Connally also loved money. After the election of 1976 he threw his enormous energy into the pursuit of wealth. At the core of his nature he was an entrepreneur, and he found himself in 1977 with the ability to generate dizzying amounts of money for virtually any enterprise he chose to bless with his presence. Major corporations far and wide wanted him on their boards. His breadth of vision and his energy and his perceived good judgment, matched with his stature as a former secretary of the treasury and his ability to compel attention at the highest levels of government, would make him a unique asset to any corporation. He chose his associations carefully for the most part. Without fail, he exceeded the expectations of the corporations he served. When Dr. Pepper put him on its board, for example, Connally was in a position to persuade the U.S. government to install the company's vending machines on U.S. military bases. As a director of Greyhound, he had the personal satisfaction of managing the nation's largest bus company, to which his father had sold his dusty stretch limousine in the mid-thirties to buy the family's Floresville ranch. For a year he was a trustee of the U.S. Trust Company in New York, and in that venerable bastion of Wall Street his presence was "awesome." In boardrooms his performance had a set pattern. For the first few meetings he was almost silent, listening and absorbing, impressive with his remarkable ability as a quick study. When he began to speak, he dominated. One denizen of the boardroom said of him, "There were twelve men in the room, and then there was John Connally." A trustee of U.S. Trust agreed: "After three meetings no one would make a move without turning to his end of the table and saying, 'What do you think, John?' "

To Vinson and Elkins, Connally was not a lawyer but a grandee. He was akin to a human cash machine, for his attractiveness as a member of corporate boards redounded handsomely to Vinson and Elkins. By 1978 Connally's salary from legal fees alone was $620,000. To that he could add $235,000 in ranch income, $286,000 in capital gains, and another $80,000 from assorted real estate ventures and speaking fees. Still, to the experts in such esoteric matters, and, more important, to Connally himself, that income did not qualify him as "Texas rich." His net worth in 1978 was only somewhat less than $4 million. His low-slung house in the River Oaks section of Houston was regarded as modest and unpretentious next to the columned mansions nearby. Connally himself was apt to point out that his suits, contrary to the pure fiction that Lyndon Johnson had promoted, were of the modest Hart Schaffner & Marx variety, and that his white Mercedes 600, that oft-noted symbol of his ostentation, was nine years old.

Most humans would be content to motor along in this fashion for a year or two before a final push for the presidency, but Connally's restlessness, his gambler's love for the still bigger deal, took him back out onto the precipice. Yes, he wanted to run for the presidency in 1980, but he lacked the cold engineer's calibration of a Jimmy Carter or the B-student doggedness of a Michael Dukakis. The presidency was a major goal of his life, but not the only goal, and he was content to let fate play the game out between his competing and often shifting interests. Becoming "Washington powerful" had to go along with becoming Texas rich, and Connally saw no reason why he had to choose between the two.

In 1977 he went into business with two Arab sheiks, and together they bought a struggling bank called the Main Bank of Houston. There was, of course, nothing wrong with that, as Connally would soon be pointing out over and over. The Main Bank was a target of opportunity; it had a modest $66 million in deposits, and it was losing $100,000 a month from bad loans and bad management. The sheiks, Ghaith Pharaon and his childhood friend, Khaled Bin Mahfouz, wanted a bank where they could deposit their oil millions and reap the highest interest by eliminating the middleman. Through the partnership the international division of the bank had the potential to bring other major deposits from the Middle East, and Connally could talk of it being a $500 million bank in a very short time. It was just routine business, he protested, but it made news partly because of the essentially xenophobic nature of Texas banking. By tradition, Texas financial institutions eschewed associations with banks outside of Texas, much less outside of America. (It was still very early in the era of holding companies.) Moreover, since Texas oil seemed to be in competition with Arab oil, an Arab connection had a slightly unpatriotic flavor.

"So what's the big deal? We bought a bank," Connally replied to inquiries.

The big deal was the appearance it created for a potential candidate for the U.S. presidency, when the United States was attempting to make itself more independent of foreign oil, when the special relationship with Israel was a cornerpiece of American foreign policy, and when an Arab oil embargo hung as a persistent threat to American society, which now drew fifty-five percent of its petroleum from abroad. Connally now had a direct, personal, financial stake in a cozy relationship with the Arab world, and it was inevitable that this relationship would be a serious, if not catastrophic, political liability. Everything Connally said about Middle Eastern policy would henceforth be put through the filter of his own personal interest and would be suspect, especially if it gave the slightest hint of being anti-Israel. He could not now claim to be a disinterested statesman in search of the best formula for peace in the Middle East. The contradiction of his situation became clear enough when he was asked if another Arab oil embargo wouldn't result in the withdrawal of Arab capital. "I am concerned that our dependence on Middle Eastern oil is great, and I think President Carter's energy policy is dangerous, because it is making us more dependent on foreign oil," he said, but of course John Connally himself had now become personally dependent on foreign oil. Taking shape in this deal was a fatal flaw of his presidential campaign.

The charge that John Connally was anti-Semitic began here. It was an unfair charge which he would deny passionately and which he resented deeply but which he should have seen as inevitable. Nothing could have been more predictable than the cartoon which resulted, showing Connally in string tie and pinstriped suit with his arms around the two sheiks in their native robes and with their swarthy faces and the headline, "John Connally—between the sheiks."

★

On January 24, 1979, more than a year before the Iowa caucuses and the New Hampshire primary, Connally announced for the presidency. The nation was strong, he told his audience at the National Press Club in Washington; "the only missing ingredient is leadership." It was a measure of the emphasis put on his own style and personal magnetism that his declaration was unextraordinary in its substance. Predictably, he attacked President Carter across a wide range—the president had scant appreciation of the "uses of power on a global scale"—and he talked of the need for a "strong president" with a "tough" policy toward the Soviet Union. He charged the administration with being asleep at the switch in the worsening Iran situation, and he proposed two constitutional amendments: a single six-year term for the presidency (a proposal President Carter himself would embrace a few months later), and the legal requirement of a balanced budget, except in a national emergency. In the press conference afterwards, Connally acknowledged the wide lead that Ronald Reagan held in the early polls—forty percent to Connally's six—but Connally had faced those odds before, and now he said, "I don't envy [Reagan] in that position." Reagan was the "incumbent challenger" who for three years had continued to build his base of strength from his presidential campaign of 1976. Inevitably, Connally's indictment in the milk fund scandal came to the fore. The candidate did his best to dismiss it as a key issue in the campaign. "I think the American people have faith in the judicial system," he scoffed. The next day the commentators and politicians dissected Connally's chances hungrily. By general agreement, he would have to build from Texas with money and solid support, broaden to the South generally, and then impress the Northeast with the force of his personality. In an editorial, as a harbinger of what was to come, the *New York Times* referred to Connally as "the Texas political chameleon."

Connally's political strategists, led by the veteran conservative operative Eddie Mahe, were far ahead of this slow take in the press. Before he had taken the job as Connally's campaign manager, Mahe had surveyed the scene and declared Connally's chances for the nomination to be excellent. In style, in substance, Connally was the best candidate the Republicans could field in 1980, Mahe felt. The governor was an exciting, dynamic, national figure, a bona fide American hero, and an unparalleled stump speaker. His ability to communicate even the most complicated economic and foreign policy questions to a general audience was as impressive as it was effortless.

The mood of America in 1979 seemed just right for John Connally as well. The country had dismissed Jimmy Carter as a nonleader, and the presidency was adrift. The spiral of inflation and rising prices and unemployment was careering out of control and remained atop the list of chief concerns in the electorate. In Connally was a former treasury secretary who understood these complicated economic forces and who had acted boldly in a similar situation eight years before. The Iranian situation presented a special circumstance where the normal discourse of civilized nations did not apply, where a spiritual leader cared nothing for his personal safety and had set upon a single-minded theocratic mission. Only a leader who understood the uses of power on a global scale, as Connally himself had termed it in his declaration for the presidency, could deal with the Iranian visionaries. And finally, related to the Iranian situation and to the economic distress, was the oil shock of 1979, when OPEC had doubled its oil prices and had caused the price of gas at the pump to rise sharply. If ever there was a candidate who understood the energy crisis and knew how to deal with greedy Arabs, it was Connally.

Mahe also found the competition wanting. He did not expect George Bush or Howard Baker to last: they were too moderate to survive the bruising, often ideological, Republican primary process. By consensus, Robert Dole, another likely candidate, had been a four-star disaster in 1976 as Ford's running mate, and he was sure to fade quickly. That left Ronald Reagan. Mahe discounted the early polls and set a realistic goal. By January 1980, one year away, and one month away from the New Hampshire primary, he wanted to pull Reagan down to the high twenties in the polls and push Connally up to the low twenties. Then he hoped to knock off Reagan in an early test—Iowa perhaps—and proceed head to head at each subsequent primary and watch the old B-grade actor wither away.

Moreover, Mahe expected Teddy Kennedy, rather than Jimmy Carter, to be the Democratic candidate in 1980. The juxtaposition of Connally and Kennedy became central to the Connally strategy from the beginning. Kennedy represented youth and dynamic energy, vibrant liberal values and the Kennedy mystique. Mahe felt that once it was clear that Kennedy would be the Democratic nominee, Republicans would have great difficulty in imagining tired, old Ronald Reagan as a viable opponent. "Ted Kennedy scared Republicans," Mahe would say later. "Carter never scared anyone, except with his incompetence." Against Ted Kennedy, Connally would be a powerful match, much more than Reagan—uniquely so because of Dallas. Connally would not be intimidated by the Kennedy magic, Mahe was sure.

Thus Reagan, and Reagan alone, was Connally's competition. Once it became a two-person contest for the Republican nomination, Mahe saw no difficulty in drawing a sharp distinction for the Republican voters. Connally's conservatism was activist. He was a fixer with conservative solutions, for his politics came from being an entrepreneur, not from being a shallow ideologue. Reagan's conservatism was passive and soft. It would not be long, Mahe felt, before the Californian would appear old and lazy, unfocused and insubstantial. When it came to a global view, between Reagan and Connally the difference was between a yokel and a cosmopolitan.

With a national and international figure like Connally, Mahe determined to run a national campaign, with organizations in every state and campaign appearances across the country—rather than a narrow campaign concentrated in a few politically important states. This was not a candidate whom you wasted in kitchen conversations or in New England town meetings, for Connally was at his best before crowds of 2,000 or more. In this, he was the antithesis of Lyndon Johnson. Johnson's aides had always been frustrated at watching Johnson fascinate and charm small, intimate gatherings and flop embarrassingly in formal speeches to large groups. With Connally, arrogance and aloofness came through in small groups, and it would be better, the national strategists agreed, to keep him away from quaint, "retail" campaigning in Iowa cornfields or New Hampshire coffee klatsches. Since the race would be money-driven in the early stage, and since it seemed as if the conventions of the largest business groups always wanted Connally above everyone as their keynote speaker, the Connally campaign was content to play to their candidate's strengths and gloss over his weaknesses.

Those weaknesses lay like a dormant virus in the nervous system of the Connally campaign. No one could be sure when they would flare up, or whether the virus could be suppressed or controlled. The symptoms were there in the first few days after Connally's declaration for the presidency: the New York Times's label of "political chameleon" characterized Connally as a turncoat. The inevitable question about his milk trial emphasized his Watergate connection. The early polls showed him, unlike the other candidates, with nearly as high an unfavorable rating as a favorable one, and it stemmed from his reputation as a "wheeler-dealer." "How do you deal with that?" Mahe would ask rhetorically. "Say you're not a wheeler-dealer? You have to ignore it." Watergate could not be ignored, however. So Connally fashioned a standard response that he was the only candidate certified as "truthful" and "innocent." "But you'd rather not have to use such a line," Mahe said wryly.

In this case there was no choice. On the party switch, he could say that Reagan had also switched parties, and that at least he, John Connally, had never been a founding member of the ultraliberal Americans for Democratic Action—but would anyone listen?

On March 20, the candidate made his first major trip to New Hampshire, and he got a frigid reception. He preached optimism, demonstrated his vigor and his decisiveness, showed off Nellie to good advantage, displayed his oratorical forcefulness before the legislature, and got panned. "I don't think he's the style of guy New

Hampshire takes to," said one old salt of Republican politics in the Granite State. But the problem was deeper than style. In New Hampshire the party switch gnawed like a festering sore upon the established, unexcitable New Englanders. This seemed to throw Connally into even higher paroxysms of self-promotion, because without the support of the party regulars, he was more than ever on his own.

The crabby curmudgeon of the conservative *Manchester Union*, William Loeb, greeted Connally's visit with a withering editorial. "Born-Again Wheeler-Dealer" was the title. After genuflections to Connally's presidential looks and his wonderful speechmaking and his nice wife, Loeb delivered a political depth charge.

> John Connally is a veteran Democrat politician of the LBJ era in Texas. This was an era of "anything goes," as long as you can make a fast buck and the devil take the hindmost. He is a wheeler-dealer on a grand scale. He wheeled and dealed himself from being a Democrat to being a Republican and joined the Nixon Administration. . . . In the last few years, Connally has done much of his wheeling and dealing with oil-wealthy Arabs of the Middle East. He might be called the Arabs' candidate for President of the United States. . . . What you have here is a wonderful impressive looking front, but it is all on the surface. Behind it, you have nothing of the character and the material which this nation needs so desperately to straighten out the sorry mess in which this country now finds itself.

As if that were not enough, the paper sicked its two ideological columnists on a few of Connally's past proposals and found them to stray from the correct line of the truth faith. Of Connally's idea of partnership between government and business, John Chamberlain wrote, "It could mean a fascistic cooperation between government bureaus and corporate management to police the industrial state. . . . We had that sort of 'cooperation' in the early New Deal days, when General 'Iron-Pants' Hugh Johnson was running the National Recovery Administration. The Supreme Court rescued us from that experiment." Of Connally's notion for compulsory national service to provide "discipline for young people," John D. Lofton, Jr., wrote, "Milton Friedman has called it a 'Hitler-youth type program' which demonstrates two things about Connally: first, he lacks a real appreciation of the meaning of freedom, and second, he is grasping at any straw that can give him what he thinks will be a popular program. . . . Connally is a wheeler-dealer in the worst sense of the phrase, a classic, old-time, all-things-to-all-people politician who lacks any principles whatever."

Connally limped out of New Hampshire feeling very much like a rogue. The party establishment rejected him; the ideological right attacked him; the dour, stingy, clamshell voters of the small towns did not take to him. If he were to make any headway at all, he would have to turn to television.

In the South his reception was considerably warmer. The Florida, South Carolina, and Alabama primaries were scheduled immediately after New Hampshire, and these Southern redoubts represented Connally's best chance to beat Reagan early. But the coin could be turned over: if he did not win decisively in the South, he was finished. When Eddie Mahe said of the Southern primaries, "They have the potential to knock some people out of the race," he knew that he could be talking about his own candidate. By May of 1979 the Southern campaign looked good. Significant politicians were defecting from Reagan to Connally. Haley Barbour, Reagan's Mississippi coordinator in 1976, came over to Connally, saying, "I was for Reagan the last time, but what is important now is timing. Not only is he [Reagan] older, but the things he's identified with, that he talked about in 1976, are not timely." That was an attitude which the Connally camp trumpeted throughout the South, and it was working. Erosion of support for Reagan in Florida, Alabama, and the Carolinas was widely reported, as Winton "Red" Blount, the former postmaster general under Nixon and an Alabamian, became Connally's Southern coordinator.

Then there was Texas. The situation there was decidedly Wild West. Someone in the Texas legislature had thought up the bright idea of moving the Texas Republican primary forward from May to March 11, thus bolstering the power and influence of Texas upon the choice of the national candidates. The notion brought to mind the action of the Texas legislature in 1960 that had blithely changed Texas law to permit Lyndon Johnson to run for both the Senate and the vice presidency simultaneously. Now it was coming to the aid of Brother Connally. If Connally needed to win an early primary to be a viable candidate, let it be Texas. The Republican governor, William Clements, supported the measure, as did the Democratic lieutenant governor, Bill Hobby. The legislation was drafted so that conservative Democrats could cross over and vote for Connally, for when it came to a Texan running for president, party should be no object. The advance of the primary to March, along with the advance of Connally's fortunes, seemed to make it a certainty.

But on May 19, when the Hobby bill came before the state senate, the desks of twelve state senators were vacant. That meant the senate did not have a quorum, and therefore could pass no legislation. Hobby was furious, and he dispatched the Texas Rangers out onto the range to find the outlaws, presumably to clap them in irons and drag them into town. The missing legislators were dubbed the "Killer Bees," and the whole state took up the fun. Liberal members of the Texas house began to wear fuzzy lapel pins, and even the sergeant at arms of the senate began to wear a T-shirt with the plaintive question WHERE THE HELL ARE THE KILLER BEES? Intelligence reports from secret informants indicated that the underground solons were holed up somewhere in the Hill Country. The fabled Rangers staked out favorite golf tournaments and chili joints, snuck around religious retreats, attended a tuna boat launching, and finally spotted the car of one bee, Raul Laugoria of Pharr, in front of a Roman Catholic church in San Juan, Texas. But the priest of the church swore that no fugitive had taken sanctuary with him. Another deadeye snatched Gene Jones of Houston, disguised with darker hair and a darker mustache, just as he was reaching for his morning paper, and spirited him to Austin, only to find out that it was not Gene Jones at all but his twin brother. It was a hoot, and it made the front page of the *New York Times* in a story that quoted a state Democratic party leader as saying that the main purpose of the Hobby bill was "to rig the 1980 Republican Presidential primary for one Republican candidate, John Connally."

In his own state, the cartoonist for the *Dallas Times Herald* portrayed Connally as a club-footed, oversized bear with his claws stuck in a honey-filled beehive and getting stung unmercifully. It was a benign and amusing episode but it did John Connally no good. It deepened the impression that Texas was zany and Connally was out there, once again, wheeling and dealing in the ethical borderland. Moreover, it was all for naught. The Killer Bees did indeed kill the Hobby-Clements-Connally measure, and the Texas primary stayed buried, late and useless, in the primary season.

Through the summer Connally coasted. He had remarked casually to an aide that he might just buy a home in New Hampshire and spend the summer months at local town meetings. At another point he mused that perhaps he and Nellie would rent a camper and crisscross the verdant grain fields of Iowa in the growing season.

But somehow these notions never materialized. He went abroad instead.

If he was coasting, he was growing increasingly impatient. He could not understand why he was not moving up in the polls, when he so palpably possessed what Jimmy Carter lacked. Carter's standing continued to plummet, and the economic downturn reflected the lack of confidence in the money markets in the United States and abroad. In early July Carter retreated to Camp David to ponder the collapse of his presidency and to address the alarming economic nervousness. He emerged on July 16 to give his famous "malaise" speech. In Kansas City, Connally watched the president on television. Carter's talk about the self-indulgence and the materialism and the spiritual emptiness in Americans touched a core of anger in Connally, and the next morning he marched into a national convention of county executives and gave a dynamic speech. Carter's "crisis in confidence" was simply a lack of confidence in the president himself, he thundered. The American people were willing to make sacrifices, but only if they were shown the way by a true leader. Little remembered from Carter's malaise speech is that its substance had to do with energy; it specifically called for a six-part energy program, designed to overcome America's dependency on foreign oil, and Connally had more stature than anyone to criticize that as well: "The Democrat-controlled Congress has not done anything except make it harder to mine and burn coal, harder to drill for oil, harder to build nuclear power plants." The audience was with him, caught up in the excitement and the force and the passion of Connally's speech, and they cheered uproariously. But something deep and angry was stirring in Connally. His superiority and his presidential value were not registering. Why was he not doing better? Why was he not being taken more seriously? He left the convention hall emotionally drained; he got into an elevator with an aide.

"How did I do, Sam?" he mumbled miserably, falling back against the elevator's paneling.

"That was great, Governor, really terrific," the aide gushed, for he thought it was the best speech of the campaign so far.

Connally turned slowly on the aide, a terrifying anger welling up from deep within. "Don't you bullshit me, Sam," he said coldly. "It was awful. Just awful. The sound system was all wrong . . . ," and his frustration poured out in numerous trivial complaints.

Carter's speech did not help the president. It was greeted as a sermon more than a speech. Wall Street was not reassured. Indeed, the market grew even more uncertain when the speech was followed by wholesale changes and firings in the cabinet and the White House staff. America was beginning to appreciate how it felt when a government fell under a parliamentary system. But still Connally did not benefit, and he could not understand why. Even when Paul Volcker was appointed to be the new chairman of the Federal Reserve Board and Wall Street suddenly felt better, no one made the point that Volcker had been Connally's undersecretary of treasury in 1971–72, when together they had devised the bold strategy to stop inflation. Nobody was making the connection that the confidence and the stability that Volcker brought, Connally could bring in spades if he were president.

Later in the summer the jets packed the airstrip at Picosa Ranch, as the campaign staff finally came together with the main fund-raisers and the media experts, and the enterprise pointed to the opening of the real political season after Labor Day. It was an eclectic group. Eddie Mahe, the campaign manager, had been chosen partly for his credentials and partly as a loyal, longstanding Republican partisan, since one of Connally's negatives, particularly in caucus states like Iowa, was his party switch. But also in attendance at Picosa was a cadre of old Connally loyalists who went back to the political wars in Texas in the 1960s. They were Johnsonian Democrats. The tension between the national Republicans from Washington and the local Democrats from Texas was present from the beginning, installed in the campaign like two cogs that did not mesh.

A number of ideas were tested at Picosa. On the media side, Connally's longtime public relations associate from Fort Worth, Julian Read, put forward some of his pet projects. Read had dusted off a concept that had worked in 1962 when Connally ran for governor of Texas as a Democrat, a series of TV spots called "Coffee with Connally," which were supposed to show off the candidate as just a regular kind of guy in an intimate down-home setting. This would cut across Connally's problem of coming off as aloof and imperious, Read argued. As Read rolled his material, the national experts rolled their eyes across the ceiling. "They were probably the worst political television that has ever been made," Mahe would say later, but New Hampshire would end up having coffee with Connally nevertheless. Mahe realized that he would have to deal with Connally's retinue from Texas, who thought that they could apply the lessons of Texas primary politics of the early 1960s to presidential politics in the late 1970s. Read also screened a promotional spot which centered on the Dallas assassination and featured Connally's bedside interview only a few days later. The effect was eerie and overwhelming, and the group agreed that the exploitation of Dallas would have to take a more quiet, subtle form at an appropriate time.

Also present at Picosa was Sam Hoskinson, Connally's issues adviser. A former CIA and National Security Council staffer, his relationship with Connally went back to the eighteen-nation trip which Connally undertook for Nixon in June 1972 and which Hoskinson, as an Alexander Haig protégé, organized. By his own admission, Hoskinson was captivated by Connally—the governor was such a refreshing, charming change from the tyranny of Henry Kissinger—and he gladly resigned from the government when he was invited to join the Connally campaign in the spring of 1979. With his widespread Washington contacts, Hoskinson exposed the candidate to a number of foreign policy and defense experts in the ensuing months. Such personages as Paul Nitze, the Washington veteran and defense expert; Admiral Thomas Moorer, former chairman of the Joint Chiefs of Staff; and William Hyland, the editor of *Foreign Affairs* magazine, came onto the periphery of the Connally circle in this way. The issues side of the campaign appealed to Connally's deepest longing: he wanted to be seen as the candidate of ideas, the figure of real presidential substance, the politician unafraid to take bold and tough positions. This longing was central to his character, and this image would contrast him advantageously to the vapid figure of Ronald Reagan. At Picosa it was agreed that early in the fall, well ahead of tradition, the candidate would give major, highly promoted policy addresses on significant issues of foreign affairs, national security, and the economy.

Only Hoskinson and Connally himself knew that a major speech was already secretly in the works. A few weeks earlier Hoskinson had been with his man in the Marriott Hotel in Chicago (and inevitably in the "presidential suite"), when together they watched Jesse Jackson and Andrew Young on television news speaking of the tension between blacks and Jews over Middle East policy. Connally saw an opportunity. "Maybe we ought to make this the subject of a major speech," he said, turning to Hoskinson. "Maybe we can divide 'em." The following day, at a private lunch, the two men developed the idea further. The Middle East fascinated them. It had been the area of Hoskinson's greatest expertise in the government, and it was Connally's prime business interest, and both tilted toward a greater accommodation of Arab interests in American policy. It was agreed that Hoskinson would get to work on a draft. This he did clandestinely, going to the length of shutting his office door and locking it whenever he set to work on the speech. By mid-September the speech had been through fifteen drafts, with Hoskinson treating the matter as if it were a black operation for the CIA. He had only a vague sense that he was playing with political dynamite, for his career had been in the civil service, and the *political* consequences of a pro-Arab appeal were supposed to be the province of the candidate. Connally had vented his impatience over the lack of dramatic movement toward him in the polls and had emphasized the need for a blockbuster that could catapult him upward. This sanctioned Hoskinson to throw caution to the winds. As the speech took shape, they joked about the coming firestorm. The speech had to be kept absolutely secret, lest through a leak they get only the firestorm without getting the speech. Taking inspiration from a Brookings Institution study, from elements of UN Resolution 242, and from their own predilections, they put three specific proposals forward.

The first dealt with a Palestinian homeland. The Israelis must withdraw from all civilian settlements in the West Bank, Gaza Strip, and the Golan Heights. They must return all land annexed in the 1967 war. The new Palestinian homeland might take shape either as an autonomous entity or, preferably, a region with self-determination within Jordan, and the Arabs should decide. On who would negotiate for the Palestinians, the speech read, "any Palestinian leader who is willing to put aside violence, sit down and work constructively on the details of a compromise peace settlement should be welcome. But any Palestinian extremist who refused to cooperate and continues to indulge in terrorism should be treated as an international outlaw by the international community. He should be given neither peace nor refuge in any land."

The second proposal was that an overall peace treaty must be negotiated between Israel, the moderate Arab states, NATO, and Japan, in which Israel's right to exist would be affirmed as the quid pro quo for the creation of a Palestinian homeland. Moderate Arab states would renounce forever any hostile actions toward the Jews and "give up the use of oil supply and prices to force political change. . . . We must secure a clear understanding from Saudi Arabia and other moderate oil-producing nations in the region that a just and comprehensive peace settlement means a return to stable oil prices in real terms. The Arabs must, in short, forsake the oil weapon in return for Israel's withdrawal from the occupied territories."

To guarantee and enforce the treaty, substantial American

military forces would be sent to the Middle East. The U.S. would lease the old Israeli airfields in the Sinai and create a new Fifth Fleet to be stationed in the Indian Ocean near the Strait of Hormuz. The Fifth Fleet idea was specifically Connally's. Hoskinson had argued against it initially because it sounded too militaristic. But Connally insisted upon it. It underscored his background as secretary of the navy.

The third and final proposal addressed Jerusalem. Within the settlement, Jerusalem's status would be negotiated with "substantial political autonomy for each of the groups within the city in the area it predominates."

As the time for delivering the speech approached, Hoskinson grew increasingly worried about the secrecy. Eddie Mahe still did not know what was brewing. Should they show the draft to Henry Kissinger? Connally vacillated. "You can't trust Henry, can you?" he remarked. No, Hoskinson replied. Every Republican candidate was courting Kissinger aggressively—George Bush had openly offered to make him secretary of state again—but Kissinger was playing the coquette. Finally, Connally decided that Kissinger should be consulted, and he authorized Hoskinson to make the contact. But appointments kept slipping, and dates kept falling through the cracks, until it was clear that Kissinger was avoiding them. At last, at Connally's prodding, Hoskinson got on a plane, flew to New York, and rang Kissinger's doorbell on East Fifty-first Street. Kissinger did not seem pleased to see Hoskinson when he opened the door, but after a grumble invited Hoskinson back into his study, where he read the speech. Unequivocally, he advised against its delivery for political reasons, fearing the reaction of the Jewish community. On substance, he made a few minor suggestions. As Hoskinson rose to leave, Kissinger took him by the arm and said, in his inimitable accent, "Make sure the governor understands I'll be behind him, even if he decides to make the speech." When Connally heard about the remark, he was amused.

Kissinger was not the only notable figure to be secretly consulted. In late September, with the final draft of the speech essentially set and having decided definitely to go forward, Connally was in New York. So was King Hussein of Jordan, who had come to address the UN General Assembly on the Palestinian question, and the king had asked to see Connally. After deliberating the appropriateness with Hoskinson and being assured that the meeting could be secret, Connally strolled into the back entrance of the Waldorf-Astoria, and had the Secret Service hold the press as he went up to the Towers for a forty-five-minute audience. Connally did not tell King Hussein what he was planning to do in a few weeks, but he questioned the king closely on an aspect of his forthcoming proposal: that Jordan accept an autonomous Palestinian state within the Jordanian kingdom. Hussein was noncommittal.

The week before the speech was to be delivered, Connally finally widened the circle of the cognoscenti to a half-dozen of his top staff. When he heard about it, campaign manager Eddie Mahe was on a brief cruise with his fundamentalist Christian wife. After reading the speech, Mrs. Mahe emerged from the cabin to announce that she could no longer support John Connally. Anybody who believed as Connally did about the Promised Land of Israel was unacceptable to her. This worried Mahe, and he fell into a round of ship-to-shore telephone calls. Ultimately he passed it. With the speech having imprints of Henry Kissinger and King Hussein, who was he to question it? When Connally's press officer, Jim Brady, read it, he pronounced it a political disaster. Even Hoskinson was shaken by the uniformly negative responses and by the predictions of dire consequences. Connally, however, had made up his mind. "John Connally really believed in that speech," Hoskinson was to say. "It was his speech. He felt that this was the most important foreign policy area we had, and, by God, we should speak out on it. He knew it was a risk, but he knew we weren't getting any contributions from the Jewish community. Prominent Jews had made promises, but they hadn't delivered."

On October 11 Connally stepped forward to the podium at the National Press Club in Washington and committed political suicide. The Middle East, he said, was the most vital and volatile part of the world, and he had come to offer a "new approach" based on American interests rather than Arab or Israeli interests. The Camp David Accords, he had concluded, did not provide the basis for successful negotiations of the remaining issues in the Middle East, and unless those remaining issues were resolved, the tension in that troubled region threatened to rend the fabric of American society, especially the relations between the blacks and the Jews. At the core of the problem was Israel's appetite for expansion, represented by its "creeping annexation of the West Bank. . . . A clear distinction must be drawn by the United States between support for Israel's security, which is a moral imperative, and support for Israel's broader territorial acquisitions." Moreover, the requirement of Israel's safety needed to be balanced against the importance of Middle East oil to Western civilization. "The oil of the Middle East is and will continue to be the life blood of Western civilization for decades to come," Connally said. "If, through a catastrophe in the Middle East, America's economy is gravely weakened, so too will be our ability to defend and support Israel."

Apart from whatever political imperatives Connally had perceived that made him be so specific, so inflammatory, and so different from all his opponents this early in the campaign, the speech must be given its due. It was courageous, sincere, and bold. In its contrast to the usual platitudes on the Middle East of other presidential candidates, it was consistent with the entire theme of the Connally campaign. This was "leadership for America"—of a sort. Contrary to Connally's representations about it, it was, however, not new. Variations of the plan had been put forward by such experts as George Ball, Andrew Young, and Zbigniew Brzezinski. In its consistency with UN Resolution 242, the speech followed the lead of the last four American presidents, as Connally would soon be protesting. There was even a bit of prescience in the speech. Only a month later Iranian militants seized the American embassy in Teheran and took American hostages. If, as a matter of fantasy, Connally's Fifth Fleet had been operational off the Strait of Hormuz and a Satan-President as wicked as Connally were in the White House, perhaps even the ayatollah would have had second thoughts about seizing American citizens.

Connally left the press club on October 11 in an expansive mood. His close aides could feel his exultation. It was as if on this fall day in Washington he had taken over the presidency. Next to Jimmy Carter's weakness and vacillation, Connally had become the U.S. president *in absentia*, showing the way for the stout-hearted to what *had* to be done. That night, in Montgomery, Alabama, he was positively bullish; his joy was palpable. He had made a score. His candidacy had grandly emerged with one lightning stroke, with a powerful, compelling pronunciamento in international affairs. This, at last, was presidential politics.

The reaction was instantaneous and visceral, but it began ironically, for it put Connally into the company of the Reverend Jesse Jackson, arguably the last person on the surface of the earth with whom Connally wanted to be associated. As Connally was speaking in Washington, Jackson was shuttling around the Middle East, embracing Yasir Arafat; meeting with Anwar el-Sadat, Hafez al-Assad, and Shimon Peres; and speaking as the self-appointed emissary of fifteen million American blacks. His people, he told the Arab leaders, would tolerate neither an American military involvement in the Middle East nor any move to crimp the flow of Arab oil to the United States, because "the people I represent would be the first ones to die and the first ones to go cold in the winter." After the Connally speech the *New York Times* chose to link Connally and Jackson in an editorial called "Merchants of Myth." Both men were proposing a "wicked" bargain, said the *Times:* a trade of the West Bank for reliable, cheap Arab oil. The editorial continued, "What makes this formula wicked is its unspoken assumption that the United States has an oil problem, mainly because American Jews somehow prevent American politicians from forcing a quick deal on Israel. What does Mr. Connally mean when he says the country must now base policy on American interests? These are ugly code words that have the effect of blaming Israel and the Jews for gas lines, escalating oil prices and the hardship they cause."

This was close to charging Connally with being anti-Semitic, and other voices deepened the impression. A conference of thirty-four Jewish organizations condemned the speech as a "disservice to the cause of peace in the Middle East" because of its criticism of the Camp David Accords, and the government of Menachem Begin, which had vowed that Israel would never give up its territorial gains, was furious. Perhaps the most savage analysis came from the *New Republic*, which raised the *ad hominem* argument of Connally's cozy business relations with Arabs and called this a tawdry grab for votes by a desperate candidate: "Whenever there has been a choice between principle and advantage, between ethics and enrichment, between honor and ambition, John Connally has been on the side of the main chance." His plan abandoned Israel, submitted to blackmail, and was "a naked trade of Israel's security for oil. . . . Doesn't John Connally know from his Saudi friends that they don't really want an independent Palestinian state in the West Bank? If he does not, he has not been listening, which makes him a bad statesman. If he does, then he is perpetuating a political fraud upon them and us for his own short term political interest."

Several weeks after the speech, Connally found himself on a plane with Joseph Kraft, a Jew himself, but a man of deep and independent global vision who had written extensively on the Middle East and whose view was informed by geopolitical rather than narrow religious perspective. Among the things they discussed was the storm Connally's speech had generated.

"You were lucky the speech drew so much hostile fire from the Israeli partisans," Kraft said. "The really strong argument against your plan is that it's unrealistic and won't work. Do you really think there's any country in the Near East that will accept an American military presence there? Do you really think Congress will send American boys to stand between Israel and the Palestinians?"

"There are American troops in Western Europe and Korea, aren't there?" Connally replied. "The Middle East is a more immediate threat to our security. I don't propose to put American troops between Israel and the PLO anyway. I'd station them in installations built by Israel in the Sinai—the ones that are now being turned back to Egypt. . . ."

"Do you have any thought that Egypt will accept an American military presence there?"

"They should. It's in their interest, and it will bring security to the area. Anyway, Joe, we paid for those bases. We ought to have the right to use them."

"It isn't like that in the Near East, Governor," Kraft snorted. "For better or for worse, the governments there don't want to be tainted as imperialist by having an overt American military presence. Look, the Saudis refused this very thing early this year when [Secretary of Defense] Harold Brown took some soundings."

"What would you do if the Russians began moving through Iraq on the Persian Gulf and the oil that is the lifeline of Western civilization was threatened?" Connally asked.

"I don't think the Russians will do that. They have their hands full in Afghanistan."

"Answer the question, Joe!"

"It would be useful to beef up the navy in the Indian Ocean."

"Exactly. I proposed that very thing in my speech. I proposed a Fifth Fleet for the Indian Ocean, and, yes, that would be useful. But we both know that wouldn't stop the Russians."

"What about Iraq?" Kraft asked. "Maybe Iraq, since it's becoming increasingly anti-Soviet, might detach from the Russian sphere."

"That's right. But you'll never do that unless you try. You'll never know what the Egyptians will accept unless you ask. You'll never know what the Saudis will accept unless you ask. I know these folks, Joe. I get on with them. I know how to deal with them."

Kraft was frankly appalled at the vanity of the man. But despite his essential opposition, he admitted to himself and confessed later in print that "if any American could assert American power credibly, it would be Connally."

The aftershock which rocked the Connally campaign would not diminish. A distinguished member of his foreign policy advisory group, the New York attorney Rita Hauser, resigned a day later. Because she had written widely on the Middle East and had been a party to the Brookings Institution study from which Connally's speech derived some inspiration, she might have expected more of a role in the speech's evolution than the mere courtesy she received. When the speech was a *fait accompli*, she had been informed of its content, and she had protested strongly against it to Connally. To her, the speech was fundamentally wrong in tone and in substance, and yet she felt it might have been recast and softened into a constructive contribution. After the speech was delivered she was swamped with disbelieving calls about how this could have happened and how she could have been a party to it. Desperate, she reached Connally and urged him to issue a clarification. He refused. She said she was in an untenable position and might have to resign. This was, she said, a "blowout for no reason." Connally grew angry, for Hauser had promised to stay regardless of the reaction, but she had not anticipated the virulence of the opposition. Later, Hauser was to see the Connally speech in character terms: "I subsequently learned that John Connally is a very impetuous man who is drawn to big, bold moves without thinking out the consequences. He was looking for a blockbuster, but why he would choose the Middle East peace process for it, I don't know. That process had gone on for years, and, regrettably, it looks as if it will go on indefinitely. His china bull approach was cuckoo." For all her disparagement of Connally's Middle East initiative in 1979, this same Rita Hauser, in 1988, would serve as an intermediary between the Reagan administration and the PLO to open serious negotiations on the very sort of plan that Connally had proposed in his presidential campaign. In 1988, she was showered with plaudits rather than brickbats for her direct talk with Yasir Arafat in Sweden.

The campaign manager, Eddie Mahe, was later to blame himself for not being more attentive to the political danger signals of the speech. He was, he would say, naive about the realities of Washington politics, particularly the power of the Jewish lobby. The purpose of the speech (like Connally's two other speeches in October on national security and the economy) had been to distinguish Connally from Reagan, and that was now happening to Connally's disadvantage. "After John Connally's speech last week supporters of Israel—along with many others concerned with noisy U.S. weakness in the face of the Soviet military and Arab economic threats—made a reassessment of Ronald Reagan and decided he looked ten years younger," William Safire of the *New York Times* wrote.

The fundamentalist Christians were the first to desert. This was a particular disappointment to Mahe for professional as well as personal reasons. The Connally campaign had worked hard to nurture a relationship in this pious corner of America. Building from Connally's friendship with Billy Graham, the campaign had invited fundamentalist leaders to Picosa Ranch, and they had declared Connally to be the leader they had prayed for. In June it was a "done deal." But now they could not associate themselves with the candidate of the infidels.

More important than this, the speech forced Connally into the posture of explanation and apology. Group after group that had promised their support asked Connally to justify himself—and, as Mahe put it, "John Connally does not do that very well." When Connally failed at this unnatural role, a team of surrogates gave interviews to the press. Jim Brady, Connally's press spokesman, tried to paint the speech as "refreshing." "It has all the makings of looking like high-risk politics," Brady said, "but it has none of the real risks. It's highly controlled, working with a net. It is to the benefit of the United States, but it is pro-Israel—when you put it under a microscope." No one was ready to be so myopic. Meanwhile, Sam Hoskinson, the ex-CIA man who had coordinated the speech, said that it was a "bum rap" to call it an anti-Israel speech. Within the campaign, Hoskinson himself quickly became the scapegoat for the disaster. Mahe professed to learn only a few days after the speech that Hoskinson was really a closet "Arabist"—a word Mahe had never heard before, and which he took to be the sinister antonym of "Zionist."

Rumors flew about uncontrollably, and even Connally's own Democratic friends sometimes promoted them. Two weeks after the speech, when Connally met with Hoskinson, he took a call from Robert Strauss, who was then President Carter's trade negotiator. The governor became visibly more and more angry as he listened. Slamming down the phone, he motioned Hoskinson to follow him into the bedroom, and there lit into Hoskinson for spreading the threat around Washington that Connally might just make a passionate defense of his Middle East speech from the very steps of the Israeli embassy! Hoskinson was mortified at this total falsehood, as Connally's rage rolled over him, and the aide found himself physically shaking with fear. After he was summarily dismissed, Hoskinson got partway down the hotel corridor when a door opened behind him. It was Connally motioning him back. Hoskinson thought he would faint. But when he was in Connally's presence again, Connally apologized. It was the only time Hoskinson had ever known him to do so.

During this difficult period there were some in the campaign who felt that they were watching the deterioration of John Connally's personality. He was becoming more and more difficult to deal with. Outbursts of temper were frequent. Nothing seemed to satisfy him. His scheduler, Dave Parker, took most of the grief, for Connally complained increasingly (and justifiably) that he was being overscheduled. Coming close to quitting on several occasions, Parker developed the practice of holding the telephone a foot from his ear as he let Connally vent his frustrations. Once, in a car on the way to yet another added-on event, Connally turned coldly to his Southern campaign director, Haley Barbour. "You son of a bitch," he hissed. "You're running a great goddamn campaign. The only problem is, when the candidate is about to be elected, he'll be dead!"

"Now, now, John," Nellie piped up, patting him on the knee. "These boys are doing the best they can."

To Connally's old friend and associate George Christian, Connally's increasing use of profanity had resonance. "Is he goddamning you a lot?" Christian asked a harried Connally aide in need. "Lyndon used to do that. I told him, if you start that goddamnin' again, I'm going to have to leave. When they start that, there's nothing you can do. You just have to back off and wait."

Haley Barbour from Mississippi could handle the abuse better than most in the campaign, because Connally reminded him of his high school football coach in Yazoo City who could "dog-cuss" him in the same way, but you knew he didn't mean it, because fifteen minutes later it was over. Moreover, Barbour loved Connally's salty side. It would come out on long campaign trips when it was just the boys, particularly the Southern boys. One of Connally's favorites, which he occasionally told with his great theatrical voice rolling down the length of his purple Lear jet, was about the two poets who were told by St. Peter that in order to get through the Pearly Gates they would have to outdo one another with a poem upon the subject of Timbuktu.

Prated the first:

> Across the burning desert sands
> Rolled the mighty caravans
> Past oases tried and true
> Winding down to Tumbuktu. . . .

The *r*s rolled out of Connally with his best Curtain Club cadence. Then a pause. The second poet, sweating, knew he was in trouble, but then got his inspiration.

Tim and I a-hunting went,
And spied three maidens in a tent
Of them was three and us but two
So I bucked one, and Tim bucked two.

To Barbour, as they sped along to the next high-toned presidential event, here was a man who hardly drank, who went to bed early, and was always a gentleman around ladies, but this—this would always be vintage John Connally.

By late October the damage of the Middle East speech was evident in the polls. The gains of a few hard-won percentage points that Connally had chipped away from Reagan stalled and were on the way down. The Gallup poll had Connally running fourth, behind Reagan, an undeclared Gerald Ford, and Howard Baker. In a hypothetical head-to-head contest among Republicans, Reagan trounced Connally 64 percent to 29 percent. Against Jimmy Carter, who had a twenty percent approval rating with the public, Connally lost by 12 percentage points, and against Teddy Kennedy, by 33 percentage points.

Even though the Connally campaign realized that it was moving into a critical, if not decisive, phase, it told itself that it was still early. The campaign had by no means used up all its "oil." More than ever, now—October and November 1979—was the time to establish the campaign as a two-man race. The basic assumption of the campaign was reviewed and reaffirmed: Connally was a national figure, and he should continue to crisscross the country in a national campaign, speaking to the large and generous audiences, irrespective of whether those audiences would ever have an opportunity to vote for Connally in the critical early primaries or whether their generosity was really helping Connally's central problem. The candidate had begun to operate under a fatal illusion: that he was running for the presidency, not for the Republican nomination.

Some very good journalists followed him through this decisive phase of his campaign. The best was the brilliant editor of the *Texas Monthly*, Paul Burka, who had an encyclopedic knowledge of Connally's past and was fascinated to observe how this latest, battle-scarred incarnation played outside Texas. Burka tagged along with the candidate to Rhode Island and to Florida. From a grocery in East Providence, to a GOP fund-raiser in Newport, to Palm Beach, to a crowd in Fort Lauderdale sprinkled with racists, Burka observed a fair sample of the Connally treatment. In the ethnic grocery of Providence, Connally's fastidiousness was on display as he bought a bunch of grapes, thus avoiding Jimmy Carter's imagery problem with a succulent peach and Gerald Ford's hot tamale. Before the old, established wealth of Newport he was wrong, all wrong. His standard phrases—"We're the most vulnerable nation on earth" and "this country is a hostage"—did not wash with the denizens of fourth-generation mansions. The audience listened in glum silence. "He's not pushing the right buttons," Burka heard one bejeweled lady whisper to her partner. After the speech the writer asked her why. "He's using fear motivation," the woman replied tartly. "That's not the way to talk to these people." The comfortable Ronald Reagan would do better here. In Palm Beach, Burka watched Connally play his sonata in both sharps and flats. Before an audience described as "everyone who is anyone in Palm Beach," he was at his best, "witty, intelligent, demagogic on occasion, in charge, yet at one with his audience," Burka would write. He was in tune because this was newer wealth, merited wealth, characterized by achievers rather than scions, and many of them were Democrats. Here Connally's activist, entrepreneurial energy showed brilliantly, and it cut across party lines. An hour later, before an older group of retired vegetative Republicans at a drab Holiday Inn, Connally was stale and indifferent. At yet another audience in Fort Lauderdale, Burka saw Connally touch the mean streak of America.

"John, there are 180 million white people in this country," said a man whom Burka took to be a character out of *Deliverance*. "When are you going to make the Negras stop stepping on us?"

Connally repeated the question as he gained himself a moment to think. "Yes, I believe in equal rights for everyone in this country," he said deftly.

Geoffrey Norman, the *Esquire* writer, followed Connally into New Hampshire and there captured the candidate's fully developed and by now richly textured reply to his central problem. The question came respectfully.

"Governor, how do you answer the charge that you are a wheeler-dealer?" Connally took it on enthusiastically, almost gratefully, as if he had planted the question.

Well, if you mean by wheeler-dealer someone who knows how to talk to congressmen and businessmen and political leaders all over the world, who knows how to compromise and horse-trade with them to get things done, who isn't afraid to negotiate and hear the other man's side, well, then, I guess I am a wheeler-dealer. You know, I've been in and out of Washington for thirty years. I've known 'em all. In the Congress. The cabinet. Business. I've been on the boards of over twenty major corporations and banks. I remember what a special thrill it was for me when I was named to the board of Greyhound. It was Greyhound that bought my daddy's little bus line from San Antonio to Corpus Christi, and the money from that sale made it possible for us to buy a little farm. So when I was named to the board of Greyhound, I felt like I had arrived. I plowed many a furrow behind a mule or a horse on that little farm we bought with the Greyhound money. And I studied many a night by a kerosene lamp. But that made it possible for me to go to college and to make something of myself. I'm grateful for that chance. I think that kind of opportunity is what made this country grow. With growth there is opportunity and with leadership in Washington we can keep on growing and keep on providing opportunity for people who want to work and take advantage of the things this country has to offer. I need your help.

This was what political operators call a "home run," but to Connally's advisers the home runs were few. At press conferences, in the age of television, Connally tended to be too verbose and didactic. He answered in paragraphs rather than short, pithy sound bites. As a consequence, he did not "edit" well on local television news shows. As the leading expert among the candidates on energy problems, he was often asked about oil, and he tended to start with the dinosaurs in the era of *Tyrannosaurus rex*. Instead of improving his rambling answers, he complained about the news media. "I'm getting so tired of the same questions over and over," he complained. When Haley Barbour, his Southern coordinator, heard that, he thought to himself, "What an opportunity! With the same questions, you can hone and hone your answers and hit a home run every time!" To Connally, it was the opposite. He did not want to give the same answer every time, because that bored him. Moreover, his media advisers realized that he was "too hot" for television. He could not keep himself from falling into his stemwinding speech, and it came across too harsh, too shrill. Particularly in a place like Iowa, the overstrong presentation amounted to a caricature of the very thing he wanted to avoid: the image of the Texas wheeler-dealer. The advisers tried vainly to get him to relax, to tone down, to control his glibness. When he did not, they concluded that he was simply undisciplined as a political candidate. The combination of his lack of discipline and his impatience was deadly.

People in the campaign talked often in the fall of 1979 about being "national," but there was another way to look at it. The campaign was money-hungry. By mid-November it had raised nearly seven million dollars, far more than any other campaign. During a two-day visit to Reagan's California alone, Connally supporters ponied up a million dollars. The presidents and chairmen of the boards of forty-one of the nation's two hundred top companies, as well as the chief executives of the major and large independent oil companies, had contributed the maximum to Connally. To say that Connally was the darling of corporate America was an understatement. The hunger had a direct effect on Connally's political schedule. Wherever a score of CEOs might gather to hear him, Connally put the highest priority on being there—and never mind that his local operatives in Iowa and New Hampshire were clamoring for his presence. His Midas touch had gone to his head. He had signed up Richard Viguerie, the genius of political direct mail, and the Viguerie effort had the money rolling in by the carload. Connally began to suggest that the $17 million limit imposed upon candidates who wanted federal matching funds was too low, and in December he announced that he would forgo matching funds altogether.

The risk was self-evident: for a candidate who labored under the image of being a high roller, this would only add to his problem. The shape of Connally's difficulty was beginning to be very clear. He was not moving up in the polls from his national campaign, and his buccaneering style was ill suited to the early primary states of Iowa and New Hampshire. If he accepted federal matching funds, he would have to accept the sublimit of spending less than $300,000 in New Hampshire. Television was becoming the last hope. Only through heavy spending on television, especially in the Boston market, did he have a chance to make a decent showing in New England before the Southern primaries.

By airing the first political commercial of the election season, Connally made news on October 30. It was a five-minute show, produced by Roger Ailes (who most recently handled Vice President Bush's media affairs in the 1988 presidential campaign), and it was aired on CBS. CBS was the only network which would sell time to presidential candidates this early. Although the network went along with Connally, it was not comfortable about it for other reasons. Already, a "CBS Reports" documentary on Teddy Kennedy was in the can and ready for broadcast on November 4, three days before Kennedy planned to announce officially for the presidency. The rumor was that the program, reported by Roger Mudd, was not entirely flattering to Kennedy, but the Connally camp could scarcely imagine how a one-hour documentary on Kennedy could fail to help the Kennedy candidacy. It continued to bank on Kennedy as the eventual Democratic nominee. "Teddy Kennedy?" Connally said with evident relish. "Now there would be a classic confrontation. There are many things—personal lives, lifestyles, family, philosophy. . . ."

He could get meaner.

On the New York radio station WINS, in late September, he had been asked if a Kennedy-Connally race would be clean, and if the milk fund would not be raised. "Milk fund scandal! Well, what about it?" Connally had fired back. "I was tried and found not guilty. I never drowned anyone. I wasn't kicked out of college for cheating. . . ." These pointed references to the Chappaquiddick incident and to Kennedy's dismissal from Harvard for cheating were meant to cast Ted Kennedy in an unfavorable light, but in the minds of the public they succeeded only in miring Connally together with Kennedy in a moral swamp. If to the Democrats Kennedy was untrustworthy because of Chappaquiddick, to the Republicans, Connally was the moral—or immoral—equivalent because of milk. A Gallup poll in November confirmed this lack of trust in Kennedy and Connally within their respective parties—the only candidates in the race who failed on this special barometer.

The CBS show "Teddy" aired on November 4, and it was devastating to Kennedy—and to Connally. When Roger Mudd asked Kennedy, after his Chappaquiddick explanation, "What guarantee does a citizen have that you wouldn't behave inexplicably again?" and the camera moved in for its relentless closeup, it was a question and a camera angle that could as easily have been turned on Connally about his milk problem. As Kennedy faded in subsequent weeks, the Connally candidacy faded proportionally.

The campaign now pointed toward the November 17 presidential straw poll in Florida. This was not a primary, but the proverbial "beauty contest"—the search for the "credible hulk," it was being called—and its result had no bearing on the delegate selection. That would not come in Florida until March 11. Nevertheless, Florida was a Southern state, where Connally had to win if he was to remain viable. That made the straw poll an attractive, indeed necessary, place to throw the weight of the Connally effort. If Connally could blunt, if not defeat, the Reagan force there, he could affect the direction of the later, more important, tests. Much was made in the Connally camp of Reagan's "suit of armor." If it could be pierced somewhere, anywhere, there would be blood everywhere.

Connally mounted a major effort in Florida, an "all-out effort," as the press portrayed it—making repeated visits to the state and sending Nellie and his children in separately. Connally poured in $300,000. The candidate himself had a personal conversation with nearly every delegate who would vote. The effort seemed to be working. The talk of Reagan's support eroding was stronger than ever. The polls showed Connally creeping up, coming at least within ten percentage points of Reagan. Connally hoped that, at worst, he would lose to Reagan by five percentage points.

In this euphoric atmosphere, Eddie Mahe, the campaign manager, urged caution. Ronald Reagan was made for Florida like a linen suit. Mahe wanted the campaign to set a modest goal, say, merely keeping Reagan under fifty percent. If they exceeded that goal, so much the better. But suddenly Nellie Connally became a factor. She was sure they were going to win. She could feel it. She wanted the campaign to make the outright claim of victory as its goal, for, as she told the campaign leaders, she owed it to their children, who had campaigned so hard. Some days before the Florida vote, at the Madison Hotel in Washington, the senior campaign staff met with the Connallys to talk about Florida. Mahe and the Southern adviser, Haley Barbour, tried desperately to argue Nellie out of her buoyancy and her determination. More was at stake here than her loyalty to her children. But she dug in her heels and her advisers failed. In the days before the vote, talk of a "major upset victory" flowed out of the Connally camp. Reagan and his staff had called the straw poll "absolutely meaningless," but it was coming only three days after his official declaration for the presidency. The high claims of Connally focused their attention. Perhaps Connally knew something they didn't know, they reasoned, and they got to work.

For his part, Eddie Mahe appreciated that the Florida vote was no pseudoevent so far as Connally was concerned. He worried about Nellie Connally's success in pressing expectations of victory. He knew that the October 11 Middle East speech had hurt them in South Florida. But Mahe did receive one piece of unexpected good news. For months he had longed—nay, would virtually have murdered—for Reagan to appear on the same podium with Connally, and now in the draw of speaking order before the Florida delegation, at long last, Connally was to go immediately after Reagan. Several days before the event, Senator Howard Baker's campaign manager called Mahe to say that Baker was going to skip the Florida speaking unless he could swap places with Connally, following Reagan, and have Connally take Baker's place as the last speaker. Mahe refused—a decision which later haunted him. He was obsessed with the back-to-back opportunity and sure that the instant comparison would redound to their benefit.

On November 17, the delegates gathered in an amusement-park atmosphere across from Disney World, outside Orlando. Robert Dole contributed a hot-air balloon, scarcely a flattering symbol for him. (Later, the results showed it.) At his hospitality suite, Reagan also accentuated his weakness rather than his strength by having a disc jockey play "golden oldies." Connally rode into town like a rhinestone cowboy, singing confidently that he was running "neck and neck" with Reagan. When the candidates fell into their twenty-minute presentations there were some surprises. On the sidelines Eddie Mahe watched with a cold, analytical eye. George Bush put on a surprising performance. Mahe considered him to be out of it. Bush was running consistently fourth or fifth, well below ten percent. Bush seemed to know he was finished—unless he reached down and somewhere found real emotional life. This he did, throwing away his dry, prepared text, and, in Mahe's view, giving the best speech of his political life. Reagan was Reagan, warm and vapid, but the magic was there, and the candidate solidified his support. That was no surprise. Then John Connally stepped forward. The phrases rolled out of him, including his most rousing line, the only line, it seemed, that his audiences remembered after a Connally performance: "We're going to say to the Japanese, 'If you don't take our citrus, if you don't take our beef, if you don't take some of our other commodities, we'd be delighted to see you sitting on the docks of Yokohama in your Toyotas, in your Datsuns, eating your oranges, watching your own television sets." Mahe listened carefully. His man was eighty percent on. The operative had heard the themes a hundred times before, and he knew and admired the style. But the tone was twenty percent off. It was that slight distortion that only the aficionado hears. There was a little too much, just a little too much, of the tone, "Vote for me—or screw you."

The vote was 36 percent for Reagan, 26 percent for Connally, 22 percent for Bush.

Around the country the interpretation was the story. "Reagan trounces Connally." "Connally finishes a distant second in Florida." "Bush makes a surprisingly strong showing." "Connally gets merely 26 percent." The Reagan staff did their best to promote the effortlessness of their victory and to dig at Connally for his poor showing despite his big money and his "all-out effort." "He spent $1,500 on every delegate he got," said one Reagan manager. "We only spent $500." Reagan was a cost-effective candidate. The *Miami Herald* portrayed Connally and his performance as "a strong, tub-thumping orator of yesteryear."

★

In the weeks after the Florida straw poll, the private life of the Connally campaign was very different from its public life. In public, life seemed to go on. Connally continued to ride the circuit with the other candidates, dispensing his strong medicine for the nation, and occasionally delivering a zinger: "If appeasement were an art form, the president would be the Rembrandt of our age," he told a South Carolina audience. In Pittsburgh he came out against affirmative action as divisive and harmful, and he hoped that this stand might countervail some of the damage of his October 11 speech among the Jews. In Washington he demanded that the president set a deadline for the release of American hostages in Iran. If Iran did not meet the deadline, the U.S. should disrupt the flow of Iranian oil to the outside world. To his aides in private, as they zipped around the country in their purple Lear jet, Connally could make their whiskers vibrate when he talked about the ayatollah. A part of Connally identified with Khomeini. As an article of faith, he felt that he had been spared in Dallas for a "greater purpose." He returned to the theme often when he was asked about that day of horror in 1963. This campaign was that greater purpose for which he had been saved. If there was physical danger in a presidential campaign, Connally was oblivious to it. He had specifically rejected Secret Service protection. Khomeini, too, had endured his years of torture and exile for a greater purpose. To his aides, Connally would say, "He [Khomeini] is not like other people. If he doesn't care for himself, you have to find something he does care about. You start killing his children or bombing his mosques."

The campaign got the most publicity in December for its decision to forgo federal matching funds. With the public perception of great wealth in the Connally camp, the commentators wrote about the "imponderable" of Connally throwing his "enormous" financial resources into the Boston television market.

In private, dejection reigned after Florida, and it began with Connally himself. As he rode back to Texas with Mahe the day after the straw poll, he talked like a candidate who was finished. It began with problems he could not control. When Iran took hostages the presidential candidates nobly ceased to criticize Carter for his Iranian policy. This robbed Connally of the opportunity both to redress the damage of October 11 and to display his knowledge of the Arab world by making other major statements on the Middle East that might get a better reception. Moreover, Teddy Kennedy was beginning to fade after the Roger Mudd interview, and Connally could not control that.

Then there was another problem he tried to control but couldn't. The Middle East speech of October was haunting him in the most unlikely places—for example, in Iowa. It was as if in the corn belt they drew the shades on Connally. Worse, it triggered the virus of Watergate, the milk fund, the Lyndon Johnson connection, the party switch, the wheeler-dealer image—all the negatives which before the October 11 speech had been ignored by the Iowa press. Suddenly, as one commentator put it, he was coming off as too "oily and noisy" for Iowa. On television his hair started to look just a little too shiny, his speech sounded a little too glib, and it all amounted to a caricature of the fast-talking Texas wheeler-dealer.

Finally there was the problem he should have controlled, but didn't. It was the fatal one. Into late January 1980 the public still labored under the impression that Connally had rafts of money. In fact, in early December the campaign went broke. No one believed it. Here was the candidate of corporate America who had raised enough money to "burn a wet mule," as his Southern campaign manager, Haley Barbour put it, who could raise a million bucks in a night, who had dismissed the $17 million federal limitation as constrictive. How could this be? The goal had been to raise $10 million by the end of the year, spend $6 million, and have $4 million or more for the crucial Southern primaries of South Carolina and Florida. Now, the Southern campaign director was told that he could have no funds remotely approaching the original projection. In South Carolina, which was supposed to be Reagan's Waterloo, the campaign would have to be run like a gubernatorial race, with billboards and signs on stakes at polling places. Among the most astonished were the business executives who had put themselves out for Connally. Now their basic business instincts took over; they had a congenital resistance to throwing good money after bad. Suddenly they turned on their prince. Their attitude became, "The big shot went out and squandered all our money—riding around in limousines and purple airplanes. He's on his own now." After the announcement in December that the campaign was strapped, the money only trickled in.

Connally retrenched. Mahe was shoved aside, and a business mogul from Phoenix named Charles Keating was brought in to take over. Keating had no campaign experience whatever, but he had been a major fund-raiser for Connally, and Connally seemed to respect that talent above all others. Keating was wooden and arrogant. As he pushed people around in the campaign and alienated the professionals with his political naiveté and his imperiousness, the campaign staff began to grumble about their "titans of industry" problem. Behind Keating came Connally's old Texas gang—Ben Barnes, Mike Myers, Wales Madden, Julian Read. It was called the Texas resurgence. They were sent into Iowa as Connally surrogates, and they were a disaster. The problem was cultural rather than political. The campaign headquarters in Des Moines put the Texas contingent in a corner and hoped the press would not get onto the power of Texas Democrats in a Republican caucus state. The press did not get onto that curiosity, but it no longer mattered. Despite a forty-two-hour blitz of Iowa in the last two days to contrast his physical prowess with Reagan's, despite a healthy dose of high-cost television, and despite even a predawn wild-game-hunt breakfast, Connally, with ten percent, finished fourth in Iowa.

He was fading. He knew it, and the press knew it. For some who watched, there was a special pleasure in it. The big, handsome money man with the high boots and the swagger and the charisma was falling. With its once-huge budget, his operation had been resented. Voters sensed his contempt, and Connally had been resented personally. George Bush was now "riding the rocket." He was first in Iowa with thirty-two percent, but he was not secure enough to be gracious. Michael Kramer of *New York* magazine was with him when the candidate passed by a television set in the Hotel Fort Des Moines as Connally came on the screen. Bush had not forgotten Connally's hand in his defeat for the Senate in 1970, but, more important now, he resented Connally's snideness not so much about his politics as about his manhood. To Texans, Connally was apt to say that Bush was all hat and no cattle. Now in front of the television screen, Bush reached out as if to shake Connally's hand through the screen.

"Thank you, sir, for all the kind things you and your friends have been saying about me," Bush said to the screen. Then he raised his hand and slammed it down on top of the set.

"That prick!" he said.

In late February, New Hampshire gave Connally two percent. A week later, Massachusetts gave him one percent, and it was on to South Carolina. "You can't come in fourth in Iowa, not even participate in New Hampshire, and expect a big win in South Carolina," Eddie Mahe was to say. "That's not the way presidential politics works." Reagan beat him nearly two to one in South Carolina, and the next day in Houston he withdrew from the race. At his press conference he drew a laugh when he said, "[To withdraw] is not to announce my withdrawal from politics," but it was. An hour later, in a more honest vein, he said he never again intended to run for political office.

Technically, after fourteen months of campaigning, and more than $11 million spent, he had won Mrs. Ada Mills of Clarksville, Arkansas, as his sole delegate to the Republican convention. Mrs. Mills worried that forever after she would be known as the $11 million delegate.

When it was over, well over, Connally found himself on a plane from Chicago to Houston one day, seated next to Sander Vanocur, the television newscaster.

"Governor," Vanocur said, "after $12 million, all those months, and only one delegate—what happened?"

Connally's gaze drifted toward the window and the distant horizon.

"I reminded everybody of Lyndon," he sighed.

★ 26 ★

Stardust

THE TEXAS TO WHICH JOHN CONNALLY RETREATED, beaten and defiant, after his political swan song was in the giddy throes of a new gilded age. In the previous decade the nation had discovered the Sun Belt, and the American population was shifting south where there were warmth and work. With the Philip Johnson and I. M. Pei towers, created by the oil giants, Houston had become the fastest growing city in America, and it was being called the "gold buckle" of the Sun Belt. In Dallas the talk was constant of salmon in aspic, raspberries in chocolate shells, gowns, jewels, wine cellars, and the Mansion on Turtle Creek. Within the oil business the hottest plays were along the Austin Chalk, that shelf of limestone 10,000 feet deep which stretched from the Mexican border to the Louisiana line and whose pockets contained oil as pure as honey and as abundant as that on the Alaskan North Slope.

The oil boom was transforming once-sleepy farming villages like Giddings and Alvin into overnight boom towns, and the day of the wildcatter was back. Deal-making was wide open; stories of mere whippersnappers becoming millionaires were widespread. "Right now is the most dynamic period the oil business has ever known," said one twenty-nine-year-old, who did not look like a man with any sense of history, from his office high in a Houston skyscraper. "There's never been a time like this."

With Jimmy Carter's partial deregulation in 1979 and Reagan's total decontrol in 1981, the price of a barrel was $37 and rising. In the final week of 1981 the rig count—the measure of prosperity, which is the number of operating wells—rose to 4,530, and the drilling of new wells had far exceeded the best days of the 1950s. Moreover, Texas banks fueled the frenzy with wide-open policies of their own. They had more money than they knew what to do with. Federal legislation had loosened restrictions on savings and loans entering the business sphere as partners in real estate and oil ventures, and Texas passed even more sweeping deregulatory provisions, so that regulation was virtually nonexistent. In the expectation of oil selling at more than $35 a barrel, fortunes were a declension of good, better, and best. Everyone could be a wildcatter, for where was the risk?

Connally wanted a piece of it. After the humiliation of his $11 million delegate, his political career was over, and he turned his back on it with a vengeance, doing nothing to retire the debt his campaign had accumulated and leaving bitterness behind with such aides as Jim Brady and David Parker, who had put tens of thousands of their modest personal savings behind the Connally campaign, only to find that, after defeat, Connally felt no obligation to them whatever. If Connally needed a final reason to turn away completely from public life, Reagan gave it to him when he chose Alexander Haig, rather than him, to be the secretary of state.

In February 1981 Connally was but a year away from mandatory retirement as a partner of the Vinson and Elkins law firm, and he did not relish being put out to pasture as a distinguished elder statesman. All his life he had been a man of action, and he had come to embrace the notion that he would never cease to work. To be sure, he had a ranch and three homes, but his stake had remained modest by Texas standards. He was worth about $6 million. He still possessed cyclonic energy, wide-ranging curiosity, and a voracious appetite for the finer things of life. It was time to start over.

Around this time an old friend reentered Connally's postpolitical life. In the eyes of many, Ben Barnes was more a godson than a friend. A product of small-town Texas like Connally, Barnes had the same drive and overpowering physical presence, as well as an engaging, boyish, glad-handing manner. Through Connally's good offices, he had in 1965 become the youngest Speaker of the Texas House in history, and together they had fashioned the program of the last years of the Connally governorship. Barnes was supposed to be the dominant political figure of the next generation down from Lyndon Johnson and Connally, and Johnson himself had once predicted that Barnes would one day rule from the White House.

But his was a story of unfulfilled promise. After Connally left the governorship Barnes had become the lieutenant governor of Texas, and then, as the Sharpstown banking scandal rocked the political establishment of Texas, Barnes ran for governor and lost. To the political observers of the state, and to Barnes himself, he had become the sad and innocent victim of a new ethos, in which his associations with the figures of the Sharpstown scandal became akin to guilt and unanswered questions about his fast lifestyle and high living became an issue. "I didn't believe that [Sharpstown] was going to rub off on me," he would say later. "I ran a campaign on the issues, instead of talking about Sharpstown. I should have talked about it every day. I should have handled it like John Kennedy handled the Catholic issue." Barnes considered himself to be a victim of Sharpstown in the way Connally considered himself a victim of Watergate, and this perception of themselves as innocents amid changing social mores deepened their bond. After his loss, Barnes had gone into business with a successful, down-to-earth builder named Herman Bennett in Brownwood, Texas, and in ten years of that association had pulled himself out of a $380,000 indebtedness into a respectable position in Texas business.

Barnes had remained a familiar figure in Texas political circles and had maintained his fast schedule in the fast lane. To his friends, he had simply shifted to a different league, but he played the game just the same. His energy was notorious—he was once compared to an oscillating fan—and so, too, was his penchant for women. To Barnes, a partnership with an established builder from an out-of-the-way place like Brownwood in solid ventures like building Holiday Inns was one thing. An alliance with his mentor was another. They would be a dream team: Barnes as the cajoling, sometimes overpowering salesman and legman, Connally as the intimidating, Olympian eminence. What they might accomplish together in a gilded age in Texas when to many they were modern Texas itself—well, it boggled the mind.

On July 9, 1981, they signed an agreement to go into business together.

A month later Connally went to the races. He was living an old pattern, which went back to his days with Sid Richardson in the 1950s—the races in the dog days of August, when it was insufferably hot back home and everyone went away. It was like sitting around the pool at the Hotel Del Charro, with Uncle Sid and J. Edgar Hoover and Clint Murchison—big rich, big powerful, big talk while they bet on the horses. This time, the spot was New Mexico, just above the

Mescalero Apache Reservation, at the resort called Ruidoso Downs, which had become a favorite watering hole for the wealthy oilmen and ranchers of West Texas, and Connally had with him a Houston developer named Joe McDermott. The parallel to his Richardson days became even more exact when Connally noticed that the old Chapperal Motel Inn, a shabby twenty-year-old motel next to the track, was up for sale. Shabby as it might be, it was situated on seventeen acres of prime land. The idea dawned on Connally, just as it had on Murchison and Richardson: a hideout near the track where their type might gather and play, away from the notice of Texas eyes. That night at midnight, in pajamas, Connally signed his first contract as a big-time developer.

In the next year and a half, Barnes/Connally exploded upon the Texas business landscape with atomic brilliance. They built apartment complexes and shopping centers and office buildings. They bought a commuter airline and an oil company to capitalize on the oil boom. Later they added a barbecue house, a Western art magazine, a title company, and an advertising company for cable television. By June 1983 the company had sixteen major construction projects, totaling $231 million. The team concentrated its efforts on projects that appealed to their expensive tastes. Besides thoroughbred horses and the Ruidoso project, now called Triple Crown Condominiums, they were behind a splashy, curvaceous condo called Sunchase IV at south Padre Island, near the Mexican border, because they loved the beach. They were constructing the first shopping center at Floresville, as well as one at Giddings to cash in on the boom that the Austin Chalk had brought to that once sleepy town. Other projects were situated along the corridor between San Antonio and Austin, upon which Connally now conferred the grand title of the Balcones Basin, and about which he spoke as the consummate politician he was: "This country has a tremendous future ahead of it. I think in the years ahead we'll see more new industries created, more new products produced, more profits made, and more prosperity than we ever dreamed of, and Texas will lead it." They put up a combined condo-office building, a concept called "pioneering" in 1982, not far from Connally's Houston neighborhood of River Oaks and away from the cluster of towers downtown and in the Oak Post district. And they purchased a massive expanse of land atop a hill overlooking Austin, to which the headquarters of their empire now moved, and planned to develop "estates" around a golf course and conference center, with a common wine cellar. In 1983 Connally stood on his company's high ground and looked to the Texas capitol far in the distance and proclaimed, "This is the prettiest office site in the state of Texas. We're beginning an era of prosperity such as America hasn't dreamed of, and Texas will be at the forefront of it!"

Theirs was a dazzling performance, which, to the casual observer, only stood to reason. With so much going for the dynamic duo, what was one to expect? Connally was experiencing a profound sense of liberation. He announced that he was having more fun than he had had in years. "Nellie and I have had the time of our life the last year and a half," he said in mid-1983. "It's been a whole different world for us, being free from the demands of public life and a structured professional life. It's wonderful to feel like an entrepreneur." And he could feel, at long last, Texas rich. He had his ranch in Floresville, his houses in Houston and Santa Fe, his penthouse on Padre Island. He was adding, if only for appearance's sake and for its pure promotional value, a condo at Ruidoso Downs and a $500,000 estate in Austin. His manored life, put on display in a glossy, elegant treatment in *Architectural Digest* in 1985, settled into a pattern. Austin was the formal residence, where Nellie's table settings for her black-tie dinner parties became renowned—English silver, Royal Crown Derby china, Villeroy & Boch stemware, amid their Oriental porcelains and her treasured Boehm birds which Jake Jacobsen had helped her acquire. The penthouse on Padre Island was their "adult beach house," where, before the soaring windows looking out to the sea, Nellie liked to sit upon their serpentine designer chairs and read a good book or just allow herself to be mesmerized by the surf. Santa Fe was for the summer and extended vacations, where Nellie drank in the scents of the desert flowers while the governor went off to the races at Ruidoso. But the ranch was home, easily reclaimed with their private plane and landing strip by the road, and it was meant to convey the openness of family life and hospitable, comfortable Texas living. To those privileged enough to share the hospitality, it felt like a museum, with its high paneled walls packed with Western art and its iron and brass railings from a London embassy, and, especially, its massive wooden dining table, surrounded by high-back Spanish wooden chairs, with a different animal carved gracefully into each. One hard-bitten Texas politician who had been often to the LBJ Ranch, but only once to Picosa, was struck by the difference. The LBJ Ranch felt like anybody's "home-place," in contrast to the *House and Garden* look of Picosa with its royal chairs. "This is him," she thought to herself as she wandered about it in awe. "*He* wouldn't have it any other way."

★

At the height of their quickly won success, Ben Barnes would speak of how he and Connally made a "good fit." Barnes saw himself as the impatient hard charger, anxious to get things done, while the governor, with his global vision, was the more analytical and meticulous type. "He doesn't mind spending hours picking out colors of glass or brick—or deciding on the interior for our buildings," Barnes said affectionately. Contrary to the way in which he was later portrayed as aloof and ill-informed, Connally was involved in the daily decisions from the beginning. He and Barnes shared a wealth of contacts from their political life, and saw no reason why the values of their political life could not work equally well in their business life. Together, they knew nearly every bank president and chairman of the board in Texas, for at the top, politics and banking were intertwined. Their two-year-old empire had been possible because of the ease with which they could quickly acquire massive amounts of cash, in the form of loans, from virtually any lending institution in Texas. Since the savings and loan institutions in the state were filthy rich, banks in Texas were simply trying to keep up with the boom. While banks and businessmen elsewhere, without the safety net of oil, had always salted their dreams with caution about a possible—indeed, inevitable—downturn, and now were contending with recession, Texas banking and business did not admit to the possibility. If Texas uniquely seemed recession-proof, Barnes/Connally was, it appeared, more bullet-proof than anybody.

As he had done at Vinson and Elkins, where he would make brief appearances with corporate clients, largely to inquire after his "carrier-interest" in the case, Connally accorded himself a magisterial presence in his own company. Hundreds of projects were put to them, and Barnes seemed ready to do them all. Barnes's sense of himself was that he could sell anything, for in politics as in business, selling was his specialty. "The things that had to be done were things I'd been trained to do," he would say. "They were political in nature." Connally waded in with an equal confidence, bred of his political rather than his business life. All his life he had admired big thinkers and big doers, and all his life he had had utter contempt for the timid and the cautious who told him that a certain grand concept was not feasible. He had never forgotten the citations of the Grand Pish-Posh in 1939 as Johnson had inducted the naysayers into his "I Can't Do It Club." Nor had he forgotten the wildcatter spirit of Sid Richardson, nor how he personally had had to sell hundreds of tickets to the Austin political banquet in November 1963 which he and John F. Kennedy never got to enjoy.

The pride and the self-confidence and the derring-do of the pair were overwhelming, and few had the courage to tell them no. "You're sitting there as a banker or a loan committee, talking to those two guys, and they will make you believe it," an executive from the early days of the company would say. They had no shame about playing to their strengths. "It was a pleasure to tell a banker you were president of Barnes/Connally investments, and you wanted to get a loan," the executive continued. "We'd say, 'If you're interested, we'd like to have the governor come by and take you to lunch.' Boy, those eyes would light up."

Connally did not seem to mind being used in this fashion. Indeed, the uses of John Connally became central to the company's business strategy, and the company went so far as to have Connally actually move into a new house or condo in a just-opened Barnes/Connally complex to make it a top address—and then to move out after a short time. Nor did Connally seem to feel that such exploitation of himself was beneath the dignity of a former governor, cabinet officer, presidential candidate, and national hero. Business was business, and he was a high-priced commodity. Soon enough, he lent himself to outside endorsements. "John Connally, the man in the Hathaway shirt," read the headlines in glossy, full-page magazine ads. There he was, eye patch and all, in full, pin-striped regalia: "Take John Connally. Dynamic, determined, a national presence in law, government, and business. And there's a Hathaway shirt and tie to match. . . ." read the copy. A few friends winced, and the *Texas Monthly* awarded him its less-than-prestigious Bum Steer Award, but more Texans admired his sense of fun. He was no run-of-the-mill elder statesman.

The company jumped from the lark of the Triple Crown Condominiums to doing five or six projects, and then it was 20. The rate of growth was phenomenal, and their projects were built for the top of the market, targeting the *mille-feuilles* of Texan society. Cash came so easily to them that they began taking loans at 100 percent, with no equity whatever required. At one point, in early 1984, they were doing twenty-eight projects at once, and pushing hard for more. If they were driven by anything besides greed, it was the fear that they might miss out on projects that would go to other big-name developers like Trammel Crow of Dallas or Houston-based

Gerald Hines, in whose league Connally now considered himself to be, even if he lacked the platoon of Harvard business school whiz kids around Hines.

Amid the bluster and the razzle-dazzle and the paper figures of robust profit, however, all was not well in the Connally principality—or in the Texas Republic at large. From its peak at the end of 1981, the rig count began to drop, as the world market became flooded with crude oil after deregulation. By May of 1982 it was in free fall, and oil prices plummeted from nearly $40 a barrel to $30, a decline more rapid than the crash of 1929. Prognosticators predicted that it would fall to $25, and at that price the crude oil business would be essentially dead. Coupled with this sharp downturn, for which Texas was totally unprepared, was a currency crisis in Mexico, where, in 1982, there were two devaluations of the peso, dropping its value by one-fourth. On the American side of the border, the first hit were border towns and fancy resorts like South Padre Island, where wealthy Mexicans had long frolicked and which was 40 percent Latin-owned. Condominiums on South Padre Island were suddenly being dumped at fire-sale prices. In the pricey Houston department store called Sakowitz, the effect was instant and cataclysmic, and its owner spoke of a double blow to his business. "Hemingway used to say that a good bull can hook you with both his left and his right horn," a dispirited Robert Sakowitz lamented. "We had a left hook with the Mexicans and a right hook with the oil industry. We were a charging bull for five years. All of a sudden, we feel dehorned."

By January 1983, economists were saying that if the price of oil fell below $25, there would be major repercussions in the region's banking system, since bankers had lent billions to oil companies upon the projection of oil at $35 a barrel. If it fell to $15, bankers and corporate presidents would be in the street. In 1982, bankruptcies in Texas had already doubled. Real estate was the next industry to be affected. Where in the past few years office buildings had been thrown up with dizzying speed, there was suddenly an office glut in places like Houston. Brokers tried to be creative, with deals like the first month rent-free, but by 1984, 21 percent of Houston's offices were vacant.

People started saying things in Texas that had never been said before—or was it that Texas had never listened before? If oil was pumped at the current rate, Texas would be pumped dry by the year 2000. The oil refineries of the "golden triangle" around Beaumont and Port Arthur were being compared to the rust belt of Pennsylvania. Experts were noticing things that they had missed before, such as the fact that in 1980 the GAO had warned against an overdependence on oil and had urged a diversification of the Texas economy. People asked whether Texas had enough time to diversify before the wells ran dry. An economist in Beaumont wondered aloud whether the state had enough adequately trained skilled workers to diversify, pointing out that college entrance scores in Texas were forty-fourth in the nation and spending in public education was well below the national average. If Connally paused long enough in his busy schedule to ponder this question, he would have appreciated the irony. For that was precisely the alarm he had raised when he was governor. To improve the educational situation would necessitate a substantial rise in state taxes, maybe even the imposition of the ultimate taboo: a personal state income tax.

In public, Connally adopted a bullish, me-first attitude as the Texas economy sagged. While interest rates were "disappointingly high" at the moment, the "excessive rates will not remain politically acceptable to the American people," he proclaimed. That was the sort of thing a politician might say, but it was scarcely something a businessman would want to bank on. As the chairman of an oil company called Chapman Energy, he boasted that "we could make money at $12 oil." Taunting as that remark was to others who were struggling to survive at $25 oil, it was all the more so for the fact that Chapman Energy was specializing in buying the reserves of companies that were in trouble or going bankrupt. The distress of others, he said openly on ABC's "Nightline," "is a bonanza for us." When the world economy recovered, the oil glut would simply disappear, he predicted, and the companies of brassy, free-wheeling independents like him would take off again, just as in the good, old days. "We have a carefully thought-out strategy of seeking to increase our reserves at minimal risk and expense," he said. This scavenging strategy, especially Connally's boasting about it, made enemies for him, as it pushed the worth of Chapman's assets from $3 million to $82 million by 1985. Still, the company's actual earnings were meager.

Connally was caught in a confusion of roles between the politician and the businessman in him. As a politician, he was a congenital optimist who was accustomed to putting a good face on a mixed situation. This was Connally the leader, bolstering others when they were down, projecting the essential Texas values of self-reliance, optimism, and risk-taking, of which he had become the very embodiment. It was not in his nature to practice caution and retrenchment.

He was not skilled at planning in good times for possible bad times ahead, and yet that ability is crucial in a good businessman. Good businessmen know, as a Houston sociologist said, that no tree grows eternally toward the sky, but what politician could make that into a winning motto? In the personal distress that lay ahead for him, Texans would maintain a strong admiration for what Connally had attempted "in retirement." This was the courageous spirit and the big dreams, they would say, that pushed America west of the Mississippi. In the next breath they would say, "John Connally should never have gone into business. He wasn't cut out for it."

As the Texas economy slid steadily downhill, the flashy manner in which Connally and Barnes did business became increasingly transparent. Their strengths were as pitchmen and deal-makers, not as sharp-eyed managers. They perceived accountants in spectacles as obstructionists, and were impatient with the details of construction and development. Selling was what they liked to do. And they did not like disagreement, even in the privacy of their own boardroom. When they encountered it, they fell back on intimidation, ignored criticism, or, in the last resort, threatened to do everything themselves. The smoky back-room approach—the "Floresville-Brownwood method," it was called—was applied to budgets and construction schedules. When a construction problem developed, Barnes's instinct was to fly off and take charge personally, but when there were twelve apartment projects and nine shopping centers going at the same time—all with crises—he could not be everywhere at once. The office environment became a "three-ring circus," where Barnes and Connally conducted business as if they were campaigning for high office. The headquarters had the flavor of a campaign center of operations, and it was seized with a crisis mentality, for they had grown too fast and did not have the solid underpinning of respected business professionals to keep on top of events. Their competitor, Trammel Crow, would say later that they were destined to fail, even if the Texas boom had continued.

Inevitably, with the get-it-built mentality, they cut corners, and they began to pay for it. They had bid too low on certain projects, and the result was sloppiness and shoddy construction. Sunchase IV on South Padre Island had to be shut down for several months when construction defects were discovered, and the cost of idleness was dear. Elsewhere, cost overruns were common, and then, in the declining economy, subcontractors went broke and walked off the job. Juggling payments from one subcontractor to another began.

When a staffer questioned the legitimacy of the practice, Barnes reacted angrily.

"Bullshit, you can do anything I tell you to do," he barked. "I'll be responsible for what happens."

At Ruidoso Downs in New Mexico, the flaw in the grand design became apparent. The company planned 104 units, abutting the odoriferous race track, where the high rollers could stay comfortably and have only a short hike to the track. Barnes and Connally proposed to build a fine restaurant and, eventually, a fourteen-story tower, accompanied by a glitzy upscale shopping center. The condominiums were priced in the $160,000 range, and yet the better units were built on four levels with daunting stairs for retirees, Jacuzzis but no showers. The neighborhood was not the classier slopelands, but the bottomland of gas stations, fast food joints, and dingy motels along a noisy four-lane commercial strip. As construction got underway in 1983, its most prominent feature was a huge gravel pit full of stagnant water, which the local people promptly dubbed as Lake Connally. A year later, when it became widely known that the project was in trouble, locals began to call it Cripple Crown instead of Triple Crown. Even though advance sales were torpid, the partners rejected proposals to scale down their dream. Only eighteen units were sold during the construction phase; by the time of the grand opening, all those sales had fallen through. As prospective buyers looked more closely, they found that behind the paint, the furnishings were cheap and the fixtures were ordinary.

Other projects began to sink into difficulty. In Houston, their office building opened without a single condominium sold; the office vacancies citywide continued to rise. As it turned out, business did not want to be separated from the frenzy of Oak Post and of the downtown. In Austin—a place where Barnes had noticed in the early eighties how real estate brokers in dark suits had become millionaires overnight—development was slowing down, and with it sales of Connally's high-priced houses in the hills began to taper off. Called Estates at Barton Creek, where you could "create your private retreat in the hills above Austin," whose acquisition "quietly bespeaks your arrival at the top," the project began to be called "Mistakes at Barton Creek."

Undaunted, Connally pressed on, seemingly oblivious to the warning signals around him. Securing the help of Charles Keating, who might be a failure as a presidential campaign manager but who still was richly successful as a business magnate, Connally bought over 3,000 more acres in rough country west of the Estates and planned to develop them as well. (The land was referred to, even by a few inside the Connally organization, as "goat country.") The need for cash was constant and unrelieved, and funding projects with a negative cash flow became a way of doing business. They were woefully undercapitalized, and the Texas bust had merely exposed that fact. The uses of John Connally began to change. Earlier, the question had been what his presence could do to secure grand new projects; now, the question became a lament: if anybody could pull the company out of disaster, it was the governor.

The governor's stake in averting disaster was greater than mere pride. The distress had gone beyond being a threat to his reputation as a success at whatever he tried. Perhaps for the first time in his life he was *personally* vulnerable. For he had put himself and his houses and his ranch and his thoroughbred horses and all his copious possessions behind his big dream of big wealth. It had not seemed like such a big deal at the time. Other big-time developers, including his competitor Trammel Crow of Dallas, had launched their companies into megaloans by making themselves personally liable (but only when it was absolutely necessary). Moreover, it was a measure of Connally's confidence and his stature and his grand sense of himself. Providing for failure was not in his makeup; it would be an admission of doubt. Money had ceased to be the object to Connally, but only a way of keeping score, and in this process of running up the score against competition he scorned as weak and timid, Connally had derived immense satisfaction. The speed with which he had proved his flight worthiness had been particularly satisfying. Making him personally liable had been the condition, seemingly the only condition, that bankers had asked of him as they shoved money his way. In this nexus of flattery and greed, small-town bankers from such places as McAllen and Belton and Alvin had treated his requests for money as a real honor. His main mistake, people began to say, was that he hadn't made all those hero-worshiping bankers into his official partners, as he had made the high flyers of Vernon Savings and Loan of Dallas into official partners in several multimillion-dollar projects.

Sunchase IV opened in May 1984, ten months late, with over $6 million in cost overruns. For the extra $6 million, the partners had borrowed, not from small-town bankers, but from Manufacturers Hanover Trust of New York, known affectionately at the outset of the relationship as "Manny Hanny." On Memorial Day the partners threw a gala for the official opening, to which 1,200 people came. As the free whiskey and champagne flowed in abundance, the Texas rich mixed with Connally's old political pals. Connally gave a talk and then conducted a tour. The governor and ex-presidential candidate showed off the bathroom fixtures and hoped his friends would buy. Two did. Others, like Cecil Burney of Corpus Christi, were amazed at the lack of prudence in the project; there had been little attention to presale, and it had not been phased in as units were sold, but simply built on the assumption that there were plenty of buyers for $300,000 sun-washed playspaces. Later, Burney was to feel that Barnes and Connally were victims more of their own impatience than of the declining Texas economy. Another old acquaintance dating back to Johnson's congressional office in 1939, Luther Jones, concluded that Connally had given himself over completely to hubris.

Not long after the unveiling of Sunchase IV, Triple Crown in New Mexico had its grand opening, and again a big, flashy party was given to which many curious came, but few bought.

Between September 1985 and September 1986 the partnership sailed into a legal quagmire, as it was buffeted by thirty-five lawsuits charging nonpayment. Officially, the total of these lawsuits amounted to $40 million, but the indebtedness was considerably higher, perhaps as high as $200 million. To his credit, Connally asserted more responsibility rather than less, becoming officially a co–managing partner with Barnes and restraining Barnes's extravagance. When Manufacturers Hanover threatened to foreclose on Sunchase IV, the company filed suit, won, and thereby bought a little time. Connally and Barnes pondered their options, such as selling off their shopping centers or refinancing the loans on their massive Austin projects. In early 1987 they narrowly avoided being locked out of their own headquarters over $37,000 in back fees. Inevitably, their misfortune became the butt of jokes for the black humorists of Austin. The most prevalent joke went around about Barnes bursting into Connally's office:

"I have good news and bad news," says Barnes excitedly.

"Just tell me the good news," Connally sighs.

"A bank has just agreed to put up $100 million in escrow against the $1 billion we owe!"

"That's fantastic," Connally replies, bolting out of his chair. "What could possibly be the bad news after that?"

"The bank wants $500 tomorrow as a down payment," Barnes replies.

With money tight or nonexistent in Texas and high interest rates the rule of the day, Connally and Barnes began to look for outside money. As they did so, they blamed their problems on the social factors. "It's the first time in Texas history it's been like this," Barnes told Peter Elkind of the *Texas Monthly.* "If anybody's to blame for our problems, it's the economy, the banks, and oil." Connally could be more global in his excuses, as he became a frequent guest on television shows exploring the downturn in Texas. If only the Reagan administration would impose a $10 per barrel import tax on foreign oil, Texas could quickly recover, he told ABC's "Nightline." Bank regulators from the Home Loan Bank Board and FDIC were unfairly focusing on Texas and Oklahoma banks, when they should be putting an equal eye on international banks, he told ABC's "Business World" program. As the partners looked outside Texas boundaries for a quick fix to their problems, buyers for their properties did not leap forward. Barnes charged publicly that "Texas was being redlined all over the country." If that was true, and it undoubtedly was in mid-1986, it was because the financial community in the rest of the nation had perceived, finally, a pattern of fast and loose activity throughout Texas banking and business that had been deep and pernicious and ingrained for decades, and which only really became clear when oil fell to $10 a barrel. At least it was clear that Barnes and Connally were being redlined, as in June 1986 Barnes spent three weeks in a New York hotel room, waiting for a lender called G. E. Capital Corporation to approve a letter of credit from an obscure offshore bank, a letter which never came through.

In their last desperate throes, they fell in with petty swindlers. Since the ersatz Churchill Downs condos at Triple Crown in New Mexico were not selling, the partners converted the project to a time-sharing arrangement and turned it over to a Las Vegas hustler named Marvin Israel, who promised spurious vacations to Hawaii and savings bonds in return for a time share. Complaints about greasy carpets, untended lawns, falling plaster, and a nonworking swimming pool began to mount, and the project began to attract the attention of law enforcement agencies. To Alan Merson, an assistant attorney general for consumer protection in New Mexico, Triple Crown had become a classic example of "four-walling," where a developer had thrown together a project "to milk the dreams of modest-income people who wanted a little place of beauty and solitude from their daily routine." Another lawyer who became involved in the case, Anita Miller, could not believe that John Connally would be in league with such a low-brow crowd, because she found it so "out of character."

Connally was apparently blind to what was happening. On one of his last trips to Ruidoso Downs, he went with Nellie and with his onetime aide during his presidential campaign. The three tarried on the balcony of Connally's condominium, looking out on empty buildings whose electricity had been turned off and which were entangled in foreclosure threats. Gazing out to the mountains across the yawning gravel pit, half full of stagnant water, Connally said expansively, "Nellie, look at that! Isn't it gorgeous!"

Meanwhile, two men from San Antonio, representing themselves as international financiers, offered, for a hefty fee, to act as agents to find millions of credit money in the Orient, and Barnes and Connally fell for it. Barnes flew off to Hong Kong, where he waited in vain for a week for a letter of credit for millions to be approved by a major Hong Kong bank—millions which would magically solve all their problems. When the bank was not interested, there seemed to be some hope from an institution called the International Bank of the South Pacific, located in the nation of Tonga, which is no more than a dot on the map halfway between Chile and New Zealand. The former secretary of the treasury surely knew what this was: a shell bank involved in very questionable activity. In this case, it turned out that the U.S. comptroller of the currency had issued an all-points bulletin to U.S. banks that the Tonga bank was operating illegally in the United States and that any information regarding its activities should be reported immediately to the comptroller's enforcement division. If Connally did not know this, he should have. A year later, the founder of the bank, an American from Oregon, turned up dead in a Las Vegas motel room. And Connally's international financiers and money scouts turned out to be a former used car salesman and an oil and gas leasing agent who ended up as fraud cases for the local San Antonio district attorney.

On July 31, after fifteen months of effort and pain and ridicule, John Connally finally declared personal bankruptcy. In a meeting with his creditors a month later, he put his debts at $93 million and announced that he had petitioned the U.S. Bankruptcy Court to allow him to hire an auctioneer for the purpose of selling off his personal possessions. Under the law, he was entitled to keep only his principal home and $30,000 worth of possessions.* In his statement to the press he again laid blame on the economic situation in Texas for

---

*The Texas Legislature had debated proposed legislation in which a bankrupt person could retain his principal residence, $30,000 in miscellaneous possessions *and his private airplane*, but the measure was defeated.

thwarting his hopes for survival, but "I willingly sacrifice [my possessions] in an attempt to repay those who had faith and confidence in me."

"The people who came to Goliad and who came to the Alamo took a few risks, and for what?" he added. "For what they thought was right. If you hope to achieve anything in life, you have to take a few risks."

★

On Westheimer Avenue, west of downtown Houston, the Hart Galleries might easily be missed in the string of restaurants, boutiques, and household appliance shops, for it is no more than a large, low-slung warehouse with a modest, inconspicuous sign. In late January 1988, however, it was the best address in town. The bidding for tickets to the Connally auction had been intense, and before the gavel came down, the line of the curious and the vulturous braving the chilly temperature stretched around the building. The extraordinary attention of the national press boosted the interest, and the Connallys professed to be surprised by all the commotion. Perhaps the media were making the sale of their life's possessions into some sort of a metaphor for the collapse of Texas, they supposed, but, of course, for them it was more personal than that.

In the afternoon of January 22, the Connallys stood in the middle of the vast showroom, surrounded by their treasures and their curios. He wore a green suit, she wore black, and, as if it were some ceremony of reaffirmation and rededication, they were photographed framed by Tanzanian elephant tusks and the felt-backed African lion-skin rug complete with its fierce-looking head.

From every direction came the accolades for the grace and dignity with which they were handling their ordeal. "He seemed to be the fulfillment of the mythology of Texas," his friend Horace Busby said wistfully, and George Christian searched for a touch of humor. "It's a stigma if you have money now," he said. "People think you are a miser and hid it somewhere."

The public quality of their divestiture was its most noteworthy aspect. They gave endless interviews, pointing to this cherished item or that sentimental memento with a sweet memory or a good story behind it. They announced that they would attend all four nights of the sale—"it never occurred to me not to be here," Nellie said. To be there was in character. All his life Connally had seen himself as larger than life, even Grecian in his proportions, as he had traveled from heights to depths, finding great happiness and now great tragedy. He was a man of immense reputation and prosperity who was neither preeminently virtuous nor essentially depraved, whose misfortune now came from an error of judgment. That fit perfectly the definition of Aristotelian tragedy. He was not about to miss the great spectacle at the end of the play, the spectacle that would inspire both pity and fear.

They stood there, hours before it would all drift away, not for a lingering last look in private but for a public attempt to define how it felt and what it meant. Their grace came from their amiability and their resignation but it also came from their humor. Nellie was asked if there were lessons to be learned.

"Not to sign any paper—and to get all property in my name," she quipped.

And he thought he might write his autobiography. What place would this episode in his life have in the book? he was asked gently.

"Chapter 11," he replied.

To some, they seemed to be wallowing in bathos. They gave the reporters a tour of their things, theirs for another few hours: the chair of his governorship, given to him by the citizens of Austin during a Southern governors' conference in 1964; a saddle, presented by the Southwest Cattlemen's Association; even a shotgun he had won in Enid, Oklahoma, in 1967 at the Grand National Quail Shoot, when he and two other Texans had competed against thirty other celebrity teams from around the nation, and Texas won.

"He needs that to prove he can shoot," Nellie needled.

The gifts, rather than the purchases, meant the most.

"This is the Lenox china that Nellie picked out as our wedding china," Connally said to camera, ". . . and the silver that she picked out, and it has our initial C on the handles."

"It's very special to me," Nellie added. "And I just hope somebody nice gets it, and it'll be special to them, too."

"You do what you have to do, do it the best way you can," Nellie said, "and then you move on." Did the process build character? someone asked. "This has made me a stronger and a better person," she replied. "I am strong—and I'm as good as I want to be."

Increasingly, Connally warmed to the notion that he was the incarnation of the Texas collapse. When he spoke of Texas, it was as if he were speaking about himself. Texas was in a down period, but it was a vibrant, resilient state. It was a state that would bounce back. Houston was a great city; it wasn't going anywhere; Dallas, too. To be sure, the state was going to change. Agriculture, oil and gas, and real estate could no longer underpin the economy, but Texas was still in competition with the rest of the world. The only difference was that the state was now going to have to compete on an equal footing. He remembered the decline of New England when the cotton mills and the shoe factories moved south, but look at New England now. When this was personalized, the same arguments came forward. "This is not the demise of Texas, nor is this the demise of John and Nellie Connally," he said. "We're not ever going to quit working. I have an insatiable curiosity. There are lots of places in the world we haven't seen. Lots of things we haven't done."

"We better hurry," Nellie interjected.

At this moment John Connally rose to a level of nobility he had never before achieved in his lifetime. His fellow Texans were taking heart from his handling of the situation. The nature of the event was humiliation and disgrace; it was proof of epic failure. The spectacle of the great and the wealthy and the proud transfixed the rest of the nation. The man had fallen so far, so fast, so publicly. Non-Texans found the display profoundly sad. This was the bottom. And yet, not sadness but celebration filled the hall. There was much talk of what might have been, those little quirks of fate and those great social forces beyond his control that had destroyed him along with so many others. As the national press surrounded Connally in platoons, they ignored Vice President Bush, who at the very same moment was on the other side of Houston, commissioning the missile cruiser U.S.S. *San Jacinto.* "He [Connally] is more qualified to run this country than any one of the candidates who are out there now," said a stranger on the edge of the crowd around Connally. "I came here as a young man twenty years ago, when John Connally was the persona of Texas. I hate to see this. It's a shame. But the spirit is amazing. He is a great man."

Connally mentioned the magic words only once that afternoon, but they were invoked to make a point that was instructive to the rest of his state, as it was difficult and traumatic for him. "Our perspective changed for all time on November 22, 1963," he said. "When you come that close to your hereafter, I assure you, you think about what's important in life. What's important are your family, your friends, your children and grandchildren, and your Maker—not material things. Money has never been an idol of mine. I've never devoted my life to making money—never will. The accumulation of wealth is not necessarily a measure of success. I know people with a lot of money. Some have inherited, some got it by good luck. Many of them—I don't have any respect for them at all. Because I don't think they've done anything with themselves or their talents. And I know a lot of people who don't have any money, who I admire greatly. They use their hearts, their minds and their God-given talents to the maximum amount they can."

In the wings, smooth-skinned and smooth-talking Jerry Hart was ready, feeling more like an executioner than an auctioneer. Hart had been having a recurring dream in the weeks before the biggest auction of his career. He imagined putting the first item of the Connally estate on the block, perhaps the silver-mounted parade saddle with the emblem of the state of Texas embossed on the sweatleathers, whereupon an Arab sheik in the middle of the huge audience would stand and inquire after the full amount of Connally's indebtedness. As auctioneer, Hart would turn to Marvin Sheinfeld, Connally's bankruptcy lawyer. "Forty-eight million," the lawyer would grumble. "Well, then," responded the sheik, "I bid $48 million for that saddle," and the auction would be over in ten minutes.

The auctioneer had had the dream in the weeks before the sale, when he had stayed at Picosa for days, identifying each item for the catalog, estimating its value and tagging it to be picked up and taken to Houston. The ranch house grew progressively emptier, until at the end the Connallys clattered around the bare rooms without floor coverings and ate in the kitchen on a simple table with everyday stainless steel utensils. On his last day there, Hart had come to the breakfast table at a brutally early hour for him and had found the governor alone with a bowl of cereal. Soon after, Nellie came through the door, back from a long walk to the gate on the crisp fall morning, bubbling about the lovely sunrise.

"You should have been with me," she uttered.

"You should have woken me," he said. "I'd love to have seen it."

Thus, in his interviews with the press, Hart made much of how bad he felt about profiting from the Connallys' misfortune. He had known the family for twenty-five years, and he knew how involved they were with their possessions. Hart could not fathom their insistence on attending the auction. What for? No form of dignity he knew required their presence.

Hart took his place upon the dais and brought the gavel down. As he peered down at the Connallys, his guilt was evident, for nothing he could say would assuage his sense of being self-serving. That afternoon, to a *New York Times* reporter, he had speculated that people would want to bid higher "just to show that they care," and he had winced inside as he said it, for he was getting a set percentage. "I care about the people whose things I sell, and whose things I buy," he began. On one of the items in this sale, he had found an inscription about how it was not the critic who counts, the man who has known neither triumph nor defeat, but the strong man who had known the dust, the sweat, the blood, the tears of the big arena and had spent himself in a worthy battle. Hart's sentimental opening felt right to the audience, but he knew he had to be careful.

For he was a conspirator in a friendly plot, peopled with white knights and lovely maidens. A persistent question to the Connallys for several months had been about what they treasured most. That afternoon, Connally had conceded to the reporters that the question had been oft asked by his friends, but that he had refused to answer. Hart knew differently. More than a hundred people, singly or in groups, had gotten together to purchase the most cherished items, especially the wedding silver, the governor's desk, and a valued shotgun, and to return them to the Connallys after a decent and legal interval—if it was legal at all—when the lawyers were sure that the items would not be repossessed and resold. Only four days before the sale, Connally had personally attended a dinner of his old college law fraternity. The purpose of the meeting was to raise money to purchase items at the sale, and the dinner raised $160,000. Hart had to be careful not to show partiality at this court-ordered sale. He was personally involved. He had contributed $8,500 of his own money to purchase Connally's law desk from Vinson and Elkins. Hart knew full well that the law of Texas allowed a bankrupt person to retain only his house and $30,000 of personal items.

Connally sat in the second row, an enormous unlit Macanudo panatella in his mouth—he reportedly owed a New York dealer $1,162.35 for cigars he had already gummed—and for a time, his immobile face masked his emotions. As he sat stoically, his dark black suit and thick black glasses against his silver hair and his white shirt made him a study in chiaroscuro. His serenity, if he was serene, might have come from the certain knowledge that he would get back his favorite things in a few months and be shed of a good deal of life's junk as well. Perhaps he no longer had use for that gold-plated belt buckle, marking his life membership in the Harris County sheriff's mounted posse. How many Homer Koon .410 gauge "snake charmers" or how many pistol-grip knives did he really need anyway?

When the gavel fell, the excitement began. In the audience of 500 that included the heart surgeon Dr. Denton Cooley, who was the other most famous bankrupt Texan, the hawkers positioned themselves and belted out the bids piercingly. The parade saddle was the first important item to go, but no Arab sheik presented himself. The opening bid was $3,000. It went to a Buick dealer for $10,000. This set the tone: bidding would be high, and would not always come from secret benefactors. In rapid succession came the plaque that had hung on his door when he was governor, a full-length signed caricature that went for $1,200, a metal star from the 1965 Fort Worth Fat Stock Show, and a pair of solid brass door hinges from the first Texas state capitol building which had been fashioned into bookends, and which were pictured in the catalogue holding the transcript of the original confirmation hearings of Edwin Pauley, the oilman who had been denied the post of undersecretary of the navy because of conflict of interest.

A convivial feeling filled the hall, as wine and barbeque were served in the back, near a framed display of ten designs for the first barbed wire of the 1880s, from Upton Snail to Smitt's Arrow Plate, and near a reproduction of the Peter Hurd and Peter Rogers mural that hung in the State Archives and chronicled Texas history from the conquistadors to Sam Houston. When a run of paintings was put on the block, most had Western and cowboy themes. A few Peter Hurds dotted the collection, and it was mentioned, though only in passing, that Hurd had been the artist for Lyndon Johnson's first official portrait, a portrait the president had rejected as "the ugliest thing I ever saw" and hired a second portraitist. At item number 39, Hart paused to lecture about the artist. It was the first of a number of paintings by Elymyr de Hory, the noted painter of fakes, whose work had fascinated the Connallys. (Also intrigued was another faker, Clifford Irving, who had written a book about de Hory.) The paintings were "highly collectible," Hart said, whereupon for the first time Connally picked up the microphone that had been put by his side, to explain that in 1983 he had located a large collection of de Hory paintings in a London apartment and had purchased the lot, fake Vermeers and Toulouse-Lautrecs, and the masterpiece, a fake Modigliani (which later went for $22,500). "It's a fascinating story," Connally told the audience, but he did not say why the fakes had fascinated him. He put forward as a recommendation the fact that SMU had had a de Hory fake hanging in a hallowed place for forty years, until its forgery was discovered.

In due course, the gorgeous Oriental rugs were brought forward, carpets that would have brought a sad smile to Jake Jacobsen's face, had he been there, and when several Audubon prints came up for sale, Hart allowed in passing that Audubon's own bankruptcy, after unsuccessful business ventures in the New World, had led to his vocation as a painter of birds.

As the evening wore on and the bidding stayed high, Connally became increasingly promotional. Frequently he picked up the microphone to give some sentimental anecdote of where he and Nellie had found that particular item and what it meant to them. Each time he did this the bidding accelerated. No one seemed to mind Connally's hawking; it made the evening more interesting. This was bankruptcy as a world-class social event. Bankruptcy was no disgrace—on the contrary. Since everyone in the room was quite sure the Connallys were going to be all right in a few months, with their most cherished possessions returned and probably with a stash of money to draw upon somewhere in the world, most likely in the Middle East—and by some clever legal maneuver, with a portion of their best things shifted into Nellie's name—it was hard to regard them as tragic. Instead, there was a bit of envy in the hall. This was supposed to be a grandiloquent metaphor for the bankruptcy of Texas, and yet, everyone in Texas who had gone bankrupt in the past six years should be so lucky as to have Connally's resources. On no one's mind were the hundreds who had gone under less elegantly as a result of Connally's business folly or high dreams and unbridled avarice.

Item 365 was a nineteenth-century engraved Khyber rebounding hammer rifle, inlaid with silver, gold, and mother-of-pearl, and when the bidding went slack at $3,000, Connally reached, once again, for the microphone. He evoked romantic visions of the British Raj in India, as the colonial troops and their colorful Sikh mercenaries rode north through the Khyber Pass to extend the empire. The weapon, he said, had been acquired in 1972 when he passed through Afghanistan on his eighteen-nation trip for Nixon, and it had been purchased with the help of Dr. Red Duke, who was then teaching in a medical school in Kabul. From the back of the room, Duke listened attentively.

"For anyone here who doesn't know," Hart interjected, "Dr. Red Duke was the doctor who saved Governor Connally's life at Parkland Hospital on November 22, 1963."

The bidding resumed, and the weapon sold for $10,000.

Just after 10:00 P.M. Connally slipped away—to the studios of ABC, where he was to appear on the "Nightline" program, and Ted Koppel would ask, with genuine deference or with wicked irony, if Connally might not consider running for governor again or perhaps for the U.S. Senate. He would consider running for governor again before he would consider the U.S. Senate, he replied, for he confessed he was not much of a "detail man." On "Nightline" Connally didn't sound like a man in barrel clothes. He allowed that some fifty business propositions had been put to him recently, that he stood on the offers of three law firms to join them, and he was considering a deal that would allow him to live in Europe for six months out of the year. A few days later he was on television again, but this time he was getting paid handsomely. He was pitching a bank called University Savings during a time-out in the Super Bowl.

"Nellie and I worked hard all of our lives to make sure our future would be financially secure," said the actor. "Well, the future is here, and things haven't quite worked out like we'd planned. But that's all right because there's no better place than Texas to start over—and to save a little."

The Aftermath of Dallas: Connally and the Conspiratorialists

NEARLY THREE WEEKS AFTER the assassination of President Kennedy, Connally began to tell his side of the story to the authorities, and from the beginning his version differed in important details from the testimony of others. On December 11, from his hospital bed in Austin (for he had developed an infection and had to be rehospitalized), he gave testimony to the FBI: "The first sense of anything unusual was when I became conscious of a shot, what sounded like a gunshot. Instinctively, I turned to my right and as I did so I sensed, more than I saw, that President Kennedy was hit." Here was a theory that was to become John Connally's alone: that Kennedy was hit by the first of Oswald's three shots. The second shot he reserved for himself. "As I turned, I realized something was amiss with President Kennedy and then I turned back to my left, and as I did so I got hit with a bullet in my right shoulder." The third bullet was the mortal blow which exploded the president's skull. Connally knew the third shot was fatal, because he was splattered with brain tissue. The size of brain parts grew in subsequent renditions until it became the size of a man's finger. The shots were "unbelievably quick," he said, snapping the fingers of his left hand three times.

By April of 1964 the Warren Commission was in full swing and taking testimony. Its central piece of evidence for sorting out the mystery of the three shots was the Zapruder film. The central witness was John Connally. Both he and Nellie Connally were due to be questioned on April 21. A week beforehand, on April 14, the commission staff met with ballistics experts and pathologists from the military to view the Zapruder film frame by frame. The conference resulted in a muddle. Perhaps, the experts hypothesized, Connally had been hit by both the first and the second bullets. Perhaps the president and Connally both had experienced delayed reactions to their wounds. "The President may have been hit as much as 36 frames [of the Zapruder film] before any visible reaction is seen," a memo on the meeting suggested. Both men may have been hit as much as two full seconds before the film shows any evidence of pain on their faces. If Connally was hit by both bullets, perhaps he only manifested a pained reaction to the second. The bullet which mysteriously dropped from Connally's stretcher was too perfect and intact to have passed through the bone of the wrist, the group asserted in what was probably its only definite conclusion, whether it was right or wrong.

Connally's surgeons at Parkland, Doctors Shaw and Gregory, were scheduled to appear before the commission immediately prior to the Connallys. They came that morning with definite opinions about how their patient had been wounded, and this, of course, was what the commission was hoping for. The doctors had spent considerable time with Governor Connally, rehashing the incident, and they had been influenced by his confident construction of the event. But before the doctors testified they were shown the frames of the Zapruder film, and it shook their certainty. To one commission member, Allen Dulles of the CIA, Dr. Shaw confessed:

"Mr. Dulles, I thought I knew just how the governor was wounded until I saw the picture today, and it becomes a little harder to explain. I felt that the wound had been caused by the same bullet that came out the chest with the governor's right arm [held close to the chest]. This is still a possibility. But I don't feel it is the only possibility."

"Why don't you think it is the only possibility?" Dulles asked.

"It is a matter of whether the wrist wound could be caused by the same bullet, and we [Dr. Gregory and he] felt that it could. But we had not seen the bullets until today. We still do not know which bullet actually inflicted the wound on Governor Connally."

"Or whether it was one or two wounds?" Dulles interjected.

"Yes."

"Or two bullets?"

"Or three."

"Why do you say three?"

"He had three separate wounds."

"You have no firm opinion that all three wounds were caused by one bullet?"

"I have no firm opinion."

Dr. Charles Gregory, who had reconstructed Connally's wrist, cast further doubt on the one-bullet theory. Arlen Specter, the staff counsel of the Warren Commission, put the possibilities to Dr. Gregory. Certainly, one bullet could have caused all three of Connally's wounds, but what if that same bullet had first passed through the strap muscle of another man's neck? Could that projectile still cause Connally's wrist wound? "I believe one would have to concede the possibility, but I believe firmly that the probability is much diminished," Gregory stated.

"Why do you say that, sir?"

"To pass through the soft tissues of the president would certainly have decelerated the missile to some extent," Dr. Gregory replied. "Having then struck the governor and shattered a rib, it is further decelerated. Yet it has presumably retained sufficient energy to smash a radius [of the wrist]. Moreover, [the bullet] escaped the forearm to penetrate at least the skin and fascia of the thigh, and I am not persuaded that this is very probable. I would have to yield the possibility." Could the bullet have passed through Kennedy's back and the governor's rib and missed his thigh and wrist? "I think that is a much more plausible probability," Dr. Gregory answered.

The combinations of possibility multiplied. Gregory had examined the pieces of bullet, other than the still well-shaped, intact bullet that had dropped from Connally's stretcher at Parkland. These were "grossly distorted" and such was the likely state of a bullet that smashed a wrist. Suddenly there was a new, even more grotesque possibility on the table: that the second bullet had penetrated Connally's chest, but fragments of the *third* bullet had ricocheted from Kennedy's skull, smashed Connally's wrist, and lodged in his thigh.

When Connally finally took the stand on April 21, 1964, it was, in many ways, the climax of the entire Warren Commission deliberations. His views carried the weight and authority of the prime survivor, as well as a further authority: he was an experienced hunter who knew well the crack of a rifle shot. He, for one, would never mistake the sound for the pop of a firecracker or a motorcycle backfire, as had a number of policemen and even an army general on the scene. Yet his view was flawed by pain and delirium and even bitterness.

His testimony was riveting. "I heard this noise which I immediately took to be a rifle shot. Instinctively, I turned to my right—and I saw nothing unusual except just people in the crowd. I didn't catch the president in the corner of my eye. The only thought that crossed my mind was that this is an assassination attempt." The beginning of his narrative was noteworthy for three things. He recognized it as a rifle shot and as an assassination attempt instantly. He turned to the right, and when he saw nothing, was in the process of turning back to the left. These very quick, rotating moves, like the juke of a basketball player, made him a moving target and in the end saved his life. If he had continued to turn right, to look all the way around over his right shoulder at President Kennedy, the bullet would have passed directly through his heart. Lastly, he never saw the president. He did not see him after the report of the first shot, which, after all, would have come to his ears after the bullet itself had found its mark. Thus, he had no basis for an opinion on whether the first bullet hit Kennedy.

"I never got far in my turn to the left. I was looking a little bit to the left of center, and then I felt like someone hit me in the back. I knew I had been shot when I looked down, and I was covered with blood, and the thought immediately passed through my mind that there were either two or three or more people involved in this or someone was shooting with an automatic-fire. These were thoughts that went through my mind because of the rapidity of the two shots. I immediately assumed, because of the amount of blood, that I had probably been fatally shot."

Twenty-five years later, with a touch of irony, he would say that at that moment, thinking he was going to die, his life flashed before his eyes and he was "not unhappy" with what he saw. He did not elaborate, but he seemed to be saying: to be killed at this triumphant moment of his life and career; perhaps to be killed with a president who, in death, would become the most popular president of the century; and, by implication, perhaps in Texas to achieve himself the same lasting glory—that was not a bad way to go. But Connally's awareness lasted longer, and as he slumped down on Nellie's lap he heard the third, fatal shot. He heard it clearly, he knew it had hit the president, and it sounded louder, for it was—figuratively, anyway.

"My God, they are going to kill us all," he had screamed. He repeated it now for the commission, and it would be repeated over and over in the years to come, as the rallying cry for the conspiratorialists. For the commission now, he permitted himself only one brief, uncharacteristic lapse into survivor's guilt:

"I have often wondered why I never had the presence of mind [to say] 'Get down in the car!' but I didn't. You just never know why you react the way you do, and why you don't do some things you ought to do."

Because Governor Connally had seen nothing, only sensed, the commission hoped the scientists and the technicians could unravel the enigma. The commission wanted to see the wounds, and Connally obliged. He did more than that. There had been confusing talk of exit wounds, of centimeters, and dehumanizing medical jargon. Now, Connally said, "If the committee would be interested, I would just as soon you look at it." He stood in the bland government hearing room, before his audience of buttoned-up, flabby men, stripped off his shirt, and stood half-naked before them. The scars were terrible. What the bullet had done was awful enough, but the marks of the rapid surgical procedures—the stab of the scalpel, undertaken with speed to save his life by getting the tube in to reinflate his lung, and then to expose the lung to remove the shrapnel of his own rib fragments—made the spectacle worse. Dr. Shaw had remained in the room for Connally's testimony and now he was called upon to describe the scars, as if this was a Goya-like seminar for students in a medical arena.

"This scar does not look quite as nice as it does during the more lateral portion of the surgically induced incision, because his skin was brought together under a little tension, and there is a little separation there," he said clinically. In short, the scar looked like hell. Before it was over, Connally had also dropped his trousers, to show them the thigh wound.

Nellie Connally followed her husband on the stand. As a witness, she had advantages and disadvantages over Connally himself, although their versions were for the most part compatible. Her main advantage was her line of sight: the president had been diagonally to her right in the limousine, and she had just turned to him to say sweetly, "Mr. President, you can't say that Dallas doesn't love you." Her disadvantage was that she was tender and feminine; she had no interest in guns nor experience in hunting. Now, she insisted, contrary to virtually every other witness and a mound of tangible evidence, that the first bullet passed through the president's neck, but not into her husband's back. "I heard a noise and not being an expert rifleman, I was not aware that it was a rifle. It was just a frightening noise and it came from the right. I turned over my right shoulder and looked back and saw the president as he had both hands at his neck. . . . He made no utterance, no cry. I saw no blood, no anything. It was just sort of nothing, the expression on his face, and he just sort of slumped down."

How fast had she reacted? The crack of the rifle shot came after the bullet had landed. Oswald's second bullet was in the chamber and being squeezed off. He could fire again in 2.3 seconds. Was the commission to believe that this genteel lady had had an instantaneous or a delayed reaction to this unfamiliar sound? Indeed, the reaction time of three passengers in the limousine now moved to the center of the investigation. The commission went back to the ultimate source, the Zapruder film.

As central as the film was, it had one critical void. A road sign had obscured President Kennedy and Governor Connally from view in the film, apparently at the very moment when the bullet or bullets found their mark. The film had to be analyzed frame by frame. Eighteen frames make up a second of time, and the principals are out of view for less than a second. The limousine and its passengers pass from view at frame number 206. Cramped with his knees against the front seat and his right side against the bulkhead of the car, Connally comes back into view at frame 223. He is turned to the right. Kennedy reemerges at frame 225. His right hand is at his chest level, moving rapidly toward his throat. He is hit. The hand arrives at the throat at frame 227. Connally now told the commission, after he studied the film frame by frame, that he thought he was hit somewhere between frames 231 and 234, or one-third of a second later than Kennedy. On the basis of that arithmetic alone, Nellie Connally's version—that the first bullet hit Kennedy and the second hit Connally—was impossible, for it took a minimum of 2.3 seconds or 41 frames of film for the same rifleman to shoot, reload, and fire again. It was impossible—unless there was more than one assassin, men firing simultaneously from about the same place. It came down to how fast and in what manner Kennedy and Connally reacted to their wounds. Kennedy's reaction was shown by his hand, Connally's from the swivel of his body.

There was one additional piece of evidence that was never considered in the analysis of the Zapruder film, as the experts looked at the way the two men responded to their wounds. That was the president's corset. Anyone who had ever stood in the president's anteroom before a formal occasion and watched his black manservant wrap the steel-rodded canvas back brace around the president's torso, fitted well above his nipples, and then watched the valet pull the straps and tighten the thongs loop by loop, as if this were Scarlett O'Hara's waistline, wondered how the man could ever turn an inch to either side. Once in it, he was planted upright, trapped and nearly bolted in a ramrod posture. In Dallas, this simple device was to impart a fate almost Grecian in its horror. When John Connally was hit, he was pivoting to his left, his lithe, athletic body in motion, and his natural course was to collapse, completing the spin, head down into Nellie's lap. But what of John Kennedy? If he had been hit by the first bullet, as Nellie Connally supposed, his body had remained upright for over six seconds, giving the assassin his second and third chances. If he had been hit by the second bullet, his head still loomed in view for nearly five full seconds—from frame 225 to the fatal frame, number 313. From frame 225 to 313, his head tilted only slightly to the left, for the corset held him erect. Thus, when Connally and a plethora of experts examined the Zapruder pictures, they did not readily consider that John Kennedy's body would not act like a normal man's body. But for that infernal corset, the force of the first bullet passing through his neck at the speed of 2,000 feet per second would surely have blown him forward and down upon the seat—and out of view of Oswald's cross hairs. The first wounding bullet had struck no bones. The president would have survived it.

The debate had shifted into the vague area of prompt or delayed reactions, both by the wounded men and by the witnesses. There was no science to it. Some doctors maintained that the reaction to a wound in the neck which hits no bones might be more delayed than the reaction to a wound which shatters a rib and collapses a lung. This was the position of Dr. Robert Shaw. "There can be a delay in sensory reaction," he testified to the Warren Commission, "an extended sensation, then just a gradual building up of a feeling of severe injury. But in the case of a wound which strikes a bony substance such as a rib, usually the reaction is quite prompt." If Kennedy and Connally were hit by the same bullet, the second, and Kennedy's hand went to his neck before Connally screamed in evident pain as he felt the punch in his back, how could this be? The conspiratorialists quickly offered the opinion that the men were hit by two separate bullets which landed at virtually the same millisecond. Not everyone felt as Dr. Shaw did. Bill Stinson, Connally's administrative aide, for example, had been a rifleman in World War II and had had his elbow shattered by shrapnel in combat. Stinson remembered his own delayed reaction had been considerable, for he had not realized he had been wounded until he could not lift his arm and aim his rifle at the onrushing enemy. Contrary to Dr. Shaw's testimony, other doctors would testify to the commission that delayed and indeed nonexistent reactions to wounds were not uncommon.*

On April 21 Connally and his surgeons left the commission with an unsolved mystery, but it would be clarified on May 6 by a very different set of doctors. These were the forensic experts from the ballistics division of Edgewood Arsenal in Maryland. They were led by a chief of the Wound Ballistics Branch at Edgewood, Dr. Alfred Oliver, who was a veterinarian by training. These experts had been ordered by the commission to make ballistics tests simulating the wounds to Connally and Kennedy.

At the commission hearing of April 21, Dr. Oliver had talked at length with Connally's surgeons, and he had received the X-rays and operative reports from Parkland Hospital. Consistent with established procedures, Oliver then conducted tests on a goat dressed in a suit, a shirt, and an undershirt, and also on a human cadaver, by firing bullets from a Mannlicher-Carcano rifle into the same places Kennedy and Connally had been shot. Working backwards from Connally's wrist wound, the Edgewood test determined that the governor's wrist could not possibly have been struck by a "pristine" bullet (or one which had not encountered some interference before its impact). Oliver concluded that the damage to Connally's wrist would have been considerably greater if the bullet had passed through only his chest and then into his wrist. Such a missile would still have had "terrific penetrating ability" and considerable "wounding potential." Most significantly, the entry wound in Connally's back—3 centimeters in diameter—did not indicate a pristine bullet either, but one which was yawing or wobbling on its axis.

What could cause such a thing? At Edgewood, the team positioned a piece of horse meat, equivalent in density to the boneless portion of a human neck, and then fired through it into the well-dressed goat. With this configuration, they found the velocity

---

*Ironically, twenty years later, in another assassination attempt on a president, the subject of delayed reaction was again a factor. For a full *fifteen minutes*, not until Ronald Reagan was in the Trauma Room of George Washington Hospital and a doctor noticed a small perforation under his arm, was it understood that the president had been shot. In the confusion after Hinckley's shots, it was several minutes before Reagan felt pain, and then it was assumed that he was having a heart attack, for he exhibited the classic symptoms of that condition. Later, it was finally appreciated that Hinckley's bullet had struck the limousine first, had flattened itself like a dime, and had entered the president's body tumbling, collapsing his lung and coming to rest in the shadow of his heart. The threats to Connally's and Reagan's lives, therefore, were remarkably similar medically.

of the bullet reduced by 200 feet per second as it passed through the horse meat, and it took on a yawing motion, passing through the goat's rib and doing an equivalent amount of damage to a simulated wrist as Connally's had suffered. To the commission or, more specifically, to four out of the seven of its members, this was the proof of the single bullet theory. This theory was bolstered by the absence of any damage to the seats of the presidential limousine from a bullet that might have penetrated the president's neck but somehow missed Connally altogether. If it had so missed, it would have had to lodge in the upholstery of the car.

John Connally would never accept it, not in 1964, not three years later when he wrote about it for *Life* magazine, not fifteen years later when he testified again about it before a select committee of the House of Representatives. He argued his position with a fervor that went beyond any possible supporting facts, as if it were a point of vanity that Lee Harvey Oswald had reserved a special bullet just for him, rather than forced him to share one with Kennedy. By November 1966, a week before the third anniversary of the calamity, the Warren Commission was under serious attack. The stock of the conspiracy industry was trading high. Thirty-four books and articles had been written challenging the commission's conclusions. Oswald had become a mystery man. There were Oswald doubles and magic bullets and whitewashes, and the testimony of Governor John Connally and his wife, Nellie, became the chief source of succor and encouragement to these alternate theories. Mark Lane's book, *Rush to Judgment*, stood atop the bestseller list. His chapter entitled "The Magic Bullet" made a farce out of the commission's theory of the second bullet, and the Connallys' testimony was the centerpiece of Lane's attack. Edward Epstein's book, *Inquest,* was the most solid of the challenges, and he reported that three of seven commission members—Senator Richard Russell, Senator John Sherman Cooper, and Congressman Hale Boggs—believed that there might have been separate bullets. Unquestionably, the debate within the commission over the wording of the final description of the single-bullet theory was spirited. "Compelling" was in the first draft. "Credible" was Senator Russell's proposal. "Persuasive" appeared in the final draft.

"The Governor flatly stated that he knew that the bullet which hit the President could not have been the one that struck him," Lane wrote. In fact, Connally had said no such thing three years before. He had not stated a certainty at all, but merely an impression, gleaned from a sixth sense, about events which took place behind his back.

In 1966, however, Connally made a gentleman out of Mark Lane. After a silence of three years Connally agreed to examine the Zapruder film for *Life* magazine. Of the theories in the wind, Connally asserted now with a boldness that verged upon arrogance, "As far as I'm concerned, there is no 'theory.' There is my absolute knowledge—and Nellie's, too—that one bullet caused the president's first wound and then an entirely separate shot struck me."

"No one will ever convince me otherwise," Nellie added.

"It's a certainty. I'll never change my mind," Connally said.

Life magazine used the Connally analysis to sound the call for a new commission of inquiry.

Logic compelled the conclusion that the governor believed in a second gunman. The conspiratorialists howled with delight. Connally had made their inferences into a declaration of belief and conferred upon them a dignity and authority they previously lacked. His testimony became their point of departure. Connally wanted it both ways. He wanted his two-bullet theory, and yet he recoiled at the notion of being in league with the likes of Mark Lane. The press clamored for a clarification, and on November 23, 1966, Connally gave one. In his opening statement he expressed shock at "journalistic scavengers" like Lane who attempt to "impugn the motives of the [Warren Commission] individually, cast doubts upon the commission as a whole, and question the credibility of the government itself." But no witness had been more important to Lane's argument than Connally, and now Connally did not shrink from his two-bullet "certainty."

In Lyndon Johnson's White House there was consternation at Connally's flamboyant challenge. As Connally proclaimed his desire not to fan the flames, his statements became a veritable bellows. Senator Richard Russell, one of the doubting commission members, finally went public with his misgivings. In an interview with an Austin paper, Russell declared his agreement with Connally on the one-bullet/two-bullet question, and cast doubts on other important elements of the commission's conclusions: the absence of a conspiracy, whether the Soviet Union had disclosed everything about Oswald's activities there between 1959 and 1962, and whether the commission knew everything about Oswald's Cuba-related activities. Senator Russell Long, whose father, Huey, had been the victim of assassination, said that "whoever fired that second shot was a better shot than Oswald." Even Malcolm Kilduff, who acted as Lyndon Johnson's press secretary in Dallas, told the press now that he agreed with Connally's rather than the commission's version of the second bullet. The brickbats came from the most unlikely redoubts. The historian Arthur Schlesinger, Jr., joined *Life* magazine in a call for a new commission.

The White House wondered what to do. In a top-secret memo to Johnson, presidential adviser Jack Valenti, just back from Europe, reported widespread disbelief in the Warren Commission findings and suspicion of either blundering or a cover-up. The consensus in Europe was that Oswald had not acted alone.

"This is not a lightly or rarely held view," Valenti wrote. "It is widening among the peoples of Western Europe. It could become so malignant as to threaten seriously the very integrity of the American Government." Valenti proposed a counterattack on the mountain of criticism by a distinguished panel of lawyers, headed by Louis Nizer. "Nizer and others ought to be unleashed *immediately* to publish a counter defense that would nail the detractors and the irresponsible nuts to the wall. The key to the whole assault on the Commission is the so-called single bullet theory. If this panel of distinguished lawyers could demolish the attack on the single bullet theory, the slanderers would be laid to rest."

Of course, Valenti was requesting LBJ to launch an attack, in essence, on his closest friend, John Connally, who might in that memo be considered a detractor at the least, and a slanderer and nut at worst. Nothing came of it, and Connally in his November 23 press conference said only that he had had "casual conversation" with Johnson about the commission findings.

Presidential consultant John P. Roche was more pointed about Connally. "The comments of Richard Russell and the Life Magazine article by Governor Connally are the two most serious blows which have yet occurred to the public credibility of the Warren Commission," Roche wrote to the president. "Paranoia is more infectious than measles. We have enough problems already with the war in Vietnam. To have the nation suddenly indulging in an orgy of sick speculation on events in Dallas could really poison the atmosphere," But the attacks on the commission could no longer be ignored, Roche wrote. He knew only what should not be done: the president should *not* reconvene the Warren Commission, and he should *not* appoint another commission. In the end, Connally himself suggested the course of action to Johnson that the president should take: a gentlemanly distance from the tempest that he, Connally, was causing.

Mark Lane, meanwhile, basked in the glory Connally had conferred upon him. He seized the moment to release a new chapter to his bestseller, which was about to be published in France. In the new material Lane unveiled a *five*-bullet hypothesis: the first to Kennedy's neck, the second to Kennedy's neck *from the front,* the third to Connally's back, the fourth to the street, and the fifth the mortal wound to the president's head. His "facts," he claimed, showed *conclusively* that bullets flew from two directions. Of Connally's *Life* article and press conference, Lane said, "Governor Connally displayed an abysmal ignorance of the implications of his own testimony. If the bullet that struck President Kennedy did not also strike Governor Connally, then there was no lone assassin."

In this point anyway, the old scavenger was dead right.

For twenty-five years, Connally's first horrible words as he was hit: "My God! They're going to kill us all!" have remained the rallying cry for the conspiratorialists.

★ NOTES ★

GUIDE TO THE NOTES

Barker Collection: Eugene C. Barker Texas History Center, University of Texas at Austin.

Ervin Committee: Select Committee on Presidential Campaign Activities. *Final Report.* Washington, D.C.: U.S. Government Printing Office, June 1974.

Ford Library: Gerald R. Ford Library, Ann Arbor, Michigan.

House Assassinations Committee: U.S. House of Representatives, Select Committee on Assassinations. [*Investigation of the Assassination of President John F. Kennedy*] *Report* and twelve volumes. Washington, D.C.: U.S. Government Printing Office, 1979.

Impeachment Inquiry: U.S. House of Representatives, Committee on the Judiciary. [The Impeachment of Richard M. Nixon] *Final Report, Hearings, and Statements of Information.* 1974.

Interviews with author: Details provided in bibliography, alphabetized by interviewee with date and place.

JFK Library: John Fitzgerald Kennedy Library, Boston, Mass.

King Library: Martin Luther King, Jr., Library, Washington, D.C.

LBJ Library: Lyndon Baines Johnson Library, Austin, Texas.

Nixon Project: Nixon Presidential Materials Project, Alexandria, Va.

Rayburn Library: Sam Rayburn Library, Bonham, Texas.

WC: Warren Commission. The President's Commission on the Assassination of President John F. Kennedy. Washington, D.C.: U.S. Government Printing Office, 1964. Twenty-six volumes.

WCR: Warren Commission. *Final Report.* Washington, D.C.: U.S. Government Printing Office. September 1964.

1. Youth

Wilson County: *Wilson County Centennial;* Jaeggli, *Court House Story.*

Connally family background: Golfrey Connally, Judge Del Cox (Connally cousin), Joe Fietsam (editor of *Floresville Chronicle Journal*), interviews with author.

Connally, Sr., as butcher: John Connally, various interviews on twenty-fifth anniversary of the Kennedy assassination, especially on the "Geraldo" Show, November 23, 1988; Manchester, *Death of a President*, and interview with author.

Connally and declamation: Golfrey Connally, interview with author.

Connally as high school actor: *Floresville Chronicle Journal* review, May 16, 1933.

Sheriff Carnes and Sam Fore, Jr.: Golfrey Connally, interview with author; Sam Fore, Jr., Mrs. Sam Fore, Jr., and Carroll Keach, oral histories, LBJ Library; Benjamin, *Germans in Texas;* Olmsted, Journey Through Texas.

Captain Will Wright: Webb, *Story of the Texas Rangers;* Dobie, *Vaquero of the Brush Country;* Caro, *Path to Power;* Del Cox and Golfrey Connally, interviews with author.

Sheriff and county clerk races in Wilson County: *Floresville Chronicle Journal*, July 1936.

Lyndon Johnson in Wilson County: Sam Fore, Jr., and Mrs. Sam Fore, Jr., oral histories, LBJ Library.

Fore's role: As Connally and Johnson rose to state and national prominence, Sam Fore watched with a certain pride of authorship. In both men, he had perceived promise early, when they were raw products of the Texas soil. Both Johnson and Connally, in turn, sought Fore's advice continually as they rose to power, especially his advice about people, for they considered him a good judge of character. The leaders shared a sentimentality about early friends, Fore in particular. When John F. Kennedy came to the LBJ Ranch, Johnson wanted Fore there to meet the president. When Governor Connally recuperated at his Picosa Ranch after his wounding in Dallas, he called Sam Fore to his bedside. Once, at a rally in Seguin, Connally told the audience that Sam Fore had done more for him in his life than anyone, apart from his own father.

For his own inauguration as president in 1964, Johnson went to great lengths to get Fore to attend, even though at the time Fore was not well. But Connally and Fore flew up to Washington together. During the festivities, there was a reception in the Mayflower Hotel for the governor of Texas, and Fore set out for it manfully on his weary, overtaxed legs. He tired along the way, and noticing an open door he walked into it. To his surprise, he found himself in the makeshift CBS television suite, where Hugh Downs had been, by chance, searching for anyone who knew the president from his youth and who could talk about his special qualities.

On television, Fore said, "We have another boy down in Texas who is going to be president some day too, and that's John Connally."

2. University of Texas

University of Texas in 1930s: Robert Eckhardt, Henry Wade, Frank Ikard, Creekmore Fath, John Henry Faulk, John V. Singleton, Jr., J. R. Parten, Maury Maverick, Jr., Joe Greenhill, Margaret Mayer, Robert Strauss, Jesse Villarreal, and Fred Schmidt, interviews with author.

Atheneum Society: Jesse Villarreal and with Creekmore Fath, interviews with author.

Revolt of the barbarians: Robert Strauss and Jake Pickle, oral histories, LBJ Library; Creekmore Fath, interview with author.

Professor Robert Montgomery: Montgomery oral history, LBJ Library;

Creekmore Fath and Fred Schmidt, interviews with author; Montgomery, *Brimstone Game.*

Student issues of 1936–38: Issues of the *Daily Texan* and the *Texas Ranger,* Barker Collection; Robert Eckhardt and Creekmore Fath, interviews with author.

Professors Edward Everett Hale and Clarence Ayres: Ayres, *Theory of Economic Progress;* Hale, "Fascism versus Communism."

Dialogue before the Caldwell Committee: Creekmore Fath, interview with author; coverage by *Daily Texan,* Barker Collection; documents from Library of the Texas State Legislature.

Connally and Nellie Brill as college actors: reviews in the *Daily Texan,* November 1937, April 1938, and September 1938, Barker Collection.

UT campus politics: Jake Pickle and Robert Strauss, oral histories, LBJ Library; John V. Singleton, Jr., Joe Greenhill, Robert Strauss, Fred Schmidt, Maury Maverick, Jr., interviews with author.

Nellie Brill as prom queen: issues of *Daily Texan,* Barker Collection; Nellie Connally file, Ex-Student Association, University of Texas; Joe Greenhill, Judge John V. Singleton, Jr., Margaret Mayer, interviews with author.

Charles Black poetry: 1937 issues of the *Ranger,* Barker Collection.

Connally statement on Studatenland: The *Cactus* (University of Texas college yearbook) 1938–39, and the *Daily Texan,* Barker Collection.

Pappy O'Daniel: Caro, *Path to Power:* Dugger, *Politician;* John V. Singleton, Jr., interview with author; home movies, produced by Lady Bird Johnson, LBJ Library.

Connally's remark about Pappy O'Daniel: John Connally, luncheon remarks at Rice University, Houston, symposium on "The World of Texas Politics," September 30, 1988, symposium files, LBJ Library.

Introduction of Connally to Johnson: J. R. Parten, interview with author and oral history, LBJ Library.

LBJ Call to Sam Fore, Jr., about Connally: Sam Fore, Jr., oral history, LBJ Library.

3. Lyndon and John

Einstein letter: Clark, *Einstein.*

Neutrality Congress: Burns, *Roosevelt;* Gunther, *Roosevelt in Retrospect;* Morgan, *FDR;* presidential statement on approval of Neutrality Legislation, August 31, 1935, FDR presidential papers; Hamilton Fish, radio address, February 9, 1937, Mutual Broadcasting Company; Senator William E. Borah, address, *Congressional Record,* October 2, 1939; Roosevelt, Fireside Chat, September 3, 1939; Roosevelt, press conference, March 7, 1939; Presidential Proclamation of Neutrality, September 5, 1939; Roosevelt, address to Joint Session of Extraordinary Session of Congress, September 21, 1939.

Lyndon Johnson as congressman: Caro, *Path to Power;* Mary Bethune, comment, LBJ Library; Luther Jones, Gene Latimer, Dorothy Jackson Nicols, John V. Singleton, Jr., Jake Pickle, Sherman Birdwell, oral histories, LBJ Library.

Creekmore Fath remark on Johnson racism: Fath, interview with author.

Garner in Uvalde: Caro, *Path to Power.*

Johnson's literary interests: Luther Jones, oral history, LBJ Library.

LBJ on loyalty: Ted Van Dyck, interview with author. When Johnson was president, and the anti-Vietnam protest was reaching a crescendo, the president called in the second rank of presidential and vice presidential assistants, of whom Ted Van Dyk was one, and told this story of Rayburn staying all night in his hospital room in 1936. Clearly, Johnson was telling the story because he was worried about possible disloyalty in the White House.

Garner and whiskey: Creekmore Fath, interview with author.

LBJ glorification of his role in Selective Service debate: Ickes, *Secret Diary.*

Dorothy Jackson's introduction to burlesque: see Dorothy Jackson Nicols, oral history, LBJ library.

Gayety Theatre: issues of the *Washington Daily News,* and clippings from the *Washington Post,* indexed at King Library.

The Dodge: Luther Jones, Gene Latimer, Dorothy Jackson Nicols, and Walter Jenkins, oral histories, LBJ Library; Henderson, *Maury Maverick;* Caro, *Path to Power;* Dugger, *Politician.*

Judge Slatton letter and LBJ letters re Connally: Connally, selected names file, LBJ Library.

LBJ's obsession with letters: Luther Jones, John V. Singleton, Jr., Gene Latimer, Sherman Birdwell, and Jake Pickle, oral histories, LBJ Library; Connally letters to LBJ, Connally, selected names file, LBJ Library; John V. Singleton, Jr., interview with author.

Johnson on cluttered desks and minds: William Stinson, interview with author.

Pish-Posh letter and the I Can't Do It Club: House papers, LBJ Library.

Norman Heine letter to Connally: Connally, selected names file, LBJ Library.

4. "If Jack Were Only Here"

Rayburn speeches: Address on NBC, February 9, 1941; addresses to Congress, June 30, 1939, and November 2, 1939, Congressional Record.

Campaign for Navy commission: Connally, select names file, LBJ Library.

Nellie Brill trip with Sugar Pickle and Lady Bird Johnson to Washington: Lady Bird Johnson, interview with author.

Harris Melasky dialogue: Raymond Buck, oral history, LBJ Library.

Home movies: "My Mother was a lady, or . . . If Jack were only Here" and "Heaven Will Protect the Working Girl," LBJ Library; Lady Bird Johnson, interview with author.

Wedding announcement: *Austin American,* December 22, 1940.

Cryptic note about delivering cash to Maverick: Caro, *Path to Power.*

Rayburn speech: NBC, Feb. 9, 1941.

LBJ address to Texas Legislature on San Jacinto Day: *Austin American,* April 21, 1941.

Election of 1941: A superb source for this is Dugger, *The Politician;* also Jake Pickle, John V. Singleton, Jr., Walter Jenkins, Raymond Buck, and Cecil Burney, Sherman Birdwell, oral histories, LBJ Library.

Nellie Connally poem: Lady Bird social file, LBJ Library.

Johnson on Hitler: *Austin American;* speeches in House Papers, LBJ Library.

Johnson campaigning in 1941: Lady Bird Johnson, narration of home movies of campaign, LBJ Library.

Victory slips away: Jake Pickle and Walter Jenkins oral histories, LBJ Library.

Ferguson bribe attempt and John Connally's reaction: Dugger, *Politician*, p. 234.

Bringing in the South Texas vote: Jake Pickle and Walter Jenkins, oral histories, LBJ Library.

Connally's retreat to Floresville after defeat: Golfrey Connally, interview with author.

Letters of recommendations for Connally commission: Connally, selected names file, LBJ Library.

LBJ speech: August 8, 1941, *Congressional Record.*

FDR "rattlesnake" speech: September 11, 1941, Roosevelt presidential papers.

Letters between LBJ and Connally: LBJ to Connally, November 13, 1941, November 22, 1941, and November 27, 1941; Connally to LBJ, December 3, 1941, December 6, 1941, and December 13, 1941, Connally, selected names File, LBJ Library.

5. First Lieutenant

Habits of Charles Marsh: Creekmore Fath, interview with author.

Marsh letter: in Marsh papers, Box 2, LBJ Library.

Connally letter to Professor James Burton: December 18, 1941, Connally, selected names file, LBJ Library.

LBJ to Connally: January 1942, House Papers, LBJ Library.

Barker memo to Forrestal re LBJ as "live wire": Navy File, LBJ Library.

Jonathan Daniels comment on LBJ: Daniels, *White House Witness.*

LBJ to Admiral John Gingrich: Navy File, LBJ Library.

Wirtz to LBJ: February 23, 1942, House Papers, LBJ Library.

Lana Turner story: Paul Healy, "Frantic Gentleman from Texas," *Saturday Evening Post,* May 19, 1951.

LBJ to Wirtz: March 14, 1942, Navy file, LBJ Library.

Charles Marsh "Dutch Harbor" statement: Dugger, *Politician*, p. 242.

Connally on House race decision: Miller, *Lyndon*, p. 101.

Johnson's claim about his mission to Pacific: James Blundell, oral history, LBJ Library.

World War II Diary: Navy file, LBJ Library. The diary is sprinkled with sexual allusions, such as "only intercourse here—social," "Plenty of prophylactics being used," and references to a mysterious "Miss Jesus" of Nourea. See Dugger, *Politician*, p. 249.

Johnson's glorification of his war experience: Twenty years later, in the White House, Johnson often dispensed copies of the book *The Mission* as gifts to his visitors. On May 13, 1966, as the Buddhists in Hué revolted against the central South Vietnamese, and as 8,000 protesters prepared to demonstrate against the war along the White House fence, Johnson launched into a discourse on his war record to several business leaders. He wondered aloud why his mission was not given equal billing to John F.

Kennedy's adventures on PT-109. A record of the president's musings was kept by a White House scribe:

"He said he didn't understand why a movie company couldn't make a film about his activities on Navy planes showing the various missions he flew. There was discussion of how the younger generation could perhaps identify with this kind of an image—the same way they did with President Kennedy—because of the youthful portrayal. The President commented that it would be very helpful for the soldiers serving in Vietnam now—and those who are probably draftees—to see that the President wasn't just talking about war games—that he had actually been in one himself and, therefore, could understand the hazards and sacrifices that are met by a soldier."

For much of his presidency, it was Johnson's custom to wear a miniature ribbon of his silver star decoration in the buttonhole of his suit. In a glamorous portrait of him in the lush LBJ Library, the ribbon is prominently represented. Occasionally, however, Johnson seemed to recognize that there was something unseemly about this vain display. Once, the authors of a book about James Forrestal wrote to ask him about his war service. The draft reply that was prepared for presidential signature contained the lines, "I was given a special assignment which took me to the Southwest Pacific on a mission for the President, for which I was awarded a silver star." But the president excised the reference to the medal in the final version. (See LBJ's letter to Duke political science professor Dr. Robert Connery, who with Robert Albion of Harvard was writing a book about James Forrestal; LBJ Library.)

But with another author, William White, Johnson carried on a lively correspondence about a gallant portrayal of his exploits in White's book *Queens Die Proudly*. In that book, the author accepted uncritically Johnson's grand memory of the events. Throughout his later life, Johnson acted toward the subject of his war record with the high sensitivity of one who was about to be found out.

Connally in the Lend-Lease office: George Ball, interview with author, and *Past Has Another Pattern*.

Lady Bird explosion about house: Dugger, *Politician*, p. 254.

Algiers in 1942: Lloyd Cutler, Eugene Rostow, and W. W. Rostow, interviews with author.

Wire from the home office: Cutler, interview with author.

Connally in Algiers, including relationship with Elliott Roosevelt: Connally letter to LBJ, June 5, 1943, LBJ Library; also Connally letter to Sam Rayburn, May 17, 1943, and William Kitrell to Rayburn, May 18, 1943, and June 7, 1943, Sam Rayburn Library.; Rayburn, *Speak, Mr. Speaker*. For the general military situation in North Africa before the invasion of Sicily, Morison, *History of U.S. Naval Operations*. For de Gaulle in Algiers: Eugene Rostow, interview with author; de Gaulle, *War Memoirs*, vol. 2, pp. 140–41. Crawley, *De Gaulle*; Ambrose, *Eisenhower*; Lyon, *Eisenhower*; Eisenhower, *Eisenhower*; Monnet, *Memoirs*; Murphy, *Diplomat Among Warriors*; Macmillan, *Blast of War*.

6. Combat

Connally's joshing note to LBJ: July 11, 1944, LBJ Library.

Buck Taylor quote: Dugger, *Politician*, p. 251.

Connally to LBJ: June 11, 1944, LBJ Library.

LBJ response: July 26, 1944, LBJ Library.

Connally's period at sea: For details of carrier strategy, Reynolds, *Fast Carriers*. For military strategy in Pacific, Costello, *Pacific War;* Brodie, *Guide to Naval Strategy.* For details of his Marine Corps service, Merrill Connally, interview with author. Also Connally to LBJ, December 4, 1944; LBJ to Connally, December 16, 1944, Connally to LBJ, December 26, 1944; 1944 letters between LBJ and Jake Pickle, House papers, all from LBJ Library.

New York Times article: "Essex Wins Glory in Pacific Battles," December 4, 1944.

The action on October 24, 1944: U.S. Navy, *Medal of Honor.*

Kamikaze information: Hoyt, *Kamikazes.*

The hit on the ESSEX, interchange between Connally and MacDonald: John Connally, interview with author.

Memorandum to LBJ re a reassignment for Connally: from J. W. Roper, January 25, 1945, House papers, LBJ Library.

Connally as flight controller: Jim Rowe letter to LBJ, June 16, 1945; LBJ to Jim Rowe, July 10, 1945; Jim Rowe to LBJ, August 15, 1945; all given to author by Elizabeth Rowe.

Nellie to LBJ: February 17, 1945, LBJ Library.

LBJ to Connally re "insurance policy": April 12, 1945, LBJ Library.

Merrill Connally actions and remarks: interview with author.

Connally letter to LBJ with oblique reference to kamikazes: Connally to LBJ, March 3, 1945; LBJ's response, April 12, 1945.

Greasy skipper story: *Austin American Statesman*, December 7, 1947.

LBJ's romantic pass at Nellie Connally: George Christian, interview with author.

Connally to LBJ on replacement: April 23, 1945, and on FDR death, Connally to LBJ, May 9, 1945, LBJ Library.

Second Bronze Star citation: September 16, 1945, with description of bravery from July 1 to August 15, 1945, U.S. Department of Navy.

Frantic wires from LBJ to Navy Department: House papers, Box 16, LBJ Library.

7. Forty-Cent Cotton & Ten-Cent Beer

The tarnish of being a wheeler-dealer: Pickle, oral history, LBJ Library. For the idea wheeler-dealer as a positive rather than a negative: Jake Jacobsen oral history, LBJ Library and interview with author.

Local hero: Austin American Statesman, December 7, 1947.

KVET founding: Merrill Connally, interview with author; *Austin American*, December 7, 1947; Alexander Stuart, "Citizen Connally: The Businessman You Never Knew," *Fortune*, July 31, 1978.

Encounter with Wade in Pacific: Henry Wade and Connally had seen one another on leave in Hawaii where the encounter with the hula dancer took place. (Henry Wade, interview with author.) Perhaps more importantly, they had had a chance encounter in a combat action. One night late in the war, Connally led a search for four downed Navy pilots off the coast of Japan, when he radioed for help to Okinawa. Henry Wade took the call.

Hollers's opening speech: House papers, Box 55, LBJ Library.

Connally to LBJ re Hollers speech: House papers, Box 55, LBJ Library.

Connally speech on LBJ war record: House Papers, Box 44, LBJ Library.

Johnson speech on KVET: Speech entitled "KVET Lies," House papers, Box 60, LBJ Library.

Misappropriation of cash by Texas politicians: John C. White, a Texas politician for thirty years, an assistant secretary of agriculture under Jimmy Carter, and former chairman of the Democratic Party, interview with author. "In the old days, $1,000 or $5,000 was really a big amount of money," White said. "It was always there in cash, and it was always there for your personal use. If you needed a new suit, it was there. I did it. Everybody did it. You were handling cash all the time. I don't know if John Connally ever took a nickel, but if he didn't, it would be unusual."

Meeting to answer Hollers charges: Jake Pickle, oral history, LBJ Library.

Connally draft rebuttal: Connally to LBJ, May 25, 1946, House papers, Box 55, LBJ Library.

Connally political reports to LBJ: May 15, 20, 24, 25, 1946, House Papers, Box 55, LBJ Library; "KVET lies", House papers, Box 60, LBJ Library.

Smear of homosexuality upon Hollers by Johnson camp: Creekmore Fath, interview with author. Fath had run for Johnson's congressional seat in 1948, and as he campaigned throughout the district, he heard the rumor that Hollers was a "queer." There could be no doubt that an orchestrated whispering campaign had been undertaken by Johnson workers, and for such a dangerous charge as this, it is inconceivable that the campaign manager did not know about it.

Watermelon battles: Jake Pickle, oral history, LBJ Library.

Steamboat whistle: Willard Deason, oral history, LBJ Library; Austin American, July 26, 1946.

Forty-cent cotton and ten-cent beer: Pickle, oral history, LBJ Library.

Hollers's Gestapo statement: *Austin American Statesman*, July 26, 1946.

8. The Burglary of 1948

Two families: During these years, the Johnson and Connally families had grown even closer together. The wives had their toddlers, and the husbands their common business and political preoccupations. Since Lady Bird's family had the money and the land, Connally was often called upon for business and legal advice. Once during this time, he accompanied her to Alabama, where she needed to sell the property of her spinster aunt, Effie. In the course of the trip, Connally and Lady Bird found themselves in a local restaurant having lunch, when suddenly there was a commotion outside, succeeded by a fast exodus from the café. Lady Bird turned to the waitress to ask what the fuss was about and was told that Clark Gable was outside, fresh from making his picture called *The Homecoming* with Lana Turner.

"Now why would everyone want to rush out to see him?" Lady Bird asked thoughtfully.

"Because he's the handsomest man in the world," replied the waitress. Then turning to Connally, she burst out, "But honey, they can all rush out there, and you and I can stay right here!" (Phil Bobbitt, interview with author.)

Jake Pickle comment on Stevenson: Pickle, oral history, LBJ Library.

Connally to Johnson, March 12, 1948: Connally, selected names file, LBJ Library.

Session under the trees at Dillman Street: Jake Pickle, oral history, LBJ Library; also Miller, *Lyndon*, p. 118. On Johnson campaign staff: Claude Wild, oral history, LBJ Library.

Gallstone episode: Warren Woodward, oral history, LBJ Library, and interview with author; also Walter Jenkins, oral history, LBJ Library.

Sporti Harvey and King Ranch anecdotes: Maury Maverick, Jr., interview with author.

Cecil Burney actions: Burney, oral history, LBJ Library, and interview with author. "While many say the Latin voter is not as intelligent as he should be, he acts pretty intelligent," Burney once observed. "He knows which side his bread is buttered on and who his friends are. He recognizes that he gets what he is entitled to from the Democratic party. When it comes time to have an election, we work especially hard in about 45 precincts, which are predominantly Latin, because we know that for every person we produce at the polls, we are going to get nine, ten more." Later Burney would often point with pride to the fact that in Johnson's 1964 presidential election, Corpus Christi exceeded by 26,000 votes the margin of victory that was needed, and thereby produced half of the margin needed to win the state of Texas. In that election, the other half was produced by the dust-blown Latin counties of the Rio Grande Valley.

Mavericks and Kildays: one member of the Kilday clan had defeated Maury Maverick, Sr., for Congress in 1938, whereas another Kilday had been fired as chief of policy when Maverick became the city's mayor in 1939.

The helicopter: Warren Woodward, oral history, LBJ Library.

Anderson interrogation of Coke Stevenson: Miller, *Lyndon*, p. 122; also Pickle, oral history, LBJ Library.

Nellie's meanness: Dugger, *Politician*, p. 319; copies of campaign mailings, LBJ Library.

Rumor about Lady Bird's unhappiness including thoughts about divorcing Johnson: Kellis Dibrell, interview with author. Dibrell had heard the rumor from Dawson Duncan of the *Dallas Morning News*. Duncan also provided the information about Johnson's expedient position on civil rights; in retrospect, Lady Bird Johnson was only truly sentimental about the losing campaign of 1941, which is demonstrated by her warm narration of home movies about that campaign (home movies, LBJ Library, and interview with author).

Letter to Connally, August 16, 1948: Connally, selected names file, LBJ Library.

San Antonio vote fraud and payoffs: Dugger, *Politician* (including the quote from Jimmy Knight), p. 321; Ruben Mungia, Jr., Maury Maverick, Jr., John V. Singleton, Jr., Franklin Spears, Kellis Dibrell, and Judge Charles Grace, interviews with author.

Defeating the voting machines: Judge Charles Grace, interview with author.

Connally's denial of knowledge or participation: Miller, *Lyndon*, p. 136.

Vote count on election night: Walter Jenkins, oral history, LBJ Library.

Connally in Alice, making deal with George Parr, week before election: Archer Parr, interview with author.

The runoff: Two counties did not even participate in the runoff, balking at the expense of it. Hansford County, a vast carpet of wheat and cotton ranches and sparsely populated by a homogeneous Anglo population, would have gone solidly for Stevenson. Kinney County, on the other hand, lying on the Mexican border along the Rio Grande, had the West Texas ranching aspect that was Stevenson's strength, but three-quarters of its population was a mixture of Mexican and Seminole Indians, and it was bracketed by counties which went to the opposite sides of the contest.

Mistaken call to Panhandle chairman: Kellis Dibrell, interview with author.

Background of the Parrs: John V. Singleton, Jr., Nago Alaniz, Lloyd Hackler, and Kellis Dibrell, interviews with author; Dugger, *Politician; Texas Observer*, "A Death in Duval," April 25, 1975; John Connally, luncheon remarks, Rice University, September 30, 1988, symposium files, LBJ Library.

Inside the Stevenson camp: Kellis Dibrell, interview with author. Dibrell provided author with transcripts of interviews conducted with Coke Stevenson on September 5, 1974, concerning his actions and his thinking during the 1948 campaign. [Stevenson tapes] Also, an account by Josh Gorce, another Stevenson aide, of 1948 actions from the Stevenson point of view was provided to the author by Kellis Dibrell.

Connally in Duval County after the election: Nago Alaniz and Loyd Hackler, interviews with author. Alaniz was a close associate of George Parr, and first told the author that Connally was right there in "the thick" of the vote fraud when the author visited him in his law office in San Diego, Texas. Alaniz also allowed that Connally and Parr met in "odd places" because they were concerned about the presence of the Stevenson men in Alice.

Parr's court: To the satraps and hangers-on around Parr, many of whom communicated with Parr in Spanish and who were scarcely able to recognize top state politicians by sight, Connally's arrival in Duval had a simple explanation: Lyndon Johnson had arrived. The man in their midst fit the description of everything they knew, which was not much, about Johnson. There was no reason for Parr—or Connally—to disabuse them of the notion. Connally was as close to being Johnson himself as any other man could get. Because he was more handsome and younger and smoother, he was a romanticization of Johnson. Given the actor in him, it was a situation Connally must have loved. The confusion between Johnson and Connally in Duval surfaced in 1984 when Luis Salas "confessed" his actions in the 1948 election and asserted that Lyndon Johnson had come to Duval County (*Corpus Christi Caller Times*, April 8, 1984). In Kahl's book *Ballot Box 13*, the possibility of the confusion between Johnson and Connally was suggested by Kahl without proof.

Connally's hand in the vote fraud: Loyd Hackler, interview with author. Hackler was the editor of the Laredo newspaper before he went to Washington as an assistant press secretary to George Christian in the Johnson White House. Some years ago, he took a long car ride to Mexico with his friend Philip Kazen. In the course of the trip, Kazen told of his and Connally's role in the vote fraud. Kazen said that most of the details of the affair had been reported, except the central fact of whose hand had actually added the names to the rolls. Hackler (from Kazen) confirmed the fact, conveyed to the author by Nago Alaniz, that many more than 202 names were added to the rolls of Jim Wells County, but that the number in Box 13 was enough to create the "landslide."

Frank Hamer as tough hombre: Frost and Jenkins, *I'm Frank Hamer*.

Stevenson in Alice: The Stevenson tapes; James M. Rowe, oral history, LBJ

Library; his unpublished manuscript, LBJ Library, and interview with author; *Texas Argus,* Spring 1964.

Pedro story: It is oft told. This version comes from Matthews, *San Antonio Lawyer.* Matthews represented Governor Stevenson in the legal wrangling in Duval County in September 1948.

Fort Worth convention: Coverage in the *Dallas Morning News;* also Vann M. Kennedy, interview with author. Kennedy was secretary of the State Democratic Executive Committee in 1948, when LBJ was certified.

Joe Hill–Creekmore Fath contretemps in the Blackstone Hotel: Fath, interview with author.

Charles Gibson: Dugger, *Politician,* p. 458n.

Trip to Judge Davidson's ranch in East Texas: Kellis Dibrell, interview with author.

Connally at the clerk's office in Fort Worth: Stevenson tapes; Dibrell, interview with author.

"God was on our side by 87 votes": Creekmore Fath, interview with author.

9. Oil, Money, and Blood

"Money, honey: Cleveland Amory, "Oil Folks at Home," *Holiday,* February, 1954; Hurt, *Texas Rich; Washington Post* series on Texas oil rich, February 13–19, 1954.

Background on wildcatters including Richardson: Olien and Olien, *Wildcatters;* Olien's interviews with Mrs. Tom Linebery and Ford Chapman provided to the author by Dr. Olien.

Richardson-Marsh arrangement: Creekmore Fath, interview with author.

Richardson on luck: Bainbridge, *Super-Americans,* p. 93; *Fort Worth Star Telegram,* October 1, 2, 3, and 4, 1959; *Oil and Gas Journal* 57:41.

Richardson-Murchison exchange on St. Joseph house: James Rowe letter to Arthur Krock, February 24, 1972, Arthur Krock Papers, Princeton University Library; James Rowe, interview with author.

Richardson-Murchison exchange on popcorn: Freeman Lincoln, "Big Wheeler Dealer from Dallas" *Fortune,* January and February 1953.

Richardson to Connally re job: Stuart, "Citizen Connally: The Businessman You Never Knew," *Fortune,* July 31, 1978.

Richardson and politics: Sherill, Oil *Follies;* Olien, *From Token to Triumph;* Flemmons, *Amon.*

Rayburn and cash: Creekmore Fath and John White, interviews with author.

No-count bull: Fath, interview with author.

Hotel Del Charro: Drew Pearson papers, LBJ Library.

Richardson barking at J. Edgar Hoover: handwritten notes in Drew Pearson papers, LBJ Library.

Richardson's lost cash: Drew Pearson papers, LBJ Library.

Letter on Boys, Inc., as gimmick: February 6, 1955, Drew Pearson papers, LBJ Library.

"Kill 'Em Keck": On his ruthlessness, J. R. Parten, oral history, LBJ Library; on his oilfield practices: Earle Loughboro, a former Keck employee, letter to Drew Pearson, January 21, 1956, Drew Pearson papers, LBJ Library;

subsequent congressional testimony concerning the Francis Case bribe attempt.

Natural Gas Scandal: Joseph and Stewart Alsop, "Natural Gas and the Democrats" December 12, 1955; "Democrat against Democrat in Fight over Gas Regulation", article, *St. Louis Post Dispatch*, December 29, 1956; Drew Pearson, "Democrats Face Hassle in Senate," column, January 4, 1956, LBJ Library; "Threat to Gas Users", editorial, *Washington Star*, January 26, 1956; "Last Chance on Natural Gas," editorial, *New York Times*, January 27, 1956; "Democrats and the Gas Lobby," editorial, *Washington Post*, January 27, 1956; Marquis Childs, column, February 15, 1956, Drew Pearson papers, LBJ Library; Eisenhower veto message, Presidential papers, February 17, 1956; James Reston, column, *New York Times*, February 20, 1956; Oil and Gas Investigation, under Senate Resolution 219, hearings and report, *Congressional Record*.

Connally involvement in natural gas scandal: Drew Pearson, handwritten personal notes, Drew Pearson papers, LBJ Library; Frank Ikard, Harold Kennedy, and Creekmore Fath, interviews with author.

Superior Oil's fine: The Kecks did not feel especially chagrined by their $10,000 fine in 1956. According to author Sherrill in *Oil Follies*, Howard Keck bragged to Congressman Wright Patman during the Democratic convention of 1960 that he had given $200,000 to the presidential campaign of Lyndon Johnson that summer, but Keck wanted his money back if Johnson was going to accept the vice presidential nomination. A Superior Oil lobbyist would only chortle to Sherrill about the odds of Keck getting his money back. The circle of oil and political money was tight indeed.

Shivers fight: Kinch and Long, *Allan Shivers;* Green, *Establishment in Texas Politics;* O. Douglas Weeks, "Texas One Party Politics in 1956," Institute of Public Affairs, University of Texas, vol. 32; Lawrence Wright, "The Tide Turns," *Texas Monthly*, January 1986; Kathleen Voigt, Fred Schmidt, interviews with author; J. R. Parten, Judge John V. Singleton, Jr., Judge Byron Skelton, Fred Schmidt, Cecil Burney, Warren Woodward, oral histories, LBJ Library.

Dialogue: Kathleen Voigt, interview with author.

Johnson's apologia to labor: Fred Schmidt, interview with author, and oral history, LBJ Library.

Johnson's remark about "cutting each other": James Blundell oral history, LBJ Library.

Letter from labor leader: George Lambert to Violet Gunther, April 10, 1956, Texas Labor Archives, University of Texas, Arlington.

Shivers lines: *Dallas Morning News*, May 2, 1956.

Nature of precinct votes and conventions in Texas: Billy Carr, Kathleen Voigt, Fred Schmidt, interviews with author.

At the LBJ Ranch before the Dallas State Convention: Kathleen Voigt and Fred Schmidt, interviews with author.

Coverage of the Dallas Convention: *Dallas Morning News*.

The estimable Frankie Randolph: Billie Carr, interview with author.

Randolph vs. B. A. Bentsen: Lloyd Bentsen, Byron Skelton, Warren Woodward, J. R. Parten, and B. A. Bentsen, oral histories, LBJ Library; Lloyd Bentsen, Billie Carr, Robert Eckhardt, Frank Ikard, interviews with author.

Connally naked with Kathleen Voigt: John V. Singleton, Jr., oral history, LBJ Library, and interview with author. (In Kathleen Voigt's interview, she did not remember Connally's indecent exposure.)

LBJ and Lady Bird thank-you letters to Connally: May 25, 1956, LBJ Library.

The September convention: New York Times, September 13, 1956; Austin American, September 11, 1956.

10. JFK . . . from Texas

Connally as vice chairman of Texas delegation in 1956: Hale Boggs oral history, JFK Library.

Johnson ladling water onto Kennedy's back: Adrian Spears oral history, LBJ Library.

Death of Kathleen: Tallahassee Democrat and Dallas Morning News, April 30, 1959; Julian Read, Billie Carr, Creekmore Fath, and John Henry Faulk, interviews with author.

Connally's work before the 1960 convention: James Blundell oral history, LBJ Library.

Rumors of Kennedy bribes in West Virginia: John Sharon oral history, JFK Library.

LBJ's personal comments on JFK: Schlesinger, Robert Kennedy; Peter Lisagor, oral history, JFK Library.

Adlai Stevenson's meeting with LBJ: John Sharon, oral history, JFK Library.

Texas pride and the Johnson campaign in 1960: Jake Jacobsen, interview with author; Jacobsen, John V. Singleton, Jr., oral histories, LBJ Library.

H. L. Hunt and the 1960 Johnson campaign: Robert Notti, oral history, JFK Library.

"Scrawny little guy with rickets": Peter Lisagor, oral history, JFK Library; India Edwards, oral history, LBJ Library.

Kennedy's Addison's disease: Telephone conversations between Don Cook and Walter Jenkins, July 5 and 6, 1960; between Cook and Johnson aide Arthur Perry; and between Charlie Kress and Walter Jenkins, July 5, 1960; between Bobby Baker and Walter Jenkins, July 6, 1960 and between Eliot Janeway and Walter Jenkins, transcripts, LBJ Library. Also Lasky, JFK: Man and Myth, p. 375.; Parmet, Jack, p. 191; Blair and Blair, In Search of JFK; Jake Jacobsen on William Manchester book, assassination file, LBJ Library; New York Times, July 5, 1960.

JFK/Johnson maneuvering at Convention: Hale Boggs, oral history, JFK Library On rumors coming to the Johnson campaign, John V. Singleton, Jr., oral history, LBJ Library.

Kennedy payoff to Arizona delegation leader: John V. Singleton, Jr., oral history, LBJ Library.

LBJ pulling in his IOUs: Jake Jacobsen, oral history, LBJ Library.

JFK appearance before the Texas delegation: Hale Boggs, oral history, JFK Library; O'Brien, No Final Victories, p. 82; Jake Jacobsen, oral history, LBJ Library; Salinger, With Kennedy.

"Pistol-whipping": Lasky, JFK: Man & Myth, p. 392.

Rayburn-Boggs dialogue: Hale Boggs, oral history, JFK Library.

Las Vegas poolside interchange: Robert Strauss, interview with author.

Herman Brown's anger: John V. Singleton, Jr., oral history, LBJ Library.

Connally-Jenkins interchange: telephone conversation, transcript, LBJ Library.

Connally rejection of Senate race: Connally luncheon remarks, Rice University, September 30, 1988, Symposium file, LBJ Library.

Connally appointment as secretary of navy: Adam Yarmolinsky, Sargent Shriver, and Lt. Governor William Hobby, interviews with author.

LBJ-JFK-Rayburn dialogue, Palm Beach: Lt. Gov. William Hobby, interview with author; Schlesinger, *Thousand Days*, p. 127.

Drew Pearson's objections to Connally: Creekmore Fath, interview with author; Pearson to Phil Graham letter, January 19, 1961, and other documents, Drew Pearson papers, LBJ Library.

The Richardson payments: Connally revealed the schedule of payments from Sid Richardson for the first time ten years after his navy confirmation hearings, when he was being confirmed as Nixon's secretary of the treasury in 1971.

Debate on secretary of navy nomination: In committee, January 21, 1961, and in full Senate, January 23, 1961; Senator William Proxmire, interview with author.

Khrushchev's and Kennedy's speeches on wars of liberation: Kaufman, *McNamara Strategy*; Kennedy, *Strategy of Peace*, p. 184.

"Dialogue of the deaf": Adam Yarmolinsky, interview with author.

Secret memo of admirals about Connally and political influence: Drew Pearson column, January 5, 1961, Drew Pearson papers, LBJ Library.

Connally and the stewards corps: Adam Yarmolinsky, interview with author.

Issues facing the navy in 1961: Arleigh Burke, chief of naval operations, testimony before House Committee on Appropriations, March 8, 1961; John Connally testimony to same committee, same day.

Connally's geopolitical view: Connally, "Communist Conspiracy," speech in Cincinnati, in *Vital Issues Magazine*, December 8, 1961.

Connally's role in Seven Days in May concept: Charles Bailey II, Fletcher Knebel, and Bill Stinson, interviews with author.

Connally's reminiscences to Knebel: Fletcher Knebel and Charles Bailey II, "Military Control: Can It Happen Here?" *Look* magazine, September 11, 1962, and also Knebel, "Boston-Austin Axis," *Look*, January 2, 1962.

4% Club: William Stinson, Julian Read, George Christian, interviews with author; On LBJ disagreement with the Connally run for governor: Jake Pickle, oral history, LBJ Library. On LBJ kidding Connally on hunt: William Hobby, interview with author.

Dallas party for Connally: Robert Strauss and Frank Ikard, interviews with author.

Port arms at Austin airport: John Connally file, Ex-Student Association, University of Texas, Austin.

Kidding about the eye patch: Bill Stinson, interview with author.

Connally as Bobby Kennedy's candidate to be assistant secretary of state: Robert Kennedy, oral history, JFK Library. In 1988, Connally made another astonishing assertion: that in 1962, Robert Kennedy had discussed with him the possibility of his replacing J. Edgar Hoover as director of the FBI. The author was able to find no corroboration of Connally's claim among Robert Kennedy's closest associates. Burke Marshall had never heard of the suggestion and found it "unlikely." Nor had Herbert J. Miller ever heard of the idea. Nicholas Katzenbach also had never heard of it and found it "incredible" and "beyond the pale of comprehension." Katzenbach added that President Kennedy and Robert Kennedy's plan was to force Hoover's retirement when he reached the age of seventy in 1965, but, given that the relationship between Connally and Robert Kennedy was "scarcely close," Connally was not a likely replacement. No record of any such possibility exists in the Robert Kennedy papers at the JFK Library. Connally's assertion is strange for another reason. One of the main reasons he was to give his closest friends for his switch to the Republican Party in 1973 was that the "Kennedy clan" would never allow Connally to capture the nomination of the Democratic party, for they harbored an eternal resentment of him over the Addison's disease controversy from the 1960 Democratic National Convention. (Burke Marshall, Herbert J. Miller, Nicholas Katzenbach, John Douglas, and Dr. Henry Gwiazda [archivist, RFK papers, JFK Library], interviews with author.

11. The Assassin

Oswald's plan to defect: Fort Worth Star Telegram: November 1, 14, and 15, 1959.

Oswald's diary: WC, vol. 16, CE 24.

Oswald in the American Embassy: Richard Edward Snyder and John A. McVickar, testimony, WC, vol. 5. Oswald's demeanor in his first appearance at the Moscow Embassy suggested to Snyder that this was the young man's "big moment in history" and that if he could stall him, Oswald would not be emotionally ready for a second performance in a few days.

Potential intelligence damage of Oswald's defection: John E. Donovan, testimony, WC, vol. 8.

Oswald's renunciation: It remains one of the ironies of history that, had the American consul, Richard Snyder, not been so sensitive about the perils of precipitous emotional renunciation of citizenship, Oswald would never have been permitted to reenter the United States. The author subscribes to this position, despite a letter Mr. Snyder wrote to the editor at *Time* magazine, after an excerpt of this book appeared in *Time* on November 25, 1988. Snyder contends as a technical matter that even if Oswald had succeeded in formally renouncing his citizenship, he could have obtained an immigrant's visa to return to "the land of his birth." The author believes that, given Oswald's fractured, emotional state of mind in 1962, he never would have pursued the bureaucratic wrangles that the application for an immigrant's visa would necessarily have entailed. (Richard E. Snyder, letter to the editor, *Time* magazine, December 1, 1988.)

Letter to Robert Oswald: November 26, 1959, WC, vol. 16, CE 295.

Russian attitude toward Oswald: Yury Nosenko (a KGB officer who later defected to the West), references in WC, including Commission Document 451, his interview by FBI, March 4, 1964; see also summation of the Nosenko testimony, House Assassinations Committee report, p. 101.

Oswald's life in Russia: His "historic" diary, WC, exhibits 24 and 101.

Letter to Robert Oswald: July 14, 1961, WC, vol. 16, CE 301.

Oswald's confession of MVD supplement: WC, CE 25.

Marguerite Oswald letter: WC, CE 270.

The entire Oswald discharge file: WC, vol. 19, Folsom Exhibit 1.

Bouhe's charity: George Bouhe, testimony, WC, vol. 8.

Oswald's antipathy to Connally: Alexandra de Mohrenshildt (Mrs. Donald Gibson), WC, vol. 11.

Oswald as welder: Tommy Bargas, testimony, WC, vol. 10.

Oswald at Jaggars-Chiles-Stovall: John G. Graef, WC, vol. 10.

General Walker assassination attempt: After an excerpt of this book appeared in *Time* magazine, November 25, 1988, the author heard from William McMahon, a former reporter for CBS and the *Philadelphia Bulletin*. McMahon related the information that after the Walker shooting, he had called the Dallas FBI and was informed that the FBI was not pursuing its investigation with any vigor. The Dallas agents had concluded that Walker had staged the assassination attempt himself to further his own political ambitions. McMahon has always felt that this was yet another cruel turn of fate, for, if the FBI had been more diligent in following up the Walker shooting, Oswald would never have had a shot at Connally and Kennedy a few months later.

Warren Commission dismissal of "Nixon Incident": WCR, pp. 175–176.

Connally's appearance on San Jacinto Day: *Dallas Morning News*, April 21, 1963.

Connally's criticism of JFK civil rights bill: *Houston Chronicle*, July 20, 1963; also see notes to chapter 14.

Oswald's speech in Mobile: WC, vol. 25, CE 2649. Exhibit 2648 comprises two letters from Oswald's cousin, Eugene Murret, one before his Mobile lecture and one afterwards. The August 22, 1963, letter shows that Oswald's speech was taken seriously and was a success. Also see FBI interview with Father Malcolm P. Mullen, S.J., professor of philosophy at Spring Hill College, who attended the Oswald lecture (WC, CE 2649). The actual quotes from Oswald's appearance come from a summary provided to the FBI by Robert Fitzpatrick, S.J., also contained in CE 2649.

The Oswalds' attitude toward Kennedy: McMillan, *Marina, and Lee*, p. 333.

De Mohrenshildt autobiography: In House Assassinations Committee supplementary material. References to Oswald's admiration of Kennedy are on p. 132.

Oswald as an agent of state violence: With such barely formed ideas, such grandiosity, such determined independence, Oswald was scarcely a good prospect to be recruited as an assassin by a foreign state. The author believes this firmly, partly from his own training in U.S. Army Intelligence in the recruitment of covert intelligence agents. If Cuba or the Soviet Union had wanted to assassinate an American president, they had far more reliable instruments of violence than Oswald.

A final note: The treatment of Oswald's motive for the assassination by both the Warren Commission and the House Assassinations Committee is woefully inadequate. The Warren Commission retreats into vague conclusions, referring to Oswald's "overriding hostility to his environment," and suggesting that the assassin was searching for "a place in history—a role as the 'great man' who would be recognized as having been in advance of his times." It also ascribes a "commitment to Marxism" as having played a part in his motivation. The House Assassinations Committee took a laundry-list approach to the motive, as it acknowledged that "finding a possible motive for Oswald's having assassinated President Kennedy was one of the most difficult issues that the Warren Commission faced." The House committee fell back on "politics" as the prime drive for Oswald's action: "It seems reasonable to conclude that the best single explanation for the assassination was his conception of political action, rooted in his twisted ideological view of himself and the world around him."

Finally, there was apparently some consideration of the possibility that Connally was Oswald's real target, as is indicated by a memo from Warren Commission assistant counsel David W. Belin to chief counsel J. Lee Rankin, January 30, 1964, entitled "Oswald's knowledge that Connally would be in the Presidential car and his intended target." Many years later, Belin would say that the commission rejected the possibility on the "common sense" grounds that if Connally was the target, Oswald would have fired as the presidential limousine approached the Book Depository rather than when it had already passed the building, and that Oswald had numerous other opportunities to kill Connally as he made public appearances around the state. (Belin interview on "U.S.A. Today on TV," February 20, 1988, and interview with author.)

The author believes there are answers to these objections. Oswald was not a stalker like, say, Governor Wallace's assailant, Arthur Bremer, and he did not have the funds to run all over the state after Connally. Moreover, the governor's travel schedule was not a matter of wide public knowledge. On November 22, Governor Connally, with President Kennedy, was coming right past the building in which Oswald worked. In addition, in the so-called "Nixon Incident," Oswald may well have strapped on his revolver to go after Connally as Connally was publicized to be in Dallas speaking to a space conference.

As for Oswald not shooting when the vehicle approached the building, this projects the discussion into the speculative realm of the criminal mind. For instance, Oswald may have felt he had a better chance of getting away if he fired when the vehicle was already past his sniper's nest than when it was approaching. Also, psychologists speak of a "motor program" that takes place in the mind of a person in a high state of excitement and anxiety, especially a life-and-death situation. Oswald was in such a state. In a "motor program," the person cannot be asked to make precise, intelligent judgments about fine points of reason and logic. It may be less important what Oswald was feeling and doing in the split seconds before he pulled the trigger than what was in his mind two days before the assassination when he settled upon his intention. (On "motor program": Dr. Thomas Gualtieri, an authority on neuropsychiatric disorders and their treatment, interview with author.)

12. Roads Taken and Not Taken
Connally's treatment of the Texas trip: Life, November 22, 1967 and his testimony to the House Assassinations Committee, 1979.

For Oswald's trip to Mexico City: For this and in much else that applies to Oswald's state of mind, I have relied on McMillan's excellent book, *Marina and Lee*. Oswald in Austin: Lee Dannelly, FBI interview, WC Exhibit 2137. William Stinson, interview with author. As Governor Connally's aide, Stinson confirmed that attempts were made to verify Oswald's presence in Austin after the assassination, but the effort did not appear to go much beyond checking to see if Oswald had signed the Governor's guest book. The *Texas Observer* also wrote about this possibility, December 27, 1963.

Dallas loves Connally: William Stinson, interview with author.

Connally loves Dallas: William Manchester, interview with author. In his interview with Connally for his book *The Death of a President*, Manchester was horrified at Connally's undemocratic instincts; the governor's attitude toward Dallas politics was the prime example. Connally's elitist instincts fit perfectly Manchester's definition of a fascist; Manchester believed that the American system was intended to exclude politicians like Connally.

The Stevenson incident: The incident in Dallas in which Adlai Stevenson was spat upon does not redound to Connally's credit, but there is a touching element in the episode. Stevenson was coming to Texas to give a speech in connection with United Nations Day on October 24. When the right-wing hotheads made a fuss about Stevenson's appearance, Connally pandered to them by declaring October 24 also to be United States Day in Texas. With this apparent official sanction, a mob surrounded Stevenson after his speech, spat upon him, and bonked him on the head with a placard.

Connally was horrified. Immediately, he issued a statement to the press decrying the incident, and wrote Stevenson a personal note of apology. On November 1, Stevenson replied, thanking the governor for his note and asserting that, but for a "minute handful," his reception in Dallas had been warm.

"After this incident, I feel all the more confident that the President's visit to Texas will be gratifying—to you as well as to him!" Stevenson wrote.

Two weeks later, on November 13, only nine days before the Dallas motorcade, Connally replied: "Of course as Governor of Texas I was distressed by what occurred, but extremely proud of you and the way you handled the entire matter both at the time and later in the press. Your graciousness is deeply appreciated. We are looking forward to the President's visit and, like you, I am confident that it will be both pleasant and rewarding."

The letter was handed to the U.N. ambassador a few minutes after he had heard the news of the shooting in Dallas.

Skelton's letters: Part of the reason why Skelton's letters about danger in Dallas were dismissed is, in my view, that he was arguing his own special interest so passionately. He wanted Kennedy to attend the dedication of the Stillhouse Hollow Dam on the Lampasas River during the President's visit to Texas, because the dam was in his Central Texas region. On May 17, he wrote to Johnson's aide Cliff Carter:

> It will be recalled that the President and the Vice President were elected by the great Central Texas area extending from Beaumont to Abilene and from Dallas to Austin by a narrow margin of 45,000 votes. Bob Poage's [the powerful congressman from Waco and chairman of the House Agriculture Committee] district alone contributed 15,000 of these votes. They did not carry Fort Worth, Dallas, San Antonio or Houston, and yet these cities have received practically every major appointment under this Administration. As you know, not a single appointment has been made of anyone in the Central Texas area. There is considerable dissatisfaction and grumbling here over this fact, and if we are now by-passed in preference to the Republican cities, which voted against us, it will be more than serious.

Fulbright as Cassandra: Senator William J. Fulbright, interview with author.

Connally's meeting with congressmen: Connally, testimony before the House Assassinations Committee, 1979; Henry Gonzalez, interview with author.

Oval office conversation between Kennedy and Connally: Connally, testimony before House Assassinations Committee, 1979.

Jarnagin: The entire dialogue that Jarnagin committed to paper is contained in the Warren Commission file as Exhibit 2821. Jarnagin appeared on "USA Today on TV" on February 20, 1988, when he again asserted that the essence of what he heard at the Carousel Club was a conversation about killing the governor of Texas. Through an attorney in San Antonio, the author also made a discreet check on Jarnagin's reputation. From a judge before whom Jarnagin had practiced law, and who knew him personally, the author gained the impression that Jarnagin, while eccentric in some of his personal habits, is a credible witness, and that his testimony deserved to be taken seriously by the Warren Commission, the Ruby trial judge, and other agencies who have looked into a possible Ruby-Oswald connection. (Shirley Ann Mauldin, also known as Miss Robin S. Hood, FBI interview, December 9, 1963, WC, Henry Wade, testimony, WC, vol. 5, and interview with author; Jarnagin, interview with author.)

LBJ attitude towards a possible Cuban conspiracy: In Johnson's CBS interview with Walter Cronkite, September 23, 1969, Johnson was asked about a possible international conspiracy behind Oswald. He replied: "I can't honestly say that I've ever been completely relieved of the fact that it might have been international connections," he replied.

"You mean you still feel that there might have been?" Cronkite asked.

"Well, I have not completely discounted it."

"What direction does your lingering suspicion lead you? To Cuba? Is that the area that you feel might have been involved?"

"Oh, I don't think we ought to discuss suspicions because there is not any hard evidence that led me to the conclusion that Oswald was directed by a foreign government or that his sympathies for other governments could have spurred him on in this effort. But he was quite a mysterious fellow, and he did have a connection that bore an examination. [On the] extent of the influence of those connections on him, I think, history will deal with much more than we are able to now."

Upon the advice of Johnson's staff, this interchange was specifically cut for "national security" reasons from the CBS broadcast; (Bob Hardesty memo and Mildred Stegall memo, April 28, 1975, LBJ Library).

A real agent of state assassination: For a contrast to Oswald, see the report of the Church Committee hearings, U.S. Senate, in 1975 on the subject of "Alleged Assassination Plots Involving Foreign Leaders." Particularly interesting is the section on Cuba and the American agent called AM/LASH, a high official in the Cuban government, who was being groomed for a possible assassination attempt on Castro, and who was being provided with poisoned cigars, poisoned pens, and other instruments of assassination.

The Church committee established that Allen Dulles, later one of the Warren Commission members, knew about the plots to assassinate Fidel Castro which were being developed within the CIA. It would not have been a huge leap of psychology for Dulles to assume that the Castro government was plotting an assassination in the same way.

On page 72 of the Church Committee report, there is this sentence: "The most ironic of these [American assassination] plots took place on November 22, 1963—the very day that President Kennedy was shot in

Dallas—when a CIA official offered a poison pen to a Cuban for use against Castro while at the same time an emissary from President Kennedy was meeting with Castro to explore the possibility of improved relations."

Connally on motorcades: Connally, testimony before the House Assassinations Committee, 1979.

Bruno references: Jerry Bruno, interview with author; his notes from the Dallas advance team and diary, JFK Library; and his testimony before the House Assassinations Committee, 1979.

Excerpts from the Bruno diary:

October 28: Talked with Senator Yarborough. The Senator was bitter because he was afraid that Connally would run the show with Lyndon Johnson and he didn't trust the two of them. Yarborough said, "They never liked Jack Kennedy—they never have and they never will. I'll give you a man in each city to help you with the details."

. . . It was obvious from talking that the problem surrounding the whole trip revolved around Don Yarborough, who indicated he would run against Governor Connally in the gubernatorial primary. Connally wanted President Kennedy to stop Yarborough by using his influence.

October 29: Met with Hank Brown, president of AFL/CIO, a liberal and a friend of Senator Yarborough. . . . He warned me that Connally would try to run the show and keep labor from participating.

October 30: [Dallas] I objected to the Trade Mart because it had four cat walks that went across the hall where it would be easy for someone to insult the President and where it would be difficult to get him off without creating a scene.

November 5: I began to find out why Governor Connally was so violently opposed to the Fair Grounds. His intention was to have two head tables, on two tiers, one which would seat the President, himself, the Vice President, and the head of the [Dallas] Citizens Council. The other would seat a Congressional delegation and would purposely eliminate Yarborough. The Fair Grounds had a low ceiling that would not accommodate Connally's plan. Connally continued to insist that if the President would not speak at the Trade Mart, he would not come to Dallas.

November 15: I met with O'Donnell and Moyers who said that Connally was unbearable and on the verge of cancelling the trip. They decided they had to let the Governor have his way.

Book Depository: The Texas State Book Depository had no particular significance for the authorities before the assassination, of course—but it should have had. The local FBI had an active case file on Oswald and it should have been even more active than it was in light of the shooting episode, involving General Walker. In early November the agent in charge knew where Oswald had gone to work. Later, the bureau would say that it had no reason to consider Oswald dangerous, but the assassination led to considerable study within security circles about the general psychological profile for potential presidential assassins.

13. November 21–22, 1963

Congressman Gonzalez on Air Force 1: Henry B. Gonzalez, interview with author.

Yarborough on Air Force 1: Ralph Yarborough, interview with author; "long knives of Austin," is from Manchester, *Death of a President*, and Jerry Bruno diary, JFK Library.

Gonzalez on "how easy it would be": Gonzalez, interview with author.

Arrival in Texas: John and Nellie Connally, testimony, WC, vol. 4, and to House Assassinations Committee, 1979.

Scene at the Rice Hotel, Houston: Ralph Yarborough, interview with author; Connally, "Why Kennedy Came to Texas," *Life* magazine, November 22, 1967.

Connally's wild ride through Houston: Judge John V. Singleton, Jr., memoir attached to his oral history, LBJ Library, and interview with author.

Houston Chronicle poll: November 22, 1963; and Ralph Yarborough, interview with author.

Johnson and Kennedy at the Rice: Manchester, *Death of the President*, p. 82.

The distaste of many intelligent women for Connally: Liz Carpenter, interview with author.

Jackie on Connally: her oral history, LBJ Library.

JFK quote on Connally-Yarborough rift and his premonition: Lawrence O'Brien, interview with author and his book *No Final Victories;* and his testimony, WC, vol. 7.

In the lobby of the Texas Hotel: Lawrence O'Brien, William Stinson, and Ralph Yarborough, interviews with author.

JFK to Connally at breakfast: Connally, *Life*, November 22, 1967; his testimony before House Assassinations Committee.

Connally's press conference in Texas Hotel: Kantor Exhibit 3, WC, vol. 20; also Charles Roberts, oral history, JFK Library. In the Roberts oral history, he is asked if he thought the trip to Texas was succeeding in patching up the feuds in the Texas Democratic party. "We were not only under that impression, we had been told by some of the principals that [the trip] was having a therapeutic effect," Roberts replied. Before leaving . . . Fort Worth, we had a quick session with Connally, and Connally gave us to understand that both the president and the vice president had pretty well impressed him [and Yarborough] with the necessity of closing ranks and burying the hatchet."

Kennedy-Johnson interchange in Fort Worth hotel: LBJ interview with Walter Cronkite, CBS, May 2, 1970.

The second premonition: Kenneth O'Donnell, testimony, WC, vol. 4; Manchester, *Death of a President*, p. 121.

Connally permission for Yarborough to sit at head table: Bishop, *Day Kennedy Was Shot*, p. 124.

The motorcade: William Stinson, Connally's aide in Dallas, drove the motorcade route with the author and provided his recollections; Stinson also took the author to Parkland Hospital. For other recollections: Ralph Yarborough and Larry O'Brien, interviews with author; Charles Roberts, oral history, JFK Library.

Dialogue in presidential limosine: Connally, "Why Kennedy Came to Texas," *Life* magazine, November 22, 1967.

Sixth floor of the depository: Roy S. Truly testimony, WC, vols. 3 and 4.

Connally's flashback to his youth: Outtakes from interview conducted by Skip Hollandsworth, "USA Today on TV," February 20, 1989, provided to the author; Connally on "Geraldo" program, November 23, 1988; Manchester, *Death of a President*, p. 160.

Nellie's remark: her testimony, before House Assassinations Committee, 1979.

Dialogue between Stinson and Dr. Red Duke: William Stinson, interview with author.

Connally's medical condition at Parkland: Dr. Charles Gregory and Dr. Robert Shaw, testimony, WC, vol. 4; William Stinson, interview with author; "Three Patients at Parkland," *Texas State Journal of Medicine*, vol. 60, January 1964.

Lyndon Johnson at Parkland: Henry Gonzalez, interview with author.

Lady Bird's comfort for Jackie and Nellie: Lady Bird memo, June 15, 1964, special file on assassination, LBJ Library and her *White House Diary;* Manchester, *Death of a President*, p. 236.

LBJ drive to Love Field: Henry Wade, interview with author. Police officers joked with Wade later about LBJ's terror and undignified behavior.

Radio traffic from Air Force One: "Angel" recording, November 22, 1963., LBJ Library.

Lady Bird's actions: Liz Carpenter, recollections of November 22, 1963, manuscript, LBJ Library.

14. Governor for Life

Old saw about legislative committees: *Time* magazine, April 15, 1966. The story was a favorite of LBJ's.

Poverty and Discrimination in Texas: Hearing before U.S. Civil Rights Commission, San Antonio, December 9–14, 1963; staff report, U.S. Civil Rights Commission: *Civil Rights, U.S.A./Public Schools, Southern States,* 1963; other commission documents: *Public Education 1963; Public Education, 1964 (Southern & Border States); Civil Rights in Texas,* 1970; *The Civil Rights Status of Spanish Speaking Americans in Kleberg, Nueces and San Patricio Counties, Texas, 1967.*

W. W. Rostow interchange with Connally: Rostow, interview with author. Connally, first message to the Legislature, *Houston Chronicle*, January 27, 1963.

Larry Temple's opposition to Connally's civil rights speech of July 19, 1963: Temple, oral history, LBJ Library.

July 19 speech: transcript, LBJ Library.

Memo re Connally speech: staff memo to LBJ, July 22, 1963, Vice Presidential Papers, LBJ Library.

Hobart Taylor, Jr., to LBJ: August 5, 1963, Vice Presidential Papers, LBJ Library.

Rauh and LBJ: Joe Rauh, interview with author; Lee C. White, memo to LBJ, December 19, 1963, LBJ Library.

Kilgore contretemps: Larry Temple, George Christian and Jake Pickle, oral histories, LBJ Library; Julian Read, George Christian, and Creekmore Fath, interviews with author. On Don Yarborough: Billie Carr, interview with author.

"Whole stake": Lady Bird Johnson, interview with author.

Yarborough comment about Connally sling: Billie Carr, interview with author.

The London suit: Frank Ikard, interview with author.

Bob Bullock remark: Ashman, Adventures of Big Bad John, pg. 284; quote confirmed in Bullock letter to author.

Connally in Laredo: confidential interview; also Loyd Hackler, interview with author.

Lady in question: confidential interviews; substance confirmed by Molly Ivins, Maury Maverick, Jr., Loyd Hackler, and Larry King.

LBJ at San Marcos: Johnson, Presidential Papers.

San Marcos situation: Sargeant Shriver and Julian Read, interviews with author.

Connally veto: Sargent Shriver letter to Johnson, May 5, 1965, LBJ Library.

Head Start figures: Marvin Watson letter to LBJ, August 31, 1965, LBJ Library.

Yarborough to U.S. Senate: August 17, 1965, *Congressional Record.*

Connally's attitude toward federal interference: Julian Read, interview with author.

Connally-Shriver meeting: Sargent Shriver, interview with author.

Connally-Watson recorded conversation: February 3, 1966, released to author after challenge of confidentiality, LBJ Library.

Skit of North Dallas women: *Texas Observer,* May 14, 1965.

Sharp contrast between Connally and LBJ on political satire: Cactus Pryor and John Henry Faulk, interviews with author.

Connally on poverty: Loyd Hackler, interview with author.

"Give 'em education': *Texas Observer* May 14, 1965.

Nellie's accomplishments with governor's mansion: Lady Bird Johnson, interview with author.

Inaugural speech and speech to legislature: *Austin American* and *Dallas Morning News,* January 27 and 28, 1965.

HemisFair: January 15, 1966 press conference at HemisFair; January 15, 1969, Report to Legislature; Sue Bitner Vickers, "HemisFair 1968," master's thesis, University of Texas at Austin, 1968; all provided to the author by Institute for Texan Cultures, San Antonio.

Connally attitude towards legislators: Connally luncheon remarks, Rice University symposium, September 30, 1988.

Cosmetology remark: Ibid.

Connally appointment of minorities: Loyd Hackler, Joe Bernal, and Ruben Mungia, Jr., interviews with author; Paul Burka article in *Texas Monthly,* November 1979, on appointment black to prison commission.

Showdown at New Braunfels: Joe Bernal, Loyd Hackler, Julian Reed, interviews with author; *Texas Observer* coverage, including transcript of roadside exchanges, August and September 1966 and June 9, 1967; U.S. Civil Rights Commission, *The Civil Rights Status of Spanish Speaking Americans in Kleberg, Nueces and San Patricio Counties, Texas, 1967.*

Manchester admiration of JFK: Manchester, *Controversy,* p. 3.

Connally on Kennedy response: Marvin Watson to LBJ, February 21, 1966, LBJ Library.

"Rift" between Johnson and Connally: *New York Times,* March 12, 1966, and June 5, 1966.

Maury Maverick remark: Robert Sherrill, "Politics on the King Ranch," *New York Times Magazine*, June 5, 1966.

Valenti-Manchester meeting: Memo for Valenti, May 10, 1965, Assassination File, LBJ Library; Manchester, interview with author.

Connally's coarse, angry epithets for LBJ: William Stinson and Loyd Hackler, interviews with author.

Rowe letter to LBJ: December 15, 1966, LBJ Library.

Jacobsen's page-by-page analysis of Manchester book: Assassination File, LBJ Library.

Connally blast at Manchester: *Dallas Times Herald*, Jan. 11, 1967.

Legislature action: *Journal of the Senate of the State of Texas*, Sixtieth Session, vol. 1, January 12, 1967.

Connally's satisfaction with blast: George Christian memo to president, January 13, 1967, LBJ Library.

Connally rendition of assassination: Connally, *Life* magazine, November 22, 1967.

Connally request for Oswald letter: George Christian letter to Paul Nitze, secretary of the navy, October 12, 1967; also *Houston Post*, November 29, 1987.

Connally's fascination with Oswald's letter may well have gone back to the very first moment he received it in 1962. His aide when he was secretary of the navy, Captain Andy Kerr, USNR (ret.) published a book in 1987 in which he asserted that Connally had, in fact, paid considerable attention to Oswald's letter when it was first received. "Connally called me . . . to ask a couple of questions about the Oswald case, which seemed to interest him," Kerr recalled about a day early in 1962. "He [felt] that the case had overtones which he wanted to be sure to understand, but after talking about it, he agreed that the referral to the Commandant [of the Marine Corps], which was basically a kiss off, was the way it should be handled, and he initialed the buck slip." Additionally, Kerr asserted that, when Connally came to Washington to testify to the Warren Commission, he made a special trip to the navy secretary's office and asked for the original of the Oswald letter. Kerr looked for the letter in the navy's files but could not find it, because, of course, it had been sent to the Warren Commission.

It remains both a mystery and a clear oversight as to why the Warren Commission did not pursue a line of questioning with Connally about the Oswald letter. (Kerr, *Journey Amongst the Good and the Great*, and his oral history, Chester W. Nimitz Library, Annapolis, Md.)

National Archives response: Marion Johnson, Warren Commission archivist, memo to archivist of United States, October 12, 1967, and archivist's negative response, National Archives; Marion Johnson, interview with author.

15. The Catalyst

Nellie's remark about the change: her testimony, House Assassinations Committee, 1979.

Connally's loss of optimism: Edward Harte, interview with author.

Safari: *Texas Magazine, Houston Chronicle*, February 11, 1968.

Johnson's mood swings: Harry McPherson oral history, LBJ Library; Goodwin, *Remembering America*.

Connally at LBJ ranch, July 31, 1967: Lady Bird Johnson, *White House Diary*, p. 567.

McNamara remark: LBJ's interview with Walter Cronkite, CBS, December 27, 1969, "Why I Chose Not to Run."

Connally-Christian in October: George Christian, oral history, LBJ Library; his book, *A President Steps Down;* interview with author; his article, "The Night Lyndon Quit," *Texas Monthly*, April 1988.

LBJ attitude toward Connally resignation: Johnson, *Vantage Point*, p. 42.

Post-Christmas visit to LBJ Ranch: Lady Bird Johnson, *White House Diary*, pp. 611–12.

Aquatic images in State of Union message: Harry McPherson, oral history, LBJ Library; Jim Jones, interview with author.

Busby memo: Container 274, LBJ Library, January 15, 1968.

State of the union night: Lady Bird Johnson, *White House Diary*, pp. 617–20.

Billy Graham recommendation: Richard V. Pierard, "Billy Graham and the U.S. Presidency", *Journal of Church and State*, vol. 22, no. 1, Winter 1980, p. 124.

Connally gala at UT: *Daily Texan*, February 28, 1968, Barker Collection.

Launching Johnson presidential campaign: Cecil Burney, interview with author.

Turning Vietnam policy around: Harry McPherson, oral history, LBJ Library.

Colloquy between Johnson and O'Brien: O'Brien, interview with author, and *No Final Victories*.

Johnson to Stinson: William Stinson, interview with author.

Reston anecdote: James Reston, interview with author.

16. A Pyrrhic Defeat

Post-March 31 jockeying: *Dallas Morning News*, April 1–7, 1968.

Barbara Jordan reaction to Connally insensitivity: Jordan, *A Self-Portrait*, and interview with author.

Allegiance of the Connally crowd: Robert Strauss, Bill Stinson, Jake Jacobsen, Jim Jones, Ted Van Dyk, and Lawrence O'Brien, interviews with author.

Connally around poor people: Jim Jones, interview with author.

Connally attitude toward Humphrey: This is clear from Connally's actions throughout this entire period and confirmed by author interview with Ted Van Dyk. Additionally, there is a historical irony here. In 1964, when Johnson was considering the choice of his running mate, Connally pushed for Eugene McCarthy rather than Hubert Humphrey to get the job (Goldman, *Tragedy of Lyndon Johnson*, p. 206).

Robert Kennedy view of LBJ as animal and perpetual liar: Robert Kennedy, oral history, JFK Library.

"Meet the Press": April 21, 1968; transcript courtesy of NBC.

Politics aboard the USS *Independence*: *Washington Post*, October 18–21, 1967.

Connally and Party: Connally would often say later, after he switched to the Republican Party that the Democratic Party had left him, not vice versa, but it was an exercise in wordplay. For ideological reasons having to do with Vietnam and Civil Rights, for deep personal reasons based upon his intimacy with Lyndon Johnson, and for the methodological reasons that the unit rule and other basic rules of old-style American politics were changing, Connally was simply left behind.

While Connally focused on national politics through the spring of 1968, he also had to keep an eye on the home front, where things were not going so well either. In May the liberals succeeded in clobbering Connally's choice for his successor as governor. That was Eugene Locke, whose main qualification for the governorship was that he had been an assistant ambassador to South Vietnam. But Locke was a terrible candidate, a man so pompous, it was said, that he was the only man in Texas who could strut while seated (Bob Armstrong, interview with author). Locke came in fifth, and the liberals were jubilant.

At the Cincinnati governors' conference, the presidential candidacy of George Wallace was the chief concern. That candidacy was showing itself to be so strong, both in the North and the South, that the topic of the moment was an initiative for a constitutional amendment to ensure that the candidate with the largest plurality would be president, even if he polled less than a majority of the popular vote. Connally refused to support the initiative. He did not believe the election would be decided in the House, and moreover, though he did not say it, he did not want to alienate the Wallace supporters who were potentially part of his constituency.

Reedy memo: George Reedy to LBJ, July 24, 1968, concerning inquiry of *U.S. News & World Report* correspondent Jack Sutherland, LBJ Library.

Kennedy's Worcester speech and its impact: McCarthy, *Year of the People;* New York Times coverage, August 22, 1968.

LBJ's temperament at the Ranch: Jim Jones, interview with author. Jones was with the president at the ranch. From electronic intercepts of diplomatic cables, the White House knew that the Russians were subject to a romantic misinterpretation of the American political system, and thus the spectacle of Chicago could have immediate foreign policy ramifications for Johnson, in Vietnam and elsewhere.

LBJ's attitude toward draft: Jim Jones, interview with author; George Christian and Larry Temple, oral histories, LBJ Library.

Slur on the Mississippi Freedom Party in 1964: Joseph L. Rauh, Jr., interview with author; also quoted in Sitkoff, *Struggle for Black Equality,* p. 182.

Rauh's threat to bolt: *Chicago Tribune,* August 21, 1968.

LBJ threat to deny Texas to Humphrey: George Ball, interview with author. Ball had resigned from his post as United Nations ambassador to become a Humphrey campaign adviser.

Humphrey and Vietnam: The Humphrey "break" with Johnson Vietnam policy did not come until September 30 in Salt Lake City, and only then when he learned that the negotiations in Paris were utterly dead. For his vacillation on this issue throughout his bid for the presidency, Humphrey is derided, even by his closest and dearest advisers. Ted Van Dyk, in author interview, said he knew that in his heart, Humphrey had wanted to break with Johnson as far back as April, but never had the courage to do so. Humphrey was, by nature, a conciliator, who shrank from confrontation. In Connally, this elicited only contempt, for he considered it simply weakness. Nevertheless, after his Salt Lake City speech, Humphrey's standing in the polls rose every day, but he had begun too late (George Ball, interview with author).

Connally incensed: William Connell, interview with author.

O'Brien-Harris meeting with Connally: O'Brien and Harris, interviews with author.

Jim Jones memos: LBJ Library.

Goodwin's meeting with Strauss and Connally: Robert Strauss and Eugene McCarthy, interviews with author.

McCarthy views contrary to Connally: Eugene McCarthy, interview with author. This story reappeared in the press in 1988 in a column by George Will, and to the author, McCarthy was intent to show that he had more views in opposition to Connally than he ever had in concert with him.

Larry O'Brien remark: :O'Brien, interview with author, and *No Final Victories*, p. 252.

Lady Bird's excitement: Lady Bird Johnson, *White House Diary*, p. 705.

Connally's visit to Humphrey headquarters: William Connell, interview with author; Solberg, *Hubert Humphrey*, p. 360.

Jesse Unruh relishing the arrival of the Great Cowboy: Chester et al., *American Melodrama*, p. 540.

Choice of running mates: The tactics of Southerners, demanding a running mate acceptable to them, had a parallel in the Republican National Convention only a few weeks before. Richard Nixon had acquiesced in that very same kind of power play when he made Spiro Agnew his running mate. This had been well reported and was now on the Democrats' minds. Herein lay the last hope of Connally, to be chosen in this year of ideas solely on the basis of the power he wielded in the South.

Last power play: Ted Van Dyk, interview with author.

17. Turning

Inside the presidential limousine: Jim Jones, interview with author.

Nixon to Haldeman re Texas vote stealing: Nixon, *RN*, p. 332.

Johnson takes charge with Strauss: Robert Strauss, interview with author.

Rumor of Connally endorsing Nixon: Ted Van Dyk, interview with author.

Luring Connally into the Nixon administration: Roy Ash, interview with author.

The Connally-Bentsen relationship: Lloyd Bentsen, interview with author.

Nofziger memo: Lyn Nofziger, interview with author.

"Exhausted volcanoes": Nixon, *RN*, p. 768; William Safire, interview with author.

Dumping David Kennedy: H. R. Haldeman, handwritten notes, Nixon Project.

No hero: Peter O'Donnell letter to Peter Flanigan, November 1, 1970; Flanigan letter to H. R. Haldeman, November 15, 1970; Flanigan letter to O'Donnell, November 16, 1970; William Timmons letter to Haldeman, December 1, 1970. To Timmons's objections, Haldeman penned the following on the Timmons memo: "This is not a major appointment [Connally's appointment to the Foreign Intelligence Advisory Board] and is not made to 'give recognition' to Connally. It is a bipartisan board with no visibility and P. needed a strong Democrat member for obvious reasons in connection with our foreign policy. Connally, as you know, was helpful in getting reorgan. passed on the Hill & can be very helpful in foreign policy areas of great importance" (Nixon Project).

Bush attitude towards Connally: Timmons memo, December 1, 1970: "As you know, John Tower and George Bush are extremely upset over the appointment of Connally. . . ." (Nixon Project).

Haldeman's handwritten notes: arranged by date, Nixon Project.

The education of John Connally: Paul Volcker, Jim Smith, and Bruce MacLaury, interviews with author;

Tutorials with William McChesney Martin: Mayer, *Fate of the Dollar,* p. 18.

Wall Street session: The dinner was hosted by New York Bankers and arranged by Hoyt Ammidon, Chairman of the Board of US Trust. Afterwards, Ammidon wrote the White House saying Connally had made a "terrific impression" (Nixon Project). Arthur Burns memo to Nixon, February 10, 1971, Nixon Project.

Preparing for confirmation: Dean, *Lost Honour;* Ehrlichman, recorded conversation with Connally, January 7, 1971, Nixon Project.

In ethical borderland: Article 4, Section 6 of the Texas constitution reads: "During the time he holds the office of Governor, he shall not hold any other office: civil, military or corporate; nor shall he practice any profession and receive compensation, reward, fee or the promise thereof for the same; nor receive any salary, reward or compensation or the promise thereof from any person or corporation for any service rendered or performed during the time he is Governor."

Connally's argument was that his Richardson work came before he was governor and was therefore exempt from this provision. The schedule of payments from the Richardson Foundation during the time he was governor was as follows:

December 31, 1964	$100,000
March 12, 1965	$100,000
April 20, 1965	$75,000
January 3, 1966	$75,000
January 3, 1967	$75,000
January 3, 1968	$75,000
January 2, 1969	$75,000

The total in fees received while governor: $575,000. (Confirmation hearings before Senate Finance Committee, February 1971.)

Senator Fred Harris at the Connally confirmation: Harris, interview with author.

18. A Most Unusual Finance Minister

Nixon memo to Haldeman: March 1, 1971, Nixon Project.

Blair House dinner: March 8, 1971, tape at Nixon Project.

Mitchell on presidential image: *Washington Post* Style section, March 8, 1971.

Haldeman action memo, March 22, 1971: Haldeman notes, Nixon Project.

"Talk to Connally. He understands me": William Safire, interview with author.

Petersen's Principle of Interlocking Neuroses: *New Republic,* July 1, 1972. Petersen came to regret the application of his principle, which he had generally reserved for marriages, to the Connally-Nixon relationship, for its publication in this *New Republic* piece had evidently caused him some embarrassment. Petersen, telephone conversation with author.

Connally takes charge: Paul Volcker, Jim Smith, Herbert Stein, William Safire, Bruce MacLaury, interviews with author.

Connally on loyalty: Bruce MacLaury, interview with author. As MacLaury listened to Connally's first major talk with his subcabinet and senior staff and heard Connally speak of loyalty in such absolute terms, he was wary. MacLaury believed that Lyndon Johnson had gotten in such trouble over Vietnam partly because many of his senior advisers and cabinet members were afraid to express their disagreement with the President. Since Connally appeared to many to be a Johnson clone, MacLaury worried about what sort of Vietnam might loom at the Treasury, where Connally would permit no dissent. As time passed, MacLaury's worries were put aside. Connally invited heated debate within the Treasury and he was often ambivalent himself on major issues, such as the Lockheed bailout. But MacLaury admired the way that Connally acted when a complicated issue was on the table. He could weigh each side openly and fairly, but when he went to the White House and a decision was made, he suspended doubts altogether and embraced the administration decision foursquare.

A new power as an old shotgun: Jim Smith, interview with author. Smith was the treasury lobbyist on Capitol Hill during Connally's tenure.

Lockheed: Connally testimony, June 7–8, 1971, before Senate Banking Committee; John Kenneth Galbraith, Alan Greenspan, David Packard, and Arthur Burns, testimony before same committee; Senator William Proxmire, Jim Smith, interviews with author.

Connally and bankruptcy: Though he could not know it, the Lockheed situation foreshadowed in macroeconomics what Connally himself was to go through fifteen years later in private business. He too would be personally guilty of mismanagement and poor investment, and he would look to government to bail him out and thereby to excuse him from the normal consequences of business failure. Texas as a whole and Connally in particular had not planned for bad economic times in the 1980s. He came to be associated with the rally call of "borrow, borrow, borrow" and the roots for this attitude extended back to his Treasury days and even before that. To his departing assistant secretary of the treasury, Bruce MacLaury, who was going into private business, Connally had one piece of advice: "Go out and borrow as much money as you can. Then you'll have to work hard to pay it off. When it's over, you'll have some assets" (MacLaury, interview with author).

To be vigorous and from Texas was to believe in an ever-rising, brilliant rocket of an economy and to ignore the warnings about gas eating at the O-rings of the economy. That very failure in his own personal business was made all the more astonishing by the fact that he had dealt with bankruptcy at the epic level of the Lockheed Corporation. In his own business life, he apparently had learned no lesson.

Goldwater position on Lockheed: contributed by Kenneth A. McLean, aide to Senator Proxmire, during author interview with Proxmire.

Bretton Woods system: Gardner, *Sterling-Dollar Diplomacy;* Harrod, *Reforming the World's Money;* Mayer, *Fate of the Dollar.*

JFK's concern about balance of payments: Schlesinger, *Thousand Days;* Ball, *Past Has Another Pattern,* and his oral history, LBJ Library.

"Bleeding gold": W. W. Rostow, interview with author.

The Munich speech: transcript, Department of Treasury Library; Paul Volcker, interview with author; Mayer, *Fate of the Dollar,* pp. 181–83.

The "Four Nos": Connally press conference, June 29, 1971, transcript, Department of Treasury Library. Nixon-Connally meeting with Congressional leaders, July 15, 1971: Nixon, RN, page 518; Herbert Stein, interview with author.

History at Camp David, August 13–15: Safire, *Before the Fall;* William Safire, Herbert Stein, Paul Volcker, W. W. Rostow, and Eugene Rostow, interviews with author.

Haldeman's stage whisper: Safire, *Before the Fall,* p. 518.

Dialogue: Safire, *Before the Fall,* and interview with author. Safire kept detailed notes of what each participant said at Camp David, for he knew he was witnessing history. But, as he told the author, he also intended the write a book later, and he suspected that there was a taping system in place at Camp David (which there was). He did not want to be proved wrong years later when those tapes were released.

Stein and Shakespeare: Stein, Presidential Economics and interview with author.

Ashes and sackcloth: Paul Volcker, interview with author.

Nixon's admiration of Connally's press conference: In *RN*, p. 519, Nixon describes Connally's performance as "brilliant."

The wisdom of wage and price controls: Eugene Rostow, interview with author and "Devaluation by Agreement, not Fiat," op-ed piece, *New York Times,* September 5, 1971; Rostow was sharply critical. In *Secrets of the Temple,* William Greider remarks: "If historians searched for the precise date on which America's singular dominance of the world economy ended, they might settle on August 15, 1971. On that day, President Nixon abruptly changed the monetary rules under which nations had traded with one another for 25 years. . . . Nixon's decision was a momentous change, sowing global controversy and economic dislocation over the next 15 years" (p. 334). By contrast, Herbert Stein, in author interview remained opposed to wage and price controls philosophically, although he felt that the country had survived the experiment, while he supported completely the closing of the gold window. Paul Volcker, in author interview, expressed nearly the opposite view. He thought wage and price controls were necessary but was not sure the closing of the gold window and the destruction of the Bretton Woods system so totally had been a good idea.

The second attempt at wage and price controls: Roy Ash and Herbert Stein, interviews with author. In his interview, Ash told of the debate over a second imposition of a milder form of wage and price controls in 1973. At that point, Connally was acting as a presidential counselor. Then, the four economic advisers were bitterly opposed to a second experiment. As Nixon went off to Key Biscayne for a weekend, he asked the four advisers and Connally and Ash to each submit a one-page statement of their views. Connally and Ash alone supported new measures, and over the opposition of his professional economists, controls were reimposed. Uniformly, the second experiment is considered a total failure.

19. The Great Jawbone

London meeting: *Wall Street Journal*, September 16, 1971.

The economists and Connally: Herbert Stein and Paul Volcker, interviews with author; Stein, *Presidential Economics*.

Kissinger on Connally: Kissinger, *White House Years* pp. 952–53.

Dialogue between LBJ and Ball: Ball, interview with author, and his book, *Past Has Another Pattern*, p. 320, 321.

Ball on Connally arrogance: Ball, *Diplomacy for a Crowded World*, p. 156.

Volcker attitude: Volcker, interview with author.

Connally-Schweitzer relationship: George Ball, interview with author and Schweitzer, letter to author, December 6, 1988.

"Dirty floats": *New York Times* and *Wall Street Journal*, October 1, 1971.

Connally in Japan: Richard Halloran, interview with author. Halloran was *New York Times* correspondent in Tokyo in 1971; *New York Times*, November 9–12, 1971.

Nixon to Kissinger: memo, November 12, 1971, Nixon Library.

Squeezing the maximum: Kissinger, *White House Years*, p. 958; Ball, *Diplomacy for a Crowded World*, pg. 156.

Rome meeting: Paul Volcker, interview with author; Mayer, *Fate of the Dollar*, pp. 199–202.

Connally's broad authority from Nixon: Roger B. Porter, "Economic Advice to the President: Eisenhower to Reagan," paper read at 81st annual meeting of American Political Science Association, New York, September 3–6, 1981.

Kissinger taking credit: *White House Years*, p. 959.

Azores meeting: Volcker, interview with author; Connally, press conference in Azores, tape, Nixon Project.

Dialogue at bipartisan meeting: Safire, memorandum, December 15, 1971, President's File, Nixon Project.

Dialogue between Connally and Shiller: Mayer, *Fate of the Dollar*, p. 200.

"Cheese became binding": Connally press conference, December 21, 1971, Nixon Project.

20. Unholy Trinity

Evening at Deason's: Margaret Mayer, interview with author.

Haldeman "action memo": February 1, 1972, Nixon Project.

"Oak-paneled rooms": Liz Carpenter, interview with author.

Connally never talking behind Nixon's back: Kissinger, *White House Years*, p. 951.

Colson "eyes only" and "personal/eyes only" memos: March 1, 1972, Nixon Project.

Nixon at Picosa: File on visit, Nixon Project; film clips and transcript of Nixon and Connally remarks, Nixon Project.

Haiphong decision: Kissinger, White House Years, pg. 1175; Nixon, RN, p. 601–604.

Connally and the use of nuclear weapons in Vietnam: Paul Volcker, interview with author.

Nixon's remarks on Haiphong: Haldeman, handwritten notes, Nixon Project.

John Reagan ("Tex") McCrary to Connally on resignation: May 16, 1972, Nixon Project.

Nixon-Connally dialogue: Nixon, *RN.*

Connally as his choice for President: Nixon, *RN.*

Fond hopes for Democrats: Robert Strauss, interview with author.

Democrats for Nixon: Folder, Nixon Project; *New York Times Magazine,* October 1, 1972; *Wall Street Journal,* September 15, 1972; Connally, appearance on "Meet the Press," July 21, 1972.

Nixon recruiting: Presidential memo, July 24, 1972, Nixon Project.

Nixon talk with LBJ, July 24: Presidential memo to Connally.

LBJ discomfort over Democratic convention: Liz Carpenter, interview with author.

"I do what I have to do": quotation relayed by George Christian, Democrats for Nixon file, Nixon Project.

Conversation of Nixon, Dean, and Haldeman: September 15, 1972, transcript, Impeachment Inquiry.

Connally and Dean: Dean, *Blind Ambition,* pp. 142–43.

Connally television address: tape, Nixon Project.

Party switch and Lady Bird: Lady Bird Johnson, interview with author.

The wry Frank Mankiewicz: Frank Mankiewicz, interview with author.

The irrepressible Liz Carpenter: Liz Carpenter, interview with author.

Connally as presidential counselor: Michael R. Gardner, interview with author. Gardner was Connally's assistant during this period.

"Burn those tapes!": Haldeman, *Ends of Power,* p. 205. Connally told the President to save the seven tapes that had been subpoenaed, and burn the rest. He did not want it done secretly, but rather he proposed a bonfire in the Rose Garden to which the press would be invited.

Implications of burning the tapes: George Frampton (ex-member of the Watergate special prosecutors staff), Leonard Garment (Nixon's lawyer), and Henry Brandon, interviews with author; Brandon article, "What if Nixon . . .," *New York Times,* August 18, 1988; Frampton and Ben-Veniste, *Stonewall.*

Almost Vice President: Sam Hoskinson and Michael Gardner, interviews with author.

Firestorm in Congress: Bryce Harlow to Rosemary Woods, October 11, 1973, Nixon Project.

Russell Long: Senator Long to Nixon, October 15, 1973, Nixon Project; Buckley comment, Harlow to Woods, Oct. 11, 1973, Nixon Project.

The gentle Ray Price: Price to Nixon, October 11, 1973, Nixon Project.

Nixon-Connally on forming a new political party: Ehrlichman, *Witness to Power.*

21. The Accuser
About Jake Jacobsen: Jacobsen, Joe Greenhill, Julian Read, Lawrence O'Brien, Milton Semer, Bob Lilly, Michael Tigar, Lynn Coleman, and Larry King, interviews with author.

The hand that fed: Christian was not the only man to benefit from Jacobsen's recommendation in high places. In the 1956 gubernatorial campaign, it was Jacobsen's recommendation to hire Jake Pickle as Price Daniel's campaign manager—an appointment of which Lyndon Johnson no doubt approved. And later, when he served Johnson in the White House, Jacobsen recommended the Austin attorney Larry Temple as a presidential assistant. That too had its irony. In the mid-1970s, Temple would join Connally and Christian to destroy Jacobsen in the milk fund case.

Jake-Connally dialogue: Jacobsen, interview with author.

Jake's comparison of Connally and Johnson on taste: When Jacobsen went to the White House, he began to advise Lyndon Johnson about his wardrobe as he had Connally, and came to be responsible for arranging for tailors and cobblers to come to the White House to fit the president. Between Connally and Johnson, Jacobsen felt Johnson had the better natural taste. Connally's bent was toward inexpensive suits and thickly knotted ties with dizzying geometric designs. As to which of the two men possessed greater vanity, Jacobsen found no difference.

Florene: Jacobsen and Greenhill, interviews with author.

LBJ-Jacobsen dialogue: Jacobsen, interview with author.

Jacobsen's influence on policy: His oral history, LBJ Library.

AMPI: Ervin Committee, Final Report, chapter 5.

AMPI and LBJ: Watergate special prosecutors' office, Milk Fund Investigation, National Archives.

Jake and AMPI: Watergate special prosecutors' Office, Milk Fund Investigation, Jacobsen file, National Archives; Bob Lilly, John White, Ted Van Dyk, and Michael Tigar, interviews with author.

Kalmbach-Semer: Ervin Committee, Final Report.

Haldeman and cash: With AMPI cash, Haldeman would soon be financing dirty tricks and black-bag jobs. He and Ehrlichman would be bankrolling the "discreet investigations" and illegal wiretaps of the absurd slapstick figure of Watergate, retired New York City cop Anthony Ulasewicz, against Democratic Party figures like Edward Kennedy and liberal columnists like Joseph Kraft, as well as providing money to White House plumbers Hunt and Liddy and pouring cash into the campaign of the opponent of Governor George Wallace of Alabama.

Jake as distinguished ex-presidential assistant: To his chronicler from the LBJ Library, in 1969, Jake philosophized about the role of the presidential aide: "An assistant should never take it on himself to block access to the president by a member of his cabinet or any other high government official," he said. "Now I don't think for a minute that I'm dumber than any one of those cabinet members. I think I've got as much sense as any one of them. That's how egotistical I am. I'm a successful businessman. I've done many things in my life. I've made lots of money, and I think that I'm just as smart as they are. But I wasn't picked to be a cabinet man. I wasn't picked to be a secretary of the treasury, although I own four banks and three savings and loans and do more financing and owe maybe $10 million. I wasn't picked to be secretary of the treasury, but Joe Fowler was—and he's the one who ought to be able to express his viewpoint to the president, not Jake Jacobsen."

Jacobsen and Cowan: Charles Ruff, former Watergate special prosecutor and Jacobsen, interviews with author; Ray Cowan file, Watergate special prosecutors' Office, National Archives.; references in the trial, *U.S. v. John Connally*, National Archives.

Jake's letter: Exhibit, *U.S. v. John Connally*, National Archives.

22. The Crime

Boehm birds: Jake Jacobsen, interview with author.

Colson to Ehrlichman, March 4, 1971: Statement of Information, Impeachment Inquiry, vol. 6. This volume, entitled "Political Contributions by Milk Producers/Cooperatives; the 1971 Milk Price Support decision," gives the best documentary narrative of the milk scandal.

Connally-Jacobsen interchange: Jacobsen, interview with author.

Congressional pressure: Nixon, and later Connally, were to speak repeatedly of the pressure from Congress. The question was, How great was the pressure? Several years later, when the milk situation loomed as a potential count for the impeachment of Nixon, the White House would assert that Congress had "put a gun" to the president's head. One hundred and twenty-five Congressmen introduced or cosponsored legislation, a White House white paper stated; thirty separate bills were introduced. This was classic Nixonian distortion, as the Senate Watergate Report would later point out. In fact, many legislators did not declare themselves at all during this March period, nor were some of the bills introduced until after the critical period. In any event, about one-fifth of the House and less than one-third of the Senate scarcely amounts to a gun at the President's temple. It was neither enough to pass a mandatory hike in the parity level nor anywhere near enough to override a presidential veto of such legislation. This was a political, not a legislative, fight.

Connally and Jacobsen before the decision: beyond the author's interview with Jacobsen, the testimonies of Connally and Jacobsen before the Senate Watergate Committee and the Watergate grand jury [such testimony is available in the National Archives] and *United States v. John Connally* were helpful.

Lilly: his testimony before the Senate Watergate Committee, and interview with author.

"In the bag": Lilly testimony, and interview with author.

Butterfield memo: March 23, 1971, Nixon Project.

Nixon to milk producers: Tape transcript, House Impeachment Inquiry, vol. 6, and in Nixon Project.

Connally in Oval Office: Tape transcript, Impeachment Inquiry, and in Nixon Project.

Three minutes: transcript, *U.S. v. Connally*, National Archives, as court exhibit.

Jacobsen and lobbying: Sixteen years later, in his bitterness and in his isolation (for he had been treated as a pariah in Texas after the Connally trial), Jake would generalize about what had transpired in the White House in 1971 and what shortly thereafter would transpire in the office of the secretary of the treasury. "How in the hell does anybody think Washington lobbyists operate?" he would say to the author. "Because he's a convincing speaker? Why, they're a dime a dozen. Say, it's a matter of right and wrong? You're not talking about someone who needs help. You're talking about a business issue! How do you convince a congressman from Utah, as a lobbyist from Washington, D.C., to do a damn thing? Or in Texas, if you're from

Austin, how do you convince someone from Lubbock to do something? You do it because you've made contributions to him or befriended him or done something for him. That's how the system operates. As a practical matter, our system of government operates on influence. With a business issue, the only way you can operate is through friendship or money—a contribution that would cause a man to want to listen to what you have to say. You hope the contribution is enough. If a politician knows the milk people are pretty free with their money, you'll be kind enough yourself."

For Connally, the $2 million was not enough. Later he would profess, under oath, both before a grand jury and would profess, under oath, both before a grand jury and before the Senate Watergate Committee, that he had no stake in campaign contributions to the Republicans, for he was a Democrat in a Republican administration, and he had been scrupulous about avoiding the appearance of political support. That is belied by the facts: by his behavior in the meeting with the president and his advisers, by his conduct in his three-minute private meeting with the president immediately thereafter, by Haldeman's note about Connally going after money, and most of all, by what was to happen next with Jacobsen.

Jake and his conscience: Jacobsen, interview with author.

End-of-year bank deposits: *Chicago Tribune*, March 18, 1974.

Connally's explanation for Jake's visit, September 24: When he was asked in court why he thought Jake happened to come by that morning, Connally surmised that perhaps Jake was anxious to know if the secretary had found out anything from the Home Loan Bank Board. If that was Jake's only interest, why couldn't he have used the telephone? Connally was asked. Connally answered with yet another remark that tried to paint Jacobsen as one of earth's strangest creatures.

Lilly cracking: John White and Bob Lilly, interviews with author; Watergate special prosecution force memorandum, November 13, 1973, James L. Quarles III interview with Lilly in San Antonio, November 2, 1973, National Archives; Lilly, testimony before the Senate Watergate Committee, November 16, 1973; Lilly grand jury testimony, October 26, 1973, exhibit, Milk Investigation, Special Watergate Prosecution Files, National Archives.

Sheraton Crest session: Jacobsen and Connally testimony, *U.S. v. Connally*, National Archives; Jacobsen, interview with author.

$10,000 for the governor: A typical reaction from those who could believe none of this took place came from Morris Jaffe, in a conversation with the author on November 2, 1987. Said Jaffe, "I can't imagine John Connally asked for $10,000. If that were true, it would be a hell of a bargain! If he had asked for $100,000 or $250,000, that would have been more realistic with his influence. One thing nobody ever accused John Connally of being is stupid, and that would have been stupid."

Rex Cauble: The National Archives released to the author the Rex Cauble file from the milk investigation of the Watergate Special Prosecutor's Office, which included a memorandum of May 12, 1975, entitled, "Activities of Rex Cauble, Denton, Texas," and a bank draft, drawn on Cauble's own bank, for $7500, on October 29, 1973. Another source was the author's interview with James Quarles III, of the special prosecutor's staff. Before he died, Leon Jaworski was to remark to a top-ranking Texas official that Cauble was the key to the cover-up side of the Connally case, and Jaworski was to say directly to Jacobsen personally, in a confidential session, that he believed Jacobsen to be telling the truth. Jaworski's view of Jacobsen's truthfulness was shared by another confidential source.

Jacobsen grand jury testimony: Exhibit, *U.S. v. Connally*, National Archives.

Connally grand jury testimony: Exhibit, *U.S. v. Connally*, National Archives.

Cauble afterwards: Lawrence Wright, "Rex Cauble and the Texas Mafia," *Texas Monthly*, November 1980.

Connally picture on Cauble's wall: *Dallas Times Herald*, August 8, 1981.

Connally as character witness at Cauble's trial: *Dallas Times Herald*, February 23, 1982.

23. The Trial

Charles Ruff's attitude: Ruff, interview with author.

Charges against Jake Jacobsen: Jacobsen file, National Archives.

Connally quote on CBS: "CBS Evening News," February 21, 1974, Fred Graham reporting.

Jacobsen psychology in winter and spring of 1974: Jacobsen and Semer, interviews with author.

Lyndon Johnson taking milk money: Watergate Special Prosecution Force memorandum, November 13, 1973, James L. Quarles III interview with Robert A. Lilly in San Antonio, November 2, 1973, National Archives. My information is that Assistant Attorney General Henry Petersen brought this evidence to the attention of Attorney General John Mitchell, and that Mitchell expressly forbade any use of it in the pretrial negotiations (Bob Lilly, James L. Quarles III, Charles Ruff, Mike Tigar, and Milton Semer, interviews with author).

Jacobsen to friend: The friend is Milton Semer; Semer, interview with author.

Special Prosecution Force pretrial thinking: Charles Ruff and James L. Quarles III, interviews with author.

Jacobsen's pretrial attitude: Jacobsen, interview with author.

Senator Lloyd Bentsen's attitude toward trial: Lloyd Bentsen and Loyd Hackler, interviews with author.

Pretrial deliberations: Transcript, *U.S. v. Connally*, National Archives.

Turkheimer memorandum on strengths/weaknesses of case: Records of Watergate Special Prosecution Force, Milk Investigation. National Archives.

Edward Bennett Williams's approach to the case: Michael Tigar and Lynn Coleman, interviews with author (both were members of the Connally defense team).

Procedural negotiations: transcript, *U.S. v. Connally*, National Archives.

The color of the trial: Larry L. King, "Williams for the Defense," *Atlantic*, July 1975; Al Reinert, "Not Guilty," *Texas Monthly*, June 1975; author interview with Larry King.

Connally comment about Jacobsen as liar: King, "Williams for the Defense."

Jury foreman's attitude: O'Toole, interview with author.

Jacobsen's emotions during cross-examination: Interview with author.

Hart-Williams colloquy: In camera deliberations, transcript, *U.S. v. Connally*, National Archives.

In Williams's mind . . . : Michael Tigar, interview with author.

Connally testimony: *U.S. v. Connally*, National Archives.

O'Toole impressions: Interview with author.

Cruelty of asking Lady Bird Johnson to testify: Liz Carpenter, interview with author.

On her testimony: Lynn Coleman and Robert Strauss, interviews with author.

Barbara Jordan testimony: Barbara Jordan, Billie Carr, Liz Carpenter, Lynn Coleman, Michael Tigar, and Robert Strauss, interviews with author.

Larry King's attitude toward Billy Graham and Barbara Jordan testimony: Interview with author.

Dialogue between Faulk and Yarborough: John Henry Faulk, interview with author.

Inside the jury deliberations: Dennis O'Toole, interview with author.

24. Rehabilitation

The hero's welcome: *Houston Chronicle*, April 19, 1975.

Interchange with a reporter: *Houston Chronicle*, June 22, 1975.

VIA: Connally's VIA was often compared to the 1973 organization of Nelson Rockefeller called the National Commission on Critical Choices, and Rockefeller's commission was also suspected of being a vehicle for Rockefeller to ride into the vice presidency. The comparison was actually backhanded flattery for Connally, because Rockefeller in 1973 was the sitting, activist governor of New York, while Connally was on the rebound from a criminal trial. The Commission on Critical Choices had started as a state study, but President Nixon, mired in Watergate, dignified the Rockefeller commission by nationalizing it and lending it presidential stature. In December 1973, just before the impeachment proceedings got underway and as the country faced the enormous problem of post-Vietnam reconstruction, a debate over critical choices before the nation was vibrant and much needed, and it was joined by the majority and minority leaders of Congress, leading scientists, educators, bankers, and academics. Connally's endeavor and his participants had no such stature.

Zale Corporation episode: Aaron Latham, "John Connally on the Comeback Trail," *New York* magazine, October 27, 1975.

Mayfield to President Ford: November 1975, Ford Library.

On turncoats: *Texas Observer*, August 20, 1976, repeating an *Observer* item from the summer of 1962.

Connally at Picosa: Walter Kennedy, interview with author (former chairman of Vermont Republican party, Kennedy was there); quotations from *New York Times Magazine*, June 8, 1976.

Wistful Ford: Ford, *Time to Heal*, p. 379.

Connally as unifier: "Meet the Press," June 15, 1976; James Wechsler, column, *New York Post*, June 15, 1976.

Stone memorandum: Clement Stone to Gerald Ford, August 7, 1976, Ford Library.

Rising opposition to Connally: *New York Times*, August 5 and 9, 1976; Railsback to Ford, August 6, 1976, Ford Library.

McCloskey actions: McCloskey letter to Ford, August 6, 1976, Ford Library;

hearings of Government Operations Subcommittee on Conservation and Natural Resources, November 5, 1971, and McCloskey speech in Congress, May 24, 1972, *Congressional Record.*

Findley letters: July 23 and August 10, 1976, Ford Library; Findley and Ford, interviews with author.

Source of Findley's passion: Findley and Ford, interviews with author.

Slur on Demetracopoulos: Elias Demetracopoulos, John Rousakis and Albert Scardino, interviews with author. As a reporter for the *Georgia Gazette,* Scardino had exposed Rousakis's fraud.

Connally's background check: President Gerald Ford and his former assistant Ed Schmults, interviews with author.

Meeting at 3 A.M.: Ford, *Time to Heal,* pp. 400–402, and interview with author. In his interview, President Ford downplayed the influence of Ronald Reagan on his choice for vice president, because he did not expect Reagan to campaign for him vigorously in the fall, which turned out to be the case. Nevertheless, for appearances sake alone, he could not afford to alienate the Reagan wing of the party.

25. Supernova

Connally as businessman: Stuart, "Citizen Connally," *Fortune,* July 31, 1978.

Connally's worth in 1978: his financial disclosure for his presidential campaign, Federal Elections Commission.

Arab deal: Robert Barnstone, "Between the Sheiks," *Texas Monthly,* November 1977.

Connally strategy: Eddie Mahe, Sam Hoskinson, Jack and Pat Ranson, Haley Barbour, and David Parker, interviews with author.

New Hampshire: "Born-Again Wheeler-Dealer," editorial, *Manchester Union-Leader,* March 20, 1979.

Killer Bees: Heard, *Miracle of the Killer Bees;* Glenn Kothmann, interview with author.

Connally, spent and angry, in Kansas City: Sam Hoskinson, interview with author; *Kansas City Star,* July 16, 1979.

Strategy at Picosa: Eddie Mahe, Haley Barbour, and Sam Hoskinson, interviews with author.

The Middle East speech: transcript, *New York Times,* October 12, 1979; Sam Hoskinson, Haley Barbour, Eddie Mahe, Jack and Pat Ranson, Paul Findley, Dr. Theodore Johnson, Rita Hauser, and George Ball, interviews with author.

Hoskinson and Kissinger: Sam Hoskinson, interview with author.

Connally elated: Haley Barbour and Sam Hoskinson, interviews with author.

"Merchants of Myth": editorial, *New York Times,* October 21, 1979 and "John Connally, Weakling," editorial, *New Republic,* October 27, 1979; James Reston, "Two Capitals," column, October 19, 1979; "Connally Speech on Israel: A Move for the Limelight," *New York Times,* October 26, 1979.

Dialogue with Joseph Kraft: Kraft, "The Politics of Vanity," *New Republic,* November 24, 1979; William Safire, "John Connally and Israel," *New York Times,* October 19, 1979.

Hauser reaction: Hauser, interview with author.

Connally declaiming on campaign plane: Haley Barbour, interview with author.

Connally in Providence and Palm Beach: Burka, "The Truth About John Connally," *Texas Monthly*, November 1979.

Corporate money: A study by Common Cause dated January 25, 1980, released the details of Connally's extraordinary backing from corporate America. Texas humorist Cactus Pryor took off from Connally's reputation as the candidate of corporate America by saying, "I think John Connally has a good shot at being president. After all, he has the support of the browns and the blacks. . . . That's Brown and Root and Black and Decker." Pryor had also remarked during Connally's milk trial: "John Connally taking $10,000 as a bribe? Why, he spends that much every week on hair spray!"

Answer to wheeler-dealer question: Geoffrey Norman, "The Canny Conservatism of John Connally," *Playboy*, March 1980; Kaye Northcott, "Connally's Last Stand . . . We Hope," *Mother Jones*, January 1980, and *Texas Observer* retrospective on Connally, March 2, 1979.

"Teddy": "CBS Reports," November 4, 1979.

"I never drowned anyone . . .": WINS, New York, September 23, 1979, reported in the *National Review*, October 12, 1979.

Florida caucus: *Orlando Sentinel, Miami Herald,* and *New York Times,* November 17–18, 1979.

Connally bombing the ayatollah's mosques: Haley Barbour, interview with author.

Fading: Theodore Johnson (Connally organizer in Iowa), Walter Kennedy (Republican Party chairman in Vermont), Haley Barbour, Jack and Pat Ranson, interviews with author.

"That prick!": Michael Kramer, "A Personal Victory," *New York* magazine, February 4, 1980.

His one delegate: *Arkansas Gazette*, March 10, 1980.

Speech to VFW: August 28, 1976, courtesy of national Veterans of Foreign Wars.

"I reminded everybody of Lyndon": Sander Vanocur, interview with author.

26. Stardust

Gilded age in Dallas: *New York Times*, May 5, 1981.

Savings and loan Practices: Continuous coverage in *New York Times*, especially June 12, 1988, "Who to Thank for the Thrift Crisis."

Connally and the Reaganites: The Reaganites were concerned that if they made Connally secretary of state, he might overshadow the president in making foreign policy and might be hard to control. The irony was that in choosing Alexander Haig, they got exactly what they feared they would get with Connally (interview with author Michael Gardner). Incidentally in his failed presidential campaign, Connally had sounded out Haig as his possible running mate. See Haig, *Caveat*, p. 4.

Connally and his campaign debt: David Parker, interview with author.

Barnes: His oral history, LBJ Library.

Barnes-Connally partnership: Peter Elkind's excellent treatment in *Texas*

Monthly, October 1986, "Barnes and Connally: Is It the End of the Trail for Their Business Empire?"

Ebullient in 1983: "What Are They Doing Now?" *Texas Business,* August 1983.

Arrival: *Architectural Digest,* July 1985.

Hard-bitten Texas politician: Billie Carr, interview with author.

Good fit: *Texas Business,* August 1983.

Carrier interest: George Ball, interview with author; Ball had discussed Connally's high price with bankers and lawyers in Houston.

Inside Barnes-Connally: Peter Elkind of the *Texas Monthly* provided the author with his complete interview notes of the principals for his 1986 article. These notes included interviews with Ed Pennington, Bryan Lewis, Ralph Wayne, Mike Crockett, and three interviews with Ben Barnes.

"It was a pleasure. . . .": Elkind interview with Pennington.

Sakowitz and Hemingway: *New York Times,* October 7, 1982.

The Decline of Texas: Paul Burka, interview with author.

Beaumont economist: Professor Bernard Weinstein, John Gray Institute, Lamar University, *New York Times,* September 16, 1984.

Me-first attitude: Connally on "Nightline," February 23, 1986, "Hard Times in Texas."

Get-it-built mentality: Ed Pennington, interview with Peter Elkind.

Personal backing behind mega-loans: Trammell Crow, interview with author.

Locked out: *Texas Business Journal,* March 1987.

Black humor in Austin: Ross Milloy, interview with author.

In league with swindlers: *San Antonio Light,* March 6, 1988; Anne Pearson and Michael Pearson (the reporters for the story), Anita Miller (a land-use attorney in New Mexico), and Alan Merson, (assistant attorney general of New Mexico), interviews with author. Also, for bulletin on Tonga Bank, Office of U.S. Comptroller of the Currency.

Bankruptcy filing and meeting with creditors: Transcript, U.S. Bankruptcy Court, September 3, 1987; AP and UPI stories on the event.

Paying debts: Connally's promise to sell all his personal assets to pay back those who had faith and confidence in him turned out not to be as total or as noble as it sounded. His personal possessions brought close to $3 million when they were put to auction, but he had another asset which was worth every bit as much as his Limoges teacups and his parade saddles: his personal papers. It would be estimated that they were worth at least $3 million. Connally attempted to hide his personal papers as an asset of worth in his initial bankruptcy filing, but when the attempted fraud was exposed, it became this author's opinion that the LBJ Library, the National Archives, the attorney general, and Comptroller of Texas, the trustee of his Texas bankruptcy estate, and the U.S. Bankruptcy Court would come to Connally's defense to keep this asset from being seized and sold for the benefit of his creditors, as he was clearly required to do under the law.

If sequestering his papers was a probable fraud on his creditors, it was also a fraud on history. Connally knew that this book was being written about him almost a year before he filed for bankruptcy, and his fight to keep his papers from being sold seemed motivated, in part, by the determination to keep the papers out of the hands of the author. The manner of his ploy illustrates the point. Only days before his filing, two trucks arrived at the LBJ Library, and the papers were unloaded. For years, Connally had refused to donate his papers to the LBJ Library or to any other library. All discussions of the question brought only contemptuous comments from Connally. To Dr. Don Carleton, the head of the Barker Collection of Texas history at the University of Texas, Connally quipped, "There aren't going to be any Connally papers." His gift now was clearly associated with his bankruptcy. A month later, a tortured deed of gift was presented to the LBJ Library, which slapped a five-year restriction on scholarly access to the papers. (The author came to refer to this as the "Reston Restriction.")

The problem for Connally was that he had no legal right to "give" anything away, even before his formal bankruptcy filing, for under the law, all property owned in the year prior to filing is considered the property of the bankrupt estate. Although no major gift of personal papers had ever before been associated with a bankruptcy, and novel legal questions were involved in the case, it seemed clear that by his filing, Connally ceased to own his own papers.

The job of the court-appointed trustee of the Connally estate was to evaluate the assets and to maximize the return that could be raised to repay the creditors. So intent was the LBJ Library to have the Connally papers, however, that it lent itself to Connally's suspect attempt, both to protect the papers from his creditors and to prevent scholarly access. After the author complained of this collusion in a possible fraud, the library adopted a waiting strategy: The library simply did not sign Connally's deed of gift but left the papers parked in its crypt in limbo, until Connally seemed to be formally discharged from bankruptcy.

Meanwhile, the author complained to the attorney general of Texas, Jim Mattox, and the comptroller of Texas, Bob Bullock, since the state of Texas, through Connally's gigantic tax liability, was a major Connally creditor. A staff attorney in Mattox's office briefed the issue and concluded that, indeed, Connally had no property right in the papers and no right to make the donation to the LBJ Library, just as the library had no right to accept the gift. Moreover, since not one document from the Connally governorship exists in the Texas State Archives—because Connally seized all his papers upon his departure—the archives had an interest in having the governorship papers.

But Mattox and Bullock met and made a cold political decision. Regardless of the law, there was no political mileage in kicking John Connally when he was down. Between the LBJ Library and the top officials of the state, the old-boy network effectively surrounded its most distinguished old boy.

One major creditor, however, was outside the network. That was the attorney general of New Mexico, who represented thousands of New Mexicans who had been bilked by the Barnes/Connally project at Ruidoso Downs. The New Mexico attorney general filed a motion with the U.S. Bankruptcy Court, demanding that the papers be appraised and sold for the benefit of the creditors. The judge in the U.S. Bankruptcy Court delegated the problem to the trustee of the Connally estate, who turned out to be more of a friend to Connally than to the creditors she was supposed to be serving. She simply did nothing.

The Auction: Author attended the auction; author conversation with Connally there.

The tour: tape of Connally's interchange with the press, provided to the author by Peter Applebome of the *New York Times;* "Nightline," ABC News, January 22, 1988.

Hart's fantasy: Jerry Hart, interview with author.

Dinner before sale: Henry Wade (who attended), Trammell Crow (who contributed), and Jerry Hart (who benefited), interviews with author.

Super Bowl pitchman: *Wall Street Journal,* January 27, 1988.

Appendix. The Aftermath of Dallas: Connally and the Conspiratorialists
"Not unhappy" and survivor's guilt: Interview on "60 Minutes," CBS, February 28, 1988.

The president's corset: Dr. Charles James Carrico and Dr. Malcolm O. Perry, testimony, WC, vol. 5; in his interview with Ralph Yarborough, the author was first alerted to the importance of the corset.

Horse meat, and the well-dressed goat: Dr. Alfred Oliver, testimony, WC, vol. 5.

Note on Reagan: John Pekkinan, an expert on the Reagan assassination attempt, interview with author.

Valenti and John P. Roche memos: Assassination File, LBJ Library; Jack Valenti, interview with author.

★ BIBLIOGRAPHY AND SOURCES ★

Abrahamsen, David, M.D.. *The Murdering Mind.* New York: Harper & Row, 1973.

Agnew, Spiro T. *Go Quietly . . . or Else!* New York: William Morrow, 1980.

Alaniz, Nago. Interview with author, San Diego, Texas, November 23, 1987.

Ambrose, Stephen. *Eisenhower.* New York: Simon & Schuster, 1983.

Anson, Robert Sam. *"They've Killed the President!": The Search for the Murderers of John F. Kennedy.* New York: Bantam, 1975.

Aristotle. *Selections.* Ed. W. D. Ross. New York: Charles Scribner's Sons, 1927.

Armstrong, Robert. Interview with author, Austin, February 7, 1987.

Ash, Roy. Interview with author, Middleburg, Va., September 5, 1988.

Ashman, Charles. *Connally: The Adventures of Big Bad John.* New York: William Morrow, 1974.

Ayres, Clarence. *The Theory of Economic Progress.* Chapel Hill: University of North Carolina Press, 1944.

Bailey, Charles, III. Telephone interview with author, November 1988.

Bainbridge, John. *The Super-Americans.* Garden City, N.Y.: Doubleday, 1961.

Ball, George W.. *Diplomacy for a Crowded World.* Boston: Atlantic Monthly Press, 1976.

———. The Past Has Another Pattern. Memoirs. New York: W. W. Norton, 1982.

———. Interview with author, Princeton, N.J., October 17, 1988.

Barbour, Haley. Interview with author, Washington, D.C., August 29, 1988.

Belin, David. *Final Disclosure.* New York: Charles Scribner's Sons, 1988.

Benjamin, Gilbert Giddings. *Germans in Texas: A Study of Immigration.* N.P.: German American Annals, vol. 7, 1909.

Bentsen, Lloyd. Interview with author, Washington, D.C., February 2, 1987.

Ben-Veniste, Richard, and Frampton, George. *Stonewall.* New York: Simon & Schuster, 1974.

Bernal, Joe. Interview with author, San Antonio, March 11, 1987.

Bernstein, Carl, and Woodward, Bob. *The Final Days.* New York: Simon & Schuster, 1976.

Bishop, Jim. *The Day Kennedy Was Shot*. New York: Funk & Wagnalls, 1968.

Blair, Joan, and Blair, Clay, Jr. *The Search for JFK*. New York: Berkley, 1974.

Bobbitt, Phil. Interview with author, Austin, October 1988.

Brammer, Bill. *The Gay Place*. Boston: Houghton Mifflin, 1961.

Brandon, Henry. *Special Relationships: A Foreign Correspondent's Memoirs from Roosevelt to Reagan*. New York: Atheneum, 1988.

——. Telephone interview with author, January 1989.

Brodie, Bernard. *A Guide to Naval Strategy*. Princeton, N.J.: Princeton University Press, 1958.

Bruno, Jerry. Telephone interview with author, May 3, 1988.

Burka, Paul. Interview with author, Austin, February 3, 1987.

Burney, Cecil. Interview with author, Corpus Christi, November 22, 1987.

Burns, James MacGregor. Roosevelt: *The Lion and the Fox*. New York: Harcourt, Brace and World, 1962.

——. Roosevelt: *The Soldier of Freedom*. New York: Harcourt Brace Jovanovich, 1970.

Caidin, Martin, and Hymoff, Edward. *The Mission*. Philadelphia and New York: Lippincott, 1964.

Caldwell, Neil. Interview with author, Angleton, Tex., June 17, 1987.

Caro, Robert A. *The Path to Power: The Years of Lyndon Johnson*. New York: Knopf, 1983.

Carpenter, Liz. Interview with author, Austin, June 18, 1987.

Carr, Billy. Interviews with author, Houston, March 17, 1987, and telephone interview, April 1989.

Chester, Lewis; Hodgson, Godfrey; and Page, Bruce. *An American Melodrama: The Presidential Campaign of 1968*. New York: Viking, 1969.

Christian, George. *A President Steps Down*. New York: Macmillan, 1970.

——. Interviews with author, Austin, February 4, 1987, June 22, 1987, & November 8, 1988.

Church, Frank; Tower, John, et al. *Alleged Assassination Plots Involving Foreign Leaders. Select Committee on Intelligence Activities*. Washington: U.S. Government Printing Office, 1976.

Clark, Ronald W. *Einstein*. New York: World, 1971.

Cohen, Richard M., and Witcover, Jules. *A Heartbeat Away: The Investigation and Resignation of Vice President Spiro Agnew*. New York: Viking, 1974.

Coleman, Lynn. Interview with author, Washington, November 23, 1987.

Connally, Golfrey. Interview with author, San Antonio, March 12, 1987.

Connally, John. Interviews with author, Houston, March 17, 1987, and January 22, 1988.

Connally, Merrill. Interview with author, Floresville, Tex., August 26, 1987.

Connell, William. Interview with author, Bethesda, Md., June 27, 1988.

Costello, John. *The Pacific War*. New York: Rawson Wade, 1981.

Cox, Del. Interview with author, Floresville, Tex., August 26, 1987.

Crawford, Ann Fears, and Keever, Jack. *John B. Connally, Portrait in Power.* Austin: Jenkins, 1973.

Crawley, Aiden. *De Gaulle.* New York: Bobbs-Merrill, 1969.

Crow, Trammell. Telephone interview with author, February 1989.

Cutler, Lloyd. Interview with author, Washington, D.C., July 24, 1987.

Daniels, Jonathan. *White House Witness: 1942–45.* Garden City, N.Y.: Doubleday, 1975.

Dallas Morning News. Texas Almanac, 1988–89. Austin: Texas Monthly Press, 1987.

Dean, John. *Blind Ambition.* New York: Simon & Schuster. 1976.

——. *Lost Honour.* Los Angeles: Stratford Press, 1982.

de Gaulle, Charles. *Unity, 1942–44, War Memoirs,* vol. 2. New York: Simon & Schuster, 1956.

Demetracopoulous, Elias. Interview with author, Washington D.C., September 1, 1988.

Dibrell, T. Kellis. Interview with author, San Antonio, June 23, 1987.

Dobie, J. Frank. *A Vaquero of the Brush Country.* Boston: Little, Brown, 1929.

Douglas, John. Telephone interview with author, February 1989.

Drew, Elizabeth. *Washington Journal, Events of 1973–74.* New York: Random House, 1974.

Dugger, Ronnie. *The Politician. The Life and Times of Lyndon Johnson.* New York: W.W. Norton, 1982.

Eckhardt, Robert. Interview with author, Washington, January 19, 1987.

Ehrlichman, John. *Witness to Power: The Nixon Years.* New York: Simon & Schuster, 1982.

Eisenhower, David. *Eisenhower at War: 1943–45.* New York: Random House, 1986.

Epstein, Edward J. *Inquest.* New York: Viking, 1966.

Fath, Creekmore. Interviews with author, Austin, February 8, 1987; June 18, 1987.

Faulk, John Henry. Interviews with author, Austin, February 4, 1987; March 15, 1987.

Fehrenbach, T. R. *Lone Star: A History of Texas and the Texans.* New York: Macmillan, 1968.

Fietsam, Joe. Interview with author, Floresville, Tex., March 12, 1987.

Findley, Paul. *They Dare to Speak Out.* Westport, Conn.: Lawrence Hill, 1985.

——. Telephone interview with author, July 1988.

Flemmons, Jerry. *Amon: The Life of Amon Carter, Sr., of Texas.* Austin: Jenkins, 1978.

Ford, Gerald. *A Time to Heal.* New York: Harper & Row, 1979.

——. Interview with author, New York, January 23, 1989.

Frampton, George. Interview with author, Washington, D.C. October 23, 1987.

Frost, H. Gordon, and Jenkins, John H., *I'm Frank Hamer: The Life of a Texas Peace Officer.* Austin: Pemberton Press, 1948.

Galbraith, John Kenneth. *A Life in Our Times: Memoirs.* Boston: Houghton Mifflin, 1981.

Gardner, Michael R. Interview with author, Washington, D.C., September 12, 1988.

Gardner, Richard N. *Sterling-Dollar Diplomacy.* New York: McGraw-Hill, 1956.

Garment, Leonard. Telephone interview with author, February 1989.

Goldman, Eric. *The Tragedy of Lyndon Johnson.* New York: Knopf, 1969.

Gonzalez, Henry B. Interview with author, Washington, D.C., February 11, 1988.

Goodwin, Richard. *Remembering America.* Boston: Little, Brown, 1988.

Grace, Charles. Telephone interview with author, June 23, 1987.

Green, George Norris. *The Establishment in Texas Politics.* Westport, Conn: Greenwood Press, 1979.

Greenhill, Joe R. Interview with author, Austin, March 9, 1987.

Greider, William. *Secrets of the Temple.* New York: Simon & Schuster. 1987.

Gualtieri, Thomas. Telephone interview with author, November 22, 1988.

Gunther, John. *Roosevelt in Retrospect.* New York: Harper, 1950.

Gwiazda, Henry. Interview with author, Boston, July 1988.

Hackler, Loyd. Interview with author, Washington, December 19, 1988.

Haig, Alexander M., Jr. *Caveat: Realism, Reagan, and Foreign Policy.* New York: Macmillan, 1984.

Haldeman, H. R., with DiMona, Joseph. *The Ends of Power.* New York: Times Books, 1978.

Hale, Edward Everett. "Fascism versus Communism." *South Western Social Science Quarterly,* June 1957.

Haley, J. Evetts. *A Texan Looks at Lyndon: A Study in Illegitimate Power.* Canyon, Tex.: Palo Duro Press, 1964.

Halloran, Richard. Interview with author, Washington, October 8, 1988.

Harris, Fred. Telephone interview with author June 1988.

Harrod, Roy. *Reforming the World's Money.* New York: Macmillan, 1965.

Hart, Jerry. Interview with author, Houston, January 22, 1988.

Hauser, Rita. Telephone interview with author, June 1988.

Heard, Robert. *The Miracle of the Killer Bees.* Austin: Honey Hill, 1979.

Henderson, Richard B. *Maury Maverick: A Political Biography.* Austin: University of Texas Press, 1970.

Hersh, Seymour. *The Price of Power: Kissinger in the Nixon White House.* New York: Summit Books, 1983.

Hightower, Jim. Interview with author. Austin, July 2, 1987.

Hobby, William P., Jr. Interview with author Austin, November 9, 1988.

Hoskinson, Sam. Interview with author, Washington, August 26, 1988.

Hoyt, Edwin. *Kamikazes.* New York: Arbor House, 1983.

Hurt, Harry, III. *Texas Rich: The Hunt Dynasty from Oil Days Through the Silver Crash.* New York: W.W. Norton, 1982.

Ickes, Harold. *The Secret Diary of Harold L. Ickes.* New York: Simon & Schuster, 1953.

Ikard, Frank. Telephone interview with author, Washington, January 30, 1987.

Jacobsen, Jake. Interviews with author, en route between Houston and Austin, August 24, 1987; Austin, August 25, 1987.

Jaffe, Morris. Interview with author, November 2, 1987.

Jaeggli, J. T., Jr. *The Court House Story.* Floresville, Tex.: 1971.

Jarnagin, Carroll. Telephone interview with author, February 1988.

Jaworski, Leon. *The Right and the Power: The Prosecution of Watergate.* New York: Reader's Digest Press, 1976.

Johnson, Claudia Alta (Taylor) (Lady Bird). *A White House Diary.* New York: Holt, Rinehart & Winston, 1970.

——. Interview with author, Austin, November 10, 1988.

Johnson, Lyndon B. *The Vantage Point: Perspectives of the President, 1963–69.* New York: Holt, Rinehart, & Winston, 1971.

Johnson, Theodore. Telephone interview with author, June 1988.

Jones, James R. Interview with author, Washington, April 25, 1988.

Jordan, Barbara. *A Self-Portrait.* Garden City, N.Y.: Doubleday, 1979.

——. Interview with author, Austin, January 1988.

Kahl, Mary. *Ballot Box 13.* Jefferson, N. C.: MacFarland, 1983.

Kaufmann, William. *The McNamara Strategy.* New York: Harper & Row, 1964.

Kearns, Doris. *Lyndon Johnson and the American Dream.* New York: Harper & Row, 1976.

Kennedy, Harold. Telphone interview with author, January, 1989.

Kennedy, John F. *The Strategy of Peace.* New York: Harper & Row, 1960.

Kennedy, Robert. *Robert Kennedy in His Own Words.* New York: Bantam, 1988.

Kennedy, Vann M. Interview with author, Corpus Christi, November 22, 1987.

Kennedy, Walter. Telephone interview with author June 1988.

Kerr, Andy. *A Journey Amongst the Good and the Great.* Annapolis: Naval Institute Press, 1987.

——. Telephone interview with author, June 1, 1989.

Kinch, Sam, and Long, Stuart. *Allan Shivers: The Pied Piper of Texas Politics.* Austin: Shoal Creek, 1973.

King, Larry L. Interview with author, Washington, November 10, 1987.

Kissinger, Henry. *The White House Years.* Boston: Little, Brown, 1979.

——. *The Years of Upheaval.* Boston: Little, Brown, 1982.

Knebel, Fletcher, and Bailey, Charles. *Seven Days in May.* New York: Bantam (paper), 1963.

Knebel, Fletcher. Telephone interview with author, November 1988.

Kothmann, Glenn. Telephone interview with author, July 1988.

Lane, Mark. *Rush to Judgment*. New York: Holt, Rinehart & Winston, 1966.

Lasky, Victor. *JFK: Man & Myth*. New York: Arlington House, 1966.

Lilly, Bob. Interview with author. Zephyr, Tex., November 21, 1987.

Lyon, Peter. *Eisenhower: Portrait of a Hero*. Boston: Little, Brown, 1974.

McCarthy, Eugene. *The Year of the People*. Garden City, N.Y.: Doubleday, 1969.

———. Interview with author, Washington, June 10, 1988.

McMillan, Priscilla Johnson. *Marina and Lee*. New York: Harper & Row, 1977.

Macmillan, Harold. *The Blast of War, 1939–1945*. New York: Harper & Row, 1968.

MacLaury, Bruce. Interview with author, Washington, November 14, 1988.

Mahe, Eddie. Interview with author, Washington, June 23, 1988.

Manchester, William. *The Death of a President*. New York: Harper & Row, 1967.

———. *The Glory and the Dream*. Boston: Little, Brown, 1974.

———. *Controversy and Other Essays in Journalism, 1950–1975*. Boston: Little, Brown, 1976.

———. Telephone interview with author, July 1988.

Mankiewicz, Frank, with Reston, James, Jr. *Perfectly Clear: Nixon from Whittier to Watergate*. New York: Quadrangle, 1973.

———. *U.S. v. Richard Nixon: The Final Crisis*. New York: Quadrangle, 1975.

———. Interview with author, Washington, January 27, 1987.

Marshall, Burke. Telephone interview with author, February 1989.

Matthews, Wilbur. *San Antonio Lawyer*. San Antonio: Corona Publishing, 1983.

Maverick, Maury, Jr. Interviews with author, San Antonio, March 11, 1987; June 23, 1987.

Mayer, Margaret. Interview with author, Washington, January 20, 1987.

Mayer, Martin. *The Fate of the Dollar*. New York: Times Books, 1980.

Merson, Alan. Telephone interview with author, March 1989.

Miller, Merle. *Lyndon: An Oral Biography*. New York: Putnam, 1980.

Monnet, Jean. *Memoirs*. Garden City, N.Y.: Doubleday, 1978.

Montgomery, R. H. *The Brimstone Game: Monopoly in Action*. New York: Vanguard, 1940.

Morgan, Ted. *FDR*. New York: Simon & Schuster, 1985.

Morison, Samuel Eliot. *History of U.S. Naval Operations in World War II*, vol. 9, *Sicily–Salerno–Anzio, January 1943–June 1944*. Boston: Little, Brown, 1954.

Muller, Herbert J. *Adlai Stevenson: A Study in Values*. New York: Harper & Row, 1967.

Mungia, Ruben. Telephone interview with author. July 24, 1987.

Murphy, Robert. Diplomat Among Warriors. Garden City: Doubleday, 1964.

New York Times. The End of a Presidency. New York: Bantam, 1974.

Nixon, Richard M. *RN: The Memoirs of Richard Nixon.* New York: Grosset & Dunlap, 1978.

Nofziger, Lyn. Telephone interview with author, October 1988.

O'Brien, Lawrence. *No Final Victories* Garden City, N.Y.: Doubleday, 1975.

———. Interview with author, New York City, April 7, 1988.

Olien, Roger M. *From Token to Triumph: The Texas Republicans Since 1920.* Dallas: S.M.U. Press, 1982.

Olien, Roger M., and Olien, Diana Davids. *Wildcatters: Texas Independent Oilmen.* Austin: Texas Monthly Press, 1984.

Olmsted, Frederick Law. *A Journey Through Texas, or A Saddletrip on the Southwestern Frontier.* New York: Edwards, 1857.

O'Toole, Dennis. Interview with author, Williamsburg, Va., December 16, 1987.

Parker, David. Interview with author, Washington, August 31, 1988.

Parr, Archer. Telephone interview with author, February 1988.

Parten, J. R. Interview with author, Madisonville, Tex., March 15, 1987.

Parmet, Herbert. *Jack: The Struggles of John F. Kennedy.* New York: Dial, 1980.

Provence, Harry. *Lyndon B. Johnson.* New York: Fleet, 1964.

Proxmire, William. Interview with author, Washington, D.C., October 3, 1988.

Pryor, Cactus. Interview with author, Austin, March 15, 1987.

Public Papers of the Presidents of the United States. John F. Kennedy, Lyndon B. Johnson, Richard M. Nixon. Washington, D.C.: U.S. Government Printing Office, 1965, 1970, 1975.

Quarles, James. Interviews with author, Washington, November 5, 1987; January 3, 1988.

Ranson, Jack, and Pat. Telephone interview with author, September 1, 1988.

Rauh, Joseph L., Jr. Interview with author, Washington, D.C., June 16, 1987.

Rayburn, Sam. *Speak, Mr. Speaker.* Ed. H. B. Dulaney, Edward Hake Phillips, and Mac Phelan Reese. Bonham, Tex.: Sam Rayburn Foundation, 1978.

Reed, Julian. Interview with author, Washington, D.C., December 14, 1988.

Reston, James. Interview with author, Washington, D.C., February 1987.

Reynolds, Clark G. *The Fast Carriers.* Huntington, N.Y.: Krieger, 1978.

Rostow, Eugene. Interview with author, Washington, April 30, 1987.

Rostow, W. W. Interviews with author, Austin, March 9, 1987; November 8, 1988.

Rousakis, John. Telephone interview with author, November 1988.

Rowe, Elizabeth. Interview with author, Washington, D.C., February 11, 1987.

Rowe, James M. Interview with author, Corpus Christi, November 22, 1987.

Ruff, Charles F. C. Interview with author, Washington, D.C., October 27, 1987.

Safire, William. *Before the Fall: An Inside View of the Pre-Watergate White House.* Garden City, N.Y.: Doubleday, 1975.

_____. Interview with author, Washington, D.C., September 22, 1988.

Salinger, Pierre. *With Kennedy*. Garden City, N.Y.: Doubleday, 1966.

Schlesinger, Arthur. *A Thousand Days: John F. Kennedy in the White House.* Boston: Houghton Mifflin, 1965.

_____. *Robert Kennedy and His Times*. Boston: Houghton Mifflin, 1978.

Schmults, Ed. Telephone interview with author, September 1988.

Schmidt, Fred. Interview with author, Fredricksburg, Tex., June 18, 1987.

Semer, Milton. Interview with author, Washington, D.C., October 1, 1987.

Sherrill, Robert. *The Oil Follies of 1970–1980*. Garden City, N.Y.: Doubleday, 1983.

Sherwood, Robert E. *Roosevelt and Hopkins: An Intimate History*. New York: Harper, 1948.

Shriver, Sargent. Interview with author, Washington, D.C., December 21, 1988.

Singleton, John V., Jr. Interview with author, Houston, June 24, 1987.

Sitkoff, Harvard. *The Struggle for Black Equality*. New York: Hill & Wang, 1981.

Smith, Jim. Interview with author, Washington, D.C., October 20, 1988.

Solberg, Carl. *Hubert Humphrey*. New York: W. W. Norton, 1984.

Spears, Franklin. Interview with author, Austin, July 1, 1987.

Stein, Herbert. *Presidential Economics*. New York: Simon & Shuster, 1984.

_____. Interview with author, Washington, September 23, 1988.

Steinberg, Alfred. *Sam Johnson's Boy*. New York: Macmillan, 1968.

Stinson, William. Interviews with author, Washington, February 29, 1988; Dallas, November 6, 1988.

Strauss, Robert. Interview with author, Washington, D.C., April 27, 1988.

Tigar, Michael. Interview with author, Austin, July 2, 1987.

U.S. Congress. Senate. Select Committee on Presidential Campaign Activities. *The Senate Watergate Report*, 1974.

_____. House. Committee on Judiciary. *Impeachment Hearings*, 1974.

U.S. Navy. *Medal of Honor, 1861–1949, the Navy*. Washington: U.S. Navy Department, 1950.

Valenti, Jack. *A Very Human President*. New York: W. W. Norton, 1976.

_____. Interview with author. Washington, March 18, 1988.

Van Dyk, Ted. Interviews with author, Washington, March 5, 1987; June 22, 1988.

Villarreal, Jesse. Telephone interview with author, June 1987.

Vizinczey, Stephen. *Rules of Chaos*. New York: McCall, 1970.

Voigt, Kathleen. Interviews with author, San Antonio, March 13, 1987; June 23, 1987.

Volcker, Paul. Interview with author, Princeton, N.J., October 17, 1988.

Wade, Henry M. Interview with author, Dallas, November 7, 1988.

Warren Commission. *President's Commission on the Assassination of President John F. Kennedy*. The Final Report and Volumes 1–26. Washington, D.C.: U.S. Government Printing Office, 1964.

Webb, Walter Prescott. *The Story of the Texas Rangers: A Century of Frontier Defense.* Austin: University of Texas Press, 1935.

White, John C. Interview with author, Washington, July 22, 1987.

White, Theodore H. *The Making of the President, 1960.* New York: Atheneum, 1961.

———. *The Making of the President, 1964.* New York: Atheneum, 1965.

———. *The Making of the President, 1968.* New York: Atheneum, 1969.

———. *The Making of the President, 1972.* New York: 1973.

———. *Breach of Faith: The Fall of Richard Nixon.* New York: Atheneum, 1975.

———. *In Search of History: A Personal Adventure.* New York: Harper & Row, 1978.

White, William S. *Queens Die Proudly.* New York: Harcourt, Brace and Co., 1943.

Williams, T. Harry. *Huey Long.* New York: Bantam (paper), 1970.

Wilson County. *Wilson County Centennial.* Floresville, Tex.: n.p. 1960.

Works Progress Administration: *Texas: A Guide to the Lone Star State.* New York: Hastings House, 1940.

Yarborough, Ralph. Interviews with author, Austin, February 5, 1987; February 25, 1988.

Yarmolinsky, Adam. Interview with author, Washington, December 17, 1988.

★ INDEX ★

affirmative action, 584
African trip, 324–25
Agnew, Spiro, 351, 380–81, 442, 443–44, 453, 457, 551
Ailes, Roger, 580–81
Albert, Carl, 364, 427, 429, 486, 490–91
Allred, James, 16, 20, 30, 56, 77, 78–79, 81, 120
AMPI [Associated Milk Producers, Inc.]: and the $2 million contribution, 485–97, 521; early investigations of, 498–512; campaign contributions of, 473–78, 482–97; Connally's early relationship with, 474–75; and Connally as treasury secretary, 482–97; in the early 1970s, 482–97; forms a national organization, 476; hires Jacobsen, 473; and the Jacobsen indictment, 514; and LBJ, 474–76, 484; and Nixon, 476–78, 482–97; and TAPE 474, 476. *See also* milk lobby/scandal; *name of specific person*
Anderson, Clinton, 165
Anderson, Jack, 136–37, 517, 553n
Anderson, Robert B., 165, 167
anti-Semitism, 53–54, 156, 463, 558, 572
Arab partnership, 557–58, 562, 572
Armco Steel Corporation, 551
Ash, Roy, 376–77, 379, 413
assassinations. *See name of specific person*

Associated Milk Producers, Inc. *See* AMPI; milk lobby/scandal
auction, bankruptcy, 603–10
Austin, Texas: and the 1948 election, 134; economy of, 598; and the JFK trip, 240–41, 244–45, 254–55, 263, 593–94; segregation in, 292

Baker, Bobby, 205
Baker, Howard, 455, 560, 577, 583
balance of payments, 394, 403–14, 416, 430
Ball, George W., 85–86, 417–19, 571
banking, 397–402, 449–51, 593, 595, 599, 601, 602
Banking Committee [Senate], 397–402
Banking and Currency Committee [House], 449–51
bankruptcy, 602–10
Barbour, Haley, 563, 576, 579, 582, 585
Barnes, Ben, 309, 311, 321, 380, 586, 589–603
Barnett, Ross, 293–94
Barth, Roger, 385, 448–49
Baskin, Robert, 460
Bennett, Herman, 590
Benton, William, 358
Bentsen, B. A., 179
Bentsen, Lloyd, 296, 377–78, 380, 382, 519
Birdwell, Sherman, 45, 52